Y0-BZU-071

FILE STRUCTURES WITH ADA

The Benjamin/Cummings Series in Computer Science

G. Almasi and A. Gottleib
Highly Parallel Computing

G. Booch
Software Engineering with Ada, Third Edition (1990)

G. Booch
Software Components with Ada

G. Brookshear
Formal Languages, Automata, and Complexity

S. Conte, H. Dunsmore, and V. Shen
Software Engineering Metrics and Models

R. DeMillo, M. McCracken, R. Martin, and J. Passafiume
Software Testing and Evaluation: A Report

R. Elmsari and S. Navathe
Fundamentals of Database Systems

D.M. Etter
Structured FORTRAN 77 for Engineers and Scientists, Third Edition

P. Helman, B. Veroff
Intermediate Problem Solving and Data Structures: Walls and Mirrors

P. Helman and B. Veroff
Walls and Mirrors: Intermediate Problem Solving and Data Structures with Modula-2

A. Kelley and I. Pohl
A Book on C, Second Edition (1990)

A. Kelly and I. Pohl
C by Dissection: The Essentials of C Programming

A. Kelly and I. Pohl
TURBO C: Essentials of C Programming

G. Luger and W. Stubblefield
Artificial Intelligence and the Design of Expert Systems

N. Miller
File Structures Using Pascal

W. Sacitch
Pascal: an Introduction to the Art and Science of Programming, Second Edition

W. Savitch
TURBO PASCAL 4.0/5.0: An Introduction to the Art and Science of Programming

M. Sobell
A Practical Guide to the UNIX System, Second Edition

R. Sebesta
Concepts of Programming Languages

D. Touretzky
Common Lisp: A Gentle Introduction to Symbolic Computation

FILE STRUCTURES WITH ADA*

Nancy E. Miller
Charles G. Petersen
Mississippi State University

*Ada is a registered trademark of the U.S. Government (AJPO)

The Benjamin/Cummings Publishing Company, Inc.
Redwood City, California • Fort Collins, Colorado • Menlo Park, California
Reading, Massachusetts • New York • Don Mills, Ontario
Wokingham, United Kingdom • Amsterdam • Bonn • Sydney
Singapore • Tokyo • Madrid • San Juan

Sponsoring Editor: *Alan Apt*
Associate Editor: *Mary Ann Telatnik*
Production Editor: *Sharon Montooth*
Copy Editor: *Bob Klinginsmith*
Composition: *Ocean View Technical Publications*
Illustration: *Merry Finley*
Manufacturing: *Casimira Kostecki*

The basic text of this book was designed using the Modular Design System, as developed by Wendy Earl and Design Office Bruce Kortebein.

Library of Congress Cataloging-in-Publication Data

Miller, Nancy E. (Nancy Ellen), 1951-
File structures with Ada.

(Benjamin/Cummings series in computer science)
Includes bibliographical references.
1. Ada (Computer program language). 2. File organization (Computer science). I. Petersen, Charles G. II. Title. III. Series.
QA76.73.A35M55 1989 005.74 89-18072
ISBN 0-8053-0440-1

2 3 4 5 6 7 8 9 10 -MU- 95 94 93 92

The Benjamin/Cummings Publishing Company, Inc.
390 Bridge Parkway
Redwood City, California 94065

Preface

MOTIVATION

After teaching file processing courses for years using COBOL as the vehicle language, we concluded that students do learn to use COBOL for a variety of file organizations (sequential, indexed sequential, and relative) but do not gain an understanding of the data structures involved in implementing the more complex file structures such as direct files and indexed sequential files. A programming language, such as Pascal, with less support than COBOL for file organizations, would allow students to gain computer science knowledge concerning the implementation of data structures on external files. Pascal is an excellent pedagogical language, but it is not in widespread use by industry as a production language. Ada, on the other hand, provides more support for files than either Pascal or COBOL. An additional plus for Ada is that it is a bona fide production language whose use is appearing more and more in software applications inside and outside the Department of Defense. Among all the commonly used production languages, Ada has the most comprehensive features for file design. Ada features, such as packages, generics, and exceptions, aid in utilizing the software engineering concepts of data abstraction and information hiding. All these features allow for the design of files that are more reliable and more easily maintained.

GOAL

This textbook meets the requirements of the Association for Computing Machinery's (ACM) course CS5 as defined in the ACM curriculum guidelines. The goal of this textbook is to study the external data structures necessary for implementing different file organizations. Ada supports sequential and random access files. The Ada programming language can be used in a more practical pedagogical way by allowing students to gain more in-depth file implementation experience as they analyze data structures for efficiency and write their own access routines.

The algorithms in this book are presented in an Ada-like pseudocode which provides students with a familiar environment in which to study the key concepts and structures necessary to implement a variety of file organizations. Data structures such as stacks, queues, linked lists, and trees are studied and analyzed for efficient use in the implementation of various file organizations. By using a superior pedagogical language such as Ada and analyzing key data structures, students will gain a better understanding of design analysis and the implementation of file organizations.

When the increased use of Ada in academia and its mandated use by the Department of Defense for all of its embedded systems are considered, it becomes apparent that there exists a need in computer science for a textbook covering file processing concepts (or file structures) using Ada instead of COBOL or PL/I.

LEVEL/AUDIENCE/MARKET

A four-year college or university with a computer science curriculum is one of the intended audiences of this book. The prerequisites are two semesters of computer programming, namely CS1 and CS2, with at least one of those semesters being devoted to Ada programming. The primary audience is third-semester computer science majors.

Many data processing applications are now being written in Ada. The professional data processor and systems analysts will find many of the concepts used in Ada to be superior to those of COBOL and PL/I. Other computing professionals involved in or interested in software contracts with the Department of Defense will find the information presented in this book to be invaluable.

ORGANIZATION AND COVERAGE

Chapter 1 presents a conceptual overview of the file-processing environment, including discussions of common file organizations, file types and characteristics, and different ways of manipulating files as factors that affect file design. Several of the examples of file applications in this chapter are referenced in later chapters.

Chapter 2 reviews the syntax for declaring and using records and record variants and for declaring and accessing text and sequential nontext files in the Ada programming language. The input-output subprograms and their associated exceptions are covered. This chapter can be omitted for those students with a very good understanding of the Ada programming language.

Chapter 3 deals with the topics of blocking and buffering of records in a file. The central theme of the chapter is the reduction in the number of I/O operations required for a program that accesses a blocked file and the reduction of the time that the CPU waits for an I/O operation to be completed when using a buffered file. Interfacing algorithms for record blocking and deblocking are also presented in this chapter. Quantitative measures of the effects of blocking and buffering are given solely in terms of the number of I/O accesses.

Chapter 4 describes external storage devices as a background for understanding the impact of storage devices on file design and manipulation. Quantitative measures of the effects of blocking and buffering (similar to those in Chapter 3) are repeated in terms of physical access time using various blocking factors and different numbers of buffers.

Chapter 5 deals with the design and maintenance of sequential files on both sequential and random-access storage devices. Algorithms for maintenance of sequential files stored on sequential devices are contrasted with algorithms for maintenance of sequential files stored on random-access devices. Sample data for a car-rental agency are used for implementing a sequential file. Quantitative measures of access times are given.

Chapter 6 describes external sort/merge techniques, which are necessary for sorting very large sequential files. Sorting is a common file-processing task, especially for manipulating sequential files. Sorting methods discussed at length are the two-way merge, the balanced *k*-way merge, and the polyphase merge. The specifications for a generic sorting package are provided. These methods are compared in terms of the number of merge cycles and external devices needed for several example data sets.

Chapter 7 begins with a discussion of the basic structures of direct files. A variety of techniques are presented for obtaining random access to data files, including the use of hashing. Examples are used to illustrate several methods for handling hashing collisions. Also included are some algorithms for creating and maintaining random-access files in the Ada programming language. In order to compare random and sequential access, the car-rental agency data used in Chapter 5 are stored in a random-access file, and quantitative measures of access times are computed.

Chapter 8 describes several types of tree structures that are used to access random-access files sequentially. The most important tree structure is the B-tree. Ways of representing and manipulating the B-tree are discussed along with accompanying algorithms. The chapter also discusses application of trees that allow sequential and random access to the car-rental agency data file created in Chapter 7.

Chapter 9 describes common implementations of indexed sequential organization, including implementations that use a tree structure, such as a B^+-tree, for the indexes. The chapter studies Scope Indexed Sequential files used on CDC computers, cylinder-and-surface-indexed sequential files (ISAM) used on IBM computers, and VSAM file organization used on IBM computers. Also included are algorithms for implementing indexed sequential files using a variety of data structures. Applications include the car-rental agency data, and access times for sequential, random, and indexed sequential files are compared.

Chapter 10 investigates other types of file organization that use linked lists or tree structures to provide multiple-key access to random-access data files. Included in this chapter is a discussion of inverted files and multilist files along with creation and manipulation algorithms. The car-rental agency data are implemented as an inverted file and multilist file to provide access by several keys. Quantitative measures of access times are given by comparing these file organizations with others discussed previously.

OUTSTANDING FEATURES

Pedagogy

Case Studies Chapter 5 introduces a case study based on an actual car-rental agency, and this case study is used throughout the book as an ongoing example illustrating practical file concepts and issues.

Additional practical, real-world case studies are presented in Chapter 2. They include discussions of an inventory of products, student class schedules, and the assignment of course grades for a class.

Examples/Illustrations Throughout the book there are a variety of examples and algorithms accompanied by numerous figures and tables. Students have found these to be very helpful for independent study.

Algorithms/Exercises Throughout this book algorithms are presented in an Ada-like pseudocode. Students learn best by working with a variety of file organizations rather than just reading about them. A variety of exercises and programming projects have been provided that illustrate the creation and manipulation of files for each type of organization. Students can implement the algorithms from the book in a hands-on file organization programming environment, thus gaining experience and greater knowledge of all key concepts. Solutions to all exercises are provided in the Solutions Manual.

Glossary/Key Terms Key terms are highlighted and defined as they occur in the text and are also included in the glossary at the end of the book.

Class Tested The non–Ada-specific material in this textbook was thoroughly class tested for six semesters in a sophomore-level file structures course. The readability of the book was greatly enhanced because of students' and reviewers' feedback over the course of several drafts.

The Use of Ada

Chapter 2 reviews the Ada syntax for declaring, using, and accessing Ada records and files. A review of Ada packages, text I/O, and exceptions is also included. This chapter can be omitted for those students with a very good understanding of the Ada programming language.

Chapter 3 introduces tasking as a tool for implementing double buffering.

Chapter 5 introduces Package Sequential_IO for creating and accessing sequential files in Ada.

Chapter 7 introduces Package Direct_IO for creating and maintaining random-access files in Ada.

Appendix A is from the Military Standard of the Ada Programming Language (ANSI/MIL-STD-1815A).

All case studies involving the car-rental agency are implemented in Ada and included as Appendix B.

SOFTWARE

All the solutions to the programming problems at the end of each chapter along with the data sets used to test these Ada programs may be purchased by adopting instructors and nonacademic professionals from the authors for a fee of $35.00. The programs have been compiled and tested with the Meridian AdaVantage compiler version 2.2 that runs under MS-DOS or PC-DOS. Please make the check or purchase order payable to "NANCY E. MILLER." Upon receipt of the fee, the purchaser will be mailed a diskette (either 5¼" (HD or DD) or 3½") that contains all the solutions and data sets in ASCII text form. Please specify the size diskette required.

Correspondence may be directed to:

Nancy E. Miller
Computer Science Department
P.O. Drawer CS
Mississippi State UNiversity
Mississippi State, MS 39762
phone: (601) 325-2756
E-MAIL: NEMILLER@MSSTATE.BITNET

SOLUTIONS MANUAL

The accompanying Solutions Manual includes:

- solutions to all exercises in the book
- guidelines for the special challenges teaching Ada assumes.

ACKNOWLEDGMENTS

We are grateful to the numerous individuals who have helped us in preparing this book. We are indebted to Meridian Software Systems, Inc. for providing the AdaVantage compiler used in testing all Ada software accompanying the book. Our thanks also go to the reviewers: Grady Booch, Victor Meyer, Charlene Hayden, and Jaime Niño.

We express our appreciation to our editor, Alan Apt, and to all those individuals at Benjamin/Cummings who have organized the reviewing and production of this book.

Contents

Chapter 8 SEARCH TREES 267

Chapter 9 INDEXED SEQUENTIAL FILE ORGANIZATION 325

Chapter 10 MULTIPLE-KEY FILE ORGANIZATION 405

Chapter 1

Overview of Files

CHAPTER CONTENTS

PREVIEW

THIS CHAPTER PRESENTS AN OVERVIEW of file organization, file types, access methods, and methods of file manipulation. It provides background information for the detailed discussions in Chapters 5 through 10. Chapters 1 through 4 describe the file processing environment which is necessary to fully understand the data structures and analyses of the traditional file organizations presented in the rest of the book.

FILE DESIGN

The study of file structures involves the investigation of data structures used to organize a large collection of data into one or more external files stored on secondary storage devices. A programmer must have a good understanding of file structures to organize data in a way that facilitates efficient storage and access. Just as the efficiency of a program depends on the choice of the structure for storing the data in internal memory, the ease of accessibility of data stored on external storage devices depends on efficient file organization.

A **file** is a collection of related data—a payroll file contains information concerning employee pay schedules, and a student file contains data about all the enrolled students. To allow easy access to all the data about one employee, all the data in the payroll file relevant to a given employee are usually stored in contiguous memory locations in a record. Figure 1.1 depicts a file and the terms used to describe the components of a file. Files of records of related data are stored on external storage devices for a number of reasons. First, the collection of data is usually too large to fit into internal memory. Second, the entire collection of data need not be stored internally since only a small portion of the file (one record of data) is accessed at a time. Third, the collection of data needs to be retained in a permanent form for access by more than one program.

It is necessary in a file of records to be able to identify a particular record. The technique for identifying a record involves choosing a data item with a unique value from the record. Such a data item is termed the **key field** of the record. For a payroll file, the key to a record of data for an employee might be the employee's social security number. Since each record has a unique key value, the file might be logically ordered in ascending key order. A library might need a more complicated arrangement for ordering records of the books in the library. A computerized library system might arrange records by the author's last name (one key) and by the subject area (a second key) so that a user could access information by author or by subject.

A programmer must consider several factors when designing a file: the organization of the file (a choice that involves selecting proper data structures); the type of function each file plays in an information system; and the characteristics of a file. A programmer must also consider the manipulations necessary to keep the file current and to extract information from it. The rest of this section presents a discussion of how these factors apply to file design.

File Organization

File organization refers to the way in which records are stored in an external file. To put it another way, the term *file organization* refers to the data structures used for organizing the data. The type of access to records available on an external file depends on file organization and storage media. This chapter presents four common file organizations that we discuss in later chapters at greater length:

1. sequential
2. random
3. indexed sequential
4. multikey

When a programmer arranges a file with **sequential file organization,** records are written consecutively—in sequence from beginning to end—and must be accessed in the same manner. The tenth record of the file can be accessed only after the first nine records have been read. Searching for a particular record requires the same process. Often the records in a sequentially organized file are stored in ascending or descending order according to a key field. The result is the ability to update the file rapidly. On the average, if records are arranged in the file by a key field, half of the records in the file must be searched in order to locate a particular record. A sequentially organized file is easier to maintain than files of other organizations, especially for adding and deleting records. However, this maintenance may take more time than that for other organizations since the entire file must be copied in order to update it. Unfortunately, the fact that a sequentially organized file can *only* be accessed sequentially means that its records cannot usually be updated in place; the user must copy the file to another file during updating. (This limitation does not apply to other file organizations.) Chapters 5 and 6 contain an extensive discussion of the manipulation of sequentially organized files.

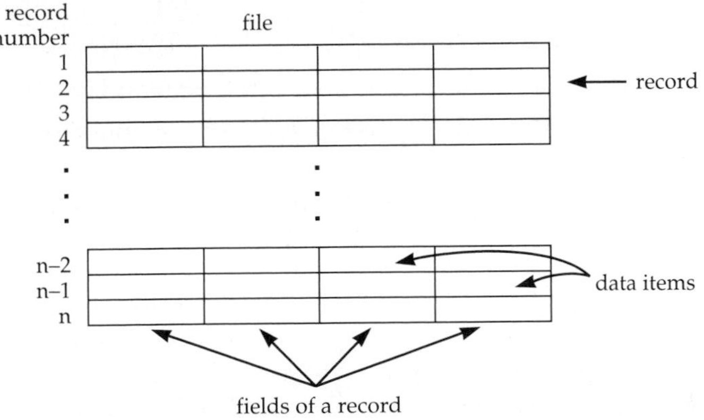

Figure 1.1
General file terms

Random file organization implies a predictable relationship between the key used to identify an individual record and that record's location in an external file. This organization is described as random because it is possible to access a record without sequentially searching through the file. Instead, a random search considers the key and directly computes the location of the record. The logical ordering of the records need not have any relationship to their physical sequence.

A **relative file** is a common implementation of random file organization available in most high-level programming languages. Once a key-position relationship is established, the position of the record in the file is specified as a record number relative to the beginning of the file. (The first record is numbered 0 or 1 depending on the implementation.) Each record's address is computed according to the following equation (assuming 1-based implementation as in Ada):

$$\text{record's address} = ((\text{relative record number} - 1) \times \text{fixed record length}) + \text{beginning of file}$$

Note that the equation specifies that the length of each record in a relative random-access file must be fixed. The limitation also imparts an advantage however: The file can be updated in place.

Relative files can also be accessed sequentially. The user specifies the relative record numbers in order from 0 or 1 (depending on the implementation) to *n*, the last record on the file. Sequential access to a relative file defines the physical ordering of records, which is usually meaningless since the record's address is computed. A retrieval of records ordered by the record keys is usually provided by some sort of index structure. Chapter 7 contains a detailed discussion of the organization and manipulation of random-access files.

Indexed sequential file organization combines sequential access and ordering with the capabilities of random access. An indexed sequential file contains two parts:

1. a collection of records stored in contiguous locations within blocks in a relative file and ordered by a key field
2. an index (a hierarchical structure of record keys and relative block numbers) to the file of ordered records

The blocks of records in the file are not necessarily stored in sequential order. The index indicates the order in which the blocks are accessed to achieve a sequential order by record keys. Since records are stored in blocks, variable-length records may be used as long as the blocks have a fixed length for random access. A search of the index of record keys retrieves the relative record number of a block containing a record, then the relative file of records is accessed randomly. Chapter 8 presents a detailed discussion of B-trees, which are the most common indexing structure used in implementing indexed sequential organization.

Table 1.1 Relationship of file organization and file access

File organization	File access	Number of key fields
sequential	sequential	one
random	sequential or random	one
indexed sequential	sequential or random	one
multikey	sequential or random	several

Indexed sequential access is relatively rapid, although it is not quite as fast as random access since the index must be searched first before the record is retrieved. The relative file can be accessed sequentially, using the index, to retrieve the file of records in order by the key field. The relative file can also be accessed randomly to update the records in place. Chapter 9 contains detailed discussions of three common implementations of indexed sequential file organization.

Multikey file organization allows access to a data file by several different key fields. A library file that requires access by author or by subject matter is a good example of a multikey file. Indexed sequential file organization uses indexes to provide random access by one key field. Multikey organization uses an indexing structure and includes the data file of records and an index for each different key field that is used to access individual records. For example, a file of employee records might be accessed by employee number, by the job code, or by the number of vacation days accumulated. Multikey organization is investigated at length and implemented using B-trees in Chapter 10. Table 1.1 relates the file organizations and file access methods discussed in this chapter.

Data File Types

The collection of data for a particular information system (a payroll information system, for example) usually resides in several types of files. The files in an information system are classified by the type of function they serve. There are six types of files in an information system:

1. master file
2. transaction file
3. table file
4. report file
5. control file
6. history file

Most files fall into only one of these six categories. A **master file** contains records of permanent information that are to be updated by adding, deleting, or changing data. For example, a payroll master file may contain an employee's social security number, the rate of pay, marital status, number of exemptions claimed, and year-to-date deductions and earnings. Individual records are added as new employees are hired, and records are deleted as employees leave. Changes to rate of pay are made as employees receive pay raises. The master file must be maintained to keep the data up to date. The process of updating a master file is called a **maintenance run**. The organization of the master file is usually sequential, random, indexed sequential, or multikey in order to provide fast and efficient access to the permanent data in that master file.

A **transaction file** contains records of changes, additions, and deletions made to a master file. One or more fields of individual records in a master file can be changed, or individual records can be added or deleted. A transaction file instead of containing updated data contains data that are often summarized or manipulated before storage in the master file. For example, a transaction file for the payroll system may contain data about hours worked during a pay period. These transactions are applied to the payroll master file to generate payroll checks and update year-to-date earnings and deductions on the master file. The number of hours worked during each pay period is not stored in the master file; rather, the data increment the year-to-date earnings field of the master file.

A **table file** consists of a table of data, such as a price list, a tax rate table, and some other forms of reference data. The data are static and are referenced by one of the other types of files. For example, a table file may contain records of product codes, product descriptions, and product prices. (Figure 1.2 shows the type of information of such a file.) Accompanying master files in this case are an inventory master file (Figure 1.3), a customer orders master file (Figure 1.4), and a manufacturing division's production master file (Figure 1.5). All the master files reference the product by product code. The table file must be referenced by all these master files in order to include product description and price on any reports. This represents a savings in space for the master file since each of the master files need not store product description and price; the master files must only store the product codes. Redundancy is eliminated, and the user makes changes in the product descriptions and prices in one place, the table file. The changes are reflected in all files that reference the table.

Figure 1.2
Sample table file

Product code	Product description	Product price

Figure 1.3
Inventory master file records

Product code	Quantity on hand	Quantity on order	Reorder point

Customer number	Customer name	Product code	Quantity ordered	Total sales

Figure 1.4
Customer orders master file records

Product code	Number made this month	Number made previous month	Number made 2nd previous month	Number made this year to date	Number made last year to date

Figure 1.5
Production master file records

Figure 1.6
Sample page of an audit listing of a maintenance run

```
Inventory Master File Maintenance Audit Listing                    Page 1

Update  Product  Quantity  Quantity  Reorder
 Code    Code    On Hand   On Order   Point    ------ACTION-------

  A     DR1112    400        50       400      Addition
  C     DR2000    350                          Change -- Qty on hand
  A     DR3814    239         0       200      Addition
  A     DR3914    150         0        50      Addition
  D     DR4000                                 Deletion
  C     GR5000              100                Change -- Qty on order
  C     GR5014                         45      Change -- Reorder point
  A     SA3012    100        25       110      Addition
  C     SA4310    125                          Change -- Qty on hand
```

Figure 1.7
Sample page of an error listing of a maintenance run

```
Inventory Master File Maintenance Error Listing                            Page 1

Update  Product  Quantity  Quantity  Reorder
 Code    Code    On Hand   On Order   Point    --------ERROR MESSAGE--------

  D     DR3000                                 Invalid Delete--Master Not On File
  C     GR5013    100                          Invalid Change--Master Not On File
  A     HM1032    125         0        75      Invalid Add--Master Already On File
  X     HM1308                                 Invalid Update Code
  Y     SA3014                                 Invalid Update Code
  A     SA4201     50         0        30      Invalid Add--Master Already On File
  D     SD1103                                 Invalid Delete--Master Not On File
```

A **report file** contains information that has been prepared for the user. This report file may be spooled to a printer to yield a hard copy, or it may be displayed on a cathode ray tube (CRT). The report file may be an audit listing of a maintenance run (Figure 1.6), an error listing of mismatches from a maintenance run (Figure 1.7), a listing of the entire master file (Figure 1.8), or a summary report of information on the master file (Figure 1.9).

Figure 1.8
Sample listing of master file

Inventory Master File Listing — Page 1

Product Code	Quantity On Hand	Quantity On Order	Reorder Point
DR1015	25	0	30
DR1112	400	50	400
DR2000	350	25	375
DR3814	239	0	200
DR3914	150	0	50
GR2001	74	10	80
GR3034	25	10	30
GR5000	500	100	525
GR5014	45	0	45
HM1032	123	0	120
HM1308	75	0	102
SA3012	100	25	110
SA4201	50	0	30
SA4310	125	0	100
SA5012	3	0	5

Figure 1.9
Sample page of summary report from a master file

Inventory Master File Listing of Records With Quantity On Hand BELOW Reorder Point — Page 1

Product Code	Quantity On Hand	Quantity On Order	Reorder Point
DR1015	25	0	30
HM1308	75	0	102
SA5012	3	0	5

A **control file** is another output from a maintenance run. The control file is very small and contains information concerning a particular maintenance run such as the date of the run; the number of master records read, added, deleted, and written; and the number of transaction records read, processed, and in error (Figure 1.10). This information is necessary to perform the two arithmetic checks that determine the success of a maintenance run. In a successful maintenance run:

1. The number of master records read minus the number of master records deleted plus the number of new master records added equals the number of master records in the new updated master file.
2. The number of transaction records read minus the number of transaction records found to be in error equals the number of transaction records processed (the number of records that caused changes to the master file).

The **history file** simply consists of all the backup master files, transaction files, and control files from past runs. The history file stores these files to provide a trail for the programmer to recreate a master file should it and all the backups be accidentally destroyed. History files are usually stored on magnetic tape reels, which are less expensive than magnetic disk packs.

```
Transactions Read            578
  Adds                       461
    Processed                446
    Invalid                   15
  Changes                     87
    Processed                 79
    Invalid                    8
  Deletions                   29
    Processed                 27
    Invalid                    2
Invalid Update Codes           1
Master Records Read       28,406
Master Records Written    28,825
```

Figure 1.10
Sample control file contents

File Characteristics

The use of a file can be characterized by the activity and the volatility of a file. The **activity** of a file is the number of records accessed during the execution of a program compared to the total number of existing records in the file. Activity is usually expressed as a percentage. The activity of a master file is the number of existing records changed during a maintenance run compared to the total number of records in the master file. A file with high activity is more efficient if it is organized sequentially (assuming that random access is not required) for two reasons. First, each record in the file is simply copied to a new file during maintenance. Second, sequential files have no indexes to be updated during maintenance as is the case for random-access files. A low-activity file is more efficient if it employs some other organization that provides random access, so that only the records to be changed are accessed and updated.

The **volatility** of a file is a measure of the number of records added and deleted compared to the original number of records. A highly volatile sequential file is updated by a procedure that merges master file records and transaction file records into a new up-to-date master file. Without the incorporation of some form of linked organization (such as a B-tree, as Chapter 8 discusses), the efficiency of a nonsequential file deteriorates with high volatility because of the extensive reorganization that takes place to accommodate additions or deletions.

Closely related to the activity and volatility of a file is the frequency of use and the required response time. The **frequency of use** is an important factor in file design and may dictate the type of access required. A file with only sequential access available requires more time to update on an hourly basis rather than once a day or once a week. The more frequent the required use of the file, the more necessary random access to the file becomes.

The **required response time** for accessing a file with queries or updates usually determines the type of access available to a file. If a response is required in seconds rather than hours, then random access will probably be the choice. Random access is not available with sequential organization. (To evaluate response time for each of the file organizations discussed in later chapters, performance of sequential files is measured in time units necessary to read a sequential file when performing a maintenance run. Performance of random-access files is measured in time units to access an individual record.)

The number of records in the file and the length of each record determine the **file size.** The record length (in bytes) is established when deciding what information is stored in each record. The length of a record equals the sum of the length (in bytes) of each field in the record. The future file size equals the number of records presently stored plus the number of additional records to be added in the future. The file size is a consideration in choosing adequate secondary storage hardware, as Chapter 4 explains.

FILES WITH ADA

Among all the commonly used production languages, Ada has the most comprehensive features for file design. Ada is a stable language and Ada programs are portable because no subset or superset compilers can pass the validation tests and still be called Ada compilers. The concept of reusable packages is one of the cornerstones of the Ada language. Predefined Ada packages (Text_IO and Sequential_IO) exist for using both text and nontext files in a sequential manner. A package for random access of nontext files (Direct_IO) is also a standard part of Ada. These packages have many procedures and functions (see Appendix A) that aid the user in file design for all of the organizations mentioned in the previous section. Ada file packages incorporate the use of generics, exceptions, and the software engineering concepts of data abstraction and information hiding. The **generic I/O packages** are templates for generating file manipulation modules that allow the user to customize packages by furnishing parameters on instantiation that are specific to the application. The wide variety of **I/O exceptions** included within the packages for detecting runtime errors associated with files provide the user with the ability to handle these exceptional situations without loss of production time. **Abstract data types** define a structure and a set of values for data objects of this type. Associated with the definition of the abstract data type is a set of operations that can be performed with data objects of this type. The definition of the abstract data type and its associated operations are visible via a **package specification.** The implementation of these operations is **encapsulated** in the package body and hidden from the user to encourage and enforce a particular abstraction. All of these features make the files created and manipulated by Ada programs more reliable and more easily maintained.

FILE MANIPULATION

Once a file is created, manipulation of that file may include querying the file to extract information, merging files of related information to produce needed reports, and maintaining the file with up-to-date data.

Queries

File queries involve searching the file for records containing certain values in particular key fields. Examples of queries to the payroll master file include:

- listing the record for a particular employee
- listing all employees that have worked more than 40 hours in the preceding week
- listing all employees within a certain department
- listing all female employees who are in managerial positions

The user queries the inventory master file (Figure 1.3) to identify all products for which the quantity on hand is less than the reorder point or to list all products for which an order has been placed. The user queries the inventory table file (Figure 1.2) to retrieve the current price to charge a customer.

File queries also involve searching the file of data for records that match a set of key values. The set of key values may contain:

- only one value in one field (a particular product code)
- several unique values in one field (all students majoring in computer science, mathematics, or statistics)
- unique values in several fields (all books in the library where author = Knuth and subject = data structures)

The program developer must anticipate the type of queries and organize the file to facilitate them.

Merging

Data often need to be extracted from more than one file of a particular information system in order to produce a summary report. A report summarizing the total inventory on hand and a listing for each product in the inventory (the product code, description, quantity on hand, and price) requires that the inventory table file, containing individual descriptions and prices, merge with the inventory master file, which contains quantity on hand. Assuming that both files are in ascending key order, the records from the two files are input and the product codes (the key) matched to produce the report. Merging these two files provides a check that determines whether each product in the current inventory has a record of data in both files (not just one file).

Maintenance

File maintenance involves updating a master file with transactions in order to keep the information in the master file up to date. Transactions consist of the addition of new records to the master file, changing data in existing records, and the deletion of existing records from the file. Typically, a one-character update code represents each type of transaction, for example: A for an add transaction, C for a change transaction, and D for a delete transaction. The transaction data need to be validated to ensure that the update code field is valid and to ensure that the transactions are in the same sequence (ascending order, in most cases) as the master file. The transaction file is edited in a separate front-end editing program prior to the execution of the master file maintenance program or as part of this maintenance program. If the editing is performed in a separate program, each record must be accessed to validate the transactions. Each valid transaction in the transaction file is accessed again by the master file maintenance program to apply the transactions to the master file. Often the master file maintenance program performs the editing as the transactions are applied to the master file so that each record in the transaction file is accessed only once instead of twice.

The **master file maintenance** program is the basic file-merging program that determines whether transactions match existing master records. If a valid transaction duplicates an existing master record, it is a change or deletion. If a valid transaction does not match existing master records, it is an addition. If no transactions apply to an existing master record, there is no change. The master file maintenance program performs a sequential update or a random update depending on the organization of the master file. In a sequential master file update, all the master records are input, matched to the transactions, and copied to a new updated master file. The transactions must be sorted in the same key sequence as the master file records. (Chapter 5 presents algorithms that describe the process of updating a sequential master file.) The master file maintenance programs perform a random master file update on files with relative and indexed sequential organization. A random update causes only the master records that match transactions to be input, modified, and rewritten to the same master file. Since the transactions are applied randomly, the transactions need not be sorted. The physical access time needed to perform the maintenance can be reduced if the transactions are sorted. (Chapter 7 presents an algorithm that describes the update of a random-access file, and Chapter 4 discusses secondary storage devices and physical access time.)

When considering file maintenance, the programmer must remember that, in many cases, permanent data are stored on several master files, not just one. For example, as Figures 1.2 through 1.5 show, an inventory information system may contain three master files of permanent data. The table file contains a product description and price information that is referenced along with the master files. The product code is listed in each master file to indicate how information that resides in four different files corresponds. The program that prints customer bills from the customer orders master file (Figure 1.4) also accesses the table file (Figure 1.2) in order to print the description and unit price. A summary report of inventory holdings might require that the table file of Figure 1.2, the inventory master file of Figure 1.3, and the production master file of Figure 1.5 all be accessed.

Multifile information systems, such as the inventory system, are designed to reduce duplication of information. The product codes, prices, and descriptions are stored in one table file. The product master files contain product codes but not prices and descriptions. Storing the price in one file makes it easier for the user to keep price information up to date.

The fact that more than one file must be accessed to retrieve all the information concerning a particular product can be a disadvantage in some cases. Each file in the multifile system has a different format, and users of the files must be aware of the file formats in order to retrieve information. The structure of records in a file (fields within a record) is usually not known to the operating system that performs the file's I/O operations. The I/O operations simply access the required number of bytes—the user must know the record format. The developer must provide special retrieval programs to access records with different record formats.

A database is a multifile system in which the user need not be aware of the different file formats. The database management system, unlike master files, does contain information pertaining to the record structures (formats) of all files within the database. The user interacts with a database management system that serves as a software interface between the master data files in the system and the user. The database management system allows the user to retrieve all the information concerning a particular product in the database without specifying which one of the several master files contains that information; the user must specify only the pertinent fields. A program that executes through the database management system may actually reference several of the permanent data files that make up the database. This book outlines the traditional file organizations used in single-file information systems; it does not cover database file designs for the implementation of multifile information systems.

SUMMARY

Files are a useful data structure for storing large collections of data on nonvolatile secondary storage devices. In designing files to match the desired access, a programmer must consider several factors:

the type of the file (master, transaction, table, report, control, history)
the organization of the file (sequential, direct, indexed sequential, multikey)
the characteristics of the file (in terms of activity and volatility)

The design of the file should also accommodate the required file manipulations: querying, file merging, and file maintenance.

Key Terms

abstract data type
activity
control file
encapsulated
file organization
file size
frequency of use
generic I/O packages
history file
indexed sequential file organization
instantiation
I/O exceptions
key field
master file
master file maintenance program
multikey organization
package body
package specification
random file organization
relative file
report file
sequential file organization
table file
transaction file
volatility

Exercises

Match the following terms with the definitions in exercises 1 through 9:

a. master file
b. transaction file
c. control file
d. table file
e. report file
f. history file
g. activity of a file
h. volatility of a file
i. file size

1. What contains updates (additions, changes, and deletions) to be applied to the master file?
2. What contains a limited number of records which are program statistics, record counts, etc., from a maintenance run?

3. What refers to the percentage of master records changed during a maintenance run?
4. What contains current permanent information?
5. What refers to the percentage of additions or deletions made to a master file during a maintenance run?
6. What is a collection of the old master files, old transaction files, and control files from past maintenance runs?
7. What is determined by the number of components in the file and the length (in bytes) of each component?
8. What contains information drawn from a master file that has been prepared for a user?
9. What contains a table of information that is static and referenced by other files?

Match the following file organizations with the definitions in exercises 10 through 13:

a. indexed sequential file organization
b. multikey file organization
c. sequential file organization
d. random file organization

10. Name an organization in which a predictable relationship exists between the key that identifies an individual component and that component's location in an external file of this organization.
11. Name an organization that combines the sequential access and ordering of components provided in sequential file organization and the random-access capabilities of random file organization.
12. Name an organization in which file components are written and accessed consecutively.
13. Which organization allows access to a data file by several different key fields?
14. What types of file organization methods are commonly available?
15. What options exist for data access? What are the differences among these access methods?
16. List reasons for structuring a collection of records as a file on a secondary storage device rather than as a data structure in main memory.
17. Why are several file organization techniques supported by most computer systems?

For each application described in questions 18 through 22, name an appropriate file organization. Justify your answers.

18. The employee payroll file is accessed once a week to calculate the company's payroll and to issue paychecks. Each record in an employee payroll master file contains the employee's identification number, pay rate, and withholding information. The master file is accessed in order by employee number. A transaction file containing data from weekly time cards will be used to update between 90 and 95 percent of the records in the master file. What organization should the employee payroll file employ?
19. An airline reservation file contains flight information used in booking passengers and issuing tickets. Each record in the airline reservation file contains a flight number, the name of the airline, the departure time, the arrival time, the maximum number of seats in the airplane, and the number of seats booked. The file is accessed by flight number. Rapid access to the file is required so that customers can receive flight information while they wait at reservation counters or on the telephone. Bookings take place immediately, and the flight records are updated as soon as passengers ask for reservations. What organization should the airline reservation file employ?
20. An inventory file contains production information about all merchandise held in stock. Each record contains a product number, a product description, a product price, the quantity on hand, and the reorder point. The inventory file is updated when an item of merchandise is withdrawn from the stock to sell to a customer and when stock is replenished with a new shipment. It is important that the updates take place immediately in order to maintain a current record of product availability. Periodic inventory reports are prepared for management. The reports are in sequence by product number and indicate the quantities of merchandise in inventory. Customers' queries about the availability of stock require that the product records be accessible immediately through on-line terminals. What organization would be best for the inventory file?
21. A table file of federal withholding tax tables is used for determining withholding amounts during payroll processing. The table file is loaded into tables in main memory when the payroll program is run. The payroll program then searches the tables in memory to locate withholding amounts. No maintenance is required since it is a reference file that is built one time at the beginning of the year. What organization should the table file employ?

22. An on-line maintenance program adds, changes, and deletes records in a master file interactively through on-line terminals. Each transaction is recorded in a transaction log file as part of the on-line master file maintenance. Each record in the log file contains the date on which the modification took place, an identification (key) of the master record that was affected, the type of maintenance activity applied (add, change, delete), and the master record field that was modified. The log file provides an audit trail through which the transaction can be traced from its point of origin through its appearance in the master file. What organization should the log file employ?

sequential file

Chapter 2

Ada Records and Files

CHAPTER CONTENTS

PREVIEW

THIS CHAPTER REVIEWS THE SYNTAX for declaring and accessing records and record variants in the Ada programming language. The chapter also reviews the syntax of external text files as used in Ada. The chapter introduces sequential nontext files. It explains the syntax for declaring files and the statements and standard subprograms for creating and accessing them. All algorithms appear in Ada-like pseudocode that employs the control structures Case, For, If, and Loop. Indentation shows the nesting of control structures and the End statements enhance readability.

RECORD DATA TYPE

Many programming languages provide data types for representing data structures. Some programming languages, such as FORTRAN and BASIC, provide little beyond arrays and files for this purpose. Other programming languages, such as COBOL, PL/1, Pascal, and Ada, provide records in addition to arrays and files as data types.

Arrays are a useful structure for storing data of the same type; a single identifier and an index are used to access an array. **Parallel arrays** are the only facility available in FORTRAN and BASIC for storing data of differing types, and accessing parallel arrays is more complicated than accessing records. Each array must be accessed separately with the same index range to retrieve related information of different types. For example, a collection of inventory data might consist of a code, description, and price for each product. (Figure 2.1 shows such a collection.)

The inventory data could not be stored using multidimensional arrays because some items are character data, some are float data, and some are integer data. By implementing parallel arrays, however, each column of inventory data becomes a single one-dimensional array, and the same index range accesses all three arrays (columns) of data.

The declarations in Ada for storing the inventory data of 50 entries using parallel arrays are as follows:

```
SUBTYPE Name_12 Is String ( 1 .. 12 );
product_code        : Array ( 1 .. 50 ) Of Integer;
product_description : Array ( 1 .. 50 ) Of Name_12;
product_price       : Array ( 1 .. 50 ) Of Float;
```

The declarations allocate the memory as shown in Figure 2.2. The 50 product codes are stored in contiguous memory locations followed by 50 product descriptions followed by 50 product prices. The ith element of each array references the data about a particular product found in the ith row of the inventory table.

The Ada statements needed to initialize the parallel arrays with the first entry of the inventory table are as follows:

```
product_code(1)          := 754;
product_description(1)   := "carburetor  ";
product_price(1)         := 12.95;
```

Figure 2.1
Collection of inventory data

Product code	Product description	Product price
754	carburetor	12.95
863	muffler	51.95
915	air filter	5.45

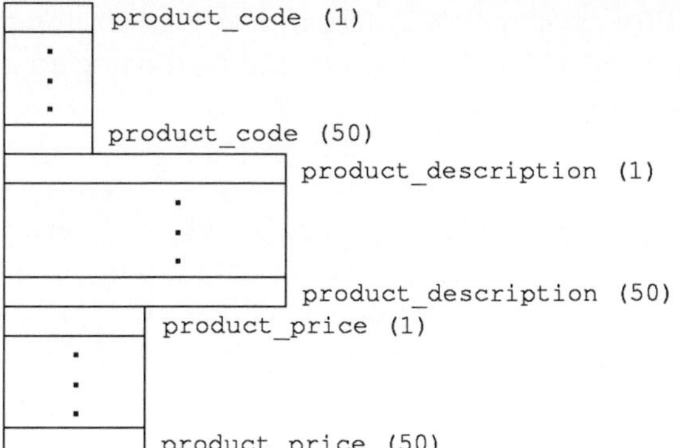

Figure 2.2
The inventory data in memory as parallel arrays

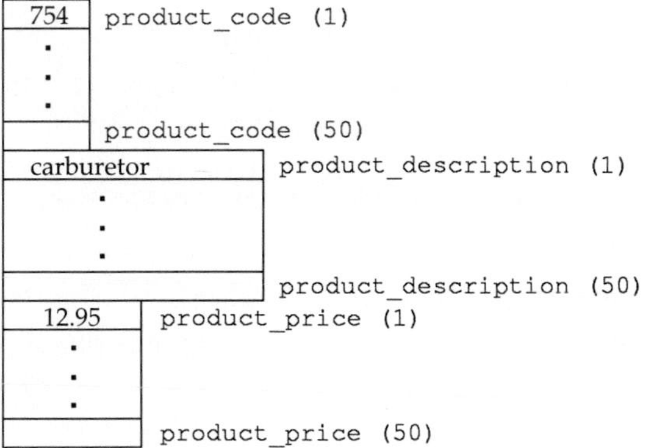

Figure 2.3
The parallel arrays with one entry

Figure 2.3 shows the result of initialization of memory. All the data in the parallel arrays are printed in columnar form by implementing the following Ada program:

```
WITH Text_IO;
PROCEDURE Print_Parallel_Arrays Is
    SUBTYPE Name_12 Is String ( 1 .. 12 );
    product_code        : Array ( 1 .. 50 ) Of Integer;
    product_description : Array ( 1 .. 50 ) Of Name_12;
    product_price       : Array ( 1 .. 50 ) Of Float;
    PACKAGE Int_IO  Is New Text_IO.Integer_IO ( Integer );
    PACKAGE Real_IO Is New Text_IO.Float_IO ( Float );
BEGIN  --Print_Parallel_Arrays
--      Array initialization
    For index In 1 .. 50 Loop
        Int_IO.Put ( product_code(index) );
        Text_IO.Put ( product_description(index) );
        Real_IO.Put ( product_price(index) );
        Text_IO.New_Line;
    End Loop;
END Print_Parallel_Arrays;
```

Since each identifier with a different data type is stored in a separate but parallel array, each identifier must be accessed using an index.

Definition

The **record data type** available in COBOL, PL/1, Pascal, and Ada allows the inventory data to be stored so that all data related to a particular product are in contiguous memory locations as one group of data. A reference to one record allows access to any piece of data about a particular product.

The **record data structure** is a collection of data items of different types accessed by a single name.

The format for the record data type in Ada is as follows:

```
TYPE Record_Name Is
        Record
            field_name_1 : type_name;
            field_name_2 : type_name;
                .
                .
                .
            field_name_n : type_name;
        End Record;
```

`Record_Name` is a valid identifier name and `field_name_i` (i = 1, . . . , *n*) is a valid identifier name (or list of identifiers) and one of the components of the record data structure. The `type_name` is any Ada type name or subtype name.

The declarations for storing the inventory data using the record data type are

```
SUBTYPE Name_12 Is String ( 1 .. 12 );
TYPE Record_Entry Is Record
                         code        : Integer;
                         description : Name_12;
                         price       : Float;
                     End Record;
product : Record_Entry;
```

Operations on Records

The general form for reference to a field of the record consists of

```
Record_Name.field_name_i
```

where `Record_Name` is a valid record name, and `field_name_i` is the name of the ith component in the record data structure known as `Record_Name`. The following Ada code references the fields within the record and initializes the record data structure:

```
WITH Text_IO;
PROCEDURE Initialize_Record Is
    SUBTYPE Name_12 Is String ( 1 .. 12 );
    TYPE Record_Entry Is Record
                             code        : Integer;
                             description : Name_12;
                             price       : Float;
                         End Record;
    product : Record_Entry;
    PACKAGE Int_IO  Is New Text_IO.Integer_IO ( Integer );
    PACKAGE Real_IO Is New Text_IO.Float_IO ( Float );
BEGIN  --Initialize_Record
    Int_IO.Get ( product.code );
    Text_IO.Get ( product.description );
    Real_IO.Get ( product.price );
--    process record
END Initialize_Record;
```

Instead of parallel arrays, an array of records is more appropriate for storing the inventory data.

```
products : Array ( 1 .. 50 ) Of Record_Entry;
```

allocates storage for an inventory table of 50 entries. As Figure 2.4 shows, each entry consists of a product code (integer), a product description (twelve characters), and a product price (float).

The general form for reference to a single record in an array

```
Array_Name(index)
```

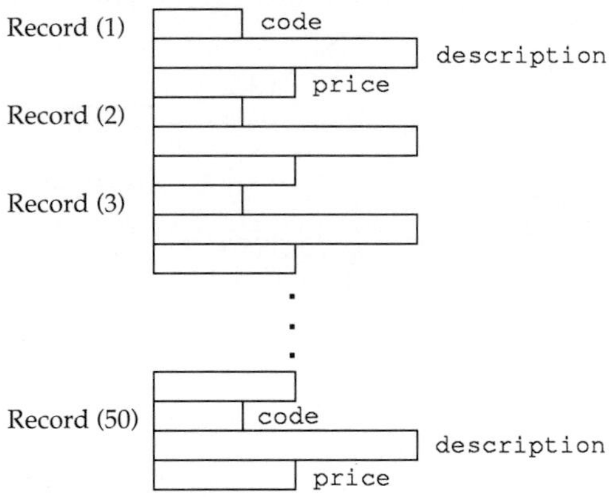

Figure 2.4
The inventory data stored as an array of records

allows access to all information about a particular product. Access to the indexth field of a single record is the result of

```
Array_Name(index).field_name_i
```

The following Ada statements initialize the first entry in the inventory table:

```
products(1).code        := 754;
products(1).description := "carburetor   ";
products(1).price       := 12.95;
```

Record aggregates is another form available in Ada for assigning values to components of a record. A **named aggregate** associates values with components of a record by specifying both the name of the component and the associated value. A **positional aggregate** associates the values with the component by positioning the value in the list of values rather than using the name. The following named aggregate initializes the first entry of the inventory table:

```
products(1) := ( description => "carburetor   ",
                 code        => 754,
                 price       => 12.95 );
```

The components in a named aggregate need not be listed in the same order as in the record description. The following positional aggregate initializes the first entry of the inventory table:

```
products(1) := ( 754, "carburetor   ", 12.95 );
```

The components in a positional aggregate must be listed in the same order as in the record description.

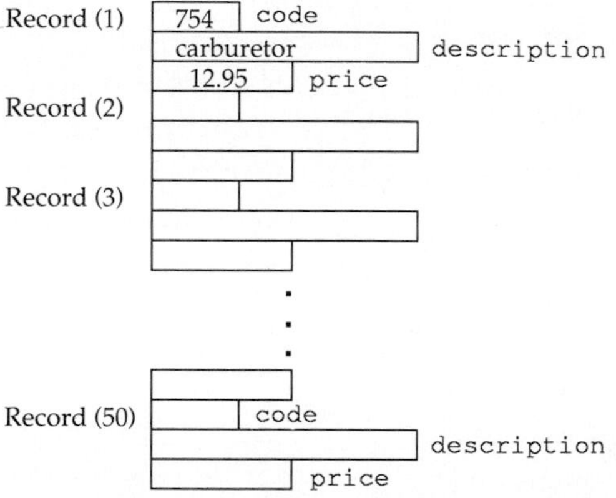

Figure 2.5
The array of records with one entry

Figure 2.5 shows the resulting memory with the first entry assigned. An array of records stores the inventory data about a product in contiguous memory locations (Figures 2.4 and 2.5). Parallel arrays store each piece of information in a different but parallel array; information is spread out over memory (Figures 2.2 and 2.3).

One of the advantages of the record data type over parallel arrays for storing the inventory data is that a record variable can be assigned to another record variable of the same type. The advantage over parallel arrays is that this can be accomplished with one assignment statement. For example, with the additional declaration

```
new_record : Record_Entry;
```

the following Ada statements input all the information concerning a new part into `new_record`:

```
WITH Text_IO;
PROCEDURE Input_New_Record Is
    SUBTYPE Name_12 Is String ( 1 .. 12 );
    TYPE Record_Entry Is Record
                              code        : Integer;
                              description : Name_12;
                              price       : Float;
                         End Record;
    products : Array ( 1 .. 50 ) Of Record_Entry;
    new_record : Record_Entry;
    PACKAGE Int_IO  Is New Text_IO.Integer_IO ( Integer );
    PACKAGE Real_IO Is New Text_IO.Float_IO ( Float );
BEGIN --Input_New_Record
    Int_IO.Get  ( new_record.code );
    Text_IO.Get ( new_record.description );
    Real_IO.Get ( new_record.price );
    products(1) := new_record;
END Input_New_Record;
```

The single assignment statement above stores the whole record of data in the first element of the array `products`. The fact that the record data type allows the user to move a group of related data with a single reference makes records one of the most commonly used data structures for storing related data.

When referencing a record from an array of records, the references and subsequent generated code can be simplified with the use of a single identifier of the record type. For example, in the following Ada code, each record in the products array is output. Notice that each Put statement requires an address computation for a field of an indexed component.

```
For index In 1 .. 50 Loop
    Int_IO.Put  ( products(index).code );
    Text_IO.Put ( products(index).description );
    Real_IO.Put ( products(index).price );
    Text_IO.New_Line;
End Loop;
```

The references in the Put statements require an address computation that includes an indexed element (`products(index)`) and an offset to a specific field of the record. These references can be simplified to an address computation for a field of a simple record using the **Renames** clause available in Ada, which provides a new name for an existing entity (in this case an array element).

```
For index In 1 .. 50 Loop
    Declare
        new_record : Record_Entry Renames products(index);
    Begin
        Int_IO.Put  ( new_record.code );
        Text_IO.Put ( new_record.description );
        Real_IO.Put ( new_record.price );
        Text_IO.New_Line;
    End;
End Loop;
```

The declaration of `new_record` makes the generated code more efficient (one index computation instead of three). The index computation of `products(index)` is made only once at the top of the loop instead of three times inside the loop. The cost is one additional storage location for the indexed address, which exists only inside the declare block.

EXAMPLE 1: RECORDS

The ABC Company wishes to keep an inventory of all the products it sells. The data to be stored for each product include a five-character product code, a 15-character product description, an integer indicating the quantity on hand, the unit price in dollars and cents, the reorder point as an integer, and an integer indicating the size of an outstanding order made to the manufacturer. A value of zero for outstanding order indicates that no outstanding order exists. The record description for each product is

```
TYPE Product Is Record
                    code                   : String ( 1 .. 5 );
                    description            : String ( 1 .. 15 );
                    quantity_on_hand       : Integer;
                    unit_price             : Float;
                    reorder_point          : Integer;
                    outstanding_order_size : Integer;
                End Record;
```

If the ABC Company sells 10,000 different products, then an array of `Product` records is needed. The following is the declaration of the array:

```
inventory : Array ( 1 .. 10_000 ) Of Product;
```

Assuming each character uses 1 byte of memory, each integer uses 2 bytes of memory, and each float uses 4 bytes of memory, each record will use the following amounts of memory:

COMPONENT	SIZE IN BYTES
code	5
description	15
quantity_on_hand	2
unit_price	4
reorder_point	2
outstanding_order_size	2
	30

Each record requires 30 bytes for each product. A total of 300,000 bytes is needed to store information for 10,000 different products. Should the storage requirement be larger than the main memory available, the programmer must store all 10,000 records on external storage devices, using files. As a result, the main memory stores only one record at a time. Files are discussed at length later in this chapter.

EXAMPLE 2: RECORDS

Suppose the record data structure is used to store data concerning college students. Data on one student may consist of the student's name, address, and phone number. A sample declaration is

```
TYPE Student Is Record
                    name         : String ( 1 .. 31 );
                    address      : String ( 1 .. 50 );
                    phone_number : Integer;
                End Record;
one_student : Student;
```

The declaration specifies: `name` containing 31 characters for last name, first name, and the middle initial; `address` containing 50 characters; and `phone_number` containing the telephone number as an integer.

Since this is information about a college student, the record would probably contain two addresses: a home address and a campus address. The declaration of address should allow both addresses to be stored, and each address should contain up to 50 characters. A record data structure is appropriate for both addresses.

```
TYPE Addresses Is Record
                    home   : String ( 1 .. 50 );
                    campus : String ( 1 .. 50 );
                End Record;
```

The record type, `Student`, now becomes

```
TYPE Student Is Record
                    name         : String ( 1 .. 31 );
                    address      : Addresses;
                    phone_number : Integer;
                End Record;
one_student : Student;
```

The home and campus addresses is accessed as a group with

```
one_student.address
```

or individually accessed with

```
one_student.address.home
one_student.address.campus
```

The record named `one_student` contains the component `address`, which in turn is a record containing the components `home` and `campus`.

The component `name` could also be viewed as a group of three components: a last name of 15 characters, a first name of 15 characters, and a middle initial. Consider substituting the following record data type for type of name:

```
TYPE Names Is Record
                  last   : String ( 1 .. 15 );
                  first  : String ( 1 .. 15 );
                  middle : Character;
              End Record;
```

The resulting description for `Student` consists of three components: `name`, `address`, and `phone_number`:

```
TYPE Student Is Record
                    name         : Names;
                    address      : Addresses;
                    phone_number : Integer;
                End Record;
one_student : Student;
```

The first two components are groups of components. The component `name`, for example, is a group containing three components: `last`, `first`, and `middle`. The following access the three components:

```
one_student.name.last
one_student.name.first
one_student.name.middle
```

The address component is a record of two components, `home` and `campus`, which are accessed by

```
one_student.address.home
one_student.address.campus
```

Some computers do not allow the data type Integer to contain the ten decimal digits necessary for the phone number. In this case the programmer declares a record to contain the three-digit area code, the three-digit exchange, and the four-digit number.

```
TYPE Phone Is Record
                  area_code : Integer Range 200 ..  999;
                  exchange  : Integer Range 200 ..  999;
                  number    : Integer Range 0   .. 9999;
              End Record;
```

The record description `Student` with the expanded phone number is

```
TYPE Student Is Record
                    name         : Names;
                    address      : Addresses;
                    phone_number : Phone;
                End Record;
```

The following are Ada references to the `phone_number` components.

```
one_student.phone_number.area_code
one_student.phone_number.exchange
one_student.phone_number.number
```

All references to components must include the record name of all nested records to produce a fully qualified reference.

To make `Student` an appropriate data structure for storing information about a college student, the programmer must allocate additional memory within the record to store the student's class schedule. Suppose that a college student can enroll for as many as six courses and that the data concerning each course include a course number (six characters), a room number (four characters), and a meeting time (an integer). An appropriate data structure for storing the class schedule is an array of six records in which each record contains data pertaining to a course. The following is a declaration for one class:

```
TYPE Class Is Record
                  course_number : String ( 1 .. 6 );
                  room_number   : String ( 1 .. 4 );
                  meeting_time  : Integer;
              End Record;
```

The class schedule could be added as the fourth component of the record `Student` in this manner:

```
TYPE Class_List Is Array ( 1 .. 6 ) Of Class;
TYPE Student Is Record
                    name          : Names;
                    address       : Addresses;
                    phone_number  : Phone;
                    classes       : Class_List;
                End Record;
one_student : Student;
```

The valid form for referencing data pertaining to the indexth course is:

```
one_student.classes(index).course_number
one_student.classes(index).room_number
one_student.classes(index).meeting_time
```

Record Size

The declaration

```
one_student : Student;
```

allocates storage for data concerning only one student but totals several bytes. Assuming each character uses 1 byte of memory and each integer uses 2 bytes of memory, the four components of `one_student` use the following amounts of memory:

COMPONENT	SIZE IN BYTES
name	31
address	100
phone_number	6
classes	72
	209

Consider the array that results if data are collected for 10,000 college students:

```
all_students : Array ( 1 .. 10_000 ) Of Student;
```

This array of 10,000 records requires 2,090,000 bytes of memory! Computers with limited memory capacities would not be able to allocate an array of 10,000 records. The programmer must use files to store the records on external storage. Only data concerning one student are brought into main memory at a time. Files would also provide permanent storage for the 10,000 records; recall that main memory is volatile. If the array of 10,000 records is not stored in files, the records will be lost after the program that allocated the array is executed.

Variant Records

Sometimes additional fields are required in some records in the file but not in others. The presence of these additional fields depends on the value of other fields within the record. For example, in Record Example 2, home address and campus address would be the same for students living at home. Why store the same address twice? For those students with the same address for home and campus, only one address need be stored; for all other students, both the home and campus addresses are required. Variant record types in Ada allow for additional fields (the **variant part** of the record) to be specified according to the value of another field in the record. A record containing a variant part is a **variant record.**

The variant part of a record, which must follow the fixed part, is specified using a version of the Case statement. The format for the variant record type in Ada is

```
TYPE Record_Name (discriminant : type_name [:= default_value]) Is
        Record
            <fixed_part>
            Case discriminant Is
                <variant_1>
                <variant_2>
                <variant_3>
            End Case;
        End Record;
```

The `discriminant` is the data object tested in the Case and determines which `variant_i` is present within the record. One or more choices followed by a list of declarations characterize `variant_i`:

```
When choice_1 [| choice_i] ... => component_list
```

A valid choice, `choice_i`, is an expression, a range, or a constant of the type of the discriminant used in the Case. The choice for the last of the variants can be `others`, which is a catchall. The word `others` stands for the values not given in the choices of the previous variants and must be included if all the possible choices have not been enumerated.

The `component_list` can be `Null` or a list of declarations, including variant record types. A record may have only one variant part; no other declaration may follow a variant part.

The record type `Addresses` from Record Example 2 is a fixed record type:

```
TYPE Addresses Is Record
                      home   : String ( 1 .. 50 );
                      campus : String ( 1 .. 50 );
                  End Record;
```

To alter `Addresses` to contain a fixed part of the home address and a variant part of the campus address is simple. In the alteration that follows, the variant part is present only if the home and campus addresses are not the same:

```
TYPE Addresses (same_as_campus : Boolean) Is
        Record
            home : String ( 1 .. 50 );
            Case same_as_campus Is
                 When TRUE  => Null;
                 When FALSE => campus : String ( 1 .. 50 );
            End Case;
        End Record;
```

The variant part depends on the value of `same_as_campus`, which is the **discriminant**. If the value of `same_as_campus` is `TRUE`, the record contains only the fixed part, `home`, as indicated by the statement `Null`; otherwise, the record contains the fixed part, `home`, and the variant part, `campus`. The discriminant, `same_as_campus`, is a component of the record and must be initialized to one of the values in the Case choice list before being written to a file. A default value may be specified for the discriminant. The value of the discriminant must be interrogated (if a default value is not given) before the fields in the variant part may be accessed.

EXAMPLE 3: RECORDS

A record structure describing people would include some fixed fields—name, sex, date of birth, number of dependents, and marital status—as well as some variant fields that are dependent on marital status. If the person is married, for example, the record might include the spouse's name. If the person is single, no fields are allocated beyond the `number_of_dependents`.

```
SUBTYPE Mmddyy Is String ( 1 .. 6 );
SUBTYPE Name_Type Is String ( 1 .. 25 );
TYPE    Status_Type Is ( DIVORCED, MARRIED, SINGLE, WIDOWED );
TYPE    Sex_Type Is ( FEMALE, MALE );
TYPE    Person ( marital_status : Status_Type := SINGLE ) Is
            Record
                name                 : Name_Type;
                sex                  : Sex_Type;
                date_of_birth        : Mmddyy;
                number_of_dependents : Integer;
                Case marital_status Is
                    When MARRIED  => spouse_name : Name_Type;
                    When DIVORCED => date_of_divorce : Mmddyy;
                    When SINGLE   => Null;
                    When WIDOWED  => date_of_death : Mmddyy;
                End Case;
            End Record;
```

The record structure determines that the description of a married person contains six elements:

1. `marital_status` = `MARRIED`
2. `name`
3. `sex`
4. `date_of_birth`
5. `number_of_dependents`
6. `spouse_name`

<table>
<tr><td rowspan="3">marital status</td><td rowspan="3">name</td><td rowspan="3">sex</td><td rowspan="3">date of birth</td><td rowspan="3">number of dependents</td><td colspan="2">spouse name</td></tr>
<tr><td>date of divorce</td><td></td></tr>
<tr><td>date of death</td><td></td></tr>
</table>

Figure 2.6
The physical view of storage for a variant record

The description of a single person contains only five elements:

1. `marital_status = SINGLE`
2. `name`
3. `sex`
4. `date_of_birth`
5. `number_of_dependents`

Figure 2.6 provides a physical view of the storage requirements for the record `Person`. Storage is allocated for every identifier in the record. The storage for each choice in the variant part of the record is overlaid to conserve storage space. As a result the discriminant must be checked before attempting to access any data. Checking the discriminant ensures that the data are interpreted as a correct type of data. In this example, a test of the discriminant, `marital_status`, would need to yield `MARRIED` before the user could reference the variant field `spouse_name`.

```
myself : Person;

myself.sex := FEMALE;
myself.marital_status := MARRIED;
Put_Line ( myself.spouse_name );
```

Notice that components of the variant part of a record in Ada are referenced using the same form as components of the fixed part of a record. Below is another form, using record aggregates, for assigning values to components of a record that includes both variant and fixed parts:

```
friend : Person;

friend := ( sex                    => MALE,
            name                   => "Poindexter ",
            date_of_birth          => "010234",
            marital_status         => DIVORCED,
            number_of_dependents   => 2,
            date_of_divorce        => "041775" );
```

CASE STUDY 2.1

Problem

Write a program that reads test scores and scores for programming assignments (programs' score) for a class. The input is in the form of student identification (four characters), exam 1 score, exam 2 score, and programs' score. A –1 for exam 1 score, exam 2 score, or programs' score indicates that the student has dropped the class. Store all of the information in an array. Include a field for total score (the sum of exam 1 score, exam 2 score, and programs' score), which your program will compute. Do not include –1 scores in the total.

Write a function that, when passed a score and an average for the total scores, returns a letter grade based on that average. Assign

A to all who are at least 13% above the average

B to those who are above the average but who do not merit A's

C to those who are above 19% below the average but who do not merit A's or B's

D to those who are above 26% below the average but who do not merit A's, B's, or C's

F to those below the D cutoff

The program should print the identification, the exam 1 score, the exam 2 score, the programs' score, the total score, and the letter grade for each student. There are no more than 200 sets of scores in the input file.

Top-Down Design

Input Input no more than 200 sets of students' scores consisting of identification, exam 1 score, exam 2 score, and programs' scores.

Output The output contains identification, exam 1 score, exam 2 score, programs' score, total score, and letter grade for each student.

Data Structures Allocate a record to store an identification, exam 1 score, exam 2 score, programs' score, and total score for one student. Define the operations to be performed on that record: get the information, add up the scores, determine grade, and print student data and grade. This data structure and these operations are encapsulated in a package. The program uses this package to allocate an array of records for student data representing all the students in a given course.

The following package specification describes the data structure for the record of student data and the operations that can be performed on that record:

```
PACKAGE Student_Package Is
    SUBTYPE Id_Type Is String ( 1 .. 4 );
    TYPE Student Is Record
                    exam_1_score,
                    exam_2_score   : Integer;
                    identification : Id_Type;
                    programs_score,
                    total_score    : Integer;
                End Record;

    PROCEDURE Get_Student_Info ( individual : Out Student );
    PROCEDURE Add_Up_Total_Score ( individual : In Out Student );
```

```
    FUNCTION Find_Grade ( score : Integer;
                          average : Float ) Return Character;
    PROCEDURE Put_Student_Info ( individual : Student;
                                 grade : Character );

END Student_Package;
```

Pseudocode

Level 0

```
sum_of_total_scores ← 0
number_of_students ← 0
Loop
    Exit When End_Of_File
    Get id, exam_1_score, exam_2_score, programs_score
    Add_Up_Total_Score
    Sum_Total_Scores
End Loop
average ← sum_of_total_scores / number_of_students
For number_of_students Loop
    Find_Grade (score, average)
    Print id, exam_1_score, exam_2_score, programs_score,
        total_score, grade
End Loop
```

Level 1

Add_Up_Total_Score

```
total_score ← 0
If exam_1_score not = –1 Then
    total_score ← total_score + exam_1_score
End If
If exam_2_score not = –1 Then
    total_score ← total_score + exam_2_score
End If
If programs_score not = –1 Then
    total_score ← total_score + programs_score
End If
```

Sum_Total_Scores

```
number_of_students ← number_of_students + 1
sum_of_total_scores ← sum_of_total_scores + total_score
```

Find_Grade (score, average)

```
If score > 13% above average Then
    grade ← 'A'
Elsif score > average Then
    grade ← 'B'
Elsif score > 19% below average Then
    grade ← 'C'
Elsif score > 26% below average Then
    grade ← 'D'
Else
    grade ← 'F'
End If
```

Solution

The following package body reflects the pseudocode in the elaboration of the operations that can be performed on the student record:

```
WITH Text_IO;
USE Text_IO;
PACKAGE Body Student_Package Is
    PACKAGE Int_IO Is New Integer_IO ( Integer );
    USE Int_IO;
    PROCEDURE Get_Student_Info ( individual : Out Student ) Is
    BEGIN
        Get ( individual.identification );
        Get ( individual.exam_1_score );
        Get ( individual.exam_2_score  );
        Get ( individual.programs_score  );
        Skip_Line;
    END Get_Student_Info;
    PROCEDURE Add_Up_Total_Score ( individual : In Out Student ) Is
        STUDENT_DROPPED : Constant Integer := -1;
        total_score : Natural := 0;
    BEGIN
        If individual.exam_1_score /= STUDENT_DROPPED Then
            total_score := individual.exam_1_score;
        End If;
        If individual.exam_2_score /= STUDENT_DROPPED Then
            total_score := total_score + individual.exam_2_score;
        End If;
        If individual.programs_score /= STUDENT_DROPPED Then
            total_score := total_score + individual.programs_score;
        End If;
        individual.total_score := total_score;
    END Add_Up_Total_Score;
    FUNCTION Find_Grade ( score : Integer;
                          average : Float )
                          Return Character Is
        float_score : Float := Float ( score );
    BEGIN  --  Find_Grade
        If float_score > 1.13 * average Then
            Return 'A';
        Elsif float_score > average Then
            Return 'B';
        Elsif float_score > average - 0.19 * average Then
            Return 'C';
        Elsif float_score > average - 0.26 * average Then
            Return 'D';
        Else
            Return 'F';
        End If;
    END Find_Grade;
```

```
    PROCEDURE Put_Student_Info ( individual : Student;
                                 grade : Character ) Is
    BEGIN
        Put ( "  " );
        Put ( individual.identification );
        Put ( individual.exam_1_score, 9);
        Put ( individual.exam_2_score, 9);
        Put ( individual.programs_score, 9);
        Put ( individual.total_score, 9);
        Put ( "        " );
        Put ( grade );
        New_Line;
    END Put_Student_Info;

END Student_Package;
```

The following program is the solution to this problem. The program uses the package specification for the student record to declare an array of records. The program also uses the operations defined for the student record.

```
WITH Text_IO, Student_Package;
USE Text_IO, Student_Package;

PROCEDURE Grading Is

    class                 : Array ( 1 .. 200 ) Of Student;
    individual            : Student;
    number_of_students    : Natural := 0;
    sum                   : Natural := 0;
    total_average         : Float;

BEGIN  --  Grading
    Loop
        Exit When End_Of_File;
        If number_of_students = class'last Then
            Put_Line ( "Number of students exceeds the class array size" ) ;
            Put_Line ( "Proceeding with the grade computations" ) ;
            Exit;
        End If;
        Get_Student_Info ( individual );
        Add_Up_Total_Score ( individual );
        sum := sum + individual.total_score;
        number_of_students := number_of_students + 1;
        class(number_of_students) := individual;
    End Loop;
    total_average := Float ( sum ) / Float ( number_of_students );
    Put_Line ( "  ID      EXAM 1  EXAM 2 PROGRAMS  TOTAL GRADE" );
    New_Line;
    For index In 1 .. number_of_students Loop
        individual := class(index);
        Put_Student_Info ( individual,
                           Find_Grade ( individual.total_score,
                                        total_average ) );
    End Loop;
END Grading;
```

In the program `Grading`, which uses an array of records, the reference to a particular record contains an index. The data are input into a simple record type (`individual`) and, at the end of the loop, stored in the array.

FILES

The amount of main memory necessary to store large amounts of data within a program is often larger than the memory available. Data that are stored in a program are volatile; the data remain in main memory only while the program is running. When the program is finished running, the memory space is allocated to another program—all data stored in the first program are lost. The amount of storage within a program is limited by the size of main memory. For these reasons, a large collection of data is often stored in **external files**, secondary storage devices that are nonvolatile. The external file is a collection of data in which each element is of the same type. External files may be thought of as arrays stored on secondary storage devices. Unlike arrays, however, only one element of the file can be accessed at a time; the number of elements in the file may vary and need not be specified in the declarations.

An Ada file is a collection of **components** having the same type and is terminated by an end-of-file marker (represented in this text as <eof>). (The actual representation of the end-of-file marker is implementation-dependent.) A file may consist of enumerations, integers, floats, arrays, or records. An Ada file is accessed (read or written) one component at a time. Two types of file access are available in Ada: sequential (`Text_IO` and `Sequential_IO`) and random (`Direct_IO`). Sequential access means that the elements of the file can only be accessed in sequential order from beginning to end. Random access means that the elements of the file can be accessed in any order. This chapter illustrates sequential access, and Chapters 5 and 6 offer detailed discussion of this concept. Chapter 7 covers random access at length.

A number of exceptions can be raised by the input-output operations. An **exception** is an error situation which may arise during execution of an Ada program. To **raise** an exception is to abandon normal program execution so as to signal that the corresponding error has taken place. Every Ada compiler is required to generate code that raises the appropriate exception if an error situation arises during program execution. I/O exceptions are declared in the package `IO_Exceptions` (Appendix A) and are used in each of the input-output packages (`Text_IO`, `Sequential_IO`, and `Direct_IO`).

An **exception handler** is a portion of a program specifying a response to the exception. The programmer has the responsibility of handling the exceptions raised by the Ada program. An exception handler is included in the end of a block of code following the term `Exception` and identifies the response to exceptions that may be raised during execution of the block. The following depicts the general form of an exception handler:

```
Begin
    --sequence of statements
Exception
    When <exception name(s)> =>
    --sequence of statements
    --(response to exception raised)
End
```

Several exception handlers can be included at the end of a block. Exception handlers can occur in a block statement or in the body of a subprogram, package, task unit, or generic unit.

Sequential Nontext Files

A sequential nontext file in Ada is defined by means of the generic package `Sequential_IO`. A skeleton of the specification part of this package is given below. The entire specification can be found in Appendix A.

```
WITH IO_Exceptions;
GENERIC
    TYPE Element_Type Is Private;
PACKAGE Sequential_IO Is
    TYPE File_Type Is Limited Private;
    TYPE File_Mode Is (IN_FILE, OUT_FILE);
    ...
    PROCEDURE Open ( file : In Out File_Type; ... );
    ...
    PROCEDURE Read ( file     : In File_Type;
                     item   : Out Element_Type );
    ...
    PROCEDURE Write ( file    : In File_Type;
                      item : In Element_Type );
    ...
END Sequential_IO;
```

The declaration of a sequential nontext file requires an instantiation of this generic package, with the type of the file element as the actual parameter. The resulting package contains the declaration of a file type (called `File_Type`) for files of such elements, as well as I/O operations for these files, such as `Open`, `Read`, and `Write` procedures.

The following

```
WITH Sequential_IO;
PROCEDURE Define_File Is
    PACKAGE File_Of_Integer Is New Sequential_IO ( Integer );
    USE File_Of_Integer;
    exam_scores : File_Type;
BEGIN --Define_File
    Null;
END Define_File;
```

creates the package File_Of_Integer that is an instance of the generic package Sequential_IO, where the element type is Integer, and the I/O operations are instantiated for this particular File_Type. The internal file name, exam_scores, is declared to be a file of this File_Type, where one element or **component** of the file is an integer representing one exam score. The declaration does not specify length as the declaration of an array does since a file is stored on secondary storage devices. In a file declaration, only the type of each component is specified.

All data types stored in an external nontext file are stored using the same format as data items stored internally in main memory. For example, if an integer data item is stored in a word of main memory, a file declared with the Element_Type of Integer has a word of storage for each file component. If a float data item occupies two words of main memory, a file declared with the Element_Type of Float has two words of storage for each file component. External nontext files are, therefore, extensions of main memory.

Operations on Nontext Files

The implementation of all input/output operations depends on the system on which Ada is running. Most implementations use a **location indicator** that specifies the current component of the file being accessed. A file is empty when created; it contains no file components, only an <eof> marker. Components may be added to the file, they may be examined, and—if random access is available—the components may be modified.

An empty file is created by the Ada procedure Create, which exists in each of the three I/O Packages (Text_IO, Sequential_IO, Direct_IO):

```
PROCEDURE Create ( file : In Out File_Type;
                   mode : In File_Mode := default_mode;
                   name : In String := "";
                   form : In String := "" );
```

The Create establishes a new external file named by name and associates this external file with the internal file named by file. The given file is left open. The mode of the given file is set to the given access mode. The default_mode for creating sequential files is the mode Out_File, meaning the file is intended for output only. The default for name, the external file name, is a null string which specifies that the file created is a temporary file and is not accessible on completion of the program containing the Create. The form specifies additional implementation-dependent file characteristics. The Create places an <eof> marker in the empty file with the location indicator positioned at the <eof> marker and allocates storage for a file buffer. The storage allocated for the file buffer is the size of one component of the file. The result of the execution of Create is shown in Figure 2.7.

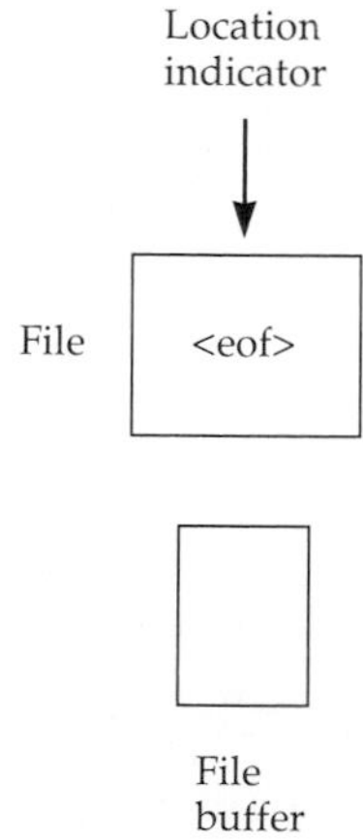

Figure 2.7
Result of Create

The exception Status_Error is raised if the file named in the Create is already open. The exception Name_Error is raised if name is not a proper string for naming an external file. The exception Use_Error is raised if the environment does not support creation of an external file with the given name and mode.

The file exam_scores declared earlier as a file of Integers is created as an empty file by the statement

```
Create ( exam_scores, OUT_FILE, "scores.exm" );
```

The external file named scores.exm is associated with the internal file name exam_scores as an output file (mode is OUT_FILE). The Create places an <eof> marker in the empty file with the location indicator positioned at the <eof> marker. If the file exam_scores was used before and contained components, the entire file contents are lost as the result of the Create command.

Create correctly positions the location indicator at the <eof> marker; the empty file is now ready for insertions. Each component is added at the end of the file immediately prior to the <eof> marker.

Adding a component to the file involves the Ada output procedure Write:

```
PROCEDURE Write ( file : In File_Type;
                  item : In Element_Type );
```

The value of item is written to the named file in a two-step process:

1. The item to be output to the file, whose type is the same as a component of the output file, is stored in the file buffer.
2. The item in the file buffer (one component in the file) is written to the external file.

The Write then advances the location indicator and places the <eof> marker at the end of the file again. Figure 2.8 depicts the movement of data to the external file. Each time a new element is written, it is written to the end of the file. The location indicator is advanced, and the <eof> marker is placed at the end of the file. The exception Mode_Error is raised if the mode is not OUT_FILE. The exception Use_Error is raised if the capacity of the external file is exceeded.

A component (the integer 92) is added to the declared file exam_scores with the statement

```
Write ( exam_scores, 92 );
```

The results are shown in Figure 2.9. The integer 92 is stored in the file.

Once the file has been created and components have been added, the file must be closed. The Close procedure

```
PROCEDURE Close ( file : In Out File_Type );
```

sets the specified file (whether an `IN_FILE` or an `OUT_FILE`) to a closed state by disassociating the internal and external file names, thus disabling further input or output associated with the file until a subsequent Open or Create is performed. The `Close` is not automatic at program termination but must be issued by the programmer. The `Close` records the file name in the file directory so that it can be located later. The exception `Status_Error` is raised if the given file is not open.

Figure 2.8
File output operation

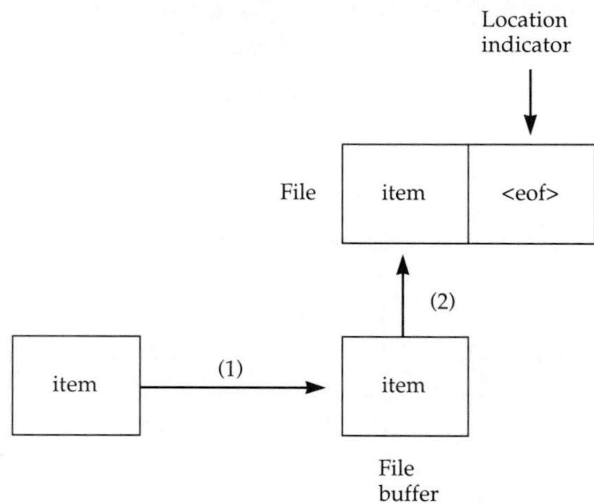

Figure 2.9
Results of output of *92* to file `exam_scores`

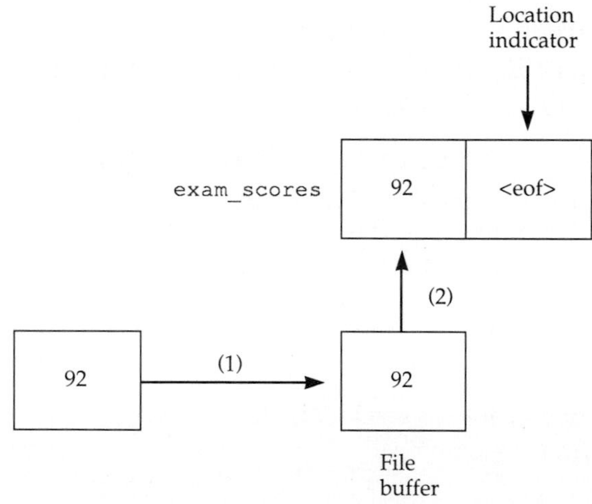

An Ada file is readied for input by calling the standard procedure `Open`:

```
PROCEDURE Open ( file : In Out File_Type;
                 mode : In File_Mode;
                 name : In String;
                 form : In String := "" );
```

The `Open` associates the internal name `file` with the external name `name`, positions the location indicator at the first component of the file, copies the first component of the file into the file buffer, and moves the location indicator to the second component. The result of the execution of the `Open` is shown in Figure 2.10. The exception `Status_Error` is raised if the given file is already open. The exception `Name_Error` is raised if no external file with the name `name` exists. The exception `Use_Error` is raised if the environment does not support opening an external file with the given `name` and `mode`.

The file `exam_scores`, which has one component (as Figure 2.9 shows), may be opened for access by the statement

```
Open ( exam_scores, IN_FILE, "scores.exm" );
```

As a result the first component of the file (92) is copied into the file buffer, and the location indicator moves to the second component (the <eof> marker). Figure 2.11 shows the result of the execution of this statement.

After a file has been opened, the file may be accessed to input one component at a time. The input operation involves two steps:

1. The contents of the file buffer in main memory are copied into an object in the program.
2. The next component from the file is copied into the file buffer.

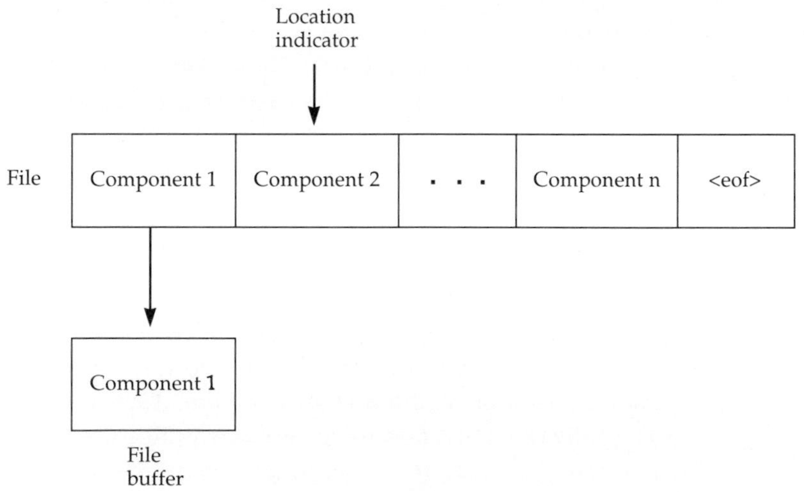

Figure 2.10
Result of `Open`

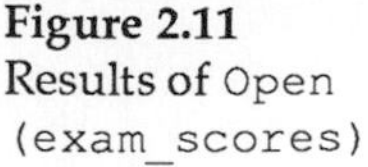

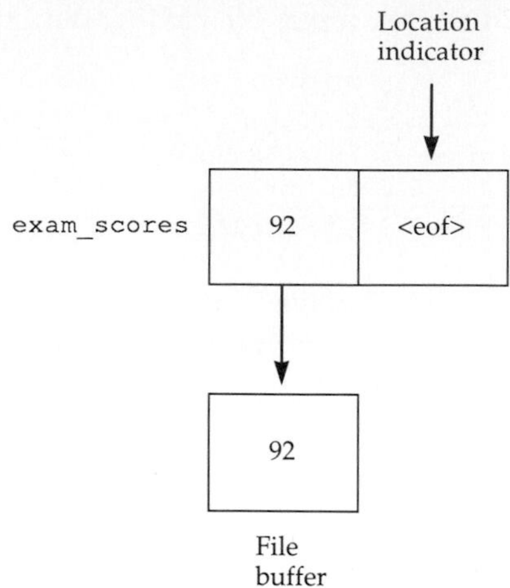

Figure 2.11
Results of `Open (exam_scores)`

The standard procedure `Read`

```
PROCEDURE Read ( file : In File_Type;
                 item : Out Element_Type );
```

inputs the component from the file buffer, returns the value in `item`, copies the component from the file indicated by the location indicator into the file buffer, and advances the location indicator to the next component. Figure 2.12 illustrates the input of data from the file. The exception `Mode_Error` is raised if the mode is not `IN_FILE`. The exception `End_Error` is raised if an attempt is made to read past the end of the file. The exception `Data_Error` is raised if the element read cannot be interpreted as a value of the type `Element_Type`.

After the file `exam_scores` has been opened, a component (an integer) is accessed with the statement

```
Read ( exam_scores, score );
```

Note that `score` must be declared an integer—the same as the file component type (`Element_Type`). The results of the execution are shown in Figure 2.13. The `Open` loads the first component of the file into the file buffer and positions the location indicator to the second component of the file. The `Read` copies the file buffer contents into the object `score`, fills the file buffer with the component pointed to by the location indicator (the second component), and advances the location indicator. If there are no more components, the location indicator points to the <eof> marker.

Figure 2.12
File input operation

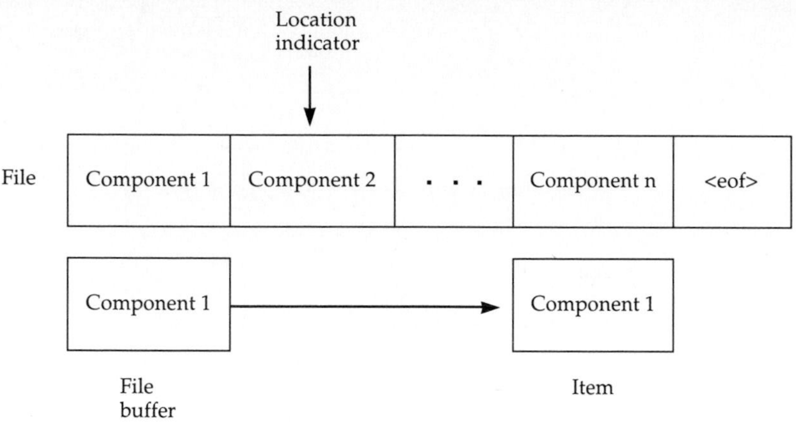

(a) First step of input operation.

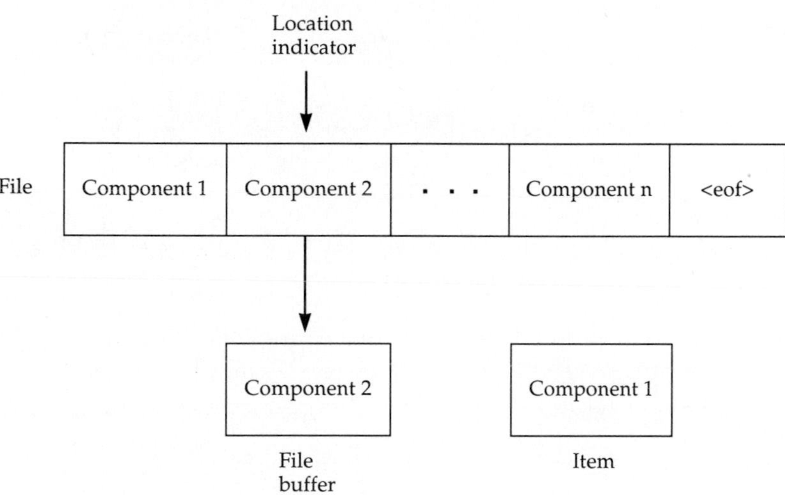

(b) Second step of input operation.

A program that reads a file needs to be able to detect when the end of the file has been reached. The Boolean function `End_Of_File` in the I/O package tests the contents of the file buffer.

```
FUNCTION End_Of_File ( file : In File_Type ) Return Boolean;
```

Figure 2.13
File input operation for file `exam_scores`

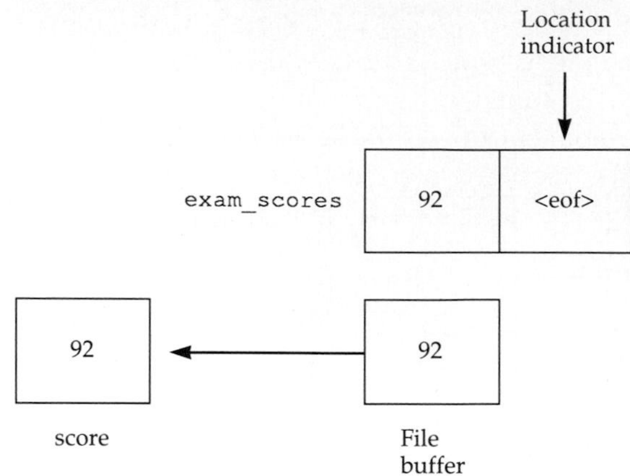

(a) First step of input operation.

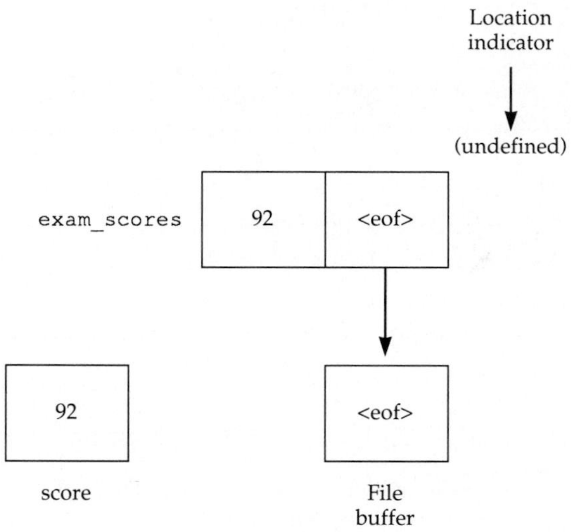

(b) Second step of input operation.

If the file buffer contains the <eof> marker, which indicates that the last component of the file has been accessed, the function `End_Of_File` returns `TRUE`; otherwise, the function returns `FALSE`. For example, in Figure 2.13, after the first component of the file `exam_scores` has been input, the file buffer contains the <eof> marker. The following program segment uses the function `End_Of_File` to determine when the last component has been accessed:

```
     WITH Sequential_IO;
     PROCEDURE Sample Is
         PACKAGE File_Of_Integer Is New Sequential_IO ( Integer );
         USE File_Of_Integer;
         exam_scores : File_Type;
         score : Integer;
     BEGIN  -- Sample
1        Open ( exam_scores, IN_FILE, "CS3533.dat" );
2        Loop
3            Exit When End_Of_file ( exam_scores );
4            Read ( exam_scores, score );
5        End Loop;
6        Close ( exam_scores );
     END Sample;
```

The `Open` in line 1 fills the file buffer with the first component (92) and positions the location indicator to the second component (<eof>). The function `End_Of_File` in line 3 tests the file buffer and does not find the <eof> marker; `End_Of_File` returns `FALSE`. The execution of the `Loop` body continues. The `Read` in line 4 inputs the file buffer contents (integer 92) into `score`, fills the file buffer with the next component (<eof>), and advances the location indicator. The function `End_Of_File` (line 3) is called again and returns `TRUE` since the file buffer does contain the <eof> marker. The `Loop` is exited.

Text Files

Ada provides facilities for input and output in human-readable form called a **text** file. The standard input file is usually the keyboard by default, and the standard output file is usually the CRT screen by default. Ada provides the declaration for the standard input and output text files, as well as I/O commands designed for use with text files in the package `Text_IO`.

For all programs that `WITH Text_IO`, the standard input and output text files are opened automatically at the beginning of program execution with the current modes of `IN_FILE` and `OUT_FILE`, respectively. The procedures `Create` and `Open` must not be used with the two standard files since these are called automatically. Procedures are provided in `Text_IO` to change the current default input and output files.

The data in a text file, regardless of data type, are stored as characters. The data stored in a **nontext** file are stored according to the internal storage formats of each data type. The characters in a text file are organized into lines that are much like the lines of data on a CRT screen. An end of line marker (<eoln>) is stored after each line of data. The end of a file is marked with the end of file marker (<eof>). That is, the last line of data is followed by an <eoln> marker, then an <eof> marker.

Additional text files may be declared using the predefined type `Text_IO.File_Type`.

```
WITH Text_IO;
PROCEDURE Sample Is
    new_text : Text_IO.File_Type;
BEGIN --Sample
--
    Null;
--
END Sample;
```

Several standard `Text_IO` procedures and functions are available in Ada for accessing text files only (for complete specification on all procedures and functions turn to Appendix A, which is Chapter 14 of the *Ada Language Reference Manual*). The specifications for some of the input and output procedures and functions for text files are shown below in template form, where brackets ([ ]) are used to indicate an option. Each option in the specifications is in reality a separate procedure or function. In other words, the procedure and function names may appear more than once; these subprogram names are said to be **overloaded**. The compiler resolves the apparent ambiguity by inspecting the number of parameters and the parameters' type.

```
PROCEDURE Put      ( [ file_identifier : In File_Type; ]
                     output_item : In <type_name> );
PROCEDURE Get      ( [ file_identifier : In File_Type; ]
                     input_item : Out <type_name> );
PROCEDURE Skip_Line [ ( [ file_identifier : In File_Type; ]
                         spacing : In Positive_Count := 1 ) ];
PROCEDURE Put_Line ( [ file_identifier : In File_Type; ]
                      string_item : In String );
PROCEDURE New_Line [ ( [ file_identifier : In File_Type; ]
                      spacing : In Positive_Count := 1 ) ];
PROCEDURE Get_Line ( [ file_identifier : In File_Type; ]
                      string_item : Out String;
                      last : Out Natural );
FUNCTION End_Of_Line [ (  file_identifier : In File_Type ) ]
                      Returns Boolean;
```

The `<type_name>` can be any scalar type such as String, Integer, or Float, or any subtype derived from these; Character; an enumeration type; or any fixed-point type. The parameter `output_item` is a single variable, constant, or expression of information to output; `input_item` is a single object (not a constant or expression) that is initialized during input.

The input_item and output_item used in the Get and Put procedures can be the types Character, String, numeric types, and enumeration types. The Get and Put for Character and String data types are procedures within Text_IO. Input and output of data of type Integer requires the instantiation of a generic package Integer_IO that is included in Text_IO. Similarly, input and output of fixed- and floating-point data values requires instantiation of the generic packages Float_IO and Fixed_IO that are included in Text_IO. The following is an example of the instantiation of all three packages:

```
WITH Text_IO;
PROCEDURE Sample Is
    Type Fixed is Delta 0.125 Range 0.0 .. 255.0;
    PACKAGE Int_IO Is New Text_IO.Integer_IO ( Integer );
    PACKAGE Flt_IO Is New Text_IO.Float_IO ( Float );
    PACKAGE Fxd_IO Is New Text_IO.Fixed_IO ( Fixed );
```

The following statements output an integer, a float, and a fixed value using the respective Put procedures.

```
BEGIN -- Sample
    Int_IO.Put ( new_text, 95 );
    Flt_IO.Put ( new_text, 23.45 );
    Fxd_IO.Put ( new_text, 125.375 );
END Sample;
```

Input and output of enumeration types uses the generic package Enumeration_IO included in Text_IO. The following statements instantiate Enumeration_IO, outputs a Boolean value, and inputs an enumerated type:

```
WITH Text_IO;
PROCEDURE Sample Is
    TYPE Status_Type  Is ( DIVORCED, MARRIED, SINGLE, WIDOWED );
    PACKAGE Bool_IO   Is New Text_IO.Enumeration_IO ( Boolean );
    PACKAGE Status_IO Is New Text_IO.Enumeration_IO ( Status_Type );
    status : Status_Type;
BEGIN -- Sample
    Bool_IO.Put ( new_text, TRUE );
    Status_IO.Get ( new_text, status );
END Sample;
```

One of the output operations for a text file in Ada is the Put procedure:

```
PROCEDURE Put ( [ file_identifier : In File_Type; ]
                output_item : In <type_name> );
```

The data written to a text file must be character data because the definition of text is a file of characters. Since the output_item listed may be any of the types mentioned above, the noncharacter data items are converted from internal form to character form before being stored in the output file. The statements

```
Create ( new_text, OUT_FILE, "data.txt" );
Int_IO.Put ( new_text, 95 );
```

create `new_text` as an empty file, automatically convert the integer **95** to the character string "95", and output "95" to `new_text` (the character 9 may be preceded by leading blanks, depending on the maximum width of the generic parameter used in the instantiation of `Integer_IO`.)

One of the input procedures for a text file in Ada is the `Get` procedure:

```
PROCEDURE Get ( [ file_identifier : In File_Type; ]
                input_item : Out <type_name> );
```

The data input from the text file are in character form and are automatically converted to internal form according to the type of `input_item`.

If the text file `new_text` is closed and opened with

```
Close ( new_text );
Open ( new_text, IN_FILE, "data.txt" );
```

the data in the file can then be accessed with the `Get` procedure:

```
Int_IO.Get ( new_text, number );
```

The object `number` must be declared as an integer. To form an integer in the object `number`, the characters are input—one at a time—from the text file and converted to internal integers until a blank or nondigit character is found. Since the data in `new_text` are the character string "95", the character '9' is input, converted to an integer 9, and then multiplied by 10. The next character, '5', is input, converted to an integer 5, added to the previous calculation to form the integer value 95 in internal format, and stored in the object `number`.

Since characters in a text file are grouped into lines of characters and terminated by <eoln>, several standard `Text_IO` procedures in Ada involve the <eoln> marker. The `New_Line` procedure

```
PROCEDURE New_Line [ ( [ file_identifier : In File_Type; ]
                     spacing : In Positive_Count := 1 ) ];
```

outputs an <eoln> marker (usually a carriage return and line feed) to the output file. This causes the next output to start on a new line in the output file. The `Put_Line` procedure,

```
PROCEDURE Put_Line ( [ file_identifier : In File_Type; ]
                     string_item : In String );
```

performs the same steps as the `Put` and `New_Line` combined but only accepts a data item of type String. The `Skip_Line` procedure,

```
PROCEDURE Skip_Line [ ( [ file_identifier : In File_Type; ]
                      spacing : In Positive_Count := 1 ) ];
```

moves the location indicator in the file past the <eoln> marker to the first character on the next line of data. Any data on the current data line are skipped in the process of moving to the next line of data. The `Get_Line` procedure,

```
PROCEDURE Get_Line ( [ file_identifier : In File_Type; ]
                     string_item : Out String;
                     last : Out Natural );
```

performs the same steps as the `Get` and `Skip_Line` combined but only accepts a data item of type String. The variable `last` is the index value of the last character replaced in `string_item`.

A program that reads a text file needs to determine when the end of a line of data has been reached. The standard `Text_IO` function `End_Of_Line`,

```
FUNCTION End_Of_Line [ ( file_identifier : In File_Type ) ]
                     Returns Boolean;
```

checks the component pointed to by the location indicator. If the location indicator points to the <eoln> or <eof> marker, which indicates that the end of this line of data has been reached, the function `End_Of_Line` returns `TRUE`; otherwise, `End_Of_Line` returns `FALSE`. The following program segment uses `End_Of_Line` to test the file `new_text` (containing 95 <eoln> <eof>) and to determine when the last character of the line has been accessed.

```
    WITH Text_IO;
    USE  Text_IO;
    PROCEDURE Sample Is
         ch       : Character;
         new_text : File_Type;
    BEGIN  -- Sample
1       Open ( new_text, IN_FILE, "DATA.TXT");
2       Loop
3           Exit When End_Of_Line ( new_text );
4           Get ( new_text, ch );
5       End Loop;
6       Close ( new_text );
    END Sample;
```

The `Open` in line 1 fills the file buffer with the first character (9) from the file and positions the location indicator at the second component (5). The function `End_Of_Line` in line 3 tests the file buffer and does not find the <eoln> marker, so it returns `FALSE`. The execution of the `Loop` body continues in line 4. The `Get` inputs the character 9 from the file buffer into the object `ch`, fills the file buffer with the next character (5), and advances the location indicator. The function `End_Of_Line` is called again (line 3), and again it returns `FALSE`. The body of the `Loop` continues with the `Get` procedure, which inputs the character 5 into the object `ch`, fills the file buffer with the <eoln> marker, and advances the location indicator to point to the <eof> marker. The function `End_Of_Line` is called, and it returns `TRUE` since the <eoln> marker has been reached. The `Loop` is exited.

A file containing several lines of data can be accessed by a program using `Open`, `Get`, `End_Of_Line`, and `End_Of_File`.

```
WITH Text_IO;
USE  Text_IO;
PROCEDURE Sample Is
    ch       : Character;
    new_text : File_Type;
BEGIN  -- Sample
    Open ( new_text, IN_FILE, "DATA.TXT");
    Loop
        Exit When End_Of_File ( new_text );
        Loop
            Exit When End_Of_Line ( new_text );
            Get ( new_text, ch );
        End Loop;
        Skip_Line ( new_text );
    End Loop;
    Close ( new_text );
END Sample;
```

`Skip_Line` is required after the `Exit When End_Of_Line` loop to skip over the <eoln> marker and to reposition the location indicator to the first character of the next line of data in the file.

Several exceptions may be raised by the `Get` and `Put` procedures. The `Status_Error` is raised by the procedures `Get`, `Get_Line`, `Put`, and `Put_Line` if the file is not open. The exception `Mode_Error` is raised by the procedures `Get` and `Get_Line` if the mode of the file is not `IN_FILE`, and by the procedures `Put` and `Put_Line` if the mode of the file is not `OUT_FILE`. The exception `End_Error` is raised by a `Get` procedure if an attempt is made to read past the end of the file. The exception `Data_Error` is raised by a `Get` procedure if the character sequence input does not correspond to the type of `input_item`.

For the standard input and output text files in Ada, the file name need not be specified. The standard input file is the default file name for `Get`, `Get_Line`, `Skip_Line`, `End_Of_Line`, and `End_Of_File`; the standard output file, is the default file name for `Put`, `Put_Line`, and `New_Line`. The programmer must specify the file name of additional external text files to override these defaults.

When using the standard input file, the calls to the procedures `Get`, `Skip_line`, and `Get_Line` and the function `End_Of_Line` can be simplified as

```
Get ( input_item );
Skip_Line;
Get_Line ( string_item, last );
End_Of_Line
```

The `Open` is performed automatically. Similarly, when using the standard output file, the calls to the procedures `Put`, `Put_Line`, and `New_Line` can be simplified as

```
Put ( output_item );
Put_Line ( string_item );
New_Line;
```

The `Create` is performed automatically.

The following program inputs exam scores from the standard input and creates a nontext file of exam scores:

```
    WITH Sequential_IO;
    WITH Text_IO;
    USE Text_IO;
    PROCEDURE Create Is
        PACKAGE File_Of_Integer Is New Sequential_IO ( Integer );
        USE File_Of_Integer;
        PACKAGE Int_IO Is New Integer_IO ( Integer );
        USE Int_IO;
        exam_scores : File_Of_Integer.File_Type;
        score : Integer;
    BEGIN  -- Create
1       Create ( exam_scores, OUT_FILE, "scores.exm" );
2       Loop
3           Exit When End_Of_File;
4           Get ( score );
5           Skip_Line;
6           Write ( exam_scores, score );
7       End Loop;
8       Close ( exam_scores );
    END Create;
```

`Get` in line 4 accepts a value in character form from the keyboard, converts it to an internal integer (using the `Int_IO.Get`), and stores it in `score`. Statement 6 writes the internal integer to the nontext file (using `File_Of_Integer.Write`).

The file `exam_scores` can be accessed and output to the CRT screen using the following program:

```
    WITH Sequential_IO;
    WITH Text_IO;
    USE Text_IO;
    PROCEDURE List Is
        PACKAGE File_Of_Integer Is New Sequential_IO ( Integer );
        USE File_Of_Integer;
        PACKAGE Int_IO Is New Integer_IO ( Integer );
        USE Int_IO;
        exam_scores : File_Of_Integer.File_Type;
        score : Integer;
    BEGIN  -- List
1       Open ( exam_scores, IN_FILE, "scores.exm" );
2       Loop
3           Exit When End_Of_file ( exam_scores );
4           Read ( exam_scores, score );
5           Put ( score );
6           New_Line;
7       End Loop;
8       Close ( exam_scores );
    END List;
```

Statement 4 inputs a score from the file `exam_scores` without conversion (`File_Of_Integer.Read`); it is already in internal form. Statement 5

(Int_IO.Put) converts the score to a character string and writes on the CRT screen.

CASE STUDY 2.2

In Record Example 2 an array of 10,000 student records required more main memory than was available. A common solution is to store the 10,000 records in an external file and access each record one at a time. The specification of a package, which describes the student record that can be used by all programs that reference a file of student records, is shown below:

```
PACKAGE Student_Data Is
   TYPE Names Is Record
                 last   : String ( 1 .. 15 );
                 first  : String ( 1 .. 15 );
                 middle : Character;
              End Record;
   TYPE Addresses Is Record
                    home   : String ( 1 .. 50 );
                    campus : String ( 1 .. 50 );
                 End Record;
   TYPE Phone Is Record
                 area_code : Integer Range 200 ..  999;
                 exchange  : Integer Range 200 ..  999;
                 number    : Integer Range   0 .. 9999;
              End Record;
   TYPE Class Is Record
                 course_number : String ( 1 .. 6 );
                 room_number   : String ( 1 .. 4 );
                 meeting_time  : Integer;
              End Record;
   TYPE Class_List Is Array ( 1 .. 6 ) Of Class;
   TYPE Student Is Record
                   name         : Names;
                   address      : Addresses;
                   phone_number : Phone;
                   classes      : Class_List;
                End Record;
END Student_Data;
```

The student file is created from a text file (standard input file) with the following program:

```
WITH Sequential_IO, Text_IO, Student_Data;
USE Text_IO, Student_Data;
PROCEDURE Create Is
   PACKAGE File_Of_Student Is New Sequential_IO ( Student );
   USE File_Of_Student;
   PACKAGE Int_IO Is New Text_IO.Integer_IO ( Integer );
   last : Natural;
   one_student : Student;
   student_file : File_Of_Student.File_Type;
```

```
PROCEDURE Input_Student_Data ( one_student : Out Student ) Is
BEGIN
    Get ( one_student.name.last );
    Get ( one_student.name.first );
    Get ( one_student.name.middle );
    Skip_Line;

    one_student.address.home := ( 1 .. 50 => ' ');
    Get_Line ( one_student.address.home, last );
    If last >= 50 Then
        Skip_Line;
    End If;
    one_student.address.campus := ( 1 .. 50 => ' ');
    Get_Line ( one_student.address.campus, last );
    If last >= 50 Then
        Skip_Line;
    End If;

    Int_IO.Get ( one_student.phone_number.area_code );
    Int_IO.Get ( one_student.phone_number.exchange );
    Int_IO.Get ( one_student.phone_number.number );
    Skip_Line;

    For index In 1 .. Class_List'Last Loop
        Declare
            one class : Class Renames one_student.classes(index);
        Begin
            Get ( one_class.course_number );
            Get ( one_class.room_number );
            Int_IO.Get ( one_class.meeting_time );
            Skip_Line;
        End;
    End Loop;
END Input_Student_Data;

PROCEDURE Print_Student_Data ( one_student : In Student ) Is
BEGIN
    Put ( one_student.name.last );
    Put ( one_student.name.first );
    Put ( one_student.name.middle );
    New_Line;
    Put_Line ( one_student.address.campus );
    Put_Line ( one_student.address.home );
    Put ( "(" );
    Int_IO.Put ( one_student.phone_number.area_code, 3 );
    Put ( ") " );
    Int_IO.Put ( one_student.phone_number.exchange, 3 );
    Put ( "-" );
    If one_student.phone_number.number > 999 Then
        Null;
    ElsIf one_student.phone_number.number > 99 Then
        Put ( "0" );
    ElsIf one_student.phone_number.number > 9 Then
        Put ( "00" );
    Else
        Put ( "000" );
    End If;
    Int_IO.Put ( one_student.phone_number.number, 1 );
```

```
        New_Line;
        For index In 1 .. Class_List'Last Loop
            Declare
                one_class : Class Renames one_student.classes(index);
            Begin
                Put ( one_class.course_number );
                Put ( "  " );
                Put ( one_class.room_number );
                Put ( "  " );
                Int_IO.Put ( one_class.meeting_time, 0 );
                New_Line;
            End;
        End Loop;
        New_Line;
    END Print_Student_Data;

    BEGIN  -- Create
        Create ( student_file, OUT_FILE, "Student.Dat" );
        Loop
            Exit When Text_IO.End_Of_File;
            Input_Student_Data ( one_student );
            Write ( student_file, one_student );
        End Loop;

        Reset ( student_file, IN_FILE );
        Loop
            Exit When End_Of_File ( student_file );
            Read ( student_file, one_student );
            Print_Student_Data ( one_student );
        End Loop;
        Close ( student_file );
    END Create;
```

Once the nontext file `student_file` is created, another program can input the file (using `Read`) and copy it to a backup file. The following program is the solution:

```
    WITH Sequential_IO, Student_Data;
    USE Student_Data;
    PROCEDURE Backup Is
        PACKAGE File_Of_Student Is New Sequential_IO ( Student );
        USE File_Of_Student;
        one_student : Student;
        backup_file,
        student_file : File_Of_Student.File_Type;
    BEGIN  -- Backup
        Create ( backup_file, OUT_FILE, "Student.Bak" );
        Open ( student_file, IN_FILE, "Student.Dat" );
        Loop
            Exit When End_Of_File ( student_file );
            Read ( student_file, one_student );
            Write ( backup_file, one_student );
        End Loop;
        Close ( backup_file );
        Close ( student_file );
    END Backup;
```

A total of 209 bytes for each record are copied from `student_file` to `backup_file` without any data conversion. The input file is a nontext file, so the input procedure `Read` in the `File_of_Student` package is used instead of the lengthy procedure `Input_Student_Data` required in the `Create` program. Both are nontext files of the same type; the transfer is simpler and more efficient (no data conversions are necessary) than it would be if these were text files.

SUMMARY

Arrays are a useful data structure for storing data of the same type. Parallel arrays are the only structure available in some programming languages for storing data of differing types. Accessing parallel arrays is more complicated than accessing records. The record data structure is a collection of data of different types accessed by a single name. Arrays of records allow related data to be stored in contiguous memory locations. The entire record of related data and any individual component of the record may be referenced. The record data structure may have nested record types and array types within it. Variant records are available in Ada. They allow the programmer to declare additional fields that depend on the values of other fields in a record.

Files are a useful data structure for storing large collections of data on nonvolatile secondary storage devices. Files allow greater flexibility in storing large data sets than arrays within a particular program. Text files in Ada store all data—numeric and nonnumeric data—in character form in lines. Nontext files in Ada store all data according to the internal storage formats for the data types. The component type of a file must be fixed, but a file may be any type available in Ada.

Key Terms

array
component
discriminant
exception
exception handler
external file
location indicator
named aggregate
nontext file
positional aggregate
raise
record aggregate
record data structure
record data type
renames clause
text file
variant part
variant record

Exercises

1. Assume that a Character scalar occupies 1 byte of memory, an Integer scalar occupies 2 bytes, and a Float scalar occupies 4 bytes. Specify the total number of bytes occupied by the data structure named `block` as declared in parts a and b.

a.
```
TYPE Block   Is Record
                    hunk_1 : Integer;
                    hunk_2 : Integer;
                End Record;
```

b.
```
TYPE Block   Is Record
                    chunk   : String ( 1 .. 10 );
                    sector  : Integer;
                    section : Float;
                End Record;
```

c.
```
TYPE Portions Is Record
                     portion_1 : Character;
                     portion_2 : Integer;
                     portion_3 : Float;
                 End Record;
TYPE Block   Is Array ( 'A' .. 'D' ) Of Portions;
```

d.
```
TYPE Part_2_Record Is Record
                          part_2_1 : Integer;
                          part_2_2 : String ( 1 .. 3 );
                      End Record;
TYPE Part_2_Array Is Array ( 1 .. 2 ) Of Part_2_Record;
TYPE Part_1_1_Record Is Record
                            part_1_1_1 : Character;
                            part_1_1_2 : Integer;
                        End Record;
TYPE Part_1_Record Is Record
                          part_1_1 : Part_1_1_Record;
                          part_1_2 : Character;
                      End Record;
TYPE Block   Is Record
                    part_1 : Part_1_Record;
                    part_2 : Part_2_Array;
                End Record;
```

2. Specify the number of bytes in `block.part_1.part_1_1` in d of question 1.

3. Specify the number of bytes in `block.part_1` in d of question 1.

4. Given the following definition and declarations

```
TYPE Period Is Record
                   month,
                   days,
                   year   : Integer;
               End Record;
```

```
TYPE Time Is Record
                 month,
                 days,
                 year   : Integer;
             End Record;
interval,
passage  : Period;
snows_of_yesteryear : Time;
```

determine if a through e are legal or illegal. Explain why a statement is illegal.

a. `Period := Time;`

b. `passage := interval;`

c. `snows_of_yesteryear := passage;`

d. `snows_of_yesteryear := interval;`

e. `passage := Period;`

5. Given the following declarations

```
TYPE Sex_Types Is ( FEMALE, MALE );
TYPE Departments Is ( ACCOUNTING, LEGAL, PRODUCTION, SALES);
TYPE Employee Is Record
                     name : String ( 1 .. 30 );
                     age  : Integer;
                     wage : Float;
                     sex  : Sex_Types;
                     dept : Departments;
                 End Record;
worker : Array ( 1 .. 100 ) Of Employee;
```

list the Ada reference and the type of data referenced for each of the descriptions below.

a. all information for employee #6

b. the age of worker #13

c. the third letter of the name of worker #62

d. the entire name of worker #71

6. Code a record structure in Ada that contains a 30-character name and a Boolean identifier named `financial_aid`. Use a variant record so that two float variables, `current` and `total` will be allocated to those records when `financial_aid` is `TRUE`.

Match the following descriptions to the appropriate term in exercises 7 through 10.

a. used to reference the entire record of information
b. a single component of a record structure
c. used to access a field within a record structure
d. a data structure in which a component of the record is an array

e. a data structure in which each element of the array is a record structure

7. record_name.field_name
8. field
9. array of records
10. record_name
11. Determine whether each statement below is true or false.
    a. A record structure declaration starts with a Begin statement.
    b. Several fields of different types may be declared within a record.
    c. The types of the fields within the record may be any standard or enumerated scalar types.
    d. The type of the fields within the record may be any data structure such as an array or record.
    e. A record structure declaration is terminated with an End Record statement.
12. Study each procedure or function below. Mark **TEXT** if the subprogram may be used with text files in Ada and mark **NONTEXT** if it may be used with nontext files. Some items can be used with both.
    a. `End_Of_File`
    b. `End_Of_Line`
    c. `Read`
    d. `Write`
    e. `Get`
    f. `Skip_Line`
    g. `Get_Line`
    h. `Open`
    i. `Create`
    j. `Put`
    k. `Put_Line`
    l. `New_Line`

Match the following terms to the appropriate statement in exercises 13 through 23:

a. file
b. text files
c. nontext files
d. file buffer

13. a file stored on an external storage device that is created and used by Ada programs only and cannot be accessed by a text editor
14. a file of characters
15. accessed by the procedures Get and Put
16. filled by the procedures Open and Create
17. a structured data type containing a sequence of elements of identical type with only one element available at a time
18. used when accessing components of files
19. a file containing numeric information in internal representation form rather than character form
20. accessed by the procedures Read and Write
21. a file in which each line of characters is separated from the next by an end of line separator
22. a file containing numeric information in character form
23. is initialized to the first component of the file by the Open procedure

Programming Problems

1. Write a program which will store and update a small telephone directory in memory in the form of a singly linked list of records. Print the original directory. Then make some insertions and deletions and print the final directory. Use any format for input and output you desire. For example, the header and the elements may be stored as follows:

	Title	**Pointer**
Header	Telephone Directory	2000

Location		**Information**		**Pointer**
2000	Abel, J. G	110 Oakleaf	236-4010	2013
2013	Baker, Sue	409 Sunset	784-1182	2026
2026	Carter, L. H.	17 Bernay	785-1365	2078
2039	Minte, Al	204 Pine	236-7295	2052
2052	Pont, M. R.	1 Market	480-1027	2065
2065	Sands, T. H.	671 First	784-8240	—
2078	Lang, Al	311 Moss	236-1111	2039

To solve the problem complete the steps that follow:

a. Input an initial list. Each record should contain:
name (last, first, middle)
street address
phone number
Store the input data in a singly linked list of records.

b. Produce an initial list in alphabetical order. Allow one line in each entry for name, street address, and phone number. Include the appropriate headings.

c. Input update records.

  code ('I' for insert, 'D' for delete)
  name (last, first, middle)
  street address
  phone number

Each record represents a change. Insert the entries in alphabetical order by last name.

d. Produce a list after update records have been processed in alphabetical order. Allow one line for each entry for name, street address, and phone number. Include the appropriate headings.

2. Implement the following improvements to the program in problem 1:

a. Use double-linked lists.

b. Add linked list for phone numbers in ascending order and list output by phone number.

c. Add linked list for each exchange and list output by exchange.

3. Write a program that, when given the taxable income for a single taxpayer, will compute the income tax for that person. Use Schedule X shown below. Assume that line 37 contains the taxable income.

SCHEDULE X Single Taxpayers

Use this Schedule if you checked File Status Box 1 on Form 1040.

If the amount on Form 1040, line 37 is over	*But not over*	*Enter on Form 1040, line 38:*	*Of the amount over*
$0	$2,300	–0–	$0
2,300	3,400	0 + 11%	2,300
3,400	4,400	$121 + 13%	3,400
4,400	8,500	251 + 15%	4,400
8,500	10,800	866 + 17%	8,500
10,800	12,900	1,257 + 19%	10,800
12,900	15,000	1,656 + 21%	12,900
15,000	18,200	2,097 + 24%	15,000
18,200	23,500	2,865 + 28%	18,200
23,500	28,800	4,349 + 32%	23,500
28,800	34,100	6,045 + 36%	28,800
34,100	41,500	7,953 + 40%	34,100
41,500	55,300	10,913 + 45%	41,500
55,300		17,123 + 50%	55,300

Example: If the individual's taxable income is $8,192, the program should use the tax amount and percent shown in column 3 of the line for amounts over $4,400. The tax in this case is

$251.00 + 0.15 (8192.00 - 4400.00) = $819.80

The input to the program is a text file (INCOME) with one individual's taxable income per line.

The output from the program should be the taxable income input and the total tax for each line input.

To solve the problem, store the tax table in a text file (TAXRATE). Set up an array of records in which each record will hold the three values from one row of the tax table: the tax base, the tax percent, and the excess base (for example, $251, 15%, $4,400). The file TAXRATE will have three values per line (base, percent, excess). Given the taxable income, search the excess values for the correct index to be used for the tax base and percentage.

4. Write a program that will input information about marital status and will store the data in an array of variant records. Input changes in marital status, and modify the data in the array. To solve the problem, complete the steps that follow:

   a. Input data in this form, storing the data in an array of variant records:

      name (20 characters)
      age (integer)
      sex ('F' or 'M')
      marital status ('M', 'D', or 'W')
      (only for married, 'M'):
         length of marriage (integer)
         number of children (integer)
         spouse's name (20 characters)

      (only for divorced, 'D'):
         divorce date (mmddyy)

      (only for widowed, 'W'):
         year of death (mmddyy)

   b. Input the following changes:

      name (20 characters)
      new status ('M', 'D', or 'W')
      (for 'M'): length, number of children, and spouse's name

(for 'D'): divorce date
(for 'W'): year of death

and make the appropriate changes to the array of records.

c. Output the array of updated information.

5. Write a program that will input student data and will store the data in an array of variant records. Input the names and graduation dates of students who have recently become seniors, and change the data in the array. To solve the problem, complete the steps that follow:

   a. Input student information in the following form:

      name (20 characters)
      sex ('F' or 'M')
      classification (1, 2, 3, or 4)
      (only if freshman, 1): date first enrolled (mmddyy)
      (only if senior, 4): graduation date (mmddyy)

   b. Update the data to input the following information about seniors:

      name (20 characters)
      graduation date (mmddyy)

   c. Output the revised array.

6. Write a program to (a) prepare a nontext file of student records from a text file, and (b) print a grade report from the nontext file.

   a. Input a text file of student data containing the following information for each student:

      student number (integer)
      student name (22 characters)
      number of courses (integer)
      course 1 information:
         course code (5 characters)
         credit hours (integer)
         grade (1 character)
      course 2 information
      course 3 information
      course 4 information
      course 5 information
      course 6 information
      course 7 information

      Output a nontext file of student records with the same data as the text file.

b. Input the nontext file created in problem 6a.

Produce a grade report that contains the student number, name, course information, and the average (float) for each student. Assign grade points to grades as follows:

A = 4
B = 3
C = 2
D = 1
F = 0

At the end of the report, print the number of students in the file, the percent who passed, the percent who failed, and the overall average.

7. Write a program to (a) prepare a nontext file of part records from a text file, and (b) print a part report from the nontext file.

   a. Input a text file of part data containing the following information for each part:

      record code (1 character)
      part number (10 characters)
      part description (26 characters)
      part price (real)

      Create the nontext file of part records with the same data as the text file but omit the record code.

   b. Input the nontext file created in problem 7a. Produce a part report listing the part number, description, and price. At the end of the report, print the number of parts in the file, the lowest price in the file, the highest price in the file, and the overall average of prices in the file.

8. Write a program that will merge the salary data from a file of male employees with the salary data from a file of female employees into a third file. Retain the ascending order of employee numbers. For each employee (component) on the two input files, include an employee number (4 digits), an employee name (20 characters), and an employee salary (a real number).

   Input a sequential file (MEN) of records with salary data and a sequential file (WOMEN) of records with salary data.

For each employee (component), create a record containing the employee number, employee name, employee salary, and a letter (F or M) indicating the sex of the employee. Output the record to a nontext file.

Produce a listing of the nontext file created with appropriate headings.

Chapter 3

Blocking and Buffering

CHAPTER CONTENTS

PREVIEW

THIS CHAPTER DISCUSSES THE EFFICIENCY of blocking and buffering. Accessing blocked files and buffered files requires fewer I/O operations and less processing time. Chapter 4 discusses the relationships among blocking and buffering, hardware, and access times. The discussion in this chapter measures efficiency only in terms of the number of I/O accesses. Chapter 3 also presents algorithms that illustrate blocking and deblocking.

BLOCKING

Components of a file are usually quite small when compared with the total capacity of most secondary storage devices. Accessing one component at a time, as directed by an Ada program, can be very inefficient for the Central Processing Unit (CPU) of the computer. The time required for the processing of a component is often much less than the amount of time needed to read it from the file or write it to the file. Accessing secondary storage takes longer than accessing main memory—even for small components. One way to improve the execution time of a program that accesses a file is by **blocking** components on a file.

A **block** is the smallest amount of data that can be read from or written to a secondary storage device at a time. A block is simply a group of data that consists of several file components of information. By grouping several components into one block—a process called **blocking** components—several components (one block) can be accessed from the file at a time. The result is that fewer accesses retrieve the entire file of components. Reducing the number of physical accesses (input or output operations to the file) reduces the execution time of a program accessing the file.

Suppose we wish to input an entire file of 10,000 components. With a block containing only one component, 10,000 input operations are required. If we employ a blocking factor of 10—a block containing 10 components—the entire file contains 1,000 blocks of 10 components each and could be input with 1,000 input operations. We could further enhance efficiency by employing a blocking factor of 100. In this case the file is input with accesses to 100 blocks of 100 components each. Of course the most efficient way of blocking the 10,000 components places all 10,000 in one block; only one input operation inputs the 10,000 components.

BLOCK SIZE LIMITATIONS

Obviously, the larger the blocking factor, the fewer the number of physical accesses necessary. A number of considerations affect block size, however. One of the primary limitations is the size of available main memory. The size of one block, which is the amount of data transferred to or from the file during an access, cannot exceed the amount of main memory available. As a result, storing all the components in one block is probably unrealistic unless the file has a small number of components.

The programs that use files constitute another important consideration. Each program requires space in main memory for internal data and instructions in addition to space for one block of data for each open file. The sum of these three cannot exceed the amount of main memory allocated for the execution of the program. Each program that accesses the file may vary greatly in the size of internal data and instructions. The program using the largest amount of main memory is a determining factor in setting the block size.

The accesses to a file constitute another consideration in determining the block size. When accessing a single component from a file of blocked components, the entire block that contains that single component must be accessed. If the component is updated, then the entire block must be output back to the external file. If the block size is large compared to the component size, this presents a disadvantage: we must access a large block of data to update one component. Suppose we plan to access several components within a short time of each other. If we group these components in one block—a practice called **clustering**—the disadvantage of accessing the entire block is diminished. When deciding whether to cluster and determining block size, consider not only the frequency of access expected for a file, but also the required response time for a given access. The time to access the next block depends on how far the next block to be read is from the last block read. Ordering accesses to match the order of components in the file can reduce access time per block.

The characteristics of the external storage devices used to store a file of blocked components is a fourth consideration for block size. Access time to a block can be improved by making one block the same size as a track of data (if cylinder-track architecture is used) or a sector of data (if sector addressing is used). External storage devices are discussed in detail in Chapter 4.

SINGLE BUFFERING

Blocking components in a file can decrease execution time because programs access a block of several components each time instead of accessing one component at a time. Blocking presents a problem when writing programs that access the blocked file since Ada programs access one component (usually a record from the file) at a time. A software interface reconciles blocked components with the processing of Ada. Employing such an interface is called **buffering**.

A buffering interface is of one of two types: a deblocking routine or a blocking routine. When reading a blocked file, a **deblocking routine** is the interface that accesses one block from the file and sends one component at a time to the program. When writing to a blocked file, a **blocking routine** stores the components from the program in a buffer in main memory. The buffer's size is the size of one block. The act of writing the components to a block-size buffer is called a **logical write**. When the buffer is full, the block is physically output to the external file in a process called a **physical write**.

Buffering Input

The deblocking routine is executed by the I/O channel of a computer. The I/O channel directs a device control unit to input or output data for the specified device. All input/output operations are handled by the I/O channel, so the CPU simply processes data and directs the I/O channel to access a particular device. The deblocking routine includes the following steps:

1. If the buffer is not empty, go to step 6.
2. The CPU issues an input request.
3. The I/O channel signals the device controller for the device specified in the input request.
4. The device controller locates the requested information and starts reading bytes from the device and sending them to the buffer in main memory.
5. The I/O channel waits until the buffer is filled, then signals the CPU that the input operation is complete. The location indicator for the buffer is set to 1.
6. The next component to which the location indicator points is sent to the program.
7. The location indicator is incremented.
8. The CPU continues to execute the program.

Each input operation performed on the file reads one block of data. Each read is termed a **physical read** since the file is physically accessed. Each input operation issued by a program logically accesses one component of the blocked file from the buffer. The input statement, Read/Get, issued by the program is termed a **logical read** since the file is not accessed physically. Rather, the next component is accessed logically from the buffer. Each input statement issued by the program is a logical read from the buffer until the buffer is empty. Then the logical read is translated to a physical read. The net effect is that every *n*th input statement (where *n* is the blocking factor) is translated to a physical read.

Suppose a file has 10 components in one block. The first input statement issued by the program accesses the buffer logically. The buffer is empty, which causes a block to be input from the file (a physical read) into a buffer in main memory. The first component in the buffer is sent to the program. Figure 3.1 shows the result of the first logical read. The next nine input statements simply retrieve the next component from the buffer in main memory as Figure 3.2 shows. This process is a memory access (a logical read) rather than a physical read from the external device. The deblocking routine keeps a location indicator, which points to the next component to be accessed from the buffer. The routine retrieves that component from the buffer, then passes it on to the program. When an input statement is issued and all the components in the buffer have been accessed, the next block of data from the file is input into the buffer in main memory, and the first component in the buffer is sent to the program (see Figure 3.3). The deblocking routine interfaces the storage of data on the file and the accesses of the program. As a result, we can block the components on the external file to save access time. In this example we use one physical read for 10 components, and the program accesses one component at a time using 10 logical reads.

Buffering Output

The blocking routine is executed similarly by the I/O channel. As a result, a program can output one component at a time to the buffer and block components in the file. The blocking routine includes the following steps:

1. The next component from the program is stored in the buffer in the space to which the number of components points.
2. Increment number of components.
3. If the buffer is not full, go to step 8.
4. The CPU issues an output request.
5. The I/O channel signals the device controller for the device specified in the output request.

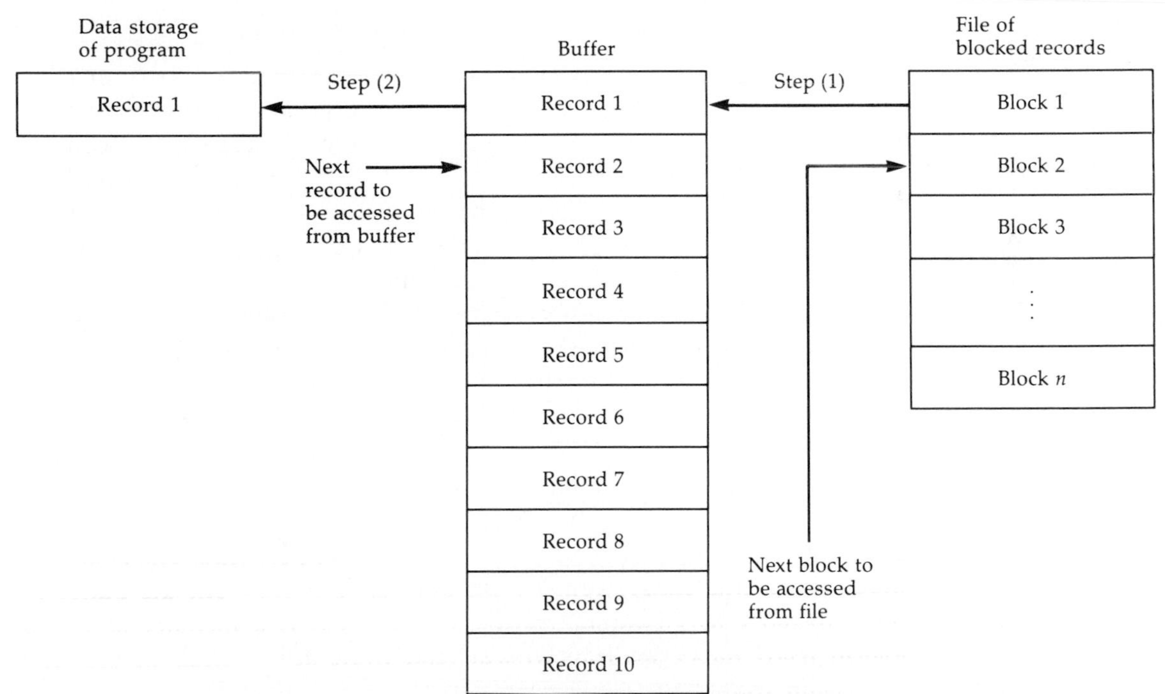

Figure 3.1
Result of first logical read issued to a blocked file

Figure 3.2
Next nine logical reads issued to a blocked file

Figure 3.3
Result of 11th logical read issued to a blocked file

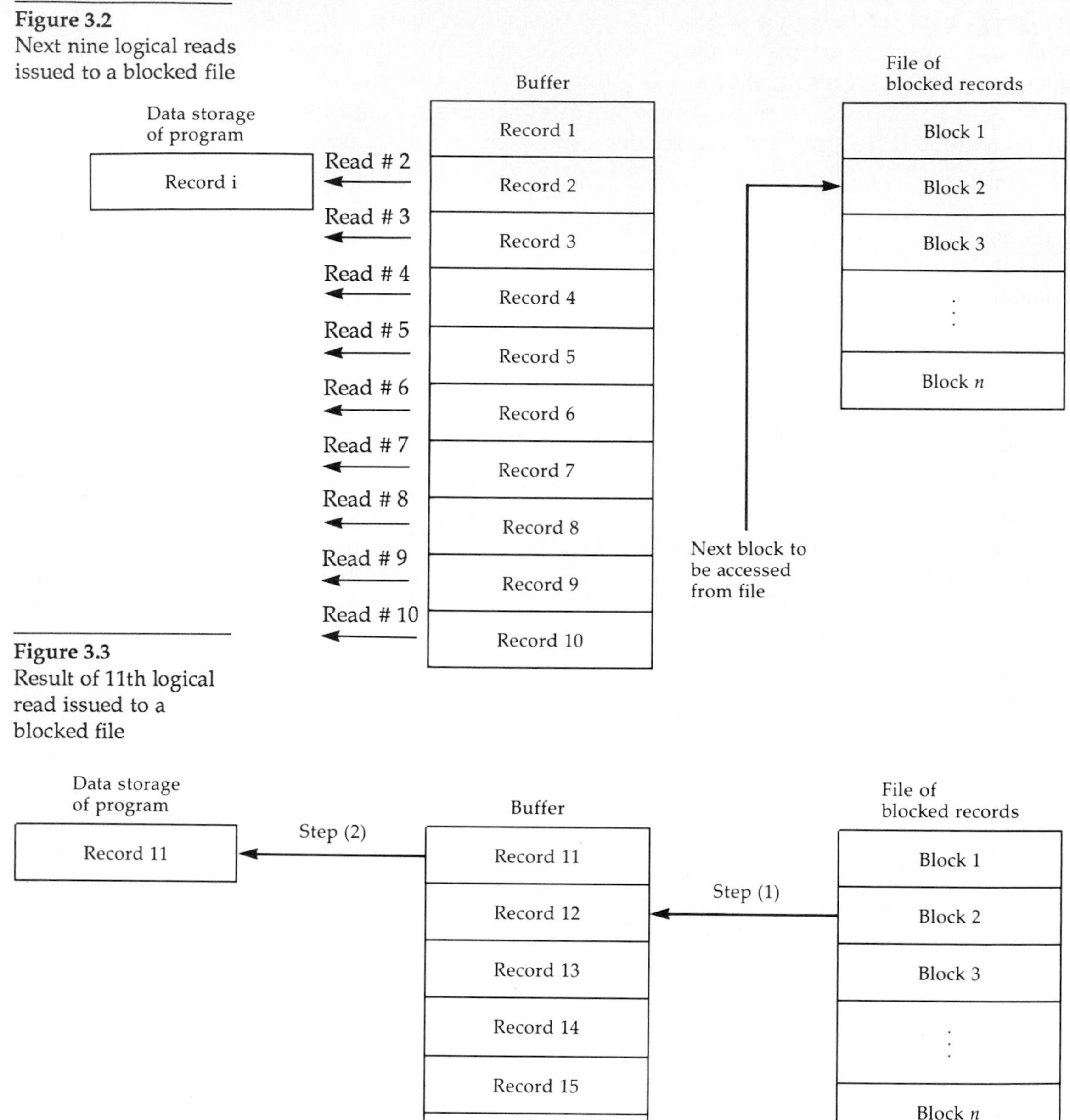

6. The device controller starts writing bytes from the buffer to the device.
7. The I/O channel waits until the entire buffer is written to the device, then signals the CPU that the output operation is complete. The number of components for the buffer is set to 1.
8. The CPU continues to execute the program.

Each output statement, Write/Put, that the program issues stores components in the buffer with a logical write; the file is not accessed physically. When the buffer becomes full, a physical write outputs the buffer's contents to the file physically.

For the file with a blocking factor of 10, the first nine output statements issued by the program logically output data to the buffer in main memory. The logical output constitutes a memory access rather than an output operation to the external file (Figure 3.4). The 10th output statement causes the block of 10 components to be physically output to the external file as Figure 3.5 shows. The 11th output statement uses a logical write to fill the buffer with a component (see Figure 3.6). Again, the program can now output one component at a time, and with the use of a blocking routine, the components can be output as blocked components on the external file to save access time to the external device. A file with a blocking factor of 10 can be created by an Ada program more efficiently than a file without blocking since one physical write occurs for every 10 logical writes.

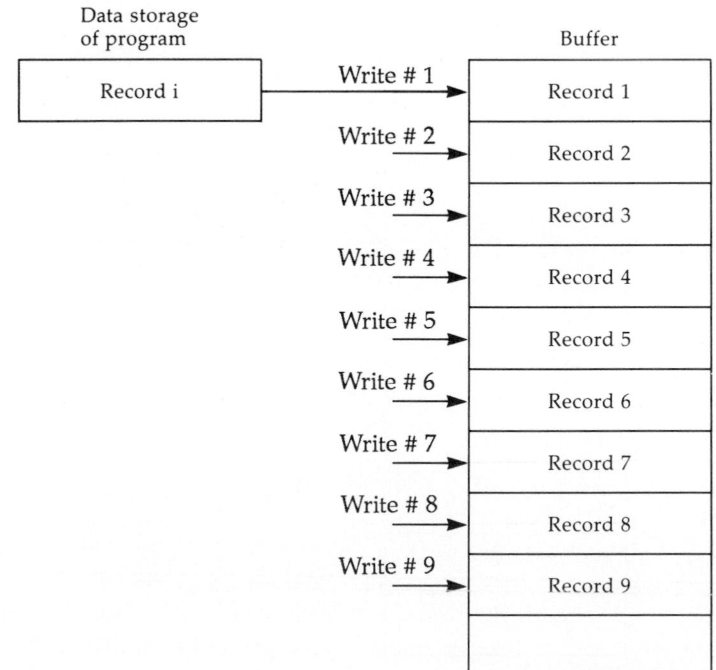

Figure 3.4
First nine logical writes issued to a blocked file

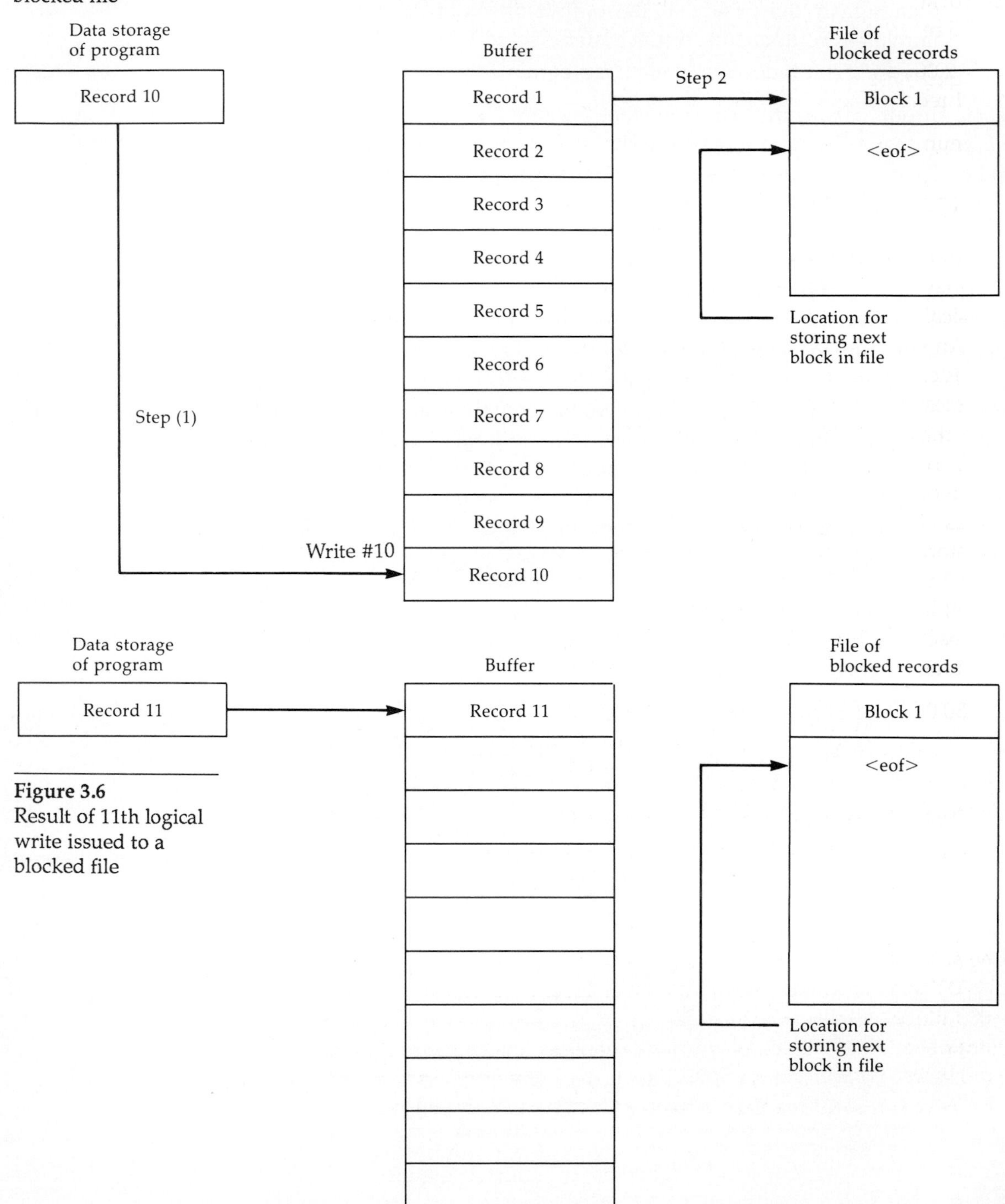

Figure 3.5
Result of 10th logical write issued to a blocked file

Figure 3.6
Result of 11th logical write issued to a blocked file

EXAMPLE 1: SINGLE BUFFERING

Suppose that 2,000 records, each 100 bytes long, are stored in file A in an unblocked manner (1 record per block). File B employs a blocking factor of 25 (25 records per block). The number of blocks in file A is

$$\frac{2{,}000 \text{ records}}{1 \text{ record/block}} = 2{,}000 \text{ blocks}$$

The number of blocks in file B is smaller.

$$\frac{2{,}000 \text{ records}}{25 \text{ records/block}} = 80 \text{ blocks}$$

The number of physical accesses necessary to input or output the entire file is equal to the number of blocks in the file. File A can be input with 2,000 physical reads, while file B can be input with only 80 physical reads.

An examination of physical reads and writes in terms of milliseconds provides a clearer understanding of why reducing the number of physical accesses is important. One second contains 1,000 **milliseconds** (ms). Suppose that 100 bytes can be transferred (from disk to CPU or vice versa) in 0.008 ms. Each physical read or write involves some overhead in addition to the 0.008 ms per 100 bytes of data. The expensive portion of a physical access is the overhead time, which varies depending on the type of secondary storage device. (Chapter 4 compares the overhead times of specific devices.) Suppose that the overhead of each physical read or write is 50 ms. As Table 3.1 indicates, each physical read or write for file A takes 50.008 ms, and each physical read or write for file B takes 50.2 ms (50 + [25 × 0.008]). The total time to access all blocks in file A is

$$\begin{aligned} 50.008 \text{ ms/block} \times 2{,}000 \text{ blocks} &= 100{,}016 \text{ ms} \\ &= 100.016 \text{ seconds (sec)} \\ &= 1.667 \text{ minutes (min)} \end{aligned}$$

The total time to access all blocks in file B is

$$\begin{aligned} 50.2 \text{ ms/block} \times 80 \text{ blocks} &= 4016 \text{ ms} \\ &= 4.016 \text{ sec} \\ &= 0.067 \text{ min} \end{aligned}$$

The access time per block is longer for file B (50.2 ms/block) than for file A (50.008 ms/block), but file B has fewer blocks (80 blocks for file B versus 2,000 blocks for file A); therefore, file B requires fewer accesses. Buffering components into a block of components helps reduce the number of physical accesses to a file of data. Reducing the number of physical accesses to the file reduces the overhead, which is the biggest portion of the total access time.

Table 3.1 Impact of blocking factor upon file access time

	File A	**File B**
Number of logical records	2,000	2,000
Record length in bytes	100	100
Blocking factor	1	25
Number of physical blocks	2,000	80
Block length in bytes	100	2,500
Time to transfer each block (ms)	0.0008	0.2
Overhead time per block (ms)		
Total access time for entire file (min)	1.667	0.067

Implementation in Ada

Programming languages such as COBOL and PL/1 have specifications that indicate block size. These languages also have preset blocking and deblocking interface routines, and they allow the program to be written to access one component at a time after the programmer indicates the blocking factor. Ada has no built-in facilities for accessing blocked files, so an Ada programmer needs to write or have access to a package of deblocking and blocking routines.

We implement blocking in Ada by storing a block of components as an array of components. Each Ada Read accesses one block of the file, which is a block of x components or an array of x components. Then the program accesses each of the x components in the block or array logically one at a time. The same is true of the action of the Write. Each component is stored logically in an array of x components until the array is full. Then an Ada Write physically writes the block of x components to the file. The last block is usually not a full block in a sequential file, but on a random file several blocks may be partially filled after updates. We implement blocking in Ada using a generic package as presented in the example below. The complete package specification is shown. The package body is described in pseudocode. The user of the package specifies the blocking factor (the number of components in a block) and the type name of the components in the block when the package is instantiated.

```
WITH Sequential_IO;
GENERIC
    BLOCK_SIZE : Positive;
    TYPE Component Is Private;
PACKAGE Blocking Is
    TYPE Buffer_Array Is Array ( Positive Range <> ) Of Component;
    TYPE Buffer_Type Is Record
                            number_of_components : Natural := 0;
                            buffer_element : Buffer_Array ( 1 .. BLOCK_SIZE );
                        End Record;
```

```
    PACKAGE Buffer_IO Is New Sequential_IO ( Buffer_Type );
    PROCEDURE Create_Blocked_File ( file_name : In Out Buffer_IO.File_Type;
                                    name : In String );
    PROCEDURE Write_To_Blocked_File ( file_name : In Buffer_IO.File_Type;
                                      data : In Component );
    PROCEDURE Close_Blocked_File ( file_name : In Out Buffer_IO.File_Type );
    PROCEDURE Open_Blocked_File ( file_name : In Out Buffer_IO.File_Type;
                                  name : In String );
    PROCEDURE Read_From_Blocked_File ( file_name : In Buffer_IO.File_Type;
                                       data : Out Component );
    FUNCTION End_Of_Blocked_File ( file_name : In Buffer_IO.File_Type )
                                 Return Boolean;
END Blocking;
```

The three algorithms that follow outline the blocking portion of buffering in Ada.

```
PROCEDURE Create_Blocked_File ( file_name : In Out Buffer_IO.File_Type;
                                name : In String )
    number_of_components ← 0
```

`Create_Blocked_File` initializes the number of components in the buffer. All blocks have a maximum of `BLOCK_SIZE` components.

```
PROCEDURE Write_To_Blocked_File ( file_name : In Buffer_IO.File_Type;
                                  data : In Component )
    If Is_Open ( file_name )
        number_of_components ← number_of_components + 1
        buffer_element(number_of_components) ← data
        If number_of_components = BLOCK_SIZE
            Output buffer to file
            number_of_components ← 0
        End If
    Else
        Raise Status_Error
    End If
```

`Write_To_Blocked_File` moves components into the buffer one at a time, filling positions 1 through `BLOCK_SIZE` of the array. When the buffer is full, it is physically written to the external file.

```
PROCEDURE Close_Blocked_File ( file_name : In Out Buffer_IO.File_Type )

    If number_of_components > 0
        Output buffer to file
    End If
    Close file
```

`Close_Blocked_File` physically writes the last nonempty block to the file.

The algorithms that follow outline the deblocking portion of the buffering:

```
PROCEDURE Open_Blocked_File (file_name : In Out Buffer_IO.File_Type;
                             name : In String )
    buffer_index ← 1

    If End_Of_File ( file_name )
        number_of_components ← 0
    Else
        Input first block from file into buffer
    End If
```

`Open_Blocked_File` initializes the buffer index and fills the buffer with the first block of components from the file (if the file is not empty).

```
PROCEDURE Read_From_Blocked_File ( file_name : In Buffer_IO.File_Type;
                                   data : Out Component )
    If Is_Open ( file_name )
        If buffer_index > number_of_components
            If End_Of_File ( file_name )
                Raise End_Error Exception
            Else
                Input next block from file into buffer
                buffer_index ← 1
            End If
        End If
        data ← buffer_element(buffer_index)
        buffer_index ← buffer_index + 1
    Else
        Raise Status_Error
    End If
```

`Read_From_Blocked_File` raises an exception if the file is not open; otherwise, it fills the buffer (if empty) with the next block of components from the file and returns a component (`data`) from the buffer.

```
FUNCTION End_Of_Blocked_File ( file_name : In Buffer_IO.File_Type )
                              Return Boolean
    Return End_Of_File ( file_name )
      And buffer_index > number_of_components
```

`End_Of_Blocked_File` is a Boolean function that checks for the end of file condition and includes a test for an empty buffer. Once the last block is input, `End_Of_File (file_name)` returns `TRUE`, but file processing is not complete, in this case, until all components in the last block in the buffer have been accessed.

DOUBLE BUFFERING

To improve the access time to an external file, most high level languages such as COBOL and PL/1 contain two buffers for each file. This attribute permits double buffering. **Double buffering** is possible when the I/O operations performed by the I/O channel and the processing operations performed by the CPU overlap in time.

Double Buffering Input

In the case of an input file, the first block from the file is input into buffer 1, the second block is input into buffer 2, and the first component from buffer 1 is passed to program storage. Figure 3.7 illustrates double buffering for an input file with 10 records to a block. When buffer 1 becomes empty while buffer 2 is still full, processing of component 11 from buffer 2 begins. The third block from the file is input into buffer 1 as Figure 3.8 shows. The effect is that the next block from the file has been physically accessed before the program directs the input; the information is waiting in one of the buffers. The program can access the waiting information in the buffer without having to wait for the information to be accessed.

Figure 3.9 illustrates the time frame that applies to single buffering. The CPU is idle while the first block is input to the buffer. In this illustration the time to input a block is 50 ms, and the time for the CPU to process a block of data is 25 ms. When the CPU finishes processing a block of data, it is idle for 50 ms while the buffer is filled with the next block of data. (This pattern yields 33 percent utilization of the CPU.) Total file-processing time is

$$(50 \text{ ms} + 25 \text{ ms})/\text{block} \times n \text{ blocks/file} = 75 \text{ ms/block} \times n \text{ blocks/file}$$

The total time to process a file with 1,000 blocks is

$$75 \text{ ms/block} \times 1{,}000 \text{ blocks/file} = 75{,}000 \text{ ms} = 75 \text{ sec}$$

Figure 3.10 illustrates the time frame that applies to double buffering. The CPU begins to process data in buffer 1 as soon as buffer 1 is filled. At the same time, buffer 2 is being filled with the next block of data. The result is that the CPU only waits 25 ms for the other buffer to be filled before continuing to process. In this situation, where access time to input one buffer from the file is longer than the process time, the implementation is said to be **I/O-bound**. The total time to process all the data in the file cannot be reduced without reducing the access time to the file. In this I/O-bound case, we have approached 50 percent utilization of the CPU. (We do not achieve 50 percent utilization because of the 50 ms necessary to fill the initial buffer.) The total time to process a file is

$$\begin{aligned}&\text{time to input the file (50 ms/block)} + 25 \text{ ms to process the last block}\\ &\qquad = (50 \text{ ms/block} \times n \text{ blocks/file}) + 25 \text{ ms}\end{aligned}$$

Double buffering, in this case, produces a savings of almost 25 ms/block over single buffering. The total time to process a file with 1,000 blocks using double buffering would be

$$\begin{aligned}&(50 \text{ ms/block} \times 1{,}000 \text{ blocks/file}) + 25 \text{ ms}\\ &= 50{,}025 \text{ ms}\\ &= 50.025 \text{ sec}\end{aligned}$$

The total time required to process a file of 1,000 blocks using double buffering is 66 percent of the total time using single buffering.

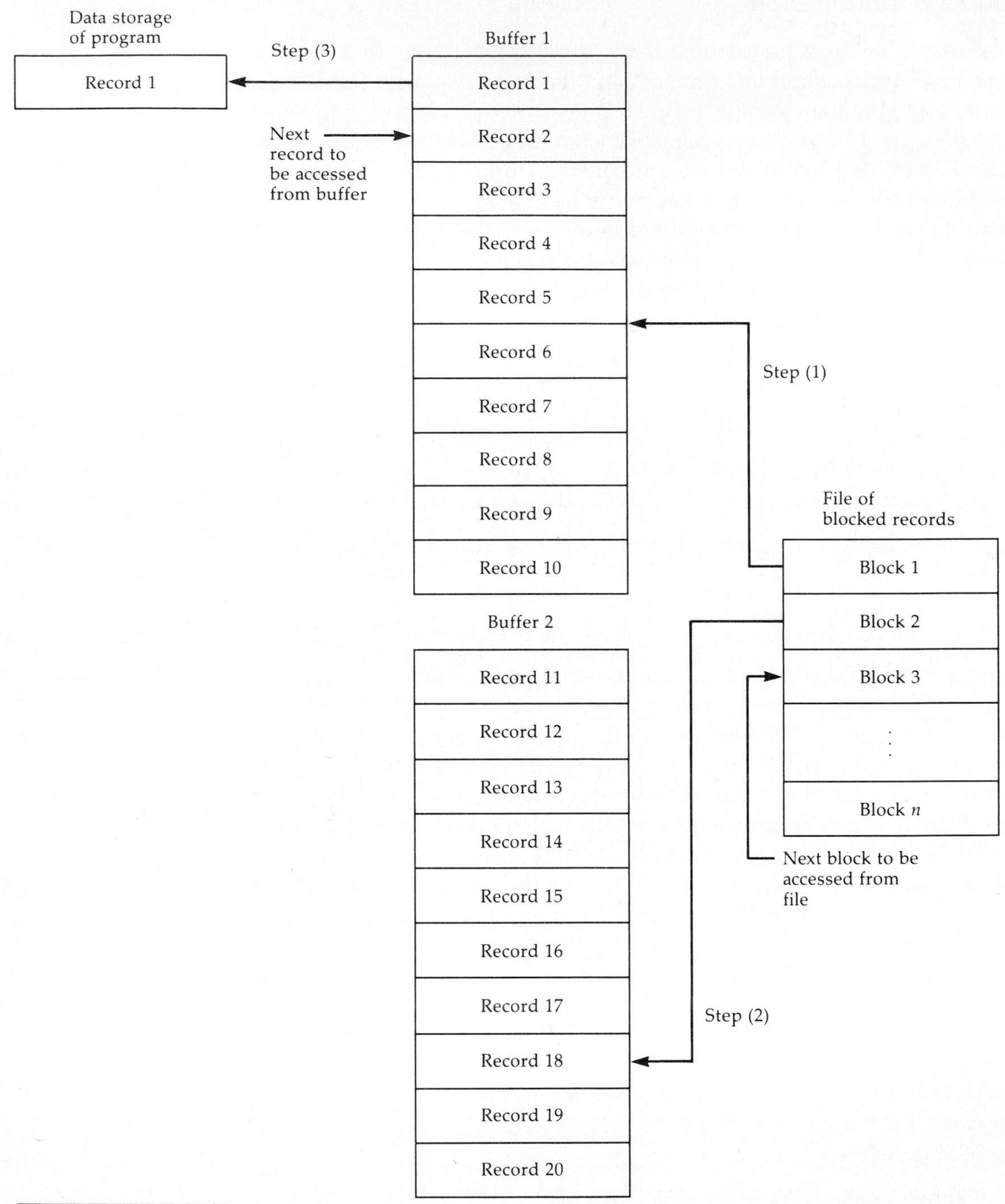

Figure 3.7
Result of first logical read issued to a blocked file using double buffering

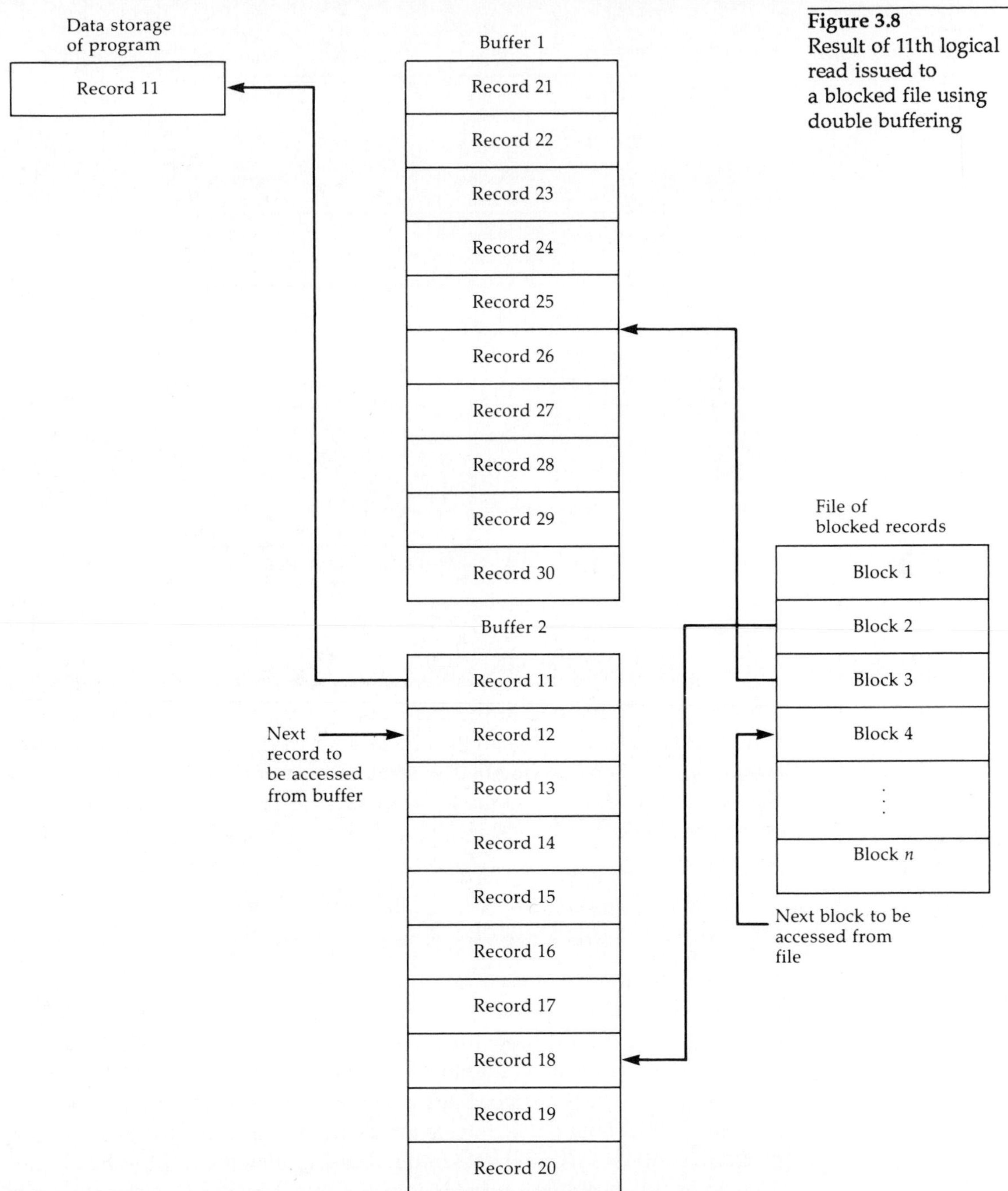

Figure 3.8
Result of 11th logical read issued to a blocked file using double buffering

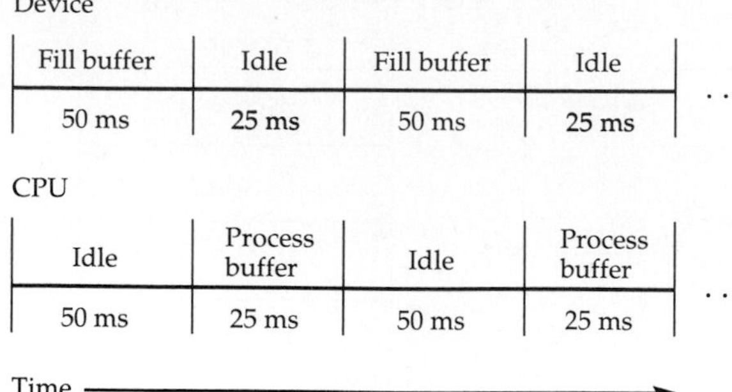

Figure 3.9
Single buffering with input

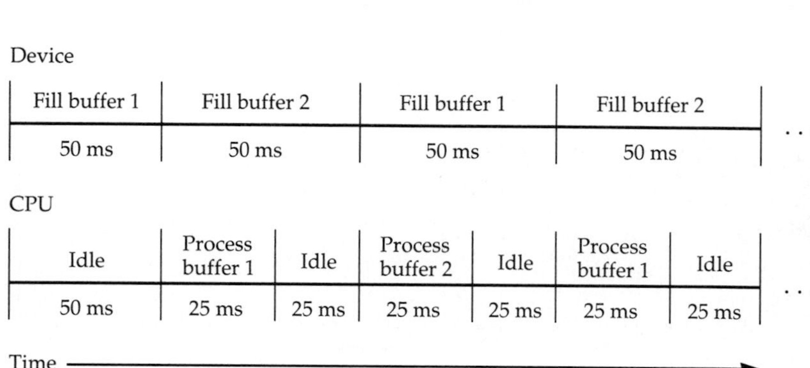

Figure 3.10
I/O-bound double buffering with input

Figure 3.11 illustrates an implementation that is **processor-bound**; to fill a buffer takes 50 ms, and to process a buffer of data takes 100 ms. Since the processing time is longer than the access time, the CPU is never idle (except while buffer 1 is being filled). The total time to process all the data in the file cannot be reduced without reducing the processing time; in other words, this processor-bound implementation represents 100 percent utilization of the CPU.

Double Buffering Output

Double buffering is also used for output files to decrease the time in which the CPU waits for a buffer to be emptied. Figure 3.12 illustrates double buffering to an output file with 10 components to a block. When buffer 1 becomes full and a physical write is issued to store buffer 1's contents physically in the file, the CPU need not wait for buffer 1 to be emptied; buffer 2 is empty. While buffer 1's contents are being stored in the external file, the program continues moving data into buffer 2 (see Figure 3.13). When buffer 2 becomes full, a physical write is issued to store buffer 2's contents in the external file while the program continues to fill buffer 1 (see Figure 3.14). The alternation between buffers 1 and 2 continues; the result is diminished waiting time for the CPU.

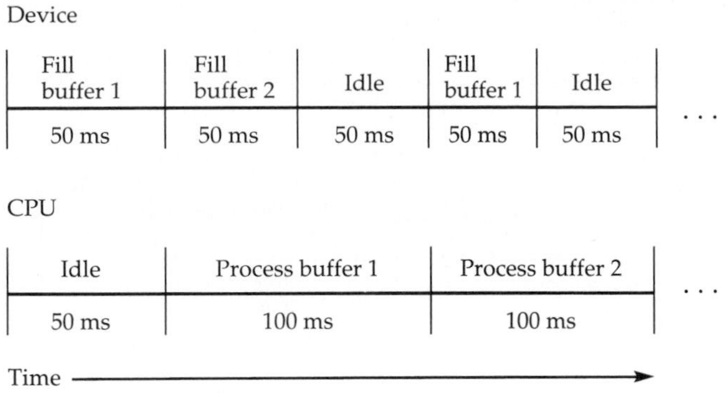

Device

Fill buffer 1	Fill buffer 2	Idle	Fill buffer 1	Idle	. . .
50 ms	50 ms	50 ms	50 ms	50 ms	

CPU

Idle	Process buffer 1	Process buffer 2	. . .
50 ms	100 ms	100 ms	

Time ⟶

Figure 3.11
Processor-bound double buffering with input

Figure 3.15 illustrates the time frame for creating an output file using only one buffer. As with the single buffering for input files, the CPU is idle while the buffer is written to the file. Double buffering for output files can improve utilization of the CPU by allowing the CPU to fill a second buffer while the first buffer is physically written to a file. Depending on the access time to write the buffer to the file and the time for the CPU to fill a buffer, the double buffering may be **I/O-bound** (see Figure 3.16) or **processor-bound** (see Figure 3.17).

Implementation in Ada

Double buffering is possible in Ada with the use of the **tasking** feature. Tasking is unavailable in most high level programming languages and is needed for real-time programming. Tasks are Ada program units that operate independently—in parallel—and have facilities for communicating with other program units. Tasks have **entries** which may be called by other program units. A task accepts a call to one of its entries by executing an **accept** statement.

A task declaration consists of a task specification and a task body, both of which must be placed in a subprogram or package to be compiled. The format for the task specification and body in Ada is as follows (the [ ] indicate optional clauses):

```
TASK [type] task_name [Is
        entry_declarations
END task_name] ;

TASK Body task_name Is
     declarations
BEGIN
     statements  --including Accept statements for entries
[Exception
     exception_handler]
END task_name;
```

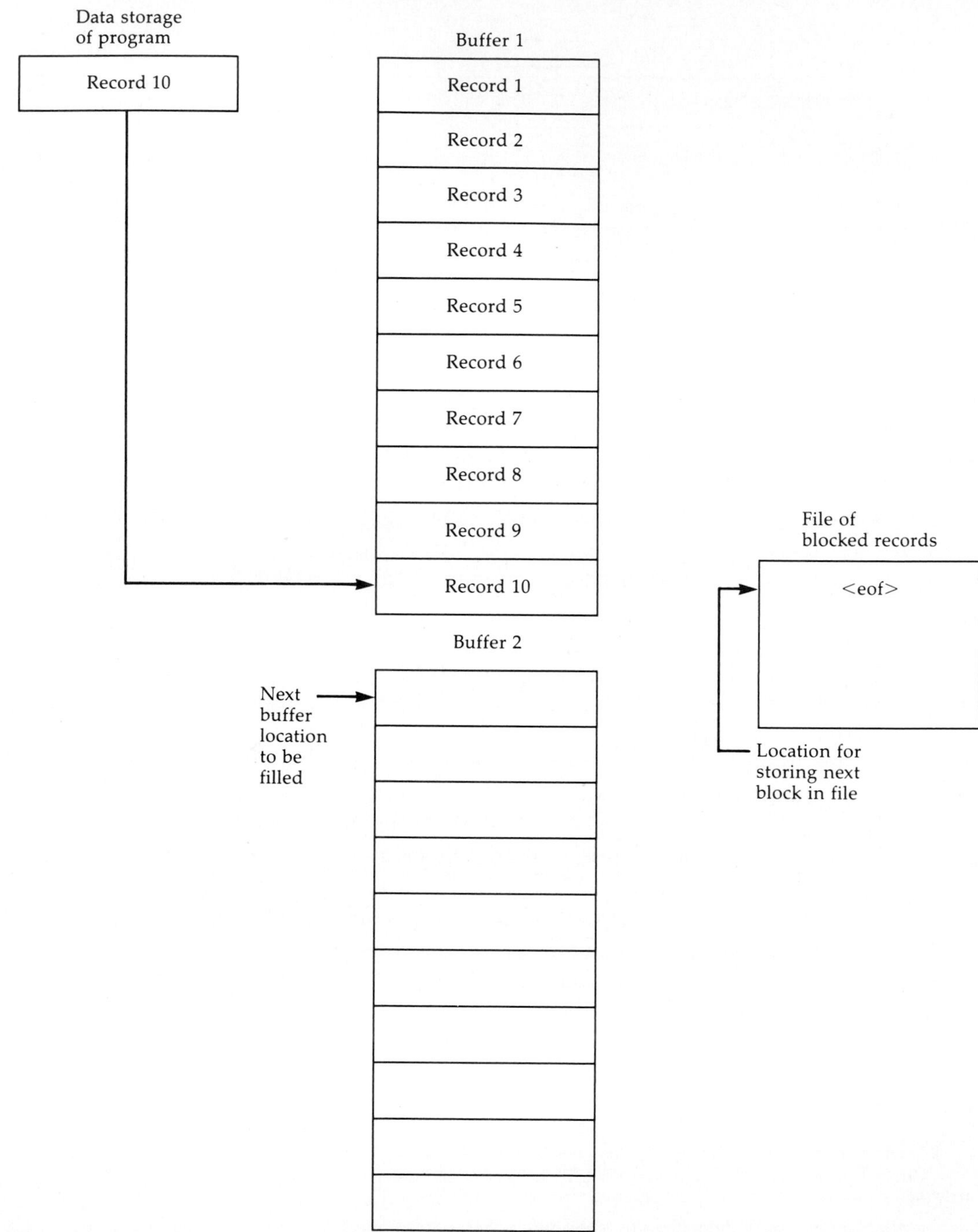

Figure 3.12
Result of first 10 logical writes issued to a blocked file using double buffering

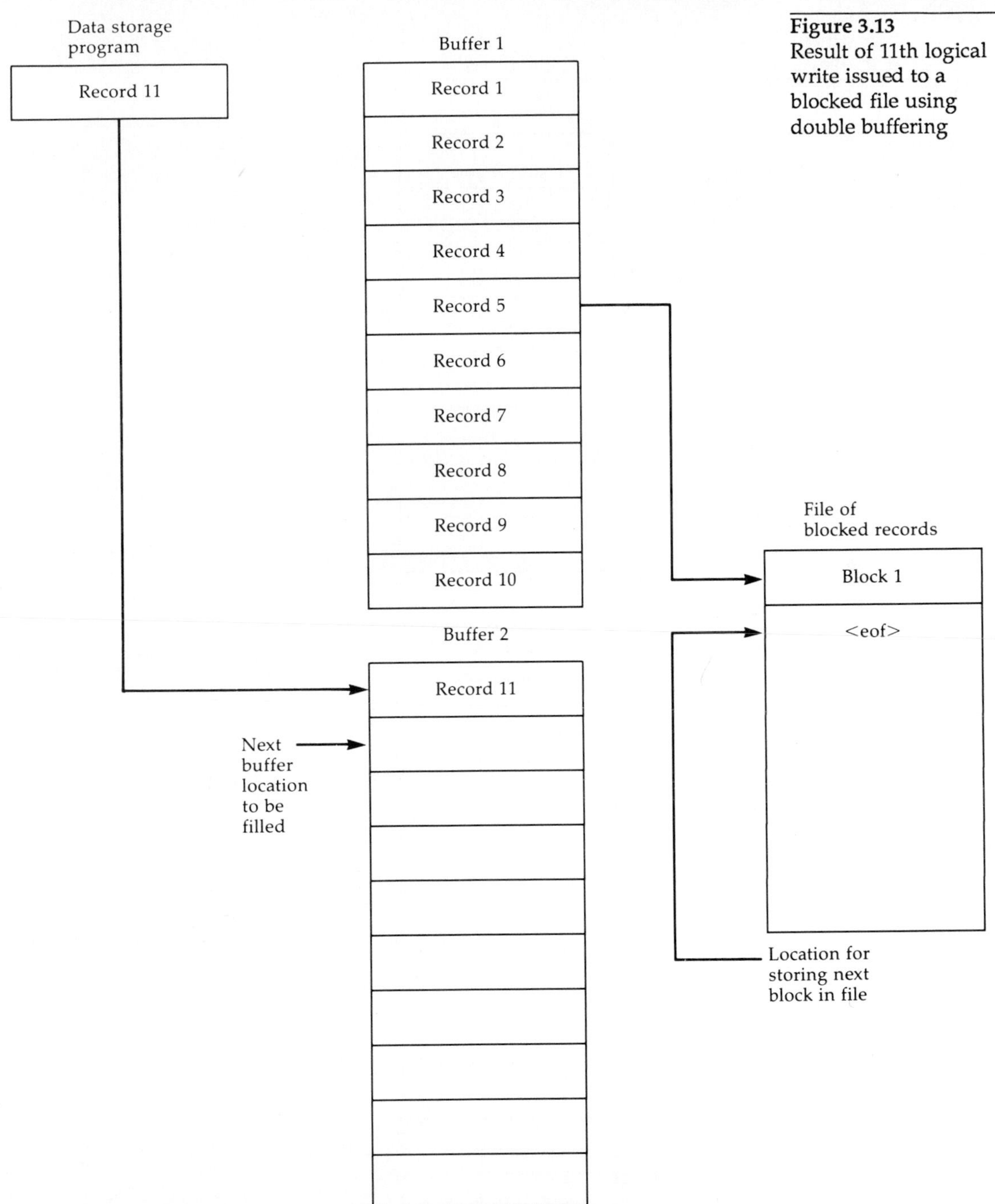

Figure 3.13
Result of 11th logical write issued to a blocked file using double buffering

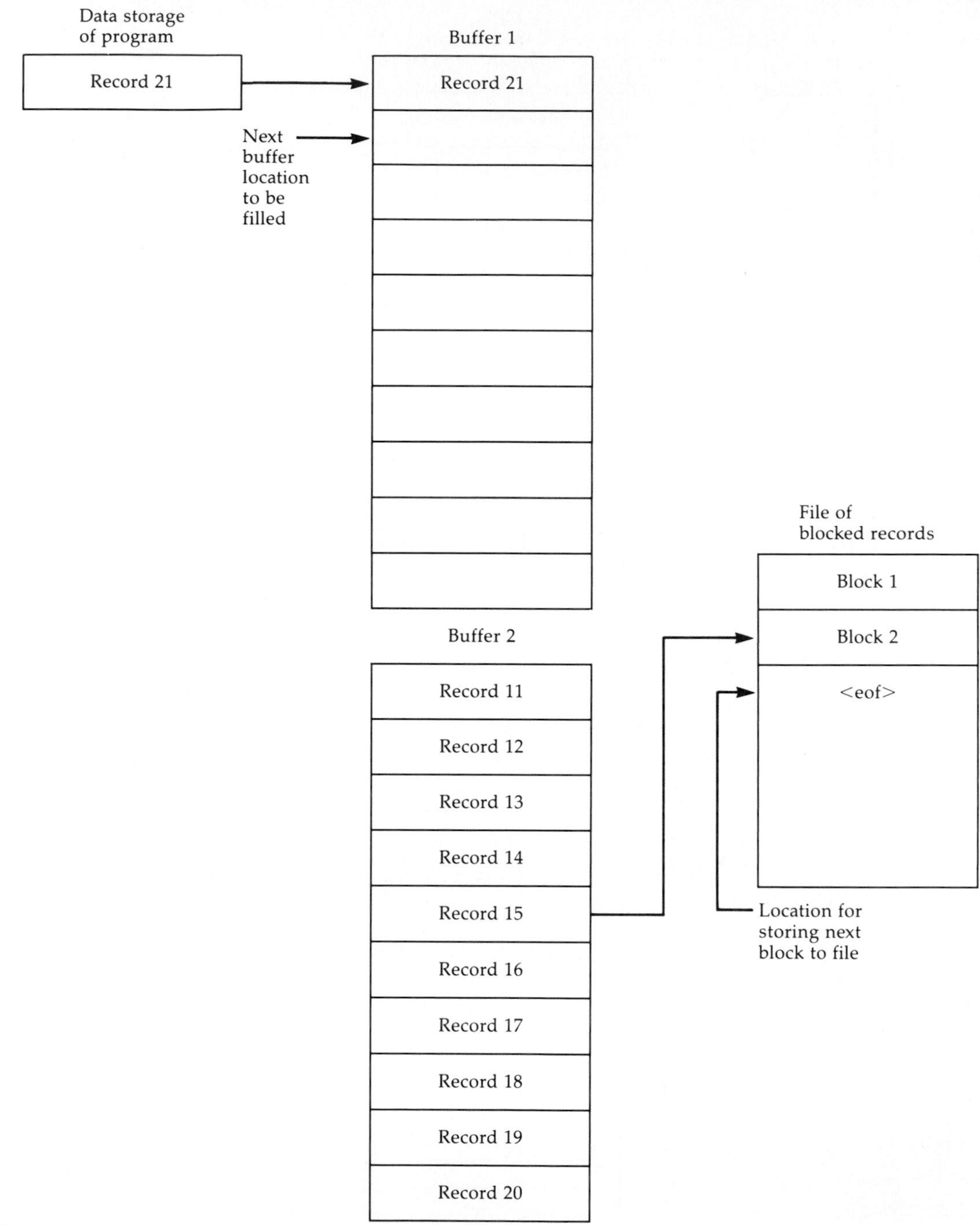

Figure 3.14
Result of issuing 21 logical writes to a blocked file using double buffering

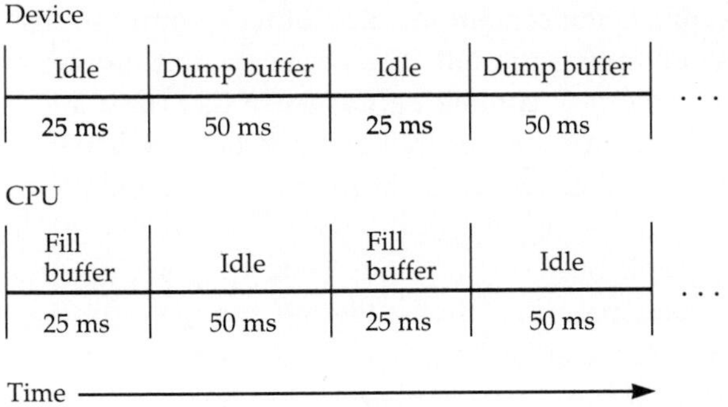

Device

Idle	Dump buffer	Idle	Dump buffer	...
25 ms	50 ms	25 ms	50 ms	

CPU

Fill buffer	Idle	Fill buffer	Idle	...
25 ms	50 ms	25 ms	50 ms	

Time →

Figure 3.15
Single buffering with output

Device

Idle	Dump buffer 1	Dump buffer 2	Dump buffer 1	...
25 ms	50 ms	50 ms	50 ms	

CPU

Fill buffer 1	Fill buffer 2	Idle	Fill buffer 1	Idle	Fill buffer 2	Idle	...
25 ms	25 ms	25 ms	25 ms	25 ms	25 ms	25 ms	

Time →

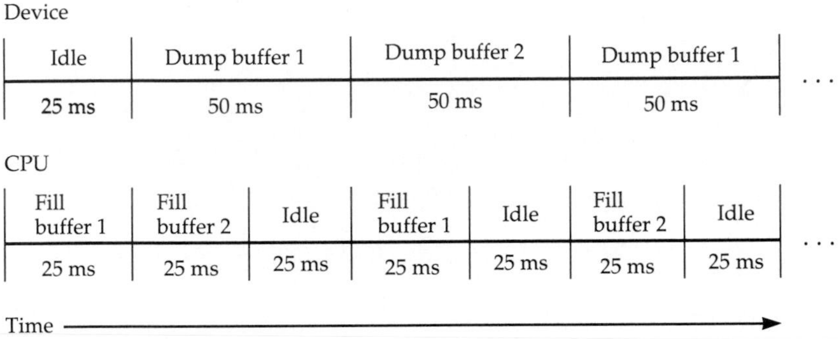

Figure 3.16
I/O-bound double buffering with output

Device

Idle	Dump buffer 1	Idle	Dump buffer 2	Idle	...
100 ms	50 ms	50 ms	50 ms	50 ms	

CPU

Fill buffer 1	Fill buffer 2	Fill buffer 1	...
100 ms	100 ms	100 ms	

Time →

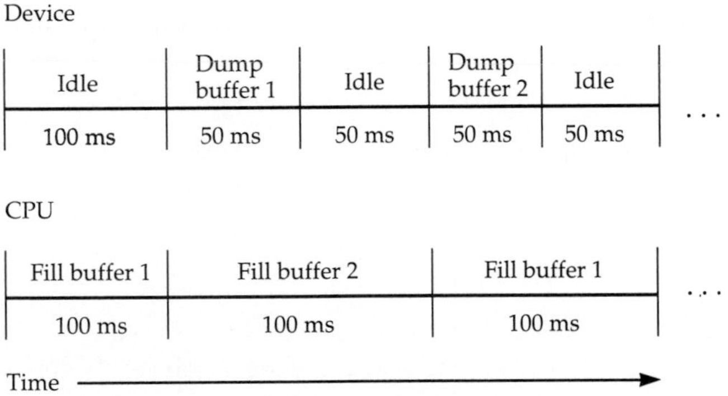

Figure 3.17
Processor-bound double buffering with output

An entry declaration consists of the keyword `Entry` followed by an entry name followed by any formal parameters. There must be an `Accept` statement in the task body for each entry listed in the task specification. The format for the `Accept` statement is as follows:

```
Accept entry_name [ (formal parameters) ] [Do
    statements
End entry_name] ;
```

The exception handler may optionally be included in the task body.

Tasks begin execution when the subprogram unit containing the task is called. If the task is in a package, the task begins execution when the package is initialized. A subprogram unit containing tasks cannot complete until all tasks declared therein have terminated. A task terminates when the execution of the task body reaches the task end.

A **rendezvous** is the synchronization of a program unit issuing an entry call and a task accepting the call. The program unit issuing an entry call is suspended until the task containing the entry has completed the execution of all the code in the `Accept` for that entry. A task is suspended in a similar manner when it reaches an accept in its body for which there has been no call.

Tasks for double buffering of input/output operations execute independently of the main program, thus allowing the overlapping of read/write operations with processing. The specifications for a package that allows double buffering of input data, which includes a task for the input operation, is presented below:

```
WITH Sequential_IO;
GENERIC
    TYPE File_Element is Private;

PACKAGE InBuffer Is
    PROCEDURE Open_Buffered_File ( file_name : String );
    PROCEDURE Close_Buffered_FIle;
    PROCEDURE Read_Buffered_File ( element : Out File_Element );
    FUNCTION End_Of_Buffered_File Return Boolean;
END InBuffer;
```

The double buffering package specification includes descriptions for all the operations normally performed on an input file: open (`Open_Buffered_File`), close (`Close_Buffered_File`), read (`Read_ Buffered_File`), and an end-of-file function (`End_Of_Buffered_ File`). The body of the double buffering package with its embedded task follows:

```
PACKAGE Body InBuffer Is
  TYPE Status_Type Is ( EMPTY, FULL );
  TYPE Buffer_Type;
  TYPE Buffer_Pointer_Type Is Access Buffer_Type;
  TYPE Buffer_Type Is Record
                        status : Status_Type;
                        element : File_Element;
                        next_buffer : Buffer_Pointer_Type;
                    End Record;
  buffer_head : Buffer_Pointer_Type;
  PACKAGE Buffer_IO Is New Sequential_IO ( File_Element );
  in_file : Buffer_IO.File_Type;

  TASK Input_Task Is          -- Task Specification
       Entry Read_Element;    -- Task Entry
  END Input_Task;

  PROCEDURE Open_Buffered_File ( file_name : String ) Is
  BEGIN
      Buffer_IO.Open ( in_file, Buffer_IO.IN_FILE, file_name );
      Input_Task.Read_Element;
      buffer_head := buffer_head.next_buffer;
      Input_Task.Read_Element;
  END Open_Buffered_File;
```

```
    PROCEDURE Close_Buffered_File Is
    BEGIN
        Buffer_IO.Close ( in_file );
        Abort Input_Task;
    END Close_Buffered_File;

    FUNCTION End_Of_Buffered_File Return Boolean Is
    BEGIN
        Return  Buffer_IO.End_Of_File ( in_file )
            And buffer_head.status = EMPTY
            And buffer_head.next_buffer.status = EMPTY;
    END End_Of_Buffered_File;

    PROCEDURE Read_Buffered_File ( element : Out File_Element ) Is
    BEGIN
        Loop
            If buffer_head.status = FULL Then
                element := buffer_head.element;
                buffer_head.status := EMPTY;
                buffer_head := buffer_head.next_buffer;
                If Input_Task'Callable Then
                    Input_Task.Read_Element;
                End If;
                Exit;
            Else
                Delay 0.1;
                If Buffer_IO.End_Of_File ( in_file )
                And Then buffer_head.next_buffer.status = EMPTY Then
                    Raise Buffer_IO.End_Error;
              End If;
            End If;
        End Loop;
    END Read_Buffered_File;

    TASK Body Input_Task Is      -- Task Body
    BEGIN
        Loop
            Accept Read_Element;   -- Task Entry
            Exit When Not Buffer_IO.Is_Open ( in_file );
            Exit When Buffer_IO.End_Of_File ( in_file );
            Declare
               buffer_to_fill : Buffer_Pointer_Type
                                Renames buffer_head.next_buffer;
            Begin
                Buffer_IO.Read ( in_file, buffer_to_fill.element );
                buffer_to_fill.status := FULL;
            End;
        End Loop;
    END Input_Task;

BEGIN  -- InBuffer
    buffer_head := New Buffer_Type;
    buffer_head.status := EMPTY;
    buffer_head.next_buffer := New Buffer_Type;
    buffer_head.next_buffer.status := EMPTY;
    buffer_head.next_buffer.next_buffer := buffer_head;
END InBuffer;
```

The data structure for the double buffering package is a circular queue of two buffers. Each buffer is a record that contains a file element, the status of the buffer (EMPTY or FULL), and a link to the next buffer in the circular queue. The buffer queue is allocated and initialized in the initialization portion of the package. The object buffer_head points to the front element of the buffer queue.

The procedure Open_Buffered_File calls the Input_Task entry Read_Element to fill both buffers. The procedure execution ends after a rendezvous of the second task entry call and the task accept. The result? The second buffer is filled in parallel with processing of the first buffer. Since the task executes independently, the user can be processing the data retrieved from the first buffer while the task is filling the second buffer.

The procedure Close_Buffered_File closes the file and ensures that the task has been terminated. The task normally terminates when the end of the input file is reached. If the user closes the buffered file before reaching the end of the file, the Abort statement terminates the active task. Aborting a terminated task has no effect.

The function End_Of_Buffered_File returns TRUE if all the components of the file have been input to the user. The test for end-of-file when double buffering is used is more complex than an end-of-file test for a non-buffered file. Finding the <eof> marker in the input file indicates that there are no more components to be input into the buffer queue. There may, however, be elements in the buffer queue that have not yet been input and processed by the user. The end of a buffered file is determined by finding the <eof> marker in the file and finding both buffers in the buffer queue empty.

The procedure Read_Buffered_File returns to the user the next file element. If an element is available (buffer_head.status = FULL), the procedure returns the element from buffer and calls the task to fill the empty buffer. If an element is not available, the procedure delays since the task may be filling the other buffer. After the delay, if the end of the file is found and the other buffer is empty, the procedure raises the exception End_Error. If no exception is raised, the procedure loops back to check whether the task finished filling the other buffer.

The task Input_Task is suspended at the Accept statement until an entry call is made by the Open_Buffered_File or Read_Buffered_ File. The body of the Accept statement is empty. The Accept in this case is used only to suspend the execution of the task waiting for an entry call. Normally the task terminates if the file is not open or if the end of the file is found. The renaming declaration in the declare block reduces the number of address computations by one. More importantly, this avoids a potential synchronization problem caused by the Read_Buffered_File procedure changing buffer_head between the filling of the element and the setting of the status in the task.

This particular example has a couple of limitations; the solutions to both are left as exercises. The first of the limitations is that the user of the package may wish to control the number of buffers to be used through a generic parameter. The implementation presented has two buffers. The second limitation is one that doesn't happen often. The implementation presented terminates the task once the file has been emptied or closed. There is no way to restart an Ada task that has terminated. If the user opens the file, reads from it, closes the file, and then tries to open the file again via the `InBuffer` package, the exception `Tasking_Error` will be raised because the task terminated by the `Close` cannot be referenced.

The authors do not pretend that the above discussion sufficiently covers the topic of Ada tasking. While tasking is an important Ada feature, tasking is not of paramount importance, except for double buffering, in a textbook on file structures. Suggested reading for a more in-depth look at tasking is *Software Engineering with Ada* and *Software Components with Ada: Structures, Tools, and Subsystems* (see Booch [1987]).

SUMMARY

Blocking information on a file reduces the number of physical accesses to the file and thereby improves the execution time of programs that access the blocked file. The block size is determined by a number of factors: the size of main memory, the size of the largest program accessing the file, the accesses to the file, and the physical characteristics of external storage devices. Buffering data to and from the file consists of blocking and deblocking interface routines to allow programs to deal logically with one component at a time while physically blocking components on the external file. Double buffering provides an added improvement in file access time for both input and output files because Ada tasking permits the overlapping of I/O and processing.

Key Terms

abort
accept
block
blocking
blocking routine
buffering
clustering
deblocking routine
double buffering
entry
I/O-bound
logical read
logical write
millisecond
physical read
physical write
processor-bound
rendezvous
task
task body
task specification

Exercises

1. Describe the difference between a logical file component and a physical file component.
2. Explain blocking of file components.
3. What is the purpose of blocking?
4. Why is blocking important?
5. What factors should be considered in determining block size?
6. Why is multiple buffering important?
7. What do the Open and Create procedures do other than just make the file available for access?
8. What are the benefits of closing a file explicitly rather than closing it implicitly at the end of program execution?
9. Does buffering use auxiliary or main storage?
10. Trace the sequence of steps involved in reading and processing a block of logical components using single buffers. How does the sequence change if double buffering is used?
11. If components are stored in a file with a blocking factor of 1, and there are *nb* blocks in the file, how many logical and physical accesses do we need to input the file?
12. If components are stored in a file with a blocking factor of *nc*, and there are *nb* blocks in the file, how many logical and physical accesses do we need to input the file? Compare the effects of this blocking factor to the effects of the blocking factor in exercise 11.
13. If a record is 120 bytes long and the blocking factor is 25, what is the block length in bytes? How large is the file buffer we need to access a file with this blocking factor using single buffering? If double buffering is used, how large must the file buffer be?
14. Determine the maximum blocking factors for each of the files listed in a through i if 38,500 bytes of main storage are available. All blocking factors should be given as integers. How many blocks (physical accesses) does each file require?

    a. a file of 100,000 records of 367 bytes accessed with single buffering.

    b. a file of 100,000 records of 367 bytes accessed with double buffering. Compare the efficiency of this buffering to the efficiency of the buffering in a.

    c. a file of 45,000 records of 417 bytes accessed with single buffering.

    d. a file of 45,000 records of 417 bytes accessed with double buffering. Compare the efficiency of this buffering to the efficiency of the buffering in c.

e. a file of 248,000 records of 860 bytes accessed with single buffering.

f. a file of 248,000 records of 860 bytes accessed with double buffering. Compare the efficiency of this buffering to the efficiency of the buffering in e.

g. a file of 75,000 logical components of 120 bytes each accessed with single buffering.

h. a file of 75,000 logical components of 120 bytes each accessed with double buffering. Compare the efficiency of this buffering to the efficiency of the buffering in g.

i. a file of 75,000 logical components of 120 bytes each accessed with triple buffering. Compare the efficiency of this buffering to the efficiency of the buffering in g and h.

15. Given the following times to input a block for each file of the corresponding letter in exercise 14 (100 bytes input in 0.008 ms), and 25 ms to process a block, compute the total time to input and process each file. The applications are I/O-bound.

    a. input time = 53.05 ms

    b. input time = 51.52 ms

    c. input time = 53.07 ms

    d. input time = 51.53 ms

    e. input time = 53.02 ms

    f. input time = 51.51 ms

    g. input time = 53.07 ms

    h. input time = 51.53 ms

    i. input time = 51.01 ms

16. Change the time to process a block in exercise 15 to 100 ms. These applications are processor-bound.

Programming Problems

1. Implement the blocking routines described in the chapter as a package. Test the package with a driver program.
2. Write the double buffering output routines described in the chapter as a package using tasking. Test the package with a driver program.
3. Modify the double buffering package to allow the user to specify the number of buffers. The number of buffers should be a generic param-

eter. The modification should include a ring buffer and a ring buffer monitor task.

4. Modify the double buffering package so that the task does not terminate when the open file is closed or is empty but rather terminates when the user specifies. (Hint: Consider a Task type.)

Chapter 4

Secondary Storage Devices

CHAPTER CONTENTS

PREVIEW

THIS CHAPTER DESCRIBES THE CHARACTERISTICS of external storage devices as a background for understanding the impact of storage devices on file design and manipulation. The chapter also presents quantitative measures of blocking and buffering in terms of physical access time and various blocking factors.

TYPES OF STORAGE DEVICES

Magnetic tapes and magnetic disks are the two most commonly used types of secondary storage devices for storing large files of data. Anyone creating or using files for programs and data needs an understanding of how data are stored on secondary storage devices and the data transfer speeds that apply. It is also important to know the types of file organizations appropriate for each secondary storage device.

MAGNETIC TAPE

Magnetic tape is a sequential-access storage device in which blocks of data are stored serially along the length of the tape and can be accessed only in a serial manner. The tape itself is a thin strip of plastic about 0.002 inch thick and about 1/2 inch wide. The plastic is coated with a magnetic oxide. The tape is usually 2,400 feet (ft) long, but the length may vary: 300-, 600-, and 1,200-foot lengths are common. Whatever the length, the tape is wound onto reels. Data are recorded as magnetic "spots" (or bits) on the magnetic oxide film in nine **tracks** that are parallel to the edges of the tape. Figure 4.1 illustrates a section of a tape with the '1' bits shown as dots.

One character (1 byte) of data is recorded across the width of the tape and uses all nine tracks. The pattern of the magnetic spots in tracks is determined by the recording format. The two most prevalent recording formats are Extended Binary Coded Decimal Interchange Code (**EBCDIC**) and American Standard Code for Information Interchange (**ASCII**). EBCDIC is an encoding scheme for representing data in which 8 bits arranged in different patterns represent any character in the character set. ASCII is a 7-bit code; 7 bits in varying patterns represent any character in the character set.

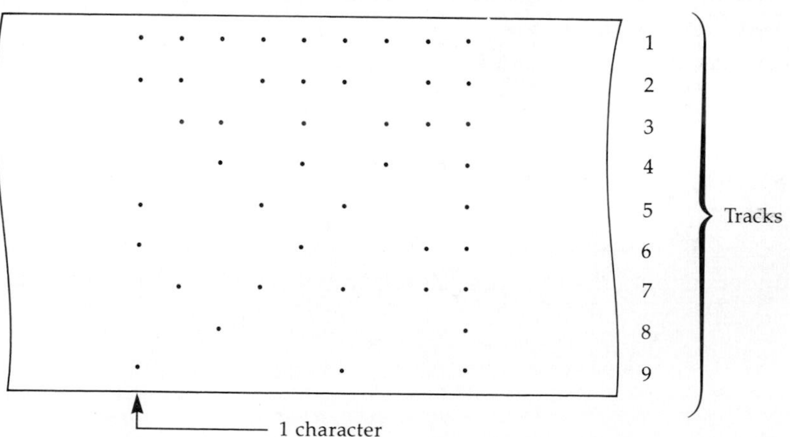

Figure 4.1
A section of magnetic tape

The characters of data are stored serially along the length of the tape as are records of data in a file.

One of the magnetic bits that compose each character on the tape is the **parity bit**, which detects errors that occur when reading or writing data. Parity is established on a tape drive as either even or odd. If the convention is odd parity, the number of 1 bits across the width of the tape must be odd. When a character is represented by an even number of 1 bits, a parity 1 bit is used to make the number of 1 bits odd. If an even number of 1 bits is read from the tape, it must be the result of an error. The convention of **even parity** employs the parity bit to make the number of 1 bits an even number and detects errors by finding odd numbers of bits.

The **recording density** of a tape is the number of characters or bytes of data that can be stored per inch. Recording densities are 200; 556; 800; 1,600; 3,200; and 6,250 characters or bytes per inch (bpi) of tape. Tapes with density ratings of 800, 1,600, and 6,250 are the most common. The higher the recording density of the tape, the higher the storage capacity.

Data can be read from or written to a tape only when the tape is moving at a specific, fixed speed past the read/write heads (see Figure 4.2). The amount of data that can be transferred at any one access is a block of data. A block of data is sometimes called a **physical record**. A block may contain one or more logical records as Chapter 3 discussed.

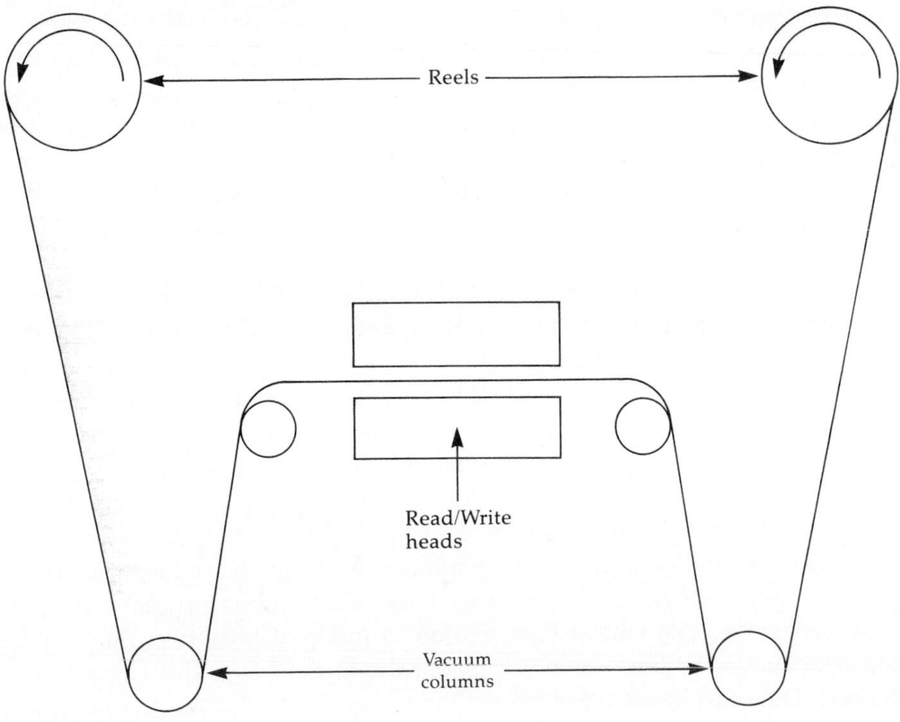

Figure 4.2
A schematic of a tape drive

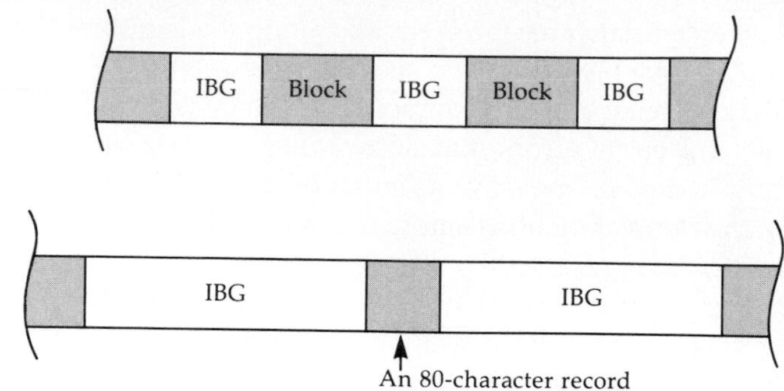

Figure 4.3
Blocks on a tape separated by interblock gaps

Figure 4.4
Size of 80 character record relative to interblock gap

When a request to read or write a block of data is issued, the tape drive must start the tape moving, accelerate to a fixed speed in order to read or write a block, and then decelerate to a stop. Physical records or blocks are separated by **interblock gaps (IBGs)** to provide space in which the tape can start and stop between read or write requests. IBGs are also called **inter-record gaps (IRGs)**. The gaps are unused spaces on the tape that pass under the read/write heads during acceleration and deceleration. As a result, the block of data passes under the read/write heads at the proper speed. Figure 4.3 depicts blocks of data separated by IBGs.

These gaps are usually between 0.6 in. and 0.75 in. in length, but the size may vary with tape densities. IBGs decrease the amount of space on the tape available for storage of data. For example, suppose 80-character records are stored on a nine-track tape with a density of 1,600 bpi and a gap of 0.6 inch. If each record is stored as one block of data, an IBG precedes and follows each record on the tape.

Figure 4.4 depicts the size of the 80-character records relative to the size of the gaps. The 80-character record uses 80/1,600 inch of the tape, or 0.05 inch of the tape. Each gap uses 0.6 inch of the tape, or 12 times the space needed for a record.

In addition to the advantages of blocking discussed in Chapter 3, blocking records on tape provides a physical advantage: It reduces the number of IBGs and allows more data to be stored on a tape. Storing 12 of these 80-character records in a block results in one gap for every 12 records rather than one gap for each record. In other words, blocking results in one-twelfth the number of IBGs or eleven-twelfths more space for data.

Figure 4.5 depicts other characteristics of magnetic tape: markers at each end of the tape and labels at the beginning of the tape and at the beginning and end of each file. The beginning of a tape has a leader section followed by a **load-point marker**, a reflective aluminum strip that the tape drive can sense. The **end-of-tape** marker is made of reflective aluminum and deactivates the tape drive to prevent the tape from unthreading from the reel. Data can be recorded on the tape after the load-point marker and before the end-of-tape marker.

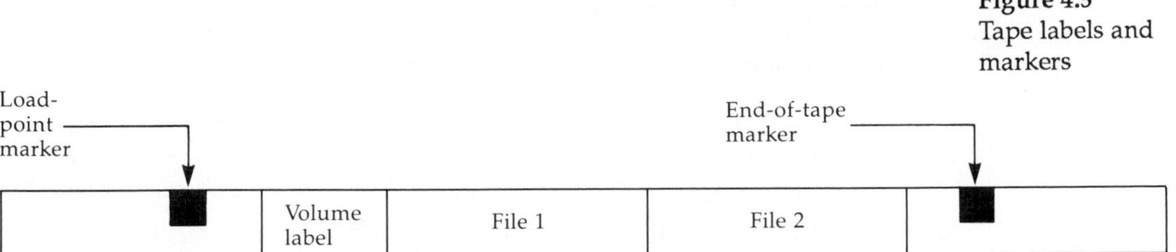

Figure 4.5
Tape labels and markers

Data file

File header label	IBG	Block 1	IBG	Block 2	. . .	Block n	IBG	File trailer label

Figure 4.6
A data file with labels

Between the tape markers the storage of data usually consists of a volume label followed by one or more files of data. The **volume label** contains the serial number of the tape and other identifying information. Each file of data is preceded by a **file header label**, which contains file identification, and succeeded by a **file trailer label**, which contains record and block counts for the file. A tape containing two files would appear as in Figure 4.5, where each file contains the information diagrammed in Figure 4.6.

Magnetic tapes can be used for files with sequential organization only. Magnetic tape reels cost less than magnetic disk packs (about 10 times less) and are more convenient to store because reels are physically smaller than disk packs. For these reasons, tapes are often used for storing backup files. Table 4.1 gives the characteristics of commercial tape drives current at the time this book was written.

Table 4.1 Characteristics of current tape drives

Manufacturer and tape model	**Speed (inches/sec)**	**Density (bpi)**	**Transfer rate**
CDC 626	75	800	120 KB/sec
CDC 679-7	200	6,250	1.25 MB/sec
IBM 3420-4	75	6,250	470 KB/sec
Telex 6420-66	125	6,250	780 KB/sec
Univac Uniservo 12	42.7	1,600	68 KB/sec

EXAMPLE 1: SPACE CALCULATION FOR TAPE

Consider a magnetic tape drive with the following characteristics:

density = 1,600 bpi
IBG length = 0.5 inch

Compute the number of inches of tape required to store 100,000 records of 100 bytes each with a blocking factor of 32.

$$\begin{aligned}\text{block length (in bytes)} &= \text{logical record length} \times \text{blocking factor}\\ &= 100 \text{ bytes/record} \times 32 \text{ records/block}\\ &= 3{,}200 \text{ bytes/block}\end{aligned}$$

Determine the number of blocks by dividing the number of records by the blocking factor.

$$\text{number of blocks} = \frac{\text{number of records}}{\text{blocking factor}}$$

$$\text{number of blocks} = \frac{100{,}000 \text{ records}}{32 \text{ records/block}}$$

$$\text{number of blocks} = 3{,}125 \text{ blocks}$$

Next divide the block length in bytes by the density (bytes/inch) to determine the length, in inches, of one block.

$$\begin{aligned}\text{block length (in inches)} &= \frac{\text{block length in bytes}}{\text{density}}\\ &= \frac{3{,}200 \text{ bytes/block}}{1{,}600 \text{ bytes/inch}}\\ &= 2.0 \text{ inches/block}\end{aligned}$$

Each block is surrounded by IBGs, so the length of tape to store the blocks is determined by assuming that there is one more IBG than there are blocks.

$$\begin{aligned}\text{tape length} &= (\text{number of blocks} \times \text{block length})\\ &\quad + (\text{number of IBGs} \times \text{IBG length})\\ \text{tape length} &= (3{,}125 \text{ blocks} \times 2 \text{ inches/block})\\ &\quad + (3{,}126 \text{ IBGs} \times 0.5 \text{ inch/IBG})\\ \text{tape length} &= (6{,}250 \text{ inches}) + (1{,}563 \text{ inches})\\ \text{tape length} &= 7{,}813 \text{ inches} = 651.083 \text{ ft}\end{aligned}$$

A 600-foot tape would not be long enough; we need a 1,200-foot tape to store the file. Note that the calculation does not include space for header and trailer labels and the volume label.

EXAMPLE 2: SPACE CALCULATION FOR TAPE

Consider a magnetic tape and tape drive with the following characteristics:

length = 2,400 ft
density = 1,600 bpi
IBG = 0.5 inch
transfer speed = 50 inches/sec
start or stop time = 10 ms (0.010 sec)

Compute the number of records that can be stored on the tape if the logical record length is 80 bytes and the blocking factor is 7 records per block. Find the block length in bytes by using the record length (in bytes) and the blocking factor.

$$\begin{aligned}\text{block length (in bytes)} &= \text{logical record length} \times \text{blocking factor}\\ &= 80 \text{ bytes/record} \times 7 \text{ records/block}\\ &= 560 \text{ bytes/block}\end{aligned}$$

Next the block length in bytes is divided by the density (bytes/inch) to determine the length, in inches, of one block.

$$\begin{aligned}\text{block length (in inches)} &= \frac{\text{block length in bytes}}{\text{density}}\\ &= \frac{560 \text{ bytes/block}}{1{,}600 \text{ bytes/inch}}\\ &= 0.35 \text{ inch/block}\end{aligned}$$

Each block is surrounded by IBGs, so the number of blocks that can be stored on a 2,400-foot tape must be one less than the number of IBGs.

$$\begin{aligned}\text{tape length} &= (\text{number of blocks} \times \text{block length})\\ &\quad + ((\text{number of blocks} + 1) \times \text{IBG})\\ 2{,}400 \text{ ft} &= (\text{number of blocks} \times 0.35 \text{ inch})\\ &\quad + ((\text{number of blocks} + 1) \times 0.5 \text{ inch})\\ 2{,}400 \text{ ft} &= (\text{number of blocks} \times 0.35 \text{ inch})\\ &\quad + (\text{number of blocks} \times 0.5 \text{ inch}) + 0.5 \text{ inch}\\ 2{,}400 \text{ ft} &= (\text{number of blocks} \times 0.85 \text{ inch}) + 0.5 \text{ inch}\end{aligned}$$

Then find the number of blocks.

$$\begin{aligned}\text{number of blocks} &= \frac{(12 \text{ inches/ft} \times 2{,}400 \text{ ft}) - 0.5 \text{ inch}}{0.85 \text{ inch/block}}\\ &= 33{,}881 \text{ blocks [33,881.764 truncated]}\end{aligned}$$

The number of blocks must be an integer because the definition of a block is the smallest amount of data the tape drive can access at any given time. Part blocks cannot be accessed.

To compute the number of records that can be stored on the tape, multiply the number of blocks by the blocking factor.

$$\begin{aligned}\text{number of records} &= \text{blocking factor} \times \text{number of blocks}\\ &= 7 \text{ records/block} \times 33{,}881 \text{ blocks}\\ &= 237{,}167 \text{ records}\end{aligned}$$

Assume the blocking factor is changed to 24 records and compute the number of records that can be stored on a 2,400-foot tape.

$$\begin{aligned}\text{block length (in bytes)} &= \text{logical record length} \times \text{blocking factor}\\ &= 80 \text{ bytes/record} \times 24 \text{ records/block}\\ &= 1{,}920 \text{ bytes/block}\end{aligned}$$

$$\begin{aligned}\text{block length (in inches)} &= \frac{\text{block length in bytes}}{\text{density}}\\ &= \frac{1{,}920 \text{ bytes/block}}{1{,}600 \text{ bytes/inch}}\\ &= 1.2 \text{ inches/block}\end{aligned}$$

$$\begin{aligned}\text{tape length} &= (\text{number of blocks} \times \text{block length})\\ &\quad + ((\text{number of blocks} + 1) \times \text{IBG})\\ 2{,}400 \text{ ft} &= (\text{number of blocks} \times 1.2 \text{ inches})\\ &\quad + ((\text{number of blocks} + 1) \times 0.5 \text{ inch})\\ 2{,}400 \text{ ft} &= (\text{number of blocks} \times 1.2 \text{ inches})\\ &\quad + (\text{number of blocks} \times 0.5 \text{ inch}) + 0.5 \text{ inch}\\ 2{,}400 \text{ ft} &= (\text{number of blocks} \times 1.7 \text{ inches}) + 0.5 \text{ inch}\end{aligned}$$

$$\begin{aligned}\text{number of blocks} &= \frac{(12 \text{ inches/ft} \times 2{,}400 \text{ ft}) - 0.5 \text{ inch}}{1.7 \text{ inches/block}}\\ &= 16{,}940 \text{ blocks [16,940.882 truncated]}\end{aligned}$$

$$\begin{aligned}\text{number of records} &= \text{blocking factor} \times \text{number of blocks}\\ &= 24 \text{ records/block} \times 16{,}940 \text{ full blocks}\\ &= 406{,}560 \text{ records}\end{aligned}$$

The blocking factor of 24 records per block allows approximately $1\frac{1}{2}$ times the number of records allowed with a blocking factor of 7 (406,560 versus 237,167 records).

EXAMPLE 3: ACCESS TIME AND TAPE

Compute the time required to read the tape in the second space calculation example with a blocking factor of 7 records per block. Assume the tape stops completely after reading each block. The **start/stop time** includes the time to traverse the IBG.

$$\begin{aligned}
\text{time to read 1 block (time 1 block)} &= \frac{\text{block length in inches}}{\text{transfer speed}} + \text{start time} + \text{stop time} \\
&= \frac{0.35 \text{ inch/block}}{50 \text{ inches/sec}} + \frac{(0.01 \text{ sec} \times 2)}{\text{block}} \\
&= (0.007 + 0.02) \text{ sec/block} \\
&= 0.027 \text{ sec/block}
\end{aligned}$$

$$\begin{aligned}
\text{time to read tape} &= (\text{time 1 block}) \times (\text{number of blocks}) \\
&= 0.027 \text{ sec/block} \times 33{,}881 \text{ blocks} \\
&= 914.787 \text{ sec} \\
&= 15.2 \text{ min}
\end{aligned}$$

Compute the time required to read the above tape with the blocking factor of 24 records per block. Assume that the tape comes to a complete stop after reading each block.

$$\begin{aligned}
\text{time to read 1 block (time 1 block)} &= \frac{\text{block length in inches}}{\text{transfer speed}} + \text{start time} + \text{stop time} \\
&= \frac{1.2 \text{ inches/block}}{50 \text{ inches/sec}} + \frac{(0.01 \text{ sec} \times 2)}{\text{block}} \\
&= (0.024 + 0.02) \text{ sec/block} \\
&= 0.044 \text{ sec/block}
\end{aligned}$$

$$\begin{aligned}
\text{time to read tape} &= (\text{time 1 block}) \times (\text{number of blocks}) \\
&= 0.044 \text{ sec/block} \times 16{,}940 \text{ blocks} \\
&= 745.360 \text{ sec} \\
&= 12.4 \text{ min}
\end{aligned}$$

The blocking factor of 24 allows $1\frac{1}{2}$ times the number of records (406,560 vs 237,167 records). The entire tape can be read in 83 percent of the time (12.4 vs 15.2 min) it takes when the blocking factor is 7 records per block.

EXAMPLE 4: BUFFERING AND TAPE

Assume single buffering for the tape file in the second space calculation example and a blocking factor of 7.

number of blocks = 33,881 blocks
time to read 1 block = 0.027 sec/block (27 ms/block)

If the processing time for one block is 25 ms, compute the total time necessary to input and process the entire file. Recall the equation for total time presented in Chapter 3.

$$\begin{aligned}
\text{total time} &= (\text{input time/block} + \text{processing time/block}) \\
&\quad \times \text{number of blocks} \\
&= (27 \text{ ms/block} + 25 \text{ ms/block}) \times 33{,}881 \text{ blocks}
\end{aligned}$$

$$
\begin{aligned}
&= 1{,}761.81 \text{ sec} \\
&= 29.36 \text{ min}
\end{aligned}
$$

Assuming double buffering, rework the same problem to compute the total time to input and process the entire file. Since the time to input one block is longer than the time to process one block, the execution is I/O-bound. Recall the equation for total time presented in Chapter 3.

$$
\begin{aligned}
\text{total time} &= (\text{input time} \times \text{number of blocks}) \\
&\quad + \text{processing time for one block} \\
&= (27 \text{ ms/block} \times 33{,}881 \text{ blocks}) + 25 \text{ ms} \\
&= 914.81 \text{ sec} \\
&= 15.25 \text{ min}
\end{aligned}
$$

Double buffering allows the entire file to be input and processed in 15.25 min versus 29.36 min using single buffering. I/O-bound double buffering is 48.1 percent faster than single buffering for this particular file.

MAGNETIC DISKS

A **magnetic disk** is a direct-access storage device (DASD) that allows a particular record to be accessed directly, without reference to preceding records. A magnetic disk can store files that employ any of the organization schemes discussed in Chapter 1 (sequential, random, indexed sequential, and multikey). Records stored on magnetic disk can be accessed sequentially or randomly, depending on file organization. Two types of magnetic disks will be discussed, hard disks and floppy disks. A **hard disk** is actually a collection of disks in a disk pack and is usually found on large scale computers. A smaller version of a disk pack is now common on many personal computers. A **floppy disk** is the flexible disk that microcomputers usually use.

Hard Disks

A **disk pack** is a collection of aluminum platters that are attached to and rotate on a center spindle. The disk pack is constantly rotating on the center spindle at a high speed, typically 3,600 revolutions per minute. A disk pack is similar to a stack of phonograph records. The upper and lower surfaces of each platter are coated with a magnetic oxide substance which serves as the recording medium. Often the outermost surfaces of the top and bottom platters are not used for storing data because they may be more easily damaged. The data are stored serially in concentric circles or tracks as shown in Figure 4.7. The number of tracks on a surface varies from 200 tracks on a surface to as many as 400 or 800 tracks per surface; the number depends on the type of pack and the drive that employs it.

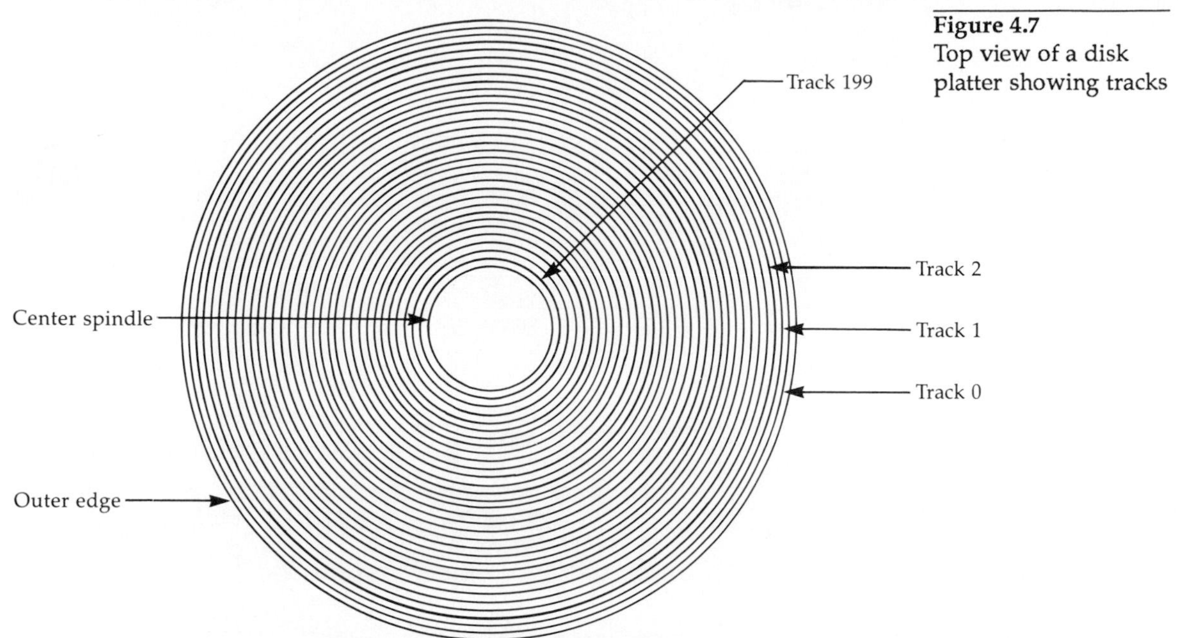

Figure 4.7
Top view of a disk platter showing tracks

The capacity of each track is usually the same regardless of the physical circumference of the tracks because the rotational velocity of the disk pack is constant (there are microcomputer systems that utilize the same recording densities on all tracks; for example, Apple Macintosh and Apple 3.5 micro disk). In order for all tracks to have the same storage capacity, the density of information on each track must be different. The storage capacity of a track is based on the maximum density allowed on the smallest track, which on a disk with 200 tracks is track 199. Different track densities allow data to pass under the read/write heads at the same rate regardless of the track being accessed. The uniform rate at which all tracks on the same disk pass under the read/write heads is called the **transfer rate**.

A disk pack may be **removable**, in that the pack may be mounted on a disk drive to access data and subsequently unmounted for storage. **Fixed** disk packs are permanently sealed in the disk drive.

Accessing Hard Disks Each platter surface of a removable disk pack has one read/write head that reads from or writes to the disk. The read/write heads are mounted on an access arm mechanism attached to the disk drive that suspends the heads a fraction of an inch from the surface of the disk as Figure 4.8 shows. Although Figure 4.8 shows 10 recording surfaces, disk packs with as many as 20 surfaces are not uncommon. The access arm mechanism moves the read/write heads across the tracks to access the data on a given track. All read/write heads move as one unit, but only one read/write head transfers data at a time. Because the read/write heads must move to a particular track to transfer data, the removable disks are also called **movable head disks**.

Figure 4.8
Side view of a disk pack

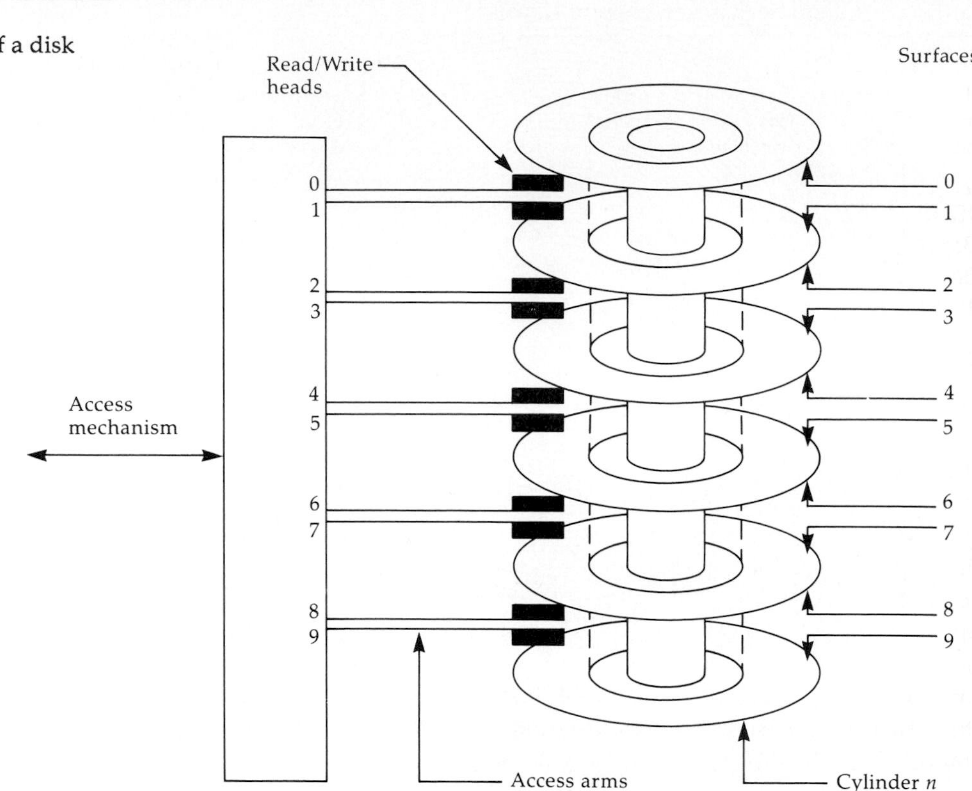

Accessing data stored on a removable disk pack involves four factors: seek time, head activation time, latency, and transfer time. The time it takes the access arm to move the read/write head to a particular track is the **seek time**. Seek time is the most significant factor. **Head activation time** is the time necessary to electrically switch on the read/write head. Head activation time is negligible relative to the other time factors. **Latency** or **rotational delay** is the time required for the beginning of the accessed block to rotate around to the read/write head. The time required for the entire block to pass under the read/write head constitutes the **transfer time**.

A disk pack with a **fixed head** is not removable; it is permanently sealed in the disk drive. Each track on every surface has a read/write head dedicated to that track. Data are stored in the same manner as with removable disks, but accessing data on a fixed-head disk is much faster than accessing data on a removable disk because the seek time is eliminated; a read/write head is already at each track. Fixed-head disks are often used in applications like airline reservation systems where several users access different parts of the disk at any one time. The access time on fixed-head disks includes head activation time, latency, and transfer time.

Table 4.2 Characteristics of current disk drives

Manufacturer and disk model	Transfer rate (byte/sec)	Avg. seek time	Cylin. per unit	Tracks per cylin.	Sectors per track	Bytes per track
Removable Disks						
DEC RP07	1.5M	23 ms	630	32	50	25,600
IBM 3330	806K	30 ms	404	19	—	13,030
IBM 3380	3M	16 ms	885	15	—	47,476
HP 3933	1.2M	24 ms	1,321	13	92	23,552
Fixed Disks						
DEC R503	250K	—	64	1	64	4,096
IBM 2305	3M	—	32	12	—	14,136
Winchester Disks						
Miniscribe 4020	500K	120 ms	480	4	56	8,192
Maxtor XT1140	500K	30 ms	918	15	56	8,192
Floppy Disks						
Shugart (8")	40K	91 ms	77	2	26	6,656
TEAC (5.25")	20K	94 ms	80	2	16	4,096
Apple (3.5")	490K	30 ms	80	2	—	5,120
Optical disks						
Sony (5.25")	510K	120 ms	18,750	2	18	18,175
Sharp (5.25")	28K	150 ms	18,750	2	18	11,800
Pinnacle (5.25")	680K	65 ms	18,751	2	17	17,408

A variation of the fixed-head disk is the **Winchester disk**. Winchester disks contain the recording surfaces, read/write heads, and the access mechanism in a sealed cartridge which may be removable or fixed in the disk drive. The densities of recorded data are much higher than for other types of disks because the sealed cartridge allows the read/write heads to float much closer to the recording surface. Table 4.2 lists the characteristics of commercial disks that are current as of the writing of this book.

EXAMPLE 5: ACCESS TIME AND HARD DISKS

The following computations require a grasp of some familiar terms and some new terms. A **kilobyte** is 1,024 bytes (i.e., 2^{10} bytes). **Minimum seek time** is the time needed to move the access arm to an adjacent track. **Maximum seek time** is the time it takes the access arm to move from the outermost or innermost track to the farthest track. Maximum seek time represents the longest possible seek time or the worst case. The law of averages says that for any given access, the access arm has to move half the distance across the tracks. We use the **average seek time** (one-half the maximum seek time) when describing random access and when the relative positions of the access arm before and after the seek are unknown. **Rotational time** is the time needed for the disk pack to make one complete revolution. Consider rotational time in relation to rotational delay. The rotational delay lies between zero delay and the rotational time. The average rotational delay is the time needed to achieve one-half a rotation. For the computations that follow, use the average rotational delay, which is one-half the rotational time.

Assume a block size of 1,000 bytes and that the blocks are stored randomly. The disk drive has the following characteristics:

minimum seek time	=	10 ms
maximum seek time	=	50 ms
average seek time	=	25 ms
rotational time	=	16.67 ms
average rotational delay	=	8.3 ms
transfer rate	=	806 KB/sec
	=	1,024 bytes/K × 806 KB/sec
	=	825,344 bytes/sec

Compute the average access time per block and the percentage of the total access time for the seek and rotational delay.

$$\begin{aligned}
\text{average access time/block} &= \text{seek} + \text{latency} + \text{transfer} \\
&= 25\text{ ms/block} + 8.3\text{ ms/block} + \frac{1{,}000\text{ bytes/bl}}{825{,}344\text{ bytes/}} \\
&= (25\text{ ms} + 8.3\text{ ms} + 1.21\text{ ms})\text{/block} \\
&= 34.51\text{ ms/block}
\end{aligned}$$

$$\begin{aligned}
\%(\text{seek} + \text{rotational delay}) &= \frac{\text{seek} + \text{rotational delay}}{\text{average access time}} \\
&= \frac{25\text{ ms} + 8.3\text{ ms}}{34.51\text{ ms}} \\
&= 96.5\%
\end{aligned}$$

As discussed earlier, the seek time is the most significant factor of the access time, and the transfer rate is the smallest factor—96.5 percent of the access time is seek time and rotational delay, and 3.5 percent is transfer time.

How would we compute access time if the disk had fixed heads? Fixed-head disks have one head per track; therefore, seek time does not apply to the access time calculation.

$$\begin{aligned}
\text{average access time} &= \text{latency} + \text{transfer} \\
&= 8.3\text{ ms} + 1.21\text{ ms} \\
&= 9.51\text{ ms}
\end{aligned}$$

The access time for fixed head disks (9.51 ms) is greatly improved over that for movable head disks (34.51 ms).

Addressing Hard Disks Two addressing methods are commonly used for accessing data on magnetic disks: the cylinder method and the sector method. In the cylinder method, data are stored on a disk using a cylinder number, a surface number, and a record number. When the access arm is positioned on a particular track, the tracks on all surfaces that are vertically aligned and have the same diameter are called a **cylinder**. A cylinder of data can be accessed each time the access arm is positioned. Cylinder *n* is pictured in Figure 4.8. If a disk pack contains 200 tracks per surface, then the disk pack has 200 cylinders. Cylinder 0 is the outermost cylinder, and cylinder 199 is the innermost cylinder. The surface number indicates which surface within the cylinder contains the data. Each track is subdivided into blocks of logical records, and the length of each block may vary from one file to another or within a file. Since each track may hold several blocks, the record number indicates a particular physical record (block) from among those stored on a track.

On disks with the sector format, each track is subdivided into fixed-length **sectors**. Each sector can contain a fixed number of characters that is determined by the manufacturer. Sectoring is a simpler form of address calculation than the cylinder method because each sector on the disk pack has a unique sector number—there is no need for surface and record numbers. The physical records of data are stored in the sectors, and, usually, no records cross sector boundaries. If the block size is larger than the size of a single sector, the block is termed a **spanned record**. Sectoring results in wasted space if the sector size is not a multiple of the record length. In addition, multiple sectors can be accessed if the physical record length is greater than the sector size.

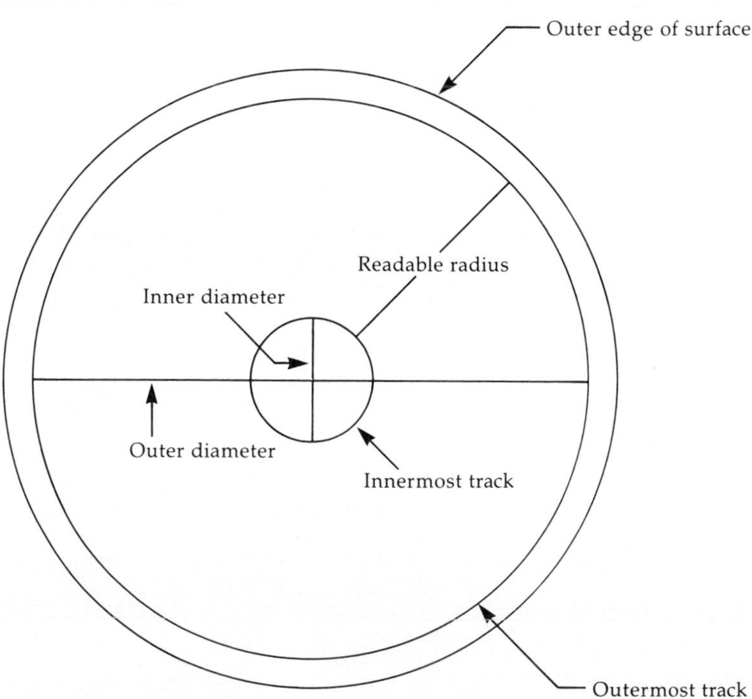

Figure 4.9
The "readable radius" of a disk surface

EXAMPLE 6: CAPACITY OF A HARD DISK

Consider the magnetic disk pack pictured in Figure 4.9. Suppose the disk is cylinder-addressable and has the following characteristics:

9 recording surfaces
surface inner diameter = 22 cm
surface outer diameter = 33 cm
maximum density = 1,600 bits/cm
minimum spacing between tracks = 0.25 mm
rotational speed = 3,600 revolutions per min

Calculate the maximum capacity of the entire disk pack in bits. First find the radius of the readable portion, or **readable radius**, of the surface. The readable radius is less than the actual radius since the outermost track cannot be on the very edge of the surface; neither can the innermost track be located on the very edge. Thus the surface inner diameter and surface outer diameter delimit the readable portion of the surface.

$$\begin{aligned}\text{readable radius} &= \frac{\text{outer diameter} - \text{inner diameter}}{2} \\ &= \frac{33\text{ cm} - 22\text{ cm}}{2} \\ &= 5.5\text{ cm}\end{aligned}$$

The number of tracks per surface depends on the minimum spacing allowable between tracks. Each surface containing n tracks also contains $n - 1$ spaces between the n tracks. Dividing the radius of a surface by the minimum spacing allowed between tracks indicates the maximum number of spacings that fit on one surface ($n - 1$). The number of tracks is one more than the number of spacings: $(n - 1) + 1$.

$$\begin{aligned}\text{tracks/surface} &= \frac{\text{readable radius}}{\text{spacing between tracks}} + 1\text{ track/surface} \\ &= \frac{5.5\text{ cm/surface}}{0.025\text{ cm/track}} + 1\text{ track/surface} \\ &= 221\text{ tracks/surface}\end{aligned}$$

$$\begin{aligned}\text{bits/track} &= \text{density} \times \text{circumference of smallest track} \\ &= \text{density} \times \text{inner diameter} \times \text{pi} \\ &= 1{,}600\text{ bits/cm} \times 22\text{ cm/track} \times 3.14159 \\ &= 110{,}583\text{ bits/track}\end{aligned}$$

$$\begin{aligned}\text{bits/pack} &= \text{bits/track} \times \text{tracks/surface} \times \text{surfaces/pack} \\ &= 110{,}583\text{ bits/track} \times 221\text{ tracks/surface} \times 9\text{ surfaces/pac} \\ &= 219{,}949{,}587\text{ bits/pack} \\ &\sim 26.2\text{ MB/pack}\end{aligned}$$

The capacity of a disk pack is usually expressed in **megabytes** (MB) where *mega* is defined as 2^{20} (1,048,576). The pack has a capacity of approximately 26.2 megabytes.

Now assume that each track in the example above is formatted into 24 sectors instead of cylinders (see Figure 4.10). Calculate the maximum capacity of the entire disk in bits.

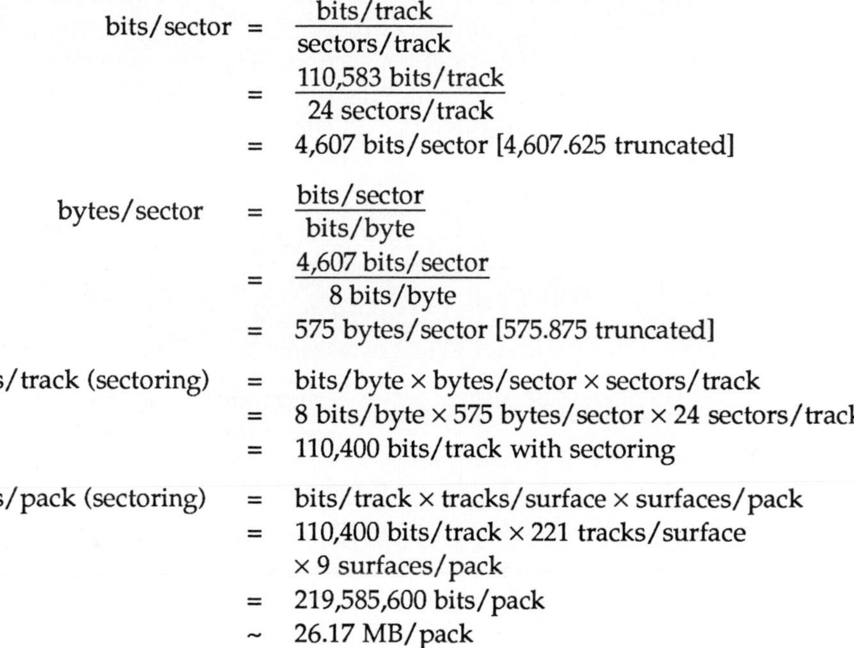

$$\begin{aligned}
\text{bits/sector} &= \frac{\text{bits/track}}{\text{sectors/track}} \\
&= \frac{\text{110,583 bits/track}}{\text{24 sectors/track}} \\
&= \text{4,607 bits/sector [4,607.625 truncated]}
\end{aligned}$$

$$\begin{aligned}
\text{bytes/sector} &= \frac{\text{bits/sector}}{\text{bits/byte}} \\
&= \frac{\text{4,607 bits/sector}}{\text{8 bits/byte}} \\
&= \text{575 bytes/sector [575.875 truncated]}
\end{aligned}$$

$$\begin{aligned}
\text{bits/track (sectoring)} &= \text{bits/byte} \times \text{bytes/sector} \times \text{sectors/track} \\
&= \text{8 bits/byte} \times \text{575 bytes/sector} \times \text{24 sectors/track} \\
&= \text{110,400 bits/track with sectoring}
\end{aligned}$$

$$\begin{aligned}
\text{bits/pack (sectoring)} &= \text{bits/track} \times \text{tracks/surface} \times \text{surfaces/pack} \\
&= \text{110,400 bits/track} \times \text{221 tracks/surface} \\
&\quad \times \text{9 surfaces/pack} \\
&= \text{219,585,600 bits/pack} \\
&\sim \text{26.17 MB/pack}
\end{aligned}$$

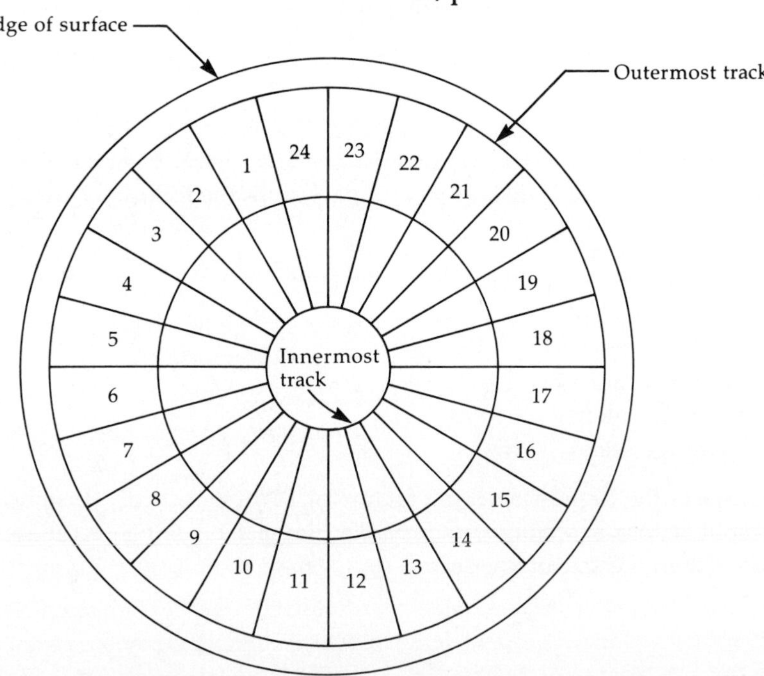

Figure 4.10
A disk surface divided into 24 sectors

The capacity of a disk pack using sectoring is approximately 26.17 megabytes, which is 358,020 bits (or 43.7 kilobytes) less than with the cylinder method. The sector-addressable disk has a smaller capacity than the cylinder-addressable disk.

Return to the cylinder-addressable disk. Calculate the data transfer rate in bytes per second (assume 8 bits per byte). Recall that the transfer rate is the speed at which the data pass by the read/write head. Two factors affect the transfer rate: the number of bytes per track and the rotational speed of the disk in revolutions (rev) per second. Since one revolution is required to read one track of data, the number of bytes per track is also the number of bytes accessed per revolution of the disk pack.

$$
\begin{aligned}
\text{bytes/track} &= \frac{\text{bits/track}}{\text{bits/byte}} \\
&= \frac{110{,}583 \text{ bits/track}}{8 \text{ bits/byte}} \\
&= 13{,}822 \text{ bytes/track} \\
&= 13{,}822 \text{ bytes/rev}
\end{aligned}
$$

$$
\begin{aligned}
\text{transfer rate} &= \text{bytes/rev} \times \frac{\text{rev/min}}{\text{sec/min}} \\
&= 13{,}822 \text{ bytes/rev} \times \frac{3{,}600 \text{ rev/min}}{60 \text{ sec/min}} \\
&= 13{,}822 \text{ bytes/rev} \times 60 \text{ rev/sec} \\
&= 829{,}320 \text{ bytes/sec} \\
&\sim 809.9 \text{ KB/sec}
\end{aligned}
$$

EXAMPLE 7: SPACE CALCULATION FOR HARD DISKS

Consider a magnetic disk drive and pack with the following characteristics:

575 bytes/sector
24 sectors/track
200 tracks/surface
20 surfaces/pack
transfer rate = 806 KB/sec
average latency = 8.3 ms
average seek = 30 ms

Compute the highest blocking factor for 80-byte records. Assume no block is split across a sector boundary. The largest blocking factor must be no larger than the size of one sector.

$$\text{blocking factor} = \frac{\text{number of bytes/sector}}{\text{number of bytes/record}} = \text{records/sector}$$

$$\text{blocking factor} = \frac{\text{575 bytes/sector}}{\text{80 bytes/record}}$$

$$= \text{7 records/block [7.1875 truncated]}$$

Now compute the number of cylinders needed for storing 33,881 blocks of seven 80-byte records.

$$\begin{aligned}\text{capacity of track} &= \text{1 block/sector} \times \text{sectors/track}\\ &= \text{1 block/sector} \times \text{24 sectors/track}\\ &= \text{24 blocks on 1 track}\end{aligned}$$

$$\begin{aligned}\text{capacity of cylinder} &= \text{blocks/track} \times \text{tracks/cylinder}\\ &= \text{24 blocks/track} \times \text{20 tracks/cylinder}\\ &= \text{480 blocks/cylinder}\end{aligned}$$

$$\begin{aligned}\text{number of cylinders} &= \frac{\text{number of blocks}}{\text{blocks/cylinder}}\\ &= \frac{\text{33,881 blocks}}{\text{480 blocks/cylinder}}\\ &= \text{71 cylinders [70.585 rounded]}\end{aligned}$$

(We stored the same file on a 2,400-foot tape in the second space calculation example earlier in the chapter.) Now investigate the time needed to input and process the entire file from a disk using single and double buffering.

EXAMPLE 8: BUFFERING AND HARD DISKS

Compute the total time necessary to sequentially input the disk file in the previous example. Assume the following parameters:

80 bytes/record
7 records/block
33,881 blocks in 71 cylinders
24 sectors/track
200 tracks/surface
20 surfaces/pack
transfer rate = 806 KB/sec
average latency = 8.3 ms
average seek = 30 ms

Once the access arm seeks a particular cylinder, each block in that cylinder can be input with only latency time and transfer time.

input time for entire file =

$$\begin{aligned}
&((\text{latency/block} + \text{transfer/block}) \times \text{number of blocks}) \\
&+ (\text{seek/cylinder} \times \text{number of cylinders}) \\
=\ &((8.3 \text{ ms/block} + \frac{560 \text{ bytes/block}}{825{,}344 \text{ bytes/sec}} \times 33{,}881 \text{ blocks}) \\
&+ (30 \text{ ms/cylinder} \times 71 \text{ cylinders}) \\
=\ &(8.3 \text{ ms/block} + 0.679 \text{ ms/block}) \times 33{,}881 \text{ blocks} + (2{,}130 \text{ ms}) \\
=\ &304.21749 \text{ sec} + 2.130 \text{ sec} \\
=\ &306.35 \text{ sec} \\
=\ &5.1 \text{ min } (9.04 \text{ ms/block average})
\end{aligned}$$

Compute the total time necessary to input the same disk file randomly. Random input requires that a seek take place for each record input.

input time for entire file =

$$\begin{aligned}
&(\text{seek} + \text{latency} + \text{transfer}) \times \text{number of blocks} \\
=\ &(30 \text{ ms/block} + 8.3 \text{ ms/block} + 0.679 \text{ ms/block}) \times 33{,}881 \text{ blocks} \\
=\ &(38.979 \text{ ms/block}) \times 33{,}881 \text{ blocks} \\
=\ &1{,}320.65 \text{ sec} \\
=\ &22 \text{ min}
\end{aligned}$$

Random input of the entire file totals to 22 min versus 5.1 min for sequential input. We will examine this difference later in terms of file design and manipulation.

Assuming single buffering for the disk file with the processing time for one block of 25 ms, compute the total time necessary to sequentially input and process the entire file. Recall the equation for total time from Chapter 3.

$$\begin{aligned}
\text{total time} &= \text{input time for entire file} \\
&\quad + (\text{processing time/block} \times \text{number of blocks}) \\
&= 5.1 \text{ min} + (25 \text{ ms/block} \times 33{,}881 \text{ blocks}) \\
&= 5.1 \text{ min} + 14.12 \text{ min} \\
&= 19.22 \text{ min}
\end{aligned}$$

Assuming double buffering, rework the same problem to compute the total time to input and process the entire file. Since the time to process one block (25 ms) is longer than the time to input one block (9.04 ms on the average), the execution will be processor-bound; therefore, we apply the equation from Chapter 3.

$$\begin{aligned}
\text{total time} &= \text{input time for first block} \\
&\quad + (\text{processing time/block} \times \text{number of blocks}) \\
&= (\text{seek} + \text{latency} + \text{transfer}) \\
&\quad + (25 \text{ ms/block} \times 33{,}881 \text{ blocks}) \\
&= (30 \text{ ms} + 8.3 \text{ ms} + 0.679 \text{ ms}) \\
&\quad + (847{,}025 \text{ ms}) \\
&= 847.064 \text{ sec} \\
&= 14.12 \text{ min}
\end{aligned}$$

Table 4.3 Tape and disk access with single and double buffering

	Disk	Tape	Disk/tape ratio
33,881 blocks	71 cylinders	2400 feet	
avg. time to read 1 block	9.04 ms	44 ms	
single buffering	19.22 min	38.96 min	49.3%
double buffering	14.12 min (processor-bound)	24.85 min (I/O-bound)	56.8%

Double buffering allows the entire file to be input and processed in 14.12 min; the single-buffered file takes 19.22 min. Processor-bound double buffering is 26.5 percent faster than single buffering for this particular file. Table 4.3 lists the processing times that apply to this example. Using single buffering, access to the disk is faster than to the tape—a fact that accounts for the smaller time for the disk file. Using double buffering, the disk processing is processor-bound and limited by processor speeds.

Magnetic disk packs and drives cost more than tape reels and drives and are usually used for files with organizations that tape will not accommodate. The advantage of the disk pack is that it rotates constantly; therefore, disk packs allow shorter access time.

Floppy Disks

A **floppy disk,** or floppy, is a single plastic platter that resembles a 45-RPM phonograph record. Floppies are usually either 8, $5\frac{1}{4}$ or $3\frac{1}{2}$ inches in diameter and are used for secondary storage for microcomputers. The floppy disk rotates and records information in concentric circles or tracks. If it contains data records on one side only, it is a **single-sided** disk. If it contains data records on both sides, it is a **double-sided** disk. There are 40 tracks on a side, which are numbered from 0 to 39 from outermost to innermost. The outside-to-inside track numbering continues from 40 to 79 on the second side of a double-sided disk.

The density of information on floppies is **single-density, double-density, quad-density,** or **high-density.** Double-density floppies can store twice as much data as single-density floppies; double density is typically 3,200 bpi. The storage capacity of a high-density floppy disk is approximately 1.2 MB. The floppy disk is usually sealed in a protective square jacket with two access holes (see Figure 4.11). The oval access hole in the middle of the lower half of the disk allows reading from and writing to the disk. When the write/protect notch in the upper right side of the disk is covered with a label, a user cannot add data to the disk, so the data already there are safe from overwriting. This statement is not true for 8-inch floppy disks. They work just the opposite of the 5.25-inch disks (i.e., the notch must be covered to write data on the disk).

Accessing Floppy Disks Single-sided floppy disk drives have one read/write head as Figure 4.12 depicts. Figure 4.13 illustrates that double-sided floppy drives have two read/write heads to access both sides of a double-sided disk. Floppies are easy to remove from and load into the disk drive.

Each track is divided into several sectors that are uniquely numbered. Floppy disks have soft sectors or hard sectors. **Hard-sectored** floppies have 10, 16, or 32 hard sectors to a side with a ring of tiny index holes (one at each sector boundary) punched near the center of the disk. A beam of light is used to sense the holes to determine the beginning of each sector. **Soft-sectored** disks have an index hole (Figure 4.11) that allows the hardware to detect the first sector of each track; computer software determines the boundaries between sectors. The number of soft sectors ranges from 9 to 26.

Data on floppies are addressed by a sector number and the track number within the sector. The track number indicates the side of a double-sided floppy. Tracks 0 through 39 are on the first side, and tracks 40 through 79 are on the second side.

Figure 4.11
A floppy disk in its protective jacket

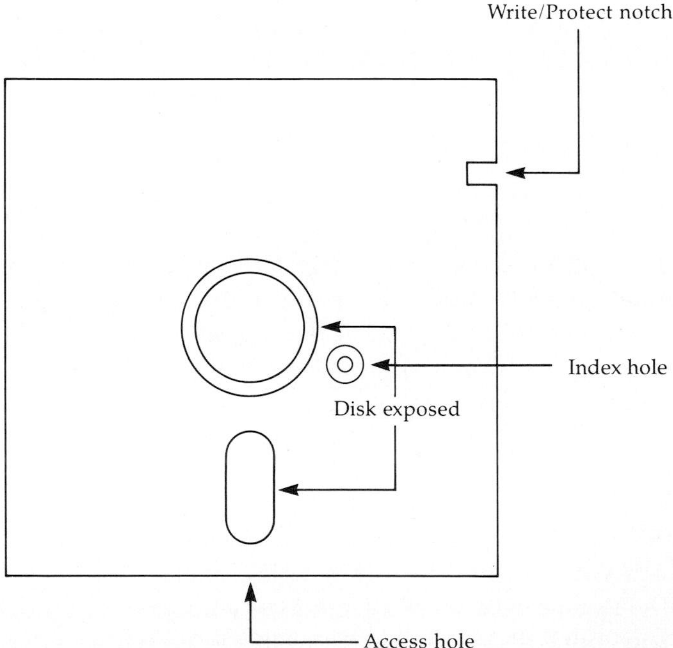

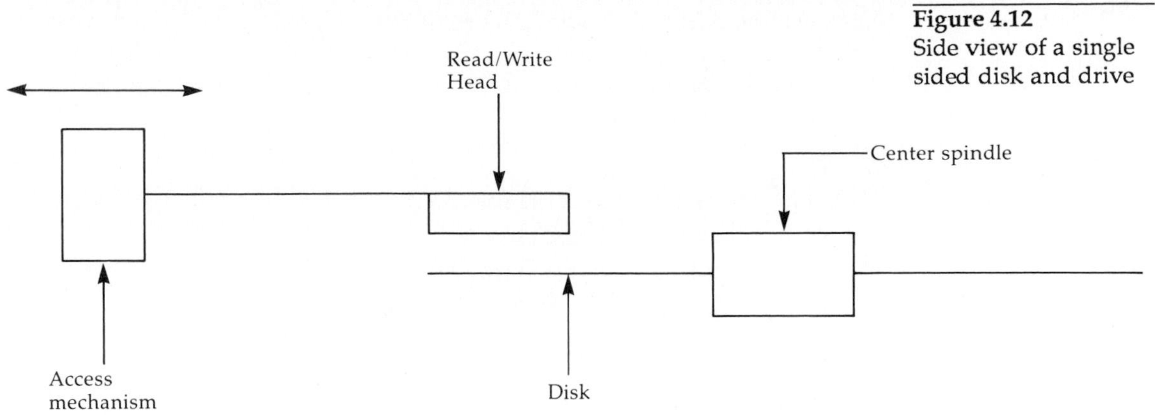

Figure 4.12
Side view of a single sided disk and drive

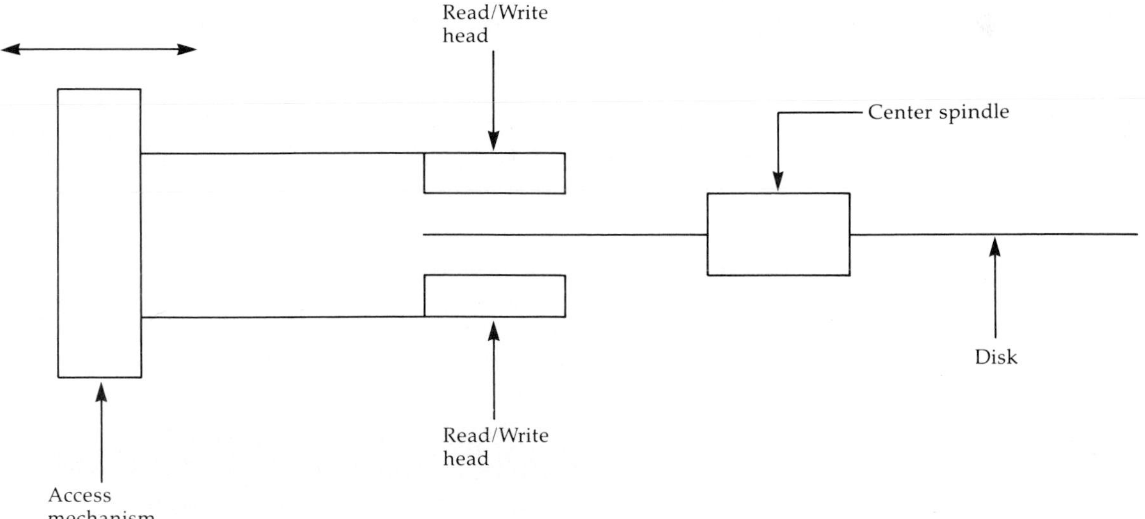

Figure 4.13
Side view of a double sided disk and drive

The access time for floppy disks is composed of seek time, **head settle time** (the time it takes the read/write heads to settle onto the disk and make contact), rotational delay, and the transfer rate.

Some microcomputers use a fixed disk (a hard disk with one or more platters). These fixed disks are sometimes called Winchester disks after the Winchester disks used on larger computers. The fixed disk is nonremovable and sealed within the disk drive. It offers higher densities, greater storage capacities (10 to 80 megabytes), and faster access than a floppy disk.

EXAMPLE 9: ACCESS TIME AND FLOPPY DISKS

Assume that the size of a block is 1,000 bytes and the blocks are stored randomly on a floppy disk with the following characteristics:

tracks = 80
average seek time = 154 ms
head settle time = 25 ms
rotation time = 166 ms/rev
transfer rate = 19.5 KB/sec (19,968 bytes/sec)

Compute the average access time per block.

$$\begin{aligned} \text{average access time/block} &= \text{seek + settle + latency + transfer} \\ &= 154\text{ ms} + 25\text{ ms} + 83\text{ ms} + \frac{1{,}000\text{ bytes/block}}{19{,}968\text{ bytes/sec}} \\ &= (154\text{ ms} + 25\text{ ms} + 83\text{ ms} + 50\text{ ms})/\text{block} \\ &= 312\text{ ms/block} \end{aligned}$$

As with hard-disk packs, seek time is the most significant factor of disk access time.

EXAMPLE 10: CAPACITY OF A FLOPPY DISK

Consider a floppy disk with the following characteristics:

tracks = 80
inner diameter = 2.648 inches
track density = 3,200 bits/inch

Compute the capacity of the entire disk in bits.

$$\begin{aligned} \text{bits/track} &= \text{density} \times \text{circumference of innermost track} \\ &= \text{density} \times \text{inner diameter} \times \text{pi} \\ &= 3{,}200\text{ bits/inch} \times (2.648\text{ inches} \times 3.14159)/\text{track} \\ &= 26{,}620\text{ bits/track} \end{aligned}$$

$$\begin{aligned} \text{bits/disk} &= \text{bits/track} \times \text{tracks/side} \times \text{sides/disk} \\ &= 26{,}620\text{ bits/track} \times 40\text{ tracks/side} \times 2\text{ sides/disk} \\ &= 2{,}129{,}600\text{ bits/disk} \\ &\sim 260\text{ KB/disk} \end{aligned}$$

The capacity of the floppy is 260 KB. The user-accessible capacity of a floppy varies from one operating system to another depending on the amount of overhead to be stored on the floppy and the type of formatting (the number of sectors). A floppy disk with 80 tracks may have only 77 user-accessible tracks since the operating system may use three tracks.

OPTICAL DISK

An **optical disk**, or CD (Compact Disk), uses light instead of magnetism. Data are recorded in tracks on disks of plastic by burning the information into the CD surface with a laser. A low intensity light is focused on a track while reading data and a sensor detects changes in the reflected light. Optical disk drives currently come in three forms. The first is optical read-only memory (OROM), which is very similar to the compact disk used for audio playback. The second is write only read many (WORM) storage devices, which requires a CD recorder (used only once for a given disk) as well as the playback capability. The third and most recent is write-many-read-always (WMRA), which is erasable and uses a technology called thermo-magnetic-optic or simply magneto-optic. This latest technology uses a different substrata that, with a laser's heat and a magnetic field, can be changed without burning actual bits in the surface as with previous technology.

The primary advantage of optical disks is the massive amounts of storage available—from 2 MB to 100 **gigabytes** (GB) where *giga* is 2^{30} (1,073,741,824). Optical disks, therefore, provide an alternative to magnetic tapes for archival storage. The data on magnetic tapes can degrade over time, whereas optical disks offer indefinite data storage. Applications of optical disks for storage of massive amounts of data include medical reference books for physicians, master listings of all books in the Library of Congress, an entire encyclopedia, and legal references for lawyers.

A second advantage of optical disks is the distance between the read heads and the disc's surface, which is a greater distance than that for magnetic disks. The greater distance provides less chance of a disk crash and subsequent data loss. Magnetic heads float less than 1 micron above the disk's surface, while optical heads are as much as 2 mm (2,000 microns) above the disk's surface. In other words, optical heads are more than 2,000 times farther from the surface than magnetic heads. Particles can interfere with the reading or writing of magnetic disks, but the optical heads are focused on the media's **substrate** (an underlying layer) rather than its surface.

A third advantage of optical disks is that digitized graphics, sound, and photographs, as well as data, can be stored on the same optical disc because of its larger storage capacity. Current research is investigating the integration of multimedia information on optical disks for use in databases and encyclopedias.

One disadvantage of optical disks is the access time, which tends to be slower than for magnetic disks. Table 4.2 includes comparison specifications for currently available optical disks.

SUMMARY

Magnetic tape is a sequential-access storage device that is compact, relatively inexpensive, and limited to sequential organization of data. Data are recorded serially along the length of the tape in various recording densities (usually 800, 1,600, or 6,250 bytes per inch). Physical records or blocks of data are separated on the tape by interblock gaps that facilitate the access of data. Several logical records can be grouped in a block to reduce the number of interblock gaps, use the tape space more efficiently, and improve access to the tape. A tape contains two physical markers (the load-point marker and the end-of-tape marker) and a number of labels (the volume label for the reel and the header and trailer labels for each file). Access time consists of the time to start the tape moving, the time to transfer data, and the time to stop the tape.

A magnetic disk is a direct-access storage device that may have movable or fixed read/write heads. Magnetic disks allow direct and sequential organization of data. A magnetic disk pack is a collection of platters on which data are recorded serially along tracks (concentric circles) on the surface of each platter. Cylinders are vertically aligned tracks. Accessing data from a magnetic disk involves seek time (for movable head disks only), head activation time (which is negligible), rotational delay, and transfer time. Magnetic disk packs are either sector-addressable (which means each track is subdivided into sectors of fixed length) or cylinder-addressable (which means each track is subdivided into blocks of fixed or variable length).

Floppy disks are flexible single-platter disks that are used for secondary storage with microcomputers. Floppy disks are single- or double-sided; they employ single-, double-, quad-, or high-density; and they are soft- or hard-sectored. Access time for a floppy disk involves seek time, head settle time, rotational delay, and transfer time. Fixed (hard) disks are also available with microcomputers. These disks are sealed and are similar to the hard Winchester disks that large computers use.

Optical disks are either read-only or write-once read-many devices that provide indefinite storage with capacity for massive amounts of mixed-media data. Access time, however, is slower than that for magnetic disks.

Key Terms

- ASCII
- cylinder
- disk pack
- double-sided floppy
- EBCDIC
- end-of-tape marker
- even parity
- file header label
- file trailer label
- fixed-head disk
- floppy disk
- gigabyte
- hard disk
- hard-sectored floppy
- head activation time
- head settle time
- interblock gap (IBG)
- interrecord gap (IRG)
- kilobyte
- latency
- load-point marker
- magnetic disk
- magnetic tape
- maximum seek time
- megabyte
- millisecond
- minimum seek time
- movable-head disks
- odd parity
- optical disk
- parity bit
- physical record
- readable radius
- recording density
- removable disk
- rotational delay
- rotational time
- sector
- seek time
- single-sided floppy
- soft-sectored floppy
- spanned record
- start/stop time
- substrate
- track
- transfer rate
- transfer time
- volume label
- Winchester disk

EXERCISES

1. Why are interblock gaps (IBGs) necessary?
2. Explain how random-access capabilities are achieved.
3. Which storage media provide random access, and which provide sequential access?
4. What is meant by the density of a tape or disk?
5. What is the difference between a fixed-head disk and a movable-head disk with respect to data access time?
6. Which of the following activities accounts for the greatest amount of time when accessing a block of data on a movable-head disk?

a. seek of a cylinder
b. head activation
c. rotational delay

7. Which of the following activities accounts for the greatest amount of time when accessing a block of data on a fixed-head disk?
   a. seek of a cylinder
   b. head activation
   c. rotational delay
8. What are the relative advantages and disadvantages of magnetic tape and magnetic disk?
9. What different types of data access exist, and what are the differences among these access methods?
10. How does file organization relate to the type of secondary storage device used?
11. Why are records blocked on magnetic tape? Consider transfer rate and tape capacity.
12. Why are records blocked on magnetic disk? Give examples in which blocked records are useful and in which blocked records are not useful.
13. Given a section of tape containing the following binary digits:

```
track 1 :   1 1 1 1 1 1 1
            1 1 1 1 1 1 1
            0 0 0 0 0 1 1
            1 0 1 0 0 0 0
            0 0 1 1 0 0 1
            1 0 0 0 0 0 0
            1 0 0 0 0 1 0
track 8 :   1 1 1 1 1 1 0
```

   What does track 9 contain if the data are recorded with even parity? With odd parity?
14. Consider a magnetic tape drive and reel with the following characteristics:

   length = 2,400 ft
   density = 1,600 bpi
   IBG = 0.5 inch

   Compute the number of 120-byte records that can be stored on the tape reel with blocking factors of:

a. 5

b. 15

c. 25

15. Compute the time required to read the files in a, b, and c of exercise 14 if:

transfer speed = 50 inches/sec
start or stop time = 10 ms (to traverse gap)

16. Distinguish between volume and file.

17. Consider a magnetic tape drive with:

density = 1,600 bpi
IBG = 0.5 inch

How many inches of tape are required to store 50,000 records, each 120 bytes long with a blocking factor of 45.

18. Assume the following parameters:

logical record length = 152 bytes
magnetic tape density = 1,600 bpi
IBG = 0.5 inch

Calculate the blocking factor so that 95 percent of the tape holds data.

19. An I/O buffer of 1,000 bytes is available for a file of logical records. Each logical record is 92 bytes long. Choose a tape recording density of either 800 or 1,600 bpi. Determine the blocking factor that yields the highest recording density. Which recording density and blocking factor yields the lowest recording density?

20. What is the cylinder size of a disk pack that has 10 platters and 200 cylinders? (Remember that the top and bottom platter surfaces are not used.) If a track stores 4,000 bytes and there are 200 tracks per surface, what is the disk capacity?

21. How many movements of the access mechanism (seeks) are required to read a sequential file stored on 21 cylinders of a disk?

22. Consider a disk with the following characteristics:

512 bytes/sector
20 sectors/track
200 tracks/surface
55 surfaces

How many 120-byte logical records can be stored on 10 cylinders of this disk, assuming that no logical record is to be split across a sector boundary?

23. Consider a disk drive with the following characteristics:

    512 bytes/sector
    20 sectors/track
    200 tracks/surface
    5 surfaces
    6,000 rev/min

    a. What is the average latency time in ms?
    b. How many sectors are there on each cylinder?

24. Explain why having one disk controller attached to three disk drives could make I/O operations too slow.

25. Distinguish between fixed-head disks and removable disks.

26. Consider a disk with the following characteristics:

    track = 10,000 bytes
    and rotation = 10 ms

    and data in which:
    block = 1,000 bytes
    IBG = 100 bytes

    a. Compute the maximum transfer rate in bytes/sec.
    b. Compute the average transfer rate in bytes/sec.

Chapter 5

Sequential File Organization

CHAPTER CONTENTS

PREVIEW

THIS CHAPTER EXAMINES THE DESIGN and maintenance of sequential files that are stored on sequential- and random-access storage devices. Algorithms for the maintenance of sequential files stored on sequential-access devices are contrasted with algorithms for the maintenance of sequential files stored on random-access devices. The chapter shows how to apply the concepts of file implementation in an example involving a car-rental agency. The chapter also presents quantitative measures of access times.

PHYSICAL CHARACTERISTICS

Sequential file organization is the oldest type of file organization. It developed in the early 1950s as a result of an association with magnetic tapes, which were the first secondary storage devices available. Today, sequential files are also stored on mass-storage, direct-access storage devices—disks—which are characterized by greater storage capacity and faster access. The physical order of records in a sequential file is the same as the logical order. The records must be accessed sequentially from the beginning of the file to the end. The nth record of the file can be accessed only after the first $n - 1$ records have been accessed. The records in a sequential file may be stored **serially** (no order assumed) or in ascending or descending order by a **key**. (A key is a field in each record that contains a unique identifying value.)

MAINTENANCE

Updating a sequential master file involves adding new records, deleting existing records, and changing information in existing records. **Adding records** to serial nonkeyed files involves appending new records at the end of the existing file. Adding new records to keyed sequential files is more complex because the ascending or descending order of the keys must be maintained. Inserting the new records requires several steps: locating the point of insertion between two existing records, copying all the records prior to the insertion point to a new file, inserting the new record on the new file, and then copying all remaining records after the insertion point to the new file.

Deleting records from a keyed sequential file is as time-consuming as inserting new records into a keyed sequential file. Deletions require the same steps as insertions; all the records except the record to be deleted must be copied to a new file to maintain the physical sequence.

Changes—changing information in existing records in a file—during a **sequential update** also require several steps: the records prior to the record to be changed are copied to a new file, the record is changed and written to the new file, and the copying continues. Some programming languages for use with direct-access storage devices allow a sequential file to be accessed randomly. These languages can change information in a record and rewrite the changed record over the existing record on the file—time-consuming copying from one file to another is eliminated. This chapter concentrates on batch processing of keyed sequential files that may be updated sequentially or randomly.

Batch processing means that updates to the master file accumulate in a **transaction file.** The transactions (updates) are sorted into the same order as the master file and applied to the master file in a **maintenance run**. Each transaction contains the key value of the corresponding master record and an update code indicating the type of update: an insertion of a new record, a deletion of an existing record, or a change to one or more fields of an existing record. Transactions that indicate an insertion also contain all the fields contained in existing master records. The change transactions contain only fields that are to be changed on the master file.

Transaction files are often edited before the maintenance run to help identify invalid data and thus avoid additional maintenance runs. Any transaction errors found during the maintenance run must be put in a new transaction file and the maintenance program run again with the new transaction file. The master file may be created by a program other than the maintenance program or by processing each record as an add transaction against an empty master file. The time that elapses between maintenance runs depends on a number of factors: the rate of change of data, the size of the master file, the need for current data in the master file, and the file activity (see Chapter 1).

As the period of time between updates becomes longer, the data on the master file become more outdated. The number of transactions becomes larger; therefore, the next maintenance run takes longer. If the master file is accessed between updates, the user should perform maintenance runs more often to keep the data current. Each maintenance run has a cost, however, and the cost must be weighed against the need for current data.

A master file is stored in ascending or descending order by a key field. During the updating process, the master file is compared to the transaction file, which has been sorted into the same key order. When a specific key value appears in both files, the maintenance run changes or deletes the record as necessary. When the maintenance run encounters a transaction record whose key value does not match any key on the master file, the record must be new; it is added to the master file. The maintenance program must detect three common errors relative to the matching process: trying to insert a record with a key that exists on the master file, trying to delete a record whose key does not exist on the master file, and trying to change data on a record whose key does not exist on the master file. Different applications handle these errors differently.

An **audit/error listing** is output as part of the maintenance run. It lists the transaction keys and update codes that summarize the additions, changes, and deletions that resulted from the maintenance run and any errors that occurred during the process. The user corrects the records that contain errors and stores the records in a new transaction file for the next update. The diagram in Figure 5.1 shows the input and output of a maintenance run.

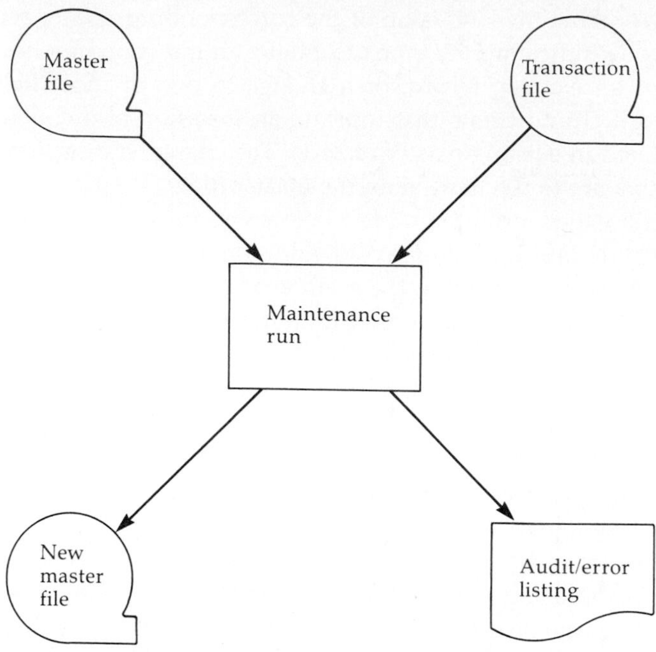

Figure 5.1
System diagram of sequential file maintenance

TRADITIONAL ALGORITHMS FOR UPDATING SEQUENTIAL FILES

The algorithm required to update a master file with a batch of transactions is the same as the algorithm for merging two files. The keys in the transaction file are compared with the keys in the master file. When the keys are the same, changes are made to the master file records; when the keys are not the same, the records are merged into a new master file.

Changes

Consider first the case of a transaction file containing only changes to existing records (no additions or deletions) and only one transaction per master file record. The logic is given in pseudocode in Algorithm 5.1. Each iteration of the `Loop` processes the record with the smaller key value regardless of whether it is in the master record or the transaction record. The algorithm employs an `Exit` at the top of the `Loop` instead of the bottom of the `Loop` so that both files can be checked for an end-of-file condition at the first iteration. The algorithm terminates in case both files happen to be empty.

```
WITH Sequential_IO;
PACKAGE Update_Objects Is
        -- This package is a shell of the necessary
        -- data types and objects
        -- to be USEd by the update algorithms
    TYPE Master_Record_Type Is Record
                                key : Key_Type;
                                -- other items
                             End Record;
    TYPE Transaction_Record_Type Is Record
                                    update_code : Code_Type;
                                    key : Key_Type;
                                    -- transactions
                                End Record;
    PACKAGE Master_IO Is New Sequential_IO (Master_Record_Type);
    new_master, master : Master_IO.File_Type;
    trans : Text_IO.File_Type;
    master_record : Master_Record_Type;
    transaction : Transaction_Record_Type;
    SENTINEL : Constant Key_Type := some_unique_value;
END Update_Objects;
```

ALGORITHM 5.1 Update_Master

```
            -- change transactions;
            -- one transaction per master record
USE Update_Objects
Get_Next_Trans ( transaction )
Get_Next_Master ( master_record )
Loop
    Exit When master_record.key = SENTINEL
          And transaction.key  = SENTINEL
          -- exit when both files end
    If master_record.key < transaction.key -- no trans for this master
        output master record to new master
        Get_Next_Master ( master_record.record )
    Elsif master_record.key = transaction.key
        make change in master record
        output master record to new master
        Get_Next_Master ( master_record )
        Get_Next_Trans ( transaction )
    Else  --  master_record.key > transaction.key
        print "no matching master record for trans key"
        Get_Next_Trans ( transaction )
    End If
End Loop
```

```
PROCEDURE Get_Next_Master ( master_record : Out Master_Record_Type )
    If End_Of_File (master)
       master_record.key ← SENTINEL
    Else
       input master record
    End If
```

```
PROCEDURE Get_Next_Trans ( transaction : Out Transaction_Record_Type )
    If End_Of_File (trans)
      transaction.key ← SENTINEL
    Else
      input transaction record
    End If
```

The primary function of the logic in Algorithm 5.1 is to compare the key of the master record with the key of the transaction record. There are three cases to consider. In the first case (lines 5 through 7), the master key is less than the transaction key; no transactions are applied to this master record, so the master record is copied to the new master. The next master record must be input and matched with the current transaction key the next time through the `Loop`. In the second case (lines 8 through 12), the master key and transaction key are the same. The specified change is made in the master record, which is then copied to the new master. The next master record and the next transaction must be input for comparison the next time through the `Loop`. In the third case (lines 14 and 15), the master key is greater than the transaction key; no master record matches this transaction key, so an error message is printed, and the next transaction record is input to compare with the current master record. If `End_Of_File` is reached on the transaction file, the `SENTINEL` (a constant value that is higher than any key occurring on either file) is moved to the transaction key. The remaining master file records are copied with no changes to the new master (according to the logic of lines 5 through 7). If `End_Of_File` is reached on the master file, the same sentinel value is moved to the master key, and error messages are printed for the remaining transaction records that did not match any master records (lines 14 and 15).

The sentinel value in `master_record.key` and `transaction.key` (rather than the functions `End_Of_File(master)` and `End_Of_File(trans)` provided in the package `Sequential_IO`) stops the main `Loop`—the ends of both of the files have been reached. The need to read another record from either file is determined by the algorithm; a read to both files does not occur each time through the loop. Therefore, a sentinel loop is needed for reading and matching the two files. Algorithm 5.1 uses the function `End_Of_File` after processing a transaction or master record, then moves the sentinel value to the key. Another approach is to add the sentinel value as the last record of the master and transaction files and repeat until the sentinels are input. Algorithm 5.1 is a simple form that assumes only one transaction per master record. This assumption is probably unrealistic because a transaction file may contain multiple changes to be applied to any given master record. The algorithm can be easily modified; by removing lines 10 and 11, the master record is not written until the transaction key changes. The resulting algorithm, Algorithm 5.2, can handle multiple transactions.

Each iteration of the `Loop` processes one record. A record is the result of an unmatched master record, an unmatched transaction record, or a transaction with the same key as the master key. When the master key and the transaction key are the same (line 8), the specified change is made in the master record (line 9), but the master record is not output to the new master file because more transactions with the same key may follow. As soon as a transaction record with a different key is found, the master key is less than the transaction key (line 5). The changed master record is written to the new master file (line 6), and the next master record is input (line 7).

ALGORITHM 5.2 Update_Master

```
                --   change transactions;
                --   several transactions per master record
   USE Update_Objects
 1 Get_Next_Trans ( transaction )
 2 Get_Next_Master ( master_record )
 3 Loop
 4      Exit When master_record.key = SENTINEL
            And transaction.key   = SENTINEL
                --   exit when both files end
 5      If master_record.key < transaction.key
                --   no transactions for this master or
                --   changes have already been made
 6           output master record to new master
 7           Get_Next_Master ( master_record )
 8      Elsif master_record.key = transaction.key
 9           make change in master record
10           Get_Next_Trans ( transaction )
11      Else    --   master_record.key > transaction.key
12           print "no matching master record for trans key"
13           Get_Next_Trans ( transaction )
14      End If
15 End Loop
```

Additions

Consider next the case of a transaction file containing additions, changes, and multiple transactions per transaction key. The possibilities are

1. one or more changes per transaction key
2. one addition per transaction key
3. several additions per transaction key
4. one addition and one or more changes per transaction key
5. several additions and one or more changes per transaction key

To keep track of the transactions that apply, the user must define a new field that specifies the updates. This field contains an `update_code` : an `A` if the transaction is an addition to the master file or a `C` if the transaction is a change to an existing master record.

Algorithm 5.2 (lines 8 through 10) handles the first possibility, that the transaction file contains one or more changes per transaction key. The second possibility, in which there is one addition per transaction key, can be processed when the master key is greater than the transaction key and the update code is A. In this situation the transaction record is output to the new master file as a new master record. The third possibility, that the transaction file contains several additions per transaction key, indicates an error in all but the first addition if all the master keys are to remain unique. In this case the first addition progresses as in situation 2 in the list above, but each of the remaining additions for the same key causes an error message.

The need for one addition and one or more changes per transaction key arises if the time between updates is so long that changes have been identified since the addition transaction was entered. To process an addition and changes to the same key, the transaction file must record the date a transaction is entered. The transactions are sorted in ascending order by entry date within each transaction key. (The keys are also sorted in ascending order.) A chronological sort ensures that transactions are processed in chronological order. Even though transactions are batched, the effect is the same as if the user performed each transaction as soon as the need arose.

The fifth possibility in the list above is a combination of situation 3 and situation 4. The first addition can be processed, all the following additions generate error messages, and the changes are processed. A transaction that contains invalid update codes (codes other than A and C) also causes an error message. Algorithm 5.3 processes all five possibilities discussed above, and it generates an error message if the file contains invalid update codes.

ALGORITHM 5.3 Update_Master

```
                --   addition and change transactions;
                --   several transactions per master record
USE Update_Objects
Get_Next_Trans ( transaction )
Get_Next_Master ( master_record )
Loop
     Exit When master_record.key = SENTINEL
            And transaction.key  = SENTINEL
                -- exit when both files end
     If master_record.key < transaction.key
                --   no transactions for this master or
                --   changes have already been made
          output master record to new master
          Get_Next_Master ( master_record )
     Elsif master_record.key = transaction.key
          Case transaction.update_code
               'A' → print "duplicate add"
                     Get_Next_Trans ( transaction )
               'C' → make change in master record
                     Get_Next_Trans ( transaction )
               Others → print "invalid update code"
                        Get_Next_Trans ( transaction )
          End Case
```

```
16      Else    --    master_record.key > transaction.key
17          Nomatch ( transaction )
        End If
    End Loop
```

```
PROCEDURE Nomatch ( transaction : In Out Transaction_Record_Type )
    new_key : Key_Type

 1  Case transaction.update_code
 2      'A' → Build new record from trans record
 3              new_key ← transaction.key
 4              Get_Next_Trans ( transaction )
 5              Loop
 6                  Exit When transaction.key = SENTINEL
 7                          Or transaction.key /= new_key
 8                  Case transaction.update_code
 9                      'A' → print "duplicate add"
10                      'C' → make change in new record
11                      Others → print "invalid update code"
                    End Case
12                  Get_Next_Trans ( transaction )
                End Loop
13              output new record to new master

14      'C' → print "no matching master record for trans key"
15              Get_Next_Trans ( transaction )

16      Others → print "invalid update code"
17                  Get_Next_Trans ( transaction )
    End Case
```

Two modifications are required to handle addition transactions that occur (1) when the master key equals the transaction key and (2) when the master key is greater than the transaction key. When the master and transaction keys are the same (line 8 of Algorithm 5.3) and the transaction is an addition (possibility number 2), the message `duplicate add` is printed (line 10 of Algorithm 5.3).

When the master key is greater than the transaction key (line 16), Algorithm 5.3 calls `Nomatch`. If the transaction is a change, the error message `no matching master record for trans key` prints, and `Nomatch` gets another transaction record (lines 14 and 15). If the transaction is an addition (situation 2), a new record is built using the data from the transaction record (line 2 of `Nomatch`). For any addition transaction that follows with the same key (situations 3 and 5), the message `duplicate add` prints (line 9 of `Nomatch`). For any change transactions that follow with the same key (situations 4 and 5), the specified changes are made in the new record (line 10 of `Nomatch`). When a different transaction key is input (line 7 of `Nomatch`), the new record is output to the new master (line 13 of `Nomatch`). The main algorithm continues to process the remaining master and transaction records.

Deletions

Consider finally the case of a transaction file containing additions, changes, deletions, and multiple transactions per transaction key. To accommodate deletion transactions, we employ Algorithm 5.4, a modification of Algorithm 5.3. Use Algorithm 5.4 in the following situations:

1. to perform one deletion per transaction key
2. to perform several deletions per transaction key
3. to perform an addition and a deletion per transaction key
4. to perform one or more changes and a deletion per transaction key
5. to perform an addition, one or more changes, and a deletion per transaction key

The update code may contain an `A` for addition, a `C` for changes, and a `D` for deletion of an existing master record. Any other update code is invalid. To implement Algorithm 5.4, which calls for three types of transactions, we sort the transactions in ascending order by entry date within each transaction key. Algorithm 5.4 applies the transactions in the order in which they occurred in real time.

One deletion per transaction key (situation 1) can be processed when the master key and the transaction key are the same. The algorithm does not copy the master record to the new master file; rather, it causes the next master record to be input. Executing several deletions per transaction key (situation 2) is similar to executing several additions per transaction key: The first deletion transaction key is processed, but the remaining deletions for the same key trigger an error message. The last three situations only occur if the time between updates is sufficient to allow changes and deletions to accumulate in the transaction file after additions to the same key.

The modified algorithm processes one addition and one deletion for the same key (situation 3) and one addition, changes, and one deletion for the same key (situation 5) as Algorithm 5.3 processes additions and changes for the same key. Assuming that an addition is entered before the deletion of the same key, the addition causes a new record to be built from the transaction record. The deletion that follows prevents the new record from being copied to the new master. Similarly, in situation 5 in the list above, an addition causes a new record to be built from the transaction record. One or more changes to the new record follow, then a deletion prevents the new record from being copied to the new master.

ALGORITHM 5.4 Update_Master

```
                    --  addition, change, and deletion transactions;
                    --  several transactions per master record
 USE Update_Objects
 Get_Next_Trans ( transaction )
 Get_Next_Master ( master_record )
 Loop
     Exit When master_record.key = SENTINEL
```

```
              And transaction.key  =  SENTINEL
                  --    exit when both files end
        If master_record.key < transaction.key
                  --    no transactions for this master or
                  --    changes have already been made
            output master record to new master
            Get_Next_Master ( master_record )
        Elsif master_record.key = transaction.key
            Case transaction.update_code
                'A' → print "duplicate add"
                      Get_Next_Trans ( transaction )
                'C' → make change in master record
                      Get_Next_Trans ( transaction )
                'D' → Get_Next_Master ( master_record )
                      Get_Next_Trans ( transaction )
                Others → print "invalid update code"
                         Get_Next_Trans ( transaction )
            End Case
        Else    --   master_record.key > transaction.key
            Nomatch ( transaction )
        End If
    End Loop

PROCEDURE Nomatch ( transaction : In Out Transaction_Record_Type )
        delete_record : Boolean
        new_key : Key_Type

        Case transaction.update_code
            'A' → build new record from trans record
                  new_key ← transaction.key
                  delete_record ← FALSE
                  Get_Next_Trans ( transaction )
                  Loop
                      Exit When transaction.key = SENTINEL
                             Or transaction.key /= new_key
                      Case transaction.update_code
                          'A' → print "duplicate add"
                          'C' → make change in new record
                          'D' → delete_record ← TRUE
                                Get_Next_Trans ( transaction )
                                Exit
                          Others → print "invalid update code"
                      End Case
                      Get_Next_Trans ( transaction )
                  End Loop
                  If Not delete_record
                      output new record to new master
                  End If
            'C'|
            'D' → print "no matching master record for trans key"
                  Get_Next_Trans ( transaction )
            Others → print "invalid update code"
                     Get_Next_Trans ( transaction )
        End Case
```

In situation 4 multiple changes to an existing record usually precede a deletion of the same record. Multiple changes are processed by the algorithm as one change transaction per execution of the inner `Loop`. The need to perform a deletion for the same key is a situation similar to situation 1: The master record, with changes, is not copied to the new master file; instead, the next master record is input.

To perform one deletion per transaction key (situation 1), the algorithm does not copy the master record to the next master file (line 14 of Algorithm 5.4). Instead it inputs the next master record. The transaction key of any deletion transactions that follow (situation 2) is lower than the remaining master record input (line 19 of Algorithm 5.4). The result is an error message (line 19 of `Nomatch`).

In situation 3, in which the transaction key of an addition is different from the key of the pending master record (line 2 of `Nomatch`) and there is a deletion for the same transaction key, `Nomatch` sets the Boolean flag `delete_record` in line 12. The `Exit` stops the `Loop` (line 14 of `Nomatch`) and prevents the newly built record from being copied to the new master file (lines 17 and 18 of `Nomatch`). In situation 4 (in which there are one or more changes and a deletion) and situation 5 (in which there are one addition, one deletion, and at least one change), the result is the same as in situation 3: The delete transaction stops the `Loop` and prevents the new record from being written to the new master. In essence the algorithm ignores all transactions for this key value.

Table 5.1 Transaction file T1, data for a car-rental agency

Code	Id no.	Make	Style	Model	Mileage	Color
A	C1	Dodge	2 DR	Omni	25,000	grey
A	C2	Dodge	2 DR	Aspen	7,000	tan
A	F1	Ford	2 DR	Escort	54,000	white
A	F2	Lincoln	4 DR	Continental	38,000	black
A	F3	Ford	2 DR	Thunderbird	35,000	blue
A	GM1	Cadillac	4 DR	Fleetwood	9,000	red
A	GM2	Oldsmobile	4 DR	Delta 88	28,050	blue
A	GM3	Chevrolet	2 DR	Camaro	33,000	silver
A	GM4	Cadillac	2 DR	Cimarron	63,000	maroon
A	GM5	Oldsmobile	4 DR	98	11,000	green
A	H1	Honda	4 DR	Accord	32,000	yellow
A	H2	Honda	2 DR HB	Accord	11,250	brown
A	T1	Toyota	2 DR HB	Celica	3,400	white

CASE STUDY 5.1

To demonstrate the effectiveness of Algorithm 5.4, consider an example involving a car-rental agency. Initially, assume the car-rental master file is empty. Table 5.1 shows Transaction File T1, which contains the data to be added to the master file. The id number is the primary key; notice that File T1 is in the order of ascending id numbers. To compare Algorithm 5.4, a traditional algorithm, to the modern algorithm presented later, we tally cases in which the operations in the traditional algorithm differ from the operations in the modern algorithm for the same transaction file. These operations are usually Boolean operators and assignment of values to flags. The operations in lines 4 (two operations), 5 (one operation), and 8 (one operation) of the main algorithm and lines 3, 4, 7, 8, and 17 (one operation each) of `Nomatch` are the operations counted. Upon execution of Algorithm 5.4, the following actions take place:

1. `Get_Next_Trans` inputs the first transaction.
2. `Get_Next_Master` finds the master file empty, so `master_record.key` is filled with the `SENTINEL` value that is higher than any transaction key.
3. In line 4 `master_record.key = SENTINEL And transaction.key = SENTINEL` is `FALSE`. The operation count = 2.
4. Since `master_record.key` contains the sentinel value, line 5 is `FALSE`. In consequence we move to line 8. The operation count = 3.
5. The result of line 8 is `FALSE` since `master_record.key` contains the sentinel. We move to line 18. The operation count = 4.
6. The main algorithm calls `Nomatch`.
7. Since `transaction.update_code` is `A`, a new record is filled with the information in the transaction record, the transaction key is saved in `new_key`, and `delete_record` is set to `FALSE`. The operation count = 6.
8. `Get_Next_Trans` inputs the next transaction record.
9. The Boolean expression in lines 7 and 8, `transaction.key /= new_key`, is `TRUE`. We move to `Nomatch`, line 17. The operation count = 8.
10. The object `delete_record` is `FALSE`, so the new record is output to the new master file. The operation count = 9.
11. The body of `Loop`, which begins in line 4 of the main algorithm, executes the last transactions. Lines 4 through 19 are repeated for each transaction until `Get_Next_Trans` finds `End_Of_File(trans)` is `TRUE`. Then `transaction.key` is filled with the sentinel value. The operation count = 9 + (10 operations × 12 transactions) = 129.
12. The next pass through line 4 evaluates to `TRUE`, and the program terminates. The operation count = 130.

Table 5.2 Car-rental agency master file after creation

Id no.	Make	Style	Model	Mileage	Color
C1	Dodge	2 DR	Omni	25,000	grey
C2	Dodge	2 DR	Aspen	7,000	tan
F1	Ford	2 DR HB	Escort	54,000	white
F2	Lincoln	4 DR	Continental	38,000	black
F3	Ford	2 DR	Thunderbird	35,000	blue
GM1	Cadillac	4 DR	Fleetwood	9,000	red
GM2	Oldsmobile	4 DR	Delta 88	28,050	blue
GM3	Chevrolet	2 DR	Camaro	33,000	silver
GM4	Cadillac	2 DR	Cimarron	63,000	maroon
GM5	Oldsmobile	4 DR	98	11,000	green
H1	Honda	4 DR	Accord	32,000	yellow
H2	Honda	2 DR HB	Accord	11,250	brown
T1	Toyota	2 DR HB	Celica	3,400	white

Table 5.3 Transaction file T2

Code	Id No.	Make	Style	Model	Mileage	Color
A	GM6	Chevrolet	4 DR	Cimarron	11,250	brown

The `Loop` satisfactorily checks for `End_Of_File` on both the master file and the transaction file. The loop terminates when both files have ended. In this case the master file was empty at the beginning of the algorithm, so all the addition transactions were written to the new master file. Table 5.2 shows the resulting master file.

The transaction file T2 in Table 5.3 contains only one record, which is applied to the master file just created. The following is the trace of Algorithm 5.4:

1. `Get_Next_Trans` inputs the first transaction.
2. `Get_Next_Master` inputs the first master record.
3. Line 4 is `FALSE`. The operation count = 2.
4. Since `master_record.key` is `C1` and `transaction.key` is `GM6`, `C1` is output to the new master file, and `C2` is input (lines 5 through 7). The operation count = 3.
5. Line 4 is `FALSE`. The operation count = 5.
6. `C2`, `master_record.key`, is less than `GM6`, `transaction.key`. As a result, `C2` is output to the new master file, and `F1` is input (lines 5 through 7). The operation count = 6.
7. Line 4 is `FALSE`. The operation count = 8.

8. `F1, master_record.key`, is less than `GM6, transaction.key`. As a result, `F1` is output to the new master file, and `F2` is input (lines 5 through 7). The operation count = 9.
9. Line 4 is `FALSE`. The operation count = 11.
10. `F2, master_record.key`, is less than `GM6, transaction.key`. As a result, `F2` is output to the new master file, and `F3` is input (lines 5 through 7). The operation count = 12.
11. Line 4 is `FALSE`. The operation count = 14.
12. `F3, master_record.key`, is less than `GM6, transaction.key`. As a result, `F3` is output to the new master file, and `GM1` is input (lines 5 through 7). The operation count = 15.
13. Line 4 is `FALSE`. The operation count = 17.
14. `GM1, master_record.key`, is less than `GM6, transaction.key`. As a result, `GM1` is output to the new master file, and `GM2` is input (lines 5 through 7). The operation count = 18.
15. Line 4 is `FALSE`. The operation count = 20.
16. `GM2, master_record.key`, is less than `GM6, transaction.key`. As a result, `GM6` is output to the new master file, and `GM3` is input (lines 5 through 7). The operation count = 21.
17. Line 4 is `FALSE`. The operation count = 23.
18. `GM3, master_record.key`, is less than `GM6, transaction.key`. As a result, `GM3` is output to the new master file, and `GM4` is input (lines 5 through 7). The operation count = 24.
19. Line 4 is `FALSE`. The operation count = 26.
20. `GM4, master_record.key`, is less than `GM6, transaction.key`. As a result, `GM4` is output to the new master file, and `GM5` is input (lines 5 through 7). The operation count = 27.
21. Line 4 is `FALSE`. The operation count = 29.
22. `GM5, master_record.key`, is less than `GM6, transaction.key`. As a result, `GM5` is output to the new master file, and `H1` is input (lines 5 through 7). The operation count = 30.
23. Line 4 is `FALSE`. The operation count = 32.
24. `H1, master_record.key`, is greater than `GM6, transaction.key`. As a result, line 19 of the main algorithm calls `Nomatch`. The operation count = 34.
25. Since `transaction.update_code` is `A`, a new record is filled with the information in the transaction record `GM6`, the transaction key is saved in `new_key`, and `delete_record` is set to `FALSE`. The operation count = 36.
26. `Get_Next_Trans` finds `End_Of_File(trans) TRUE`; therefore, `transaction.key` is filled with the sentinel value.

27. The Boolean expression in lines 7 and 8 of `Nomatch`, `transaction.key /= new_key`, is `TRUE`. We move to line 17 of `Nomatch`. The operation count = 38.
28. The object `delete_record` is `FALSE`, so the new record `GM6` is output to the new master file. The operation count = 39.
29. The `Exit When`, which begins in line 4 of the main algorithm, is `FALSE`. The operation count = 41.
30. `H1`, `master_record.key`, is less than `transaction.key` (the sentinel), so `H1` is output to the new master file, and `H2` is input (lines 5 through 7). The operation count = 42.
31. Line 4 is `FALSE`. The operation count = 44.
32. `H2`, `master_record.key`, is less than `transaction.key` (the sentinel), so `H2` is output to the new master file, and the id `T1` is input (lines 5 through 7). The operation count = 45.
33. Line 4 is `FALSE`. The operation count = 47.
34. `T1`, `master_record.key`, is less than `transaction.key` (the sentinel), so the id `T1` is output to the new master file, and `Get_Next_Master` finds `End_Of_File(master) TRUE`; `master_record.key` is filled with the sentinel value (lines 5 through 7). The operation count = 48.
35. The next pass through line 4 evaluates to `TRUE`, and the algorithm terminates. The operation count = 50.

The `Exit When` checks for `End_Of_File` on both the master file and the transaction file, and the algorithm terminates when both files have ended. In this case the master file records were copied to the new master file until the proper order for the addition of transaction `GM6`, at which time the addition took place. The algorithm found no more transactions, so the rest of the master file was copied to the new master file. Table 5.4 shows the resulting master file.

Table 5.4 Car-rental agency master file after update

Id no.	Make	Style	Model	Mileage	Color
C1	Dodge	2 DR	Omni	25,000	grey
C2	Dodge	2 DR	Aspen	7,000	tan
F1	Ford	2 DR HB	Escort	54,000	white
F2	Lincoln	4 DR	Continental	38,000	black
F3	Ford	2 DR	Thunderbird	35,000	blue
GM1	Cadillac	4 DR	Fleetwood	9,000	red
GM2	Oldsmobile	4 DR	Delta 88	28,050	blue
GM3	Chevrolet	2 DR	Camaro	33,000	silver
GM4	Cadillac	2 DR	Cimarron	63,000	maroon
GM5	Oldsmobile	4 DR	98	11,000	green

Id no.	Make	Style	Model	Mileage	Color
GM6	Chevrolet	4 DR	Cimarron	11,250	brown
H1	Honda	4 DR	Accord	32,000	yellow
H2	Honda	2 DR HB	Accord	11,250	brown
T1	Toyota	2 DR HB	Celica	3,400	white

Table 5.5 Transaction file T3

Code	Id no.	Make	Style	Model	Mileage	Color
D	F1					
A	GM7	Pontiac	2 DR	Fiero	1,250	orange
C	GM7				5,000	
D	GM7					
A	GM7	Pontiac	2 DR	Fiero	1,500	navy
D	H3					
C	T1				7,800	
D	T1					

The transaction file T3 in Table 5.5 illustrates a set of transactions that includes an addition, a change, a deletion, and a subsequent addition for the same key. `GM7` is added to the fleet, the mileage is updated later, the car is subsequently wrecked and deleted from the fleet, and a navy Fiero is assigned the same key, `GM7`. (In this application deleted keys are reassigned when the cars are replaced by new ones.) The process of applying T3 to the master file is as follows:

1. `Get_Next_Trans` inputs the first transaction.
2. `Get_Next_Master` inputs the first master record.
3. Line 4 is `FALSE`. The operation count = 2.
4. Lines 4 through 7 are repeated for master records `C1` through `C2`. The operation count = 6.
5. Line 4 is `FALSE; master_record.key, F1,` is the same as `transaction.key`. The `transaction.update_code` is `D`, so `Get_Next_Master` inputs `F2`, and `Get_Next_Trans` inputs the code `A` and the id `GM7`. The operation count = 10.
6. Lines 4 through 7 are repeated for master records `F2` through `GM6`, the point that `master_record.key = H1` and `transaction.key = GM7`. The operation count = 10 + (3 operations × 8 transactions) = 34.
7. Line 4 is `FALSE; master_record.key, H1,` is greater than `transaction.key, GM7`. As a result, main algorithm line 19 calls `Nomatch`. The operation count = 38.
8. Since the `transaction.update_code` is `A`, a new record is filled with the information in the transaction record `GM7`, the id number currently assigned to the orange Fiero. The transaction key is saved in

new_key, and delete_record is set to FALSE. The operation count = 40.

9. Get_Next_Trans inputs the code C and the id GM7.
10. The Boolean expression in lines 7 and 8 of Nomatch is FALSE. As a result, the mileage change is made to GM7, and Get_Next_Trans inputs the code D and the id GM7. The operation count = 42.
11. Lines 7 and 8 of Nomatch evaluate to FALSE, so delete_record is set to TRUE, and Get_Next_Trans inputs the code A and the id GM7. The operation count = 44.
12. We exit the loop and move to line 17.
13. The object delete_record is TRUE, so we move to line 4 of the main algorithm. The operation count = 45.
14. Line 4 evaluates to FALSE. The operation count = 47.
15. H1, master_record.key, is greater than GM7, transaction.key (the second A). As a result, main algorithm line 19 calls Nomatch. The operation count = 49.
16. The transaction.update_code is A, a new record is filled with the data about the navy Fiero, GM7 is saved in new_key, and delete_record is set to FALSE. The operation count = 51.
17. Get_Next_Trans inputs the code D and the transaction involving H3.
18. Lines 7 and 8 of Nomatch, transaction.key /= new_key, is TRUE, so we move to line 16. The operation count = 53.
19. The object delete_record is FALSE, so the new record GM7, data about the navy Fiero is output to the new master file. The operation count = 54.
20. Lines 4 through 7 of the main algorithm are repeated for master records H1 and H2. The operation count = 60.
21. In line 4, master_record.key = T1 and transaction.key = H3; the line is FALSE, so the main algorithm calls Nomatch. The operation count = 64.
22. The transaction.update_code is D, so the error message no matching record for trans key is output.
23. Get_Next_Trans inputs the code C and the transaction involving T1.
24. In line 4 of the main algorithm, master_record.key = T1, and transaction.key = T1. Because line 4 is FALSE, the algorithm changes the mileage. The operation count = 68.
25. Get_Next_Trans inputs the code D and the transaction involving T1.
26. Line 4 is FALSE; master_record.key and transaction.key are the same (T1). Because the transaction.update_code is D, line 14 calls Get_Next_Master, which sets master_record.key to the sentinel value and calls Get_Next_Trans (line 15). Get_Next_Trans sets transaction.key to the sentinel value. The operation count = 72.

27. Line 4 evaluates to `TRUE`, and the program terminates. The operation count = 74.

Table 5.6 shows the resulting master file. The only error message printed on the audit/error list refers to the code `D` and the id `H3`. The error in the transaction should be corrected and applied during the next maintenance run.

Table 5.6 Master file after update with transaction file T3

Id no.	Make	Style	Model	Mileage	Color
C1	Dodge	2 DR	Omni	25,000	grey
C2	Dodge	2 DR	Aspen	7,000	tan
F2	Lincoln	4 DR	Continental	38,000	black
F3	Ford	2 DR	Thunderbird	35,000	blue
GM1	Cadillac	4 DR	Fleetwood	9,000	red
GM2	Oldsmobile	4 DR	Delta 88	28,050	blue
GM3	Chevrolet	2 DR	Camaro	33,000	silver
GM4	Cadillac	2 DR	Cimarron	63,000	maroon
GM5	Oldsmobile	4 DR	98	11,000	green
GM6	Chevrolet	4 DR	Cimarron	11,250	brown
GM7	Pontiac	2 DR	Fiero	1,500	navy
H1	Honda	4 DR	Accord	32,000	yellow
H2	Honda	2 DR HB	Accord	11,250	brown

The control file for the maintenance run traced above contains the following totals:

Master records read	=	14
Valid additions	=	2
Invalid additions	=	0
Valid changes	=	2
Invalid changes	=	0
Valid deletions	=	3
Invalid deletions	=	1
Master records written	=	13

The following calculation allows the user to check the control totals to make sure the maintenance program performed correctly:

	Master records read	14
+	Valid additions	2
−	Valid deletions	3
	Master records written	13

The master file in Table 5.6 does indeed contain 13 records.

Each execution of the body of the `Loop` in Algorithm 5.4 processes one matching transaction record or one unmatched master record, or it processes one group of unmatched transactions. If there are multiple matching transactions (changes or deletions to existing master records) or a key, the algorithm must make several passes through the body of the loop to process them.

Each pass through for multiple matching transactions entails evaluation of three Boolean expressions in lines 4, 5, and 8:

```
4   Exit When master_record.key = SENTINEL
         And  transaction.key = SENTINEL        : FALSE
5   If master_record.key < transaction.key      : FALSE
8   Elsif master_record.key = transaction.key   : TRUE
```

(The modern algorithm, which the next section examines, contains an improvement: A loop in line 8 processes all transactions of the same key, so each transaction can be applied with the evaluation of one Boolean expression [line 8] rather than three.)

When transaction keys do not match the master keys and the main algorithm calls `Nomatch`, three different updates (addition, change, and deletion) are allowed. A key cannot be added more than once; a key can be added and have several changes; a key can be added with 0 to n changes followed by only one deletion:

addition $(\text{change})_n$ (deletion)

Once a key has been deleted, it may be assigned to another item. Algorithm `Nomatch` processes all additions and changes for a key that does not match, or it processes transactions through the first deletion transaction only. In some applications, keys are unique and are not reassigned once deleted. Other applications, such as the car-rental agency example, allow keys to be deleted and then reassigned to another entity. These applications are limited by the restriction that Algorithm 5.4 places on the number of updates. If an addition follows a deletion for the same key (as in the application of transaction file T3 above), Algorithm `Nomatch` is called to process all transactions through the first deletion. The main algorithm continues executing the transaction, and `Nomatch` is called again with the second addition. Returning to the main program and reentering `Nomatch` to continue processing transactions for the same key is inefficient. The modern algorithm for a sequential file update uses a loop to process multiple matched transactions of the same key more efficiently and allows any number of addition, change, and deletion transactions for the same key in any order (although they are usually ordered by date of entry into the transaction file).

MODERN ALGORITHMS FOR UPDATING SEQUENTIAL FILES

The traditional algorithms for sequential file update contain inefficiencies and put more emphasis on unmatched transactions and unmatched master records than on matched transactions. The most important function of the update is the handling of matched transactions. An algorithm that is more efficient than the traditional algorithms was invented by Feijen and discussed by Dijkstra and Dwyer (see Bibliography). Those transactions that match records in the master file have primary importance, although the algorithm successfully handles unmatched transactions as well as master records that have no changes. Each iteration of the main loop processes all transactions for a given key by:

1. finding the master record that matches the transaction key
2. applying all transactions that are ordered by entry date
3. recording the updated master record

Step 2 applies the transactions if the master record for that key is found, it prints error messages if the transactions are changes or deletions and the master record is not found, or it processes additions if the master record is not found. The emphasis is on applying these transactions, whatever the outcome.

The details of applying the transactions are hidden at a lower level of the program design so that they may vary depending on the type of secondary storage being used for storing the master file. The modern algorithm easily allows for the sequential file to be stored on either magnetic tape or disk. In the case of magnetic disk, the details of applying transactions may be conveniently modified to produce an algorithm that updates the master file randomly. In a random update the matching master record is located, the transactions are applied to the master record, and the updated master record is rewritten to the original location. (The capacity to rewrite to the original locations is unique to random-access devices such as disks.) The savings that the random update realizes result from the fact that the entire master file need not be read and copied to another file; only the master records that matched transactions are read and written back to their original locations.

The next section presents the modern algorithm as a sequential update algorithm. The succeeding section changes the modern sequential update algorithm to perform random updates.

Sequential Update

Algorithm 5.5 presents the modern sequential update algorithm. The `master_record.key` and the `transaction.key` are assigned a sentinel value upon reaching the end of the file. The sentinel value is higher than any value found in the master file and the transaction file.

ALGORITHM 5.5 Modern_Sequential_Update

```
                    --  addition, change, and deletion transactions in
                    --  order (ordered by entry time); several
                    --  transactions per master record
USE Update_Objects
current_key : Key_Type
hold_master : Master_Record_Type
master_allocated : Boolean
Get_Next_Trans ( transaction )
Get_Next_Master ( master_record ) -- same as for traditional algorithm
Choose_Smaller_Key ( transaction.key, master_record.key, current_key )

Loop
    Exit When current_key = SENTINEL
    Check_Initial_Status_Of_Master ( current_key, master_record,
                                     hold_master, master_allocated )
    Loop
        Exit When transaction.key /= current_key
        Process_One_Transaction ( master_allocated, transaction,
                                  hold_master )
    End Loop
--  should record be output?
    Check_Final_Status_Of_Master ( master_allocated, hold_master )
    Choose_Smaller_Key ( transaction.key, master_record.key,
                         current_key )
End Loop

PROCEDURE Choose_Smaller_Key ( trans_key,
                               master_key : IN Key_Type,
                               current_key : OUT Key_Type )
--  between trans_key and master_key
If trans_key < master_key
    current_key ← trans_key -- trans_key < master_key
Else
    current_key ← master_key -- trans_key >= master_key
End If

PROCEDURE Check_Initial_Status_Of_Master
            ( current_key      :  IN Key_Type,
              master_record    :  IN OUT Master_Record_Type,
              hold_master      :  OUT Master_Record_Type,
              master_allocated :  OUT Boolean )
-- for current key

If master_record.key = current_key
    hold_master ← master record
    master_allocated ← TRUE
    Get_Next_Master ( master_record )
Else
    master_allocated ← FALSE
End If
```

```
PROCEDURE Check_Final_Status_Of_Master
            ( master_allocated :   IN Boolean,
              hold_master      :   IN Master_Record_Type )
 1 If master_allocated
 2     output hold_master to new master file
 3 End If

PROCEDURE Process_One_Transaction
            ( master_allocated :   IN OUT Boolean,
              transaction      :   IN OUT Transaction_Record_Type,
              hold_master      :   IN OUT Master_Record_Type )
 1 If master_allocated
 2     Case transaction.update_code
 3         'A' → output "duplicate add" error
 4         'C' → change master record
 5         'D' → master_allocated ← FALSE
                   -- so it will not be output in
                   -- Check_Final_Status_Of_Master
       End Case
 6 Else
 7     Case transaction.update_code
 8         'A' →   -- build new master record from transaction
 9                 hold_master ← transaction record
10                 master_allocated ← TRUE
11         'C'|
12         'D' → output "no matching master record" error
       End Case
   End If
13 Get_Next_Trans ( transaction )
```

Algorithm 5.5 starts the sentinel loop by reading in the first transaction and the first master record (lines 1 and 2). `Choose_Smaller_Key` sets current key to the smaller of `transaction.key` and `master_record.key`. The smaller key is the next to be processed. The main `Loop` continues until the current key contains the sentinel value. (If the current key is the smaller of `transaction.key` and `master_record.key`, and the current key contains the sentinel, then both files have been emptied.) The main `Loop` (lines 4 through 11) processes the record with the key of `current_key` whether the current key be a master record with no updates, a pair of matching master and transaction records, or an unmatched transaction.

`Check_Initial_Status_Of_Master` checks whether a master record exists for the current key and sets a Boolean `master_allocated` accordingly. If the master record for the current key exists, the master record is saved in `hold_master`, and the next master record is read. Any matching transactions use `hold_master` when making updates. The Boolean `master_allocated` is checked by `Check_Final_Status_Of_Master` after matching transactions are applied to determine whether a record is to be written to the new master file.

If the master record for the current key exists but there are no matching transactions for the current key, `Check_Initial_Status_Of_Master` holds the master record and advances the master file, zero iterations of `Pro-`

cess_One_Transaction occur, and Check_Final_Status_Of_Master copies the master record to the new master file. In this case the master key is the smaller key, so the master record is processed, then the next master record is input.

When the master record for the current key exists and has a matching transaction, Process_One_Transaction is performed—it applies the transaction and inputs the next transaction for all matching transactions that follow. The Boolean master_allocated is used within Process_One_Transaction to indicate whether a matching master record exists. (TRUE means the matching record exists, and FALSE means it does not.) For example, if master_allocated is FALSE, then an addition transaction is valid and causes master_allocated to be changed to TRUE as a new record is created. Any change transactions that follow are applied to the hold_master. A deletion transaction that follows sets master_allocated back to FALSE, which indicates that hold_master is inactive. There is no limit to the number or order of addition, change, and deletion transactions that may be applied for a single key. The final status of master_allocated indicates whether anything is to be written to the new master file for the current key.

Comparison to Traditional Algorithm 5.4

The car-rental agency transaction files that were used to demonstrate the traditional algorithms can also demonstrate the efficiency of the modern sequential update algorithm. Operations in line 3 (two operations), line 5 (one operation), line 6 (two operations), lines 8, 9, and 10 (one operation each), and line 11 (two operations) of the modern algorithm are counted. Assume the car-rental master file is empty. Apply transaction file T1 (Table 5.1) to the empty master file. Upon execution of Algorithm 5.5, the following actions take place:

1. Get_Next_Trans inputs the first transaction.
2. Get_Next_Master finds the master file empty, so the master_record.key is filled with the sentinel value, which is higher than any transaction key.
3. Choose_Smaller_Key sets current_key to transaction.key since master_key has the sentinel value. The operation count = 2.
4. In line 5 current_key = sentinel is FALSE. The operation count = 3.
5. In line 6 Check_Initial_Status_Of_Master sets master_allocated to FALSE. The operation count = 5.
6. In line 8 transaction.key /= current_key is FALSE, so Process_One_Transaction is called. The operation count = 6.
7. Since master_allocated is FALSE and the transaction.update_code is an A, a new record is built in hold_master, and master_allocated is set to TRUE. The operation count = 7.

8. `Get_Next_Trans` inputs the next transaction record, which is different from the last one input. We return to the main program.
9. Line 8 is `TRUE`, so we move to line 10. The operation count = 8.
10. `Check_Final_Status_Of_Master` finds `master_allocated TRUE`, so the new record built is output to the new master file. The operation count = 9.
11. `Choose_Smaller_Key` sets `current_key` to `transaction.key`. The operation count = 11.
12. The algorithm continues to the body of `Loop`, which begins in line 4. Lines 4 through 11 are repeated for each transaction until in line 11 the `current_key` is assigned the `transaction.key`, which is the sentinel value. The operation count = 11 + (9 operations × 12 transactions) = 119.
13. The next execution of line 5 evaluates to `TRUE`, and the program terminates. The operation count = 120.

The `Loop` checks for the end of both the master file and the transaction file, and it terminates when both have ended. In this case the master file is empty at the beginning of the algorithm, so all the addition transactions are written to the new master file. The resulting master file is the same as for the traditional algorithm (Table 5.2).

The operation count for modern algorithm 5.5 when applying transaction file T1 is 120 operations; the operation count for the traditional algorithm 5.4 is 130 operations. Transaction file T1 consists solely of additions, and the traditional algorithm 5.4 checks for `master_record.key < transaction.key` first. If the condition is not met, it checks `master_record.key = transaction.key`, and—failing again—it finally calls `Nomatch` to handle the additions. More operator evaluations take place in the traditional algorithm 5.4 for each addition than in the modern algorithm. The modern algorithm 5.5 emphasizes *processing* transactions; the traditional algorithm 5.4 emphasizes *copying master records* and *matching transactions* with master records during the copying process. The modern algorithm 5.5 appears to be more efficient in creating the master file.

Transaction file T2 (Table 5.3) illustrates a transaction file with only one transaction. The trace of the execution of Algorithm 5.5 using the master file that was just created in Table 5.2 and transaction file T2 follows:

1. `Get_Next_Trans` inputs the first transaction.
2. `Get_Next_Master` inputs the first master record.
3. `Choose_Smaller_Key` sets `current_key` to `master_record.key`, which is `C1`. The operation count = 2.
4. In line 5 `current_key = sentinel` is `FALSE`. The operation count = 3.
5. In line 6 `Check_Initial_Status_Of_Master` stores master record `C1` in `hold_master`, and sets `master_allocated` to `TRUE`; and

Get_Next_Master inputs the next master record. The operation count = 5.

6. In line 8 transaction.key /= current_key is TRUE, so we move to line 10. The operation count = 6.
7. Check_Final_Status_Of_Master finds master_allocated TRUE, so the record in hold_master is output to the new master file. The operation count = 7.
8. Choose_Smaller_Key sets current_key to master_record.key. The operation count = 9.
9. Lines 4 through 11 are repeated for master records C2 through GM5; Choose_Smaller_Key sets current_key to transaction.key (GM6) rather than master_record.key (H1). The operation count = 9 + (7 operations × 9 transactions) = 72.
10. Line 5 is FALSE. The operation count = 73.
11. Check_Initial_Status_Of_Master sets master_allocated to FALSE for current_key (GM6). The operation count = 75.
12. In line 8 transaction.key /= current_key is FALSE, so Process_One_Transaction is called. The operation count = 76.
13. Since master_allocated is FALSE and the transaction.update_code is an A, a new record is built in hold_master, and master_allocated is set to TRUE. The operation count = 77.
14. Get_Next_Trans sets transaction.key to the sentinel.
15. Line 8 is TRUE, so we move to line 10. The operation count = 78.
16. Check_Final_Status_Of_Master finds master_allocated TRUE, so the record in hold_master is output to the new master file. The operation count = 79.
17. Choose_Smaller_Key sets current_key to master_record.key since transaction.key has the sentinel. The operation count = 81.
18. The algorithm continues with the beginning of the body of the Loop in line 4. Lines 4 through 11 are repeated for each master record until in line 11 the current_key is assigned the transaction.key, which is the sentinel value. The operation count = 81 + (7 operations × 3 transactions) = 102.
19. In the next pass, line 5 evaluates to TRUE, and the program terminates. The operation count = 103.

Algorithm 5.5 performs satisfactorily for a transaction file of only one transaction. The resulting master file is the same as the result of Algorithm 5.4 (Table 5.4). The operation count for the modern algorithm 5.5 is 103 operations versus 50 operations for traditional Algorithm 5.4 when applying transaction file T2 (which contains only one transaction, an addition). Since the traditional algorithm emphasizes copying the master file and processing transactions during the copying process, only three operations are required for each master record copied unchanged to the new master file.

The modern algorithm, on the other hand, emphasizes processing transactions; seven operations occur for each master record copied unchanged to the new master file.

The advantages of the modern algorithm 5.5 over the traditional algorithm 5.4 can be seen from applying transaction file T3, which contains a number of additions, changes, and deletions in multiples. The modern algorithm 5.5 is especially useful when an addition follows a deletion and when there are multiple changes to an existing master record. The trace of applying T3 to the master file in Table 5.4 follows:

1. `Get_Next_Trans` inputs the first transaction.
2. `Get_Next_Master` inputs the first master record.
3. `Choose_Smaller_Key` sets `current_key` to `master_record.key`, which is `C1`. The operation count = 2.
4. In line 5 `current_key = sentinel` is `FALSE`. The operation count = 3.
5. In line 6 `Check_Initial_Status_Of_Master` stores master record `C1` in `hold_master`, and sets `master_allocated` to `TRUE`; `Get_Next_Master` inputs the next master record. The operation count = 5.
6. In line 8 `transaction.key /= current_key` is `TRUE`, so we move to line 10. The operation count = 6.
7. `Check_Final_Status_Of_Master` finds `master_allocated TRUE`, so the record in `hold_master` is output to the new master file. The operation count = 7.
8. `Choose_Smaller_Key` sets `current_key` to `master_record.key`. The operation count = 9.
9. Lines 4 through 11 are repeated for master record `C2`. `Choose_Smaller_Key` sets `current_key` to `master_record.key (F1)` since `transaction.key` is not smaller. The operation count = 16.
10. Line 5 is `FALSE`. The operation count = 17.
11. `Check_Initial_Status_Of_Master` moves master record `F1` to `hold_master` and sets `master_allocated` to `TRUE`. `Get_Next_Master` inputs `F2`. The operation count = 19.
12. In line 8 `transaction.key /= current_key` is `FALSE`; so `Process_One_Transaction` is called. The operation count = 20.
13. Since `master_allocated` is `FALSE` and the `transaction.update_code` is `D`, `master_allocated` is changed to `FALSE` to prevent `hold_master` from being copied to the new master file. The operation count = 21.
14. `Get_Next_Trans` inputs the code `A` and the id `GM7`.
15. Line 8 is `TRUE`, so we move to line 10. The operation count = 22.

16. `Check_Final_Status_Of_Master` does nothing since `master_allocated` is `FALSE`. The operation count = 23.
17. `Choose_Smaller_Key` sets `current_key` to `master_record.key` (`F1`) since `transaction.key` is `GM7`. The operation count = 25.
18. Lines 4 through 11 are repeated for master records `F2` through `GM6`. `Choose_Smaller_Key` sets `current_key` to `transaction.key` (`GM7`), which is smaller than `master_record.key` (`H1`). The operation count = 25 + (7 operations × 8 transactions) = 81.
19. Line 5 is `FALSE`. The operation count = 82.
20. `Check_Initial_Status_Of_Master` sets `master_allocated` to `FALSE` for `current_key` (`GM7`). The operation count = 84.
21. In line 8 `transaction.key /= current_key` is `FALSE`, so `Process_One_Transaction` is called. The operation count = 85.
22. Since `master_allocated` is `FALSE` and the `transaction.update_code` is an `A`, a new record is built in `hold_master`, and `master_allocated` is set to `TRUE`. The operation count = 86.
23. `Get_Next_Trans` inputs the code `C` and the id `GM7`.
24. In line 8 `transaction.key /= current_key` is `TRUE`, so `Process_One_Transaction` is called. The operation count = 87.
25. Since `master_allocated` is `TRUE` and the `transaction.update_code` is a `C`, `hold_master` is changed. The operation count = 88.
26. `Get_Next_Trans` inputs the code `D` and the id `GM7`.
27. In line 8 `transaction.key /= current_key` is `FALSE`, so `Process_One_Transaction` is called. The operation count = 89.
28. Since `master_allocated` is `TRUE` and the `transaction.update_code` is a `D`, `master_allocated` is changed to `FALSE`. The operation count = 90.
29. `Get_Next_Trans` inputs the second code `A` and id `GM7`.
30. In line 8 `transaction.key /= current_key` is `FALSE`, so `Process_One_Transaction` is called. The operation count = 91.
31. Since `master_allocated` is `FALSE` and the `transaction.update_code` is an `A`, a new record is built in `hold_master`, and `master_allocated` is set to `TRUE`. The operation count = 92.
32. `Get_Next_Trans` inputs the code `D` and the id `H3`.
33. Line 8 is `TRUE`, so we move to line 10. The operation count = 93.
34. `Check_Final_Status_Of_Master` finds `master_allocated TRUE`, so the record in `hold_master` (`GM7`) is output to the new master file. The operation count = 94.
35. `Choose_Smaller_Key` sets `current_key` to `master_record.key` (`H1`), which is smaller than `transaction.key` (`H3`). The operation count = 96.

36. Lines 4 through 11 are repeated for master records H1 through H2. Choose_Smaller_Key sets current_key to transaction.key (H3), which is smaller than master_record.key (T1). The operation count = 96 + (7 operations × 2 transactions) = 110.
37. Line 5 is FALSE. The operation count = 111.
38. Check_Initial_Status_Of_Master sets master_allocated to FALSE for current_key (H3). The operation count = 113.
39. In line 8 transaction.key /= current_key is FALSE, so Process_One_Transaction is called. The operation count = 114.
40. Since master_allocated is FALSE and the transaction.update_code is a D, the message no matching master record is output. The operation count = 115.
41. Get_Next_Trans inputs the code C and the id T1.
42. Line 8 is TRUE, so we move to line 10. The operation count = 116.
43. Check_Final_Status_Of_Master finds master_allocated FALSE, so nothing happens. The operation count = 117.
44. Choose_Smaller_Key sets current_key to master_record.key (T1) since transaction.key (T1) is not smaller. The operation count = 119.
45. Line 5 is FALSE. The operation count = 120.
46. Check_Initial_Status_Of_Master moves master record T1 to hold_master and sets master_allocated to TRUE. Get_Next_Master sets master_record.key to the sentinel. The operation count = 122.
47. In line 8 transaction.key /= current_key is FALSE, so Process_One_Transaction is called. The operation count = 123.
48. Since master_allocated is TRUE and the transaction.update_code is a C, hold_master is changed. The operation count = 124.
49. Get_Next_Trans inputs the code D and the id T1.
50. In line 8 transaction.key /= current_key is FALSE, so Process_One_Transaction is called. The operation count = 125.
51. Since master_allocated is TRUE and the transaction.update_code is a D, master_allocated is changed to FALSE. The operation count = 126.
52. Get_Next_Trans sets transaction.key to the sentinel.
53. Line 8 is TRUE, so we move to line 10. The operation count = 127.
54. Check_Final_Status_Of_Master finds master_allocated FALSE, so nothing happens. The operation count = 128.
55. Choose_Smaller_Key sets current_key to master_record.key (sentinel) since transaction.key (sentinel) is not smaller. The operation count = 130.

56. Line 5 is `TRUE`, so the program terminates. The operation count = 131.

Transaction file T3 contains a variety of transactions: the deletion of an existing master record (`F1`); an addition, change, deletion, and subsequent addition of a new key (`GM7`); the deletion of a nonexistent master record (`H3`), and finally the change and deletion of an existing master record (`T1`). The resulting master file is the same as for the traditional Algorithm 5.4 (Table 5.6).

Each execution of the main `Loop` (lines 4 through 11) processes all records for a single key value. For multiple matching transactions, there are three Boolean expressions evaluated in the main `Loop` when the first transaction is processed:

```
5 Exit When current_key = sentinel            : FALSE
6 If master_record.key = current_key          : TRUE
8 Exit When transaction.key /= current_key    : FALSE
```

For each transaction that follows with the same key, there is only one Boolean expression evaluated in the main `Loop`:

```
8 Exit When transaction.key /= current_key    : FALSE
```

The modern algorithm performs seven operations when processing the transactions for an existing master record (`T1`); the traditional Algorithm 5.4 performs eight operations. Only two transactions are processed here, but the savings are greater for a larger number of transactions for a single key. The modern sequential update algorithm is more efficient than the traditional Algorithm 5.4 for multiple transactions for the same key because it contains fewer Boolean expressions to evaluate.

When the transactions do not match, any number of additions, changes, and deletions may be applied in any order. The flag `master_allocated` is checked after all transactions have been applied to determine the final status of the applications (whether a record is to be output to the new master file, for example). Three Boolean expressions are evaluated for the first of unmatched transactions:

```
5 Exit When current_key = SENTINEL            : FALSE
6 If master_record.key = current_key          : FALSE
8 Exit When transaction.key /= current_key    : FALSE
```

For each transaction that follows with the same key, there is only one Boolean expression evaluated in the main `Loop`:

```
8 Exit When transaction.key /= current_key    : FALSE
```

For processing the transactions for `GM7`, the traditional Algorithm 5.4 performed 16 operations, but the modern algorithm processed only 15 operations. The number of Boolean expressions evaluated for unmatched transactions is fewer in the modern algorithm than for the traditional Algorithm 5.4. Why? Because Algorithm `Nomatch` of the traditional Algorithm 5.4 returns to the main program when each deletion is encountered. The modern algorithm handles multiple transactions more easily. It is more efficient and simpler than the traditional Algorithm 5.4 when performing maintenance on a master file with high activity and/or high volatility, and it is also shorter in terms of the number of lines in the algorithm. Table 5.7 summarizes the operation counts for both algorithms for application of all three transaction files.

Table 5.7 Operation counts for modern and traditional algorithms

Transaction file	Modern algorithm	Traditional algorithm
T1	120	131
T2	103	51
T3	131	80

Algorithms 5.4 and 5.5 have been implemented in Ada for the car-rental agency data and are presented in Appendix B. Figure 5.2 graphically illustrates the interfacing of program components with each other and the external I/O files. The nongeneric package `Ch5Struc` encapsulates the data structures used by both the traditional (`Alg5_4`) and the modern (`Alg5_5`) algorithms.

Random Update

Algorithm 5.6 presents the modern random update algorithm. The changes needed to convert Algorithm 5.5, a sequential update, to a random update are few. Algorithm 5.6 inputs the first transaction but not the first master record. In the random update, the transaction file is the primary force behind the main `Loop`. Notice in line 2 that `current_key` is set to the `transaction.key`. The main `Loop` is the same as in the sequential update. Only `Check_Initial_Status_Of_Master` and `Check_Final_Status_Of_Master` differ.

`Check_Initial_Status_Of_Master` retrieves a master record from the master file that matches `current_key`, if one exists. The process of retrieving a matching master record differs from one application to another; it involves either a sequential read or a random access (see Chapter 7). If a matching master record is retrieved, the master record is stored in `hold_master`, and `master_allocated` is set to `TRUE`. In a similar fashion `Check_Final_Status_Of_Master` checks the status of the Boolean `master_allocated`. It writes the record in `hold_master` either as a new record in the current master file or as a replacement for the existing record in the original location from which it was read.

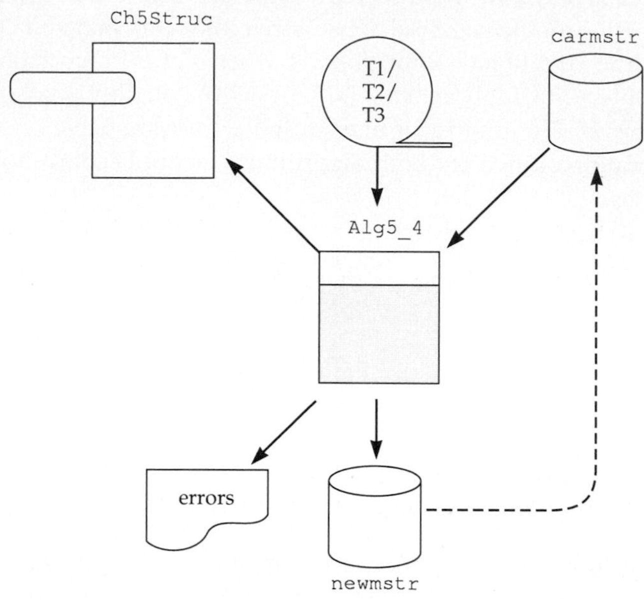

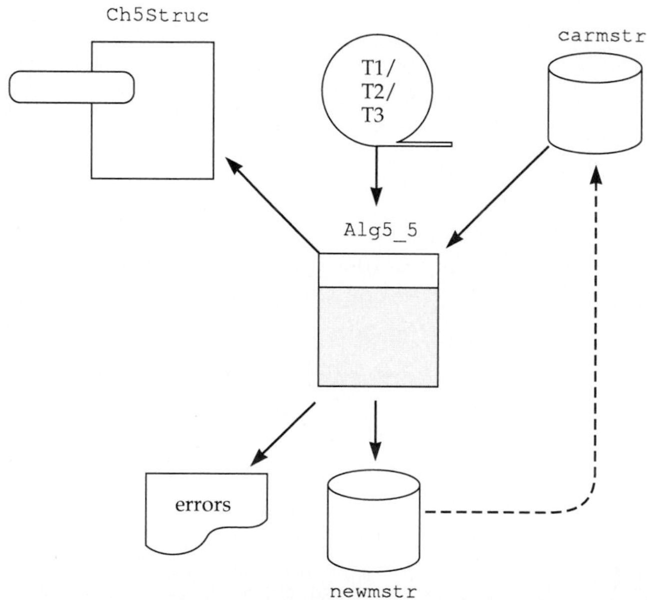

Figure 5.2
Case study 5.1 interfaces

ALGORITHM 5.6 Modern_Random_Update

```
                    -- addition, change, and deletion transactions in
                    -- order (ordered by entry time); several
                    -- transactions per master record
   USE Update_Objects
   current_key  : Key_Type
   hold_master  : Master_Record_Type
   master_allocated : Boolean

   Get_Next_Trans ( transaction )
   current_key ← transaction.key   -- rather than Choose_Smaller_Key
   Loop
       Exit When current_key = sentinel
            -- same as for Modern Sequential Update
       Check_Initial_Status_Of_Master ( current_key, hold_master,
                                         master_allocated )
       Loop
           Exit When transaction.key /= current_key
           Process_One_Transaction (  master_allocated, transaction,
                                      hold_master )
       End Loop
       -- should record be output?
       Check_Final_Status_Of_Master ( master_allocated, hold_master )
       current_key ← transaction.key -- rather than Choose_Smaller_Key
   End Loop

PROCEDURE Check_Initial_Status_Of_Master
                    ( current_key        : IN Key_Type,
                      hold_master        : OUT Master_Record_Type,
                      master_allocated   : OUT Boolean )
--  for current_key
   If current_key exists in master file
       input master record with current_key into hold_master
       master_allocated ← TRUE
   Else
       master_allocated ← FALSE
   End If

PROCEDURE Check_Final_Status_Of_Master
                    (   master_allocated :   IN Boolean,
                        hold_master      :   IN Master_Record_Type )

   If master_allocated
   output hold_master to new master file
              -- either a new record or replaces old record
   End If
```

A random update requires that random access be available, and random access is available only on magnetic disk. A random update is more efficient since only the master records that have matching transactions are input and updated within the current master file; it does not copy all master records to a new master file.

The number of input/output operations for the random update is greatly reduced from that of the sequential update. The number of input/output operations for the sequential update using transaction file T3 is

Master records read	=	14
Master records written	=	13
Transaction records read	=	8
Total I/O operations	=	35

Only the changed master records or additions are output to the master file for the random update:

Reads attempted to master file	=	4	(F1, GM7, H3, T1)
Master records written	=	3	(D F1, A GM7, D T1)
Transaction records read	=	8	
Total I/O operations	=	15	

The algorithm makes four attempts to input a record from the master file. Only two of those four attempts are successful (F1, and T1). Both records were subsequently "deleted," requiring that the records be written over rather than actually being physically deleted. The third output operation to the master file adds GM7. The random update has a total of 15 input/output operations; the sequential update has 35 input/output operations. Since each input or output operation may be 30 to 40 milliseconds, the random update represents quite a savings in access time (provided that random access is available).

SUMMARY

Sequential organization of data files is the oldest type of file organization. Updating a sequential file involves the addition of new records, the changing of information on existing records, and the deletion of existing records. Additions and deletions involve inserting records into or deleting records from a file in such a way that the order of keyed records within the file is maintained. Without direct-access storage devices, the updating of a sequential file requires the copying of the existing file to another file.

A master file may be created by a special creation program or by application of each transaction as an addition in the maintenance program. A batch maintenance run requires that transactions be sorted into the same order (by ascending entry date within ascending transaction key) as the master file. The length of time between maintenance runs depends on the rate of change of data, the size of the master file, the need for current data on the master file, and the file activity.

During the maintenance run, the keys of the master records are matched with the keys of the transaction records, producing a new master file and an audit/error report. When transaction records have keys that match master record keys, one of three actions occurs: (1) addition transactions cause error messages, (2) change transactions modify the master record, or (3) deletion transactions prevent the copying of the master record to the new master file. When transaction records have keys that do not match keys on the master file: (1) additions cause new records to be built for the new master file, (2) changes with keys matching previous additions cause changes to the new record, (3) deletions with keys matching previous additions prevent the new record from being output to the new master file, and (4) changes and deletions with keys that do not match previous additions generate error messages. The chapter presents several algorithms: The traditional algorithms, which are used when sequential storage devices (magnetic tapes) are available, and a modern algorithm, which is easily modified for either sequential or random update when using direct-access storage devices (magnetic disks).

Key Terms

adding records
audit/error listing
batch processing
changes
deleting records
editing
key
maintenance run
random update
sentinel value
sequential file organization
sequential update
serially
transaction file
update code

Exercises

1. An installation has two tape drives and one disk drive. An application program requires access to three sequential files: an old master file, a transaction file, and an updated master file. Each file should be on a different device. Which file should be stored on the disk?
2. Consider a master file of 10 records and the following batch of transactions to be processed:

Transactions file		**Master file**
Code	*Key*	*Key*
C	0196	0195
A	0196	0196
D	0196	2000

Transactions file		**Master file**
D	2111	2111
A	2111	2150
D	2111	2473
C	3342	2732
A	4000	3340
C	4000	3342
		4000

What is the file activity ratio?

3. Consider a master file of 10 records and the following batch of transactions to be processed:

Transaction file		**Master file**
Code	*Key*	*Key*
C	0196	0195
A	0196	0196
D	0196	2000
D	2111	2111
A	3310	2150
D	3310	2473
C	3342	2732
A	4200	3340
C	4200	3342
		4000

What is the file activity ratio? What is the file volatility ratio?

4. Suppose the transaction file in exercise 3 were in the following order:

Code	*Key*
D	2111
D	0196
A	0196
A	4200
C	0196
C	3342
C	4200
A	3310
D	3310

If the master file were to be stored on tape, would it be possible to update the master file with the transaction file in this order? If the master file were stored on disk, would it be possible?

5. What factors should be considered in determining how frequently a sequential master file should be updated?

6. Discuss the limitations of sequential files.

7. What is the major disadvantage of batch processing?

8. A sequential file is to be created containing records describing potential new acquisitions for a library. The author's surname will be the key to accessing information concerning a new book. Are there any advantages to ordering the file by the surname assuming that:

   a. search requests are not batched?

   b. search requests are batched?

9. How can updating a master file stored on magnetic disk differ from updating a master file stored on magnetic tape?

10. How does a file update differ from a file merge?

Programming Problems

1. Write a program to create a sequential payroll file where each record contains the following information:

   employee number (the key)
   employee name
   employee salary
   social security number
   tax exemption amount
   insurance premium
   parking fee
   association dues

2. Write a program to print or display the contents of the sequential payroll file created in problem 1.

3. Write a program that updates the sequential payroll file created in problem 1 and creates a new version of the file. Accommodate record additions, changes, and deletions by employing the following:

Update Code		**Information**
A (addition)	—	all the information listed in problem 1
C (change)	—	employee number
	—	one or more field identifiers and changes: N and new name S and new salary X and new tax exemption I and new insurance premium P and new parking fees D and new association dues
D (Deletion)	—	employee number

   Assume that there will be a maximum of one transaction applied to a master file record.

4. Repeat problem 3 with the assumption that there may be up to five transactions per master record. The transactions are to be processed in the order in which they are received.

5. Write a program to update an input sequential part master file that contains data about an inventory of parts with input transaction records. (The input transaction file has been sorted.) You will produce an output updated sequential part master file on disk and an audit/error list.

   Input the master file in which the key field is a part number. The file is a nontext file and contains the following in each record:

   part number (10 characters)
   part description (26 characters)
   part price (real)

   Input the transaction file in which the major key field is a part number and the minor key field is the entry date. A text file of update information contains several different formats:

   a. additions:
      update code (A)
      part number (10 characters)
      part description (26 characters)
      part price (real)
   b. changes:
      description
         update code (C)
         part number (10 characters)
         change id (D)
         new description (26 characters)
      price:
         update code (C)
         part number (10 characters)
         change id (P)
         new price (real)
   c. deletions:
      update code (D)
      part number (10 characters)

   Output an updated master file. Also output an audit/error list with the following information for each transaction:
   update code
   part number
   error message (if any)

The program should perform the following operations:

a. Without using keyboard input, validate each transaction to ensure that it contains one of the following update codes:
   A for add
   C for change
   D for delete

b. Create a master record for each valid add transaction.

c. Change the appropriate master field for each valid change transaction.

d. Delete the master record for each valid delete transaction.

e. Identify the following error conditions:

Error Condition	**Error Message**
Add a transaction that is already on master file	INVALID ADD-ALREADY ON MASTER
Change a transaction that is not on master file	INVALID CHANGE-NOT ON MASTER
Delete a transaction that is not on master file	INVALID DELETE-NOT ON MASTER
Invalid update code	INVALID UPDATE CODE

f. Indicate on the audit/error list what field was changed (price or description) and print the new field. For additions, print price and description of new record added.

g. Tally master- and transaction-record counts and print the tally after the audit/error list.

h. Input the new part master file and print the contents to make sure the information is right.

i. Count the number of lines output on the page and reprint headings at the top of each new page. Do not print across the page perforations. Also print page numbers at the top of each page.

6. Write a program to update an input sequential vendor master file that describes various vendors by inputting vendor transaction records. The input transaction file has been sorted in a prior program step. You will output an updated sequential vendor master file on disk and print an audit/error list.

   Input the master file in which the major key field is a vendor number and the minor key is the date the product is due. The file is a nontext file and contains the following in each record:

vendor number (8 characters)
vendor date due (yymmdd)
vendor name (20 characters)
vendor amount due (real)

Input a transaction file in which the major key field is a vendor number and the minor key field is the date due. A text file of update information contains several different formats:

a. additions:
   update code (A)
   vendor number (8 characters)
   vendor date due (yymmdd)
   vendor name (20 characters)
   vendor amount due (real)

b. changes:
   name
      update code (C)
      vendor number (8 characters)
      vendor date due (yymmdd)
      change id (N)
      new name (20 characters)
   amount due
      update code (C)
      vendor number (8 characters)
      vendor date due (yymmdd)
      change id (A)
      new amount due (real)

c. deletions:
   update code (D)
   vendor number (8 characters)
   vendor date due (yymmdd)

Output an updated vendor master file. Also print an audit/error list with the following information for each transaction:
update code
vendor number
vendor date due
error message (if any)

Repeat each of the program operations you completed in problem 5 using the data about vendors.

Chapter 6

External Sort/Merge Algorithms

CHAPTER CONTENTS

PREVIEW

THIS CHAPTER EXAMINES SEVERAL external sort/merge algorithms used for sorting large data files that exceed the main memory of a computer. Algorithms are presented for the two-way sort/merge, the balanced two-way sort/merge, the balanced *k*-way sort/merge, and the polyphase sort/merge. An algorithm is also presented for the Fibonacci distribution that is used in the polyphase sort/merge only. The sort/merge routines discussed are compared for efficiency in numerous examples.

TWO-WAY SORT/MERGE

One of the requirements of the sequential file maintenance algorithms presented in Chapter 5 is that the transaction file of updates be sorted by the key into the same order (ascending or descending) as that of the master file. Often a transaction file is so large that the whole file will not fit into main memory; in these cases an internal sort is inappropriate. Sorting is common for maintenance of not only sequential files but also other types of file organization. Sorting transactions to match the key order of the master file can reduce the time required to locate a matching master record. Transactions must be sorted for sequential file maintenance; sorted transactions can improve the maintenance of master files with other types of file organization. Many reports generated from files require that the file be sorted by certain fields other than the key. External sort/merge algorithms are the most common method for sorting data files that are larger than main memory.

A simple sort/merge algorithm involves two phases:

1. The records in the file to be sorted are divided into several groups. Each group is called a **run**, and each run fits into main memory. An internal sort is applied to each run, and the resulting sorted runs are distributed to two external files.
2. One run at a time from each of the external files created in phase 1 merge into larger runs of sorted records. The result is stored in a third external file. The data are distributed from the third file back into the first two files, and the merge continues until all records are in one large run.

Figure 6.1 illustrates the sort/merge process.

The external storage devices used for storing the three files of the sort/merge algorithm may be either magnetic tape or magnetic disk. Each file needs to be on a separate device to allow easy access during the merge phase.

EXAMPLE 6.1

Suppose a file of records to be sorted contains the following keys in this order:

50 110 95 10 100 36 153 40 120 60 70 130 22 140 80

Assume the size of a run is three records; that is, main memory can hold only three records at a time to be sorted. In phase 1, groups of three records are read into main memory, sorted using some internal sort, and alternately written to one of two external files. Figure 6.2 shows the results after each step of the merge. After phase 1 (Figure 6.2(a)), file 1 contains run 1 (keys 50 110 95 in sorted order), run 3 (keys 153 40 120 in sorted order), and run 5 (keys 22 140 80 in sorted order). File 2 contains run 2 (keys 10 100 36 in sorted order), and run 4 (keys 60 70 130 in sorted order). Consecutive runs are alternately stored in files 1 and 2 so the two files contain the same number of runs for the merge phase. (At worst, one of the files may have one more run than the other.)

In phase 2, the first run in file 1 is merged with the first run in file 2 to produce a sorted run containing six records in file 3. The second run in file 1 is merged with the second run in file 2 to produce a second sorted run of six records in file 3. This merging is continued until files 1 and 2 are empty (Figure 6.2(b)). The runs in file 3 are now redistributed alternately to files 1 and 2. After the redistribution file 3 is empty, and files 1 and 2 contain the records (Figure 6.2(c)). The process is ready to start merge 2. The merging phase is repeated until all records are in one run. The second merge stores two runs in file 3 as shown in Figure 6.2(d). Redistributing the two runs to files 1 and 2 (Figure 6.2(e)) and merging a third time leaves all records in one run (Figure 6.2(f)).

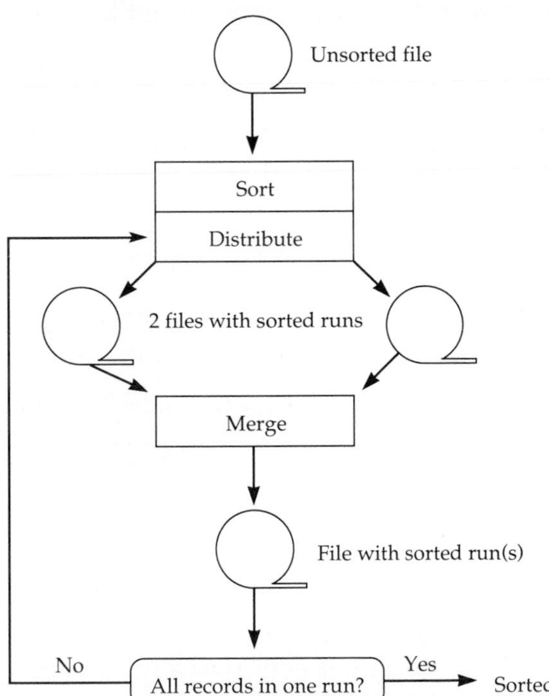

Figure 6.1
Flow of control in sort/merge algorithm

Figure 6.2
Two-way sort/merge—
Example 6.1

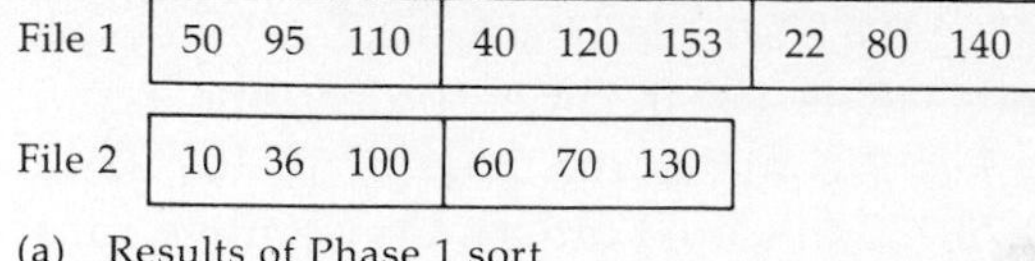

(a) Results of Phase 1 sort

File 1 Empty

File 2 Empty

File 3 | 10 36 50 95 100 110 | 40 60 70 120 130 153 | 22 80 140

(b) Result of merge 1

File 1 | 10 36 50 95 100 110 | 22 80 140

File 2 | 40 60 70 120 130 153

File 3 Empty

(c) Results of redistribution after merge 1

File 3 | 10 36 40 50 60 70 95 100 110 120 130 153 | 22 80 140

(d) Results of merge 2

File 1 | 10 36 40 50 60 70 95 100 110 120 130 153

File 2 | 22 80 140

(e) Results of redistribution after merge 2

File 3 | 10 22 36 40 50 60 70 80 95 100 110 120 130 140 153

(f) Results of merge 3

EXAMPLE 6.2

Suppose the initial file to be sorted is

50 110 95 10 100 36 153 40 120 60 70 130

The number of runs is even (12 records ÷ 3 records/run = 4 runs on 2 files). Files 1 and 2 contain the same number of runs after the sorting phase (Figure 6.3(a)). The first execution of the merge phase merges the first run of both files, producing a sorted run in file 3, then merges the second run of both files and produces a second sorted run in file 3 as shown in Figure 6.3(b). Since both input files are now empty, the runs from file 3 are redistributed to files 1 and 2 (Figure 6.3(c)) in order to merge again. The resulting file contents from the second execution of the merge pass are shown in Figure 6.3(d).

Figure 6.3
Two-way sort/merge—
Example 6.2

File 1	50 95 110	40 120 153
File 2	10 36 100	60 70 130

(a) Results of phase 1 sort

File 1 Empty

File 2 Empty

File 3	10 36 50 95 100 110	40 60 70 120 130 153

(b) Results of merge 1

File 1	10 36 50 95 100 110
File 2	40 60 70 120 130 153

(c) Results of redistribution after merge 1

File 1 Empty

File 2 Empty

File 3	10 36 40 50 60 70 95 100 110 120 130 153

(d) Results of merge 2

Phase 1 (the **sort phase**) of the sort/merge sorts the records into runs of a specified length and distributes the runs alternately to two external files. Once phase 1 is complete, phase 2 (the **merge phase**) merges runs into larger runs. The merge phase repeatedly redistributes and merges runs until all records are in one run.

A variety of merge algorithms are available. Example 6.2 is an example of a two-way sort/merge that merges runs from two input files into one output file. The algorithm for the **two-way sort/merge** is presented in pseudocode in Algorithm 6.1.

ALGORITHM 6.1 Two-way Sort/Merge

```
                        --Sort Phase
initial distribution
                        --Merge Phase
TYPE File_Array Is Array ( 1 .. 3 ) Of File_Type
file             : File_Array
infile_index     : Integer
number_of_runs   : Integer
```

```
Loop
    open input files
    create output file
    number_of_runs ← 0
    Loop -- merge next runs from 2 input files
        input first record from file 1
        input first record from file 2
        Exit When End_Of_Both_Files ( file )
        Loop -- output record with smaller key to file(3)
            infile_index ← Smallest_key ( file )
            output record from file(infile_index) to file(3)
            input next record from file(infile_index)
            Exit When End_Of_Run_On_Both_Files ( file )
        End Loop
        output end-of-run-marker to file(3)
        increment number_of_runs by 1
        Exit When End_Of_Both_Files ( file )
    End Loop
    close all files
    If number_of_runs > 1
        Distribute ( file )
    Else
        Exit -- sorted file in file 3
    End If
End Loop

FUNCTION End_Of_Run_On_File ( file : In File_Type ) Return Boolean
    Return next_record ( file ) = end-of-run-marker

FUNCTION Smallest_Key ( file : In File_Array ) Return Integer

    If End_Of_Run_On_File ( file(1) )
    Or End_Of_File ( file(1) )
        Return 2 -- file 2
    Elsif End_Of_Run_On_File ( file(2) )
    Or End_Of_File ( file(2) )
        Return 1 -- file 1
    Elsif key 1 < key 2
        Return 1 -- file 1
    Else
        Return 2 -- file 2
    End If

FUNCTION End_Of_Run_On_Both_Files ( file : In File_Array )
        Return Boolean

    Return End_Of_Run_On_File ( file(1) )
       And End_Of_Run_On_File ( file(2) )

FUNCTION End_Of_Both_Files ( file : In File_Array ) Return Boolean
    Return End_Of_File ( file(1) ) And End_Of_File ( file(2) )

PROCEDURE Distribute ( file : In File_Array )

    open file(3)
    create file(1) and file(2)
    alternate_file ← 0
```

```
For run_index ← 1 .. number_of_runs Loop
    Loop
        input record from run(run_index) of file(3)
        output record to file(1 + alternate_file)
        Exit When End_Of_Run_On_File ( file(3) )
    End Loop
    alternate_file ← 1 – alternate_file
End Loop
close all files
```

Each pass of the two-way sort/merge doubles the size of each run, thus cutting the number of runs in half. Two runs of one record each merge into one run in one pass. Three runs of one record each merge into two runs (two records in the first run and one record in the second run) during the first pass, then into one run in the second pass. Four runs of one record each merge into two runs of two records each in the first pass, then one run of four records in the second pass. The total number of passes through the two-way sort/merge (Algorithm 6.1) is $\lceil \lg NR \rceil$, if $NR > 1$ and NR is the number of runs produced during the initial sorting phase. (The notation *lg NR* means the *logarithm to the base 2 of NR*, and the symbol $\lceil x \rceil$ means the *ceiling of x*.) For example, two runs take $\lceil \lg 2 \rceil = 1$ pass. Three runs take $\lceil \lg 3 \rceil = 2$ passes. Four runs take $\lceil \lg 4 \rceil = 2$ passes. Each pass of the two-way sort/merge transmits each record to the output file during the merging portion, then transmits each output record back to one of the original input files during the distribution procedure. Therefore, each pass of the merge phase of Algorithm 6.1 transmits each record twice. As a result, the number of passes through the file of records is $2\lceil \lg NR \rceil - 1$ for the merge phase plus one for the sort phase—a total of $2\lceil \lg NR \rceil$ passes.

BALANCED TWO-WAY SORT/MERGE

An improvement for the two-way sort/merge algorithm is to increase the number of files available for the merge. Instead of merging two input files into one output file, the **balanced two-way sort/merge** algorithm merges two input files and stores the merged runs alternately on two output files. Increasing the number of output files to the same number of input files eliminates the need to redistribute the runs to the two input files before the merge can be repeated. The I/O time it takes to simply read and copy runs in order to distribute them into two files is a needless waste that the balanced algorithm avoids. The balanced two-way sort/merge algorithm merges runs from files 1 and 2, storing the merged runs in files 3 and 4; it then inputs files 3 and 4, merging runs and storing merged runs in output files 1 and 2, and continues until all records are merged into one run.

EXAMPLE 6.3

Consider the file of records used in Example 6.1:

50 110 95 10 100 36 153 40 120 60 70 130 22 140 80

In the first execution of the merge phase of the balanced two-way sort/merge, runs from files 1 and 2 (Figure 6.4(a)) merge to yield the file contents shown in Figure 6.4(b). Files 3 and 4 are input files for the next execution of the merge phase that stores the merged runs in output files 1 and 2 (Figure 6.4(c)). One more merge pass is necessary to merge all records in one run (Figure 6.4(d)).

Figure 6.4
Balanced two-way sort/merge—Example 6.3

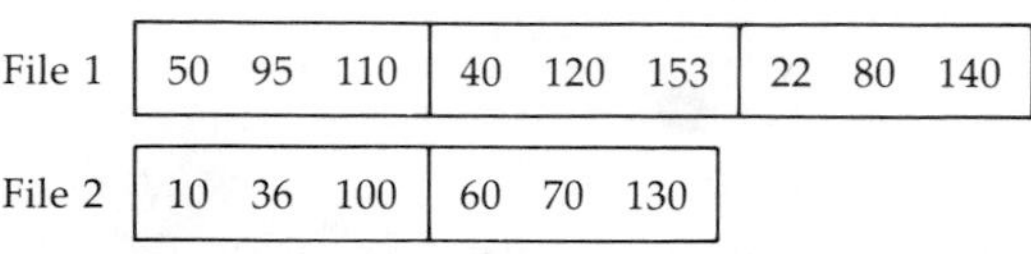

(a) Results of the phase 1 sort

File 1 Empty

File 2 Empty

File 3 | 10 36 50 95 100 110 | 22 80 140 |

File 4 | 40 60 70 120 130 153 |

(b) Results of merge 1

File 1 | 10 36 40 50 60 70 95 100 110 120 130 153 |

File 2 | 22 80 140 |

File 3 Empty

File 4 Empty

(c) Results of merge 2

File 1 Empty

File 2 Empty

File 3 | 10 22 36 40 50 60 70 80 95 100 110 120 130 140 153 |

File 4 Empty

(d) Results of merge 3

EXAMPLE 6.4

In this example the initial file is the same as that of Example 6.2:

50 110 95 10 100 36 153 40 120 60 70 130

In contrast to Example 6.3, the number of runs on each file after the sort phase is even. After the sorting phase, files 1 and 2 contain the same number of runs (Figure 6.5(a)). The first execution of the merge phase merges runs from files 1 and 2 and stores the merged runs alternately in files 3 and 4; the results are shown in Figure 6.5(b). Files 3 and 4 are input files for the next execution of the balanced merge phase, which alternately stores the merged runs in output files 1 and 2. The results of the second execution of the balanced merge phase are shown in Figure 6.5(c).

The two-way sort/merge performs a merge of two input files to one output file, distributes the runs back to the two input files, and repeats until all records are in one run. The balanced two-way sort/merge performs a merge of runs from files 1 and 2 to files 3 and 4, merges runs from files 3 and 4 back to files 1 and 2, and repeats until all records are in one run. The savings in execution time provided by the balanced two-way sort/merge result from the elimination of the redistribution of runs between merges.

File 1	50 95 110	40 120 153
File 2	10 36 100	60 70 130

(a) Results of phase 1 sort

File 1 Empty

File 2 Empty

File 3	10 36 50 95 100 110
File 4	40 60 70 120 130 153

(b) Results of merge 1

File 1	10 36 40 50 60 70 95 100 110 120 130 153

File 2 Empty

File 3 Empty

File 4 Empty

(c) Results of merge 2

Figure 6.5
Balanced two-way sort/merge—Example 6.4

Algorithm 6.2 presents the balanced two-way sort/merge algorithm that applies to cases in which the number of output files is the same as the number of input files.

ALGORITHM 6.2 Balanced Two-way Sort/Merge

```
--                       Sort Phase
initial distribution
--                       Merge Phase
number_of_output_files : Constant Integer ← 2
TYPE File_Array Is Array ( 1 .. 3 ) Of File_Type
TYPE File_Indexes Is Array ( 1 .. number_of_output_files ) Of Integer
file             : File_Array
hold             : Integer
in_file          : File_Indexes ← ( 1, 2 )
infile_index     : Integer
number_of_runs   : Integer
out_file         : File_Indexes ← ( 3, 4 )
outfile_index    : Integer
Loop
    open input files
    create output files
    number_of_runs ← 0
    Loop          -- perform 2-way merge on files(in_file(1))
                  -- and (in_file(2)) evenly distributing output
                  -- to files(out_file(1)) and (out_file(2))
        input first record from each input file
                  -- The remainder of runs/number_of_output_files will
                  -- be 0 or 1 for 2 output files. So the remainder
                  -- + 1 will select output file 1 or 2 alternately.
        outfile_index ← number_of_runs Mod number_of_output_files + 1
        Loop      --output record with smaller key
            infile_index ← Smallest_key ( file, in_file )
            output record from file(infile_index)
                           to file(out_file(outfile_index))
            input next record from  file(in_file(infile_index))
            Exit When End_Of_Run_On_Both_Files ( file, in_file )
        End Loop
        output end-of-run-marker to file(out_file(outfile_index))
        increment number_of_runs
        Exit When End_Of_Both_Files ( file, in_file )
    End Loop
    close all files
    If number_of_runs > 1 Then
        For file_index ← 1 .. 2 Loop
            hold ← in_file(file_index)
            in_file(file_index) ← out_file(file_index)
            out_file(file_index) ← hold
        End Loop
    Else
        Exit

    End If
End Loop
```

```
FUNCTION End_of_Run_on_File ( file : In File_Type ) Return Boolean

    Return next_record of file = end-of-run-marker

FUNCTION Smallest_Key ( file : In File_Array;
                        in_file : In File_Indexes ) Return Integer

    If End_Of_Run_On_File ( file(in_file(1)) )
    Or  End_Of_File ( file(in_file(1)) )
        Return in_file(2)
    ElsIf End_Of_Run_On_File ( file(in_file(2)) )
    Or End_Of_File ( file(in_file(2)) )
        Return in_file(1)
    ElsIf key ( in_file(1) ) < key ( in_file(2) )
        Return in_file(1)
    Else
        Return in_file(2)
    End If

FUNCTION End_Of_Run_On_Both_Files ( file : In File_Array;
                                    in_file : In File_Indexes ) Return Boolean

    Return End_Of_Run_On_File  ( file(in_file(1)) )
       And End_Of_Run_On_File ( file(in_file(2)) )

FUNCTION End_Of_Both_Files ( file : In File_Array;
                             in_file : In File_Indexes ) Return Boolean

    Return End_Of_File  ( file(in_file(1)) )
       And End_Of_File ( file(in_file(2)) )
```

Each pass of the merge phase of the balanced two-way sort/merge cuts the number of runs in half, so the number of passes of the merge phase required are $\lceil \lg NR \rceil$. (*NR* is the number of runs produced during the initial sorting phase.) The number of passes through the merge phase of the balanced two-way sort/merge is the same as the number through the two-way sort/merge. The difference is that each pass of the merge phase of the balanced two-way sort/merge transmits each record of the file once. Each pass of the merge phase of the two-way sort/merge transmits each record of the file twice. The number of passes through the file for the balanced two-way sort/merge is roughly half ($\lceil \lg NR \rceil + 1$) that of the two-way sort/merge ($2\lceil \lg NR \rceil$).

BALANCED *k*-WAY SORT/MERGE

The balanced two-way sort/merge algorithm improved on the two-way sort/merge by increasing the number of output files to the same number of input files. The result is the elimination of the redistribution of merged runs back to two files. By merging runs from two input files and storing merged runs on two output files, the next merge pass reverses the use of the input and output files; the two nonempty files merge to the two empty files. An obvious improvement is to increase the number of files available for the sort/merge to k input files and k output files. By increasing the number of input and output files, each file contains fewer runs, with the result that fewer merges have to be performed. The merging process is more complicated with k input files because a *k-way* merge needs to distribute merged runs into k output files.

EXAMPLE 6.5

Consider the initial file used in Examples 6.1 and 6.3:

50 110 95 10 100 36 153 40 120 60 70 130 22 140 80

Assume that there are three input files and three output files. The sort phase produces the result illustrated in Figure 6.6(a). The merge phase now performs a three-way merge of files 1, 2, and 3, then stores merged runs alternately in files 4, 5, and 6. The file contents in Figure 6.6(b) result. (File 6 is empty because of the small number of runs in files 1, 2, and 3.) The second execution of the merging operation merges files 4, 5, and 6 (if 6 is not empty) and stores merged runs in files 1, 2, and 3. The process is repeated until all runs are in one file (in this case, a second merge is all that is necessary). The resulting file contents are pictured in Figure 6.6(c).

For this file of data, the balanced two-way sort/merge performed the merge phase three times to merge all the runs into one run in one file. Using the balanced three-way sort/merge, the same file of data is merged into one run with only two executions of the merge phase. Ideally, if each sorted run from the sort phase (phase 1) is stored in a separate file (each requiring a separate external device), then one merge cycle merges all runs into one run; a total of only $k + 1$ files are needed—that is, k input files and 1 output file.

EXAMPLE 6.6

Use the same data:

50 110 95 10 100 36 153 40 120 60 70 130 22 140 80

Allocating each sorted run from the sort phase to a separate file results in the file contents in Figure 6.7(a). Now the merge phase performs a five-way merge; it merges runs from files 1, 2, 3, 4, and 5 and stores merged runs in file 6 (Figure 6.7(b)).

Figure 6.6
Balanced k-way sort/merge—Example 6.5

File 1	50 95 110	60 70 130
File 2	10 36 100	22 80 140
File 3	40 120 153	

(a) Results of phase 1 sort

File 1	Empty
File 2	Empty
File 3	Empty
File 4	10 36 40 50 95 100 110 120 153
File 5	22 60 70 80 130 140
File 6	Empty

(b) Results of merge 1

File 1	10 22 36 40 50 60 70 80 95 100 110 120 130 140 153
File 2	Empty
File 3	Empty
File 4	Empty
File 5	Empty
File 6	Empty

(c) Results of merge 2

The realistic sort/merge situation is somewhere between the balanced two-way merge, which merges two input files into two output files, and the idealistic k-way sort/merge, which uses k input files for k runs and merging to one output file. The **balanced k-way sort/merge** algorithm presented in Algorithm 6.3 uses k input files and k output files to perform an extended version of the balanced two-way sort/merge presented in Algorithm 6.2.

Figure 6.7
5-way sort/merge—
Example 6.6

ALGORITHM 6.3 Balanced *K*-way Sort/Merge

```
                     -- Sort Phase
initial distribution
                     -- Merge Phase
number_of_files           : Constant Positive ← k
maximum_number_of_files: Constant Positive ← 2 * k
TYPE File_Array Is Array ( 1 .. maximum_number_of_files ) Of File_Type
file              : File_Array
first_in          : Positive ← 1
first_out         : Positive ← k + 1
hold, infile      : Positive
number_of_runs    : Natural
outfile : Positive
Loop
    open input files
    create output files
    number_of_runs ← 0
    Loop  -- merge next runs from k input files
        input first record from each input file
        outfile ←  number_of_runs Mod number_of_files + first_out
        Loop    -- output record with smaller key to file
            infile ← Smallest_Key ( file, first_in )
            output record from file(infile) to file(outfile)
            input next record from file(infile)
            Exit When End_Of_Run_On_All_Files ( file, first_in )
        End Loop
```

```
        output end-of-run-marker to file(outfile)
        number_of_runs ← number_of_runs + 1
        Exit When End_Of_All_Files ( file, first_in )
    End Loop
    close all files
    If number_of_runs > 1  -- first_out is k + 1 or 1
        hold ← first_in
        first_in ← first_out
        first_out ← hold
    Else
        Exit
    End If
End Loop

FUNCTION End_of_Run_on_File ( file : In File_Type ) Return Boolean

    Return next_record on file = end-of-run-marker

FUNCTION Smallest_Key ( file : In File_Array
                        first_input_file : In Positive ) Return Integer
     max_file        : Natural ← first_input_file + number_of_files − 1
     first_file      : Natural
     second_file     : Natural
     first_file ← Find_Nonempty_File ( first_input_file, max_file )
     Loop
         second_file ← Find_Nonempty_File ( first_input_file, max_file )
         Exit When second_file = 0
         If key ( first_file ) > key ( second_file )
             first_file ← second_file
         End If
     End Loop
     Return first_file

FUNCTION Find_Nonempty_File ( input_file    : In Positive
                              max_file      : In Natural ) Return Natural
    file_index : Natural ← input_file
    Loop
        Exit When file_index > max_file
        If End_Of_Run_On_File ( file(file_index) )
        Or End_Of_File ( file(file_index) )
            increment file_index
        Else
            Return file_index
        End If
    End Loop
    Return 0

FUNCTION End_Of_Run_On_All_Files ( file        : In File_Array
                                   first_in    : In Positive ) Return Boolean
    test_end : Boolean ← TRUE

    For lcv ←  first_in .. first_in + number_of_files − 1
        test_end ← test_end And End_Of_Run_On_File ( file(lcv) )
    End Loop
    Return test_end
```

```
FUNCTION End_Of_All_Files ( file      : In File_Array
                            first_in  : In Positive ) Return Boolean
    test_end : Boolean ← TRUE
    For lcv ← first_in .. first_in + number_of_files – 1
        test_end ← test_end And End_Of_File ( file(lcv) )
    End Loop
    Return test_end
```

Each pass of the merge phase of a two-way sort/merge cuts the number of runs to one-half the number of runs for the start of that phase. Each pass of the merge phase of a three-way sort/merge cuts the number of runs to one-third the number of runs for the start of that phase—that is, the number is reduced by a factor of three. Each pass of the merge phase of a four-way sort/merge cuts the number of runs to one-fourth the number of runs for the start of that phase; the number is reduced by a factor of four. So, in general, the number of passes for the merge phase of a k-way sort/merge is $\lceil \log_k NR \rceil$. The variable k is the number of files to be merged and is also the number of output files, and NR is the number of runs produced during the initial sorting phase.

For example, when $NR = 36$, a three-way sort/merge requires $\lceil \log_3 36 \rceil = 4$ passes of the merge phase. A four-way sort/merge requires $\lceil \log_4 36 \rceil = 3$ passes of the merge phase. Since each pass of the merge phase transmits each record of the file once, the number of passes through a file to be sorted is one more than the number of passes through the merge phase.

POLYPHASE SORT/MERGE

Close examination of the balanced two-way sort/merge algorithm indicates the need for two improvements: the reduction of copying when the number of runs is not a multiple of the number of files being merged and the reduction of the number of output files required. Example 6.7 explains how an algorithm with these improvements, the polyphase sort/merge, works.

EXAMPLE 6.7

Consider the records to be sorted:

50 110 95 10 100 36 153 40 120 60 70 130 22 140 80

The number of runs in file 1 after the sort phase is greater than the number of runs in file 2 (Figure 6.8(a)). After the first two pairs of runs are merged from files 1 and 2, file 2 is empty, but file 1 still has one unprocessed run (Figure 6.8(b)). The balanced two-way sort/merge algorithm and the balanced k-way sort/merge algorithm simply copy the last run from file 1 into the output file.

An improved algorithm reduces the copying of runs at the end of a file in this manner: When an input file becomes empty, file 1 still has an unprocessed run, while the output file 3 has two merged runs. To maximize the merging phase, files 1 and 3 could be merged into file 2 (which is empty). Figure 6.8(c) shows the resulting file contents. Now file 1 is empty, file 2 (the output file) has one run, and file 3 still has one run. Files 2 and 3 can be merged into the empty file 1 to produce one run containing all the records (Figure 6.8(d)). In effect, the improved algorithm performs a two-way sort/merge until one of the input files becomes empty—the end of a merge pass. The empty file is the one output file to receive runs merged from the other two files. Table 6.1 summarizes the number of runs on each file after the sort phase and after each pass of the merge phase.

Figure 6.8
Polyphase sort/merge—Example 6.7

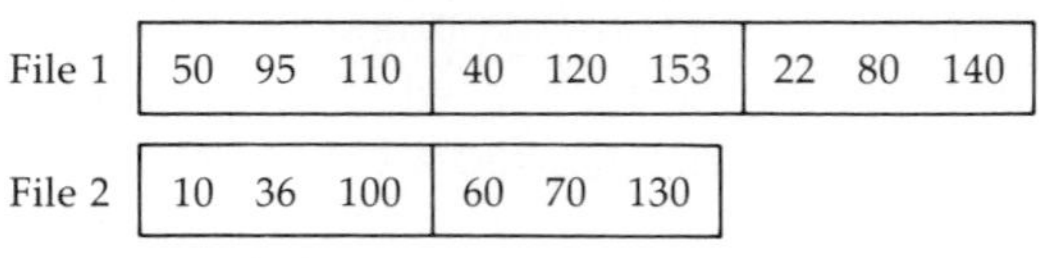

(a) Results of phase 1 sort

File 1 | 22 80 140

File 2 Empty

File 3 | 10 36 50 95 100 110 | 40 60 70 120 130 153

(b) Results of merging first two pairs of runs in merge 1

File 1 Empty

File 2 | 10 22 36 50 80 95 100 110 140

File 3 | 40 60 70 120 130 153

(c) Results of merge 2

File 1 | 10 22 36 40 50 60 70 80 95 100 110 120 130 140 153

File 2 Empty

File 3 Empty

(d) Results of merge 3

Table 6.1 Summary of polyphase sort/merge using Example 6.1 data

	Number of runs on:		
	File 1	**File 2**	**File 3**
Sort phase	3	2	0
Merge pass 1	1	0	2
Merge pass 2	0	1	1
Merge pass 3	1	0	0

The process uses only three files ($k + 1$), where the balanced two-way sort/merge algorithm used four files ($2k$), but it performs a k-way merge only until one input file is empty. Then it merges k input files into one output file until all records are in one run. The merge process discussed here is the polyphase sort/merge algorithm. The sort phase distributes sorted runs into k files, then the merge phase merges k input files into one output file. The first input file emptied in each merge phase becomes the output file for the next phase. The improvement realized is that a k-way merge is performed requiring $k + 1$ files. (The balanced k-way sort/merge algorithm requires $2k$ files.) The improved algorithm, the **polyphase sort/merge** algorithm, is presented in Algorithm 6.4.

ALGORITHM 6.4 Polyphase Sort/Merge

```
empty_file    : Natural
end_of_a_file: Boolean
maximum_number_of_files : Positive ← k + 1
TYPE File_Array Is Array ( 1 .. maximum_number_of_files ) Of File_Type
file: File_Array
infile: Positive
number_of_files  : Positive ← k
TYPE Runs_Array Is Array ( 1 .. maximum_number_of_files ) of Natural
number_of_runs  : Runs_Array
outfile: Positive ← maximum_number_of_files
                    -- Sort Phase
--initial distribution
--and initialization of number_of_runs array
--to initial number of runs in each file
                    -- Merge Phase
open input files
create file(outfile)
Loop    -- continue until all files are merged
    number_of_runs(outfile) ← 0
    Loop    -- merge next runs from k input files
        input first record from each input file
        increment number_of_runs(outfile)
        Loop    -- output record with smaller key
            infile ← Smallest_Key
            output record from file(infile) to file(outfile)
            input next record from file(infile)
            Exit When End_Of_Run_On_All_Files
        End Loop
```

```
        For lcv ← 1 .. maximum_number_of_files
            If lcv /= outfile
                decrement number_of_runs(lcv)
            End If
        End Loop
        output end_of_run_marker to file(outfile)
        Check_For_End_Of_A_File ( end_of_a_file, empty_file )
        Exit When end_of_a_file
    End Loop
    If Total_Runs ( number_of_runs ) = 1
        close all files
        Exit
    Else
        close file(outfile)
        open file(outfile)
        close file(empty_file)
        create file(empty_file)
        outfile ← empty_file
    End If
End Loop
FUNCTION Total_Runs ( number_of_runs : In Runs_Array ) Return Natural
    total : Natural ← 0
    For lcv ← 1 .. maximum_number_of_files
        total ← total + number_of_runs(lcv)
    End Loop
    Return total
FUNCTION Smallest_Key Return Natural
    file_index  : Positive ← 1
    first_file, second_file     : Natural
    Find_Nonempty_File ( first_file, file_index )
    Loop
        Find_Nonempty_File ( second_file, file_index )
        Exit When second_file = 0
        If key ( first_file ) > key ( second_file )
            first_file ← second_file
        End If
    End Loop
    Return first_file

PROCEDURE Find_Nonempty_File ( nonempty : Out Natural
                               file_index : In Out Positive )
    Loop
        Exit When file_index > maximum_number_of_files
        If file_index /= outfile
            If Not End_Of_Run_On_File (file(file_index) )
            And Not End_Of_File (file(file_index) )
                nonempty ← file_index
                increment file_index
                Return
            End If
        End If
        increment file_index
    End Loop
    nonempty ← 0
```

```
FUNCTION End_of_Run_on_File ( file : In File_Type ) Return Boolean

    Return next_record on file = end-of-run-marker

FUNCTION End_Of_Run_On_All_Files Return Boolean
    test_end : Boolean ← TRUE

    For lcv ← 1 .. maximum_number_of_files
        If lcv /= outfile
            test_end ← test_end
                             And End_Of_Run_On_File ( file(lcv) )
        End If
    End Loop
    Return test_end

PROCEDURE Check_For_End_Of_A_File (end_of_a_file : Out Boolean
                                   empty_file    : Out Natural )

    For lcv ← 1 .. maximum_number_of_files
        If lcv /= outfile
        And Then End_Of_File ( file(lcv))
            empty_file ← lcv
            end_of_a_file ← TRUE
            Return
        End If
    End Loop
    end_of_a_file ← FALSE
    empty_file ← 0
```

An extensive analysis of the polyphase sort/merge found in Knuth (1973) is summarized in Table 6.2. The polyphase sort/merge that uses a perfect Fibonacci distribution with $k = 2$ (a two-way merge) requires approximately 1.04 lg NR + 0.99 passes through the data. (The variable k indicates the number of files to be merged. NR is the number of initial runs after the sort phase.) This characteristic makes it competitive with the balanced two-way sort/merge (passes = $\lceil \lg NR \rceil + 1$), and the polyphase sort/merge needs only three files instead of four.

For a three-way merge, the polyphase sort/merge makes 0.703 lg NR + 0.96 pass over the data. For a file of 36 initial runs ($NR = 36$), the balanced three-way merge makes four passes over the data and requires six files; the polyphase sort/merge makes 5.178 passes over the data but requires only four files. An additional pass over the data is a small price to pay to reduce the number of files required by one-third (from six files to four files). Note that the number of passes through the data decreases as the number of files increases. The balanced k-way sort/merge makes $\lceil \lg NR \rceil + 1$ passes through the data. The number of passes for the polyphase sort/merge is $1/NR$ times the total number of initial runs processed during the initial distribution and merge phases. The polyphase sort/merge is more efficient than the balanced k-way sort/merge whenever the number of files being merged (k) is greater than three.

Table 6.2 Analysis of polyphase sort/merge

K	**Number of passes**	
2	1.504 ln NR + 0.992	(= 1.040 lg NR + 0.99)
3	1.015 ln NR + 0.965	(= 0.703 lg NR + 0.96)
4	0.863 ln NR + 0.921	
5	0.795 ln NR + 0.864	
6	0.762 ln NR + 0.767	
7	0.744 ln NR + 0.723	
8	0.734 ln NR + 0.646	
9	0.728 ln NR + 0.568	
19	0.721 ln NR – 0.030	

Legend:
k = number of files to be merged
NR = number of initial runs after sort phase

Fibonacci Distribution

The basic principle behind the efficiency of the polyphase sort/merge algorithm is the unbalanced distribution of initial runs from the sort phase. Unbalanced distribution ensures that one file ends before any of the other files, so fewer passes over the data are required. R. L. Gilstad, who developed the polyphase sort/merge in 1960, found that an unbalanced distribution of initial runs, using the **perfect Fibonacci distribution**, provided a much improved performance over a balanced distribution (see Knuth, 1973).

The perfect Fibonacci distribution maximizes the merge phase by reducing the copying of runs, thus reducing the number of merge cycles. The ***k*th_order_Fibonacci_series** is used to distribute runs to each file. The variable *k* indicates both the number of files to be merged and the order of the Fibonacci series to be used. The runs are distributed to *k* files and merged *k*-way into one output file.

The *k*th order Fibonacci series is defined as:

$$F_n^{(k)} = 0 \text{ for } 0 \le n \le k - 2$$
$$F_n^{(k)} = 1 \text{ for } n = k - 1$$
$$F_n^{(k)} = F_{n-1}^{(k)} + F_{n-2}^{(k)} + \ldots + F_{n-k}^{(k)} \text{ for } n \ge k$$

The F represents a value from a Fibonacci sequence. The superscript specifies the order of the sequence and the subscript specifies the position of the value in that sequence.

When $k = 2$, $F_0^{(2)} = 0$ and $F_1^{(2)} = 1$, this is the usual Fibonacci sequence:
$F_{n+1}^{(2)} = F_n^{(2)} + F_{n-1}^{(2)}$

Each next item in the series is the sum of the previous two items in the series. For $k = 3$, the kth order Fibonacci series computes each item in the series as the sum of the previous three items in the series.

Consider the case where $k = 3$. Three files are used for the initial distribution, and a three-way merge is performed; a total of four files are required. If 17 runs are sorted, the perfect Fibonacci distribution is seven runs on file 1, six runs on file 2, and four runs on file 3. Table 6.3 illustrates the number of runs on each file after the sort and merge phases of the polyphase sort/merge for 17 runs. Merge pass 1 merges four runs from files 1, 2, and 3. File 3 becomes empty, leaving three runs on file 1, two runs on file 2, and the four merged runs on file 4. Merge pass 2 merges two runs from each of three files when file 2 becomes empty. A file of 17 runs requires four passes of the merge phase.

Table 6.3 Summary of polyphase sort/merge on 17 runs

	Number of runs on: File 1	File 2	File 3	File 4
Sort phase	7	6	4	0
Merge pass 1	3	2	0	4
Merge pass 2	1	0	2	2
Merge pass 3	0	1	1	1
Merge pass 4	1	0	0	0

The polyphase merge is more efficient than the balanced three-way sort/merge in that the number of runs merged in the polyphase for 17 runs is never less than three. (Table 6.4 shows the results of the balanced three-way sort/merge on 17 runs.) Since the number of runs in the balanced three-way merge is not a multiple of three, the last merged run produced by each merge phase of the balanced three-way sort/merge is a merge of two runs (the only two runs left). The polyphase maximizes the merging process by stopping the merge pass when a file empties and ensures that k files are merged in each pass.

Table 6.4 Summary of balanced two-way sort/merge on 17 runs

	Number of runs on: File 1	File 2	File 3	File 4	File 5	File 6
Sort phase	6	6	5	0	0	0
Merge pass 1	0	0	0	2	2	2
Merge pass 2	1	1	0	0	0	0
Merge pass 3	0	0	0	1	0	0

The distribution of runs among the nonempty files after each merge pass is a perfect **Lth-level distribution**; one file always ends before all the other files, and the last merge pass merges one run from each of the nonempty files into the empty file. A perfect Fibonacci distribution ensures that the polyphase sort/merge always has one run on each of k files to be merged during the last pass of the merge phase.

Look from the bottom up at Table 6.3, the distribution of runs on the files—the zeroth-level distribution for $k = 3$. The table reads 1, 0, 0, 0, which indicates that the sort/merge is finished. The first-level distribution of runs on the nonempty files is 1, 1, 1; the level indicates that one pass of the merge phase is required to merge the runs into one run. The second-level distribution is 1, 2, 2, which indicates that two merge passes are required to merge all runs into one run. The third-level distribution is 3, 2, 4, which indicates that three merge passes are required to merge all runs into one run.

When $k = 3$ files are merged, the third-order Fibonacci series is used for initial distribution of runs from the sort phase. The Lth-level indicates the number of merge passes that are required to merge all runs into one run. The first six terms of the third-order Fibonacci series are computed as:

$$
\begin{array}{llrcl}
0 \le L \le k-2: & 0 \le L \le 1: & L & = & 0;\ F_L^{(3)} = F_0^{(3)} = 0 \\
 & & L & = & 1;\ F_1^{(3)} = 0 \\
L = k-1: & L = 2: & L & = & 2;\ F_2^{(3)} = 1 \\
L \ge k: & L \ge 3: & L & = & 3;\ F_3^{(3)} = F_2^{(3)} + F_1^{(3)} + F_0^{(3)} \\
 & & & = & 1 + 0 + 0 \\
 & & & = & 1 \\
 & & L & = & 4;\ F_4^{(3)} = F_3^{(3)} + F_2^{(3)} + F_1^{(3)} \\
 & & & = & 1 + 1 + 0 \\
 & & & = & 2 \\
 & & L & = & 5;\ F_5^{(3)} = F_4^{(3)} + F_3^{(3)} + F_2^{(3)} \\
 & & & = & 2 + 1 + 1 \\
 & & & = & 4
\end{array}
$$

The third-order Fibonacci series is computed by summing the three previous terms. The result is

0, 0, 1, 1, 2, 4, 7, 13, 24, 44, 81, ...

When using a k-way polyphase merge, the number of runs r distributed to a given file f is specified by the formula below. L specifies a level value that starts at 1 and goes up until the total number of runs distributed over all k input files at a given level is greater than or equal to the total number of runs to be merged. Level 0 is defined as 1 for file 1 and 0 for all other files.

$$r = \sum_{i=0}^{k-f} F^{k}_{L+f+i-2}$$

The subscripts indicate which consecutive Fibonacci terms must be summed in order to determine the number of runs on the kth file (the subscripts are never negative).

For $L = 1$, file 1 ($f = 1$) contains:

$$r = \sum_{i=0}^{3-1} F^{(3)}_{1+1+i-2} = F^{(3)}_0 + F^{(3)}_1 + F^{(3)}_2 = 0 + 0 + 1 = 1 \text{ run}$$

File 2 contains:

$$r = \sum_{i=0}^{3-2} F^{(3)}_{1+2+i-2} = F^{(3)}_1 + F^{(3)}_2 = 0 + 1 = 1 \text{ run}$$

File 3 contains one run.

$$r = \sum_{i=0}^{3-3} F^{(3)}_{1+3+i-2} = F^{(3)}_2 = 1 \text{ run}$$

For $L = 2$, file 1 ($f = 1$) contains:

$$r = \sum_{i=0}^{3-1} F^{(3)}_{2+1+i-2} = F^{(3)}_1 + F^{(3)}_2 + F^{(3)}_3 = 0 + 1 + 1 = 2 \text{ runs}$$

File 2 contains:

$$r = \sum_{i=0}^{3-2} F^{(3)}_{2+2+i-2} = F^{(3)}_2 + F^{(3)}_3 = 1 + 1 = 2 \text{ runs}$$

File 3 contains:

$$r = \sum_{i=0}^{3-3} F^{(3)}_{2+3+i-2} = F^{(3)}_3 = 1 \text{ run}$$

For $L = 3$, file 1 contains:

$$r = \sum_{i=0}^{3-1} F^{(3)}_{3+1+i-2} = F^{(3)}_2 + F^{(3)}_3 + F^{(3)}_4 = 1 + 1 + 2 = 4 \text{ runs}$$

File 2 contains:

$$r = \sum_{i=0}^{3-2} F^{(3)}_{3+2+i-2} = F^{(3)}_3 + F^{(3)}_4 = 1 + 2 = 3 \text{ runs}$$

File 3 contains:

$$r = \sum_{i=0}^{3-3} F^{(3)}_{3+3+i-2} = F^{(3)}_4 = 2 \text{ runs}$$

For $L = 4$, file 1 contains:

$$r=\sum_{i=0}^{3-1} F^{(3)}_{4+1+i-2} \quad = \quad F^{(3)}_3 + F^{(3)}_4 + F^{(3)}_5 = 1 + 2 + 4 = 7 \text{ runs}$$

File 2 contains:

$$r=\sum_{i=0}^{3-2} F^{(3)}_{4+2+i-2} \quad = \quad F^{(3)}_4 + F^{(3)}_5 = 2 + 4 = 6 \text{ runs}$$

File 3 contains:

$$r=\sum_{i=0}^{3-3} F^{(3)}_{4+3+i-2} \quad = \quad F^{(3)}_5 = 4 \text{ runs}$$

Table 6.5 presents the Lth-level perfect Fibonacci numbers for three files ($k = 3$, which signifies a three-way merge into one file). The table indicates the distribution of runs on the three nonempty files that is "perfect" at the Lth-level, where L indicates the number of passes of the merge phase that are required to merge all runs into one run. For 17 runs with $k = 3$, the initial perfect Fibonacci distribution is seven runs, six runs, and four runs on three files as computed earlier. After the first merge pass, the number of runs is nine distributed as four runs, three runs, and two runs. After merge pass 2, the number of runs is five distributed as two, two, and one. The next merge pass leaves three runs with one on each file, so the final merge pass merges the three remaining runs into one run to complete the polyphase sort/merge.

Consider the data in Example 6.1 that produced five sorted runs for the merging phase. The Fibonacci distribution sort distributes the runs "perfectly" with one run on file 1, two runs on file 2, and two runs on file 3 as shown in Figure 6.9(a). The first execution of the merging phase merges files 1, 2, and 3 into output file 4; file 1 is emptied (Figure 6.9(b)). File 1 now becomes the output file for the next merge pass, in which the remaining runs on files 2 and 3 are merged with the run on file 4. As a result all records are in one run on one file (Figure 6.9(c)).

For this file of data, the balanced two-way sort/merge performs the merge phase three times to put all the records in one run, and the process requires three files. The balanced three-way sort/merge executes the merge phase twice and requires six files. The polyphase sort/merge, using a perfect Fibonacci distribution, performs the merge phase twice and requires only four files. The efficiency of the balanced k-way merge is achieved, and the number of files is reduced from $2k$ to $k + 1$.

Table 6.5 *L*th-level perfect Fibonacci numbers for $k = 3$

Level *L*	**File** 1	2	3	**Total No. of runs**
0	1	0	0	1
1	1	1	1	3
2	2	2	1	5
3	4	3	2	9
4	7	6	4	17
5	13	11	7	31
6	24	20	13	57
7	44	37	24	105
8	81	68	44	193
L	a_L	b_L	c_L	t_L
$L+1$	$a_L + b_L$	$a_L + c_L$	a_L	$t_L + 2a_L$

Figure 6.9
Polyphase sort/merge of Example 6.1 data

File 1 [50 95 110]

File 2 [10 36 100] [40 120 153]

File 3 [60 70 130] [22 80 140]

(a) Results of phase 1 sort on Example 6.1 data

File 1 Empty

File 2 [40 120 153]

File 3 [22 80 140]

File 4 [10 36 50 60 70 95 100 110 130]

(b) Results of merge 1

File 1 [10 22 36 40 50 60 70 80 95 100 110 120 130 140 153]

File 2 Empty

File 3 Empty

File 4 Empty

(c) Results of merge 2

To develop an algorithm for initially distributing runs using the Fibonacci series, assume three files store sorted runs from the sort phase. The first cycle of the distribution algorithm distributes runs in a "perfect" fashion for level 1— namely, one run on the first file. Assuming that the numbers of runs on files 1 through *k* are a_L, b_L, c_L, ..., respectively, at the *L*th-level of distribution (Table 6.5), where $a_L \geq b_L \geq c_L \geq ...$, the distribution at the L + 1st level can easily be computed using the number of runs in the *L*th-level:

> level = $L + 1$
> file 1 = $a_L + b_L$ runs
> file 2 = $a_L + c_L$ runs
> file 3 = a_L runs
> total runs (t_{L+1}) = $t_L + 2a_L$ runs

The Fibonacci distribution used in the sort phase to distribute sorted runs to the files is presented in Algorithm 6.5.

For example, assume nine runs are to be distributed using Algorithm 6.5. The first pass of the `Loop` loads run 1 (R1) on file 1 as shown by Table 6.6. The second pass of the `Loop` stores run 2 (R2) on file 2 and stores run 3 (R3) on file 3. The result is a perfect distribution—1, 1, and 1—at level 1. The third pass of the `Loop` loads run 4 (R4) to file 1 and loads run 5 (R5) to file 2. The result is a perfect second-level distribution—2, 2, and 1. The fourth pass through the `Loop` continues through the file to put run 6 (R6) and run 7 (R7) on file 1, run 8 (R8) on file 2, and run 9 (R9) on file 3. The result is a perfect third-level distribution—four, three, and two runs.

Table 6.6 Distribution of runs produced by Algorithm 6.5

	Contents of File 1	**File 2**	**File 3**
Pass 1 of outer Loop adds:	R1		
Pass 2 of outer Loop adds:		R2	R3
Pass 3 of outer Loop adds:	R4	R5	
Pass 4 of outer Loop adds:	R6 R7	R8	R9
Total runs of each file	4	3	2

ALGORITHM 6.5 Fibonacci Distribution Sort

```
fib_1              : Natural
level              : Positive ← 1
number_of_files  : Positive ← k
maximum_number_of_files : Positive ← k + 1
TYPE Runs_Array Is Array ( 1 .. maximum_number_of_files ) of Natural
fib                : Runs_Array ← (1, Others → 0)
number_of_runs  : Runs_Array ← (Others → 0)
TYPE File_Array Is Array ( 1 .. maximum_number_of_files ) Of File_Type
file : File_Array
```

```
open original_file  -- file to be sorted
create input files
Loop
    Exit When End_Of_File ( file(original_file) )
    For file_number ← 1 .. number_of_files
        Loop
            Exit When End_Of_File ( file(original_file) )
            Exit When number_of_runs(file_number)
                    = fib(file_number)
            write a sorted run on file(file_number)
            increment number_of_runs(file_number)
        End Loop
    End Loop
                -- compute L + 1st-level distribution
    Exit When End_Of_File ( file(original_file) )
    fib_1 ← fib(1)
    For file_number ← 1 .. number_of_files – 1
        fib(file_number) ← fib_1 + fib(file_number + 1)
    End Loop
    fib(number_of_files) ← fib_1
End Loop
close all files
```

EXAMPLE 6.8

The polyphase merge performs most efficiently if the number of runs of records to be sorted coincides exactly with a perfect Fibonacci distribution. When the number of runs does not agree, the polyphase merge can still be used, although the merge is somewhat less efficient. By adding **dummy runs** (also called null runs and empty runs), we can obtain the required number of runs on each file.

Suppose seven runs are distributed instead of the nine runs distributed above. The distribution is four runs (file 1), two runs (file 2), and one run (file 3)—not a perfect Fibonacci distribution. Two dummy runs (D1 and D2) are loaded to files 2 and 3 in place of the missing runs (R8 and R9). The dummy runs make the files have the correct number of runs even though some runs are empty. This ensures that only one file ends before the rest of the files and that the one empty file at the end of each merge pass is subsequently the output file of the next merge pass.

Table 6.7 shows the contents of each file after each merge pass. The initial distribution is four, three, and two runs. After merge pass 1, the distribution is two, two, and one. After merge pass 2, the distribution is one, one, and one, and merge pass 3 merges all runs into one run on file 2.

Table 6.7 File contents of polyphase sort/merge with dummy runs

	Number of runs on File 1	File 2	File 3	File 4
Sort phase	R1	R2	R3	—
	R4	R5	D2	
	R6	D1		
	R7			
Merge pass 1	R6	D1	—	R1+R2+R3
	R7			R4+R5+D2
Merge pass 2	R7	—	R1+R2+R3+R6+D1	R4+R5+D2
Merge pass 3	—	ALL RUNS	—	—

Algorithm 6.5 must be modified to write dummy runs to the files with less than the perfect number of runs. The modified Algorithm 6.5 is presented in Algorithm 6.6, with the modified lines beginning with a plus sign. The dummy runs are written to the end of all files not containing a perfect number of runs since the number of records to be sorted is not known in advance. Algorithm 6.6 does not produce an optimal distribution of dummy runs, but Tremblay and Sorenson (1984) found that this distribution allows the polyphase sort to perform only 2 percent to 3 percent below the optimum. (Knuth [1973] presented the optimal distribution, in which dummy runs are artificially inserted at the beginning of all files—a procedure that is more complex.)

ALGORITHM 6.6 Modified Fibonacci Distribution Sort

```
fib_1 : Natural
level : Positive ← 1
number_of_files : Positive ← k
maximum_number_of_files : Positive ← k + 1
TYPE Runs_Array Is Array ( 1 .. maximum_number_of_files ) of Natural
fib : Runs_Array ← (1, Others → 0 )
number_of_runs : Runs_Array ← (Others → 0)
TYPE File_Array Is Array ( 1 .. maximum_number_of_files ) Of File_Type
file : File_Array
open original_file -- file to be sorted
create input files
Loop
    Exit When End_Of_File ( file(original_file) )
    For file_number ← 1 .. number_of_files
        Loop
            Exit When End_Of_File ( file(original_file) )
            Exit When number_of_runs(file_number)
                    = fib(file_number)
            write a sorted run on file(file_number)
            increment number_of_runs(file_number)
        End Loop
    End Loop
```

```
                  -- compute L + 1st-level distribution
     Exit When End_Of_File ( file(original_file) )
     fib_1 ← fib(1)
     For file_number ← 1 .. number_of_files - 1
          fib(file_number) ← fib_1 + fib(file_number + 1)
     End Loop
     fib(number_of_files) ← fib_1
+                   --add dummy runs if necessary
+    For file_number ← 1 .. number_of_files
+         Loop
+              Exit When number_of_runs(file_number)
+                             = fib(file_number)
+              output end_of_run_marker to file(file_number)
+              increment number_of_runs(file_number)
          End Loop
     End Loop
End Loop
close all files
```

ADA SORT_A_FILE PACKAGE

A generic package for sorting files can be specified that is appropriate for any of the sort/merge techniques described in the chapter. The specifications for the package do not change; only the implementation within the package body reflects a specific sorting and merging algorithm. The user instantiates the package and calls the procedure `Sort`, passing the external name of the file to be sorted. The sorted file is returned to the original file when the `Sort` is completed.

```
GENERIC
     TYPE Key_Type Is Private;
     TYPE File_Component_Type Is Private;
     number_of_files : Positive;
     WITH FUNCTION Key_Of ( file_component : File_Component_Type )
                              Return Key_Type;
     WITH FUNCTION ">" ( left_operand, right_operand : Key_Type )
                          Return Boolean;
PACKAGE Sort_A_File Is
     PROCEDURE Sort ( original_file_name : String );
END Sort_A_File;
```

The generic parameters of the package require the user to specify the type of the key on which the sort is performed. The type of the key is one of the user's own choosing. The user also specifies the type of the file component for the file to be sorted. The next generic parameter is the number of temporary files to be output by the sort phase and subsequently input to the merge phase. The package specification does not restrict the records in the original unsorted file that have the key as the first component of the record. The package specification does require that the user write, and pass as a generic parameter, the function `Key_Of`.

```
FUNCTION Key_Of ( data : File_Component_Type ) Return Key_Type Is
Begin
    Return data.key_field;
End Key_Of;
```

The user must identify the key_field by the specific field name in the user's definition of `File_Component_Type`. The last generic parameter is the ">" function. This function is predefined for any scalar type and arrays with discrete components. If the user has a key for which the ">" is not defined, the user must write the function and include it in the program that instantiates the sorting package.

```
WITH Sequential_IO;
PACKAGE Body Sort_A_File Is

     PACKAGE Sort_IO Is New Sequential_IO ( File_Component_Type );
--   maximum_number_of_files : Positive := 2 * number_of_files;
--   maximum_number_of_files : Positive := number_of_files + 1;
--                implementation dependent
     file : Array ( 1..maximum_number_of_files ) Of Sort_IO.File_Type;
     PROCEDURE Sort ( original_file_name : String ) Is
          PROCEDURE Sort_Phase Is
          Begin
                -- implementation dependent
          End Sort_Phase;
          PROCEDURE Merge_Phase Is
          Begin
                -- implementation dependent
          End Merge_Phase;
     Begin  -- Sort
          Sort_Phase;
          Merge_Phase;
     End Sort;
End Sort_A_File;
```

The skeleton package body presents two expressions for the initial value of the object `maximum_number_of_files`. The initial value used is dependent on the implementation in the **Merge_Phase**. The expression

2 * number_of_files

is required for the balanced *k*-way merge. The expression

number_of_files + 1

is required for the two-way and the polyphase merges. This information is hidden from the user because it is strictly dependent on the kind of merge that is implemented.

An example user's program showing the instantiation of the package `Sort_A_File` is presented:

```
WITH Sort_A_File;
PROCEDURE Sort_Program Is
    SUBTYPE Name_Type Is String ( 1 .. 10 );
    TYPE Info_Type Is Record
                          i : Integer;
                          f : Float;
                          s : Name_Type;
                          c : Character;
                      End Record;
    FUNCTION Key ( data : In Info_Type ) Return Float Is
    Begin
        Return data.f;
    End Key;
    PACKAGE Sort_It Is New Sort_A_File
                          ( Float, Info_Type, 2, Key, ">" );
BEGIN
    Sort_It.Sort ( "example.fil" );
END Sort_Program;
```

The type name `Info_Type` is the `File_Component_Type`. The sort key is defined by the function `Key` to be the second field (named `f`) in the record. The instantiation of the package `Sort_It` lists five generic parameters. The first, `Float`, is the type of the sort key. The second, `Info_Type`, is the `File_Component_Type`. The maximum number of temporary files, `2`, to be used in the sort is listed third. `Key`, the name of the function that defines the field in the record on which the file is sorted, is the fourth generic parameter. Lastly is the function `">"` (no definition of ">" by the user is necessary since `">"` is predefined for the type `Float`).

PHYSICAL ASPECTS OF SORTING

The number of passes through the data is not the only means of measuring the time necessary to perform an external sort/merge. The physical characteristics of the external storage device used for storing the files during the merge phase also have a large impact on the total time required to sort a file.

If the files used for the sort/merge are stored on magnetic tape reels, which can be accessed only sequentially, each file needs to be on a separate reel. A balanced three-way sort/merge requires six tape reels and—for maximum efficiency—six tape drives. If there are fewer than six tape drives, the six tape reels have to be switched a number of times.

Another factor in the total sorting time is the time needed to rewind the tape when the end of a file is reached. In all the sort/merges discussed, when all the runs from a file have been input, the tape must be rewound to the beginning of the file to serve as an output file for the next cycle of the merge phase. (Some tape drives have a high-speed rewind that reduces the rewind time.)

Data may be in multireel files (files that require more storage space than a single tape can provide). In this case the sort proceeds one reel at a time. Then all sorted reels merge onto reel 1 until it is full, then they merge onto reel 2, and so on, until all the sorted reels have been merged.

The fact that magnetic disks can be accessed randomly makes it possible to store all the files used in a sort/merge on one disk. (The deciding factor is the size of the files.) To perform the balanced three-way sort/merge, six files stored on one disk require only one disk drive. The reduction in the number of physical devices (one disk rather than six tape drives) is not without additional cost, however. The disk input/output operations necessary to access an individual run for a particular file are characterized by more overhead (seek time + latency time) than that required for tape input/output operations (start time + stop time). As a counter to this additional cost in time, the data transfer rate is much faster for disk than for tape.

The access overhead of seek and latency can be reduced by distributing the files to more than one disk so the input/output operations of different disks overlap. (Each disk must have a separate disk controller.) Several disks serviced by one controller device yield the same results as storing all files on one disk—that is, the controller can access only one device at a time. With a separate controller for each disk drive, input/output requests are directed to a file on each disk in parallel and the buffers fill in parallel. As with the tape reels, one file per disk is the arrangement that yields optimal sort time, but this arrangement is possible only as long as the resources are available. The discussion here assumes that only one user is applying the sort/merge at a time. In a multiuser environment each user is competing with other users for disk access.

SUMMARY

External sort/merge algorithms are necessary for sorting large data files that exceed the main memory of the computer. The external sort/merge algorithm consists of two phases: a sort phase and a merge phase. The sort phase inputs a portion of the file to be sorted into main memory, it sorts these records with an internal sort algorithm, and it distributes the sorted runs on one or more output files. The output files from the sort phase are input to the merge phase, in which runs from the input files are merged into larger runs and stored in one or more output files.

The two-way sort/merge algorithm merges two input files into one output file, then redistributes the runs from the output file back to the two input files. The merge continues until all records are in one file. The balanced two-way sort/merge algorithm merges two input files by alternately storing merged runs into one of two output files. The advantage of the balanced two-way sort/merge over the two-way sort/merge is that the redistribution of runs from the output file back to the two input files is eliminated. When one merge cycle is completed, the two output files become input files, and records are merged and stored in the two empty files.

The balanced *k*-way sort/merge algorithm allocates 2*k* files for the merge phase to reduce the number of cycles of the merge phase. The *k* input files are merged with the merged runs stored in *k* output files. At the end of one cycle, the output files become the input files for the next cycle, and the input files become the output files for the next cycle. The polyphase sort/merge algorithm requires that the sort phase distribute runs on *k* files using a perfect Fibonacci distribution so the number of runs on the *k* files is unbalanced (unlike the balanced *k*-way sort/merge). The polyphase sort/merge algorithm then merges *k* input files and stores merged runs on only one output file until one of the input files becomes empty. The empty input file becomes the output file for the next merge cycle. The merge algorithm continues merging the unprocessed runs on the *k* nonempty files and stores merged runs in the empty file.

For further information, the reader can consult the following sources:

Knuth, Donald E. *The Art of Computer Programming. Vol 3, Sorting and Searching.* Reading, MA: Addison-Wesley, 1973.

Tremblay, Jean-Paul, and Sorenson, Paul G. *An Introduction to Data Structures with Applications.* New York: McGraw-Hill, 1984.

Key Terms

balanced *k*-way sort/merge
balanced two-way sort/merge
dummy runs
merge phase
*L*th-level distribution
perfect Fibonacci distribution
polyphase sort/merge
*k*th order Fibonacci series
run
sort phase
two-way sort/merge

Exercises

1. Show the distribution of 33 runs to five files using Algorithm 6.6. Remember to add dummy runs to provide a "perfect" distribution.
2. Create a table similar to Tables 6.3 and 6.4 that shows the number of runs on each file after the sort and after each merge phase of the distribution in exercise 1 and the polyphase sort/merge ($k = 5$).
3. Create a table similar to Tables 6.3 and 6.4 that shows the number of runs on each file after the sort and after each merge phase for sorting 31 runs using the:

a. two-way sort/merge with two input files

b. balanced two-way sort/merge with two input files

c. balanced k-way sort/merge ($k = 3$)

d. polyphase sort/merge ($k = 3$)

4. Compute the number of passes through the data for each of the four sort/merge algorithms in exercise 3.
5. Given that each time a disk access is made the seek time is 50 ms, the latency time is 20 ms, and the transfer time is 1 ms/record, compute the total time to input and output the records being sorted in exercise 3.
6. Compute the Fibonacci distribution of 25 runs onto four files.
7. Repeat exercise 3 but show the number of runs per file for sorting 25 runs. Use $k = 4$ for part c and $k = 4$ for part d.
8. Compute the number of passes through the data for each of the four sort/merge algorithms in exercise 7.
9. Why are external sort/merge algorithms analyzed in terms of the number of passes through the data rather than the number of comparisons made?
10. Contrast the two-way sort/merge and the balanced two-way sort/merge.
11. Contrast the balanced k-way sort/merge and the polyphase sort/merge.
12. Consider the following record keys:

    6 29 1 10 23 48 17 13 16 12 11 7 2 3

    Show the file contents after the sort phase and after each merge phase of each of the following algorithms. Assume that the initial runs contain only one record.

    a. two-way sort/merge

    b. balanced two-way sort/merge

    c. balanced k-way sort/merge ($k = 3$)

    d. polyphase sort/merge ($k = 3$)

Programming Problems

1. Write an Ada program to perform the sort phase used by the two-way and balanced k-way sort/merge algorithms in the chapter. Use a run size and internal sort of your choice.

2. Write an Ada program to implement the two-way sort/merge in Algorithm 6.1. Use the program in problem 1 as the sort phase.
3. Write an Ada program to implement the balanced two-way sort/merge in Algorithm 6.2. Use the program in problem 1 as the sort phase.
4. Write an Ada program to implement the balanced *k*-way sort/merge in Algorithm 6.3. Use the program in problem 1 as the sort phase.
5. Vary the value of *k* in the program in problem 4 and measure the time it takes to sort a file of data.
6. Write an Ada program to implement the modified Fibonacci distribution sort in Algorithm 6.6.
7. Write an Ada program to implement the polyphase sort/merge in Algorithm 6.4. Use the Fibonacci distribution sort routine of problem 6 as the sort phase.
8. Vary the value of *k* in the program in problem 7 and measure the time it takes to sort a file of data.
9. Use a variety of values for *k* in the programs in problems 4 and 7. Measure and compare the time it takes to sort the same file of data with the two sort/merges.

Chapter 7

Relative File Organization

CHAPTER CONTENTS

PREVIEW

THIS CHAPTER BEGINS WITH A DISCUSSION of the basic structures of random-access files. Random-access file organization is an indexing technique that allows a user to locate a record in a file with as few accesses as possible (ideally, only one). As a result, random-access files provide faster access than sequential files. A random-access file has two components: an indexing scheme used to locate a record in the data file and a physical organization of the data records. (The organized records are called the data file.) The indexing scheme allows the user to determine the location in the data file of the record to be accessed, then the user interrogates the location. Chapter 5 already explored one physical organization: sequential organization. Another physical organization presented in this chapter is relative file organization. The remaining chapters explore several indexing techniques: direct addressing (absolute addressing and relative addressing), hashing, binary search trees, B-trees, and multiple-key indexing. These indexing techniques usually employ relative file organization. Relative file organization is the physical organization on which all indexing techniques discussed in Chapters 7, 8, 9, and 10 are based. Direct addressing and a variety of randomizing (hashing) schemes for obtaining random access to data files (including prime-number division, digit extraction, folding, radix conversion, and perfect hashing) are presented in Chapter 7. Binary search trees and B-trees are discussed in Chapter 8. Three common, commercially available indexing implementations that use trees are investigated in Chapter 9. Chapter 10 presents two indexing techniques for providing access to the data file by multiple keys.

All the nonperfect hashing schemes presented cause collisions. The chapter contains several examples that illustrate methods for handling hashing collisions (linear probing, separate overflow area, double hashing, synonym chaining, bucket addressing, and dynamic hashing). Algorithms for creating and maintaining random-access files in Ada are included. The car-rental agency data used in Chapter 5 are stored in a random-access file, and quantitative measures of access times are computed for comparison of the random and sequential access.

DIRECT ADDRESSING

Sequential file organization limits the user to serial access of the records in the file. Maintenance of sequential files most often consists of batching transactions to be applied periodically to the master file. During the maintenance run, all the records in the master file must be read—whether a change is in order or not—and copied to a new master file.

With **direct file organization** there exists a predictable relationship between the key used to identify an individual record and that record's **absolute address** on an external file. Direct file organization allows access to a record directly by the key of the record; the position of the record in the overall key sequence is not a consideration. The logical ordering of the records need not have any relationship to their physical sequence on the file, so the file is sometimes characterized as having random access. The absolute address of the record is a machine-dependent address consisting of cylinder-number, surface-number, and record-number if cylinder addressing is used (Figure 7.1). Using sector addressing, the absolute address consists of sector-number and record-number (Figure 7.2). Absolute addressing is device-dependent and requires that the user know exactly how the data are stored physically. Relocation of a direct file to another part of the disk requires changing the absolute addresses.

Relative file organization is a common implementation of direct file organization using relative addressing (Figure 7.3). Once a key-location relationship is established, the position of the record in the file is specified as a record number relative to the beginning of the file, where the first record is record number 1. A relative file with space for N records contains locations with relative record numbers 1, 2, . . . , N where the ith record has the relative record number i. Relative file organization is a machine-independent implementation of direct file organization that is supported in several high-level programming languages: Ada, COBOL, FORTRAN, PL/1, and many versions of Pascal. Maintenance of a relative file involves processing one transaction at a time rather than batching transactions to be applied to the master file. The record in the relative file to be modified is accessed randomly, the change is made to the record, and the modified record is written back to the relative file in the same position in the file from which it was read. Only those records in the relative file that have matching transaction records need be input and modified—a definite advantage over sequential organization.

The key-position relationship must be a predictable relationship so that random access to the record is possible once it is stored in the relative file. The relationship is a mapping function from the key values to the addresses in the external file, and it is designated when the relative file is established. One of the simplest mapping functions is one in which the key value for the record is the same as the record's relative address or position in the external file. For a file of N records, the key values supplied by the user are in the range of 1 to N. The primary advantage to this approach is that there is no processing time needed to determine the record's relative address in

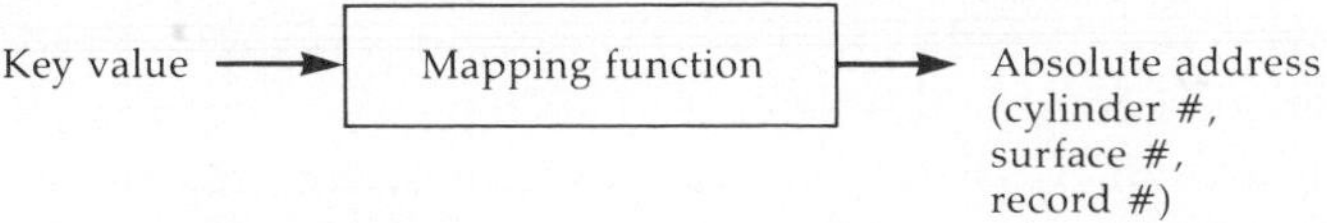

Figure 7.1
Key-position relationship with direct organization on cylinder-addressable devices

the file when the record is to be accessed. For example, for a relative file that contains 5,000 part numbers in the range of 1 to 5000 (called **dense keys** because the values of consecutive keys differ by only one), a relative file of 5,000 record locations (1 through 5000) is established, and part number 2534 is stored in the position in the file with a relative record number 2534. Accessing the record later is as easy as specifying the part number.

For a range of key values that do not start with 1, such as 5,000 numbers of parts in inventory in the range of 10001 to 15000 (dense keys), the address is the part number less the constant 10,000. A part number in the range of 10001 to 15000 is stored in relative record positions 1 through 5000.

For data with a large range of key values that are not dense, such as employee data with social security numbers as the key values, the programmer may have to allocate a large relative file to use the key as the relative record number. As a result, a high percentage of the file space may be wasted, or empty. For example, the use of social security numbers as the key and the relative record number requires the allocation of a file with 999,999,999 records. If the lowest social security number is 100-00-0000, the data are stored in record 100000000; the positions with relative record numbers 1 to 099999999 are never used—they are wasted. If the file contains data for 10,000 employees with keys (social security numbers) in the nondense range of 1 to 999999999, only 10,000 locations, or 0.001 percent of the file, are used; 99.999 percent of the file is empty. The employee data are easy to access since the key is the relative record number, but a great deal of space is wasted.

Figure 7.2
Key-position relationship with direct organization on sector-addressable devices

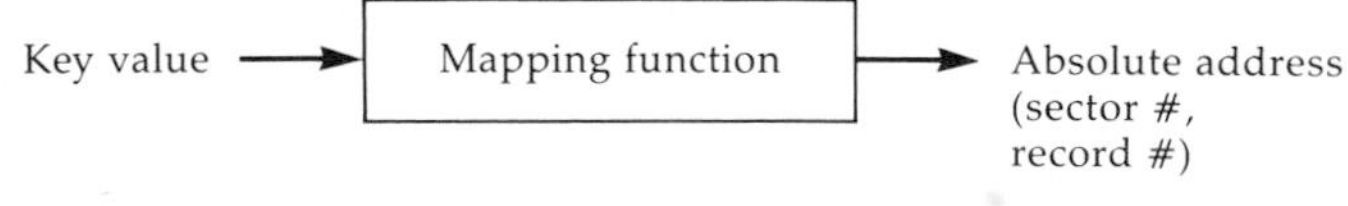

Figure 7.3
Key-position relationship with relative organization

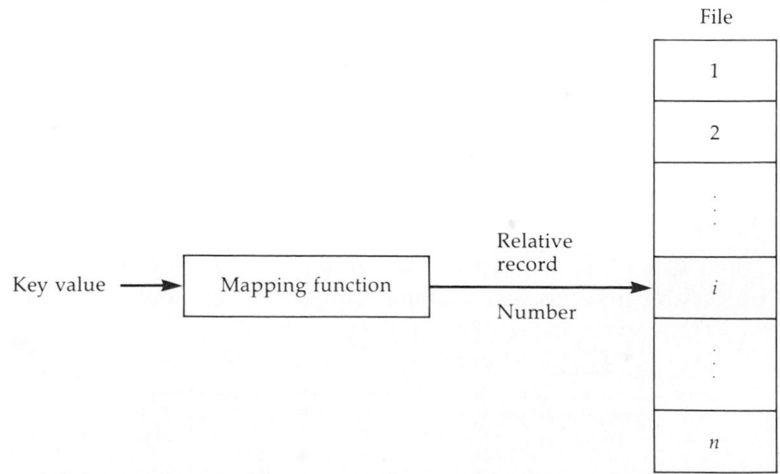

A common solution to the wasted space of random addressing is to map the large range of nondense key values into a smaller range of record positions in the file. With the use of a mapping scheme, the key is no longer the address of the record position in the file where the record with this key is found. Table 7.1 illustrates the need for an indexing technique for determining the address of a record if the key is given. A number of mapping schemes have been applied to a set of five-digit keys. Notice that the keys are listed in key order in the table, but the corresponding record locations where each key is stored is definitely not in order. Therefore, several indexing techniques have been used to recall the key and the corresponding record position address for each record in the file. These indexing techniques include hashing, binary search trees, B-trees, index tables, inverted files, and multilist files.

Table 7.1 5 hashing functions applied to file positions 0 through 99

	Hashing functions				
Key values	**1**	**2**	**3**	**4**	**5**
24964	35	49	13	56	16
25936	37	69	95	50	49
32179	72	91	0	25	89
38652	46	26	38	58	25
40851	14	18	59	57	25
53455	8	54	89	5	25
53758	20	87	95	0	25
54603	89	36	49	59	0
63388	47	83	21	36	44
81347	61	73	60	3	56
Number of synonyms	0	0	1	0	3

Hashing function legend:

1 = Prime-number division remainder (divisor = 97)
2 = digit extraction (fifth and third positions)
3 = Folding (123 + 45)
4 = Radix conversion (base = 12)
5 = Mid-square (234 squared)

Hashing, which provides sequential access according to the physical order of records, or random access, is discussed in this chapter. B-trees, which provide sequential access of records by key order as well as random access, are discussed in Chapter 8; index tables, which provide sequential access by key order, or random access, are presented in Chapter 9; and inverted files and multilist files, which provide access by more than one key per record, are investigated in Chapter 10.

HASHING

A common approach to establishing a key-position relationship that does not waste space is to perform a calculation on the key value that results in a relative record number. **Hashing** is the application of a function to the key value that results in mapping the range of possible key values into a smaller range of relative addresses. For the data that use the social security numbers of 10,000 employees as keys, the hash function needs to map the range of key values (1 to 999999999) into 10,000 relative positions (1 to 10000). The hash function must map a large range of values, where not all values in the range are used (the values are not dense), into a smaller range of relative addresses. The hashing function may also be referred to as a **randomizing scheme** since the function randomly selects a relative address for a specific key value without regard to the physical sequence of records in the file. Random access to the records in the file—not sequencing records in the file—is the intent.

Many times a key value contains characters that make it difficult to manipulate the key to compute an address. A nonnumeric key value must be converted to a numeric value before applying a hashing function that involves using any numeric operation to the key. This conversion can be done easily using the ordinal position of a character (`Character'Pos` in Ada). The primary problem with most hashing functions is that the function does not always produce unique relative addresses. When the hashing function for two different keys results in the same relative address, a **collision** occurs; only one record may be stored in a single relative address. The two different keys that hash to the same relative address are termed **synonyms**.

Most hashing functions can be improved by allocating more file space than the minimum needed to store the number of keys. The relationship between the file space and the number of keys is described by three terms that mean the same thing: **load factor**, packing factor, and packing density. The load factor is the ratio of the number of key values to be stored versus the number of file positions:

$$\text{load factor} = \frac{\text{number of key values}}{\text{number of file positions}}$$

Twenty percent of a file with a load factor of 80 percent is empty. Such an arrangement reduces the number of collisions over a file with a load factor of 100 percent since the range of key values is mapped into a larger file space. The number of file positions needed for a load factor of 80 percent is

$$0.80 \times \text{number of file positions} = \text{number of key values}$$

or

$$\text{number of file positions} = \frac{\text{number of key values}}{0.80}$$

or number of file positions = 1.25 × number of key values.

The smaller the load factor, the less dense the file is, and the less chance of collisions. The disadvantage of a low load factor (less than 50 percent) is the great amount of file space that is wasted by being empty. A balance must be achieved between the number of collisions and the amount of file space wasted. Descriptions of a number of the more common hashing functions follow.

Prime-Number Division Remainder

A number of randomizing schemes are available for transforming the key value into a relative record number. The most common randomizing scheme is called the **prime-number division remainder method**. If the key value is divided by a number (*N*), the remainder of the division is a number in the range of 0 to $N - 1$. This method can be used to map the keys into *N* record positions by choosing the divisor to be the number of relative positions in the file (*N*). The remainder is the relative address of the record with the key. Since a large range of key values is being mapped into a smaller range of record positions, collisions may occur between keys that yield the same remainder. The divisor should also be chosen to reduce the number of collisions. Buchholz (1963) showed that an even divisor is a poor choice and that a prime divisor is better than an even divisor. Lum (1971 to 1973) found that any divisor performs sufficiently as long as the divisor does not contain prime factors less than 20. Researchers generally find that choosing a prime number that is close to the number of record positions in the file results in relative addresses that are less prone to collision. The prime-number division remainder method preserves the uniformity of the key set. Keys that are close are mapped to close but unique positions. Collisions occur when keys divided by the number of file positions yield the same remainder, but choosing a prime number close to the number of file positions reduces collisions.

Another factor that affects the probability of collisions is the load factor of the file. As the load factor increases, the probability of collisions rises drastically. A load factor of 70 percent to 80 percent is generally considered the maximum for reasonable performance. If space is available for a smaller load factor, the probability of collisions is reduced. The prime-number division remainder hashing scheme is generally preferred if the distribution of key values is unknown.

Digit Extraction

Another randomizing scheme is **digit extraction**. The distribution of this hashing function is dependent on the distribution of the key values. The key values are analyzed to determine which digit positions of the key are more evenly distributed. The more evenly distributed digit positions are assigned from right to left. The digit values in the chosen digit positions are extracted, and the resulting integer is used as the relative address. If none of the digit positions has a uniform distribution, more collisions occur.

Suppose, for example, that analysis of nine-digit key values reveals that the four more evenly distributed digits are the ninth, seventh, fifth, and second digit positions. For a key value of 546032178, the relative address is 8134. The digit extraction scheme maps key values into a range of 0 to 9999. This capability makes it a viable approach for storing the employee data using social security numbers as keys. The scheme requires that the key values be known in order to determine the digit positions for extraction.

The skeleton of a program that uses a hashing function and a key that is a string of nine characters follows. The hashing function is an implementation of the digit extraction described above. A different hashing function requires that only the function body change.

```
WITH Direct_IO;
PROCEDURE Hashing Is
    SUBTYPE Key_Type Is String (1..9);
    TYPE Record_Type Is Record
                            key : Key_Type;
                            -- other fields
                        End Record;
    PACKAGE Dir_IO Is New Direct_IO ( Record_Type );
    address : Dir_IO.Positive_Count;
    a_record : Record_Type;
    char_zero : Constant Integer := Character'Pos ('0');
    FUNCTION Hash ( key : In Key_Type )
             Return Dir_IO.Positive_Count Is
    BEGIN  --  Hash function for digit extraction
        Return Dir_IO.Positive_Count (
               ( Character'Pos ( key (9) ) - char_zero ) * 1000 +
               ( Character'Pos ( key (7) ) - char_zero ) * 100  +
               ( Character'Pos ( key (5) ) - char_zero ) * 10   +
               ( Character'Pos ( key (2) ) - char_zero ) + 1 );
    END Hash;
BEGIN -- Hashing
    address := Hash ( a_record.key );
END Hashing;
```

Folding

Another randomizing scheme involves **folding**. To form the relative address, the key value is split into two or more parts and then summed, or subjected to `And` or `Xor`, as if each part were an integer. If the resulting address contains more digits than the highest address in the file, the excess high-order digits are truncated. Suppose an eight-digit key is mapped into a relative file with addresses in the range of 0 to 9999. For the key value 25936715, folding in half (splitting the key into two parts and summing) yields 2593 + 6715, or 9308, as the relative address. Folding in thirds (splitting the key into three parts and summing) yields 259 + 36 + 715, or 1010, as the relative address. Folding alternate digits (digits in the odd positions form one part, and digits in the even positions form the other part) yields 2961 + 5375, or 8336, as the relative address.

Folding is useful for converting keys with a large number of digits (larger than can be stored in a word of memory) to a smaller number of digits so the address fits into a word of memory (for faster access). Folding (shown below) is easier to compute than some of the other hashing schemes, but it can produce erratic results.

```
FUNCTION Hash ( key : In Key_Type )
         Return Dir_IO.Positive_Count Is
BEGIN  --  Hash function for folding with the first four
       --  digits added to the last four digits
    Return Dir_IO.Positive_Count (
        (  ( Character'Pos ( key (1) ) - char_zero ) * 1000 +
           ( Character'Pos ( key (2) ) - char_zero ) * 100  +
           ( Character'Pos ( key (3) ) - char_zero ) * 10   +
           ( Character'Pos ( key (4) ) - char_zero ) + 1
           +  -- add the first four digits to the last four
           ( Character'Pos ( key (6) ) - char_zero ) * 1000 +
           ( Character'Pos ( key (7) ) - char_zero ) * 100  +
           ( Character'Pos ( key (8) ) - char_zero ) * 10   +
           ( Character'Pos ( key (9) ) - char_zero ) + 1 )
           Rem 10_000 ); -- The Rem operation truncates the
                         -- value to four digits.
END Hash;
```

Radix Conversion

Radix conversion is another randomizing scheme. The key value is interpreted as having a different base or radix and is converted to a decimal number. (Excess high-order digits are truncated.) Consider a five-digit key and a relative file with an address range of 0 to 9999. The decimal key value 38652 is considered a value in base 11; it is converted to a decimal, and the conversion yields the following relative address:

$$3 \times 11^4 + 8 \times 11^3 + 6 \times 11^2 + 5 \times 11^1 + 2 \times 11^0 = 55354$$

Since the result of the conversion from base 11 to a decimal is a five-digit integer, truncate the high-order 5 to yield 5354, which is a four-digit integer in the range of addresses in the relative file.

```
FUNCTION Hash ( key : In Key_Type )
         Return Dir_IO.Positive_Count Is
    RADIX : Constant Integer := 11;
BEGIN  --  Hash function for radix conversion
    Return Dir_IO.Positive_Count (
        ( ( Character'Pos ( key (5) ) - char_zero ) * RADIX ** 4 +
            ( Character'Pos ( key (6) ) - char_zero ) * RADIX ** 3 +
            ( Character'Pos ( key (7) ) - char_zero ) * RADIX ** 2 +
            ( Character'Pos ( key (8) ) - char_zero ) * RADIX      +
            ( Character'Pos ( key (9) ) - char_zero ) ) Rem 10_000 );
END Hash;
```

Mid-Square

Another randomizing scheme is the **mid-square**. The middle *n* digits are extracted from the key value and squared to form a relative address. The value of *n* (the number of middle digits extracted) depends on the required size of the resulting address. Excess high-order digits of the squared result are truncated. Consider a relative file with an address range of 0 to 9999 and a nine-digit key. Suppose the middle three digits are extracted from the key and squared. For the key value 29615834, the middle three digits are 158, and the square of 158 is 24964. Truncating the high-order 2 yields a relative address of 4964. The mid-square hashing function works well if the keys do not have several leading or trailing zeros and if low load factors are used.

```
FUNCTION Hash ( key : In Key_Type )
         Return Dir_IO.Positive_Count Is
BEGIN   --  Hash function for mid-square
        --  extracting the middle three digits
    Return Dir_IO.Positive_Count (
        ( ( Character'Pos ( key (4) ) - char_zero ) * 100 +
          ( Character'Pos ( key (5) ) - char_zero ) * 10  +
          ( Character'Pos ( key (6) ) - char_zero ) ) ** 2
          Rem 10_000 );
END Hash;
```

This section has presented just a few of the many possible hashing schemes. For thorough performance analysis of many hashing functions with various load factors, see the list of references at the end of the summary of this chapter.

EXAMPLE 7.1

Table 7.1 includes a list of key values that have been used with the five hashing functions that have been discussed. The table reports the number of synonyms generated for these 10 key values by each hashing function. The prime-number division remainder uses a prime divisor of 97. Analysis of the digit extraction reveals that positions 3 and 5 are the more evenly distributed. The folding scheme sums the first three digits as one integer and the last two digits as another integer and truncates the sum to two digits. The base for radix conversion is base 12. The mid-square uses digit positions 2, 3, and 4 as the integer that is squared, then truncates to two digits.

The prime-number division remainder scheme, digit extraction, and radix conversion yield the fewest synonyms (none) for this small set of 10 keys. Folding yields one synonym. (The distribution and combination of digits in the third and fifth positions produced the last digit of the address.)

The mid-square yields three synonyms that are a result of several keys having the same digit in position 4, the rightmost digit of the integer squared. (The digit 5 occurs in position 4 a total of four times.)

Table 7.2 illustrates the occupied file locations (in ascending order) for each of the five hashing functions listed in Table 7.1. The prime-number division remainder scheme yields the most uniform distribution, with digit extraction close behind. The folding hashing function produces a synonym at position 95, and it tends to have three of the 10 records clustered around locations 89 through 95.

Table 7.2 Occupied file positions for Table 7.1

Hashing functions				
1	**2**	**3**	**4**	**5**
8	18	0	0	0
14	26	13	3	16
20	36	21	5	25
35	49	38	25	25
37	54	49	36	25
46	69	59	50	25
47	73	60	56	44
61	83	89	57	49
72	87	95	58	56
89	91	95	59	89

Hashing function legend

1 = Prime-number division remainder (divisor = 97)
2 = Digit extraction (fifth and third positions)
3 = Folding (123 + 45)
4 = Radix conversion (base = 12)
5 = Mid-square (234 squared)

The radix conversion scheme clusters one-half of the records in positions 50 through 59, which leaves empty locations for synonyms in positions 60 through 99. The key values are not uniformly distributed throughout the file, so the empty locations are not uniformly distributed.

The mid-square produces four synonyms for location 25, with 90 percent of the keys in locations 0 through 56. Again, like the radix conversion, most of the empty locations tend to be in the back half of the file.

Conduct an analysis such as this on a sample of key values (if available) to determine the best hashing function for this particular application. If a sample of key values is not available, the prime-number division remainder method is usually the best scheme for uniform distribution using a load factor less than 100 percent.

Perfect Hashing

A hashing function that provides a one-to-one mapping from a key into a position is termed a **perfect hashing** function since no collision occurs. A perfect hashing function requires the knowledge of the set of key values in order to generate a perfectly uniform distribution of addresses. Perfect hashing functions could be applied to a table lookup for reserved words in compilers, filtering high-frequency words in natural-language processing, or a table lookup for month abbreviations used in dates. Several perfect hashing functions are reviewed here. For algorithms and analysis of each of the perfect hashing schemes discussed, see the sources listed at the end of the summary for this chapter.

Quotient Reduction The perfect hashing function known as **quotient reduction** was introduced by Sprugnoli (1977) and is defined by the following formula:

$$\text{hash}(w) = (w + s)/N$$

The variable w is the key value being hashed, and s and N are constants in the set of generated addresses. This method assumes the set of keys are in ascending order, so that:

$$\text{hash (first key)} = 0$$

The constants s and N are used to adjust the other key values to different intervals based on the differences between key values in the ascending set. For example, for the set of key values {1, 3, 8, 14, 17, 23}, the quotient-reduction algorithm produces the hashing function:

$$\text{hash}(w) = (w + 3)/5$$

The respective hashed addresses that are generated are {0, 1, 2, 3, 4, 5}. The hashing function is unique to the static set of keys, and it hashes the key values to a minimal range of addresses. The quotient-reduction method works well when the set of key values is uniformly distributed.

Remainder Reduction Sprugnoli also introduced the perfect hashing function known as **remainder reduction.** Remainder reduction is similar to the quotient reduction method except that the set of key values does not have to be uniformly distributed; they are scrambled using modular arithmetic before the quotient-reduction algorithm is applied. The formula for the remainder reduction method is

$$\text{hash}(w) = ((d + wq) \text{ Mod } M)/N$$

As with the quotient-reduction method, the constants d, q, N, and M must be chosen via an extensive algorithm for this particular key set.

Associated Value Hashing Cichelli presented a hash function known as **associated value hashing** that works well for characters. The formula for the hash function has the form:

hash(key) = key length +
associated value of the key's first character +
associated value of the key's last character

Cichelli's hashing function involves extensive searching of the words in the set of keys in order to assign an associated value to each letter that is either the first character or the last character of a key. The associated value is based on the frequency of use of each letter in either the first or last character position of the word. Once the associated values for all possible letters have been computed, the hashed address for each key in the set is simple to compute.

Cichelli's hashing function, since it assumes the key values are characters, is an application to reserved word lookup in compilers, for month abbreviations, or for frequently occurring English words in natural-language processing.

Reciprocal Hashing Introduced by Jaeschke (1981), **reciprocal hashing** involves finding constants c, d, and e. The hashing function is

$$\text{hash}\ (w) = \text{c}/(\text{d}w + \text{e})\ \text{Mod}\ n$$

The variable n is the number of keys in the set. The constants c, d, and e must be determined with special algorithms, as with the quotient reduction and remainder reduction. The constant c is determined so that (c/w) Mod n is different for each key (w) in the set of keys. The constants d and e are determined so that $\text{d} \times (w) + \text{e}$ are pairwise relatively prime for all keys (w) in the set of key values. The constants d and e are used to transform the set of key values into a set of keys that are relatively prime to each other. Then the relatively prime keys are mapped into unique addresses.

Ordered Minimal Perfect Hashing An **ordered minimal perfect hashing** scheme devised by Chang (1984) is a modification of reciprocal hashing:

$$\text{hash}\ (w) = \text{c Mod p}(w)$$

The constant c is the same constant computed in reciprocal hashing, and $\text{p}(w)$ is a prime-number function. The keys in the static key set can be stored in ascending order by ordering the keys and then applying Chang's hashing method to each key.

Most perfect hashing functions require extensive manipulations of the key sets and apply to static key sets only. In most file processsing environments where data files are not static but updated to keep current, perfect hashing functions are not applicable.

TECHNIQUES FOR HANDLING COLLISIONS

Even with a load factor less than 100 percent, collisions occur. Several techniques are available for handling collisions and synonyms. Two classes of collision-handling techniques exist: open addressing and chaining. Both classes are described with several variations of each class of techniques. For all techniques examined, n locations are allocated in the file (numbered $1, \ldots, n$) where each position contains a flag, which is initialized to **empty**. The flag indicates that nothing has yet been stored in that position. Once data have been stored in a particular position in the file, the flag is changed to **occupied**.

Linear Probing

One of the simplest techniques for resolving collisions is **linear probing**, in which the file is scanned sequentially as a circular file and the synonym is stored in the nearest available space to the hashed address. Locating a record involves hashing the key, accessing the hashed address (i) to determine whether the data in the hashed address are or are not the record being sought. If not, a sequential search through positions $i + 1, i + 2, \ldots, n, 1, 2, \ldots, i - 1$ of the file is in order.

The file is searched as a circular file to use as many empty positions as possible. In a search of a noncircular file, a key hashes to position i, which is occupied, and positions $i + 1, \ldots, n$ are searched for an empty location. The back portion of the file tends to fill up, leaving more empty locations at the front portion of the file. In a search of a circular file, the entire file could be searched, starting at position $i + 1$, and the synonyms are distributed throughout the file, not clustered at the back portion. Storing the synonym in the nearest available location is simple, but accessing the synonym later may require a sequential search of the entire file.

EXAMPLE 7.2

Suppose that a set of words are to be stored in a relative file using the hash function formed by the exclusive or (`Xor`) of the bit strings of the decimal position of each letter of the word as it appears in the alphabet. An *A* is in position 1 of the alphabet or the bit string *1*, *B* is in position 2 of the alphabet or the bit string *10*, and so on to *Z*, which is in position 26 of the alphabet or bit string *11010*. A string of 5 bits is needed to assign unique representations to all 26 letters of the alphabet. The `Xor` of the bit strings of each letter of the word results in a string of five bits representing 32 different binary values (0 through 31). So the file size is 32 positions. This hashing function, when applied to the word THE, results in the following address computation:

$$\text{hash (THE)} = 10100_2 \text{ Xor } 01000_2 \text{ Xor } 00101_2 = 11001_2 = 25_{10}$$

Linear probing is used to resolve collisions in the following example. The set of words and the hashed values for each word are presented in Table 7.3. The relative file after the first six additions is presented in Figure 7.4. THE, OF, AND, TO, A, and IN have been added to the file, and the next word added, THAT, causes a collision with position 9. Since THAT collides with OF, which is already in position 9, THAT is stored in the nearest available location, position 10. Then IS, WAS, and HE are added before a collision occurs again (as a result of attempting to add FOR in position 27). Figure 7.5 illustrates the relative file just before the second collision occurs.

Table 7.3 Set of words with hashed positions

WORD	hash (WORD)	WORD	hash (WORD)
THE	25	AT	21
OF	9	BY	27
AND	11	I	9
TO	27	THIS	6
A	1	HAD	13
IN	7	NOT	21
THAT	9	NO	1
IS	26	TON	21
WAS	5	SAYS	24
HE	13	ARE	22
FOR	27	BUT	3
IT	29	FROM	22
WITH	2	OR	29
AS	18	HAVE	26
HIS	18	AN	15
ON	1	THEY	0
BE	7		

FOR is stored in the next location, position 28. IT, WITH, and AS are added to the relative file (Figure 7.6), but HIS collides with AS in position 18. HIS is stored in the nearest available location, position 19 (Figure 7.7).

The next word to be added, ON, collides with A in position 1. Position 2 is occupied with the word WITH, so ON has a secondary collision with the word WITH in the attempt to store ON in the nearest available position. A sequential search of the file from position 2 to position 3 continues until an available position is found. Since position 3 is available, ON is stored in position 3, two locations away from the hashed address (position 1). Accessing ON later means searching from position 1 to position 3 to find the word.

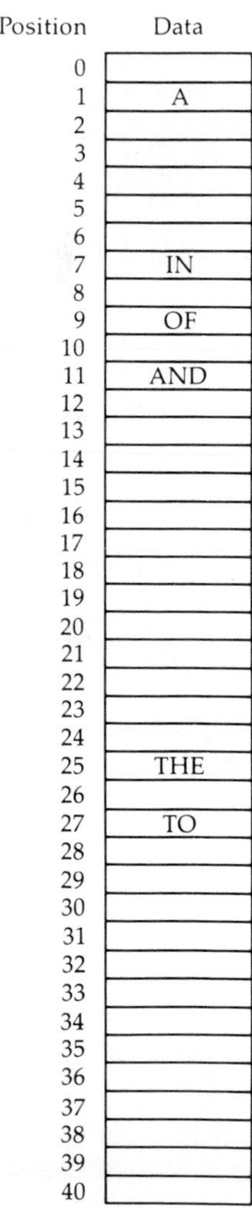

Position
Data
0
1 A
2
3
4
5
6
7 IN
8
9 OF
10
11 AND
12
13
14
15
16
17
18
19
20
21
22
23
24
25 THE
26
27 TO
28
29
30
31
32
33
34
35
36
37
38
39
40

Figure 7.4
Direct file with first six additions

Position	Data	
0		
1	A	
2		
3		
4		
5	WAS	
6		
7	IN	
8		
9	OF	
10	THAT	Synonym of 9
11	AND	
12		
13	HE	
14		
15		
16		
17		
18		
19		
20		
21		
22		
23		
24		
25	THE	
26	IS	
27	TO	
28		
29		
30		
31		
32		
33		
34		
35		
36		
37		
38		
39		
40		

Figure 7.5
Direct file just before the second collision occurs

Position	Data	
0		
1	A	
2	WITH	
3		
4		
5	WAS	
6		
7	IN	
8		
9	OF	
10	THAT	Synonym of 9
11	AND	
12		
13	HE	
14		
15		
16		
17		
18	AS	
19		
20		
21		
22		
23		
24		
25	THE	
26	IS	
27	TO	
28	FOR	Synonym of 27
29	IT	
30		
31		
32		
33		
34		
35		
36		
37		
38		
39		
40		

Figure 7.6
Direct file when third collision occurs

Position	Data	
0		
1	A	
2	WITH	
3		
4		
5	WAS	
6		
7	IN	
8		
9	OF	
10	THAT	Synonym of 9
11	AND	
12		
13	HE	
14		
15		
16		
17		
18	AS	
19	HIS	Synonym of 18
20		
21		
22		
23		
24		
25	THE	
26	IS	
27	TO	
28	FOR	Synonym of 27
29	IT	
30		
31		
32		
33		
34		
35		
36		
37		
38		
39		
40		

Figure 7.7
Direct file with HIS

BE collides with IN in position 7, so it must be stored in position 8. The word AT is stored in position 21 without any collisions (Figure 7.8). BY hashes to position 27 but collides with TO in position 27, FOR in position 28, and IT in position 29, so BY must be stored in location 30. I collides with OF in position 9, THAT in position 10, and AND in position 11, so the nearest available location is position 12. THIS is stored in position 6 with no collisions (Figure 7.9).

HAD collides with HE in position 13, so it is stored in position 14. NOT collides with AT in position 21, so it is stored in position 22. NO hashes to position 1 but is stored in the nearest available position, which is position 4. TON collides with AT in position 21 and NOT in position 22, so it must be stored in position 23. SAYS hashes and is stored in position 24 (Figure 7.10).

Position	Data	
0		
1	A	
2	WITH	
3	ON	Synonym of 1
4		
5	WAS	
6		
7	IN	
8	BE	Synonym of 7
9	OF	
10	THAT	Synonym of 9
11	AND	
12		
13	HE	
14		
15		
16		
17		
18	AS	
19	HIS	Synonym of 18
20		
21	AT	
22		
23		
24		
25	THE	
26	IS	
27	TO	
28	FOR	Synonym of 27
29	IT	
30		
31		
32		
33		
34		
35		
36		
37		
38		
39		
40		

Figure 7.8
Direct file with ON, BE, and AT

Position	Data	
0		
1	A	
2	WITH	
3	ON	Synonym of 1
4		
5	WAS	
6	THIS	
7	IN	
8	BE	Synonym of 7
9	OF	
10	THAT	Synonym of 9
11	AND	
12	I	Synonym of 9
13	HE	
14		
15		
16		
17		
18	AS	
19	HIS	Synonym of 18
20		
21	AT	
22		
23		
24		
25	THE	
26	IS	
27	TO	
28	FOR	Synonym of 27
29	IT	
30	BY	Synonym of 27
31		
32		
33		
34		
35		
36		
37		
38		
39		
40		

Figure 7.10
Direct file with HAD, NOT, NO, TON, and SAYS

Position	Data	
0		
1	A	
2	WITH	
3	ON	Synonym of 1
4	NO	Synonym of 1
5	WAS	
6	THIS	
7	IN	
8	BE	Synonym of 7
9	OF	
10	THAT	Synonym of 9
11	AND	
12	I	Synonym of 9
13	HE	
14	HAD	Synonym of 13
15		
16		
17		
18	AS	
19	HIS	Synonym of 18
20		
21	AT	
22	NOT	Synonym of 21
23	TON	Synonym of 21
24	SAYS	
25	THE	
26	IS	
27	TO	
28	FOR	Synonym of 27
29	IT	
30	BY	Synonym of 27
31		
32		
33		
34		
35		
36		
37		
38		
39		
40		

Figure 7.9
Direct file with BY, FOR, IT, I, and THIS

The next word to be added is ARE, which hashes to position 22. Position 22 holds NOT, however, which hashed to position 21 and collided with AT. The situation presented here is one of the major disadvantages with linear probing: **displacement**. ARE is displaced from position 22 by a word that hashed to another address, but because linear probing is used, position 22 was available. A linear search finally finds that position 31 is the nearest available location to position 22 for storing ARE.

BUT collides with ON in position 3 and collides with words in positions 4 through 14. BUT is finally stored in position 15. FROM collides with NOT in position 22 and collides with words in locations 23 through 31; FROM is stored in position 32. OR collides with IT in position 29. After a linear search OR is placed in position 33 (Figure 7.11).

HAVE hashes to position 26, which is occupied by IS. A linear search through locations 27, 28, 29, 30, 31, 32, . . . reveals that the nearest available position is 34, nine positions away from the hashed address. AN hashes to position 15 and is displaced by BUT, so AN is stored in position 16. THEY hashes to position 0. Figure 7.12 presents the relative file with all the words added.

One of the problems with linear probing is the number of positions that must be searched (or probed) before a synonym is located. The word HAVE hashed to position 26, but the first available location nearest the hashed address was position 34. The lookup process for accessing HAVE involves three steps:

1. The hash: hash (HAVE) = 26
2. Access the hashed location—26
3. HAVE is not in location 26, so the algorithm sequentially searches the file until HAVE is located or until an empty location is found or until the entire file is searched.

HAVE is located after searching locations 26 through 34—a total of nine probes. If a word is stored in its hashed position, the number of probes is one.

The second problem with linear probing is the number of probes necessary to discover that a word is not present. Searching for a word that is not present in the file involves:

1. hash (WORD) = 15
2. Access hashed location 15; the word is not found.
3. Serially search positions 16 and 17 until an empty location is found.

Knuth (1973) states that the formula for the average number of probes for an unsuccessful search is

$$\frac{1}{2}\left[1+\frac{1}{(1-a)^2}\right]$$

The variable a is the load factor. For a load factor of 80 percent, the average number of probes for an unsuccessful search is 13 probes. The formula for the average number of probes for a successful search is

$$\frac{1}{2}\left[1+\frac{1}{(1-a)}\right]$$

For a load factor of 80 percent, the average number of probes for a successful search is three probes. Table 7.4 lists the average number of probes for successful and unsuccessful searches through a file using linear probing for a variety of load factors.

Position	Data	
0		
1	A	
2	WITH	
3	ON	Synonym of 1
4	NO	Synonym of 1
5	WAS	
6	THIS	
7	IN	
8	BE	Synonym of 7
9	OF	
10	THAT	Synonym of 9
11	AND	
12	I	Synonym of 9
13	HE	
14	HAD	Synonym of 13
15	BUT	Hashes to 3
16		
17		
18	AS	
19	HIS	Synonym of 18
20		
21	AT	
22	NOT	Synonym of 21
23	TON	Synonym of 21
24	SAYS	
25	THE	
26	IS	
27	TO	
28	FOR	Synonym of 27
29	IT	
30	BY	Synonym of 27
31	ARE	Hashes to 22
32	FROM	Synonym of 22
33	OR	Synonym of 29
34		
35		
36		
37		
38		
39		
40		

Figure 7.11
Direct file with ARE, BUT, FROM, and OR

Position	Data	
0	THEY	
1	A	
2	WITH	
3	ON	Synonym of 1
4	NO	Synonym of 1
5	WAS	
6	THIS	
7	IN	
8	BE	Synonym of 7
9	OF	
10	THAT	Synonym of 9
11	AND	
12	I	Synonym of 9
13	HE	
14	HAD	Synonym of 13
15	BUT	Hashes to 3
16	AN	Hashes to 15
17		
18	AS	
19	HIS	Synonym of 18
20		
21	AT	
22	NOT	Synonym of 21
23	TON	Synonym of 21
24	SAYS	
25	THE	
26	IS	
27	TO	
28	FOR	Synonym of 27
29	IT	
30	BY	Synonym of 27
31	ARE	Hashes to 22
32	FROM	Synonym of 22
33	OR	Synonym of 29
34	HAVE	Synonym of 26
35		
36		
37		
38		
39		
40		

Figure 7.12
Direct file with the entire set of words

Another problem with linear probing is the fact that storing the synonym in the nearest available location (i) may displace another record added later that hashes to position i but is not a synonym of the record in position i. The displacement of records from the hashed address causes more records to be stored away from the hashed address and leads to more extensive linear probing to access records later.

Table 7.4 Number of probes for linear probing

Load factor	Average no. of successful probes	Average no. of unsuccessful probes
.10	1.056	1.118
.20	1.125	1.281
.30	1.214	1.520
.40	1.333	1.889
.50	1.500	2.500
.60	1.750	3.625
.70	2.167	6.060
.80	3.000	13.000
.90	5.500	50.500
.95	10.500	200.500

Two-Pass File Creation with Hashing

The displacement problem of linear probing usually occurs when the relative file is initially created with a one-pass algorithm. A one-pass algorithm hashes the key of each record to be loaded to the relative file. It stores a record in the hashed address, if empty, and stores synonyms in the first available location nearest the hashed address. A two-pass algorithm reduces the displacement problem by loading hashed positions in the first pass and loading synonyms in the available positions in the second pass. The first pass of the two-pass algorithm hashes the key of each record to be loaded to the relative file and stores the record in the hashed address, if empty. The synonyms are stored in an output file that is used during the second pass. The second pass inputs the synonyms separated by the first pass, hashes the key of each record, and stores the synonym in the first available position nearest the hashed address.

The two-pass algorithm allows more records to be stored in the positions to which they were hashed, thereby reducing the amount of linear probing that must be done later to access any record without synonyms. The two-pass algorithm works well if the set of key values is known before the file is created. Any additions to the file after the initial loading may produce displacement problems similar to those produced by the one-pass algorithm. Table 7.5 indicates that three words were displaced by synonyms of other words. The two-pass algorithm eliminates the displacement of records from their hashed addresses. The words that are synonyms are separated to the right column for the second pass.

Figure 7.13 shows the relative file contents after the first pass. The second pass adds the synonyms that were skipped during the first pass; the resulting file contents are shown in Figure 7.14. The three words displaced during the one-pass loading algorithm in the previous example (ARE, BUT, and AN) are stored in their respective hashed addresses; access to these records is direct. Linear probing is used only for those records that hashed to a location that was already occupied.

Table 7.5 Hashed positions for a two-pass algorithm

First pass WORD	Hash (WORD)	Second pass WORD	Hash (WORD)
THE	25		
OF	9		
AND	11		
TO	27		
A	1		
IN	7		
		THAT	9 (synonym)
IS	26		
WAS	5		
HE	13		
		FOR	27 (synonym)
IT	29		
WITH	2		
AS	18		
		HIS	18 (synonym)
		ON	1 (synonym)
		BE	7 (synonym)
AT	21		
		BY	27 (synonym)
		I	9 (synonym)
THIS	6		
		HAD	13 (synonym)
		NOT	21 (synonym)
		NO	1 (synonym)
		TON	21 (synonym)
SAYS	24		
ARE	22*		
BUT	3*		
		FROM	22 (synonym)
		OR	29 (synonym)
		HAVE	26 (synonym)
AN	15*		
THEY	0		

* Would have been displaced by a nonsynonym in the one-pass algorithm

Table 7.6 lists the hashed location for each word in the discussion of the one-pass and two-pass algorithms as well as the actual position in which each word was stored during the algorithms. The table compares the algorithms by including the number of probes necessary to locate each word in the file. The one-pass algorithm displaces two words (ARE and BUT) several positions away from their hashed positions; it takes several probes to locate them (10 and 13 probes, respectively). Displacement does not occur with the two-pass algorithm. The access is the same on the average. Some of the synonyms are farther away from their hashed positions as a result of eliminating displacements, but the average number of probes for all words in the file is 2.97. Words added after the file is created with the two-pass algorithm could result in displacement.

Position	Data
0	THEY
1	A
2	WITH
3	BUT
4	
5	WAS
6	THIS
7	IN
8	
9	OF
10	
11	AND
12	
13	HE
14	
15	AN
16	
17	
18	AS
19	
20	
21	AT
22	ARE
23	
24	SAYS
25	THE
26	IS
27	TO
28	
29	IT
30	
31	
32	
33	
34	
35	
36	
37	
38	
39	
40	

Figure 7.13
Direct file of words in Table 7.3 after first pass

Position	Data	
0	THEY	
1	A	
2	WITH	
3	BUT	
4	ON	Synonym of 1
5	WAS	
6	THIS	
7	IN	
8	BE	Synonym of 7
9	OF	
10	THAT	Synonym of 9
11	AND	
12	I	Synonym of 9
13	HE	
14	HAD	Synonym of 13
15	AN	
16	NO	Synonym of 1
17		
18	AS	
19	HIS	Synonym of 18
20		
21	AT	
22	ARE	
23	NOT	Synonym of 21
24	SAYS	
25	THE	
26	IS	
27	TO	
28	FOR	Synonym of 27
29	IT	
30	BY	Synonym of 27
31	TON	Synonym of 21
32	FROM	Synonym of 22
33	OR	Synonym of 29
34	HAVE	Synonym of 26
35		
36		
37		
38		
39		
40		

Figure 7.14
Direct file after second pass

Position	Overflow Data
0	THAT
1	FOR
2	HIS
3	ON
4	BE
5	BY
6	I
7	HAD
8	NOT
9	NO
10	TON
11	FROM
12	OR
13	HAVE
14	
15	
16	
17	
18	
19	
20	
21	
22	
23	
24	
25	
26	
27	
28	
29	
30	

Figure 7.15
Overflow area for direct file in Figure 7.13

Table 7.6 Comparison of one-pass and two-pass algorithms

WORD	Hash (WORD)	One-pass location	No. of probes	Two-pass location	No of probes
THE	25	25	1	25	1
OF	9	9	1	9	1
AND	11	11	1	11	1
TO	27	27	1	27	1
A	1	1	1	1	1
IN	7	7	1	7	1
THAT	9	10	2	10	2
IS	26	26	1	26	1
WAS	5	5	1	5	1
HE	13	13	1	13	1
FOR	27	28	2	28	2
IT	29	29	1	29	1
WITH	2	2	1	2	1
AS	18	18	1	18	1
HIS	18	19	2	19	2
ON	1	3	3	4	4 (+1)
BE	7	8	2	8	2
AT	21	21	1	21	1
BY	27	30	4	30	4
I	9	12	4	12	4
THIS	6	6	1	6	1
HAD	13	14	2	14	2
NOT	21	22	2	23	3 (+1)
NO	1	4	4	16	16 (+12)
TON	21	23	3	31	11 (+8)
ARE *	22	31	10	22	1 (–9)
BUT *	3	15	13	3	1 (–12)
FROM	22	32	11	32	11
OR	29	33	5	33	5
HAVE	26	34	9	34	9
AN *	15	16	2	15	1 (–1)
THEY	0	0	1	0	1
Average number of probes			2.97		2.97

* Displaced during the one-pass algorithm

Separate Overflow Area

Another alternative to the two-pass algorithm for loading the relative file initially is storing synonyms sequentially in a **separate overflow area.** Using a separate overflow area eliminates the displacement problem altogether and allows use of the one-pass loading algorithm. Accessing synonyms entails sequentially searching all the records in the overflow area, which is probably not as large as the hashed positions of the relative file. Depending on the size of the overflow area, the searching time for locating synonyms could be lengthy. For the example set of words in Table 7.3, the first-pass loading algorithm resulted in the storage presented in Figure 7.13. The synonyms are stored sequentially in an overflow area as indicated in Figure 7.15. Accessing a record that is not in the hashed address involves sequentially searching the overflow area for the record.

The average number of probes for a file with synonyms stored in a separate overflow area depends on the number of synonyms. Table 7.7 lists the number of probes for the file of words in Figures 7.13 and 7.15. The average number of probes for this file is 4.28—considerably worse than either the one-pass or two-pass algorithms, which do not employ a separate overflow area.

Table 7.7 Separate overflow area reduces probes for words in Tbl 7.3

WORD	No. of probes	WORD	No. of probes
THE	1	BE	6
OF	1	AT	1
AND	1	BY	7
TO	1	I	8
A	1	THIS	1
IN	1	HAD	9
THAT	2	NOT	10
IS	1	NO	11
WAS	1	TON	12
HE	1	ARE	1
FOR	3	BUT	1
IT	1	FROM	13
WITH	1	OR	14
AS	1	HAVE	15
HIS	4	AN	1
ON	5	THEY	1
Average number of probes			4.28

Double Hashing

When a separate overflow area is established for synonyms, the synonym is stored in the next available overflow position. Rather than sequentially searching for a next available overflow position or sequentially searching for the synonym later, the synonym is often hashed to an overflow record position. Hashing synonyms to an overflow area using a second hash function is **double hashing**. The record is initially hashed to a relative file position. If the hashed address is not available, a second hash function is applied and added to the first hashed value, and the synonym is hashed to the overflow area. If the hashed overflow area is not available, a **secondary collision** occurs; then linear probing is used. The access to synonyms is more direct than searching the overflow area sequentially. The synonyms involved in secondary collisions are the only records that have to be accessed sequentially.

Reconsider the set of words in Example 7.2. Suppose that the synonyms are hashed to an overflow area using a second hash function, which is defined as the remainder of the division of the bit string of the letters in the word by the constant 31. Therefore,

$$\text{hash2 (THE)} = 101000100000101_2 \text{ MOD } 31 = 20741_{10} \text{ MOD } 31 = 2$$

The resulting value of the second hash function is an integer in the range of 0 through 30. The hashed position for storing the synonym in the overflow area is the sum of the results of the two hash functions. If the sum is greater than 30 (the largest numbered position in the file), the remainder of the division of the sum by 31 is the position number in the range of 0 through 30. The second hash function values for the synonyms are presented in Table 7.8.

The relative file can be loaded with a one-pass algorithm by hashing a record to a position in the prime or home area of the file as before. If the hashed address is occupied, the synonym is hashed using the second hash function value added to the first hash function value as shown in the table. If the resulting double-hashed address in the overflow area is not occupied, the synonym is stored in the double-hashed overflow address. If the double-hashed address is occupied, then linear probing of the overflow area is applied as before.

The words THAT, FOR, HIS, ON, and BE are stored in their respective double-hashed addresses as shown in Figure 7.16. The next word to be added that is a synonym of a home address is BY, which double hashes to overflow position 23. Position 23 is occupied by HIS. Linear probing is applied to store BY in the nearest available position, namely overflow position 24. The words I, HAD, and NOT are added to the file in their respective overflow positions. A secondary collision occurs when NO double hashes to overflow position 30, which is occupied by ON. A circular search of the file ensues from position 30 to position 0 before an empty location is found. TON also collides with NOT in position 8 and is stored in position 9. FROM and OR are double-hashed to their respective overflow positions (Figure 7.17).

The last word to be added that is a synonym of a home address, HAVE, collides with NO in position 0 and OR in position 1. HAVE must be stored in overflow position 2. The prime or home area is as in the previous example. The relative file overflow area is shown in Figure 7.18.

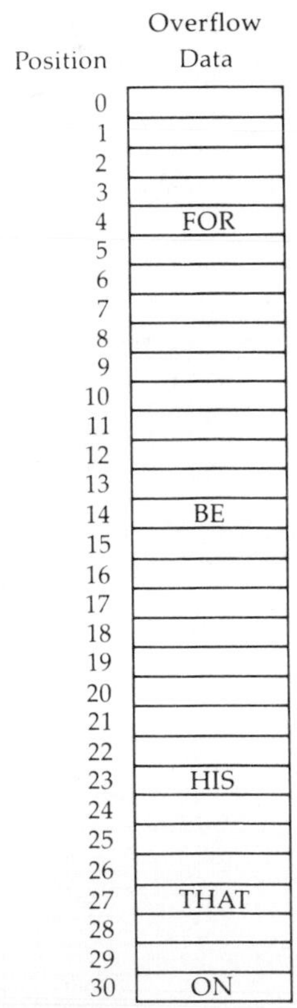

Position
Overflow Data
0 1 2 3 4 5 6 7 8 9 10 11 12 13 14 15 16 17 18 19 20 21 22 23 24 25 26 27 28 29 30
FOR
BE
HIS
THAT
ON

Figure 7.16
Overflow area for file in Figure 7.13 after double hashing

Table 7.8 Using double hashing to organize words from Ex. 7.2

WORD	hash1 (WORD)	hash2 (WORD)
THE	25	
OF	9	
AND	11	
TO	27	
A	1	
IN	7	
THAT	9	(synonym) +18 =27
IS	26	
WAS	5	
HE	13	
FOR	27	(synonym) +8 = 35 MOD 31 =4
IT	29	
WITH	2	
AS	18	
HIS	18	(synonym) +5 = 23
ON	1	(synonym) +29 =30
BE	7	(synonym) +7 = 14
AT	21	
BY	27	(synonym) +27 =54 MOD 31 =23 (synonym)
I	9	(synonym) + 9 = 18
THIS	6	
HAD	13	(synonym) + 13 = 26
NOT	21	(synonym) + 18 = 39 MOD 31 = 8
NO	1	(synonym) + 29 = 30 (synonym)
TON	21	(synonym) + 18 = 39 MOD 31 = 8 (synonym)
SAYS	24	
ARE	22	
BUT	3	
FROM	22	(synonym) + 21 = 43 MOD 31 = 12
OR	29	(synonym) + 2 = 31 MOD 31 = 0
HAVE	26	(synonym) + 5 = 31 MOD 31 = 0 (synonym)
AN	15	
THEY	0	

Position	Overflow Data
0	NO
1	OR
2	
3	
4	FOR
5	
6	
7	
8	NOT
9	TON
10	
11	
12	FROM
13	
14	BE
15	
16	
17	
18	I
19	
20	
21	
22	
23	HIS
24	BY
25	
26	HAD
27	THAT
28	
29	
30	ON

Figure 7.17
Overflow area after 13 additions

Table 7.9 lists the number of probes for each of the words stored in a separate overflow area using double hashing (Figure 7.18). The average number of probes for a successful search of this file is 1.63 where the load factor is 50 percent—an average that is comparable to linear probing at the same load factor.

Table 7.9 Probes of separate overflow area using double hashing

WORD	No. of probes	WORD	No. of probes
THE	1	BE	2
OF	1	AT	1
AND	1	BY	3
TO	1	I	2
A	1	THIS	1
IN	1	HAD	2
THAT	2	NOT	2
IS	1	NO	4
WAS	1	TON	3
HE	1	ARE	1
FOR	2	BUT	1
IT	1	FROM	2
WITH	1	OR	2
AS	1	HAVE	4
HIS	2	AN	1
ON	2	THEY	1

Average number of probes 1.63

The formula for determining the average number of probes using double hashing for a successful search is

$$\left[-\frac{1}{a}\ln(1-a)\right]$$

The formula for determining the average number of probes using double hashing for an unsuccessful search is

$$\left[\frac{1}{1-a}\right]$$

Table 7.10 gives a summary of the average number of probes for a variety of load factors. For a load factor of 80 percent, the average number of probes for a linear probe is 3.000 (see Table 7.4), but it is 2.012 for double hashing. For a load factor of 95 percent, the double hashing method is more efficient for successful searches (3.153 probes) than the linear probing method (10.5 probes) and even more efficient for unsuccessful searches (20.0 probes for double hashing versus 200.5 probes for linear probing).

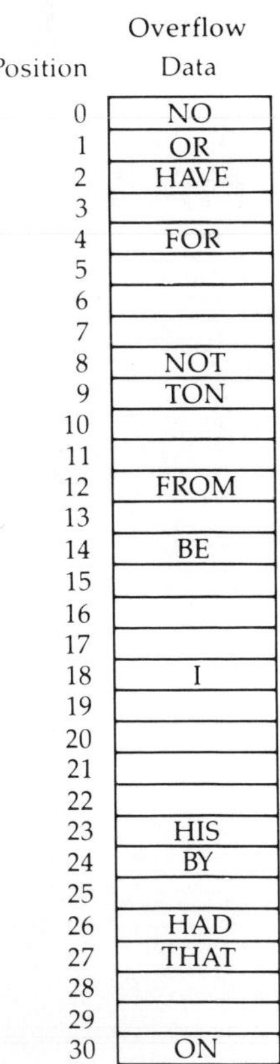

Figure 7.18
Complete overflow area

Table 7.10 Number of probes for double hashing

Load factor	Average no. of successful probes	Average no. of unsuccessful probes
.10	1.054	1.111
.20	1.116	1.250
.30	1.189	1.429
.40	1.277	1.667
.50	1.386	2.000
.60	1.527	2.500
.70	1.720	3.333
.80	2.012	5.000
.90	2.558	10.000
.95	3.153	20.000

Synonym Chaining

Synonym chaining is a technique used with and without a separate overflow area to reduce the number of records examined when searching for a synonym. The initial creation of the relative file that uses synonym chaining involves hashing the key of the record to be loaded and retrieving the record in the hashed address. If the hashed address is occupied, then the synonym is stored using one of the techniques discussed above. The record in the initial hashed address contains a link to the position containing the synonym. If several synonyms hash to one address, all the synonyms are linked together even though the synonyms are not physically stored in contiguous positions in the file. The access to any synonym involves searching only the linked synonyms rather than searching the whole file (if linear probing is used) or the whole overflow area (if a separate overflow area is used). Each record is enlarged to include a link field, but the access of a synonym record is more direct than any of the techniques previously discussed.

Given the set of words used in Example 7.2, synonym chaining could be used in resolving collisions. The use of a separate overflow area for storing synonyms eliminates the displacement problem found in the linear probing example. Each position in the home and overflow areas in the relative file contains a link field that contains the address of the next synonym in overflow in addition to the other information. The relative file must be allocated with the number of necessary positions, an empty value must be recorded in each position, and a null value (-1, for example) must be recorded in the link field of each record. Each record that hashes to an occupied home address is stored in the next available position in the overflow area (allocating the next available location sequentially), and a link field is maintained from the home address to the synonym in overflow. Each later record that is a synonym of a home address is stored in the next available position in overflow and included in the linked list of all synonyms that hashed to this particular home address.

The relative file in Figure 7.19 shows the words THE, OF, AND, TO, A, and IN stored in their respective locations, with THAT being the first synonym encountered. THAT hashes to home position 9, which is occupied by OF, so THAT is stored in the first overflow position. Home position 9 retains a link (in the form of the relative position number of overflow) to overflow position 0.

The words IS, WAS, and HE are stored in the home area, but FOR is a synonym for home position 27, so it is stored in overflow position 1. Home position 27 is linked to overflow position 1. IT, WITH, and AS reside in home positions, while HIS is a synonym for home position 18, ON is a synonym for home position 1, and BE is a synonym for home position 7. The file contents are shown in Figure 7.20.

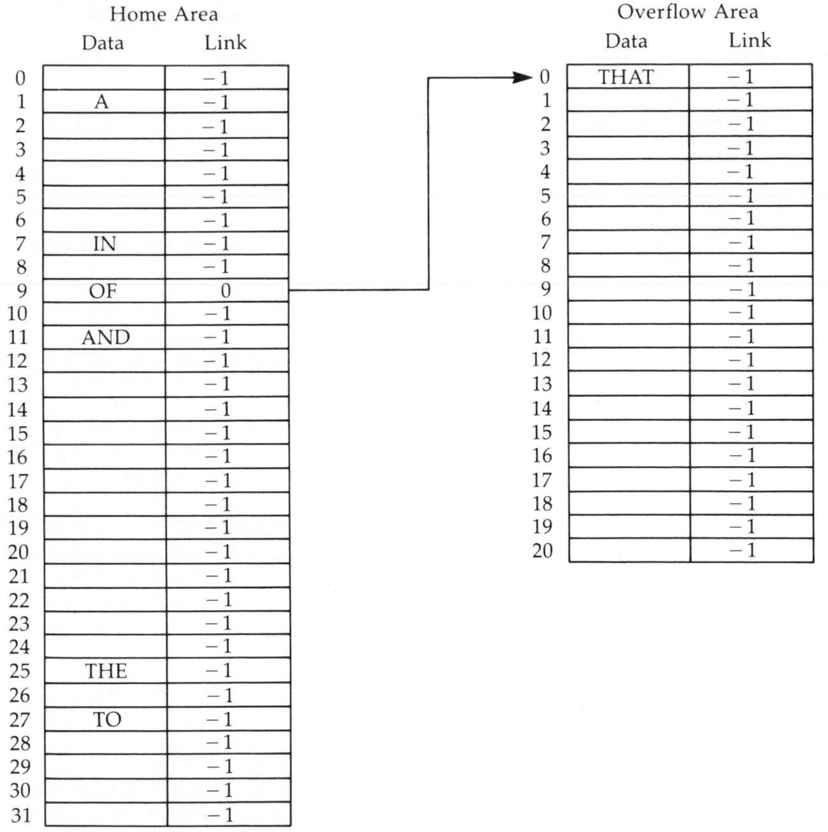

Home Area

	Data	Link
0		−1
1	A	−1
2		−1
3		−1
4		−1
5		−1
6		−1
7	IN	−1
8		−1
9	OF	0
10		−1
11	AND	−1
12		−1
13		−1
14		−1
15		−1
16		−1
17		−1
18		−1
19		−1
20		−1
21		−1
22		−1
23		−1
24		−1
25	THE	−1
26		−1
27	TO	−1
28		−1
29		−1
30		−1
31		−1

Overflow Area

	Data	Link
0	THAT	−1
1		−1
2		−1
3		−1
4		−1
5		−1
6		−1
7		−1
8		−1
9		−1
10		−1
11		−1
12		−1
13		−1
14		−1
15		−1
16		−1
17		−1
18		−1
19		−1
20		−1

Figure 7.19
Direct file using synonym chaining

Figure 7.20
Synonym chaining after 13 additions

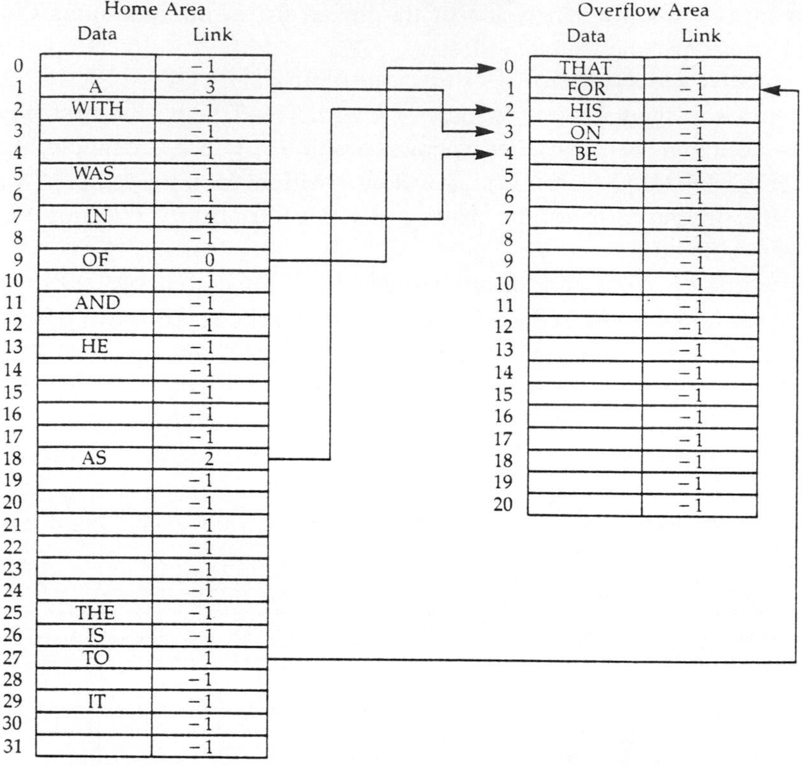

Home Area

	Data	Link
0		−1
1	A	3
2	WITH	−1
3		−1
4		−1
5	WAS	−1
6		−1
7	IN	4
8		−1
9	OF	0
10		−1
11	AND	−1
12		−1
13	HE	−1
14		−1
15		−1
16		−1
17		−1
18	AS	2
19		−1
20		−1
21		−1
22		−1
23		−1
24		−1
25	THE	−1
26	IS	−1
27	TO	1
28		−1
29	IT	−1
30		−1
31		−1

Overflow Area

	Data	Link
0	THAT	−1
1	FOR	−1
2	HIS	−1
3	ON	−1
4	BE	−1
5		−1
6		−1
7		−1
8		−1
9		−1
10		−1
11		−1
12		−1
13		−1
14		−1
15		−1
16		−1
17		−1
18		−1
19		−1
20		−1

Figure 7.21
Direct file from Figure 7.20 with three additions

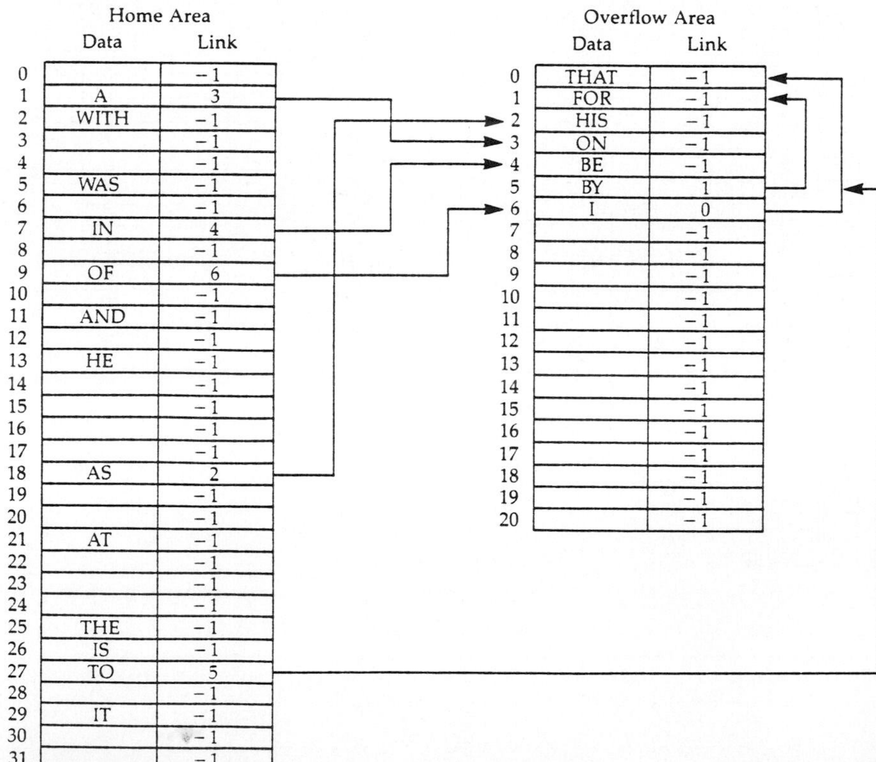

Home Area

	Data	Link
0		−1
1	A	3
2	WITH	−1
3		−1
4		−1
5	WAS	−1
6		−1
7	IN	4
8		−1
9	OF	6
10		−1
11	AND	−1
12		−1
13	HE	−1
14		−1
15		−1
16		−1
17		−1
18	AS	2
19		−1
20		−1
21	AT	−1
22		−1
23		−1
24		−1
25	THE	−1
26	IS	−1
27	TO	5
28		−1
29	IT	−1
30		−1
31		−1

Overflow Area

	Data	Link
0	THAT	−1
1	FOR	−1
2	HIS	−1
3	ON	−1
4	BE	−1
5	BY	1
6	I	0
7		−1
8		−1
9		−1
10		−1
11		−1
12		−1
13		−1
14		−1
15		−1
16		−1
17		−1
18		−1
19		−1
20		−1

Then AT is stored in home position 21. BY is a synonym for home position 27, which is linked to overflow position 1 (which holds FOR). BY is stored in the next available overflow position, and the content of the link field of the home position 27 (1) is recorded in the link field of BY. BY links with the previous synonym FOR, so the address of BY (5) is stored in the link field of the home position. As a result, home area 27 (TO) has the address of the last synonym added (BY in overflow position 5), and BY has the address of the previous synonym (FOR in overflow position 1).

Similarly, I hashes to home position 9, which is linked to overflow position 0. I is added in overflow position 6, so overflow position 6 now has a link to overflow position 0, and home position 9 has the address of I (6) (Figure 7.21). The rest of the words in the set are added in a similar manner to result in the relative file contents presented in Figure 7.22.

Table 7.11 lists the number of probes for each of the words in the file stored in the overflow area of Figure 7.22. The average number of probes for a successful search of this file is 1.563 where the load factor is 60 percent—a number comparable to the average for double hashing at the same load factor.

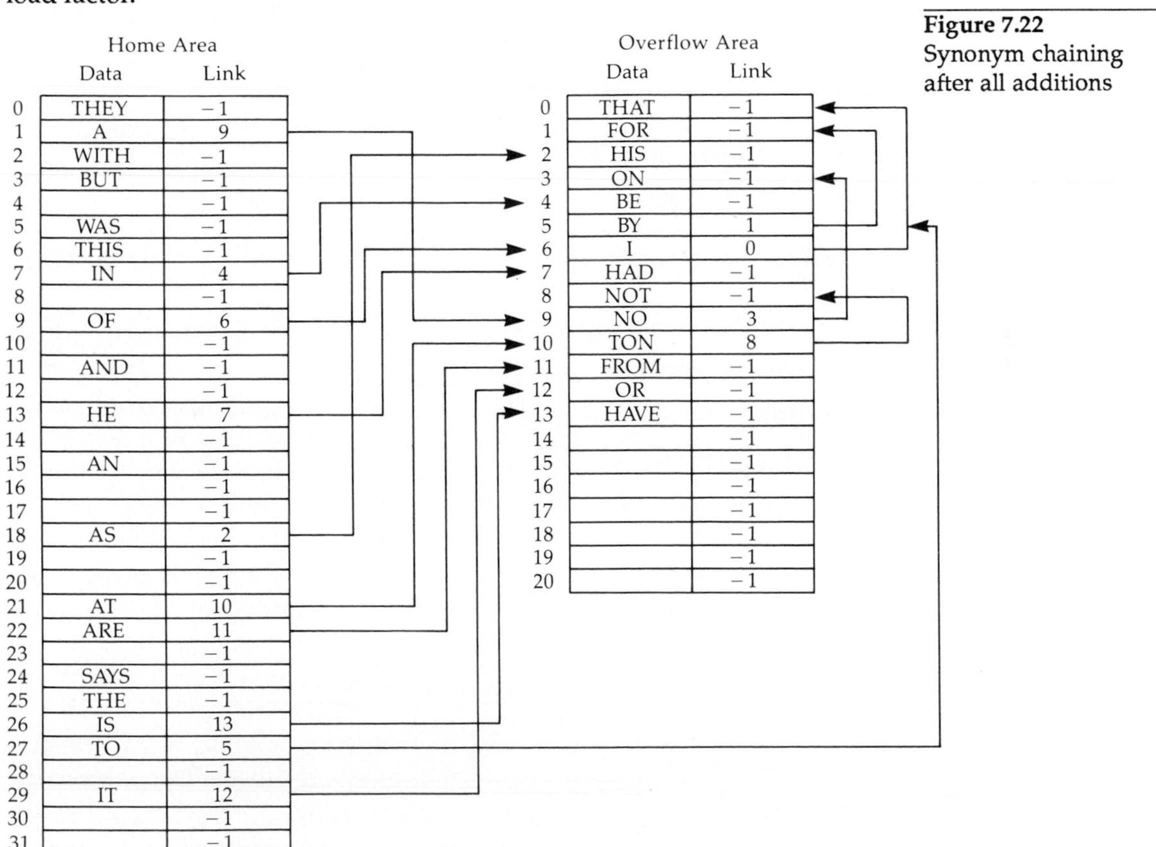

Home Area

	Data	Link
0	THEY	−1
1	A	9
2	WITH	−1
3	BUT	−1
4		−1
5	WAS	−1
6	THIS	−1
7	IN	4
8		−1
9	OF	6
10		−1
11	AND	−1
12		−1
13	HE	7
14		−1
15	AN	−1
16		−1
17		−1
18	AS	2
19		−1
20		−1
21	AT	10
22	ARE	11
23		−1
24	SAYS	−1
25	THE	−1
26	IS	13
27	TO	5
28		−1
29	IT	12
30		−1
31		−1

Overflow Area

	Data	Link
0	THAT	−1
1	FOR	−1
2	HIS	−1
3	ON	−1
4	BE	−1
5	BY	1
6	I	0
7	HAD	−1
8	NOT	−1
9	NO	3
10	TON	8
11	FROM	−1
12	OR	−1
13	HAVE	−1
14		−1
15		−1
16		−1
17		−1
18		−1
19		−1
20		−1

Figure 7.22
Synonym chaining after all additions

Table 7.11 Probes for words in overflow area of Figure 7.22

WORD	No. of probes	WORD	No. of probes
THE	1	BE	2
OF	1	AT	1
AND	1	BY	2
TO	1	I	2
A	1	THIS	1
IN	1	HAD	2
THAT	3	NOT	3
IS	1	NO	2
WAS	1	TON	2
HE	1	ARE	1
FOR	3	BUT	1
IT	1	FROM	2
WITH	1	OR	2
AS	1	HAVE	2
HIS	2	AN	1
ON	3	THEY	1
Average number of probes			1.563

The formula for the average number of probes in a successful search using synonym chaining into a separate overflow area is

$$\left[1+\frac{a}{2}\right]$$

The formula for determining the average number of probes in an unsuccessful search of the same kind is

$$[a+e^{-a}]$$

Table 7.12 summarizes the average number of probes for a variety of load factors. For a load factor of 80 percent, the average number of probes for linear probing is 3.000 (see Table 7.4), for double hashing is 2.012 (see Table 7.10), and for synonym chaining is 1.4. For a load factor of 95 percent, the average numbers of probes for a successful search are

linear probing = 10.500 probes
double hashing = 3.153 probes
synonym chaining = 1.475 probes

With the same load factor, the average numbers of probes for unsuccessful searches are

linear probing = 200.500 probes
double hashing = 20.000 probes
synonym chaining = 1.337 probes

The average number of probes for a successful search is not much improved by synonym chaining, but a great reduction in the number of probes can be realized by using chaining during an unsuccessful search.

Table 7.12 Number of probes for synonym chaining

Load Factor	Average no. of successful probes	Average no. of unsuccessful probes
.10	1.050	1.005
.20	1.100	1.019
.30	1.150	1.041
.40	1.200	1.070
.50	1.250	1.107
.60	1.300	1.149
.70	1.350	1.197
.80	1.400	1.249
.90	1.450	1.307
.95	1.475	1.337

Bucket Addressing

Bucket addressing involves allocating a group of record positions, termed a **bucket**, to be associated with a particular hash address. The primary idea behind bucket addressing is to allocate the bucket size of each hash address so it is as large as the maximum number of synonyms for any hash address. All the synonyms for a particular hash address are then stored sequentially in the bucket for the particular hash address. Accessing a record in a relative file that uses bucket addressing involves hashing the key, then sequentially searching the bucket of records at the hashed address. The number of records that must be examined to find a record is limited by the bucket size; the algorithm does not have to search the whole file or the whole overflow area.

The major problem with bucket addressing as a technique for resolving hashing collisions is the amount of space wasted if the number of synonyms for any one hashed address varies greatly. Since the bucket size is determined by the maximum number of synonyms for any hashed address (each hashed address has the same size bucket), those hashed addresses having a lower number of synonyms also have buckets with unused space —space that is wasted. A secondary problem in using bucket addressing is determining the bucket size. Suppose that data in a relative file are unavailable for analysis prior to creation of the relative file and that the bucket size is smaller than the maximum number of synonyms as a result. All the synonyms that hash to a bucket address cannot be stored in the bucket, so hashing collisions must be resolved using one of the techniques discussed above. To prevent the problem, the programmer could set a very large bucket size, but this solution is at the expense of wasted space.

For the set of words used in Example 7.2, the maximum number of synonyms for any one hashed address is three, so the bucket size is three. (In other words, each hashed address holds three records.) All the synonyms are stored in the bucket in the hashed address. Accessing a record involves sequentially searching the bucket in the hashed address. The relative file with a bucket size of three for the set of words of Table 7.3 has the contents shown in Figure 7.23.

Position	Bucket size of 3		
0	THEY		
1	A	ON	NO
2	WITH		
3	BUT		
4			
5	WAS		
6	THIS		
7	IN	BE	
8			
9	OF	THAT	I
10			
11	AND		
12			
13	HE	HAD	
14			
15	AN		
16			
17			
18	AS	HIS	
19			
20			
21	AT	NOT	TON
22	ARE	FROM	
23			
24	SAYS		
25	THE		
26	IS	HAVE	
27	TO	FOR	BY
28			
29	IT	OR	
30			
31			

Figure 7.23
Words in Table 7.3 in a direct file with a bucket size of 3

Position	Bucket size of 2		
0	THEY		
1	A	ON	
2	WITH	**NO**	
3	BUT		
4			
5	WAS		
6	THIS		
7	IN	BE	
8			
9	OF	THAT	
10	**I**		
11	AND		
12			
13	HE	HAD	
14			
15	AN		
16			
17			
18	AS	HIS	
19			
20			
21	AT	NOT	
22	**TON**	ARE	
23	**FROM**		displaced from 22 by TON
24	SAYS		
25	THE		
26	IS	HAVE	
27	TO	FOR	
28	**BY**		
29	IT	OR	
30			
31			

Figure 7.24
Direct file with a bucket size of 2 using consecutive spill addressing

One solution to hashing collisions in bucket addresses is **consecutive spill addressing.** If a hashing collision occurs with bucket addressing, the nearest bucket with available space is used to store the synonym. The term *spill addressing* is derived from the fact that when a bucket becomes full, the full bucket spills over into the next bucket. Searching for the synonym later involves the same problems encountered with linear probing: The synonym is not located in the hashed addresses, so a sequential search of consecutive buckets must take place. Figure 7.24 illustrates the use of the bucket size of 2 and consecutive spill addressing. The third synonym that hashes to a bucket is stored in the next bucket with available space. For example, TON is stored in the next bucket (bucket 22), displacing FROM, which hashes to 22. The words that are not stored in their hashed locations are in bold type in the figure (NO, I, TON, FROM, and BY).

Maintaining a directory of free space for the file aids in locating the next bucket with available space. The directory improves spill addressing greatly. It identifies all the buckets containing available space, so the bucket with available space nearest the hashed address can be determined by probing the directory.

Another solution to hashing collisions in bucket addressing is **bucket chaining.** If a hashing collision occurs, an overflow bucket is allocated to store the synonym, and the primary bucket is chained to the new overflow bucket. If the overflow bucket fills, another overflow bucket is allocated and chained to the other buckets with synonyms. With bucket chaining, the file can be expanded without rehashing all the records into a larger file. The overflow bucket usually holds only one key rather than being the same size as the home bucket.

Figure 7.25 illustrates the relative file of words with a bucket size of 2 for the home area and an overflow area with bucket size 1. The two areas would have the same bucket size if the overflow area were in the same file as the home area. When a word hashes to a full bucket, the word is stored in the next available overflow area (allocated sequentially as needed); the home bucket has the address of the overflow bucket. Should the overflow bucket fill, it would spill into another overflow bucket and be linked together. The chaining of buckets reduces the number of probes it takes to locate all the synonyms of an address.

The primary disadvantage to bucket chaining is the number of buckets that must be accessed to locate a record. All the buckets chained to a hashed address may have to be searched to find a record. Fewer probes are required if the bucket size is large enough to hold all synonyms.

Table 7.13 lists the number of probes for each of the words stored using bucket addressing with home buckets chained to overflow buckets. The average number of probes for a successful search of this file is 1.125 where the load factor is 60 percent—bucket chaining is an improvement over synonym chaining (a special case of bucket sizes of 1).

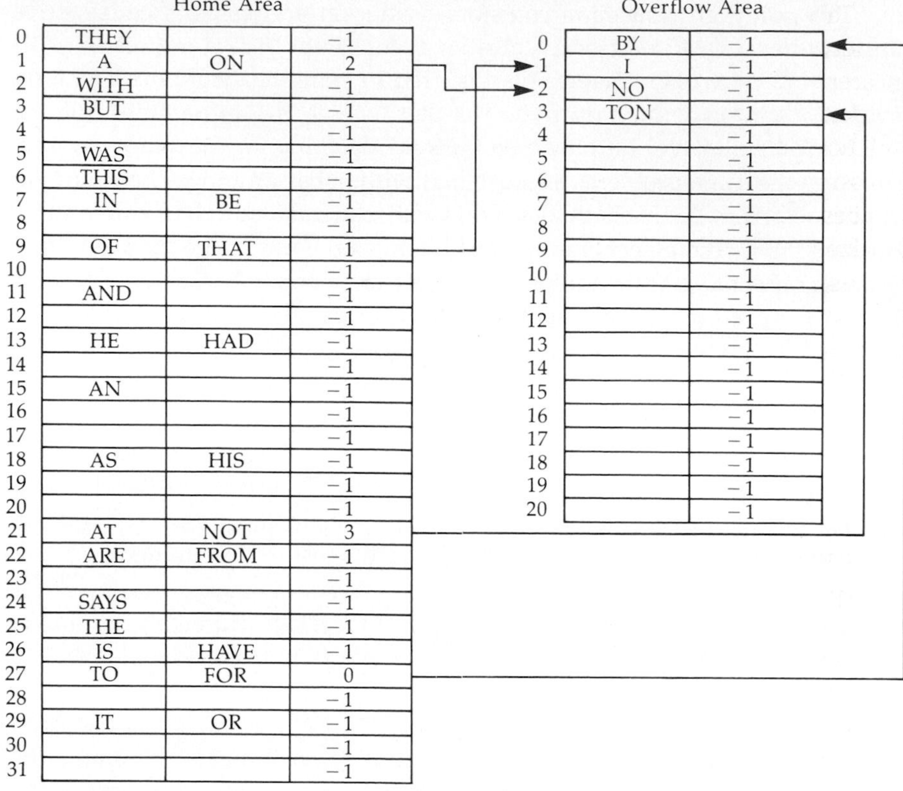

Figure 7.25
Direct file with bucket size of 2 using bucket chaining

Table 7.13 Probes for words in Table 7.3*

WORD	No. of probes	WORD	No. of probes
THE	1	BE	1
OF	1	AT	1
AND	1	BY	2
TO	1	I	2
A	1	THIS	1
IN	1	HAD	1
THAT	1	NOT	1
IS	1	NO	2
WAS	1	TON	2
HE	1	ARE	1
FOR	1	BUT	1
IT	1	FROM	1
WITH	1	OR	1
AS	1	HAVE	1
HIS	1	AN	1
ON	1	THEY	1
Average number of probes			1.125

*Probes for words in Table 7.3 in separate overflow area using bucket chaining

Table 7.14 gives a summary of the average number of probes for a variety of load factors for bucket sizes of 2 and 50. For a load factor of 80 percent, the average number of probes for a successful search is lower for bucket addressing using buckets of size 2 (1.299) than for any of the other methods discussed in this chapter. Unsuccessful searches using bucket addressing and chaining to a separate overflow area actually require fewer probes than successful searches up to the 70 percent load factor. For a bucket size of 50, the number of probes for successful and unsuccessful searches is close to 1 until a load factor of 95 percent.

Table 7.14 Number of probes for bucket chaining

	Bucket size of 2		Bucket size of 50	
Load Factor	Average no. of successful probes	Average no. of unsuccessful probes	Average no. of successful probes	Average no. of unsuccessful probes
.10	1.006	1.001	1.000	1.000
.20	1.024	1.009	1.000	1.000
.30	1.052	1.027	1.000	1.000
.40	1.088	1.058	1.000	1.000
.50	1.132	1.104	1.000	1.000
.60	1.182	1.164	1.000	1.001
.70	1.238	1.238	1.001	1.018
.80	1.299	1.327	1.015	1.182
.90	1.364	1.428	1.083	1.920
.95	1.400	1.500	1.200	2.700

DYNAMIC HASHING

One of the problems with conventional hashing is that the number of records to be stored in the file must be known before the file is initially created. Each time the file becomes full, the entire file can be rehashed into a larger file using a different hashing function. **Dynamic hashing** is a technique used to dynamically change the hashing function to access a hashed file that increases in size as records are added. A hash table is created as an index to the hashed file. Suppose that the words in Table 7.3 are stored in a file with a bucket size of 2. Figure 7.26 shows the file when the first collision occurs. When an overflow occurs with bucket addressing (BY is added, hashing to position 27), a new hashing function is applied to all records within the bucket and to the synonym being added to split the records between the addressed bucket and a new overflow bucket. At the same time, the entry in the hash table for bucket 27 becomes a binary tree that chains to the two buckets as a result of the split. If the binary representation of the key used by the hashing function is available, all keys with a zero bit in the first position stay in the primary bucket, and all keys with a one bit in the first position are moved to a new overflow bucket. In this case the key is character data, so any randomizing function can be applied to the first character of the key to randomly split the records between the two buckets.

In this example, all keys starting with the characters *A* through *O* stay, but all keys starting with *P* through *Z* move to a new overflow bucket. The primary bucket is chained to the new overflow bucket. The entry in the hash table for position 27 becomes the root of a binary tree containing the two bucket addresses as a result of the split bucket. Figure 7.27 presents the file and hash table after the split. Figure 7.28 shows the file and hash table after all the words have been added.

Figure 7.26
Dynamic hashing with bucket size of 2 when first bucket overflow occurs

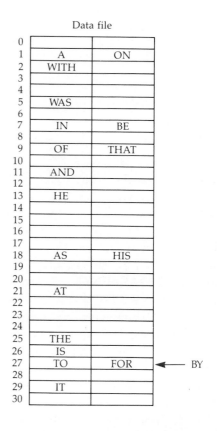

Hash table

	Hash table
0	0
1	1
2	2
3	3
4	4
5	5
6	6
7	7
8	8
9	9
10	10
11	11
12	12
13	13
14	14
15	15
16	16
17	17
18	18
19	19
20	20
21	21
22	22
23	23
24	24
25	25
26	26
27	27
28	28
29	29
30	30

Data file

	Data file		
0			
1	A	ON	
2	WITH		
3			
4			
5	WAS		
6			
7	IN	BE	
8			
9	OF	THAT	
10			
11	AND		
12			
13	HE		
14			
15			
16			
17			
18	AS	HIS	
19			
20			
21	AT		
22			
23			
24			
25	THE		
26	IS		
27	TO	FOR	← BY
28			
29	IT		
30			

Hash table

0	0
1	1
2	2
3	3
4	4
5	5
6	6
7	7
8	8
9	9
10	10
11	11
12	12
13	13
14	14
15	15
16	16
17	17
18	18
19	19
20	20
21	21
22	22
23	23
24	24
25	25
26	26
27	
28	28
29	29
30	30

First character tree

A–O	27
P–Z	31

Data file

0		
1	A	ON
2	WITH	
3		
4		
5	WAS	
6		
7	IN	BE
8		
9	OF	THAT
10		
11	AND	
12		
13	HE	
14		
15		
16		
17		
18	AS	HIS
19		
20		
21	AT	
22		
23		
24		
25	THE	
26	IS	
27	FOR	BY
28		
29	IT	
30		
31	TO	

Figure 7.27
Dynamic hashing after first split

Suppose that the word TAN (hashing to position 27) is added to the file. Entry 27 in the hash table has the address of bucket 27 for those words with the first letter less than or equal to *O* and the address of bucket 31 for all other synonyms. TAN starts with a *T*, so bucket 31 is searched for an available slot in which to store TAN. Since bucket 31 contains only one word, TAN is added (Figure 7.29). When LOX is added and it hashes to position 27, the hash table indicates that bucket 27 should be searched. An overflow occurs with bucket 27 and the contents are split according to the second letter of the words (since this is the second split for synonyms of bucket 27). The node in the binary tree pointing to bucket 27 becomes the root of a subtree that indicates that bucket 27 has words with the first two letters in the range of *AA* through *OO* and that bucket 33 has words with the first two letters in the range of *AP* through *OZ*. Figure 7.30 has the resulting file contents and hash table.

A better distribution for splitting words between buckets is to use the *i*th letter (depending on the level in the hashing tree) and perform a hashing function on that letter. Simply using the letter to split the bucket may leave the words in a bucket that is not large enough to hold them all.

As long as the hashing tree is held in main memory, all words can be accessed with one file access. The number of file accesses for a successful probe increases if any part of the hashing tree is accessed from external storage.

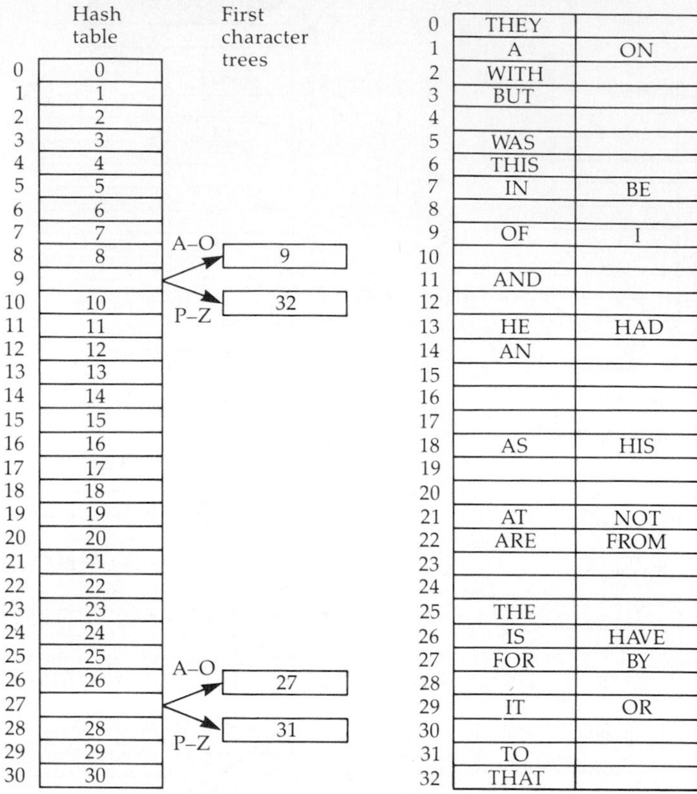

Figure 7.28 Complete dynamic hashing file

RANDOM-ACCESS FILES IN ADA

Random-access files in Ada are those files used for random (or direct) access. The file is viewed as a set of elements occupying consecutive positions in linear order. Data can be transferred to or from an element of the file at any selected position. The position of an element is specified by its index, which is a number of subtype `Positive_Count`, defined in the package `Direct_IO`, that is in the range of `1..Count'Last`. `Count` is also defined in `Direct_IO` and is `0..`*`implementation_defined`*. Neither of these types is compatible with `Positive` or `Natural`, respectively. There are no operations defined for `Count` and subsequently none for `Positive_Count`. Therefore, random-access files in Ada (termed **direct** files in Ada) are organized as relative files where the relative record number (termed the index in Ada) of the first element is one. The index of the last element of a direct file is called the `current_size`; the `current_size` is zero if there are no elements. The `current_size` is a property of the external file. An open direct file in Ada has a current index, much like the location indicator used for sequential files. The `current_index` is the index that is used by the next read or write operation to indicate the position in the file for access. When a direct file is opened, the `current_index` is set to one. The `current_index` of a direct file is a property of a file object, not of an external file.

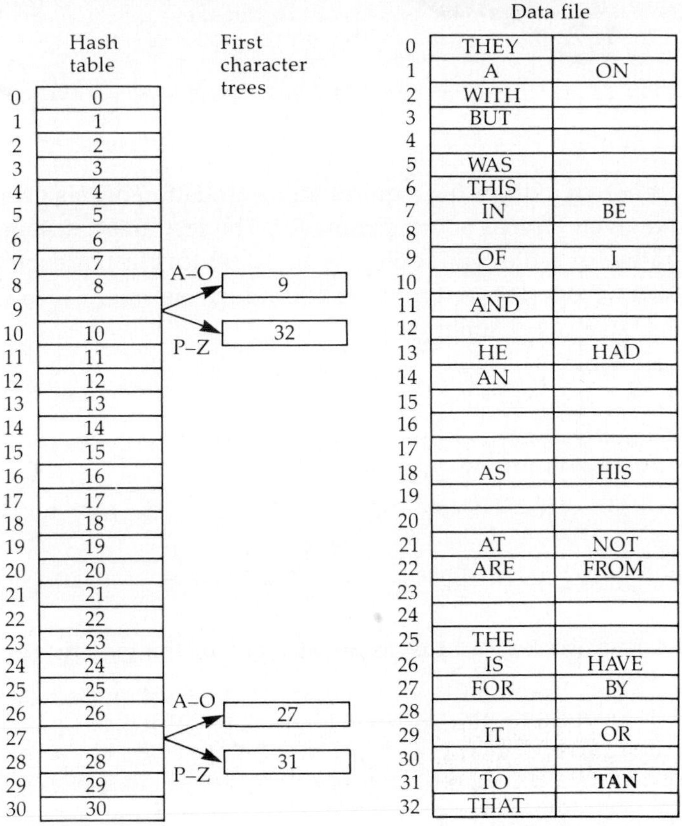

Hash table

0	0
1	1
2	2
3	3
4	4
5	5
6	6
7	7
8	8
9	
10	10
11	11
12	12
13	13
14	14
15	15
16	16
17	17
18	18
19	19
20	20
21	21
22	22
23	23
24	24
25	25
26	26
27	
28	28
29	29
30	30

First character trees

Hash entry	Branch	Bucket
9	A–O	9
9	P–Z	32
27	A–O	27
27	P–Z	31

Data file

0	THEY	
1	A	ON
2	WITH	
3	BUT	
4		
5	WAS	
6	THIS	
7	IN	BE
8		
9	OF	I
10		
11	AND	
12		
13	HE	HAD
14	AN	
15		
16		
17		
18	AS	HIS
19		
20		
21	AT	NOT
22	ARE	FROM
23		
24		
25	THE	
26	IS	HAVE
27	FOR	BY
28		
29	IT	OR
30		
31	TO	**TAN**
32	THAT	

Figure 7.29
Dynamic hashing file after TAN is added

A direct file in Ada is defined by means of the generic package `Direct_IO`. A skeleton of the specification part of this package is given below.

```
WITH IO_Exceptions;
Generic
    TYPE Element_Type Is Private;
PACKAGE Direct_IO Is
    TYPE File_Type Is Limited Private;
    TYPE File_Mode Is ( IN_FILE,INOUT_FILE, OUT_FILE );
    TYPE Count Is Range 0 .. implementation_defined;
    SUBTYPE Positive_Count Is Count Range 1 .. Count'Last;
    ...
    PROCEDURE Read ( file : File_Type;
                     item : Out Element_Type );
    ...
    PROCEDURE Read ( file : File_Type;
                     item : Out Element_Type;
                     from : Positive_Count );
    ...
    PROCEDURE Write ( file : In File_Type;
                      item : Element_Type );
    ...
    PROCEDURE Write ( file : In File_Type;
                      item : Element_Type;
                      to   : Positive_Count );
    ...
```

```
    PROCEDURE Set_Index ( file : In File_Type;
                          To   : In Positive_Count );
    ...
    FUNCTION Index ( file : In File_Type ) Return Positive_Count;
    ...
END Direct_IO;
```

The declaration of a direct file requires an instantiation of this generic package, with a given type as actual parameter. The resulting package contains the declaration of a file type (called `File_Type`) for files of such elements, as well as I/O operations for these files, such as `Open`, `Read`, `Write`, `Set_Index`, and `Index` subprograms.

The following

```
WITH Direct_IO;
PROCEDURE Skeleton Is
    TYPE Relative_Record_Type Is Record
                                 key  : Integer;
                                 info : String ( 1 .. 20 );
                             End Record;
    PACKAGE Key_IO Is New Direct_IO (Relative_Record_Type );
    relative_file : Key_IO.File_Type;
```

creates the package `Key_IO` that is an instance of the generic package `Direct_IO`, where the element type is the record `Relative_Record_Type`, and the I/O operations are instantiated for this particular `File_Type`. The internal file name, `relative_file`, is declared to be a file of this

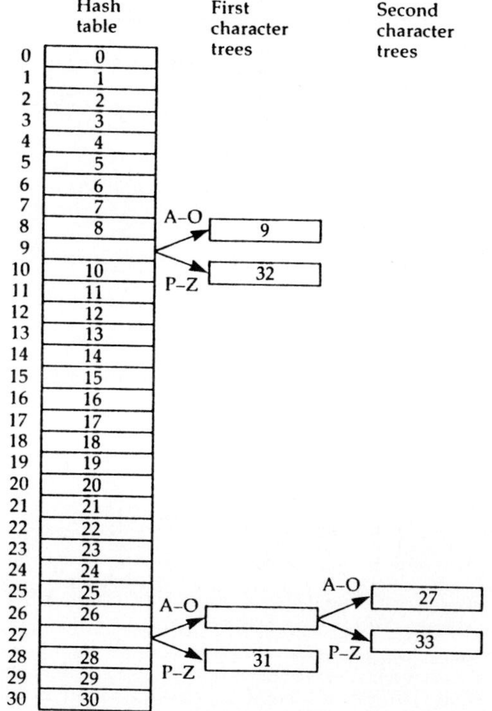

Figure 7.30
Dynamic hashing file after LOX is added

	Data file	
0	THEY	
1	A	ON
2	WITH	
3	BUT	
4		
5	WAS	
6	THIS	
7	IN	BE
8		
9	OF	I
10		
11	AND	
12		
13	HE	HAD
14	AN	
15		
16		
17		
18	AS	HIS
19		
20		
21	AT	NOT
22	ARE	FROM
23		
24		
25	THE	
26	IS	HAVE
27	FOR	**LOX**
28		
29	IT	OR
30		
31	TO	TAN
32	THAT	
33	BY	

File_Type, where one element or component of the file is a record containing an integer key field and an information field (info). Such a file is stored on secondary storage devices; the declaration does not specify length as the declaration of an array does. In a file declaration only the type of each component is specified.

The operations described in Chapter 2 for nontext files (Create, Open, and Close) are the same whether the nontext file is accessed sequentially or randomly. The default access mode for the procedure Create is the mode INOUT_FILE for Direct_IO. The physical size of the created direct file is *implementation-dependent*. The six operations available for direct input and output are described in this section.

Output to a direct file involves the Ada output procedure Write, of which there are two forms:

```
PROCEDURE Write ( file : In File_Type;
                  item : Element_Type );

PROCEDURE Write ( file : In File_Type;
                  item : Element_Type;
                  to   : Positive_Count );
```

The second form sets the current index of the given file to the index value specified by the parameter to. Then, for both forms of the Write, the value of item is written to the file named into the position specified by the current_index. Finally the current_index is increased by one. The first form of the Write is the same as for sequential nontext files. The second form allows the current_index to be modified before the contents of item are output. The exception Mode_Error is raised if the mode is IN_FILE. The exception Use_Error is raised if the capacity of the external file is exceeded. The exception Status_Error is raised if the file is not open.

Input from a direct file in Ada involves the procedure Read, of which there are two forms:

```
PROCEDURE Read ( file : File_Type;
                 item : Out Element_Type );
PROCEDURE Read ( file : File_Type;
                 item : Out Element_Type;
                 from : Positive_Count );
```

The second form sets the current_index of the given file to the index value specified by the parameter from. Then, for both forms, the Read inputs the element from the file in the position specified by the current_index and returns the data in item. Finally the current_index is increased by one. The first form of the Read is the same as for sequential nontext files. The second form allows the current_index to be modified before the element in position current_index is input. The exception Mode_Error is raised if the mode is OUT_FILE. The exception End_Error is raised if the index to be used exceeds the size of the external file. The exception Data_Error is raised if the element read cannot be interpreted as a value of the type Element_Type; however, an implementation is allowed to omit this check if performing the check is too complex. The exception `Status_Error` is raised if the file is not open.

The `current_index` of a direct file can be set by the procedure `Set_Index`:

```
PROCEDURE Set_Index ( file : In File_Type;
                      to : In Positive_Count );
```

`Set_Index` operates on a file of any mode, and it sets the `current_index` of the given file to the index value specified by the parameter `to` (which may exceed the `current_size` of the file). The exception `Status_Error` is raised if the file is not open.

The function `Index` interrogates the value of `current_index`.

```
FUNCTION Index ( file : In File_Type ) Return Positive_Count;
```

`Index` operates on a file of any mode, and it returns the `current_index` of the file named in the parameter `file`. The exception `Status_Error` is raised if the file is not open.

The function `Size` interrogates the value of `current_size`:

```
FUNCTION Size ( file : In File_Type ) Return Count;
```

`Size` operates on a file of any mode, and it returns the `current_size` of the file named in the parameter `file`. The exception `Status_Error` is raised if the file is not open.

A program that is reading a direct file in a sequential fashion (using the first form of the `Read`) needs to be able to detect when the end of the file has been reached. The function `End_Of_File` checks the `current_index` of a file.

```
FUNCTION End_Of_File ( file : In File_Type ) Return Boolean;
```

`End_of_File` operates on a file of mode `IN_FILE` or `INOUT_FILE`. If the `current_index` of the file named in the parameter `file` exceeds the size of the external file, the function returns `TRUE`; otherwise, the function returns `FALSE`. The exception `Status_Error` is raised if the file is not open.

A direct file may be created using sequential access or random access. When using sequential access, the records of data are written to the direct file in a sequential order; the first record is stored in position 1, the second record is stored in position 2, the third record is stored in position 3, and so on. This scheme for creating the file is often used when a directory is to accompany the file to provide indirect access.

When building a direct file using random access, the key of the record is hashed to a random position; records can be inserted in random order. However, for hashed files, the direct file must first be skeletonized with dummy records; this is usually done in a sequential fashion. The skeletonization of the direct file with dummy records involves initializing the record with dummy information. For example, character fields might be filled with spaces, and numeric fields and link fields for chaining synonyms might be filled with zeros. The dummy record is written to each record position in the file of n record positions. The skeletonization ensures that the empty record positions can be recognized because the fields in the record have spaces and zeros. Once the file has been skeletonized, records can be stored randomly in the file.

Algorithm 7.1 creates a direct file by using random access. It is a one-pass algorithm that uses a separate overflow area for storing synonyms. Algorithm 7.1 also uses the chaining method to link all synonyms—including the record in the hashed position and all synonyms in the overflow area.

`Direct_IO` can never be instantiated with an unconstrained record. The synonym field of the record for the direct file should be of subtype `Positive_Count` since that is the data type of the address of a synonym. However, `Positive_Count` does not exist as a subtype until the package `Direct_IO` is instantiated. Therefore, the synonym field cannot be subtype `Positive_Count`. The synonym field is, instead, type `Integer`, which must be converted to subtype `Positive_Count` before use as an index in a subsequent Read or Write to the direct file. Algorithm 7.1 contains conversions between type `Integer` and subtype `Positive_Count` where necessary.

ALGORITHM 7.1 Direct File Creation

```
TYPE InputFile_Record_Type Is Record
                                          -- specification of fields
                                          -- including key : Key_Type
                                      End Record
TYPE Direct_File_Record_Type Is Record
                                             info : InputFile_Record_Type
                                             synonym : Integer
                                         End Record
PACKAGE Seq_IO Is New Sequential_IO ( InputFile_Record_Type )
PACKAGE Dir_IO Is New Direct_IO ( Direct_File_Record_Type )
direct_file : Dir_IO.File_Type
dummy_record : Direct_File_Record_Type
inputfile : Seq_IO.File_Type
inputfile_record : InputFile_Record_Type
number_of_records : Positive
random_record : Direct_File_Record_Type
record_index : Dir_IO.Positive_Count
                           -- skeletonize the direct file

     Create ( direct_file )
     Initialize dummy_record to spaces and zeros
     dummy_record.synonym ← −1
     set number_of_records in direct_file
     For i ← 1 .. number_of_records Loop
          Write ( direct_file, dummy_record )
     End Loop
     Close ( direct_file )
     Open ( direct_file )
```

```
Open ( inputfile )
Loop
     Exit When End_Of_File ( inputfile )

                    -- input each record from inputfile, hash the key
                    --  and store in the relativefile

     Get_a_record_from_inputfile
     record_index ← Hash ( key_from_inputfile_record )
     Read ( direct_file, random_record, record_index )

                    -- if the random_record is a dummy record
                    -- the hashed position is empty and the
                    -- inputfile_record can be put into this empty
                    -- position

     If random_record = spaces and zeros
          random_record.info ← inputfile_record
          Write ( direct_file, random_record, record_index )

     Else
                    -- the hashed position is full so call
                    -- procedure Overflow to store the synonym in
                    -- the next available position in the overflow
                    -- area and link the record with all other
                    -- synonyms of this hashed address

           Overflow
        End If
End Loop
Close ( direct_file )

PROCEDURE Overflow
     next : Integer ← Integer ( Dir_IO.Size ( direct_file ) ) + 1

     hold_record : Direct_File_Record_Type ← ( inputfile_record, random_record.synonym
     random_record.synonym ← next

                    -- store relative_record back to hashed address
                    -- with link changed to include new record

     Write ( direct_file, random_record, record_index )

                    -- store the hold_record (new record) in
                    -- position next and increment next

     Write ( direct_file, hold_record, Dir_IO.Positive_Count ( next ) )
```

Once the direct file is created, the direct file can be accessed sequentially to list the contents by using a counter that takes on the values 1 through *n*. Listing the contents of the direct file after the creation is an excellent test to make sure the program performed properly. Algorithm 7.2 is the pseudocode for listing the file contents.

ALGORITHM 7.2 Listing

```
Open ( direct_file )
Loop
    Exit When Eof ( direct_file )
    Read ( direct_file, random_record )
    If random_record /= spaces and zeros

            -- skip dummy records

        print fields of relative_record
    End If
End Loop
Close ( direct_file )
```

Retrieving a record from the file entails checking the hashed address, and if the record in the hashed address is not the one being sought, a search of the linked list of synonyms is in order. The algorithm for finding a record in the direct file created previously (in Algorithm 7.1) is presented in Algorithm 7.3. The call to the procedure `Findrecord` is

```
previous ← 0
record_index ← Hash ( key )
Findrecord ( key, random_record, record_index, previous, found )
```

In this procedure `key` is the key of the record being sought, and if the key is found, the contents of the file location are returned by the procedure in `random_record`. The object `record_index` is the address of the home position. The object `previous` is returned by the procedure as the address of the record that is the predecessor of the record being sought (it aids in maintaining the file; `previous` facilitates deleting records, for example). The object `found` returns `TRUE` if the record being sought is not on file; otherwise, `found` returns `FALSE`.

ALGORITHM 7.3 Findrecord

```
PROCEDURE Findrecord ( key : In Key_Type
                       random_record : In Out Direct_File_Record_Type
                       record_index : In Out Dir_IO.Positive_Count
                       previous : In Out Dir_IO.Positive_Count
                       found : In Out Boolean )

Read ( direct_file, random_record, record_index )
If random_record.info.key = key
    found ← TRUE
Elsif random_record.synonym = –1
    found ← FALSE
Else
    previous ← record_index
    record_index ← Dir_IO.Positive_Count ( random_record.synonym )
    Findrecord ( key, random_record, record_index, previous, found )
End If
```

Updating the direct file with additions, changes, and deletions is simpler than updating a sequential file in that the direct file can be accessed directly. Each transaction key is hashed, a call to `Findrecord` is made, and if `found` returns `FALSE`, the record is not on file. In this case the addition transaction may be processed, but change and deletion transactions cannot be processed. On the other hand, if `found` returns `TRUE`, change and deletion transactions can be processed because the record has been found; addition transactions cannot be processed because the record exists already.

Deletion transactions require that the master record to be deleted be "marked" as inactive. (The master file is not copied during the maintenance run because it is in sequential files, so the record cannot actually be deleted.) The easiest way to mark a record for deletion is by returning that position to a dummy record as initially skeletonized; those positions can then be reused for later additions. Some methods of collision resolution may require an additional field in every record that is a delete flag, which indicates whether the record is active or marked as deleted. If a record contains the delete flag that is marked for deletion, the search procedure skips the record.

The transaction file and the direct master file do not have to be matched sequentially as with the sequential file. In direct files, transactions for a given transaction key are processed independently. If several transactions have the same transaction key, the transactions need to be sorted according to the entry date of the transaction. Algorithm 7.4 updates the direct master file.

ALGORITHM 7.4 Relative File Update

```
TYPE TransFile_Record_Type Is Record
                                        trans_key : Key_Type
                                        update_code : Character
                                        -- specification of other fields
                                    End Record
TYPE Direct_File_Record_Type Is Record
                                        info : InputFile_Record_Type
                                        synonym : Integer
                                    End Record
PACKAGE Seq_IO Is New Sequential_IO ( TransFile_Record_Type )
PACKAGE Dir_IO Is New Direct_IO ( Direct_File_Record_Type )
direct_file : Dir_IO.File_Type
dummy_record : Direct_File_Record_Type ← ( spaces & zeros, –1 )
random_record : Direct_File_Record_Type
home,
position,
previous : Dir_IO.Positive_Count
transactionfile : Seq_IO.File_Type
transfile_record : TransFile_Record_Type
                    -- input the next available overflow address
    Open ( direct_file )
    Open ( transactionfile )
```

```
Loop
    Exit When End_Of_File ( transactionfile )
    Get_next_trans
    position ← Hash ( trans_key )
    home ← position
    previous ← 0
    Findrecord ( trans_key, random_record, position, previous, found )
    Case update_code
        'A' → If found   -- record found
                   Write ( error_file, "duplicate add" )
              Else         -- record not found
                   Add_new_record
              End if
        'C' → If found   -- record found
                  Change_record
              Else         -- record not found
                  Write ( error_file, "not on file" )
              End if
        'D' → If found   -- record found
                  Delete_record
              Else         -- record not found
                  Write ( error_file, "not on file" )
              End if
        Others → print "invalid update code"
    End Case
End Loop
Close ( direct_file )
Close ( transactionfile )
```

```
PROCEDURE Add_New_Record

    If random_record.info.key = spaces
        random_record.info ← transfile_record
        Write ( direct_file, random_record, home )
    Else
        Overflow
    End If
```

```
PROCEDURE Overflow
    next : Integer ← Integer ( Dir_IO.Size ( direct_file ) + 1 )
    Read ( direct_file,  random_record, home )
    hold_record : Direct_File_Record_Type ← ( transfile_record, random_record.synonym )
    random_record.synonym ← next

              -- store random_record back with link field changed

    Write ( direct_file, random_record, home )

              -- store hold_record into position next

    Write ( direct_file, hold_record, Dir_IO.Positive_Count ( next ) )
```

```
PROCEDURE Change_Record

    make transaction change in random_record
    Write ( direct_file, random_record, position )
```

```
PROCEDURE Delete_Record
    previous_record : Direct_File_Record_Type
    If position = home
        If random_record.synonym = -1

                -- delete home position with no synonyms

            Write  ( direct_file, dummy_record, home )
        Else
                -- delete home position that has synonyms
                -- by moving first synonym from overflow
                -- to the home position

            position ← random_record.synonym
            Read ( direct_file, random_record, position )
            Write ( direct_file, random_record, home )
            Write ( direct_file, dummy_record, position )
        End If
    Else
                -- delete a synonym that is in overflow

        Read ( direct_file, previous_record, previous )
        previous_record.synonym ← random_record.synonym
        Write ( direct_file, previous_record, previous )
        Write ( direct_file, dummy_record, position )
    End If
```

CASE STUDY 7.1: THE CAR-RENTAL AGENCY

The data from the car-rental agency case study examined in Chapter 5 are used to create the direct master file using Algorithm 7.1, which stores the synonyms in a separate overflow area and chains them together. The data to be stored in the master file initially are listed in Table 5.1. Since the key (id number) is character data, the first letter and the last digit form the numeric key to be hashed, where the ordinal position of the first letter in the type `Character` is substituted for the first letter.

Thirteen records are to be loaded initially to the file, and some additions will be made later. A load factor near 80 percent is desired—13 divided by 80 percent equals 16.25. The prime-number division remainder method is used, and the divisor is 17 (the largest prime number close to the number of positions). Seventeen positions are allocated for the home area, and overflow positions are added to the file later as needed. The positions bear the indexes 1 through 17. The hashing function

hash (key) = (numeric key MOD 17) + 1

hashes the records into positions 1 through 17. Synonyms will be stored in the overflow area (starting in position 18 of the file), and the load factor is 76 percent.

Table 7.15 lists the keys and the hashed addresses of the records to be loaded to the master file initially. Notice that there are three synonyms for location 9—they will be linked together. The first step is to skeletonize the direct file with dummy records as in Figure 7.31. Dummy records include blanks in all fields except the link fields, which are initialized to –1 to indicate that the record has no other synonym.

Table 7.15 Car-rental agency data: Keys with hashed positions

Key	Numeric key	Hash (key)
C1	671	9
C2	672	10
F1	701	5
F2	702	6
F3	703	7
GM1	711	15
GM2	712	16
GM3	713	17
GM4	714	1
GM5	715	2
H1	721	8
H2	722	9
T1	841	9

Car-Rental Agency Direct Master File

	Id no.	Make	Style	Model	Mileage	Color	Link
1							–1
2							–1
3							–1
4							–1
5							–1
6							–1
7							–1
8							–1
9							–1
10							–1
11							–1
12							–1
13							–1
14							–1
15							–1
16							–1
17							–1

Figure 7.31 Skeletonized direct master file

Figure 7.32
Car-rental agency direct master file after creation

Car-Rental Agency Direct Master File

	Id no.	Make	Style	Model	Mileage	Color	Link
1	GM4	Cadillac	2 DR	Cimarron	63,000	maroon	–1
2	GM5	Oldsmobile	4 DR	98	11,000	green	–1
3							–1
4							–1
5	F1	Ford	2 DR HB	Escort	54,000	white	–1
6	F2	Lincoln	4 DR	Continental	38,000	black	–1
7	F3	Ford	2 DR	Thunderbird	35,000	blue	–1
8	H1	Honda	4 DR	Accord	32,000	yellow	–1
9	C1	Dodge	2 DR	Omni	25,000	grey	19
10	C2	Dodge	2 DR	Aspen	7,000	tan	–1
11							–1
12							–1
13							–1
14							–1
15	GM1	Cadillac	4 DR	Fleetwood	9,000	red	–1
16	GM2	Oldsmobile	4 DR	Delta 88	28,050	blue	–1
17	GM3	Chevrolet	2 DR	Camaro	33,000	silver	–1
18	H2	Honda	2 DR HB	Accord	11,250	brown	–1
19	T1	Toyota	2 DR HB	Celica	3,400	white	18

The result of creating the master file with linked synonyms is shown in Figure 7.32. Notice that the records are not stored in order by the key as they were in the sequential file. The order of records in the file is dependent on the hashing function. Each transaction record is input, the key is hashed, the record in the hashed position is read. If the record in the hashed position contains a dummy record, the transaction record is stored in the hashed position. Each transaction record—with the exception of the two synonyms that are not stored in the hashed position—causes one input access and one output access to the direct master file. H2, the first synonym, causes the following I/O accesses:

1. Hashed position 9 is input and is found to be occupied.
2. The link field of location 9 (-1) is stored in the link field of H2, which is written to position 18.
3. The link field of the home position (9) is changed to 18 and written back to the file.

Similarly, T1 causes the following I/O accesses:

1. Hashed location 9 is input and is found to be occupied.
2. The link field of position 9 (18) is stored in the link field of T1, which is written to position 19.
3. The link field of the home position (9) is changed to 19 and written back to the file.

Creating the car-rental direct master file takes two accesses for each of the 11 nonsynonyms and three accesses for each of the two synonyms. Therefore, the total number of input/output accesses to the master file is 28. To create the sequential file for the case study in Chapter 5 required 13 input/output operations. If each access requires 35 ms, the total time to access the direct car-rental master file during creation is 0.980 second; it takes 0.455 second total access time to create the sequential master file.

Transaction file T2 in Table 5.3 contains only one transaction, an addition of key GM6. The key GM6 hashes to position 3. The direct master update algorithm performs the following I/O operations to process the transaction:

1. Position 3 is input and found to be empty.
2. Transaction GM6 is written to position 3.

These two operations each take 35 ms or 70 ms total access time to add one record to the direct car-rental agency master file. The sequential file update requires 29 operations and a total access time of 1.015 seconds (1015 ms). In cases with a low volatility ratio, direct files with random access require less access time to make additions or deletions than sequential files. Figure 7.33 shows the direct car-rental master file after applying transaction file T2. The added record is shown in bold.

Transaction file T3 in Table 5.5 contains a number of transactions, including a group for one key. The deletion transaction F1 requires that the hashed position 5 be input and that a blank record be written back to the file into position 5 (two accesses).

Car-Rental Agency Direct Master File

	Id no.	Make	Style	Model	Mileage	Color	Link
1	GM4	Cadillac	2 DR	Cimarron	63,000	maroon	–1
2	GM5	Oldsmobile	4 DR	98	11,000	green	–1
3	**GM6**	**Chevrolet**	**4 DR**	**Cimarron**	**11,250**	**brown**	**–1**
4							–1
5	F1	Ford	2 DR HB	Escort	54,000	white	–1
6	F2	Lincoln	4 DR	Continental	38,000	black	–1
7	F3	Ford	2 DR	Thunderbird	35,000	blue	–1
8	H1	Honda	4 DR	Accord	32,000	yellow	–1
9	C1	Dodge	2 DR	Omni	25,000	grey	19
10	C2	Dodge	2 DR	Aspen	7,000	tan	–1
11							–1
12							–1
13							–1
14							–1
15	GM1	Cadillac	4 DR	Fleetwood	9,000	red	–1
16	GM2	Oldsmobile	4 DR	Delta 88	28,050	blue	–1
17	GM3	Chevrolet	2 DR	Camaro	33,000	silver	–1
18	H2	Honda	2 DR HB	Accord	11,250	brown	–1
19	T1	Toyota	2 DR HB	Celica	3,400	white	18

Figure 7.33
Direct master file after applying T2

The first addition, A GM7, inputs the hashed position (hash (GM7) = 4). The hashed position contains a blank key, so transaction GM7 is stored in position 4 (two accesses). The transaction C GM7 causes position 4 to be input in order to change the mileage and subsequently write the changed record back to position 4 (two accesses). The transaction D GM7 inputs position 4, and writes a blank record back to position 4 (two accesses). The second transaction, A GM7, performs as the first (two accesses). Processing a group of transactions for the same key turns out to be the same as processing independent transactions. Each transaction causes the input of one or more records and the output of at least one record. Each transaction is independent of the preceding or succeeding transactions.

The transaction D H3 is hashed to position 10, and position 10 is input to find key C2. Since H3 is not found in the hashed position, the link field of position 10 indicates where any synonyms are located. The link field of position 10 is –1, which indicates that there are no synonyms for this position in the file. An error message is output, indicating that H3 was not found. An invalid deletion causes one access to the master file.

The final two transactions, C T1 and D T1, cause two accesses each to first change record T1, then replace the key with a dummy key. Figure 7.34 shows the file contents after applying transaction file T3. The modifications made to the master file are highlighted in bold.

Figure 7.34
Car-rental agency direct master file after applying transaction file T3

Car-Rental Agency Relative Master File

	Id no.	Make	Style	Model	Mileage	Color	Link
1	GM4	Cadillac	2 DR	Cimarron	63,000	maroon	–1
2	GM5	Oldsmobile	4 DR	98	11,000	green	–1
3	**GM6**	**Chevrolet**	**4 DR**	**Cimarron**	**11,250**	**brown**	**–1**
4	**GM7**	**Pontiac**	**2 DR**	**Fiero**	**1,500**	**navy**	**–1**
5		**Ford**	**2 DR HB**	**Escort**	**54,000**	**white**	**–1**
6	F2	Lincoln	4 DR	Continental	38,000	black	–1
7	F3	Ford	2 DR	Thunderbird	35,000	blue	–1
8	H1	Honda	4 DR	Accord	32,000	yellow	–1
9	C1	Dodge	2 DR	Omni	25,000	grey	18
10	C2	Dodge	2 DR	Aspen	7,000	tan	–1
11							–1
12							–1
13							–1
14							–1
15	GM1	Cadillac	4 DR	Fleetwood	9,000	red	–1
16	GM2	Oldsmobile	4 DR	Delta 88	28,050	blue	–1
17	GM3	Chevrolet	2 DR	Camaro	33,000	silver	–1
18	H2	Honda	2 DR HB	Accord	11,250	brown	–1
19		**Toyota**	**2 DR HB**	**Celica**	**3,400**	**white**	**18**

The total number of accesses to the direct master file is 15. Each access requires 35 ms, so the total access time to apply transaction file T3 is 525 ms. To perform 27 accesses in the sequential file update takes 945 ms (almost double the direct update access time). For a low volatility ratio (42 percent), the direct file with random access requires much less time than the sequential file with sequential access.

The Ada implementations of Algorithm 7.1 and Algorithm 7.4 are presented in Appendix B. Figure 7.35 graphically illustrates the interfacing of the program components with each other and the external I/O files. The data structures, the instantiation of `Direct_IO`, and the hash function are encapsulated in a nongeneric package (`Ch7Struc`). `Ch7Struc` is shared by `Alg7_1` and `Alg7_4`. The use of a common package ensures that the exact same data structures and hashing function are used by both the create (`Alg7_1`) and the update (`Alg7_4`) algorithms.

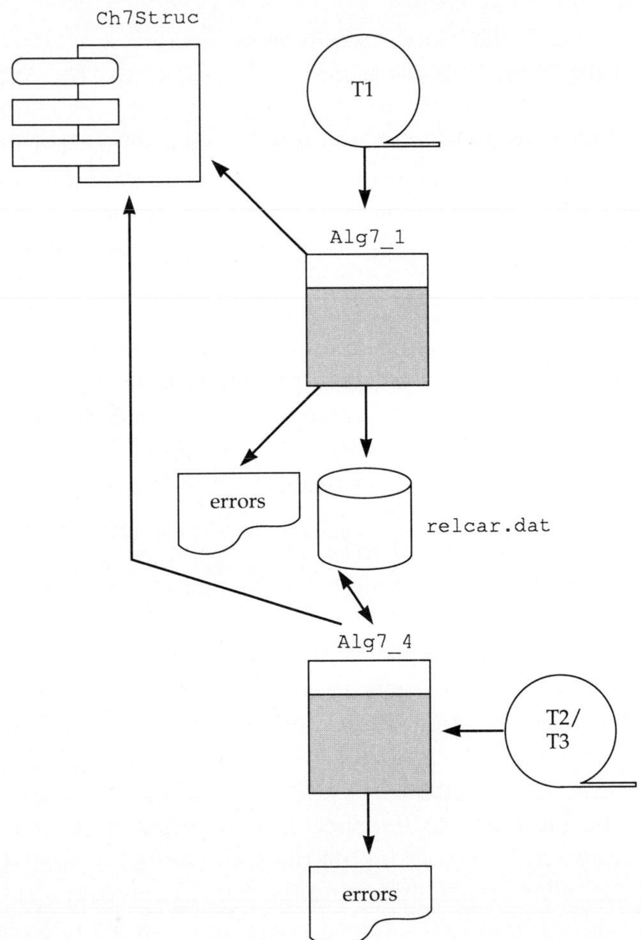

Figure 7.35
Case Study 7.1 interfaces

SUMMARY

Direct file organization exhibits a predictable relationship between the key used to identify an individual record and that record's absolute address on an external file. Relative file organization is a common implementation of direct file organization that uses relative addressing. Relative addressing refers to the address of a record in the file that is in the form of an integer record number relative to the beginning of the file. The first record in the file is usually numbered 0 or 1.

Relative file organization is a machine-independent implementation of direct file organization that is supported in several high-level programming languages: Ada, COBOL, FORTRAN, PL/1, and many versions of Pascal. Maintaining a relative file is simpler than maintaining a sequential file in that each transaction is processed independently; the transactions are not applied to the master file in batches.

Direct addressing is the most direct way of locating a record in a file since the key is the address of the record's location in the file. When the range of key values is larger than the range of record positions in the file, indexing techniques such as hashing, trees, index tables, inverted files, and multilist files determine the record's location given the key of the record.

Hashing is an indexing technique that allows sequential access by physical ordering of records (not key order). A hashing function is applied to the key value of the record in order to map the range of possible key values into a smaller range of relative addresses. A number of hashing techniques were discussed: prime-number division remainder, digit extraction, folding, radix conversion, mid-square, and perfect hashing.

The primary problem with all hashing functions is that the function does not always produce unique relative addresses. Hashing collisions are the result of this limitation. A number of techniques resolve hashing collisions: linear probing, establishing a separate overflow area for synonyms, double hashing into a separate overflow area, synonym chaining, bucket addressing, consecutive spill addressing, and bucket chaining into a separate overflow area.

Dynamic hashing is a technique that dynamically changes the hashing function to enlarge the file more easily. Each entry of the hash table containing bucket addresses is modified into a binary tree that contains the two bucket addresses when a bucket is split.

Relative (direct) files in Ada use `Read`, `Write`, and `Set_Index` procedures to move the file index to the specified record as indicated by the record index parameter. The `Read` inputs the record into the record object that is a parameter, after optionally setting the `index`. The `Write` stores the contents of the record object in the record position in the file referenced by the `index`, after optionally setting the `index`. The Set_Index sets the `index` to the value of the index parameter. To create a direct hashed file in random fashion, the file must first be skeletonized with dummy records (records that contain spaces and zeros for all fields) in each record location of the file. When the file has been created, a call to Close is made to keep the file on the disk. The algorithm for updating the file involves hashing the key of the transaction record, retrieving the record from the direct file (if the record exists), making a change to the record, and storing the changed record in the same position from which it was retrieved. The car-rental agency data used in Chapter 5 were stored in a direct file, and quantitative measures of random-access times were compared to access times of a sequential file with sequential access.

For further information and thorough performance analyses of hashing functions, the reader should consult the following sources:

Buchholz, W. "File organization and addressing," *IBM Systems Journal*, 2, 86–91, June 1963.

Chang, C. C. "The study of an ordered minimal perfect hashing scheme," *Communications of the ACM*, 27(4):384–387, April 1984.

Cichelli, R. J. "Minimal perfect hash functions made simple," *Communications of the ACM*, 23(1):17–19, January 1980.

Cook, C. R. "A letter oriented minimal perfect hashing function," *Sigplan Notices*, 17(9):18–27, September 1982.

Fagin, R., et al. "Extendable hashing: A fast access method for dynamic files," *ACM Transactions on Database Systems*, 4(3):315–344, September 1979.

Ghosh, S. P., and V. Y. Lum. *An analysis of collisions when hashing by division*, IBM Research Report RJ1218, May 1973.

Guibas, L. U. "The analysis of hashing techniques that exhibit k-ary clustering," *Journal of ACM*, 25(4):544–555, October 1978.

Jaeschke, G. "Reciprocal hashing: A method for generating minimal perfect hashing functions," *Communications of the ACM*, 24(12):829–833, December 1981.

Jaeschke, G., and G. Osterburg. "On Cichelli's minimal perfect hash functions method," *Communications of the ACM*, 23(12):728–729, December 1980.

Jensen, Kathleen, and Nicklaus Wirth. *Pascal User Manual and Report*. Third Edition. Revised by Andrew B. Mickel and James F. Miner. New York: Springer-Verlag, 1985.

Knott, G. D. "Hashing functions," *Computer Journal*, 18(3):265–278, August 1975.

Knuth, Donald E. *The Art of Computer Programming. Vol. 3, Sort and Searching*. Reading, MA: Addison-Wesley, 1973.

Litwin, W. "Virtual hashing: A dynamically changing hashing," *Proceedings of the Fourth Conference on Very Large Databases*, West Berlin, September 1978, pp. 517–523.

Lum, V. Y. "General performance analysis of key-to-address transformation methods using an abstract file concept," *Communications of the ACM*, 16(10):603–612, October 1973.

Lum, V. Y., and P. S. T. Yuan. "Additional results on key-to-address transform techniques," *Communications of the ACM*, 15(11):996–997, November 1972.

Lum, V. Y., P. S. T. Yuan, and M. Dodd. "Key-to-address transform techniques," *Communications of the ACM*, 14(4):228–229, April 1971.

Maurer, W. D., and T. G. Lewis, "Hash table methods," *ACM Computing Surveys*, 7(1):5–20, March 1975.

Scholl, M. "New file organization based on dynamic hashing," *ACM Transactions on Database Systems*, 6(1):194–211, March 1981.

Sprugnoli, R. "Perfect hashing functions: A single probe retrieving method for static sets," *Communications of the ACM*, 11(10):841–850, November 1977.

Key Terms

absolute address
associated value hashing
bucket addressing
bucket chaining
collision
consecutive spill addressing
current index
current size
dense keys
digit extraction
direct file organization
displacement
double hashing
dynamic hashing
folding
hashing
linear probing
load factor
mid-square
packing density
packing factor
perfect hashing function
prime-number division remainder method
quotient reduction
radix conversion
randomizing scheme
reciprocal hashing
relative file
relative record number
remainder reduction
secondary collision
separate overflow area
synonym
synonym chaining

Exercises

1. Using the prime-number division remainder method of hashing with $N = 101$ and assuming an EBCDIC representation, compute the hash addresses for the following set of keys:

   PAY

   AGE

   RATE

   NUMBER

2. Repeat exercise 1 using the ASCII representation of the keys.
3. Using an open addressing method of collision resolution with linear probing, obtain the file contents for the following set of keys:

   PAY and RATE mapped into 1

   TAX mapped into 2

   PENSION mapped into 4

   DEDUCT, STATUS, DEPENDENTS, SEX, SALARIED mapped into 8

   Apply the prime-number division remainder method of hashing with $N = 11$, and assume that the insertions are performed in the following order: PAY, RATE, TAX, PENSION, DEDUCT, STATUS, DEPENDENTS, SEX, SALARIED.
4. Describe the problems with linear probing.
5. Describe the problems in bucket addressing with consecutive spill addressing.
6. Compare the relative advantages and disadvantages of absolute addressing and relative addressing.
7. Discuss the advantages and disadvantages of a directory lookup table in memory for locating data in a relative file.
8. What factors affect the performance of a hashing function?
9. How is the performance of a hash function evaluated?
10. Compare the complexity of the nonperfect hashing functions presented in the chapter.
11. If information about a set of key values is not available, which type of hashing function performs the best?
12. What is the maximum optimum load factor?
13. Why does synonym chaining into a separate overflow area prevent displacement?
14. Describe the primary purpose of each of the following terms:
    a. hashing function

b. linear probing

c. double hashing

d. synonym chaining

e. bucket addressing

15. Explain two methods of collision resolution for bucket addressing.
16. Can a bucket size greater than 1 allow for variable-length records? Explain.

Programming Problems

1. Write a program that creates a direct master file using the prime-number division remainder hashing function and linear probing.
2. Write a program to update the master file created in problem 1. Count the number of accesses to update the file.
3. Write a program that creates a direct master file using the prime-number division remainder hashing function, linear probing, and synonym chaining (without a separate overflow area). Use the same data as in problem 1.
4. Write a program to update the master file created in problem 3 using the transaction file in problem 2. Count the number of accesses to update the file.
5. Compare the number of accesses computed in problems 2 and 4. Which storage method resulted in the fewest number of accesses to update the master file?
6. Create a directly accessed part master file that describes an inventory of parts from a nontext sequential part master file. Use Algorithm 7.1 to create the master file. The sequential master file has the following characteristics:

   key field = part number

   a nontext file of part data containing the following in each record:

   part number (10 characters)

   part description (26 characters)

   part price (float)

   The direct master file should have these characteristics:

   Key field = part number.

   Record positions 1 through 59 should be allocated for the prime data area of home addresses.

Record positions 60 through 99 should be allocated for the overflow data area.

Your program should perform the following operations:

a. Apply the prime-number division remainder as a randomizing (hashing) routine. Use the formula (key MOD 59) + 1 = range of 1, . . . , 59).

b. Use a linked list to link all synonyms, storing the first synonym in the home address, and all other synonyms in the next available position in overflow. The link field contains the index of the position of the next synonym or 0 if there is no next synonym.

c. Before attempting to write any information to the file, initialize the entire file of 99 record locations to a file of dummy records. Use blanks for part number and description and zeros for price and link field.

Use the following declarations in Ada:

```
SUBTYPE Key_Type Is String ( 1 .. 10 );
TYPE Part_Record_Type Is Record
                                  part_number      : Key_Type;
                                  part_description : String ( 1 .. 26 );
                                  part_price       : Float;
                                  synonym          : Integer;
                              End Record;
```

Here are some hints to help you achieve exemplary program style and clarity:

Output the new direct master file on the printer using Algorithm 7.2 to make sure the information is right. Be sure to skip over dummy records and not print them!

Print headings at the top of each new page. Do not print across the page perforations.

Tally the number of records input from the sequential master file and the number of records output to the direct master file.

7. In problem 7, you will randomly update the direct master file you created for problem 6 with input transaction records using Algorithms 7.3 and 7.4. Use a synonym link (integer). The input transaction file has already been sorted. Produce an updated direct master file (on disk) and an audit/error list (on the printer).

   The transaction file consists of:

   a. key fields = part number (major)
      update code (minor)

   b. a text file of update information containing several different formats:

- additions
  - update code (A)
  - part number (10 characters)
  - part description (26 characters)
  - part price (float)
- changes
  - description
    - update code (C)
    - part number (10 characters)
    - change id (D)
    - new description (26 characters)
  - price
    - update code (C)
    - part number (10 characters)
    - change id (P)
    - new price (float)
- deletions
  - update code (D)
  - part number (10 characters)

The output files should consist of:

a. direct master file (updated)

b. audit/error list with the following information for each transaction:
   update code
   part number
   error message (if any)

Your program should perform the following operations:

a. Read each input transaction record (without using standard input). Validate each transaction to ensure that it contains one of the three update codes.

b. Create a master record for each valid add transaction.

c. Change the appropriate master field for each valid change transaction.

d. Delete the master record for each valid delete transaction.

e. Identify the following error conditions:

Error condition	Error message
An add transaction that is already on master file	INVALID ADD-ALREADY ON MASTER
A change transaction that is not on master file	INVALID CHANGE-NOT ON MASTER
A delete transaction that is not on master file	INVALID DELETE-NOT ON MASTER
Invalid update code	INVALID UPDATE CODE

Here are some hints to help you achieve exemplary program style and clarity:

Tally the master and transaction record counts and print after audit/error list.

Using Algorithm 7.2, print the updated direct master file to make sure the information is right.

Print headings and page numbers at the top of each new page. Do not print across the page perforations.

8. You will create a direct master file from a nontext sequential part master file. The sequential master file has the following components:

   key field = part number

   A nontext file of part information containing the following in each record:

   part number (10 characters)
   part description (26 characters)
   part price (float)

   The direct master file has the same components as the master file in problem 6.

   Follow the hints listed in problem 7 and use the following Ada declarations:

```
SUBTYPE Key_Type Is String ( 1 .. 10 );
TYPE Part_Record_Type Is Record
                                part_number      : Key_Type;
                                part_description : String ( 1 .. 26 );
                                part_price       : Float;
                                synonym          : Integer;
                            End Record;

TYPE Hash_Table_Entry Is Record
                                part_number : Key_Type;
                                synonym : Integer;
                            End Record;
TYPE Hash_Table Is Array ( 1 .. 100 ) Of Hash_Table_Entry;
```

Your program should include the following operations:

a. Apply prime-number division as a randomizing (hashing) routine in creating the direct master file. Use the formula (key MOD 59) + 1 = range of 1, . . . , 59).

b. Use a linked list to link all synonyms, storing the first synonym in the home address and all other synonyms in the next available position in overflow. The link field contains the index of the position of the next synonym or 0 if there is no next synonym.

c. Before attempting to write any information to the file, initialize the entire file of 99 record locations to a file of dummy records. Use blanks for part number and description and zeros for price and link field.

d. As the direct file is created, create an internal hash table that contains part number and synonym for each record position in the file. As records are linked, also record the part number and synonym fields in the hash table to correspond to the direct file. The hash table will allow faster access to the record being sought and will use only one Read. The subscript for an entry in the hash table is the same as the record number where the part number can be found.

9. In problem 9, you will randomly update a direct master file with input transaction records. The input transaction file has been sorted. Produce an updated direct master file (on disk) and an audit/error list (on the printer). Use the direct master file that you created in problem 8. Use the descriptions for the transaction file and output files that you used in problem 7. Follow the hints listed in problem 7.

   Your program should include the following operations:

   a. Sequentially read the entire direct file and store the part number and synonym from each record in the corresponding position of a hash table as used in problem 8. The hash table will be used to chase links to locate a record to allow only one Read.

b. Read each input transaction record from a file. Validate each transaction to ensure that it contains one of the three update codes.

c. Create a master record for each valid add transaction.

d. Change the appropriate master field for each valid change transaction.

e. Delete the master record for each valid delete transaction.

f. Identify the error conditions listed in the table in problem 7.

Chapter 8

Search Trees

CHAPTER CONTENTS

PREVIEW

MOST HASHING FUNCTIONS RANDOMIZE KEYS to a file in a random (nonsequential) fashion, so sequentially accessing a random file from record 1 to record *n* does not indicate any ordering of keys. This chapter provides a description of several types of tree structures that are useful in sequentially accessing random-access (hashed) files. Binary search trees, AVL trees, *m*-way search trees, B-trees, B^+-trees, and B^*-trees are discussed. Of all the tree structures discussed, the B-tree (and varieties thereof) is the only external tree structure. B-trees are important because they allow efficient searching and updating of large data files. This chapter discusses the representation and manipulation of B-trees along with algorithms that describe the manipulation. The application of trees that allow sequential and random access to the hashed car-rental agency file created in Chapter 7 is presented.

BINARY SEARCH TREES

A **binary search tree** provides the flexibility of a linked list and allows quicker access to any node than a linked list. With a linked list each node contains one pointer to another node that follows as illustrated in Figure 8.1. With a binary search tree, each node contains two pointers to two other nodes: the left pointer to a subtree containing values less than the current node and a right pointer to a subtree containing values greater than the current node (Figure 8.2). A search through the binary tree in Figure 8.2 is as efficient as a binary search through an array in terms of the number of nodes that are visited.

Since values are ordered in the tree from the left subtree to the right subtree, we can reference the immediate predecessor and immediate successor of a node. The **immediate predecessor** of a node is the largest value in the left subtree. The immediate predecessor is located by choosing the left pointer and chasing right pointers until a node is reached with a null right pointer. For example, the immediate predecessor of node 50 can be found by choosing the left pointer to 30, then chasing right pointers until a node contains a null right pointer. The value 40 is the largest value in the left subtree and thus the immediate predecessor of 50.

Figure 8.1
A linked list

Figure 8.2
Binary tree

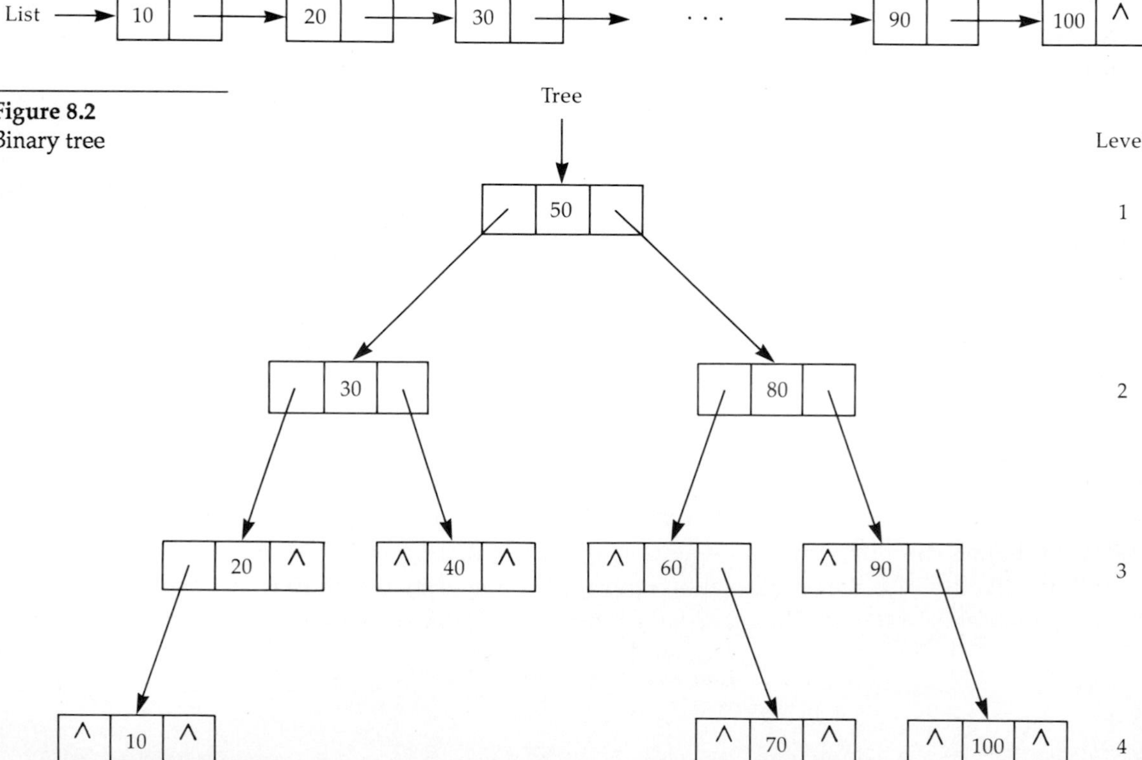

The **immediate successor** of a node is the reverse of the predecessor. The immediate successor is the smallest value in the right subtree. Locate it by choosing the right pointer of a node, then chase left pointers until a node is reached with a null left pointer. Using this method, 60 is the immediate successor of node 50. If the tree is traversed **inorder**, we visit the left subtree, visit the root, and then visit the right subtree; 40 immediately precedes 50, and 60 immediately succeeds 50.

The **root** of a tree is the top node that is pointed to by no other node except an external pointer. `TREE` is the external pointer in the tree in Figure 8.2—it points to the root node 50. The root node 50 is the **parent** of node 30 and node 80; similarly, any node in the tree is the parent of all nodes pointed to by the node. Node 80 is the parent of node 60 and node 90. Nodes that point to no other node are **leaf nodes** or **terminal nodes**. Nodes 10, 40, 70, and 100 are leaf or terminal nodes. Nodes 20 and 40 are **sibling nodes** since both have the same parent (both are pointed to by the same node). Node 50 is an **ancestor** of all other nodes in the tree. Node 20 is a **descendant** of node 50. A node that is neither a root nor a terminal node is the **root of a subtree**—it contains all descendants and is at the same time the **child** of its parent node. For example, node 30 is the root of the subtree containing nodes 30, 20, 40, and 10 and is at the same time the left child of node 50.

The **level** on which any node resides is the distance the node is from the root of the tree. The root of a tree is on level 1. The children of the root of a tree are on level 2 of the tree. Nodes 30 and 80 in the tree in Figure 8.2 are on level 2, and nodes 20, 40, 60, and 90 are on level 3. (The distance is three levels down when starting at the root.) The maximum number of nodes for a binary tree of level h is $2^h - 1$. The **height** (h) of a tree is the number of levels of nodes contained in the tree. The height of the tree in Figure 8.2 is 4, and the height of the subtree whose root is 30 is 3.

The **degree of a node** is the number of subtrees pointed to by the node. The degree of a nonterminal node of a binary tree may be a maximum of 2 since the node may contain pointers to at most two other nodes. The degree of a terminal node of a binary tree is 0 since the node contains null pointers. The degree of node 80 is 2, while the degree of node 60 is 1. The **degree of a tree** is the maximum degree of the nodes in the tree. The degree of a binary tree is 2, which is the maximum number of pointers a node may contain.

The height of a tree is the most important characteristic since the height indicates the maximum number of nodes that must be visited (or compared) to locate a value in a tree. The height of a binary tree may vary depending on the order in which values are added to a tree. If the values from the binary tree in Figure 8.2 are inserted in ascending order, the resulting tree (Figure 8.3) is **skewed** to the right of the root. The height of the tree in Figure 8.3 is 10; the height of the tree in Figure 8.2 is 4. When searching for a value of 100, only four nodes need to be visited in the balanced tree in Figure 8.2; all ten nodes need to be visited in the skewed tree in Figure 8.3.

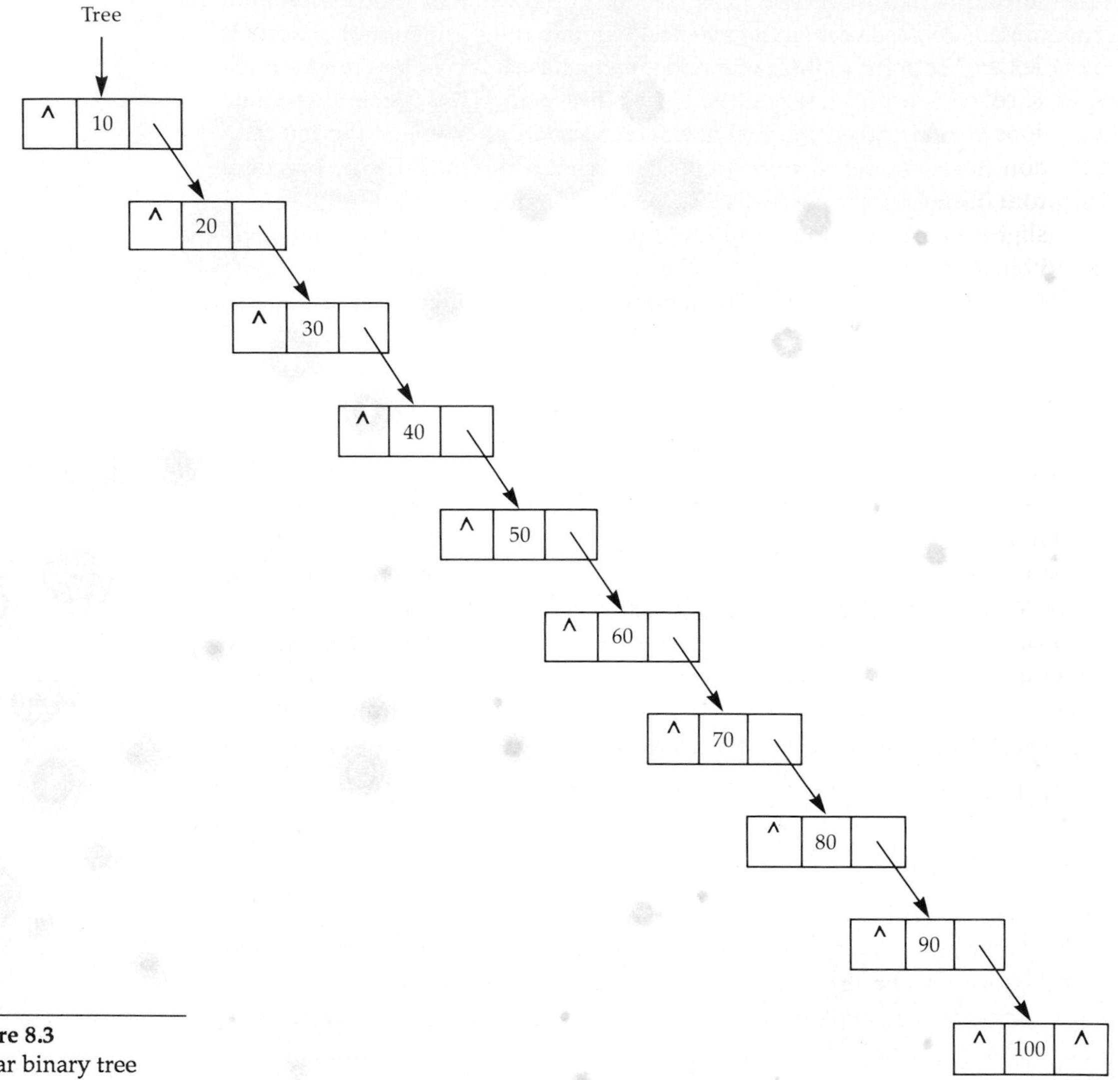

Figure 8.3
Linear binary tree

The maximum number of nodes, N, in the trees is related to the height as presented earlier:

$$N = 2^h - 1$$

Balancing a binary tree minimizes the height of the tree, making the tree more efficient to search. The minimum height, h, of a binary tree may be computed for a given number of nodes, N, by solving the equation above for h:

$$N \le 2^h - 1$$
$$N + 1 \le 2^h$$
$$h \le \lceil \lg (N + 1) \rceil$$

A **balanced tree** is one in which the height is a minimum for the number of nodes. Maintaining a balanced tree for dynamic insertions and deletions is complex and costly. On the other hand, balanced binary trees work well for a static set of values for which the balanced tree is initially built, where no insertions or deletions are made; search times are of the order lg(*N*). A variation of the balanced binary search tree that prevents the shape of the tree from becoming too far out of balance and that provides an access time only slightly less than that of a balanced binary search tree is a height-balanced binary tree.

HEIGHT-BALANCED BINARY SEARCH TREES

A binary tree structure that is balanced with respect to the heights of subtrees is a **height-balanced binary tree**, which was introduced by Adelson-Velskii and Landis in 1962 (see Knuth (1973)). This type of tree is usually termed an **AVL tree** for the authors' initials. The purpose of the AVL tree is to monitor the shape of the search tree and keep it close to a perfectly balanced tree (to provide a more efficient search time) without rebalancing the entire tree. If an insertion or deletion causes the tree to become too far out of balance, the tree is rebalanced. The definition of an AVL tree follows.

A nonempty binary tree T is height balanced when:

1. T_L is the tree whose root is the left subtree (left child) of T.
2. T_R is the tree whose root is the right subtree of T.
3. T_L and T_R are height balanced.
4. h_L is the height of T_L.
5. h_R is the height of T_R.
6. $|h_L - h_R| \leq 1$.

An AVL tree is simply a tree in which the heights of the subtrees of each node never differ by more than one level. Consider the tree in Figure 8.2: Node 50 is the root, node 30 is the root of the left subtree (T_L), and node 80 is the root of the right subtree (T_R). The height of the left subtree whose root is 30 ($h_L(30)$) is 2. In addition:

1. The subtrees with roots 10, 70, and 100 are height balanced since the left and right subtrees are empty.
2. $h_L(20) = 1$; $h_R(20) = 0$ and $|h_L(20) - h_R(20)| = 1$, so the subtree with root 20 is height balanced.
3. $h_L(40) = 0$; $h_R(40) = 0$ and $|h_L(40) - h_R(40)| = 0$, so the subtree with root 40 is height balanced.
4. $h_L(60) = 0$; $h_R(60) = 1$ and $|h_L(60) - h_R(60)| = 1$, so the subtree with root 60 is height balanced.

5. $h_L(90) = 0$; $h_R(90) = 1$ and $|h_L(90) - h_R(90)| = 1$, so the subtree with root 90 is height balanced.
6. $h_L(30) = 2$; $h_R(30) = 1$ and $|h_L(30) - h_R(30)| = 1$, so the subtree with root 30 is height balanced.
7. $h_L(80) = 2$; $h_R(80) = 2$ and $|h_L(80) - h_R(80)| = 0$, so the subtree with root 80 is height balanced.
8. $h_L(50) = 3$; $h_R(50) = 3$ and $|h_L(50) - h_R(50)| = 0$, so the tree with root 50 is height balanced.

Since the AVL trees are height balanced, random retrievals can be performed in O[lg(*N*)] time (the time is on the Order of [lg(*N*)]) if the tree has *N* nodes. A new node can be inserted into or deleted from the tree in time O[lg(*N*)], and the tree remains height balanced. To see the rebalancing that must take place after an insertion to keep a tree height balanced, consider the tree with one node in Figure 8.4. If the value 20 is inserted, the tree still meets the requirements of an AVL tree (Figure 8.5).

The insertion of the value 30 leaves the tree skewed to the right (Figure 8.6). The height of the left subtree of the root is 0, and the height of the right subtree of the root is 2; the tree is no longer height balanced. A simple rotation makes the tree height balanced again. The rotation is termed an **RR rotation** since the insertion has been made in the **R**ight subtree of the **R**ight subtree of the root causing the height to become too large.

Node a in Figure 8.6 represents the node nearest the insertion point where subtree heights differ by more than one level. Node b represents the child of node a in the direction of the insertion, and node f (which is null in this case, and not shown in the figure, since ais the root of the tree) is the parent of node a. Using these definitions, an RR rotation is defined as:

```
a.rightchild ← b.leftchild      -- rightchild of 10 is ^
b.leftchild ← a                 -- leftchild of 20 is 10
If f = null
      b is the new root of the tree -- 20 is new root
Else
      f.rightchild ← b
```

The tree at the bottom of Figure 8.6 is the result of the RR rotation. Node b is the new root, and the tree is height balanced.

The insertion of the value 40 in Figure 8.7 leaves the tree height balanced even though the subtrees have different heights. The insertion of the value 50 (Figure 8.8) leaves the tree skewed to the right, so an RR rotation is applied to the subtree that is not height balanced (the subtree with the root 30). The resulting AVL tree is shown at the bottom of Figure 8.8.

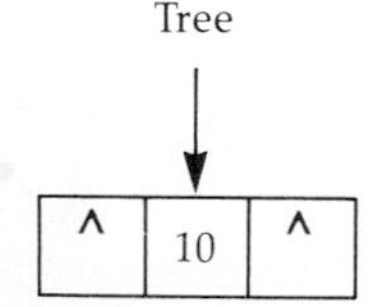

Figure 8.4
AVL tree with one node

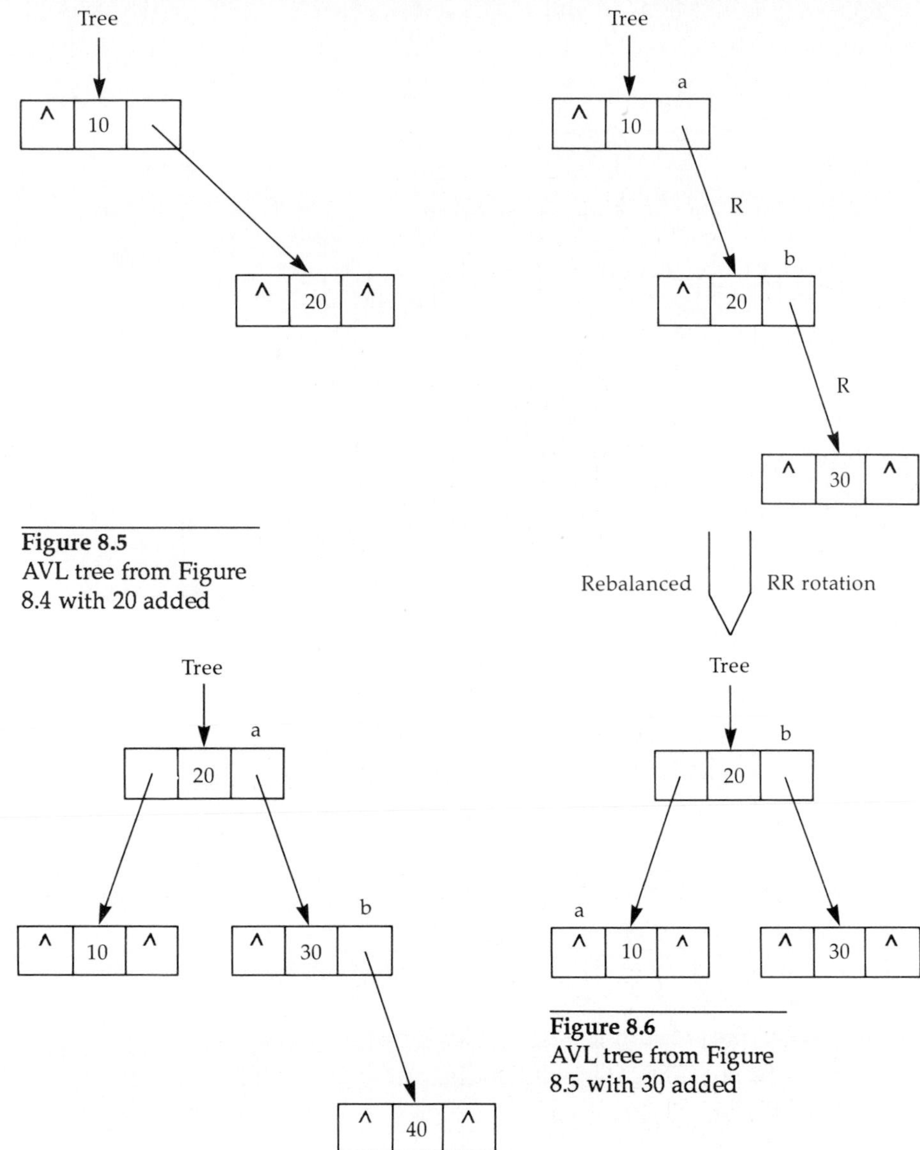

Figure 8.5
AVL tree from Figure 8.4 with 20 added

Figure 8.6
AVL tree from Figure 8.5 with 30 added

Figure 8.7
AVL tree from Figure 8.6 with 40 added

The insertion of the value 70 (Figure 8.9) again leaves the tree skewed to the right with labels a and b having the same definitions as before. Even though the tree after the RR rotation looks more complex than the RR rotations in previous figures, the same steps are involved. The immediate successor of node a becomes the right child of a, and node a becomes the left child of node b to move two nodes to the left subtree of the root; the tree is height balanced.

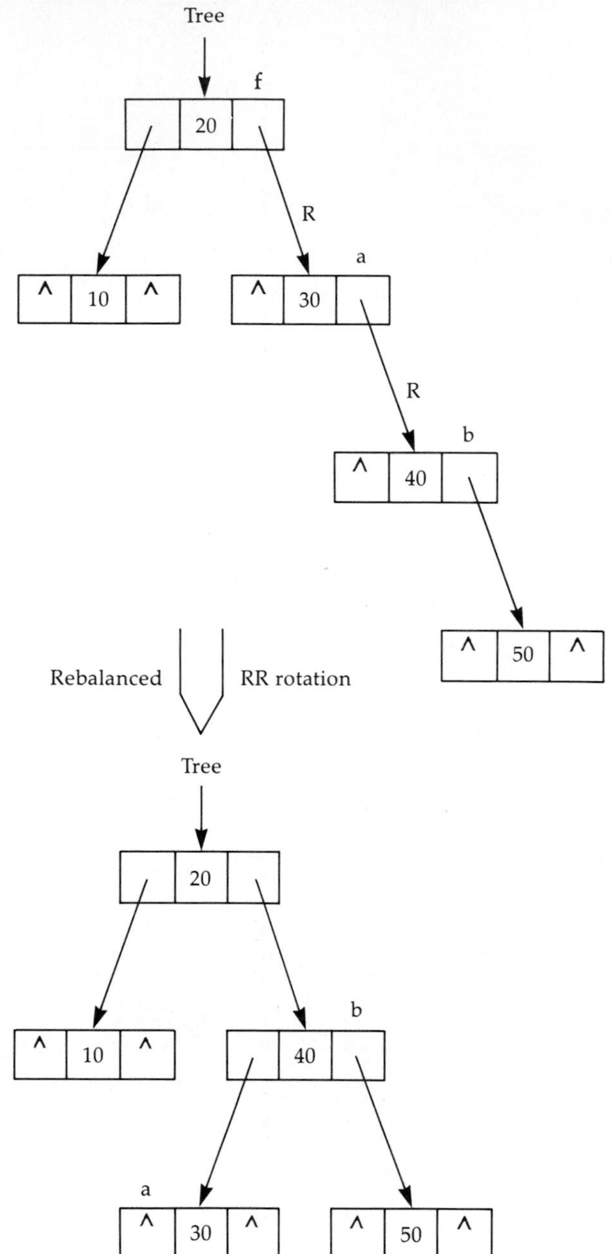

Figure 8.8
AVL tree from Figure 8.7 with 50 added

A more complex rotation is the **RL rotation**, in which the insertion is made in the **L**eft subtree of a node that is the **R**ight child of its parent (Figure 8.10). The insertion of the value 60 leaves the subtree with root 50 no longer height balanced. The nodes in the subtree with root 50 are rotated using the more complex RL rotation. The RL rotation requires that node `b` be the right child of node `a` (the R in RL) and that node `c` be the left child of node `b` (the L in RL). The steps of the RL rotation are

```
b.leftchild ← c.rightchild        -- leftchild of 70 is ^
a.rightchild ← c.leftchild        -- rightchild of 50 is ^
c.rightchild ← b                  -- 70 is successor of 60
c.leftchild ← a                   -- 50 is predecessor of 60
If f = null
    c is the new root of the tree
Else
    f.rightchild ← c              -- rightchild of 40 is 60
```

All insertions that leave the tree skewed to the right may be rebalanced using either the RR or RL rotation.

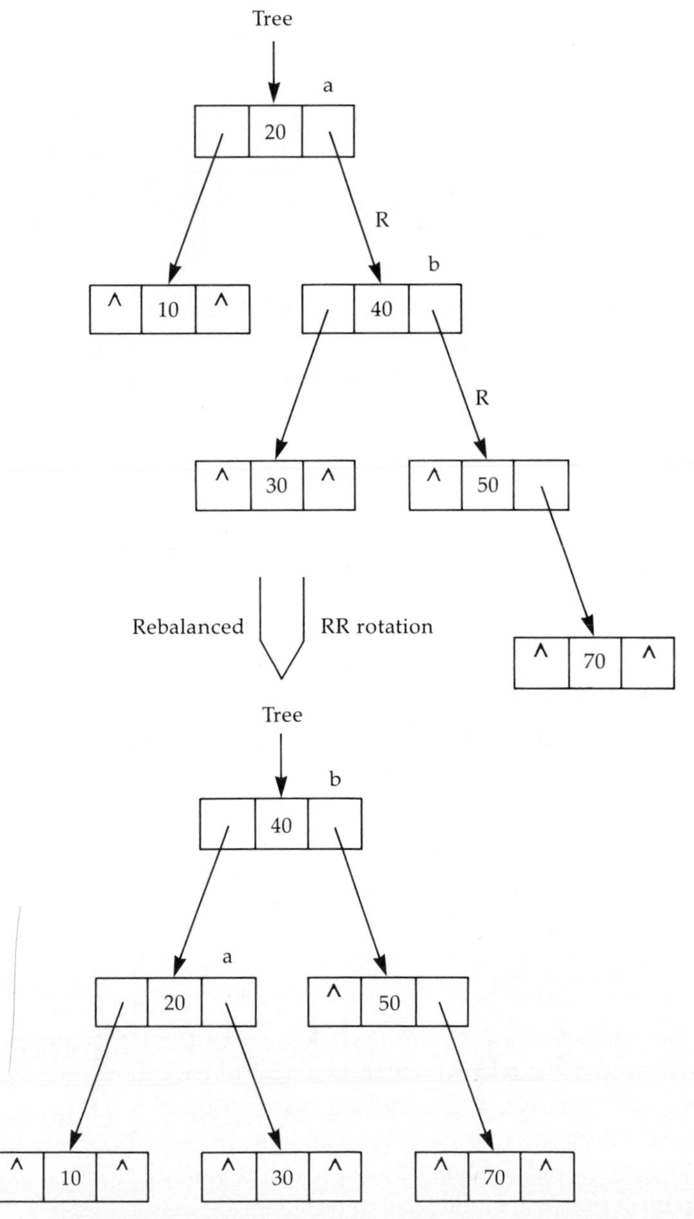

Figure 8.9
AVL tree from Figure 8.8 with 70 added

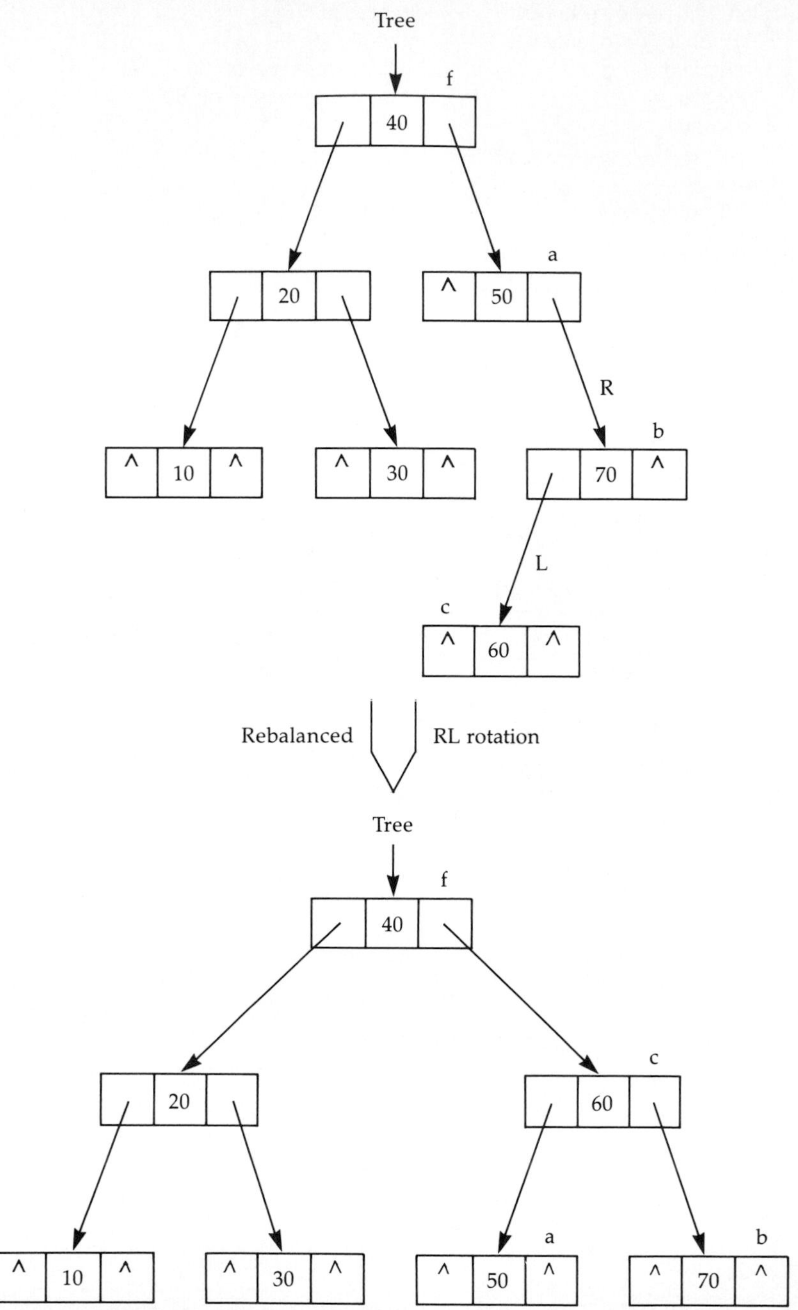

Figure 8.10
AVL tree from Figure 8.9 with 60 added

An insertion that leaves the tree skewed to the left requires rotations symmetric to the RR and RL rotations. The left rotations are LL and LR. Beginning with an AVL tree with two nodes (Figure 8.11), the insertion of the value 2 leaves the tree skewed to the left (Figure 8.12). An LL rotation makes 50 the new root, leaving the tree height balanced. The steps of an **LL rotation** are symmetric to the RR rotation and are defined as:

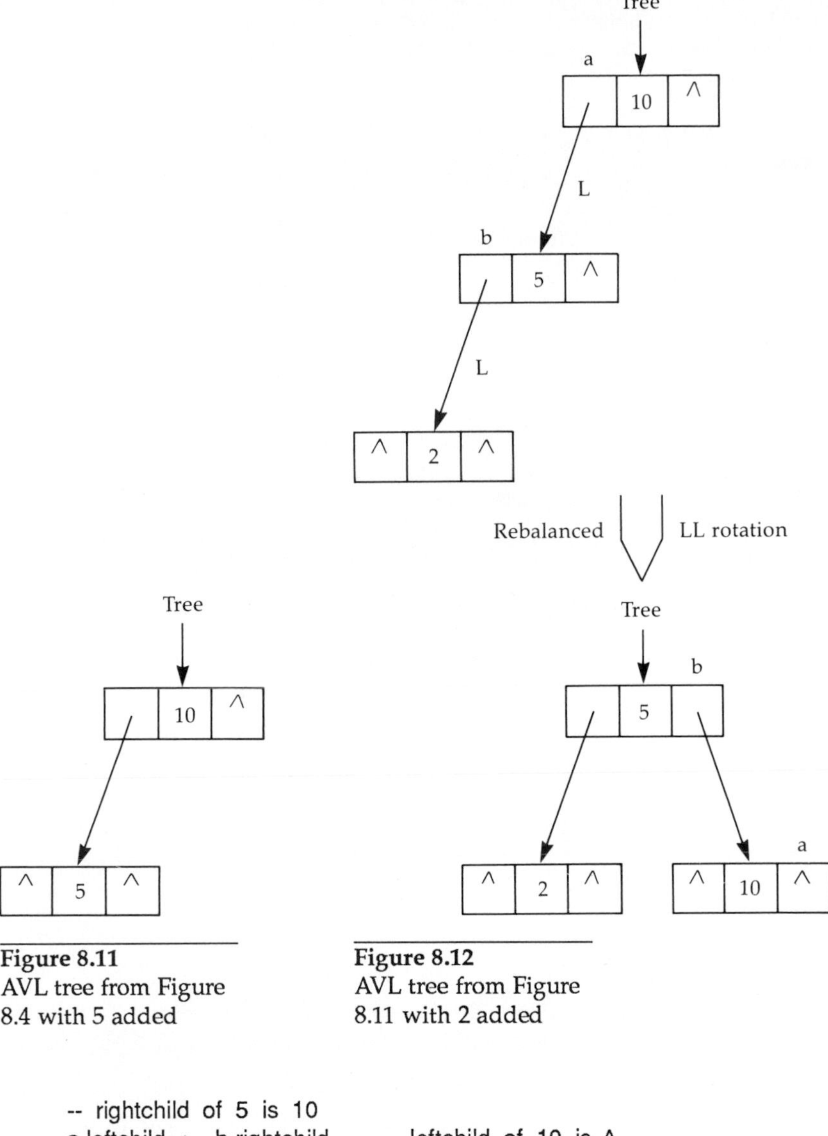

Figure 8.11
AVL tree from Figure 8.4 with 5 added

Figure 8.12
AVL tree from Figure 8.11 with 2 added

```
-- rightchild of 5 is 10
a.leftchild ← b.rightchild      -- leftchild of 10 is ^
b.rightchild ← a                -- rightchild of 5 is 10
If f = null
    b is the new root of the tree   -- 5 is new root
Else
    f.leftchild ← b
```

Adding the value 4 to the AVL tree in Figure 8.12 results in the tree remaining height balanced as shown in Figure 8.13. The further addition of the value 3 leaves the tree skewed to the left (Figure 8.14). The path is the **Right** child of the **Left** child of the root **(LR rotation)**. The LR rotation is more complex than but is symmetric to the RL rotation. The LR rotation is defined as:

```
b.rightchild ← c.leftchild        -- rightchild of 2 is 3
a.leftchild ← c.rightchild        -- leftchild of 5 is ^
c.leftchild ← b                   -- 2 is predecessor of 4
c.rightchild ← a                  -- 5 is successor of 4
If f = null
    c is the new root of the tree -- 4 is new root
Else
    f.leftchild ← c
```

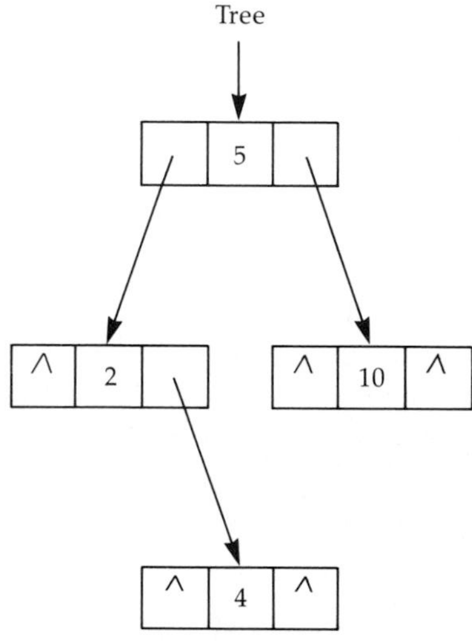

Figure 8.13
AVL tree from Figure 8.12 with 4 added

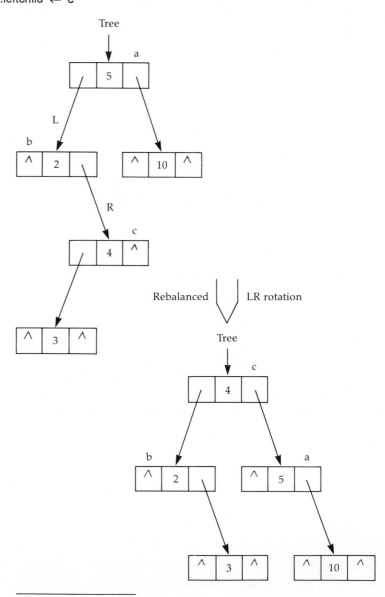

Figure 8.14
AVL tree from Figure 8.13 with 3 added

The four rotations presented rebalance the subtree containing the newly inserted value to keep the entire tree height balanced after each insertion. The same rotations are used for rebalancing the tree after deletions that leave the tree no longer height balanced. The tree is prevented from becoming too far out of balance to keep the access time to a minimum. Adelson-Velskii and Landis proved that a height-balanced tree is never more than 45 percent higher than a perfectly balanced tree with the same number of nodes. The height of the AVL tree has been proved to be

$$h \leq 1.4404\ [\lg(N + 2)] - 0.328$$

or O(1.4[lg(N)]). By rebalancing a subtree after each insertion or deletion, the number of nodes accessed to locate a value (height) is slightly more than the number accessed in a perfectly balanced tree (O[lg(N)])—all without the expense of rebalancing the entire tree.

The AVL trees that have been presented in this chapter are internal structures (that is, they reside in main memory). If the AVL tree is used to store keys of a random file, the tree must be built in main memory from the random file before lg(N) accesses could be realized. Building the tree each time the random file needs to be accessed could become expensive. An alternative is to store the AVL tree on disk. Then each node accessed from the tree is a retrieval from disk, and the maximum number of disk accesses for an AVL tree of N nodes is the maximum height of an AVL tree with N nodes ($\lceil 1.4[\lg(N)] \rceil$). If an AVL tree contains a million nodes that represent a million key values in the random file, the maximum number of node accesses (disk accesses) is 28. This small number of disk accesses is a lot better than sequentially searching the random file for a key value—the worst case of the sequential search is a million accesses to the random file!

Main memory is not always large enough to build a tree. Some structures contain a large number of key values, such as the tree in the previous example with one million. A special class of tree structures, called ***m*-way search trees**, addresses the class of trees that are too large to build in main memory or take too long to build in order to access a file. When a tree is stored externally, the number of disk accesses (the number of nodes visited) must be kept to a minimum or the access time becomes intolerable. Reduction in the number of disk accesses to tree structures stored externally can be realized with the use of a balanced *m*-way search tree instead of a height-balanced binary search tree (an AVL tree).

m-WAY SEARCH TREES

A balanced search tree in which all nodes are of degree *m* or less is an *m*-way search tree. Thus each node in an *m*-way search tree contains 0 to *m* pointers to other nodes. An m-way search tree T has the following characteristics:

1. Each node in the tree T contains the following information:
   n,
   S_0,
   $(K_1, A_1, S_1), \ldots, (K_n, A_n, S_n)$
2. n is the number of key values, $1 \leq n < m$.
3. $K_i (1 \leq i \leq n)$ is a key value, where $K_i < K_{i+1}$ for $1 \leq i \leq n\text{-}1$.
4. S_0 is a pointer to a subtree containing key values less than K_1.
5. $S_i (1 \leq i < n)$ is the pointer to a subtree containing key values between K_i and K_{i+1}.
6. S_n is a pointer to a subtree containing key values greater than K_n.
7. $S_i (0 \leq i < n)$, is a pointer to an m-way search tree.
8. $A_i (1 \leq i \leq n)$ is the address in the file of the record with key K_i.

Figure 8.15(a) is an example of a three-way search tree represented in diagram form; Figure 8.15(b) is the same tree showing the format of each node. To locate any key value, `search_value`, in the tree, the root node `a` is first examined for the value of i so that K(i) ≤ `search_value` < K(i + 1). In this case K(0) is a constant smaller than all legal keys (0 in this case), and K(n + 1) is a value larger than all legal keys (999 in this case). If `search_value` = K(i), then the address of the record containing K(i) is returned (A(i)). If `search_value` ≠ K(i), then the subtree S(i) needs to be searched for the value `search_value`. For example, if `search_value` = 60, the root node `a` is examined to find 30 < 60 < 70. `search_value` is not equal to 30, so subtree `c`, S(1), is searched for the value `search_value`. The node `c` is examined to find `search_value` larger than the largest key value, K(2), in the node: 50 < `search_value` < 999, so the subtree `e`, S(2), is searched next. In examining node `e`, 60 is found to be the only key value, so the search is complete. The address of the record in the file containing the key value 60, A(1), is returned.

Algorithm 8.1 searches m-way search tree `p` for key value `search_value` using the scheme discussed above.

ALGORITHM 8.1 Search

```
PROCEDURE Search ( search_value : In Key_Type
                   p : In Access_Node_Type
                   address : Out Natural
                   parent_node : In Out Natural )
index : Positive ← 1
If  p = Null  -- tree is empty
   address ← 0
Else
   Loop
       Exit When index > p.n
       If search_value > p.K(index)
```

```
            index ← index + 1
        Elsif search_value = p.K(index)
            address ← p.A(index)
            Return
        Else  -- search_value < p.K(index)
                -- Search subtree pointed to by S(index – 1)
            parent_node ← p
            Search ( search_value, p.S(index – 1), address, parent_node )
            Return
        End If
    End Loop
        -- Search subtree pointed to by S(n)
    parent_node ← p
    Search ( search_value, p.S(n), address, parent_node )
End If
```

The algorithm to search an *m*-way search tree is called with the following calling routine:

```
parent_node ← 0
p ← root of m-way search tree to be examined
search_value ← the key value to be located
Search ( search_value, p, address, parent_node )
```

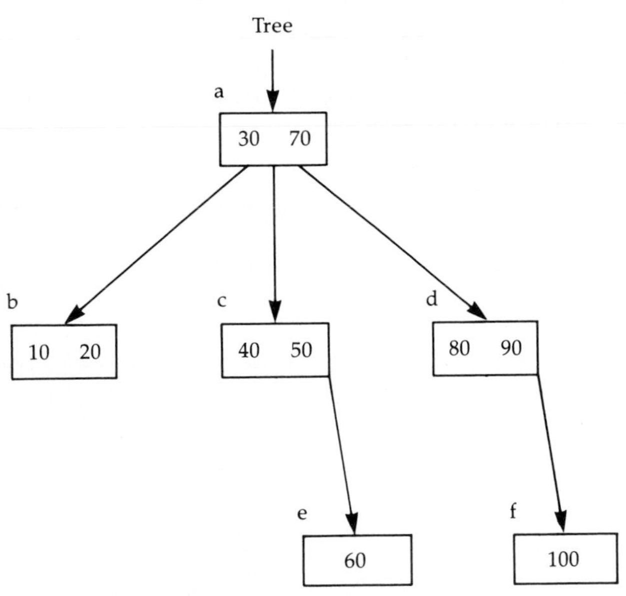

(a) Diagram form of a three-way search tree

Node	Format
a	2, b, (30, addr[30], c), (70, addr[70], d)
b	2, 0, (10, addr[10], 0), (20, addr[20], 0)
c	2, 0, (40, addr[40], 0), (50, addr[50], e)
d	2, 0, (80, addr[80], 0), (90, addr[90], f)
e	1, 0, (60, addr[60], 0)
f	1, 0, (100, addr[100], 0)

(b) Format of each node in (a)

Figure 8.15 Diagram (a) and format of nodes (b) for a three-way search tree

The value returned by the algorithm `Search` is either (1) the address of the record in the file (A(*i*)) that contains the key value located or (2) 0 if the key value is not found in the tree. If the address is 0, `p` = Null, but `parent_node` is a pointer to the node last examined when it was determined that the key value did not exist in the tree. When the key value does not exist, an insertion can be made into position `i` of `parent_node`.

The search for 60 reveals that `p` = node `e`, `i` = position 1 (K (1)), and `parent_node` = node `c`. The search for 45 reveals `p` = Null (45 is not found), `parent_node` = node `c`, and `i` = 2 (45 < K (2)). Since 45 was not found in the tree, 45 can be added (node `g`) as a child of `parent_node` (node `c`), with the address of node `g` being S(*i* – 1) or S(1). Node `c` now contains the following information:

2, 0, (40, addr(40), g), (50, addr(50), e)

Node `g` contains the following information:

1, 0, (45, addr(45), 0)

The tree with 45 added is presented in diagram form in Figure 8.16.

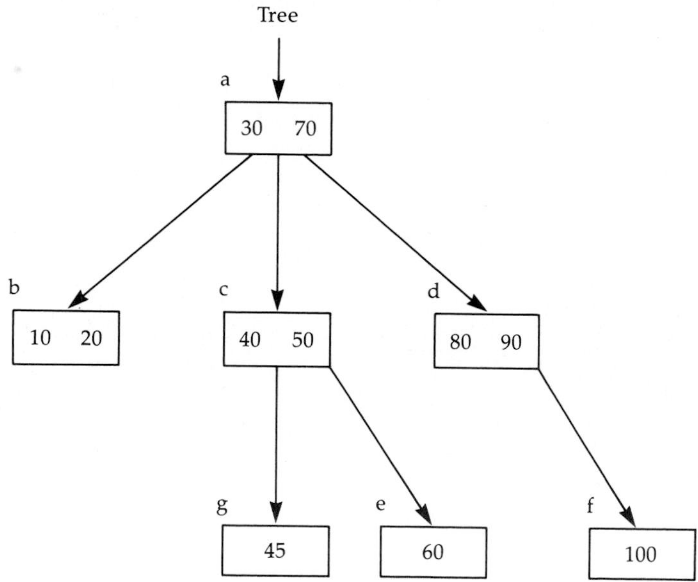

Figure 8.16
Diagram form of three-way search tree with 45 added

In analyzing the m-way search tree, the maximum number of disk accesses is equal to the height (h) of the tree. So the size of m needs to be increased to keep the height as small as possible. The maximum number of key values in an m-way search tree of height h is $m^h - 1$. The maximum number of key values in a three-way search tree of height 3 is 27 – 1 or 26 values. For a 200-way search tree with a height of 3, the maximum number of key values is $8 \times 10^6 - 1$. For a large m and small h, each access of a node from the tree requires the buffer for the file to be large enough to hold all the data in one node. For a 200-way search tree, the buffer must be large enough to hold n, S_0, and 199 tuples (a **tuple** contains the three values of (K_i, A_i, S_i)).

B-TREES

To give the best performance, an m-way search tree must be balanced. One type of balanced m-way search tree is a **B-tree** (named for one of its authors, Bayer, from Bayer and McCreight (1972)), which has the following characteristics:

1. A B-tree is an m-way search tree that is either empty or has a height ≥ 1.
2. The root node has at least two children; therefore, it has at least one value.
3. All nonterminal nodes other than the root node (with $S_i \neq 0$) have at least $\lceil m/2 \rceil$ children; therefore, they have at least $\lceil m/2 \rceil - 1$ values. ($\lceil x \rceil$ is the ceiling of x.)
4. All terminal nodes (with $S_i = 0$) are at the same level.
5. All nonterminal nodes with k S_is have $k - 1$ keys.

A B-tree of order 3 (degree of 3) must have a height of at least 1 and a root node with at least two children, and all nonterminal nodes (without any 0 subtree addresses) must have at least $\lceil m/2 \rceil$ (or at least two) children and as many as three children. The three-way search tree of Figure 8.16 is not a B-tree since nodes with $S_i = 0$ occur on levels 2 and 3. This violates the definition above. A B-tree of order 3 containing the data in Figure 8.16 is shown in Figure 8.17. The B-tree of Figure 8.17 has one more node than the three-way search tree of Figure 8.16, but the height of both trees is 3, which indicates that the greatest number of disk accesses for either tree is three. The B-tree is balanced with all 0 subtree addresses (S_i) on the same level. The three-way search tree has only two nodes with less than the maximum number of keys, but the B-tree has four nodes with less than two keys. These four nodes with less than the maximum number of keys allow for easy insertion of new key values without increasing the height of the B-tree.

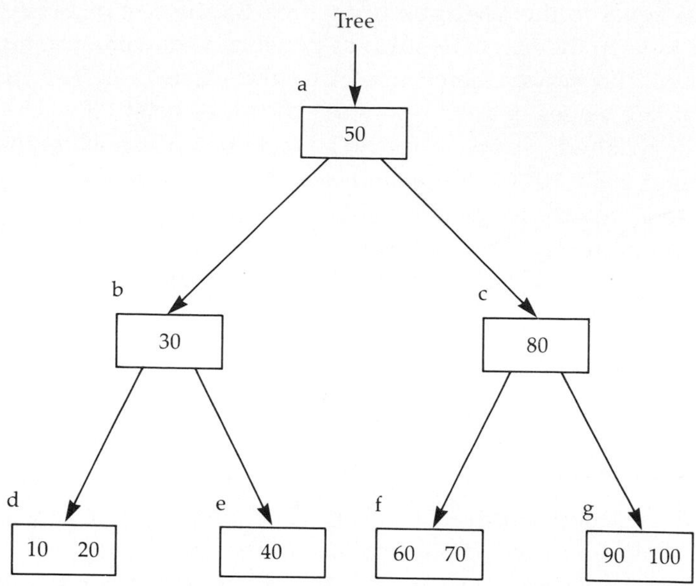

Figure 8.17
Diagram form of B-tree of order three for data in Figure 8.16

The B-tree is maintained in a balanced fashion so that after inserting and deleting key values, the B-tree always adheres to the properties listed in the definition. The B-tree is always the most efficient form for use as an indexing structure for a file where the *m*-way search tree could be unbalanced after several insertions.

The utilization of storage is an important advantage offered by the externally stored B-tree. Each node is at least half-full of key values. At worst a B-tree containing a total of N keys requires $1 + \log_{\lceil m/2 \rceil}((N + 1)/2)$ node accesses. If each node requires a disk access, the worst case is $1 + \log_{\lceil m/2 \rceil}((N + 1)/2)$ disk accesses—a number of accesses comparable to a perfectly balanced tree. These advantages allow for simple search, insertion, and deletion algorithms.

Insertions

Inserting 75 into the tree in Figure 8.17 calls for an attempt to add 75 into node `f`, which is already full. When 75 is added to node `f`, the information in the node becomes:

3, 0, (60, addr[60], 0), (70, addr(70), 0), (75, addr(75), 0)

Each node can hold only two tuples, so the node is split into two nodes of at least $\lceil m/2 \rceil$ key values. The $m = 3$ key values are equally distributed (split) between the current node and the new node. Since one node is split in two, an additional key needs to be inserted into the parent node to adhere to the requirements of the B-tree (two key values in node `c` for three child nodes). The middle key of the *m* keys is extracted and added to the parent node, and the two nodes after the split become children. The three keys in node `f` are split so that the keys lower than the middle key stay in node `f`:

1, 0, (60, addr(60), 0)

The keys higher than the middle key are split into node `h`:

1, 0, (75, addr(75), 0)

Nodes `f` and `h` become the children of node `c`. Then the tuple

(70, addr(70), h)

which is the middle key, is added into the parent of `f` or into node `c`. Since node `c` has only one tuple (80), the tuple (70, addr(70), h) can be added to node `c` as shown in Figure 8.18.

Inserting 55 into the tree in Figure 8.18 entails simply adding a tuple with (55, addr(55), 0) to node `f`, which has only one tuple (60, addr(60), 0). Figure 8.19 shows the tree after 55 has been added.

Inserting 57 into the tree in Figure 8.19 calls for 57 to be inserted in node `f` between 55 and 60. Node `f` contains the following data:

3, 0, (55, addr(55), 0), (57, addr(57), 0), (60, addr(60), 0)

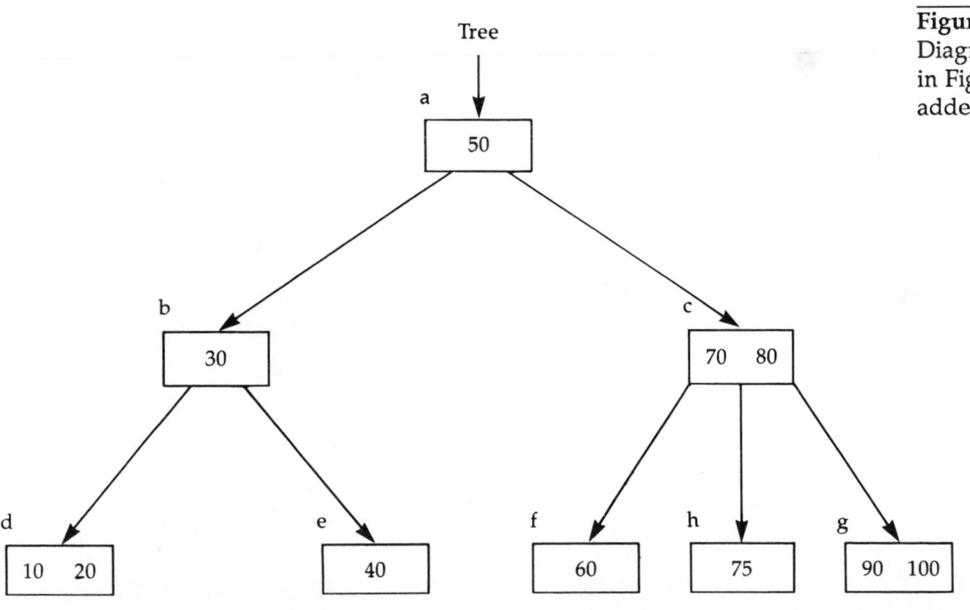

Figure 8.18
Diagram form of B-tree in Figure 8.17 with 75 added

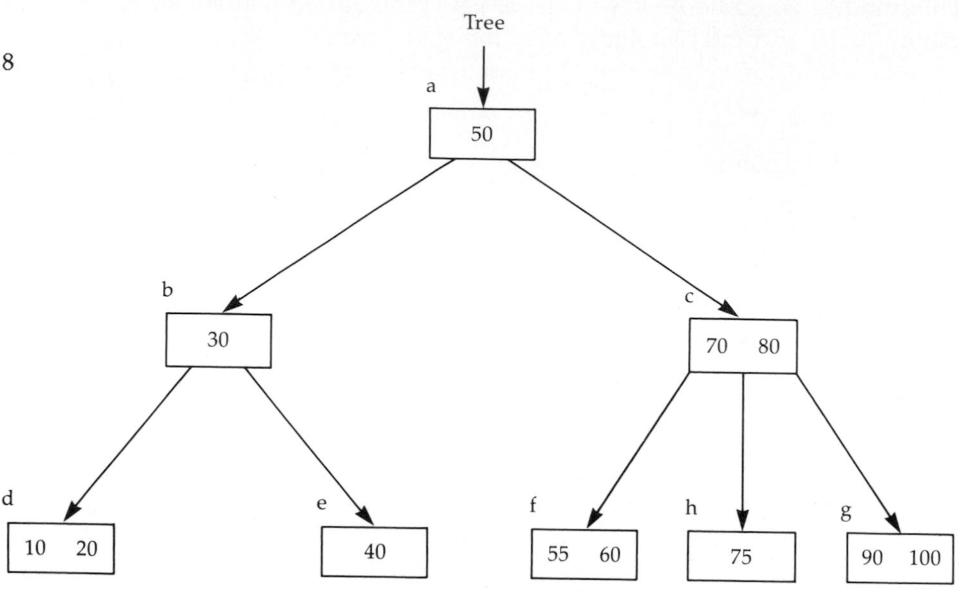

Figure 8.19
Diagram form of B-tree in Figure 8.18 with 55 added

In this case node `f` contains three tuples instead of two. Therefore, node f is split as before:

3, 0, (55, addr(55), 0), (57, addr(57), 0), (60, addr(60), 0)
    +++++++++++   ******************

New node `f` contains the tuples 1 through $\lceil m/2 \rceil - 1$ (underlined with plus (+) signs):

1, 0, (55, addr(55), 0)

A new node `i` with tuples $\lceil m/2 \rceil + 1$ through n (underlined with asterisks (*) above):

1, 0, (60, addr(60), 0)

and the tuple (57, addr(57), i) is inserted into the parent of `f` (node `c`).

Node `c` already contains the two tuples

3, f, (57, addr(57), i), (70, addr(70), h), (80, addr(80), g)
    +++++++++++   ******************

Inserting (57, addr(57), i) causes node `c` to be split into a new node `j`. Node `c` contains the data underlined with +:

1, f, (57, addr(57), i)

The new node `j` contains the data underlined with *:

1, h, (80, addr(80), g)

The two new nodes c and j are children of node a, and the tuple (70, addr(70), j) is added to the parent node a. Since node a contains only one tuple

1, a, (50, addr(50), c)

the node a now contains

2, a, (50, addr(50), c), (70, addr(70), j)

The resulting tree with the addition of the value 57 is shown in Figure 8.20.

The last type of change that results from an insertion is the growth of the height of the tree. Consider the insertion of 95, 85, and 87, in that order. The insertion of 95 into the B-tree in Figure 8.20 results in node g being split, 90 in node g, 100 in new node k, and the middle value, 95, promoted to the parent node j as shown in Figure 8.21. The insertion of 85 into the B-tree (Figure 8.22) fills node g with 85 and 90. Finally, the insertion of 87 into the B-tree causes the splitting of node g, with 85 remaining in node g, 90 being moved to a new node l, and the middle value, 87, being promoted to the parent node j (Figure 8.23). Node j has three values, which is more than the maximum number of two, so node j is split. The value 80 remains in node j, 95 moves to new node m, and 87 moves up to the parent node a (Figure 8.24). Node a is now above the maximum capacity, so the root node, a, is split: 50 remains in node a, 87 is moved to new node n, and the middle value (70) is promoted (Figure 8.25). Since node a has no parent (node a is the root), a new root is formed with 70 as the root. The new node n is the right child of the new root, and the old root is the left child of the new root. The tree has grown to a height of 4.

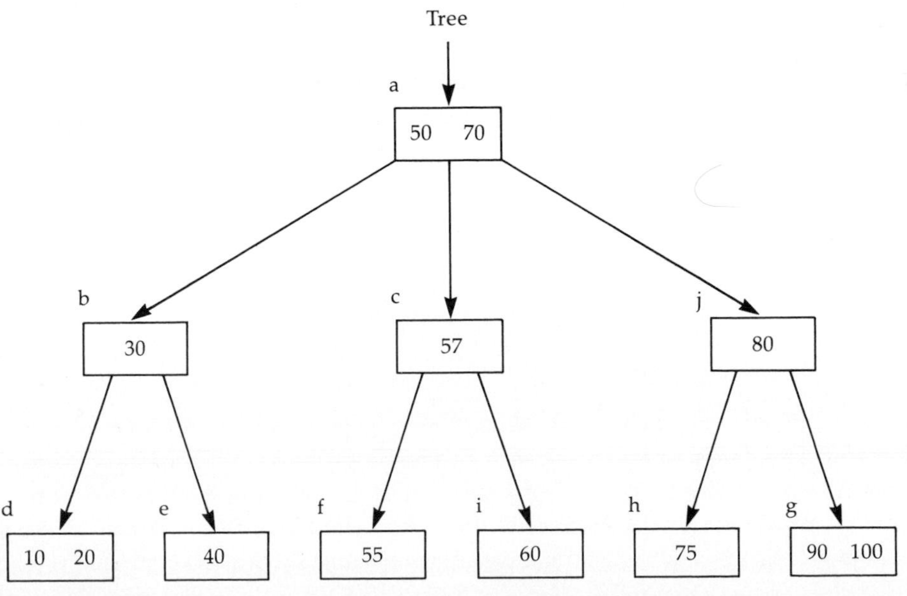

Figure 8.20
Diagram form of B-tree in Figure 8.19 with 57 added

Figure 8.21
Diagram form of B-tree in Figure 8.20 with 95 added

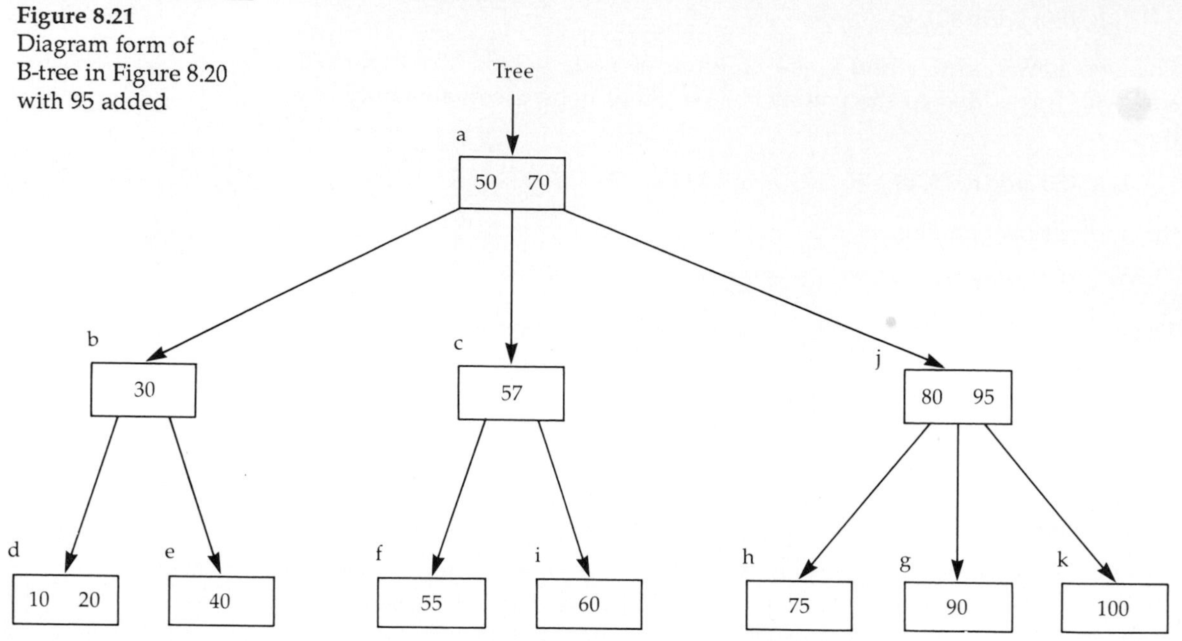

Figure 8.22
Diagram form of B-tree in Figure 8.21 with 85 added

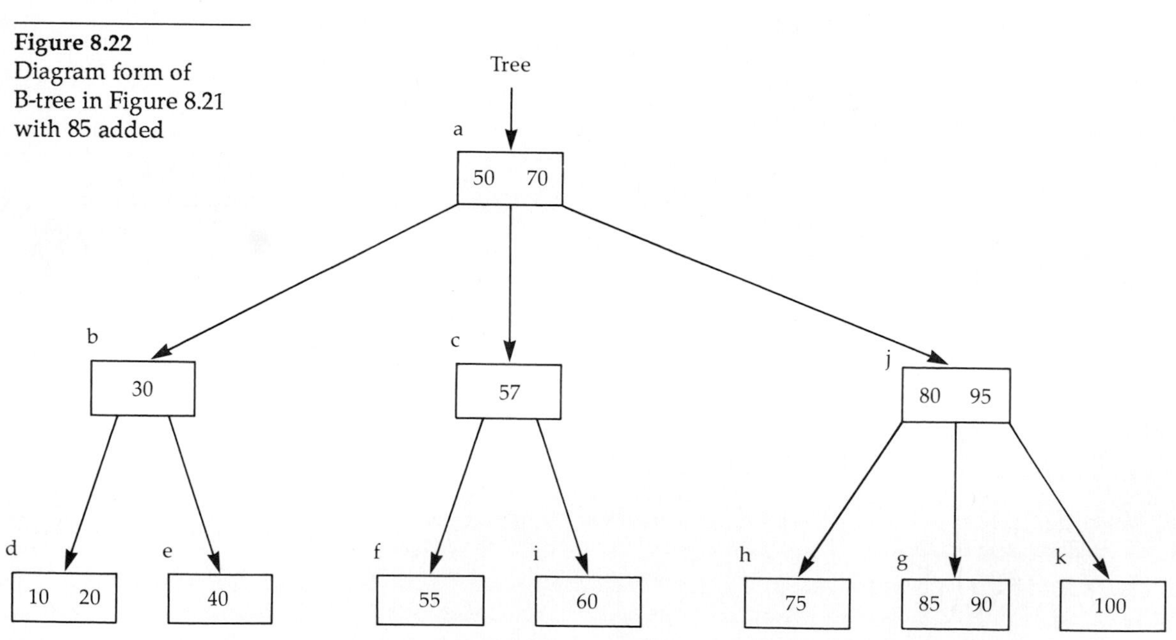

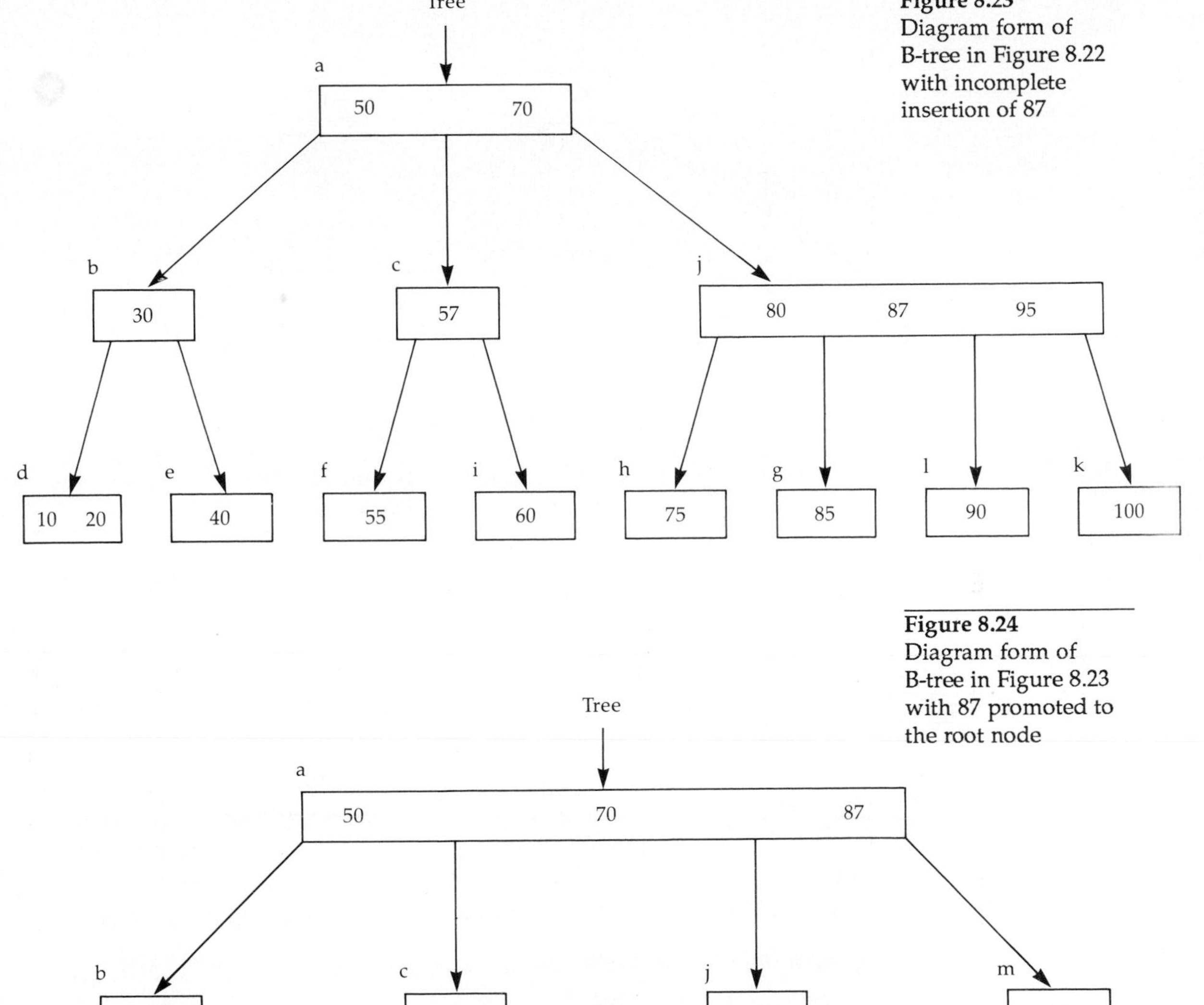

Figure 8.23
Diagram form of B-tree in Figure 8.22 with incomplete insertion of 87

Figure 8.24
Diagram form of B-tree in Figure 8.23 with 87 promoted to the root node

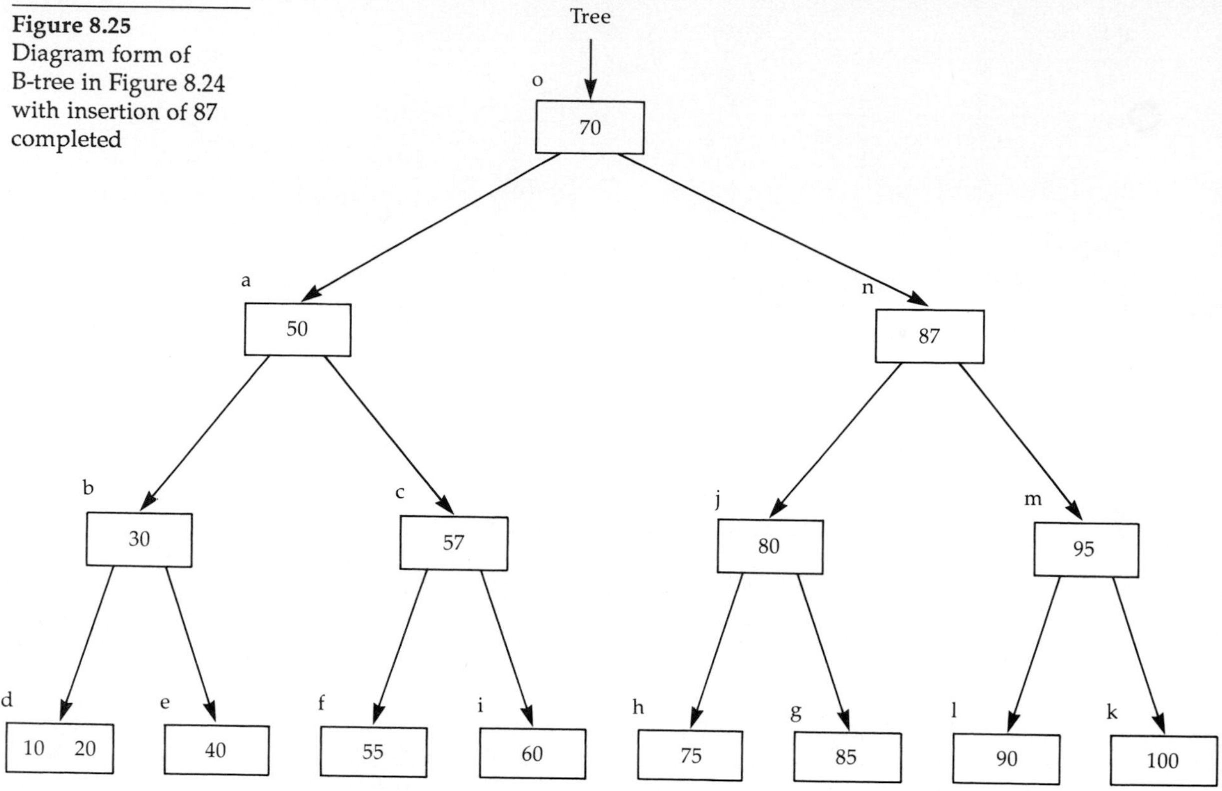

Figure 8.25
Diagram form of B-tree in Figure 8.24 with insertion of 87 completed

Algorithm 8.2 inserts a tuple `Key, addr` into B-tree `p` using the scheme described above. As a node is split, the middle tuple key value is withdrawn with the address of the new tuple containing the second half of the split node. It is inserted into the parent of the node that was split. To access the parent of the split node, procedure `Find_Node` is called recursively.

ALGORITHM 8.2 Insertion

```
TYPE A_Tuple Is Record
                    key : Key_Type
                    addr : Positive
                    s : Natural
                End Record
TYPE Tuple_Array Is Array ( Integer Range <> ) Of A_Tuple
TYPE Node_Type Is Record
                    n : Natural
                    s0 : Natural
                    tuple : Tuple_Array ( 1 .. degree - 1 )
                End Record
TYPE BigNode_Type Is Record
                    n : Natural
                    s0 : Natural
                    tuple : Tuple_Array ( 1 .. degree )
                End Record
TYPE Operation_Type Is ( INSERT_KEY, DELETE_KEY, NIL, SEARCH_KEY )
```

```
    PACKAGE B_Tree_IO Is New Direct_IO ( Node_Type )
    b_tree_file : B_Tree_IO.File_Type
    hold_tuple : A_Tuple
    key_found : Exception
    next : Positive;

PROCEDURE Insert ( key : In Key_Type
                   addr : In Positive )
    address_of_root_node,
    new_root_node : Node_Type
    operation : operation_Type ← INSERT_KEY
                   -- B-tree has been created with a null value
                   -- of 0 for the address of the root node being
                   -- stored in the field n
    hold_tuple ← ( key, addr, 0 )
    Input ( b_tree_file, address_of_root_node, 1 )
    Find_Node ( hold_tuple, address_of_root_node.n, operation )
    If operation = INSERT_KEY
                   -- hold_tuple becomes the new root of the tree
                   -- with the old root as its left child (s0)
                   -- as in Figure 8.25, where old root is node a
                   -- and new root is node o
        new_root_node.n ← 1
        Input ( b_tree_file, address_of_root_node, 1 )
        new_root_node.s0 ← address_of_root_node.n
        new_root_node.tuple(1) ← hold_tuple
        next ← Size ( b_tree_file ) + 1
        Output ( b_tree_file, new_root_node, next )
        address_of_root_node.n ← next
        Output ( b_tree_file, address_of_root_node, 1 )
    End If
EXCEPTION
    When key_found → Raise key_not_inserted
        -- key_found is raised by Find_Node
        -- if the key already exists in the tree

PROCEDURE Find_Node ( hold_Tuple : In Out A_Tuple
                      p : In Natural
                      operation : In Out Operation_Type )
    index : Positive

    If p = 0
        Return
    Else
        Input ( b_tree_file, node, p ) -- node ← contents of p
        If hold_tuple.key > node.tuple(node.n).key
            -- larger than the largest key in node
            index ← node.n + 1     -- search the nth subtree
            Find_Node ( hold_tuple, node.tuple(node.n).s, operation )
            If operation = INSERT_KEY
                Insert_Tuple ( hold_tuple, index, node, operation )
                    -- insert hold_tuple into position index of node
            End If
        Else     -- hold_tuple.key ← node.tuple(node.n).key
            index ← 1
```

```
                Loop
                    If hold_tuple.key > node.tuple(index).key
                        index ← index + 1
                    Elsif hold_tuple.key = node.tuple(index).key
                        hold_tuple.addr ← node.tuple(index).addr
                        Raise key_found
                    Else  -- hold_tuple.key < node.tuple(index).key
                        If index = 1
                           Find_Node ( hold_tuple, node.s0, operation )
                        Else
                           Find_Node ( hold_tuple, node.tuple(index - 1).s, operation
                        End If
                        If operation = INSERT_KEY
                           Insert_Tuple ( hold_tuple, index, node, operation )
                              -- insert hold_tuple into position index of node
                        End If
                        Exit
                    End If
                End Loop
            End If
        End If
PROCEDURE Insert_Tuple (hold_tuple : In Out A_Tuple
                        index : In Positive
                        node: In Out Node_Type
                        operation : In Out Operation_Type )
    -- Insert_Tuple is internal to Find_Node
    If node.n < degree - 1  -- resulting node is large enough for addition
        operation ← NIL
        For count In Reverse index .. node.n Loop
            node.tuple(count + 1) ← node.tuple(count)
        End Loop
        node.n ← node.n + 1
        node.tuple(index) ← hold_tuple
        Output ( b_tree_file, node, p )
    Else
        -- node is full so addition will cause a split
        Split
    End If
PROCEDURE Split  --internal to Insert_Tuple
    big_node : Big_Node_Type

    big_node ← node
    For count In Reverse  index .. node.n Loop
        big_node.tuple(count + 1) ← big_node.tuple(count)
    End Loop
    big_node.tuple(index) ← hold_tuple
    big_node.n ← node.n + 1

    middle ← ( degree - 1) / 2 + 1

    -- split lower values into node
    For count In 1 .. middle - 1 Loop
        node.tuple(count) ← big_node.tuple(count)
    End Loop
    node.n ← middle - 1
```

```
-- move middle tuple into hold_tuple
hold_tuple ← big_node.tuple(middle)
next ← Size ( b_tree_file ) + 1
hold_tuple.s ← next
-- split higher values into new_node
new_node.s0 ←  big_node.tuple(middle).s
index ← 0
For count In middle + 1 .. big_node.n Loop
     index ← index + 1
     new_node.tuple(index) ← big_node.tuple(count)
End Loop
new_node.n ← index
Output ( b_tree_file, newnode, next )

Output ( b_tree_file, node, p )
-- operation remains INSERT_KEY upon return
```

Searches

Searching for values in the B-tree involves a simple modification of `Find_Node` to eliminate all calls to `Insert_Tuple`. The search algorithm calls `Find_Node`, and `Find_Node` returns normally if the key is not found; `Search` then raises the `key_not_found` exception. A `key_found` exception is raised by `Find_Node` if the key is found, so the search algorithm can retrieve the address (`addr`) of the record with the search key value. Algorithm 8.3 searches the B-tree built with Algorithm 8.2 using the scheme discussed above.

ALGORITHM 8.3 Search

```
PROCEDURE Search ( key : In Key_Type; addr : In Out Positive )
    hold_tuple : A_Tuple
    operation  : Operation_Type ← SEARCH_KEY
    root_node : Node_Type
    Input ( B_Tree_File, root_node, 1 )
    hold_tuple ← ( key, 1, 0 )
    Find_Node ( hold_tuple, root_node.n, operation )
    Raise key_not_found
EXCEPTION
    When key_found → addr ← hold_tuple.addr
        -- exception raised by Find_Node
```

Deletions

Deletions of values from the B-tree may involve merging values from two nodes into one node rather than splitting values into two nodes to ensure that the tree maintains the characteristics of a B-tree. Deleting a value from a leaf node simply involves removing the tuple with that value from the node. Given the B-tree of order 5 in Figure 8.26, deleting 250 from node `k`, which contains more than the minimum number of tuples, is the simplest deletion (Figure 8.27). Note that node `e` stores data in format form:

2, 0, (40, addr(40), 0), (50, addr(50), 0)

Deleting 50 from the B-tree leaves node `e` with only one value:

1, 0, (40, addr(40), 0)

Node e now contains fewer than the minimum number of tuples ($\lceil m/2 \rceil - 1$). The algorithm for deletion in this situation requires that the nearest right sibling with > $\lceil m/2 \rceil$ tuples be located. Node `f` is the nearest right sibling of node e with more than the minimum number of tuples. The parent node b

2, d, (30, addr(30), e), (60, addr(60), f)

of node e has a value K(i) = 60 (the immediate successor of 50), and S(i – 1) = e. The relationship of the value to be deleted (50) to the value K(i) in the parent node (60) to K(1) of the nearest right sibling (70) is 50 < 60 < 70. Since node `f` contains more than the minimum tuples for a node, rotation of these three values takes place so that the immediate successor of 50 (K(i) = 60, underlined in the following with +) in the parent node and S(0) (underlined in the following with *) from the right sibling node `f` are moved into node e:

2, 0, (40, addr(40), 0), (60, addr(60), 0)
+++++++++ *

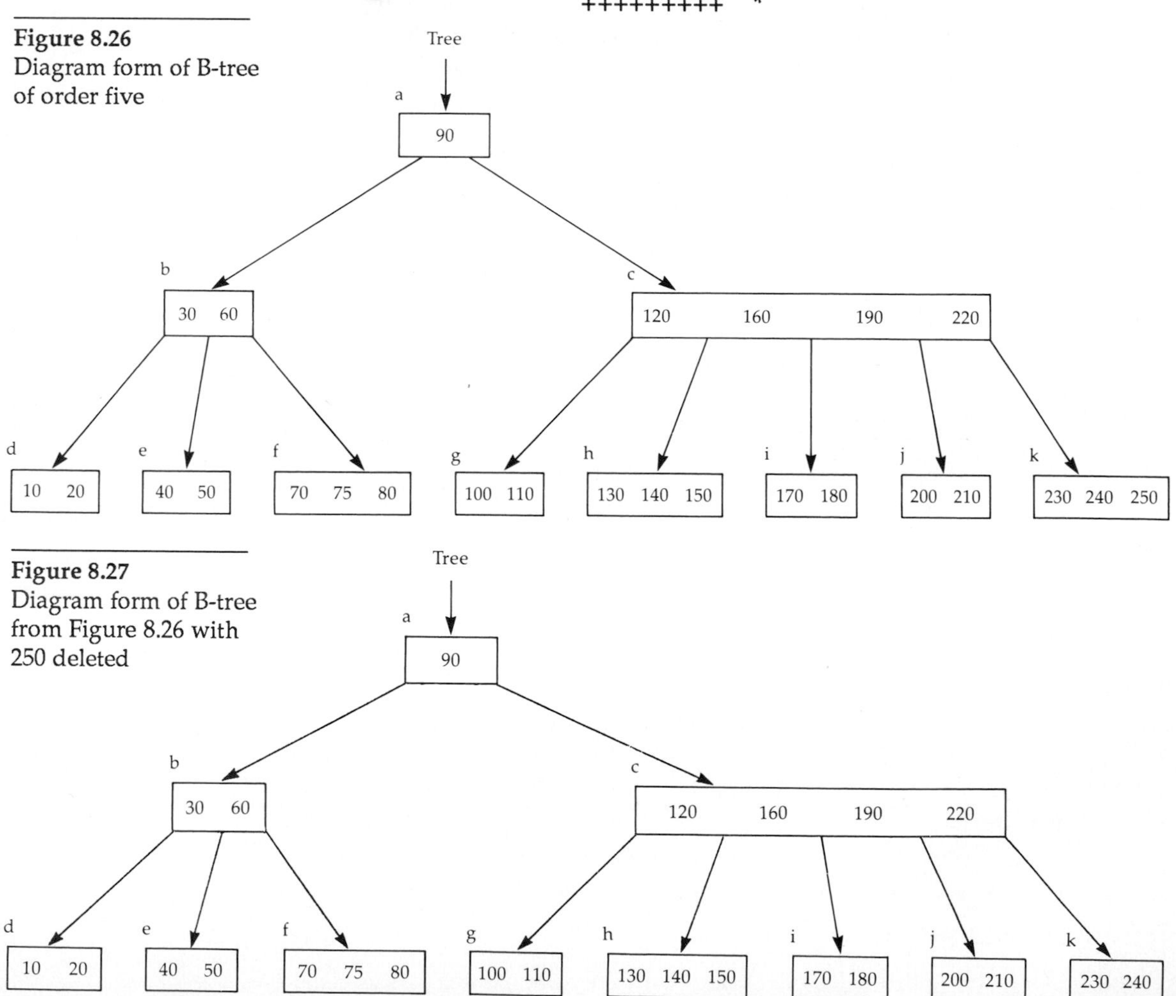

Figure 8.26
Diagram form of B-tree of order five

Figure 8.27
Diagram form of B-tree from Figure 8.26 with 250 deleted

The value K(1), which is underlined in the following with +, is moved from node `f` into node `b`:

2, d, (30, addr(30), e), (70, addr(70), f)
                              +++++++++++

The resulting B-tree with the value 50 deleted is illustrated in Figure 8.28.

If the nearest right sibling had not had more than the minimum number of tuples in the node, the nearest left sibling and the immediate predecessor in the parent node (the key K(*i*)) could have been used as well. The next deletion illustrates the algorithm if both the nearest siblings have exactly the minimum number of tuples.

Deletion of the value 20 from the B-tree in Figure 8.28 causes a merger of values from three nodes since the nearest right sibling (node `e`) contains the minimum of two tuples (40 and 60), and node `d` has no left sibling. The immediate successor of 20 is K(*i*) = 30 with S(*i* – 1) = `d` from node `b`:

2, d, (30, addr(30), e), (70, addr(70), f)

The nearest right sibling, node `e`, contains K(1) = 40. Deleting the value 20 from node `d` leaves it with less than the minimum number of tuples:

1, (10, addr(10), 0)

The remaining values in node `d`, the immediate successor K(*i*) = 30, and the nearest right sibling, node `e` (underlined by +), are merged into node `d`:

4, 0, (10, addr(10), 0), (30, addr(30), 0), (40, addr(40), 0), (60, addr(60), 0)
                                                  +++++++++++++++++++++++

Node `b` is left with only one tuple:

1, d, (70, addr(70), f)

Node `e` is discarded because it has been emptied of all information. The B-tree of Figure 8.29 is the resulting tree.

Node `b` has only one tuple (the minimum number of tuples is two), so the process is repeated. The successor value merges from the parent node `b` (90) and the first subtree pointer of the nearest right sibling (the pointer to `g`) into node `b`:

2, d, (70, addr(70), f), (90, addr(90), g)

The K(1) from node `c` moves into the node vacated by the value 90 (node `a`). The B-tree after complete deletion of the value 20 is shown in Figure 8.30.

Deletion of values from nonleaf nodes requires that an immediate successor (or predecessor) be located and moved into the place left by the deleted value. To illustrate, suppose the value 160 is deleted from the B-tree in Figure 8.30. The deletion of 160 causes a rotation from the predecessor node `h`, which has more than the minimum number of tuples. The immediate predecessor of 160 is 150, so 150 moves into the spot left by the deletion of 160 (Figure 8.31).

Figure 8.28
Diagram form of B-tree from Figure 8.27 with 50 deleted

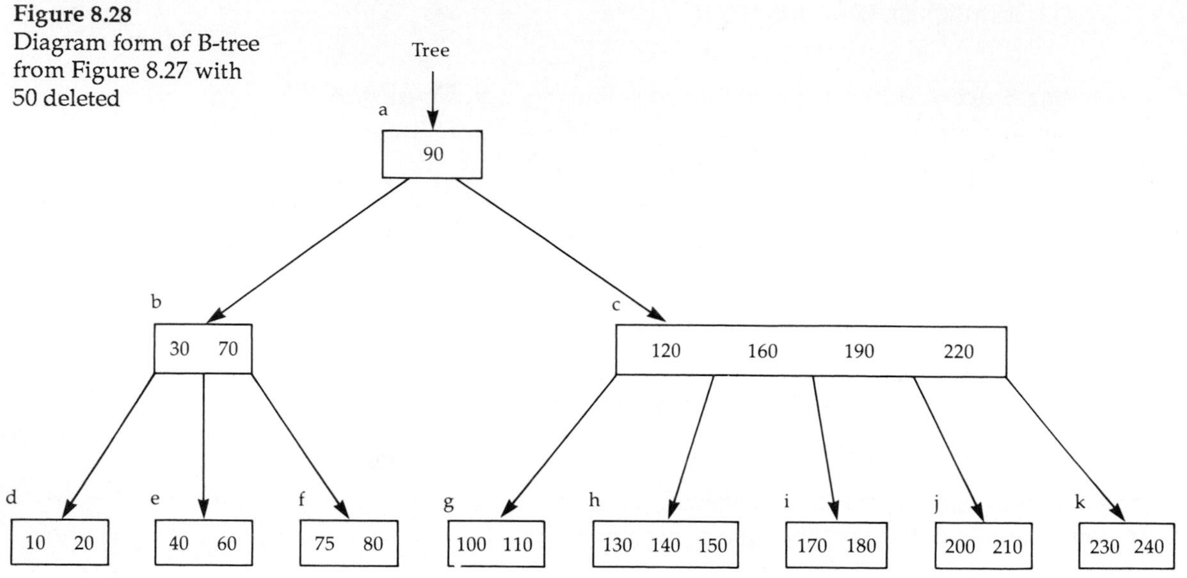

Figure 8.29
Diagram form of B-tree from Figure 8.28 with incompleted deletion of 20 nodes d and e with parent combined into node d)

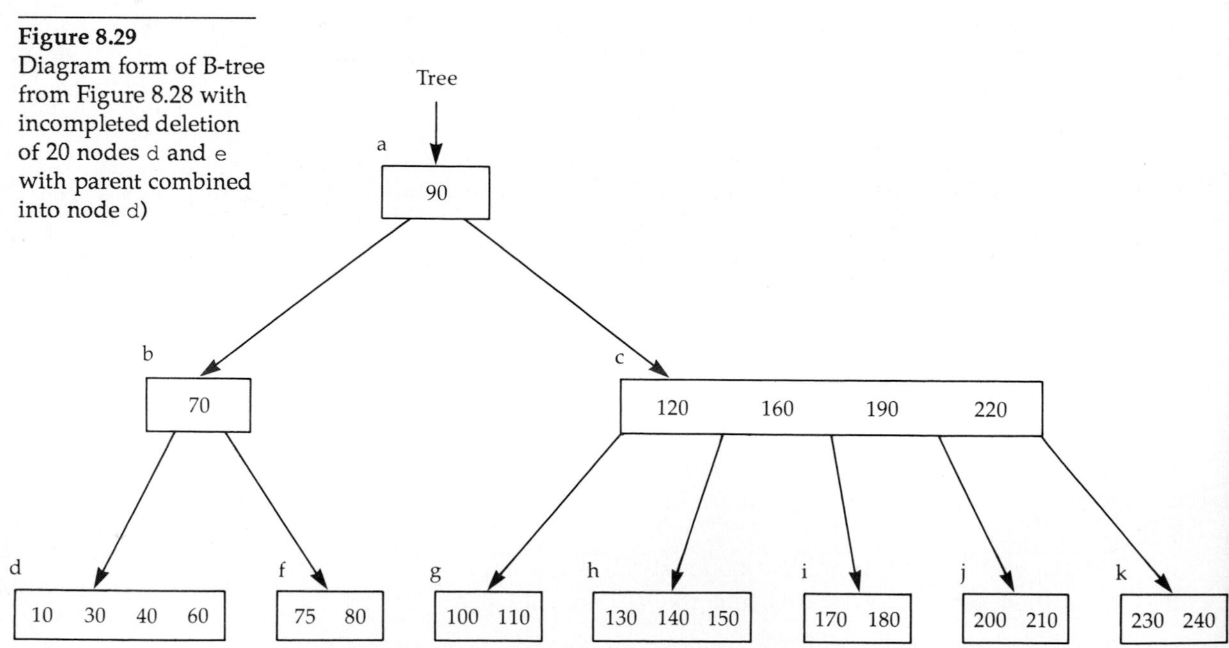

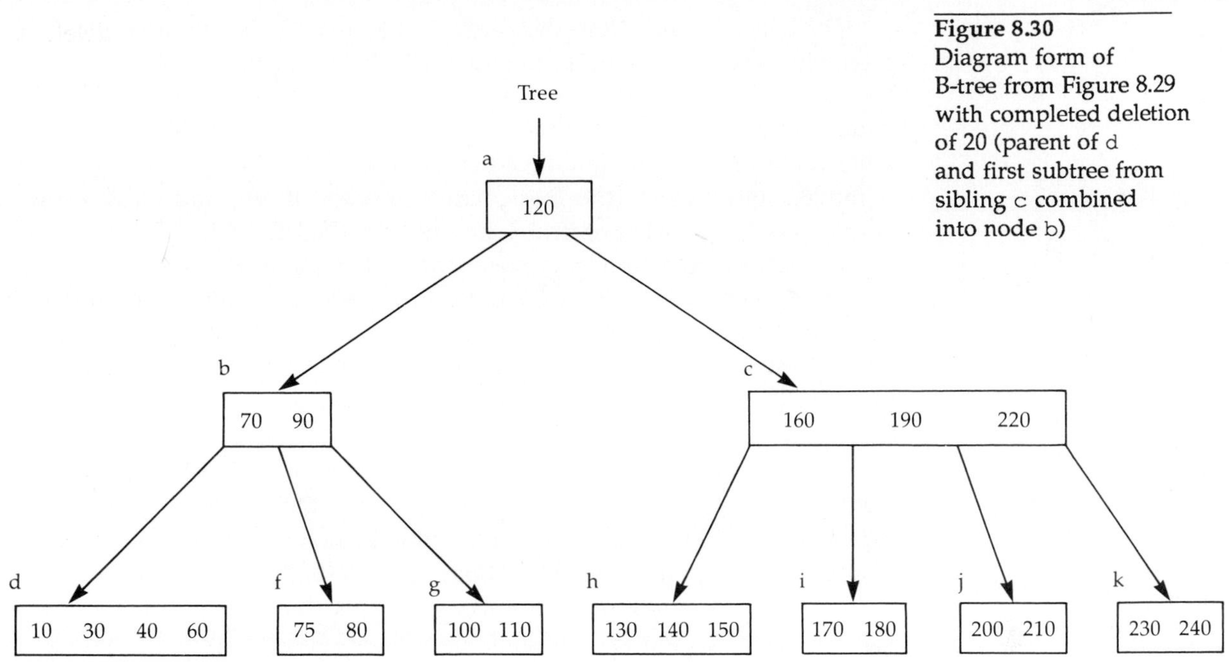

Figure 8.30
Diagram form of B-tree from Figure 8.29 with completed deletion of 20 (parent of `d` and first subtree from sibling `c` combined into node `b`)

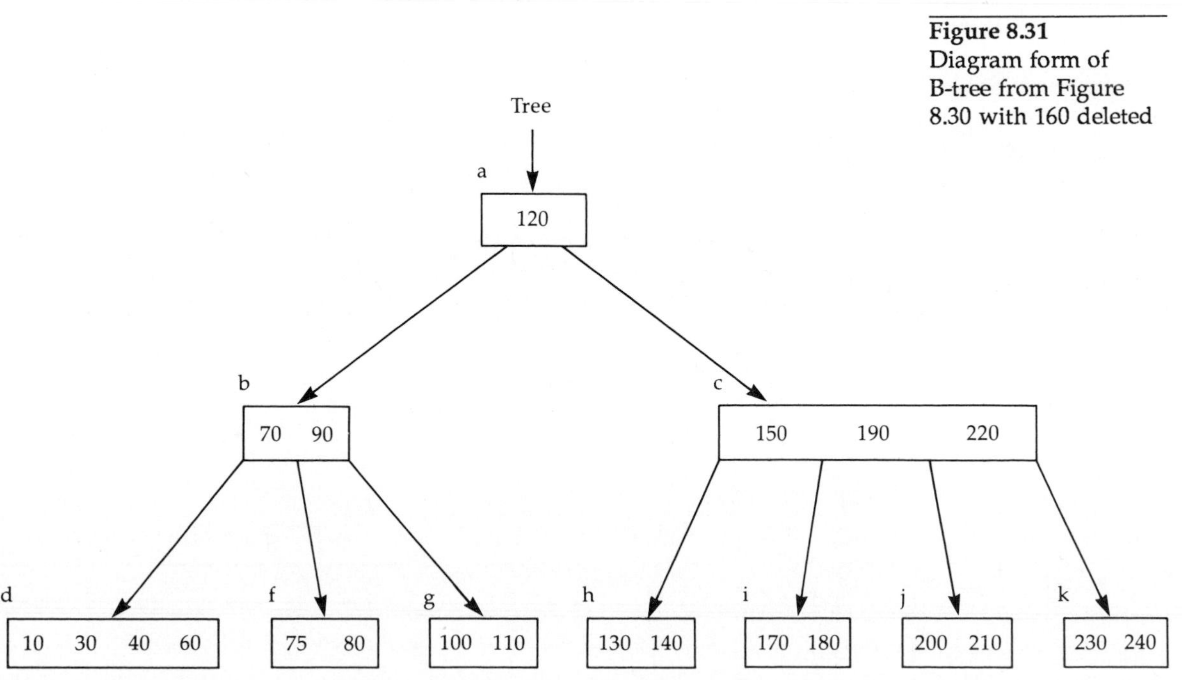

Figure 8.31
Diagram form of B-tree from Figure 8.30 with 160 deleted

The deletion of 90 from the B-tree in Figure 8.31 causes the immediate predecessor 80 to move up to the parent node `b` (Figure 8.32), leaving node `f` with less than the minimum number of tuples. The nearest right sibling of node `f` (node `g`) has only the minimum contents, but the left sibling of node `f` has more than the minimum contents, so the value 70 of the parent node is moved into node `f` (the immediate successor of 70), and 60 (from the nearest left sibling, node `d`) moves into node `b` (Figure 8.33).

The last two deletion examples involve deletion of the one tuple in the root node and the deletion of a tuple in a node with minimum contents. The latter causes the height to decrease because all the children, siblings, and parent nodes are also in a minimum state. The deletion of the only tuple in the root node, 120, brings the immediate predecessor, 110, up into the spot vacated by the tuple 120 (Figure 8.34). Moving 110 to the root node leaves node `g` with a subminimum number of tuples. Node `g` has no right siblings, and its left sibling, node `f`, has only the minimum number of tuples. The contents of node `g` and the immediate predecessor in the parent node `b` (80) merge into the left sibling, node `f` (Figure 8.35). Node `b` is left with less than the minimum number of tuples. As a result, the successor value from the parent node of node `b` (110) and S(0) (the pointer to node `h`) from node `b`'s sibling node `c` are merged into node `b`. K(1) (150) moves to node `a` into the tuple position vacated by the value 110 (Figure 8.36).

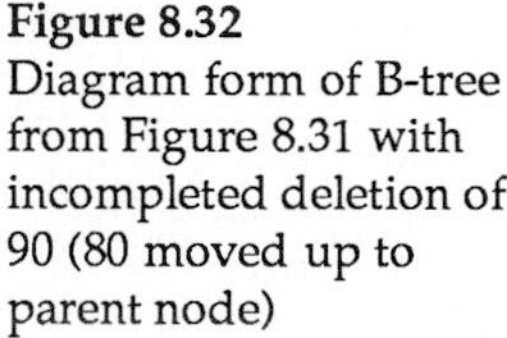

Figure 8.32
Diagram form of B-tree from Figure 8.31 with incompleted deletion of 90 (80 moved up to parent node)

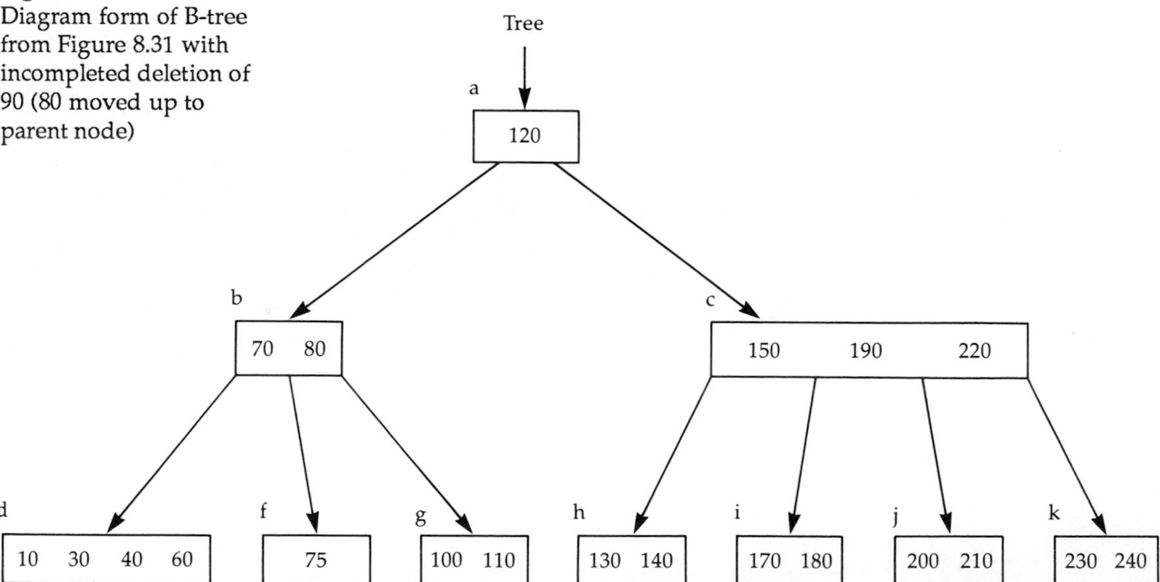

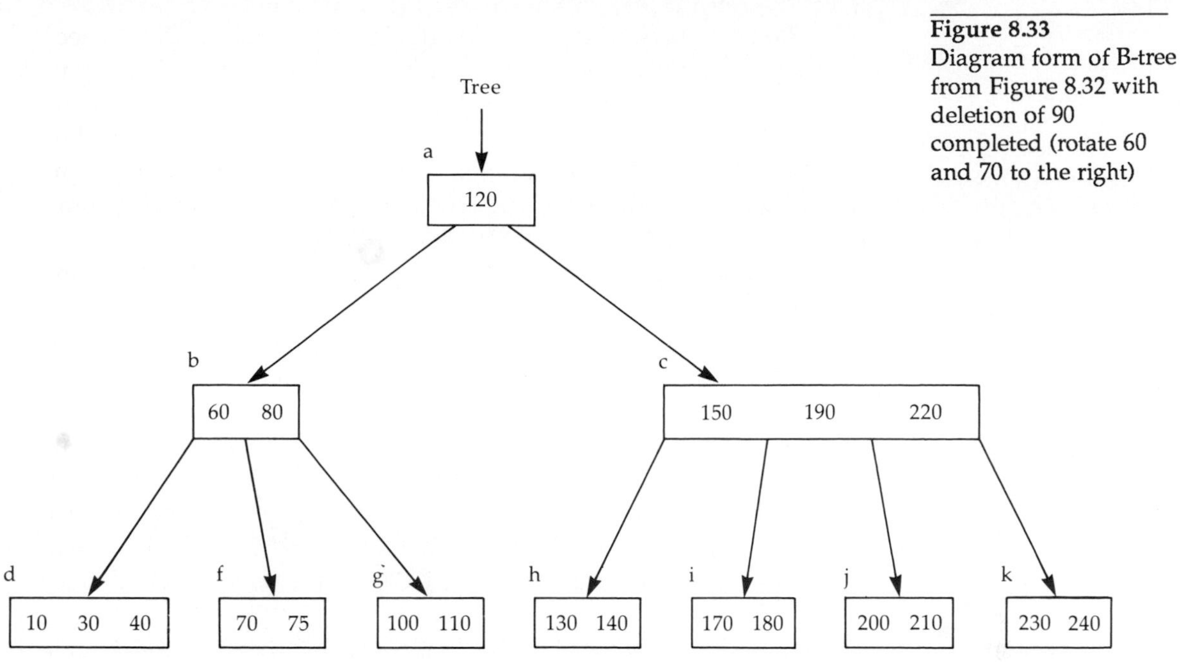

Figure 8.33
Diagram form of B-tree from Figure 8.32 with deletion of 90 completed (rotate 60 and 70 to the right)

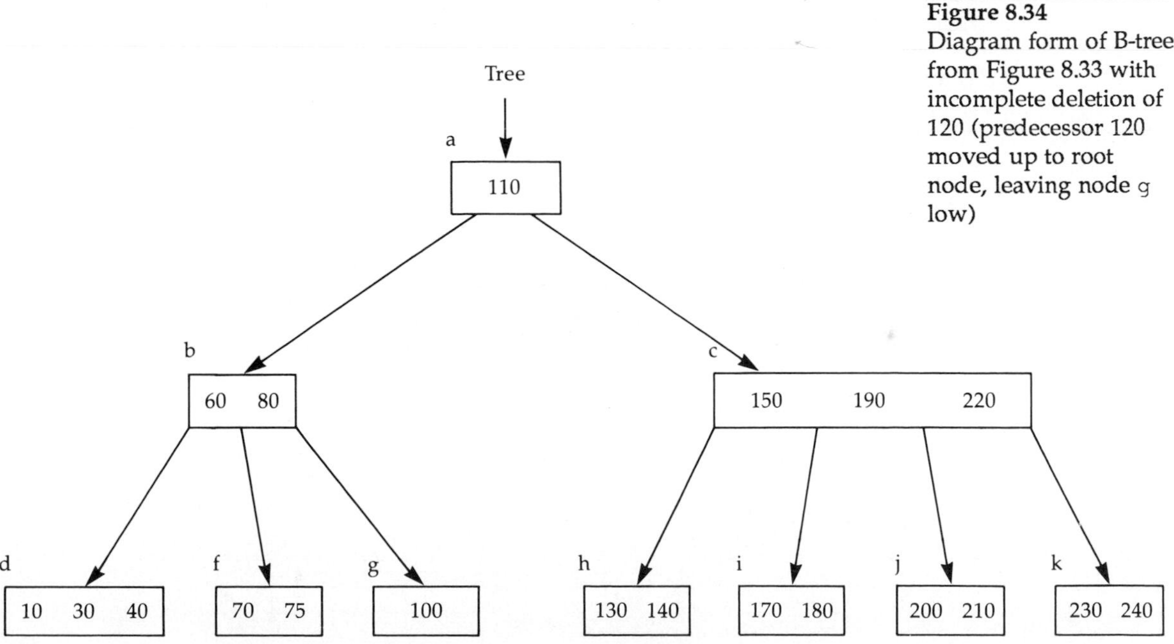

Figure 8.34
Diagram form of B-tree from Figure 8.33 with incomplete deletion of 120 (predecessor 120 moved up to root node, leaving node g low)

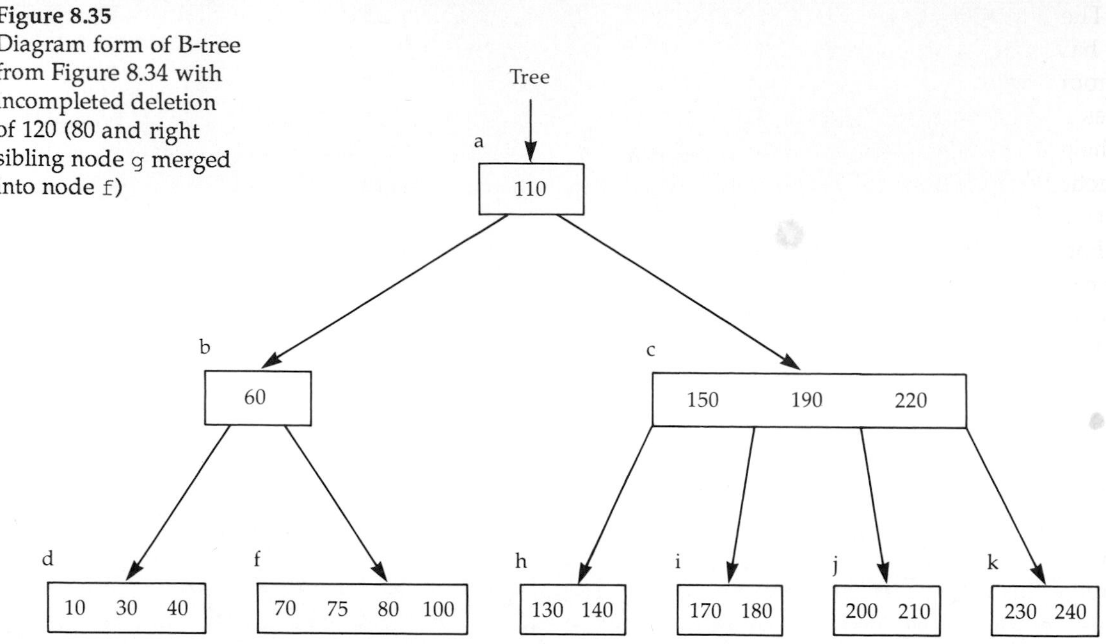

Figure 8.35
Diagram form of B-tree from Figure 8.34 with incompleted deletion of 120 (80 and right sibling node `g` merged into node `f`)

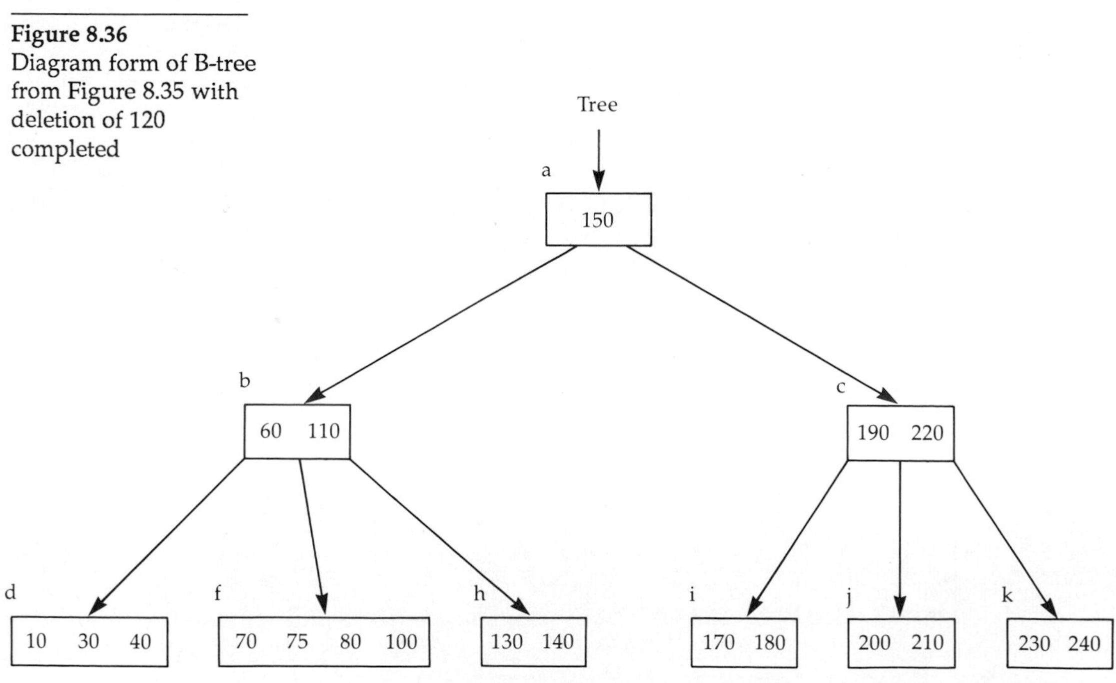

Figure 8.36
Diagram form of B-tree from Figure 8.35 with deletion of 120 completed

The B-tree in Figure 8.36 now has nodes in the right subtree of the root that have minimum contents. If a value is deleted from the right subtree of the root, the tree attempts to rotate a value from a sibling. A deletion from nodes `i`, `j`, or `k` causes a merging of nodes, which results in the reduction in the height of the tree. Similarly, the deletion of a value from node `c` causes a reduction in height since the left (and only) sibling of node `c` and the parent (root) node have only minimum contents.

For example, the deletion of the value 190 from the B-tree in Figure 8.36 first causes a rotation of the predecessor to replace 190; 180 is moved from node `i` into the spot vacated by 190 in node `c` (Figure 8.37). Now node `i` has less than the minimum number of tuples, so the parent value 180 and the right sibling, node `j`, are merged into node `i`, which deletes node `j` (Figure 8.38). This leaves node `c` with less than the minimum contents. Node `c` has no right sibling. Its parent node, `a`, has the minimum contents for a root node, and its left sibling has only the minimum contents. Therefore, a merge takes place: The subminimum node `c` and the parent value, node `a`, merge into the left sibling, node `b` (Figure 8.39). Node `c` is deleted entirely and so is node `a`, which is empty. Node `b` becomes the new root of the B-tree, which now has a height of only 2. The number of tuple values has decreased to the point that the height of the tree can be reduced, leaving a more efficient search tree. The number of nodes in the tree has been reduced from nine nodes in Figure 8.36 to only six nodes in Figure 8.39.

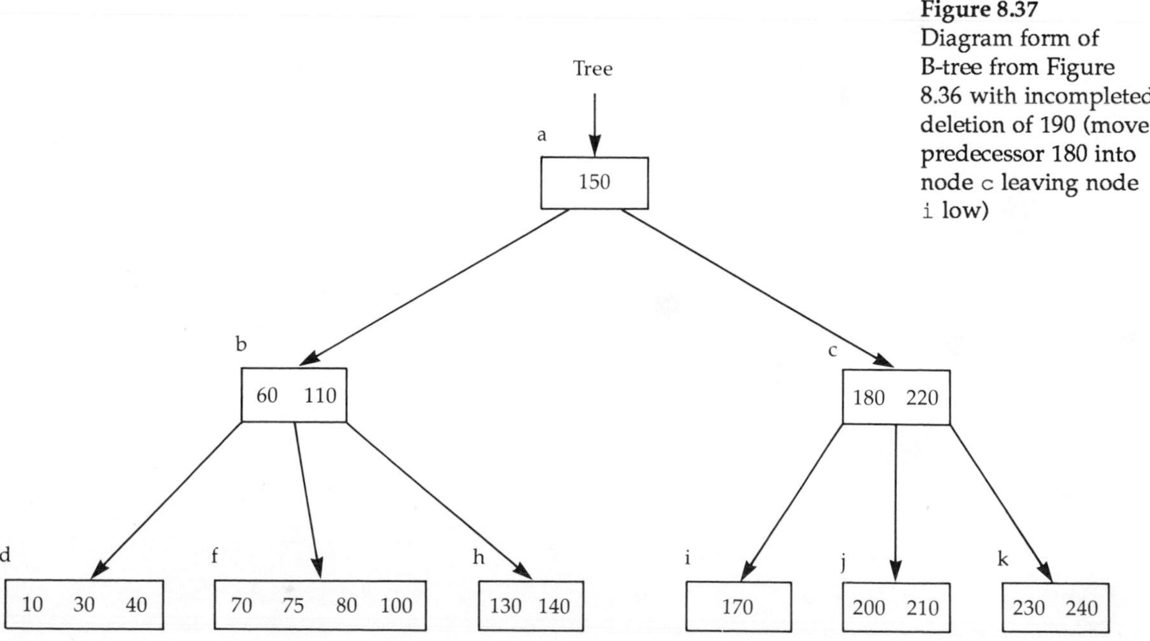

Figure 8.37
Diagram form of B-tree from Figure 8.36 with incompleted deletion of 190 (move predecessor 180 into node `c` leaving node `i` low)

Figure 8.38
Diagram form of B-tree from Figure 8.37 with incompleted deletion of 190 (merge parent value 180 and right sibling into node `i`)

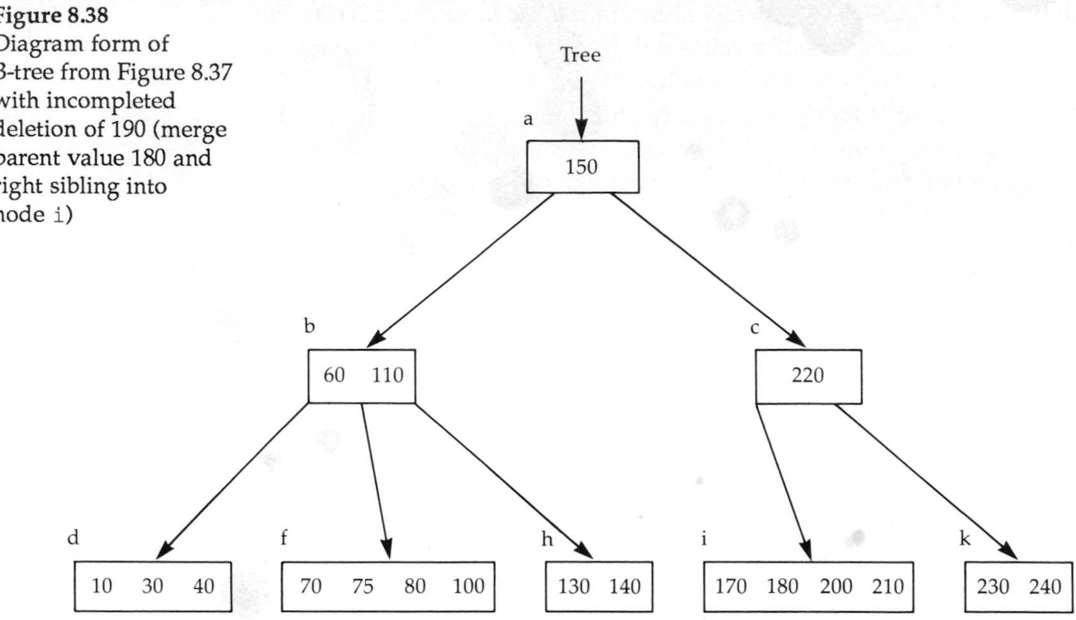

Figure 8.39
Diagram form of B-tree from Figure 8.38 with deletion of 190 completed

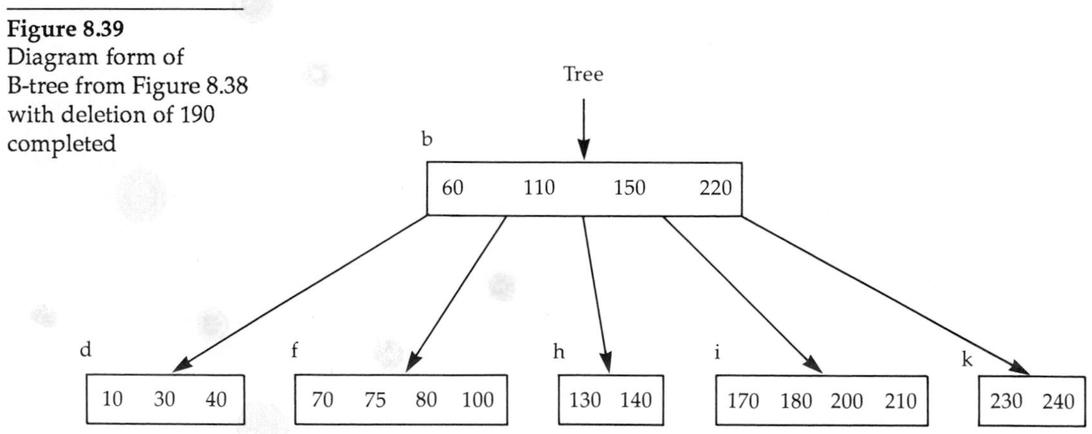

Algorithm 8.4 deletes a tuple (`delete_value`) from B-tree `p` using the scheme discussed above. Deletion from a nonleaf node is performed first so that after the predecessor is moved up in the tree, the deletion of the predecessor from a leaf node follows.

ALGORITHM 8.4 Deletion

```
PROCEDURE Delete ( delete_value : In Key_Type )
    address_of_root_node : Node_Type
    maximum,
    minimum : Natural
    node_undersized : Boolean ← FALSE
    root_address : Natural

    minimum ← Ceiling ( degree / 2 ) – 1
    maximum ← degree – 1
    Input ( b_tree_file, address_of_root_node, 1 )
    root_address ← address_of_root_node.n
    Delete_Tuple ( delete_value, root_address, node_undersized )
    If node_undersized
        If root_node.n = 0   -- all tuples have been deleted from root_node
            address_of_root_node.n ← root_node.s0
            -- reducing the height of the B-tree
            Output ( b_tree_file, address_of_root_node, 1 )
        End If
    End If
EXCEPTION
    When key_not_found → Raise key_not_deleted
         -- key_not_found is raised by Delete_Tuple
         -- if the key is not in the tree

PROCEDURE Delete_Tuple ( delete_value : In Key_Type
                         p : In Natural
                         node_undersized : In Out Boolean )
    child_address : Natural
    index : Natural
    node : Node_Type

    -- search node with address p for key
    If p = 0       -- not found
        Raise key_not_found
    Else
        Input ( b_tree_file, node, p ) -- node ← contents of p
        If delete_value > node.tuple(node.n).key
            -- larger than the largest key in node
            index ← node.n
            child_address ← node.tuple(node.n).s
            Delete_Tuple ( delete_value, child_address, node_undersized )
            If node_undersized
                -- node at child_address is under minimum;
                -- child_address is field s in tuple(index) of parent p
                Under_Flow ( p, child_address, index, node_undersized )
            End If
        Else
            index ← 1
```

```
            Loop
                If delete_value > node.tuple(index).key
                    index ← index + 1
                Elsif delete_value = node.tuple(index).key
                    Found_Delete_Value
                    Exit
                Else -- delete_value < node.tuple(index).key
                    If index = 1
                        child_address ← node.so
                    Else
                        child_address ← node.tuple(index - 1).s
                    End If
                    -- search down another level in B-tree
                    Delete_Tuple ( delete_value, child_address, node_undersized )
                    If node_undersized
                        -- as in Figure 8.28 where node b is under the minimum
                        -- node at child_address is under minimum;
                        -- child_address is field s in tuple (index - 1) of parent
                        Under_Flow ( p, child_address, index - 1, node_undersiz
                    End If
                    Exit
                End If
            End Loop
        End If
    End If

PROCEDURE Found_Delete_Value  -- internal to Delete_Tuple

    If index = 1
        child_address ← node.s0
    Else
        child_address ← node.tuple(index - 1).s
    End If
    If child_address = 0
        -- delete key(index) from leaf node
        -- as in Figure 8.28 where 50 is deleted from node e
        -- and control returns recursively to parent b (at this point,
        -- parent b is determined to be undersized)
        node.n ← node.n - 1
        node_undersized ← node.n < minimum
        For count In index .. node.n Loop
            node.tuple(count) ← node.tuple(count + 1)
        End Loop
        Output ( b_tree_file, node, p )
    Else  -- delete key(index) from nonterminal node;
          -- find predecessor to replace key(index)
        Find_Predecessor ( child_address, node_undersized )
        If node_undersized
            -- node at child_address is under minimum;
            -- child_address is field s in tuple(index - 1) of parent p
            Under_Flow ( p, child_address, index - 1, node_undersized )
        End If
    End If
```

```
PROCEDURE Find_Predecessor ( descendant_address : In Positive
                             node_undersized : In Out Boolean )
   -- internal to Found_Delete_Value; global references made to node, index
   descendant_node : Node_Type
   q: Natural
   Input ( b_tree_file, descendant_node, descendant_address )
   q ← descendant_node.tuple(descendant_node.n).s
   If q = 0    -- descendant_node is a leaf node so choose largest key in
               -- descendant_node as the predecessor to replace the
               -- deleted key in node.tuple(index)
      descendant_node.tuple(descendant_node.n).s ← node.tuple(index).s
      node.tuple(index) ← descendant_node.tuple(descendant_node.n)
      descendant_node.n ← descendant_node.n − 1
      node_undersized ← descendant_node.n < minimum
      Output ( b_tree_file, node, p )
      Output ( b_tree_file, descendant_node, descendant_address )
   Else  -- descendant_node is a nonterminal node so look deeper in
         -- B-tree for predecessor
      Find_Predecessor ( q, node_undersized )
      If node_undersized
         -- node at address q is under minimum;
         -- q is field s in last tuple of parent descendant_address
         Under_Flow ( descendant_address, q, descendant_node.n, node_undersized )
      End If
   End If

PROCEDURE Under_Flow ( parent_address, child_address : In Positive
                       tuple_index : In Out Natural
                       node_undersized : Out Boolean )
   -- node at child_address is under minimum;
   -- child_address is field s in tuple(tuple_index) of parent node at parent_address
   child_node : Node_Type
   left_address : Positive
   left_extras : Integer
   parent_node : Node_Type
   right_address : Positive
   right_extras : Integer
   right_node : Node_Type
   -- child_node ← contents of child_address
   Input ( b_tree_file, child_node, child_address )
   -- parent_node ← contents of parent_address
   Input ( b_tree_file, parent_node, parent_address )

   If tuple_index < parent_node.n  -- a right sibling exists
      tuple_index ← tuple_index + 1
      right_address ← parent_node.tuple(tuple_index).s
      -- right_node ← contents of right_address
      Input ( b_tree_file, right_node, right_address )
      -- right_extras is the number of tuples over the minimum
      -- that can be balanced between child_node and right_node
      right_extras ← ( right_node.n − minimum + 1 ) / 2
      -- child_node is undersized since Find_Predecessor pulled
      -- largest key out earlier; or deleted key from leaf node;
      -- so now replace predecessor of node where key deleted to original
      -- location in child_node;
```

```
            -- as in Figure 8.27 where 60 from parent node b is moved into
            -- child_node e to restore to minimum as in Figure 8.28
            child_node.n ← child_node.n + 1
            child_node.tuple(child_node.n) ← parent_node.tuple(tuple_index)
            child_node.tuple(child_node.n).s ← right_node.s0

            If right_extras > 0   -- move extras number of tuples from right_node
                                  -- to child_node
                Balance_From_Right
            Elsif tuple_index /= 0    -- left sibling exists
                Choose_Left_Sibling
                If left_extras > 0
                    Balance_From_Left
                Else   -- left sibling has no extras so merge child_node
                       -- and right_node into child_node (now contains maximum tuples
                    Merge_With_Right
                End If
            Else    -- left sibling does not exist so merge child_node and
                    -- right_node into child_node (node contains maximum tuples)
                Merge_With_Right
            End If
        Else  --  no right sibling exists; choose left sibling
            Choose_Left_Sibling
            If left_extras > 0
                Balance_From_Left
            Else    -- right sibling does not exist and left sibling has no extras,
                    -- so merge left_node and child_node
                    -- into left_node (now contains maximum tuples)
                Merge_With_Left
            End If
        End If

PROCEDURE Balance_From_Right -- internal to Underflow
    -- move extra tuples from right_node to child_node
    -- as in Figure 8.28 where child_node now has 40 and 60, but parent_node
    -- is below the minimum and needs the one extra tuple the right sibling,
    -- node f, can spare;
    -- the one extra tuple from right_node f is used to fill b to a minimum;
    -- since balancing from the right, pull the lowest key (70) from the
    -- right sibling to fill the parent_node
    For count In 1 .. right_extras - 1 Loop
        child_node.tuple(child_node.n + count) ← right_node.tuple(count)
    End Loop
    parent_node.tuple(tuple_index) ← right_node.tuple(right_extras)
    parent_node.tuple(tuple_index).s ← right_address

    right_node.s0 ← right_node.tuple(right_extras).s
    right_node.n ← right_node.n - right_extras

    For count In 1 .. right_node.n Loop
        right_node.tuple(count) ← right_node.tuple(right_extras + count)
    End Loop
    child_node.n ← minimum - 1 + right_extras
    node_undersized ← FALSE
```

```
    Output ( b_tree_file, child_node, child_address )
    Output ( b_tree_file, left_node, left_address )
    Output ( b_tree_file, parent_node, parent_address )

PROCEDURE Choose_Left_Sibling  -- internal to Underflow

    If tuple_index = 1
        left_address ← parent_node.s0
    Else
        left_address ← parent_node.tuple(tuple_index – 1).s
    End If
    Input ( b_tree_file, left_node, left_address )
    -- left_node ← contents of left_address
    left_extras ← ( left_node.n – minimum + 1 ) / 2

PROCEDURE Merge_With_Right -- internal to Underflow
    -- merge  child_node and right_node into child_node
    -- as in deletion of 20 from Figure 8.28; child_node d is left below the
    -- minimum; so the 30 from the parent_node has been moved into child_node;
    -- now merge all tuples from right_node into child_node
    For count In 1 .. minimum Loop
        child_node.tuple(minimum + count) ← right_node.tuple(count)
    End Loop
    For count In tuple_index .. parent_node.n – 1 Loop
        parent_node.tuple(count) ← parent_node(count + 1)
    End Loop
    child_node.n ← maximum
    parent_node.n ← parent_node.n – 1
    node_undersized ← parent_node.n < minimum

    Output ( b_tree_file, child_node, child_address )
    Output ( b_tree_file, parent_node, parent_address )
    -- Dispose ( right_node )
    right_node.n ← 0
    Output ( b_tree_file, right_node, right_address )

PROCEDURE Balance_From_Left -- internal to Underflow
    -- move extra number of tuples from left_node to child_node
    -- as in Figure 8.32 where child_node has only 75, (is below the
    -- minimum) and the right sibling is at a minimum;
    -- the tuples in child_node are moved to the right left_extra places
    -- to make room for the additions;
    -- the next lower key in the parent node (70) is moved into child_node;
    -- the largest tuple, the left sibling, is used to fill parent node b

    For count In Reverse  1 .. minimum Loop
        -- move tuples over "left_extras" places
        -- to make room for tuples at lower end
        child_node.tuple(count + left_extras) ← child_node.tuple(count)
    End Loop
    child_node.tuple(left_extras) ← parent_node.tuple(tuple_index)
    child_node.tuple(left_extras).s ← child_node.s0
    left_node.n ← minimum + 1

    For count In Reverse  1 .. left_extras – 1 Loop
        child_node.tuple(count) ← left_node.tuple(left_node.n + count)
    End Loop
```

```
    child_node.s0 ← left_node.tuple(left_node.n).s
    parent_node.tuple(tuple_index) ← left_node.tuple ( left_node.n )
    parent_node.tuple(tuple_index).s ← child_address
    left_node.n ← left_node.n – 1
    child_node.n ← minimum – 1 + left_extras
    node_undersized ← FALSE

    Output ( b_tree_file, child_node, child_address )
    Output ( b_tree_file, left_node, left_address )
    Output ( b_tree_file, parent_node, parent_address )
PROCEDURE Merge_With_Left
    -- internal to Underflow
    -- merge left_node and child_node into left_node
    -- as in Figure 8.34; child_node g is left below the minimum;
    -- so the 80 from the parent_node has been moved into the right end of
    -- left_node;
    -- now merge all tuples from child_node into left_node

    left_node.n ← left_node.n + 1
    left_node.tuple(left_node.n) ← parent_node.tuple(tuple_index)
    left_node.tuple(left_node.n).s ← child_node.s0

    For count In 1 .. child_node.n Loop
        left_node.tuple(left_node.n + count) ← child_node.tuple(count)
    End Loop
    left_node.n ← maximum
    parent_node.n ← parent_node.n – 1
    node_undersized ← parent_node.n < minimum
    Output ( b_tree_file, left_node, left_address )
    Output ( b_tree_file, parent_node, parent_address )
    -- Dispose ( child_node )
    child_node.n ← 0
    Output ( b_tree_file, child_node, child_address )
```

ADA B-TREE PACKAGE

A generic package for creating, inserting, deleting, and searching B-trees can be specified that includes the techniques described in this chapter. The specifications for the B-tree package list the different procedures and functions available for B-tree manipulation. The user instantiates the package and calls the procedure `Create_B_Tree`, `Open_B_Tree`, or `Close_B_Tree`, passing the external name of the B-tree file. The user calls the subprograms `Insert`, `Delete`, passing the key and the address of the record with that key in the data file to be inserted or deleted. The user calls the procedure `Search`, passing the key to be searched, and the package returns the address of the key when found.

```
GENERIC
    degree : Positive;
    TYPE Key_Type Is Private;
    WITH Function ">" ( left_operand, right_operand : Key_Type )
                        Return Boolean;
```

```
PACKAGE B_Tree Is
    PROCEDURE Create_B_Tree ( external_b_tree_filename : String );
    PROCEDURE Open_B_Tree ( external_b_tree_filename : String );
    PROCEDURE Insert ( key : Key_Type; key_position : Positive );
    PROCEDURE Delete ( key : Key_Type );
    PROCEDURE Search ( key : Key_Type; key_position : Out Positive );
    PROCEDURE Close_B_Tree;
    key_not_found,
    key_not_inserted,
    key_not_deleted : Exception;
END B_Tree;
```

The generic parameters of the package require the user to specify the degree of the B-tree be manipulated. The type of the degree is a `Positive` value. The user also specifies the type of the key on which all searching, inserting, and deleting is performed. The type of the key is one of the user's own choosing. The last of the generic parameters is the `">"` function. This function is predefined for any scalar type and any array with discrete components. If the user has a key for which the `">"` is not defined, the user must write the function and include it in the program that instantiates the B-tree package. The B-tree package is an indexing package for a data file, but the package has no knowledge of the format of the record in the data file. The B-tree package only needs to know the degree of the B-tree, the type of the key, and the address where the record with that key can be found in the data file.

An example user's program showing the instantiation of the package B_Tree is presented:

```
WITH B_Tree;
PROCEDURE Use_B_Tree Is
     SUBTYPE Name_Type Is String ( 1..20 );
     key_name : Name_Type;
     key_position : Positive;
     PACKAGE User_B_Tree Is New B_Tree ( 3, Name_Type, ">" );
BEGIN
     User_B_Tree.Open_B_Tree ( "user-bt.fil" );

     User_B_Tree.Insert ( key_name, key_position );

     User_B_Tree.Close_B_Tree;
END Use_B_Tree;
```

The degree of the B_Tree in `"user-bt.fil"` is three. The key_name is a `String`. The function `">"` is already defined for strings, so no further definition in the user's program is required. The instantiation of the package `User_B_Tree` lists the three generic parameters. The first, 3, is the degree of the B-tree. The second, `Name_Type`, is the type of the key name. Lastly is the function `">"`. The skeleton program `Use_B_Tree` shows the use of the procedures that open a B-tree file (`Open_B_Tree`), insert a key in the B-tree file (`Insert`), and close the B-tree file (`Close_B_Tree`).

B^*-TREES

Bayer and McCreight (1972) applied a modification to the B-tree known as the **overflow technique**, which improves the insertion algorithm by using local rotation to cause keys to overflow from a full node into a sibling node that is less than full. The net effect is that every node is at least two-thirds full rather than half-full as in B-trees. Keeping the nodes two-thirds full uses the available space more efficiently and also reduces the number of nodes necessary to hold a fixed number of keys. The search time is improved over that for the B-tree. The tree that employs the overflow technique is the **B^*-tree**, and it has the following characteristics:

1. It is an m-way search tree that either is empty or has a height ≥ 1.
2. The root node has at least two children (therefore at least one value) and a maximum of $2\lfloor(2m-2)/3\rfloor + 1$. ($\lfloor x \rfloor$ is the floor of x.)
3. All nonterminal nodes (with $S_i \neq 0$) other than the root node have at least $\lceil(2m-1)/3\rceil$ children (and therefore at least $\lceil(2m-1)/3\rceil - 1$ values. ($\lceil x \rceil$ is the ceiling of x.)
4. All terminal nodes (with $S_i = 0$) are at the same level.
5. All nonterminal nodes with k S_is have $k-1$ keys.

The primary difference between the B-tree and the B^*-tree is that the interior nodes of a B-tree are at least half-full of tuples, and the interior nodes of a B^*-tree is at least two-thirds full of tuples. Fewer nodes are necessary with the B^*-trees to store the same number of keys.

For example, consider trees of order 7. The minimum and maximum number of children and keys for a B-tree of order 7 is ($m = 7$):

root node	–	$(2, m)$	$= 2 \leq \text{children} \leq 7$
			$= 1 \leq \text{keys} \leq 6$
interior nodes	–	$(\lceil m/2\rceil, m)$	$= 4 \leq \text{children} \leq 7$
			$= 3 \leq \text{keys} \leq 6$

The minimum and maximum number of children and keys for the B*-tree of order 7 is

root node	$-(2, 2\lfloor(2m-2)/3\rfloor + 1)$	$= 2 \leq \text{children} \leq 9$
		$= 1 \leq \text{keys} \leq 8$
interior nodes –	$(\lceil(2m-1)/3\rceil, m)$	$= 5 \leq \text{children} \leq 7$
		$= 4 \leq \text{keys} \leq 6$

Notice that interior nodes (nonterminal nodes except the root) of a B-tree of order 7 are half-full, which translates to a minimum of three keys. The maximum number of keys in the root node is twice the minimum number of keys for the interior node, so when an insertion into a full root ($m-1$ keys) occurs, a split occurs, leaving a minimum number ($\lceil m/2\rceil - 1$ keys) in each of two nodes that are children of the root node. The root node now has only one key. For example, Figure 8.40(a) shows a B-tree of order 7 after six keys have been inserted. The root node is full with $m - 1$, or six, keys. If the key 70 is inserted, the root node is split, leaving the middle key in the root node and $\lceil m/2 \rceil - 1$, or three, keys in each of the children (Figure 8.40(b)).

The interior nodes of a B*-tree of order 7 are two-thirds full, so the minimum number of keys is four. For the same situation to occur with B*-trees, the root node has to have enough keys to allow a split that leaves each of the two children two-thirds full. The root node for a B*-tree has to allow a maximum of twice the minimum number of keys in an interior node ($2\lfloor(2m-2)/3\rfloor$). When an insertion causes a split of the root node, the root node has the middle key, and the two children are two-thirds full ($\lceil(2m-1)/3\rceil - 1$).

Figure 8.41 illustrates a B*-tree with a full root node. When the key 90 is inserted, the root node retains the middle key, 50, and each of the children has the minimum number of keys (Figure 8.41(b)). As the keys 100 and 110 are inserted into the B*-tree in Figure 8.41, and the right child of the root fills, the insertion of key 120 causes a split in a B-tree node. In a B*-tree, insertions into a full node cause a local rotation to a sibling that is not full. Figure 8.42(b) presents the B*-tree after insertions of keys 100, 110, 120, and 130. A local rotation with the left sibling involves moving the parent value to the left sibling node and moving the first key in the full node to the parent node to make room for insertion of a key into a full node. The B*-tree has two leaf nodes that are full with a total of 13 keys in the tree of three nodes (Figure 8.42(b)). The same 13 keys inserted in order into a B-tree (Figure 8.42(a)) require a total of four nodes; the B-tree uses more space.

The insertion into a full node of a B*-tree with full sibling nodes causes a split of the keys in the two sibling nodes into three sibling nodes. For example, the insertion of the key 140 into the B*-tree in Figure 8.42(b) causes a split of node `c`—a rotation cannot be done because node `b` is also full. However, moving the middle key (110) to the parent node and splitting the remaining keys into two nodes leaves only three keys in each of the split nodes—a number below the minimum of two-thirds. A split for a node in a B*-tree must involve splitting the keys from the full node that requires the insertion (node `c`, with m keys after the insertion) and a full sibling (node `b`, with $m - 1$ keys) into three nodes, each of which is at least two-thirds full with ($\lfloor(2m-2)/3\rfloor$, $\lfloor(2m-1)/3\rfloor$, and $\lfloor 2m/3 \rfloor$ keys, respectively.

Where key_{parent} is the key in the parent node that separates the two siblings, the equations for determining the number of keys to be stored in each node are as follows:

1. node `b` has lowest $\lfloor(2m-2)/3\rfloor$ keys or
   $key_1 \ldots key_{\lfloor(2m-2)/3\rfloor}$ from original node `b`
   $= key_1 \ldots key_4$ from original node `b`
2. parent node of `b` has key $_{\lfloor(2m-2)/3\rfloor+1}$ = key $_{\lfloor(2m+1)/3\rfloor}$ or
   $= key_5$ from original node `b`

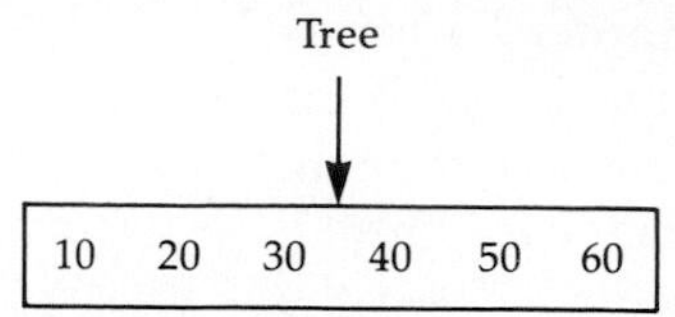

(a) Diagram of B-tree of order 7 with full root node

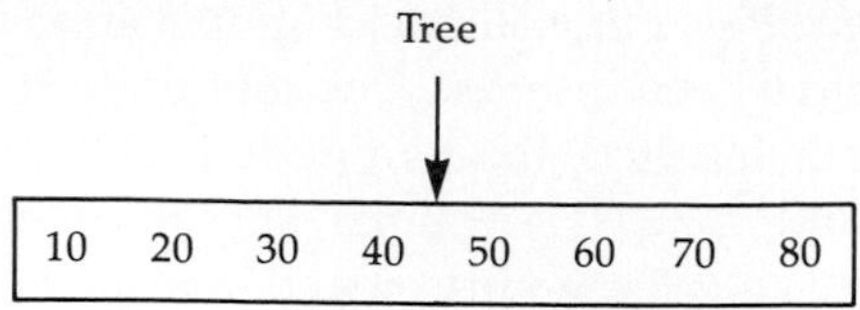

(a) Diagram of B*-tree with full root node

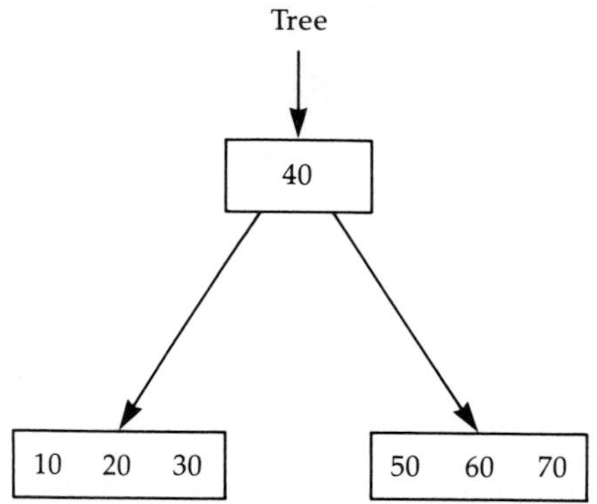

(b) Diagram of B-tree of order 7 when the value 70 is inserted

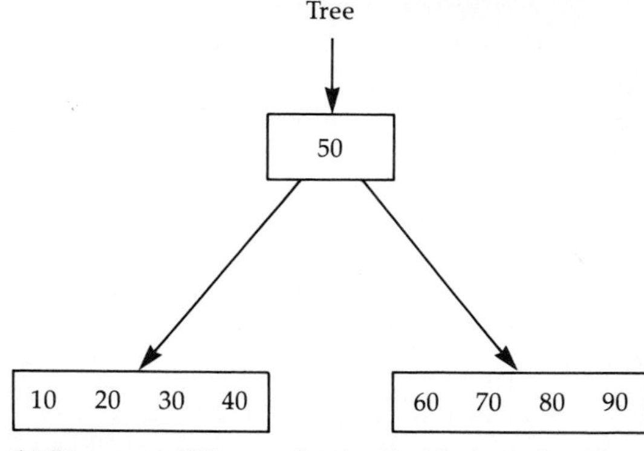

(b) Diagram of B*-tree of order 7 with the value 90

Figure 8.40
B-tree during insertion of keys when first split occurs

Figure 8.41
B*-tree during insertion of keys when first split occurs

Figure 8.42
B-tree and B*-tree from Figures 8.39 and 8.40 with insertions so that leaf nodes of B*-tree are full

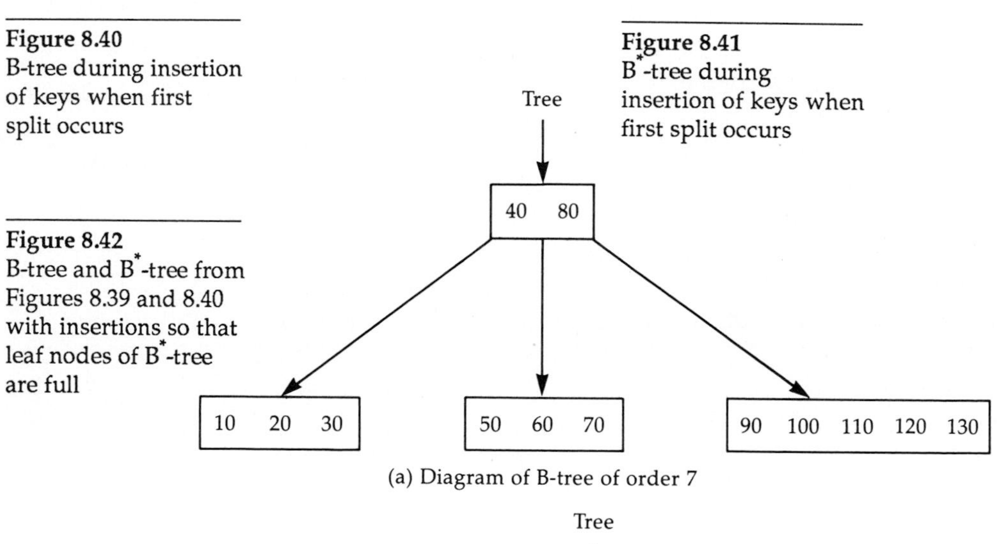

(a) Diagram of B-tree of order 7

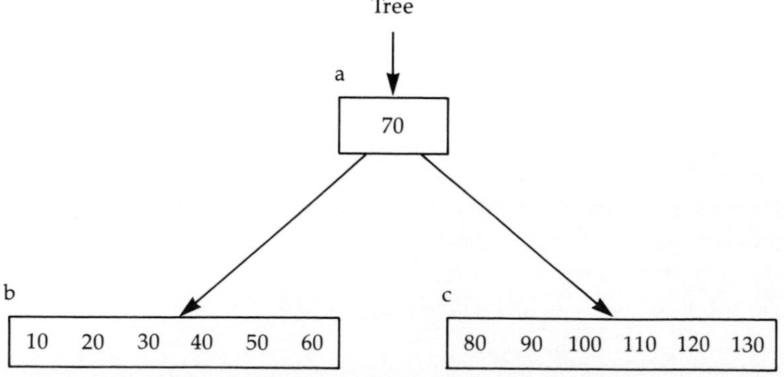

(b) Diagram of B*-tree of order 7 with full leaf nodes

3. node c has next $\lfloor(2m - 1)/3\rfloor$ keys or
   = $key_{\lfloor(2m-2)/3\rfloor} + 2 \ldots key_{m-1}$ from original node b,
   key_{parent} and
   $key_1 \ldots key_{\lfloor(m-1)/3\rfloor}$ from original node c
   = key_6 from original node b, 70, and
   = $key_1 \ldots key_2$ from original node c
4. parent node of c has $key_{\lfloor(m-1)/3\rfloor+1}$ from original node c
   = key_3 from original node c
5. node d has last $\lfloor 2m/3\rfloor$ keys or
   $key_{\lfloor(m-1)/3\rfloor+2} \ldots key_m$ from original node c
   = $key_4 \ldots key_7$ from original node c

If the original node has no left sibling, the right sibling can be used in the same way. Figure 8.43(b) illustrates the B*-tree after nodes b and c have been split into nodes b, c, and d. A B-tree with the same keys is shown in Figure 8.43(a). Notice that both trees now have the same number of nodes; the B-tree has two leaf nodes at a minimum level and one leaf node at a maximum level, and the B*-tree has all leaf nodes at a minimum level. Insertions of keys larger than 140 cause a split in the B-tree but not in the B*-tree.

Figure 8.43
B-tree and B*-tree with 140 added so that B*-tree splits two nodes into three nodes

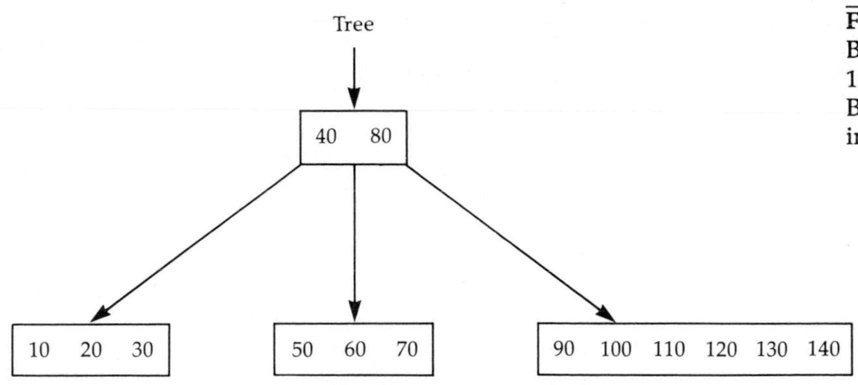

(a) Diagram of B-tree of order 7

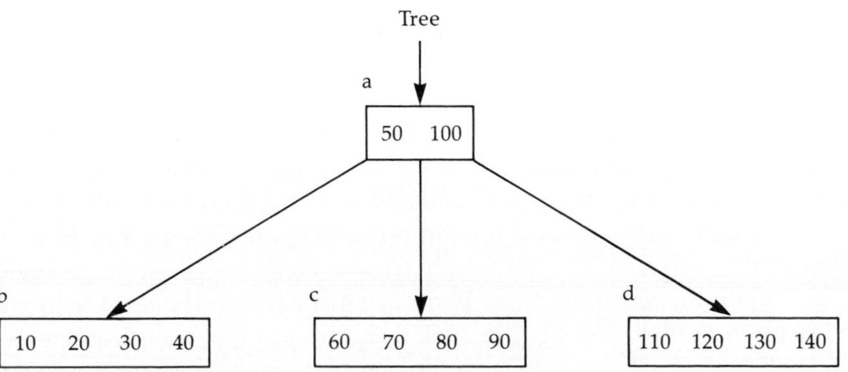

(b) Diagram of B*-tree of order 7, split from two into three nodes

Figure 8.44
B-tree and B*-tree with 150, 160, 170, 180 added

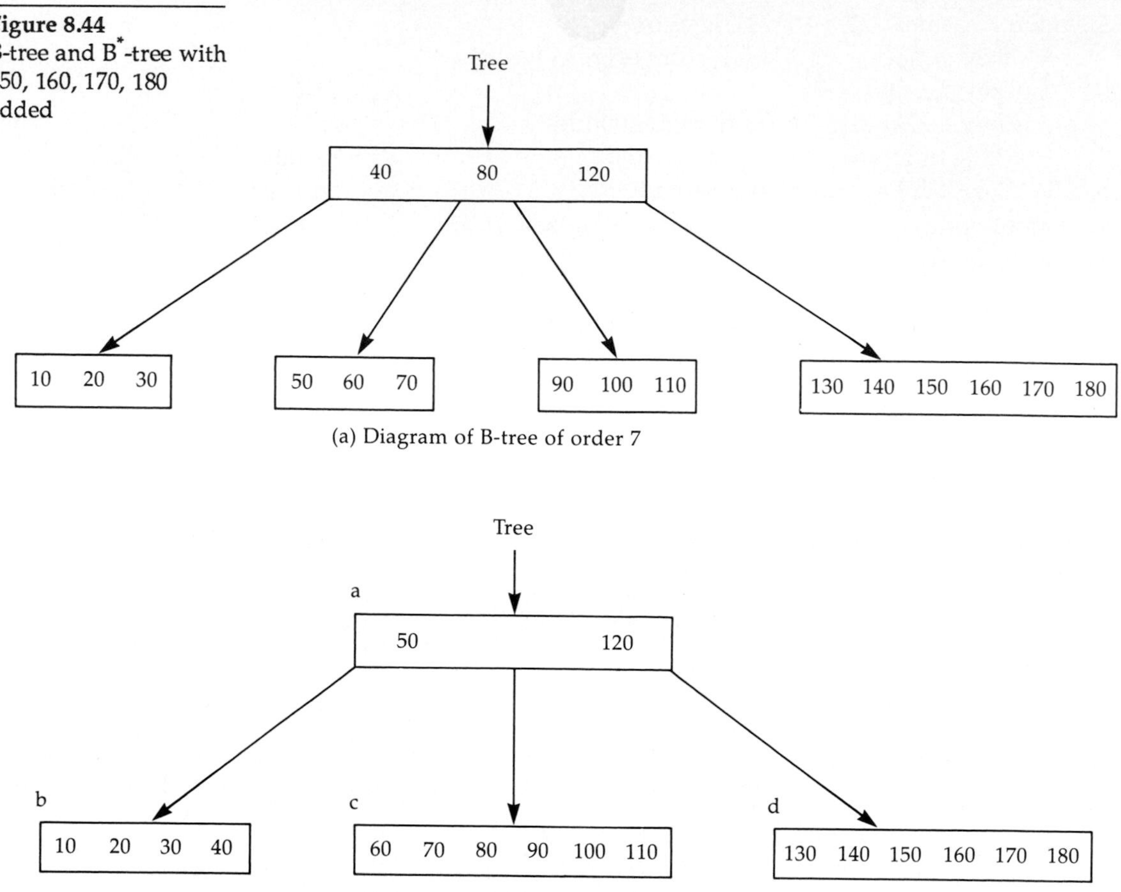

Figure 8.44 shows both trees after the insertion of keys 150, 160, 170, and 180. The rotation of keys from node `d` into sibling node `c` allows the insertions without splitting. The B*-tree still has four nodes after the insertions. The same cannot be said for the B-tree (Figure 8.44(a)), which now has five nodes.

The important characteristic of B*-trees is that each node except the root is at least two-thirds full rather than half-full. This improves the search time so that a B*-tree of order m with N keys requires at worst $1 + \log_{\lceil (2m-1)/3 \rceil - 1} ((N + 1)/2)$ node accesses (disk accesses).

B^+-TREES

A **B^+-tree** is similar to a B-tree with each node at least half-full, except that interior nodes have only keys (no addresses to the records in the data file) and subtree pointers to other nodes. The leaf nodes of a B^+-tree are the only nodes that contain addresses of records in the data file, and all keys appear in the leaf nodes. In addition the leaf nodes are linked in key sequence to facilitate rapid sequential accessing. The nonterminal nodes can contain more keys in the same amount of space than B-trees, so that the height decreases for a large number of keys—a characteristic that leads to shorter search times (fewer disk accesses).

Figure 8.45 shows a B-tree of order 3. The dashed lines indicate addresses of records in the data file. Each tuple contains a key (K), an address (A) of the record in the file with that key, and a subtree pointer (S). If the A's are deleted from each tuple, each nonterminal node could easily hold one more tuple. The terminal nodes still hold a maximum of two tuples, with the format:

$$S_0, (K_1, A_1, S_1), (K_2, A_2, S_2)$$

The nonterminal nodes contain three tuples of the form:

$$S_0, (K_1, S_1), (K_2, S_2), (K_3, S_3)$$

S_{i-1} points to a subtree with keys less than or equal to K_i, and S_n points to a subtree with keys greater than K_n. Each K_i in the nonterminal nodes indicates the largest key value in the child node addressed by S_{i-1}. A B^+-tree in the format described above with the same key values as the B-tree in Figure 8.45 is shown in Figure 8.46. Notice that node b contains two keys and two subtree pointers and that node c contains two keys and three subtree pointers. This is a unique characteristic of B^+-trees that does not occur with B-trees. Since the nonterminal nodes can contain three tuples instead of two, the height of the B^+-tree does not increase as fast as the height of the B-tree as keys are inserted.

The disadvantage of the B^+-tree is that each search must continue to a terminal level before locating a key. The search of the B-tree locates the key value 50, for example, in the root node; the search of the B^+-tree has to visit a node on all levels to locate 50. The countering advantage is that the B^+-tree usually contains fewer levels than a B-tree.

The B^+-tree structure is a common structure for storing an index to a data file where each terminal node is a block of records in a data file and the nonterminal nodes constitute the index for the data file. The nonterminal nodes are usually stored in an index file separate from the data file. Examples of the use of the B^+-tree for indexing a data file are SIS files used on CDC machines and VSAM files used on IBM machines. Both examples are described in detail in Chapter 9.

Figure 8.45
Diagram form of B-tree of order three as an index to a data file

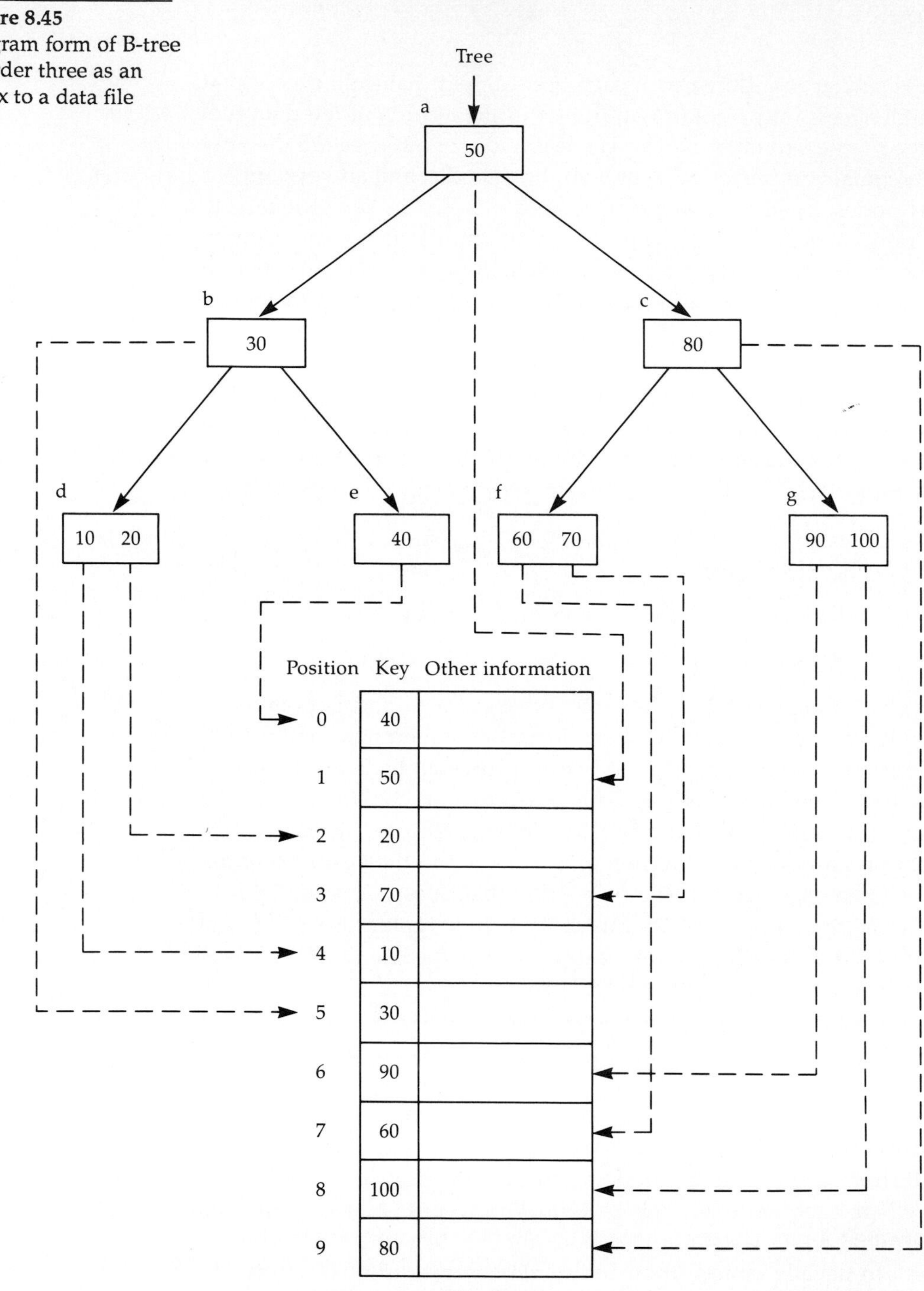

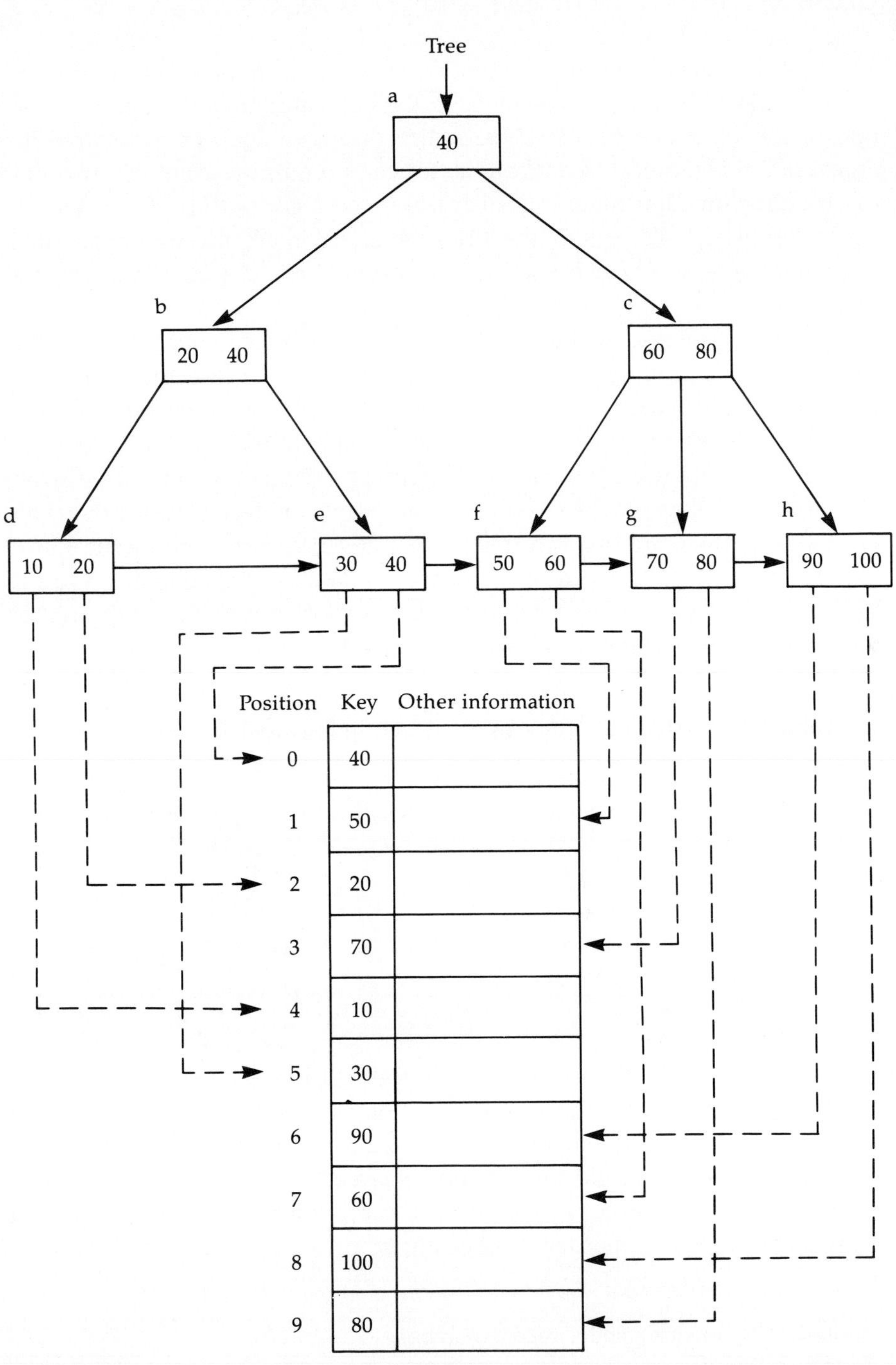

Figure 8.46
Diagram form of B^+-tree of order three as an index to a data file

CASE STUDY 8.1: THE CAR-RENTAL AGENCY

The car-rental agency relative master file created in Chapter 7 allowed rapid access to individual records by hashing the key value to determine the position of the record in the file. One major disadvantage of the relative file organization is that the records are no longer stored physically in key order; the hashing function randomly distributes the records throughout the file space. Sequential listings of the file in key order are no longer possible. Sequential access to keys is sacrificed to provide rapid access to individual records.

A B-tree structure of the key values provides a sequential index to the records in the car-rental agency stored sequentially in a direct master file. A B-tree of order 5 requires that interior nodes have a minimum of three children or two keys. Table 5.1 in Chapter 5 is a listing of the transaction file T1 used to create the car-rental agency direct master file. The B-tree structure of order 5 that provides sequential access to the records consists of the key values, which are inserted into the B-tree as each record is written into the direct master file. The resulting B-tree is illustrated in diagram form in Figure 8.47, and the file containing the nodes of the B-tree with subtree pointers (subtree pointer S) is listed in Table 8.1.

Table 8.1 B-tree file of nodes for B-tree in Figure 8.47

	n,	S_0,	(K_1,	A_1,	S_1),	(K_2,	A_2,	S_2),	(K_3,	A_3,	S_3),	(K_4,	A_4,	S_4)
1	4													
2	2	0	C1	9	0	C2	10	0						
3	2	0	F2	6	0	F3	7	0						
4	3	2	F1	5	3	GM1	15	5	GM4	1	6			
5	2	0	GM2	16	0	GM3	17	0						
6	4	0	GM5	2	0	H1	8	0	H2	18	0	T1	19	0

The address of the root node is stored in the first integer field of record 1 in the file (4 indicates that the root is in record 4). The root node (record 4) points to subtree nodes in positions 2, 3, 5, and 6. The B-tree is stored externally in the B-tree file, and the nodes are accessed as needed. An inorder traversal of the nodes in the B-tree file provides a sequential listing of the records in the file in order by key values:

```
PROCEDURE Inorder_Traversal ( record_number : In Natural )

Input ( b_tree_file, node, record_number)
p ← node.s0
If p /= 0
    Inorder_traversal ( p )
End If
```

```
For i In 1 .. node.n Loop
    Output ( node.tuple(i).key )
    If node.tuple(i).s /= 0
        Inorder_traversal ( node.tuple(i).s )
    End If
End Loop
```

In this case the traversal is called initially with the root as the parameter:

```
Input ( b_tree_file, head_node, 1 )
root ← head_node.n
Inorder_traversal ( root )
```

Transaction file T2 (Figure 5.3) is applied next to the car-rental agency direct master file. As GM6 is added to the direct master file in position 14, it is also added to the B-tree file, resulting in the B-tree structure shown in Figure 8.48 and corresponding file contents in Table 8.2. The key value GM6 is added to node 6, which causes a split into node 7, adding key H1 to the parent node 4. The B-tree file must keep current with the contents and locations of keys in the direct master file so that the data file may be listed sequentially after each update run.

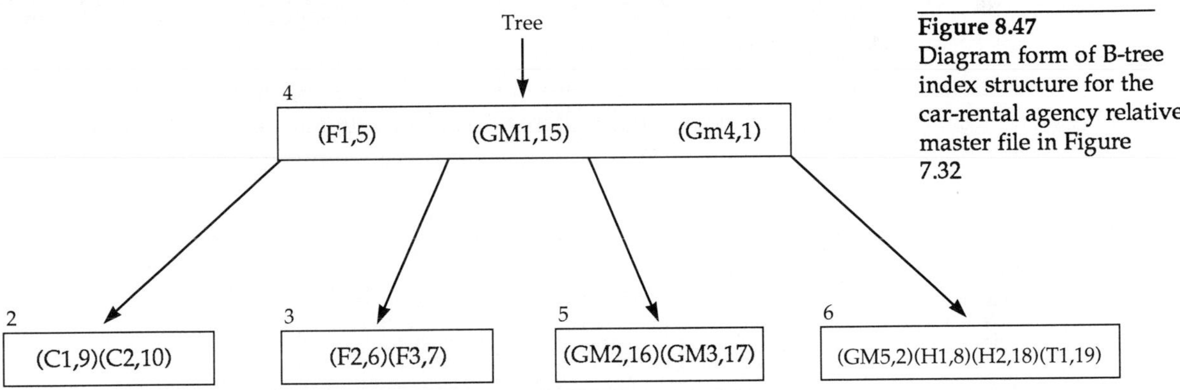

Figure 8.47
Diagram form of B-tree index structure for the car-rental agency relative master file in Figure 7.32

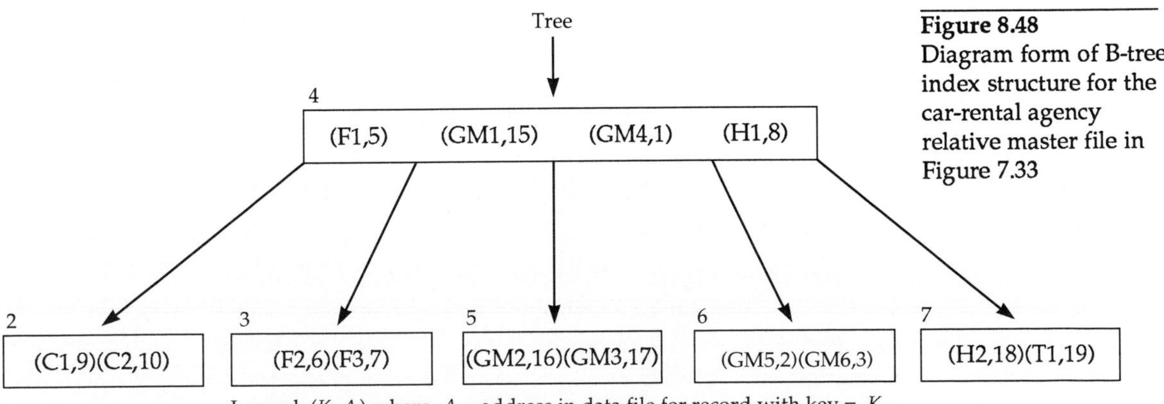

Figure 8.48
Diagram form of B-tree index structure for the car-rental agency relative master file in Figure 7.33

Table 8.2 B-tree file of nodes for B-tree in Figure 8.48

	n,	S_0,	(K_1,	A_1,	S_1),	(K_2,	A_2,	S_2),	(K_3,	A_3,	S_3),	(K_4,	A_4,	S_4)
1	4													
2	2	0	C1	9	0	C2	10	0						
3	2	0	F2	6	0	F3	7	0						
4	3	2	F1	5	3	GM1	15	5	GM4	1	6	H1	8	7
5	2	0	GM2	16	0	GM3	17	0						
6	4	0	GM5	2	0	GM6	3	0						
7	2	0	H2	18	0	T1	19	0						

The last transaction file, T3 (Table 5.5), is applied to the direct master file. As the additions and deletions are made to the direct master file, they must also be made to the B-tree file. Figure 8.49 and Table 8.3 represent the B-tree after deleting F1, adding GM7, and deleting T1. The deletion of F1 with two child nodes—at a minimum—causes nodes 2 and 3 to be merged into node 2, leaving node 3 empty. The addition of GM7 causes the tuple with GM7 to be added to node 6, but the subsequent deletion of T1 leaves node 7 with less than the minimum number of keys. As a result, the parent value, H1, is moved into node 7, and the key, GM7, is moved to the parent node. The update routine for the relative master file takes a little longer to execute since changes are made to both the direct master file and the B-tree file. The benefit of the longer execution is that the direct master file may be accessed randomly by searching the B-tree as well as sequentially by traversing the B-tree inorder.

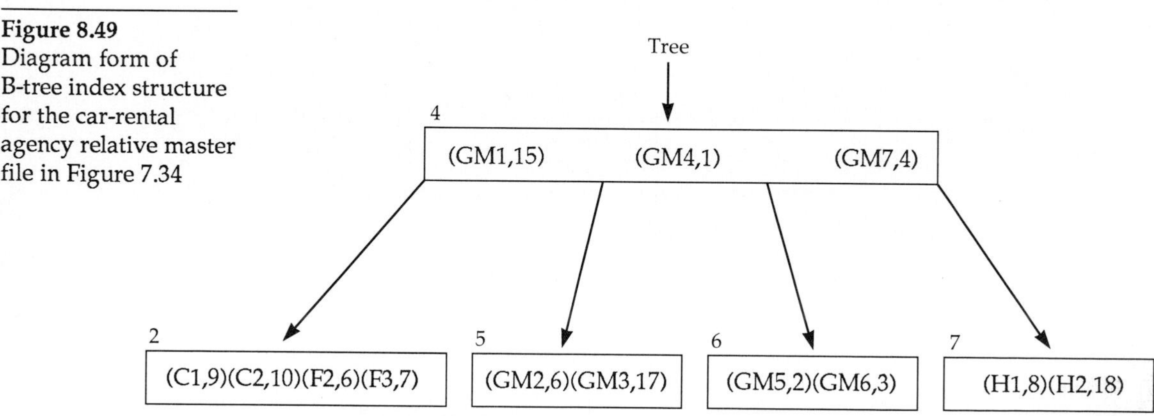

Figure 8.49 Diagram form of B-tree index structure for the car-rental agency relative master file in Figure 7.34

Table 8.3 B-tree file of nodes for B-tree in Figure 8.49

	n,	S_0,	(K_1,	A_1,	S_1),	(K_2,	A_2,	S_2),	(K_3,	A_3,	S_3),	(K_4,	A_4,	S_4)
1	4													
2	4	0	C1	9	0	C2	10	0	F2	6	0	F3	7	0
3	0	0												
4	3	2	GM1	15	5	GM4	1	6	GM7	4	7			
5	2	0	GM2	16	0	GM3	17	0						
6	4	0	GM5	2	0	GM6	3	0						
7	2	0	H1	8	0	H2	18	0						

The Ada implementations of Algorithm 8.2 and Algorithm 8.3 are presented in Appendix B. Figure 8.50 graphically illustrates the interfacing of the program components with each other and the external I/O files. The data structures shared by Algorithm 8.2 (`Create`) and Algorithm 8.3 (`Update`) are encapsulated in a nongeneric package, `Ch5Struc`. The generic `B_Tree` package, also used by both algorithms, encapsulates the operations on the B-tree file while hiding the data structures that define the file components. The hiding of these data structures from the instantiator of the `B_Tree` package prohibits tampering with file components by the user, thus ensuring the integrity of the B-tree.

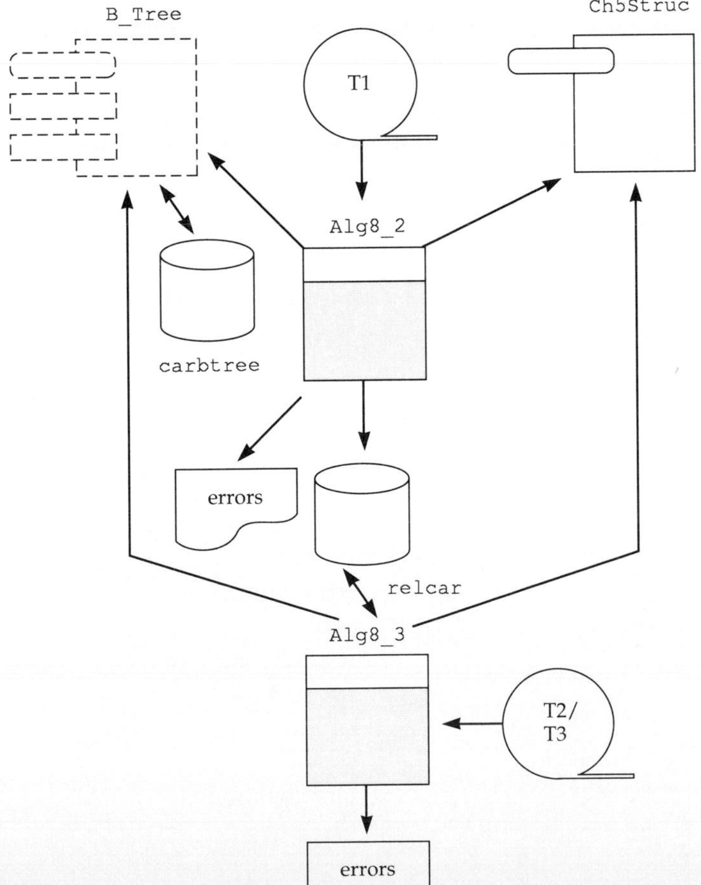

Figure 8.50 Case study 8.1 interfaces

SUMMARY

A binary search tree provides the flexibility of a linked list for inserting and deleting nodes and allows access to any node in the tree almost as quickly as a binary search through an array (allowing for disk accesses for each node visited). AVL trees are height-balanced binary trees with random retrievals occurring in O[lg(n)] time for a tree of n nodes. Further reduction in the number of accesses can be realized with the use of an m-way search tree, which is an m-way (instead of binary) AVL tree. The chapter also discusses a B-tree structure that is a balanced m-way search tree that guarantees that each node is at least half-full of key values. Improvements to the B-tree structure known as B^*-trees (which keep each node at least two-thirds full) and B^+-trees (which store only key values and subtree pointers in nonterminal nodes) are discussed. The B^+-tree structure is the common structure for providing indexing to data files (for example, with SIS and VSAM files) that allow both random and sequential access. Algorithms (originally designed by Wirth) for searching an m-way search tree, inserting nodes into a B-tree, and deleting nodes from a B-tree were presented in the chapter. A B-tree external file was built for the car-rental agency case study and modified as the master file was updated.

For further reading on B-trees see:

Bayer, R., and McCreight, E. "Organization and maintenance of large ordered indexes," *Acta Informatica*, 1(3):173–189, 1972.

Knuth, Donald E. *The Art of Computer Programming. Vol. 3, Sorting and Searching*. Reading, MA: Addison-Wesley, 1973.

Key Terms

ancestor
AVL tree
B-tree
B^*-tree
B^+-tree
balanced tree
binary search tree
child
degree of a node
degree of a tree
descendant
height
height-balanced binary tree
immediate predecessor
immediate successor
inorder
leaf nodes
level
LL rotation
LR rotation
m-way search trees
overflow technique
parent
RL rotation
root
root of a subtree
RR rotation
sibling nodes
skewed
terminal nodes

Exercises

1. Describe the difference between a binary search tree and an *m*-way search tree.
2. If an AVL tree is a balanced binary search tree, what is a balanced *m*-way search tree?
3. A 16-way search tree contains how many keys and how many subtree pointers?
4. For a B-tree of order 9, what are the minimum and maximum number of key values in the root node?
5. For a B-tree of order 9, what are the minimum and maximum number of key values in the nonterminal nodes?
6. What is the maximum number of nodes in a B-tree of order 5 with a height of 3? What is the maximum number of keys?
7. How many nodes need to be visited in the worst case to find a key in a B-tree of order 4 with 243 keys?
8. Draw the B-tree of order 6 after each insertion of the following keys: 25, 26, 24, 39, 32.
9. Insert the following keys into the B-tree in exercise 8: 9, 28, 45, 13. Show the tree structure after each insertion.
10. Insert the following keys into the B-tree in exercise 9: 41, 5, 23, 19, 27, 6, 14, 34, 21, 31, 11, 29. Draw the tree after each insertion.
11. Using the B-tree in exercise 10, draw the tree after deletion of each of the following keys: 26, 21, 11, 9, 45, 13, 39, 6, 14.
12. Repeat exercises 8 through 11 for a B^*-tree of order 6.
13. Describe the difference between a B-tree, a B^*-tree, and a B^+-tree.
14. Write an algorithm to perform the overflow technique used by B^*-trees when a node becomes full and has a sibling node that is not full.
15. Write the algorithm to perform the three-way split of key values from two full nodes of a B^*-tree into three nodes. The node with *m* keys has a full left sibling node.
16. Describe which keys are split into which nodes for the three-way splitting technique explained in the chapter where the node with *m* keys (more than maximum) has a right sibling node that is full. (In the chapter the node with *m* keys had a left sibling node that was full.) The process is symmetric to the one described in the chapter.
17. Repeat exercise 15 for the symmetric process described in exercise 16.

Programming Problems

1. Write a program that builds a B-tree of order 3 (stored externally) for a sequence of key values.
2. Write a program that lists the key values in the B-tree built in problem 1 in sequential order.
3. Write a program that searches the B-tree built in problem 1.
4. Write a program that performs insertions in and deletions from the B-tree built in problem 1.
5. Write a program to implement the overflow algorithm written in exercise 14.
6. Write a program to implement the three-way splitting technique for B^*-trees written in exercise 15.
7. Write a program to input the hashed file created in programming problem 6 or 8 from Chapter 7 (input in sequential order by relative record number) and build the three-way B-tree to be used in listing the part numbers in sequence. Each node of the B-tree should have the following contents:

   n = the number of key values

   S_0 = the record number of the subtree with values less than K_1

   Two tuples of the form (K_i, A_i, S_i) where $i = 1, \ldots, n$

   K_i = a part number
   A_i = the relative record number within the hashed file where part number K_i can be found
   S_i = the record number of the subtree with values greater than K_i

   M = 3, so the maximum value of n is $M - 1$ or 2, so each node may have as many as two key values (K_i) and three subtrees (S_i)

8. Input the three-way B-tree created in problem 7, then output it, listing the contents of the file.
9. Use the B-tree to print an inorder traversal that results in a sequential listing of the relative file.
10. Apply the instructions in problems 7 through 9 to a B-tree of order 7.

Chapter 9

Indexed Sequential File Organization

CHAPTER CONTENTS

PREVIEW

SEQUENTIAL FILE OPERATION is limited to sequential access of the records in the file. Sequential files do not provide direct access to individual records in the file. Relative file organization provides rapid access to individual records in the file by establishing a predictable relationship between the key used to identify an individual record and that record's relative address on the file. Sequential access of a relative file may or may not be meaningful, depending on the physical ordering of the records in the file. Hashing is usually used to randomly access records on a relative file, resulting in no relationship between the logical ordering and physical ordering of records in the file. The B-tree structure for a hashed file provides indexed random files whereby the key is hashed to randomly access the record, or the B-tree is accessed as the index for the hashed file to access the file sequentially. The chapter that follows looks at several ways of providing both sequential and random access to a data file.

This chapter contains a comprehensive description of common implementations of indexed sequential organization, in which records are stored sequentially in data blocks and an index is used to access the data blocks either randomly or sequentially. Included in the discussion are implementations that use a tree structure, such as the B^+-tree, for storing the indexes. Those implementations studied include SIS files (used on CDC computers) that use a B^+-tree with no minimum restrictions for the index, ISAM file organization (used on IBM computers) that uses a static structure for the index, and VSAM file organization (more commonly found on IBM computers today) that uses a B^+-tree for the indexes.

STRUCTURING INDEXED SEQUENTIAL FILES

Indexed sequential file organization for a collection of records in a file provides sequential access to the records by one primary key field as well as random access to an individual record by the same primary key field. An indexed sequential file provides the sequential access available with sequential files by storing the records physically in order by a primary key. An indexed sequential file makes random access available in relative files by including an index of pointers to the sequential data file.

Two common methods exist for structuring indexed sequential files: (1) the index-and-data-blocks method and (2) the cylinder-and-surface indexing method. The index-and-data-blocks method is used on CDC (Control Data Corporation) computers and in VSAM on IBM (International Business Machines) computers; the cylinder-and-surface indexing method is used in ISAM on IBM computers.

INDEX-AND-DATA-BLOCKS METHOD

The **index-and-data-blocks method** used on CDC computers is known as **Scope Indexed Sequential (SIS) file organization.** An SIS file is a collection of data blocks and index blocks. Each data block or index block is transferred by a single I/O instruction. The data blocks are a fixed size and contain a header for the block, a number of logical records, and a number of keys corresponding to the logical records in the data block. The information is arranged as shown in Figure 9.1, where each Ri is a logical record of the file and each key i is the primary key value for each corresponding record Ri.

Header	R1	R2	R3	. . . Padding . . .	Key 3	Key 2	Key 1

Figure 9.1
Format of a data block on CDC computers

3	101 Jane Doe	104 John Smith	106 Sally Adams		106	104	101

Figure 9.2
Data block containing three records and keys

2	101 Jane Doe	106 Sally Adams		106	101

Figure 9.3
Data block after deletion of one record

The logical records are stored in contiguous positions at one end of the data block and physically ordered by key values to provide sequential access to the data. The keys corresponding to the logical records in the data block are stored in contiguous positions at the other end of the data block. The data block is, therefore, filled from the two ends toward the middle of the block. This allows all unused space (padding) within the block to be in one area. As deletions are made from the data block, records and keys are moved to maintain the records in contiguous positions at one end, keys in contiguous positions at the other end, and unused space in the middle. For example, consider the data block containing three logical records and three keys in Figure 9.2. The deletion of record 2 (104 John Smith) causes record 3 and key 3 to move to respective ends of the data block, so all unused space is in the middle (Figure 9.3). The number of entries in the header is changed from three to two records.

Each record may be fixed or variable in length because each record is preceded by a header word (not shown in previous diagrams) that defines the record length in bytes. The size of the keys is fixed and is stored in the header for the block along with the number of entries (record-key pairs) in the data block.

SIS files contain one or more index blocks to provide rapid access to the data blocks. The index blocks are all of a fixed size and contain a header and pairs of keys and addresses corresponding to the data blocks. Each index block in an SIS file has the format shown in Figure 9.4. The data blocks and index blocks are organized in a B$^+$-tree.

Header (no. of entries)	
Key 1	Address 1
Key 2	Address 2
Key 3	Address 3
⋮	⋮
Key i	Address i
⋮	⋮
Key n	Address n
padding	

Figure 9.4
Format of an index block on CDC computers

Each key *i* is the lowest key value in data block *i*, each address *i* is the pointer to data block *i*, and

key 1 < key 2 < . . . < key *i* < . . . < key *n*

In this case there are *n* entries in the index block. The number of entries (key-address pairs) in the index block is stored in the header for the index block. The key-address pairs are maintained in ascending order by key values to provide rapid searching during random access. The data blocks are linked in sequential order to provide fast sequential access. Figure 9.5 is an example of an SIS file with three data blocks and one level 0 index block.

To access a record randomly with key *k*, the entries in the level 0 index block are scanned until the first key in the index block larger than the key *k* is located. The previous entry points to the data block that should contain the record with key *k*. The data block pointed to by the entry in the level 0 index block is accessed, and the logical records are scanned for the record with key *k*. To access the SIS file sequentially, the data blocks are accessed in order of the key-address entries in the level 0 index blocks from key-address 1 to key-address *n*. As each data block is accessed, the logical records within are accessed in physical order.

Suppose that the record with key 109 in Figure 9.5 is to be accessed. The level 0 index block is scanned starting with key 101. The first key value in the level 0 index block larger than key 109 is 111. The key previous to 111 is 107, which points to the second data block and should contain the record with key 109 if it is present. The second data block is accessed, and the keys of the data block are searched to locate key 109. Key 109 is found to be the second key, so the second record is the record being sought, namely: 109 Pete Lama.

Figure 9.5
SIS file with three data blocks and one level 0 index block

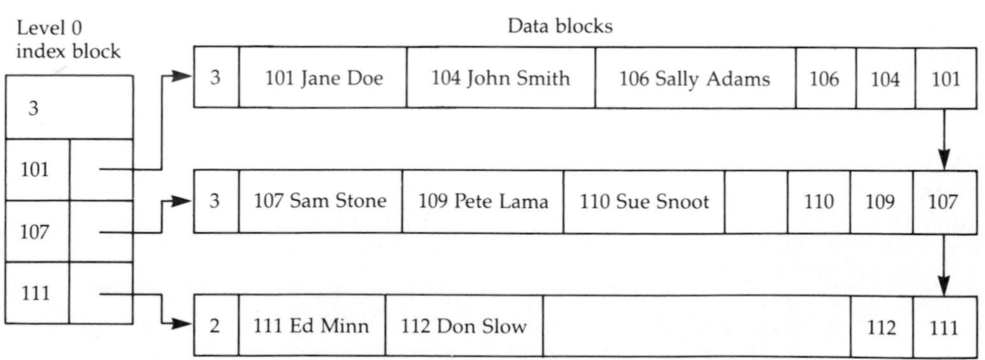

When updating the SIS files, logical records are maintained in sequence by ascending key values within the data blocks, and entries are maintained in sequence by ascending key values within the level 0 data block. Additions of logical records to the SIS file may cause a data block to fill by using all the padding space in the middle of the data block. When attempting an addition to a full data block, the data block is split into two data blocks to allow for the expansion.

During a **data block split**, roughly one-half of the original logical records in the data block remain along with the corresponding keys, and the number of entries recorded in the data block header is changed. The other remaining logical records from the original data block are written to a new data block with the number of entries being recorded in the header for the new data block. The lowest key value in the new data block and a pointer to the new data block form a new entry that is inserted into the level 0 index block in sequence by the keys. The data blocks do not necessarily have to be in contiguous positions; the level 0 index block stores the keys and pointers of the data blocks in sequence to allow either random or sequential access to the data blocks.

The number of logical records that remain in the data blocks is described above as roughly one-half because the decision concerning where the data block is to be split is actually based on where the new record should be inserted in sequence. For the SIS file in Figure 9.5, suppose that a record with the data

105 Hal Hacker

is added to the file. The search routine is used to see whether the record exists in the file. The last data block accessed, if the search fails, is the place where the new record is added. If the record with key value 105 is present, it resides in the first data block with the lowest key of 101. The new record should then be added to the same data block since the lowest value of the next data block is larger than 105 (107). Data block 1 is accessed, found to be full, and split into two data blocks to allow for the addition of record 105 in key sequence. The records with keys 101 and 104 remain in the original data block, but the last record has a key higher than 105 (106). Record 105 is inserted at the beginning of a new data block, then record 106 is moved from the original data block and stored in the contiguous location following record 105. No shifting of records within a block is necessary to store the records in key sequence. A new key-address entry for the new data block must be added to the index block. The resulting SIS file is shown in Figure 9.6.

By making the split at the insertion location rather than splitting half the records to a new data block, then moving to allow an addition of a new record, the movement of records is minimized. By inserting the record 105 in a new data block instead of following 104, free space is available in both blocks for further additions.

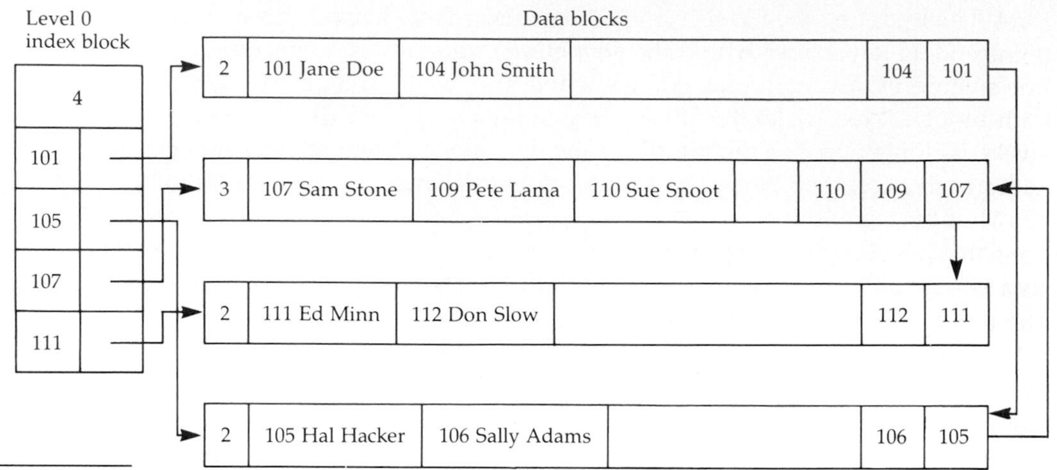

Figure 9.6
SIS file with record 105

If enough new data blocks are added to the SIS file to fill up the space in the level 0 index block, the level 0 index block is split in much the same manner. Part of the original entries remain in the level 0 index block, and the other entries move to a new level 0 (sibling) index block. The location of the split actually depends on where the new entry should be inserted in the key sequence. Since there are now two level 0 index blocks, a new and higher level 1 index block is added which contains an entry for each level 0 index block. The first entry is the lowest key value in the original level 0 index block and a pointer to the index block. The second entry is the lowest key value in the new level 0 index block and a pointer to the index block. When the level 1 index block fills, the split of the level 1 index block occurs, causing the addition of a level 2 index block.

Suppose that a record with the following data

108 Larry Loper

is added to the SIS file in Figure 9.6. A search of the level 0 index block yields a pointer to the data block beginning with key 107 because it is the block for inserting record 108. Since the data block is full, it must be split with record 107 remaining in the data block and record 108 being inserted into a new data block. Records 109 and 110 are copied to the new data block. The data blocks now contain data as shown in Figure 9.7.

An entry for the new data block with 108 as the lowest key should be added to the level 0 index block. If the level 0 index block is full, it is split at the first key entry larger than 108, entry 108 is moved to a new level 0 index block, and entry 111 is moved to follow 108. Figure 9.8 presents the new SIS file with two level 0 index blocks and a level 1 index block. Since two level 0 index blocks exist, a level 1 index block is created with the same format as the level 0 index block of key-address pairs, except that the address in each entry is a pointer to a level 0 index block with the corresponding key. In the level 1 index block in Figure 9.8, the first entry is key value 101 with a pointer to the level 0 index block, which contains the lowest key value 101. The second entry is key value 108 with a pointer to the level 0 index block with the lowest key value 108. (We assume, in this case, that each of the level 0 index blocks can point to as many as four data blocks as illustrated in Figures 9.7 and 9.8.)

The SIS method of indexed file organization allows for dynamic additions to and deletions from the file without much reorganization since the data blocks and index blocks are not necessarily in contiguous positions. The time it takes to retrieve data from the data blocks is not affected by the splitting of index blocks as long as the primary level of index blocks (where the level 0 index blocks are at the lowest level) remains only one index block.

To access an SIS file with several levels of index blocks, the primary level is searched to find a pointer to the level $n - 1$ index block. The level $n - 1$ index block is scanned to locate a pointer to the level $n - 2$ index block. The process continues until the level 0 index block (found by chasing pointers) is scanned to locate a pointer to the one data block that should contain the desired data.

Deletions of logical records from a data block may empty the data block of all logical records and keys, in which case the data block is freed (or chained to other free data blocks for use later). The entry for this data block in the level 0 index block is removed. Should this entry be the first entry in the level 0 index block, a modification to the level 1 index block is in order.

To illustrate the changes necessary as a result of deletions from the file, suppose that the record with key 107 is deleted from the SIS file in Figure 9.8. Since 107 is the only record in the data block, the number of entries in the header for the data block becomes 0, the data block is freed, and the key-address entry for 107 in the level 0 index block is removed. If there were key-address entries in the level 0 index block below entry 107, they would be moved up so all the empty space would be in contiguous locations. The number of entries in the header of the level 0 index block is decremented to two. The resulting contents of index and data blocks after the deletion of 107 are illustrated in Figure 9.9.

A number of changes must take place during the deletion of the first record from a data block that is the first block referenced in a level 0 index block. For example, if the record with the key 101 is deleted from the file in Figure 9.9, the other records and keys in the data block move toward the ends of the data block (Figure 9.10), and the number of entries in the header becomes 1. Since 101 was the first record in the data block, the key-address entry for the block starting with 101 in the level 0 index block must be changed to reveal that 104 is the starting record in the data block. Similarly, since 101 is the first key-address entry in the level 0 index block, and it is changed to 104, the level 1 index block that is the parent must have the corresponding entry changed from 101 to 104. All levels of index blocks that contain record 101 must be changed to 104 to indicate the deletion of 101 from the data file.

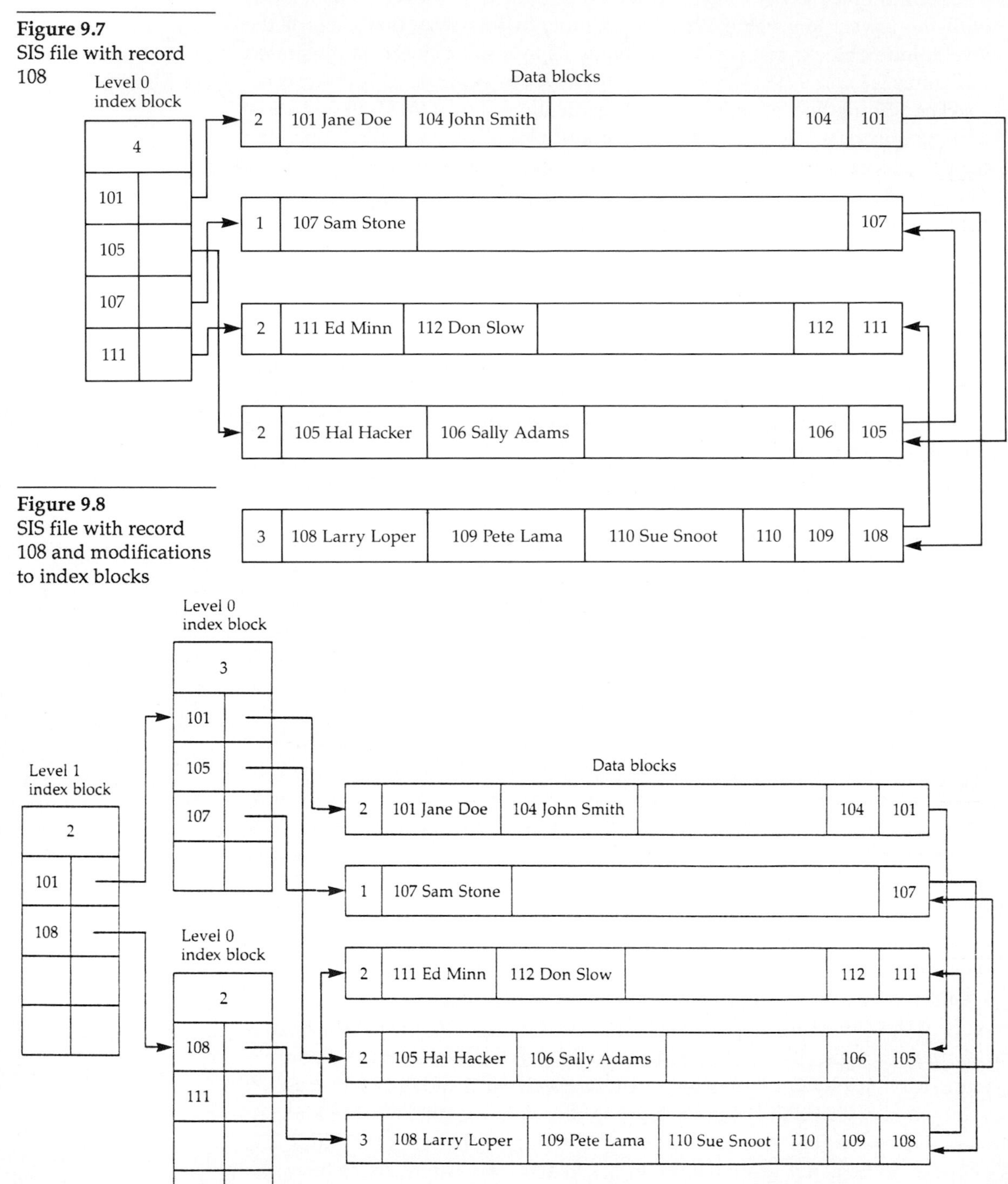

Figure 9.7
SIS file with record 108

Figure 9.8
SIS file with record 108 and modifications to index blocks

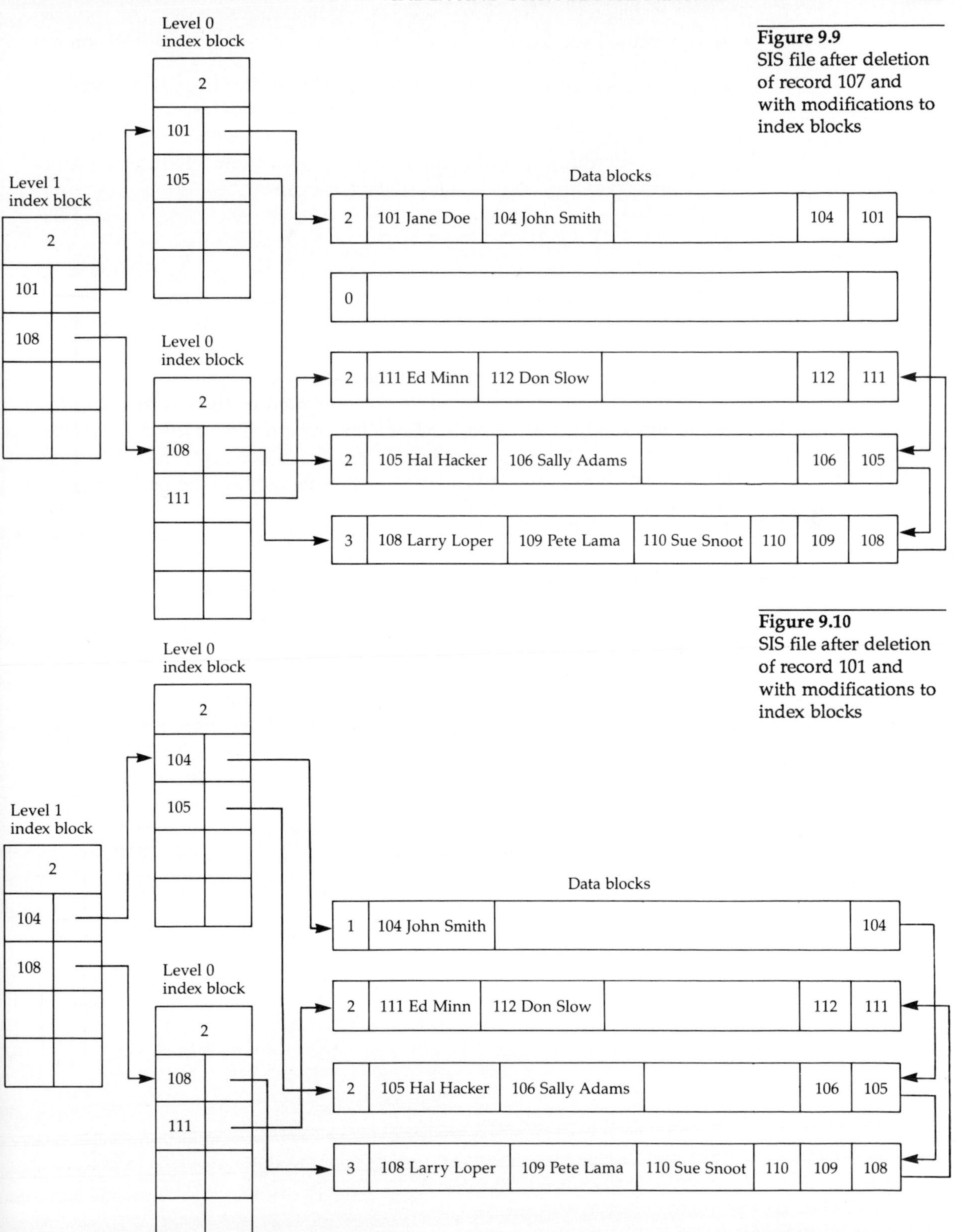

Figure 9.9
SIS file after deletion of record 107 and with modifications to index blocks

Figure 9.10
SIS file after deletion of record 101 and with modifications to index blocks

Ada BPlus-Tree Package

A generic package for creating, inserting, adding, deleting, and searching B^+-trees can be specified that includes the techniques described in the chapter. The specifications for the `BPlus_Tree` package, which follow, list the different procedures available for B^+-tree manipulation. The user instantiates the package and calls the procedure `Create_BPlus_Tree`, `Open_BPlus_Tree`, or `Close_BPlus_Tree` passing the external name of the B^+-tree file and the data blocks file. The user calls the procedures `Insert` (passing the data record to be inserted) and `Delete` (passing the key to be deleted) to add a new record or remove an old one, respectively. The exception `key_not_inserted` is raised by the `Insert` procedure if the key in the data record already exists. The exception `key_not_deleted` is raised by the `Delete` procedure if the key is not in the tree. The user calls the procedure `Retrieve` passing the key to be used in a search of the indexes, and the procedure returns the corresponding data record if it is in the file. The exception `key_not_found` is raised if the `Retrieve` cannot find the key in the file. All of these exceptions are visible to the user via the package specification. The `Replace` procedure is used to replace the data record in the file that has the same key as the data record passed in by the procedure. The `Replace` procedure also raises the exception `key_not_found` if the data record's key is not in the file. A combination of `Retrieve` and `Replace` can be used in tandem if only part of the data record is to be updated.

The generics of the package require the user to specify the size of an index block in the index blocks file (the degree of the B^+-tree to be manipulated) and the size of a data block in the data blocks file. The type of both is `Positive`. The B^+-tree package is an indexing package for a data file, but it has no knowledge of the format of the record in the data file. The function `Key_Of` must be elaborated by the user so the package can have access to the key without knowing the key's specific type nor the key's position within the data record. The user must also specify the function `">"`—this requires no work at all on the part of the user if the key's type is discrete or an array with discrete components.

```
With Text_IO;
Generic
    INDEX_BLOCK_SIZE : Positive;
    DATA_BLOCK_SIZE : Positive;
    Type Key_Type Is Private;
    Type Record_Info Is Private;
    With FUNCTION Key_Of ( a_record : Record_Info ) Return Key_Type;
    With FUNCTION ">" ( left_operand, right_operand : Key_Type )
                        Return Boolean;
Package BPlus_Tree Is
    PROCEDURE Create_BPlus_Tree ( external_bplus_tree_filename,
                                  external_data_block_file : String );
    PROCEDURE Open_BPlus_Tree ( external_bplus_tree_filename,
                                external_data_block_file : String );
```

```
    FUNCTION Insert ( data_record : Record_Info ) Return Boolean;
    FUNCTION Delete ( key : Key_Type ) Return Boolean;
    PROCEDURE Retrieve ( key : Key_Type; data_record : Out Record_Info);
    PROCEDURE Replace ( data_record : Record_Info );
    PROCEDURE Close_BPlus_Tree ( external_bplus_tree_filename,
                                 external_data_block_file : String );
    key_not_found : Exception;
    key_not_inserted : Exception;
    key_not_deleted : Exception;
End BPlus_Tree;
```

Implementation in Ada

The implementation of indexed sequential files in Ada through the index-and-data-blocks method requires the use of direct files, which allow rapid access to individual records. The addresses of data blocks or surfaces are stored in the indexes in terms of a record index.

The data records are fixed in size, so separate and corresponding key fields for each record in the data block are unnecessary. Each data block contains a fixed number of fixed-size data records. Each index block contains a fixed number of entries. Without knowing how many data records there will be in the file, the number of levels of index blocks could continue to grow beyond storage capacity. As the indexed sequential file is created, storing data records in data blocks, the index blocks are created as well. As a data block fills, an entry is stored in an index block. As the data blocks are stored in the file, the B^+-tree of index blocks grows with the address of the root saved in memory until the file is built. Then the address of the root is stored in location 1 of the B^+-tree file.

Figure 9.11 is a diagram of data structures of index blocks and data blocks as an indexed sequential file is being created. The data blocks are labeled DB*d*, where *d* indicates the location where the block will be stored in the relative data file. The index blocks are labeled IB*i*, where *i* indicates that the index block is written to location *i* of the index block file. The address of the index block at the root of the index structure is written to location 1 of the index blocks file for easy retrieval.

The maximum number of entries for each data block is three. The maximum number of entries for each index block is two, and each entry has a key field and an address field as shown in Figure 9.12. As each data block is filled, the first key in the data block and the address of the data block form the key-address entry, which is added to the tree structure of index blocks. The index block structure is basically a B^+-tree with no minimum requirements for the number of entries in the index blocks. As index blocks fill, a split occurs at the point where the last key-address is inserted, and a sibling level 0 index block is created.

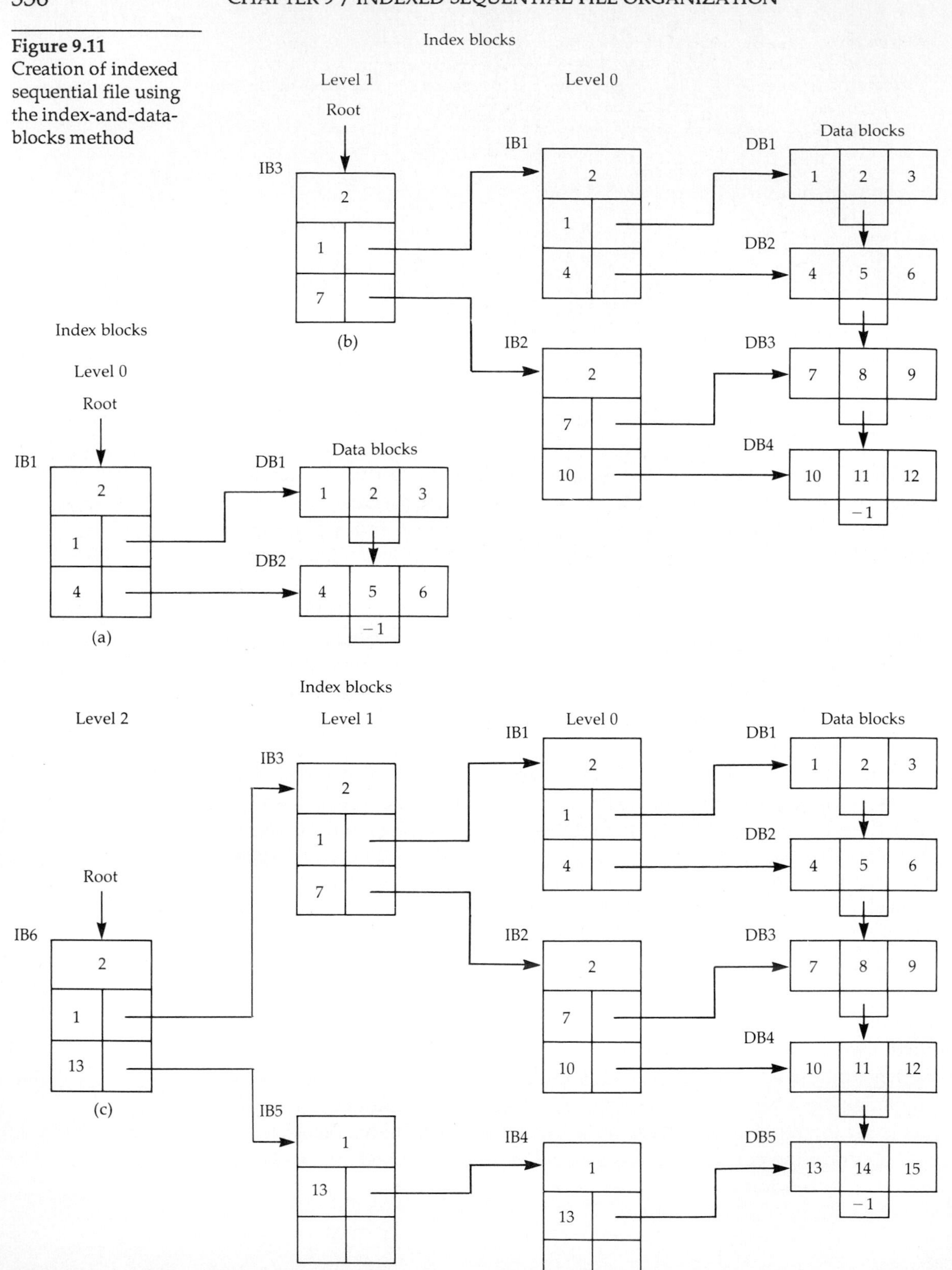

Figure 9.11
Creation of indexed sequential file using the index-and-data-blocks method

Index blocks

Level 2 Level 1 Level 0 Data blocks

IB6 IB3 IB5 IB1 IB2 IB4 DB1 DB2 DB3 DB4 DB5 DB6

Root

(d)

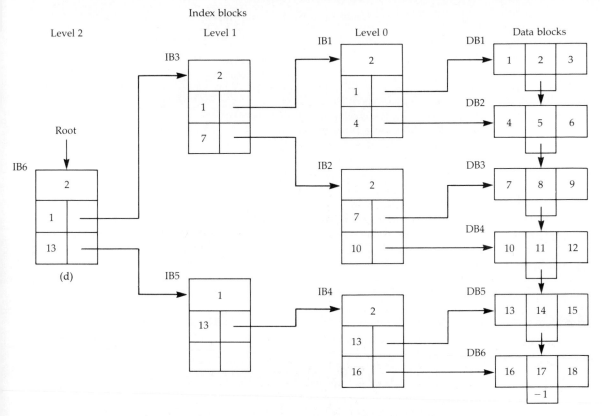

Figure 9.11(a) illustrates the data and index blocks created after two data blocks have been written to the file. Figure 9.11(b) shows the indexed sequential file after four data blocks have been created. The index structure now has two levels. As the fifth data block is written to the data file (Figure 9.11(c)), a new level 0 index block is created, causing a new index block at level 1 (IB5) and level 2 (IB6). Adding a sixth data block to the file (Figure 9.11(d)) adds a new key-address entry to the level 0 index block, and the index structure retains the same number of blocks.

The pseudocode for creating an indexed sequential file using the index-and-data-blocks method is presented in Algorithm 9.1. The routine `Insert_Into_Index_Blocks` is a modification of the insertion algorithm for B-trees.

Index block

Index_entries

key address

key address

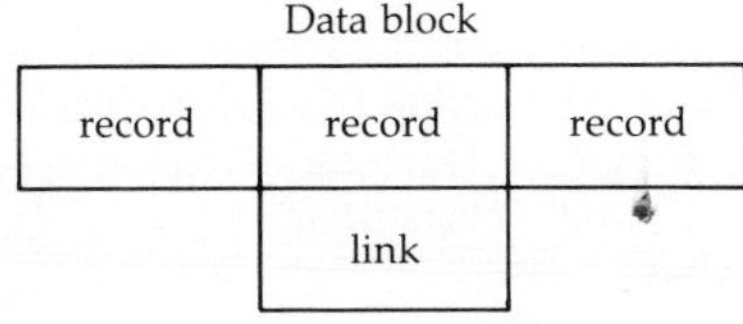

Figure 9.12
Index block and data block layout

ALGORITHM 9.1 Create Indexed Sequential File

```
    TYPE Index_Entry Is Record
                                  key : Key_Type
                                  address : Positive
                              End Record
    TYPE Index_Tuple Is Array ( 1 .. INDEX_BLOCK_SIZE ) Of Index_Entry
    TYPE Level_Indicator Is ( DATA, INDEX )
    TYPE Index_Node Is Record
                                  entries : Natural
                                  level   : Level_Indicator
                                  tuple   : Index_Tuple
                              End Record
    TYPE Data_Tuple Is Array ( 1 .. DATA_BLOCK_SIZE ) Of Record_Info
    TYPE Data_Block_Type Is Record
                                       entries    : Natural
                                       tuple      : Data_Tuple
                                       link       : Natural
                                   End Record
    Package Block_IO Is New Direct_IO ( Data_Block_Type )
    data_blocks_file : Block_IO.File_Type
    Package Index_IO Is New Direct_IO ( Index_Node )
    index_blocks_file : Index_IO.File_Type

PROCEDURE Insert ( data_record : In Record_Info )
    data_block : Data_Block_Type
    data_block_number : Natural
    hold_tuple : Index_Entry
    location : Natural
    new_block : Data_Block_Type
    successful : Boolean
    Find_Node ( data_record.key, data_block_number, location,
                data_block, successful )
    If successful
        Raise key_not_inserted  -- key already exists
    End If
    If data_block_number = 0  -- no root exists, the tree is empty
        data_block_number ← 1
        hold_tuple ← ( data_record.key, 1 )
        New_Root ( hold_tuple )
    End If
    If data_block.data_entries = DATA_BLOCK_SIZE -- data block is full
        new_block.tuple(1) ← data_record
        Split_Data_Block ( data_block, location, new_block )
    Else -- data block has room for insertion
        data_block.entries ← data_block.entries + 1
        For lcv In Reverse  location + 1 .. data_block.entries Loop
            data_block.tuple(lcv) ← data_block.tuple(lcv - 1)
        End Loop
        data_block.tuple(location) ← data_record
    End If
      -- clear the stack, built by Find_Node
    Output ( data_blocks_file, data_block,
             Block_IO.Positive_Count ( data_block_number ) )
```

```
PROCEDURE Find_Node ( key : In Key_Type
                      data_block_number : In Out Natural
                      location : Out Natural
                      data_block: In Out Data_Block_Type
                      successful : In Out Boolean )
    first_node : Index_Node
    root_address : Natural
    Input ( index_blocks_file, first_node, 1 )
    root_address ← first_node.entries
    Search_Indexes ( key, root_address, successful, data_block_number )
    If successful
        Input ( data_blocks_file, data_block,
                Block_IO.Positive_Count ( data_block_number ) )
        Search_Data_Block ( key, data_block, location, successful )
    Else
        data_block.data_entries ← 0
        data_block.link ← 0
        location ← 1
    End If

PROCEDURE Search_Indexes ( key : In Key_Type
                           index_block_address : In Natural
                           successful : Out Boolean
                           data_block_number : Out Natural )
    found : Boolean ← FALSE
    index_block : Index_Node
    lcv : Natural
    If index_block_address = 0   -- the tree is empty
        successful ← FALSE
        data_block_number ← 0
    Else
        Input ( index_blocks_file, index_block,
                Index_IO.Positive_Count ( index_block_address ) )
        lcv ← 1
        Loop
            Exit When lcv > index_block.entries
            If key > index_block.tuple(lcv).key
                lcv ← lcv + 1
            Elsif key = index_block.tuple(lcv).key
                found ← TRUE
                Exit
            Else
                found ← TRUE
                lcv ← lcv − 1
                Exit
            End If
        End Loop
        If lcv > index_block.entries
          -- key  was  > last key in index_block so look in
          -- last address
            found ← TRUE
            lcv ← lcv − 1
        End If
```

```
        Push ( lcv )
        Push ( index_block_number )
        successful ← found
        If found
            If lcv = 0
              -- key was < first key in index_block so is not
              -- in the file
                data_block_number ← 0
                found ← FALSE
                successful ← found
            Else -- search next level down
                 If index_block.level = DATA
                 -- next level down is a data block
                 data_block_number ← index_block.tuple(lcv).address
                Else -- Else next level down is an index block
                  Search_Indexes ( key, index_block.tuple(lcv).address
                                   successful, data_block_number )
                End If
            End If
        End If
    End If

PROCEDURE Search_Data_Block ( key : In Key_Type
                              data_block_number : In Data_Block_Type
                              location : Out Natural
                              successful : Out Boolean )
    lcv : Natural ← 1
    successful ← FALSE
    Loop
        Exit When lcv > data_block.entries
        If key > data_block.tuple(lcv).key
            lcv ← lcv + 1
        Elsif key = data_block.tuple(lcv).key
            successful ← TRUE
            Exit
        Else -- key < data_block.tuple(lcv).key
            Exit
          -- key not found in data block so return lcv as the
          -- location of the first entry > key.
          -- key belongs immediately prior to location lcv
        End If
    End Loop
    location ← lcv

PROCEDURE Split_Data_Block ( data_block : In Out Data_Block_Type
                             location : In Positive
                             new_block : In Out Data_Block_Type )
    entry_position : Positive ← 1
    next_data_location : Natural

    For lcv In location .. data_block.entries Loop
        entry_position ← entry_position + 1
        new_block.tuple(entry_position) ← data_block.tuple(lcv)
    End Loop
```

```
    new_block.entries ← entry_position
    data_block.entries ← location - 1
    new_block.link ← data_block.link
    next_data_location ← Size ( data_blocks_file ) + 1
    data_block.link ← next_data_location
    Output ( data_blocks_file, new_block,
             Block_IO.Positive_Count ( next_data_location ) )
    Insert_Into_Index_Blocks ( new_block.tuple(1).key,
                               next_data_location )

PROCEDURE Insert_Into_Index_Blocks ( key : In Key_Type
                                     address : In Positive )
    TYPE Operation_Type Is ( INSERT_KEY, NIL )
    hold_tuple : Index_Entry
    index, index_block_address : Positive
    node : Index_Node
    operation : Operation_Type ← INSERT_KEY
    hold_tuple := ( key, address )
    Loop
        Exit When stack_empty  -- pop off ancestors
        Pop ( index_block_address )
        Pop ( index )
          -- index_block_address is the address of the index_block
          -- at the next higher level; insert into position index + 1
        If operation = INSERT_KEY
            Input ( index_blocks_file, node,
                    Index_IO.Positive_Count ( index_block_address ) )
            Insert_Tuple ( hold_tuple, node, index_block_address,
                           index, operation )
        End If
    End Loop
    If operation = INSERT_KEY
      -- new root contains hold_tuple with old root as
      -- tuple(1); tuple = (key, addr(key))
      New_Root ( hold_tuple )
    End If

PROCEDURE Insert_Tuple ( hold_tuple : In Out Index_Entry
                         node : In Out Index_Node
                         index_block_address : In Positive
                         index : In Positive
                         operation : In Out Operation_Type )
    If node.entries < INDEX_BLOCK_SIZE -- resulting node is large enough for addition
        operation ← NIL
        For count In Reverse index + 1 .. node.entries Loop
            node.tuple (count + 1) ← node.tuple (count)
        End Loop
        node.entries ← node.entries + 1
        node.tuple (index + 1) ← hold_tuple
        Output ( index_blocks_file, node,
                 Index_IO.Positive_Count ( index_block_address ) )
```

```
    Else   --  node is full so addition will cause a split
         Split
       -- operation retains INSERT_KEY upon return
    End If

PROCEDURE Split  -- internal to Insert_Tuple
        -- splits an index block into two index blocks
    j : Natural ← 1
    new_node : Index_Node
    next_index_location : Positive
    new_node.tuple(1) ← hold_tuple
    For count In index + 1 .. node.entries Loop
         j ← j + 1
         new_node.tuple(j) ← node.tuple(count)
    End Loop
    new_node.entries ← j
    new_node.level ← node.level
    node.entries ← index
    next_index_location ← Positive ( Size ( index_blocks_file ) + 1 )
    hold_tuple ← ( new_node.tuple(1).key, next_index_location )
    Output ( index_blocks_file, newnode,
             Index_IO.Positive_Count ( next_index_location ) )
    Output ( index_blocks_file, node,
             Index_IO.Positive_Count ( index_block_address ) )

PROCEDURE New_Root ( hold_tuple : In Index_Entry )
    -- called from Insert_Into_Index_Blocks
    -- if the root index block is split.
    -- A new root is created
    first_node : Index_Node
    next_index_location : Positive
    new_node : Index_Node
    root_address : Natural
    root_node : Index_Node
    Input ( index_blocks_file, first_node, 1 )
    root_address ← first_node.entries
    If root_address = 0    -- no root exists yet
         new_node.level ← DATA
         new_node.tuple (1) ← hold_tuple
         new_node.entries ← 1
    Else
         Input (  index_blocks_file, root_node,
                  Index_IO.Positive_Count ( root_address ) )
         new_node.level ← INDEX
         new_node.tuple(1) ← ( root_node.tuple(1).key, root_address )
         new_node.tuple(2) ← hold_tuple
         new_node.entries ← 2
    End If
    next_index_location ← Positive ( Size ( index_blocks_file ) + 1 )
    Output ( index_blocks_file, newnode,
             Index_IO.Positive_Count ( next_index_location ) )
    first_node.entries ← next_index_location
    Output ( index_blocks_file, first_node, 1 )
```

To search the indexed sequential file created by Algorithm 9.1, the top-level index block is input and scanned first to locate the address of the next lower-level index block. The next lower-level index block is input, and index blocks are scanned until the lowest-level index block is searched and yields the address of a data block. The data block is input and searched for a particular record. The index block numbers and the particular entry selected for moving on to a lower-level index block are pushed onto a stack. (Each level of the index is being scanned in case changes need to be made in the index blocks.) By stacking the index block numbers and entry values, the search routine (`Find_Node`) can be used by an insertion routine or a deletion routine to modify all index nodes on the path to a selected record in a data block. Algorithm 9.2 presents the search routine, `Retrieve`, in pseudocode, that calls `Find_Node` and either returns the record found or raises the exception `key_not_found`.

ALGORITHM 9.2 Search Algorithm for Locating a Record in File

```
PROCEDURE Retrieve ( key : In Key_Type
                     data_record : Out Record_Info )

    data_block : Data_Block_Type
    data_block_number : Natural
    location : Natural
    successful : Boolean

    Find_Node ( key, data_block_number, location, data_block, successful )
      -- clear the stack
    If successful
        data_record ← data_block.tuple(location)
    Else
        Raise key_not_found
    End If
```

Maintenance of the indexed sequential file involves changes to existing records, additions of new records to the file, and deletions of existing records. Changes to existing records require that: (1) the record to be changed be located through the use of Algorithm 9.2, (2) the data block containing the located record be input, (3) the specified changes be made to the record, and (4) the data block containing the record changed be output back to the same location in the data file from which the record was input. Algorithm 9.2, `Retrieve`, performs steps one and two above. The pseudocode for changing existing records, `Replace`, in the indexed sequential file built in Algorithm 9.1 is presented in Algorithm 9.3.

ALGORITHM 9.3 Change Indexed Sequential File Created in Algorithm 9.1

```
PROCEDURE Replace ( data_record : In Record_Info )

    data_block : Data_Block_Type
    data_block_number,
    location : Natural
    key : Key_Type
    successful : Boolean

    key ← data_record.key
    Find_Node ( key, data_block_number, location, data_block, successful )
      -- clear the stack
    If successful
        data_block.tuple(location) ← data_record
        Output ( data_blocks_file, data_block,
                 Block_IO.Positive_Count ( data_block_number ) )
    Else
        Raise key_not_found
    End If
```

Algorithm 9.4 is an expansion of Algorithm 9.3. It allows additions to the existing file as well as changes to existing records. The `Insert` procedure described in Algorithm 9.1 is called to apply additions to the existing B^+-tree file. Algorithm 9.4 presents the user program to change and add records in the indexed sequential file created in Algorithm 9.1.

ALGORITHM 9.4 User Program to Change and Add Records in Indexed Sequential File Created in Algorithm 9.1

```
    Loop
        Exit When End_Of_File ( transfile )
        Input ( transfile, trans_record )
        Case update_code
            'C' → Retrieve ( trans_key, hold_record )
                    -- Make_Changes_In_Data_Record ( hold_record,
                    --                               trans_record )
                  Replace ( hold_record )

            'A' → Insert ( trans_record )
                  Output ( "add successful" )
        End Case
    EXCEPTION
        When key_not_found → Output ( "No matching record" )
            -- key_not_found raised by Retrieve or Replace

        When key_not_inserted → Output ( "duplicate add transaction" )
            -- key_not_inserted raised by Insert
    End Loop
```

Deletion of records from the data blocks only affects the index blocks if the first record in a data block is deleted or if a record that is the only record in a data block is deleted. If the first record in a data block is deleted, the key in the index blocks is replaced by the key of the next record in the data block. If the record deleted is the only record in a data block, the key entry is removed from all index blocks that contain that key.

For example, consider the index blocks and data blocks from Figure 9.11(d). If the record with key 12 is deleted, no change occurs in the index blocks (Figure 9.13(a)). On the other hand, if the record with key 7 is deleted, all key-address entries in the index blocks that reference key 7 must be changed to reflect the new lowest key in the data block. Key 8 is now the lowest key in data block 3, so the first entry in index block 2 (IB2) references key 8 in data block 3 (DB3), and the second entry in index block 3 (IB3) references key 8 in index block 2 (IB2). Figure 9.13(b) illustrates the index blocks and data blocks after deleting key 7.

Figure 9.13
Deletion of records from an indexed sequential file

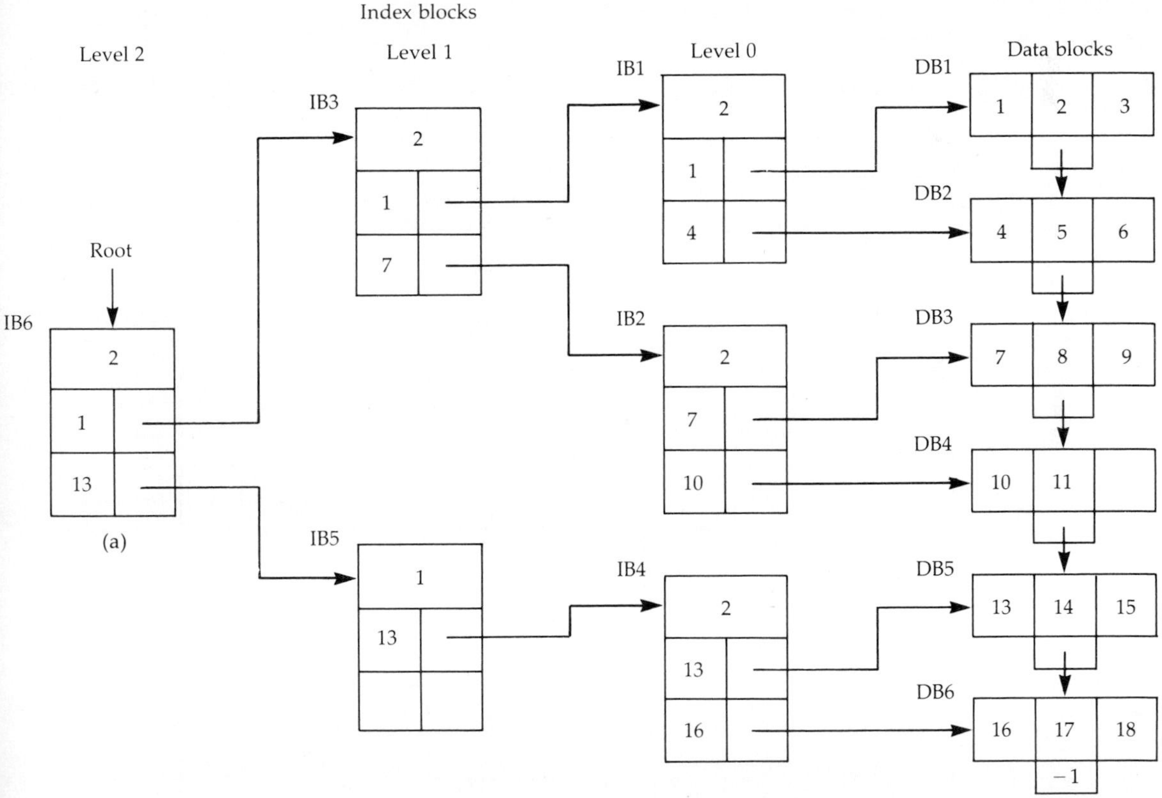

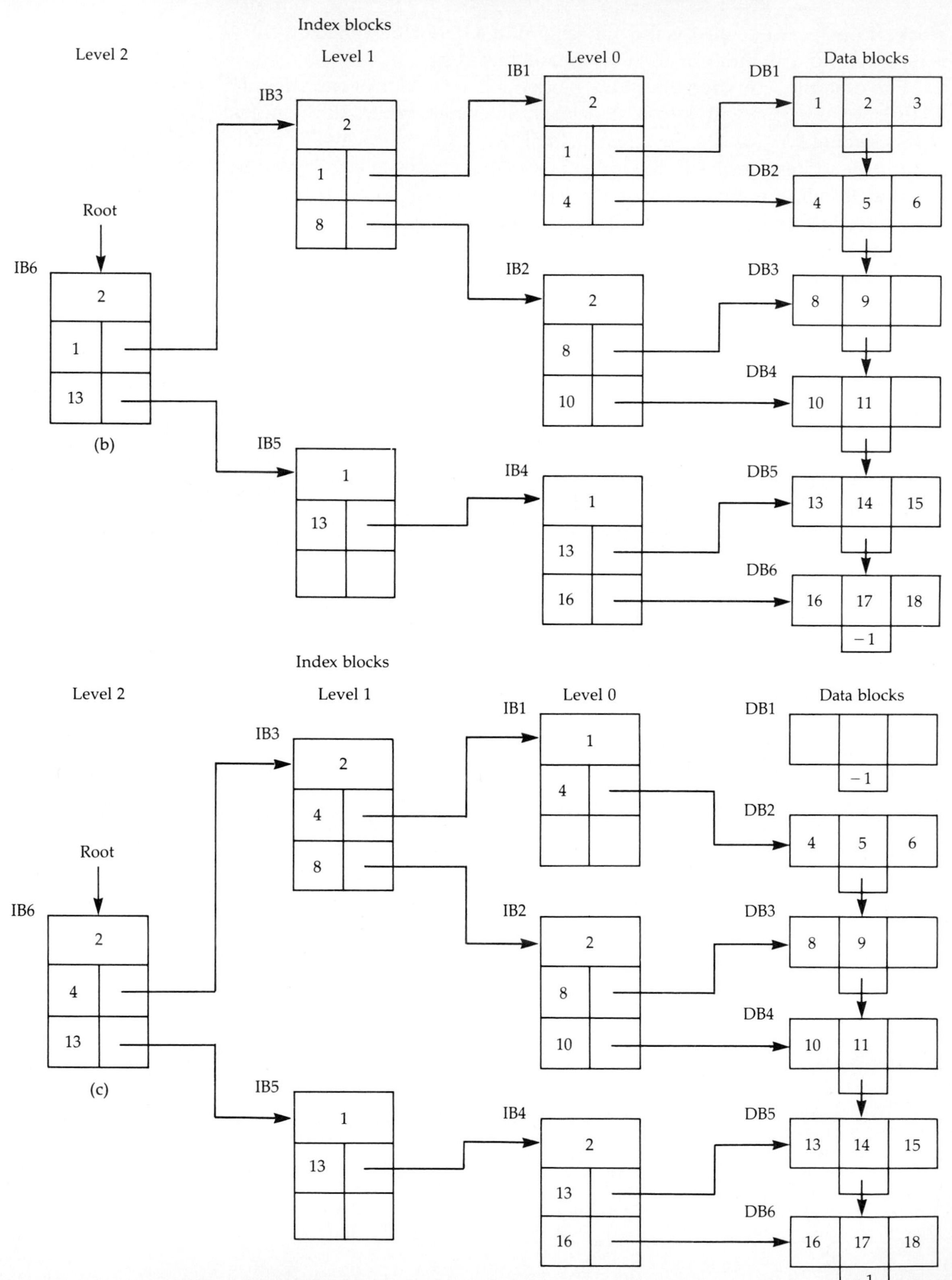
Index blocks
Level 2
Level 1
Level 0
Data blocks
Root
IB6
IB3
IB5
IB1
IB2
IB4
DB1
DB2
DB3
DB4
DB5
DB6
(b)
Index blocks
Level 2
Level 1
Level 0
Data blocks
Root
IB6
IB3
IB5
IB1
IB2
IB4
DB1
DB2
DB3
DB4
DB5
DB6
(c)

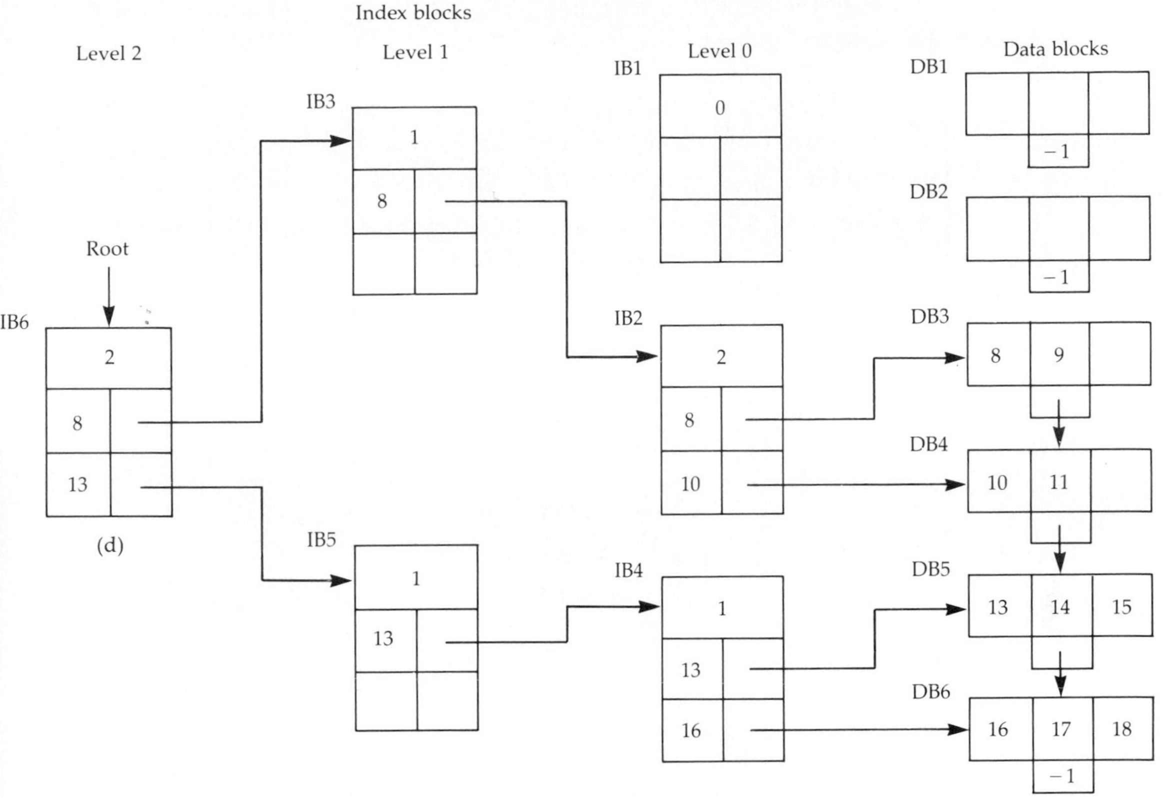

If the records with keys 1, 2, and 3 are deleted from the data blocks file, data block 1 (DB1) is left empty. The first entry in the level 0 index block (IB1) that references DB1 is deleted, leaving only one entry in the index block to DB2 (Figure 9.13(c)). Since the first entry of IB1 has been deleted, the first entry in level 1 index block IB3 must be changed to reference the new first entry in IB1, namely key 4. Similarly, the first entry in level 2 index block (and root) IB6 must be replaced by a reference to key 4.

Consider the situation where enough deletions have been made to delete all entries from an index block. Suppose that the records with keys 4, 5, and 6 have been deleted from the data blocks file. The single entry in level 0 index block IB1 is now empty. The first key-address entry in level 1 index block IB3 is removed, leaving only a single reference to key 8 in IB3. Since the first entry in IB3 was removed, the reference to key 4 in level 2 index block (the root) must be replaced with the new first entry of IB3, namely a reference to the key 8. The results of deleting the records with keys 4, 5, and 6 are shown in Figure 9.13(d). The information from the index blocks could be stored in fewer index blocks, but the SIS file organization refrains from moving data around any more than necessary. After a number of deletions, the indexed sequential file may need to be reorganized by listing all the listing all the records in sequential order and recreating a new SIS file with full data and index blocks.

Algorithm 9.5 is an expansion of Algorithm 9.4, with new statements indicated with a + to the left for the `Delete` routine. Algorithm 9.5 allows deletions from and changes to existing records as well as additions to the existing file.

ALGORITHM 9.5 User Program to Change, Add, and Delete Records in Indexed Sequential File Created in Algorithm 9.1

```
     Loop
          Exit When End_Of_File ( transfile )
          Input ( transfile, trans_record )
          Case update_code
             'C' → Retrieve  ( trans_key, hold_record )
                      -- Make_Changes_In_Data_Record ( hold_record,
                      --                                trans_record )
                   Replace   ( hold_record )

             'A' → Insert    ( trans_record )
                   Output    ( "add successful" )

+            'D' → Delete    ( trans_key )
+                  Output    ( "delete successful" )
          End Case
     EXCEPTION
          When key_not_found → Output ( "No matching record" )
            -- key_not_found raised by Retrieve or Replace
          When key_not_inserted → Output ( "duplicate add transaction" )
            -- key_not_inserted raised by Insert
          When key_not_deleted → Output ( "no matching record" )
            -- key_not_deleted raised by Delete
     End Loop

+ PROCEDURE Delete ( key : In Key_Type )
+      TYPE Operation_Type Is ( REPLACE, DELETE, NIL )
+      action : Operation_Type
+      data_block : Data_Block_Type
+      data_block_number : Natural
+      first_key : Key_Type
+      hold_tuple : Index_Entry
+      location : Natural
+      successful : Boolean

+      Find_Node ( key, data_block_number, location, data_block,
+                  successful )
+      If successful
+           first_key ← data_block.tuple(1).key
+           If data_block.entries = 1   -- delete only entry
+                action ← DELETE
+                Delete_Index_Entry ( action, key, hold_tuple )
+
```

```
+           Else
+               For lcv In location + 1 .. data_block.entries Loop
+                     data_block.tuple(lcv - 1) ← data_block.tuple(lcv)
+               End Loop
+               data_block.entries ← data_block.entries - 1
+               Output ( data_blocks_file, data_block,
+                        Block_IO.Positive_Count ( data_block_number ) )
+
+               If location = 1  --  delete first entry
+                   hold_tuple ← (data_block.key(1).key, data_block_number)
+                 -- replace key with hold_tuple entry in parent
+               End If
+               action ← REPLACE
+               Delete_Index_Entry ( action, key, hold_tuple )
+           End If
+             -- clear the stack
+       Else
+           Raise key_not_deleted
+       End If
+ PROCEDURE Delete_Index_Entry ( action : In Out Operation_Type
+                                key : In Key_Type
+                                hold_tuple : In Out Index_Entry )
+       index,
+       index_block_address : Positive
+       index_block : Index_Node
+       predecessor_found : Boolean
+
+       Loop
+           Exit When stack_empty
+           Pop (index_block_address)
+           Pop ( index )
+           Input ( index_blocks_file, index_block,
+                   Index_IO.Positive_Count ( index_block_address ) )
+           Case action
+               REPLACE → Replace_Entry ( key, hold_tuple, index_block,
+                                         index_block_address, index, action )
+
+               DELETE  → Delete_Entry ( index_block, index_block_address,
+                                        index, action, predecessor_found )
+               NIL     → Null
+           End Case
+       End Loop
+       If action = DELETE   -- last data block has been deleted
+           index_block.entries ← 0
+           Output ( index_blocks_file, index_block, 1 )
+       End If
+ PROCEDURE Replace_Entry ( key : In Key_Type
+                           hold_tuple : In Out Index_Entry
+                           index_block : In Out Index_Node
+                           index_block_address : In Positive
+                           index : In Positive
+                           action : In Out Operation_Type )
```

```
+       If index_block.tuple(index).key = key
+            index_block.tuple(index) ← hold_tuple
+            Output ( index_blocks_file, index_block,
+                      Index_IO.Positive_Count ( index_block_address ) )
+       End If
+       If index = 1
+            hold_tuple ← ( index_block.tuple(1).key,
+                           index_block_address)
+          -- action remains REPLACE
+       Else
+            action ← NIL
+       End If
+
+ PROCEDURE Delete_Entry ( index_block : In Out Index_Node
+                          index_block_address : In Positive
+                          index : In Positive
+                          action : In Out Operation_Type
+                          predecessor_found : In Out Boolean )
+       key : Key_Type
+       previous : Natural
+
+       key ← index_block.tuple(1).key
+       If index_block_level = DATA
+            If index = 1
+                 predecessor_found ← FALSE
+            Else  -- link around deleted data block
+                 previous ← index_block.tuple(index – 1).address
+                 Input ( data_blocks_file, data_block,
+                         Block_IO.Positive_Count ( previous ) )
+                 data_block.link ← index_block.tuple(index + 1).address
+                 Output ( data_blocks_file, data_block,
+                          Block_IO.Positive_Count ( previous ) )
+                 predecessor_found ← TRUE
+            End If
+       Else  -- index_block.level = INDEX
+            If Not predecessor_found And index > 1
+                 Locate_Predecessor ( index – 1 )
+                 predecessor_found ← TRUE
+            End If
+       End If
+       If index_block.entries = 1    -- delete only entry
+            Return
+       Else
+            index_block.entries ← index_block.entries – 1
+            For count In index .. index_block.entries Loop
+                 index_block.tuple(count) ← index_block.tuple(count + 1)
+            End Loop
+            Output ( index_blocks_file, index_block,
+                      Index_IO.Positive_Count ( index_block_address ) )
+            If index = 1
+                 hold_tuple ← (index_block.tuple(1).key,
+                               index_block_address)
+                   -- replace key with hold_tuple entry in parent
```

```
+               action ← REPLACE
+           Else
+               action ← NIL
+           End If
+       End If
+
+ PROCEDURE Locate_Predecessor ( previous : Positive )
+       data_block : Data_Block_Type
+       hold_address : Natural
+       index_block : Index_Node
+       next_block : Data_Block_Type
+       next_block_address : Natural
+
+       hold_address ← index_block.tuple(previous).address
+       Input ( index_block_file, index_block,
+               Index_IO.Positive_Count ( hold_address ) )
+       Loop
+           Exit When index_block.level = DATA
+           hold_address ← index_block.tuple(index_block.entries).address
+           Input ( index_blocks_file, index_block,
+                   Index_IO.Positive_Count ( hold_address ) )
+       End Loop
+       hold_address ← index_block.tuple(index_block.entries).address
+       Input ( data_blocks_file, data_block, hold_address )
+       next_block_address ← data_block.link
+       Input ( data_blocks_file, next_block,
+               Block_IO.Positive_Count ( next_block_address ) )
+       data_block.link ← next_block.link
+       Output ( data_blocks_file, data_block, hold_address )
```

CASE STUDY 9.1: THE CAR-RENTAL AGENCY

The same data used in previous chapters are stored in an SIS file for comparison. The transaction file T1 in Table 5.1 contains the initial records to be loaded to the file. The records are in sequential order and are loaded to data blocks of size 3 with index blocks holding three entries. Figure 9.14 shows three snapshots of loading the records to the SIS file. Any record can be accessed by first retrieving the root from location 1 of the index blocks file, then retrieving and searching two levels of index blocks, and executing a final retrieval of a data block. The search for a record that does not exist in the SIS file involves the same process.

The transaction file T2 contains only a single addition of the record with key GM6. The key GM6 should be inserted into data block 4, which is already full (Figure 9.14(c)). As a result, data block 4 is split into data block 6 at the point of insertion, causing a new entry to be added to parent index block IB2 (Figure 9.15).

Figure 9.14
Creation of car-rental agency indexed sequential master file using the index-and-data blocks method

Index block

Level 0

Root

IB1

2	
C1	→ DB1
F2	→ DB2

Data blocks

DB1

C1	Dodge	2 DR	Omni	25,000	grey
C2	Dodge	2 DR	Aspen	7,000	tan
F1	Ford	2 DR HB	Escort	54,000	white

DB2

F2	Lincoln	4 DR	Continental	38,000	black
F3	Ford	2 DR	Thunderbird	35,000	blue
GM1	Cadillac	4 DR	Fleetwood	9,000	red

−1

(a) Data blocks 1 and 2 are full

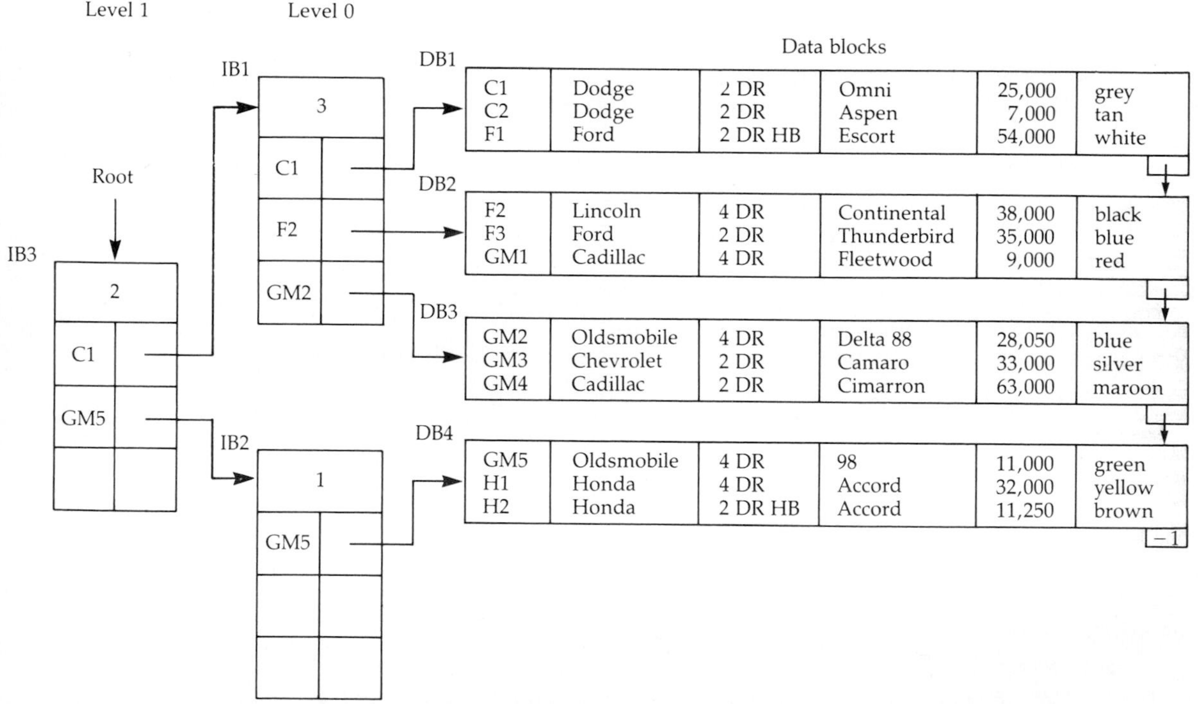

(b) Four full data blocks

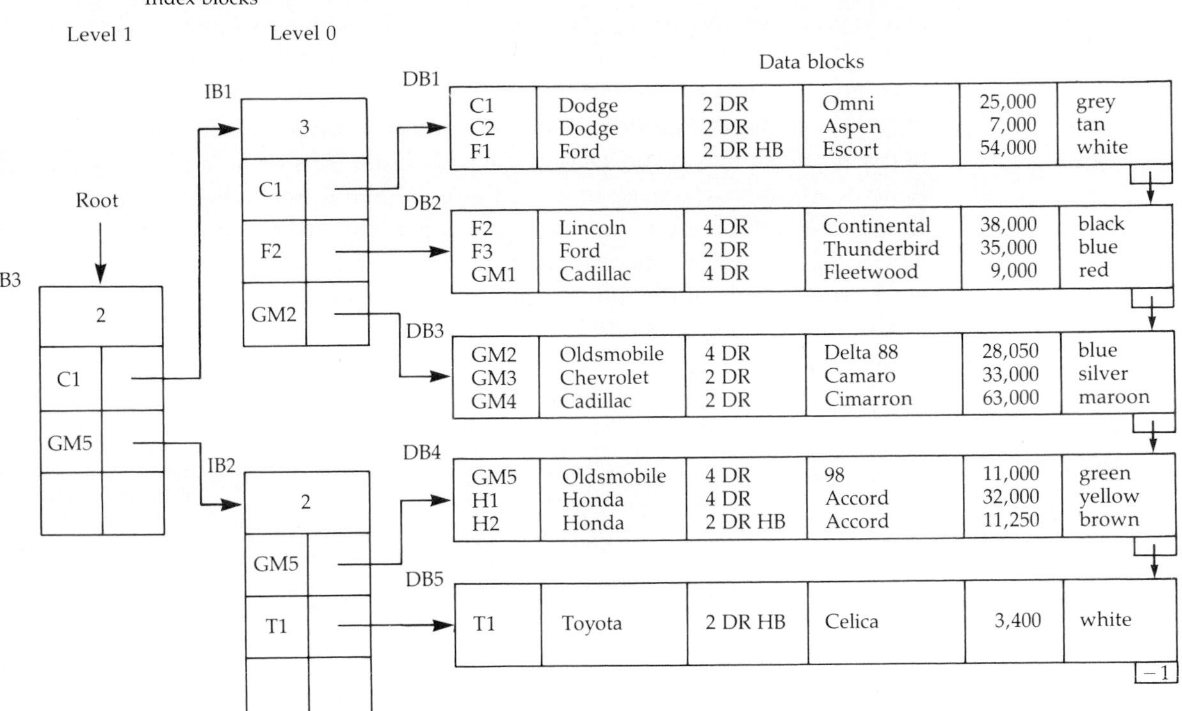

(c) Five data blocks and three index blocks

Transaction file T3 contains several transactions, the net effect of which is shown in Figure 9.16. The record with key F1 is deleted from data block 1, which causes no change in the index block structure. The addition of GM7 into data block 6, which is full, causes a split into data block 7. The key GM7 is inserted into index block 2, causing a split into index block 4 of keys GM7 and T1, with the key GM7 also being inserted into the root index block. A subsequent deletion of GM7 causes H1 and H2 to move up one location in DB7 and the corresponding index entry in IB4 to change to H1 in data block 7. The second addition of GM7 into data block 6 causes no change in the indexes. The deletion of the record with the key T1 leaves index block 4 with only one entry and data block 5 empty. Figure 9.16 shows the results of applying transaction file T3.

The car-rental agency master file in Figure 9.16 has two levels of index blocks. Searching for a record in the file involves an input operation to retrieve the location of the root of the index blocks structure, an input operation for an index block on each of the two levels of the structure, and a fourth input operation to input a data block. Therefore, the search time for accessing a record in the file involves four input operations from secondary memory. Sequentially accessing the indexed file to list the car records in sequence by key involves a traversal of the linked list of data blocks. One of the major advantages of the indexed sequential file organization over relative file organization (in addition to the fact that indexed sequential organization provides both sequential and random access to the data) is that data records are stored in data blocks rather than one data record per record location. The data in the indexed sequential file in Figure 9.16 can be retrieved in sequential order with only six input operations (one input operation per data block). The relative file in Figure 7.34 (which contains the same data) can be retrieved sequentially using the B-tree in Figure 8.49 with 13 input operations (one input operation per record). Of course the index blocks of the index tree need to be input with one input operation per index block, which adds to the number of input operations. But clearly, the structure of indexed sequential files allows the use of blocking, which improves the access time.

Figure 9.15
Car-rental agency indexed sequential master file after applying transaction file T2

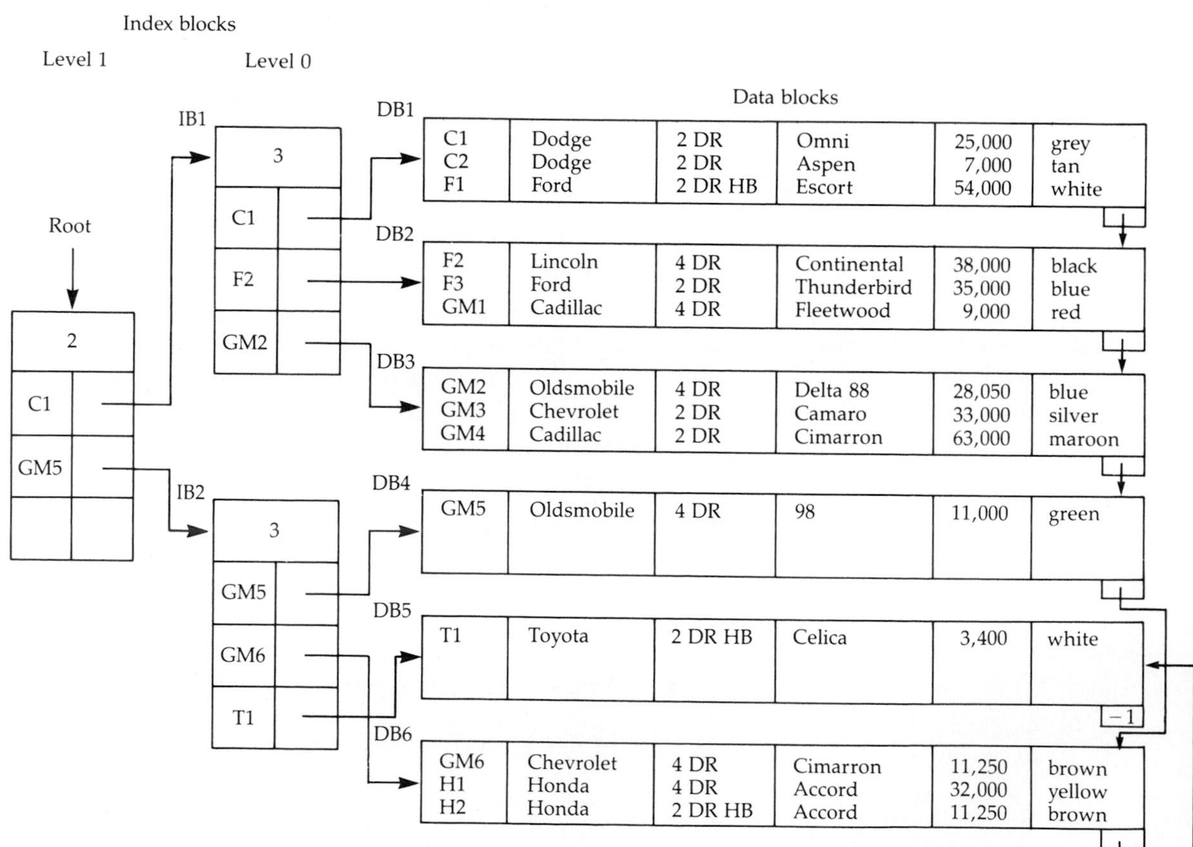

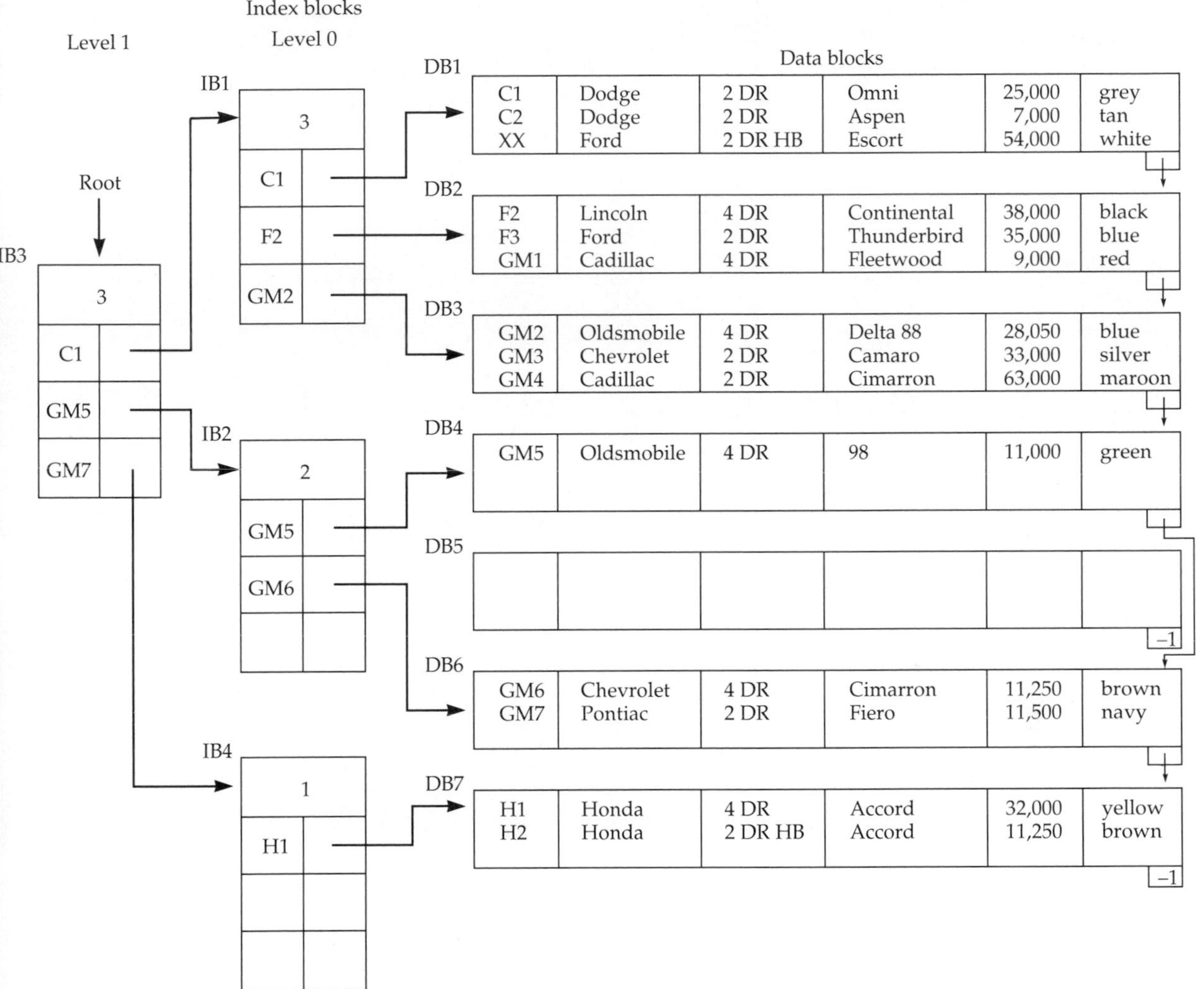

Figure 9.16
Car-rental agency indexed sequential master file from Figure 9.15 after applying transaction file T3.

The Ada implementations of Algorithm 9.1 and Algorithm 9.5 are presented in Appendix B. Figure 9.17 graphically illustrates the interfacing of the program components with each other and the external I/O files. The data structures shared by Algorithm 9.1 (`Create`) and Algorithm 9.5 (`Update`) are encapsulated in a nongeneric package, `Ch5Struc`. The generic `B_Plus_Tree` package, also used by both algorithms, encapsulates the operations on the B-plus-tree file while hiding the data structures that define the file components. The hiding of these data structures from the instantiator of the `B_Plus_Tree` package prohibits tampering with file components by the user, thus ensuring the integrity of the B-plus-tree. The `B_Plus_Tree` package also instantiates a generic stack package to store the parent nodes as the b-plus-tree is searched. The parent nodes on the stack are updated in the case of an insertion or a deletion.

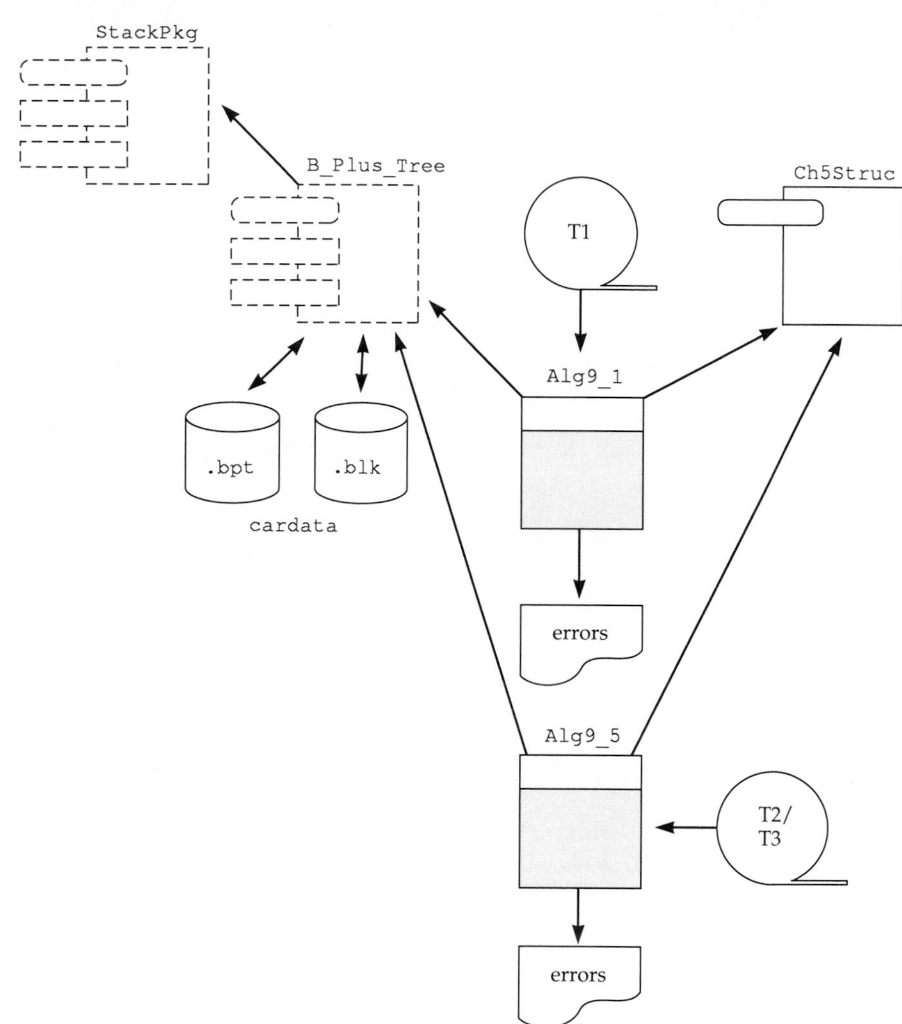

Figure 9.17 Case study 9.1 interfaces

CYLINDER-AND-SURFACE INDEXING METHOD

The **cylinder-and-surface indexing method** used on IBM computers is known as Indexed Sequential Access Method **(ISAM) file organization** and is based on the physical characteristics of a magnetic disk. An ISAM file consists of three areas: (1) an index area containing an index to the cylinders of data, (2) a prime data area containing data records, and (3) an independent overflow area. The data of the ISAM file are stored in several cylinders, each consisting of a **surface index** (secondary-level index) to data records stored within the cylinder, a **prime data area** of data records stored sequentially by a primary key, and a **cylinder overflow area**. The surface index is usually stored on surface 0, the prime data area is usually stored on surfaces 1 through $n - 1$, and the cylinder overflow area is usually surface n of the cylinder. Each surface of the prime data area is fixed in size and contains data records stored in ascending order by a primary key value. The first cylinder of the ISAM file contains only the **cylinder indexes** (top-level indexes), and the last cylinder contains the **independent overflow area**. The prime data area resides between the first and last cylinders. Figure 9.18 is a layout of an ISAM file on a disk with six surfaces per cylinder and three records per surface. The file consumes 14 cylinders. Only the key values are shown for the data records stored in the prime data area.

The cylinder overflow area at the end of each cylinder is reserved for overflow of records from the prime area caused by the addition of new records. The cylinder overflow area, also termed **embedded overflow** (since the overflow area is embedded within prime data areas of the file), eliminates many of the problems associated with adding new records to a sequential file. The addition of a record to a full track in the prime data causes the last record on the track to be moved to the cylinder overflow area to allow the records on the prime data track to be stored in sequential order. The record moved to overflow is linked with the prime data track from which it was moved in the cylinder and track overflow indexes. Should the cylinder overflow area fill up, an independent overflow area (independent since it follows the prime data areas) is usually reserved.

The advantage of the cylinder (embedded) overflow area is that the area is on the same cylinder as the prime data area from which the overflow occurs; no additional seeks are necessary to access the embedded overflow. The disadvantage is that the embedded overflow area is usually the same for all cylinders (usually one or two tracks), even though the number of additions to all cylinders may not be the same. Some cylinders are used, while others are empty and just waste space.

The advantage of the independent overflow area is that the last one or two tracks of each cylinder do not have to be reserved for possible overflow. As a result all additions can be made to the independent overflow area at the end of the file (on the last cylinder). The disadvantage of the independent overflow area is that an additional seek is necessary each time the area is accessed. The common approach is a compromise whereby cylinder overflow areas are reserved for the average number of overflows to the cylinder, and an independent overflow area is reserved in case the cylinder overflow areas become full.

The records in the first cylinder of the prime data area all have lower key values than those in the second cylinder of the prime data area. When the ISAM file is created, the data records are stored in contiguous locations on contiguous surfaces within the prime data area of the first cylinder. After the prime data area of the first cylinder is full, the prime data area of the second cylinder is filled in the same manner. The physical ordering of the records in the prime data area along with the surface indexes allows the sequential access of data from the file.

The surface index for a cylinder contains two index entries (normal and overflow) for each surface of the prime data area of the cylinder. Each normal entry indicates the address of a surface in the prime data area and the highest key of all the records on that surface. Each overflow entry indicates the address of the next overflow record in sequence (if any) for that prime data area surface and the highest key of all the records in overflow assigned to that surface. The key in the normal entry is lower than the key in the overflow entry for any surface and

$$\text{Nkey } 1 < \text{Okey } 1 < \text{Nkey } 2 < \text{Okey } 2 < \ldots < \text{Nkey } n < \text{Okey } n$$

Nkey i is the key of the normal entry, and Okey i is the key of the overflow entry for prime data surface i. In searching for a particular record, the keys Nkey i and the keys Okey i are scanned in sequence as shown above until the first key larger than the key of the record being sought is found. Assuming the cylinder overflow areas are empty, the surface index (also called **track index**) for cylinder 101 of the ISAM file from Figure 9.18 is presented in Figure 9.19. (Si is surface i.) Data records are maintained in sequence by ascending key values on a surface and within the prime data areas. Additions of records to a surface cause the expansion of records from the surface into the cylinder overflow area. The overflow entry, when different from the normal entry for a surface, indicates that an expansion of the surface has occurred and shows where the records that overflowed from the surface may be found.

The cylinder index for an ISAM file consists of an entry for each cylinder of the prime data area. Each entry consists of the highest key in the cylinder and the address of the cylinder. The cylinder index of the ISAM file of 14 cylinders from Figure 9.18 is presented in Figure 9.20. (Ci is cylinder i.) To access a record randomly with key k, the entries in the cylinder index are scanned until the first key larger than key k is located. The corresponding address indicates the cylinder to be scanned. The normal and overflow entries of the surface index of the cylinder are scanned until the first key larger than key k is found. The corresponding address is the surface on which the record with key k should be found. The surface is scanned sequentially to locate the record.

Given the cylinder index shown in Figure 9.20, suppose a record with key 105 is added to the file. To decide where the record should be added, the searching routine used to locate an existing record is performed. The first key in the cylinder index larger than 105 is the first entry with a key of 121 and an address of cylinder 101.

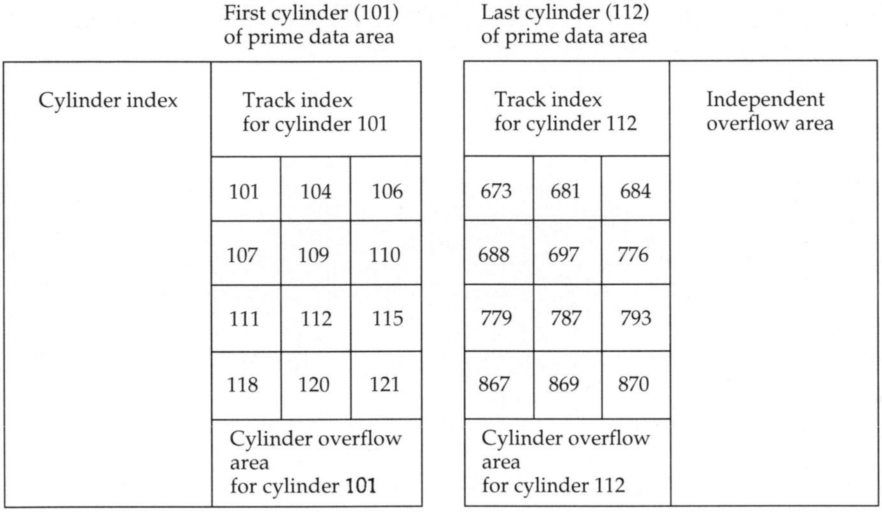

First cylinder (101) of prime data area

Last cylinder (112) of prime data area

Cylinder index	Track index for cylinder 101			Track index for cylinder 112			Independent overflow area
	101	104	106	673	681	684	
	107	109	110	688	697	776	
	111	112	115	779	787	793	
	118	120	121	867	869	870	
	Cylinder overflow area for cylinder 101			Cylinder overflow area for cylinder 112			

Figure 9.18
Layout of ISAM file of 14 cylinders (six surfaces per cylinder and three records per surface)

Surface index for cylinder 101

Normal entry		Overflow entry	
Highest key	Address	Highest key	Address
106	S1	106	S1
110	S2	110	S2
115	S3	115	S3
121	S4	121	S4

Figure 9.19
Surface index for cylinder 101 of Figure 9.17

Cylinder index

Highest key	Address
121	C101
⋮	⋮
870	C112

Figure 9.20
Cylinder index for the ISAM file

A search of the cylinder 101 surface index (Figure 9.21) determines that surface 1 has keys as large as 106, so 105 should be stored on surface 1 if there is room. Because the file was created by storing records in contiguous locations, surface 1 is full. To maintain the sequence of records by key values on a surface, record 105 should be stored between record 104 and record 106. The last record on the surface is moved to the cylinder overflow area (surface 5, record 0), and the overflow entry for surface 1 becomes 106, S5R0. Record 105 is stored in sequence at the end of the surface. The normal entry for surface 1 becomes 105, S1. Cylinder 101 with the specified changes is presented in Figure 9.22.

Figure 9.21
Cylinder 101 of the ISAM file

Surface index for cylinder 101

Normal entry		Overflow entry	
Highest key	Address	Highest key	Address
106	S1	106	S1
110	S2	110	S2
115	S3	115	S3
121	S4	121	S4

Prime data area for cylinder 101

S1	101	104	106
S2	107	109	110
S3	111	112	115
S4	118	120	121
(Overflow) S5			

Figure 9.22
Cylinder 101 with record 105

Surface index for cylinder 101

Normal entry		Overflow entry	
Highest key	Address	Highest key	Address
105	S1	106	S5R0
110	S2	110	S2
115	S3	115	S3
121	S4	121	S4

Prime data area for cylinder 101

S1	101	104	105
S2	107	109	110
S3	111	112	115
S4	118	120	121
(Overflow) S5	106		

Suppose a record with the key 108 is added to the ISAM file in Figure 9.22. A search of the cylinder index yields cylinder 101 as the cylinder for inserting the record 108. A search of the cylinder 101 surface index yields surface 2 as the location for inserting the record 108. Surface 2 is full with keys 107, 109, and 110. The record with key 108 should be stored between record 107 and record 109. The last record on the surface is moved to the next available location in the cylinder overflow area (surface 5, record 1), and the overflow entry for surface 2 becomes: 110, S5R1. Record 109 is moved to the end of the surface to allow record 108 to be stored in sequence. The normal entry for surface 2 becomes 109, S2. Cylinder 101 now contains the data presented in Figure 9.23.

Notice that the records stored in the cylinder overflow area are expansions from all of the surfaces in the prime data area. The physical ordering of the records in the overflow area has no meaning, but the records in overflow are referenced from the surface indexes. Each record that is moved to the cylinder overflow area as a surface is expanded and linked in a list to allow sequential access of all records in the ISAM file by the primary key value.

To illustrate the linked list of records in the cylinder overflow area, suppose that a record with key 102 is added to the ISAM file in Figure 9.23. A search of the cylinder index determines that cylinder 101 is where the insertion should take place. A search of the cylinder 101 surface index indicates that surface 1 has keys as large as 105, so record 102 should be inserted on surface 1. A scan of surface 1 indicates that record 102 should be inserted between records 101 and 104. The last record on the surface (105) is moved to the next available location in the cylinder overflow area (surface 5, record 2). Record 105 contains a pointer to record 106, which is also in overflow, and the overflow entry for surface 1 becomes 106, S5R2. The overflow entry indicates that surface 1 has been expanded into the cylinder overflow area with records with keys as large as 106 and that the linked list of all records expanded from surface 1 begins in location surface 5, record 2. Record 104 is moved to the end of the surface to allow record 102 to be stored in sequence between record 101 and record 104. The normal entry for surface 1 is changed to reflect the new highest key on the surface: 104, S1. The new cylinder 101 is presented in Figure 9.24.

Should another record be added to cylinder 101, the cylinder overflow area is full, and the independent overflow area in the last cylinder would be used to expand the cylinder overflow area. The overflow entry for an expanded surface contains CcSsRr as the address, which indicates cylinder c, surface s, record r.

Deletion of records from an ISAM file does not cause the records to be physically removed. Instead deletion causes the record to be "marked" as deleted. The deleted record may be marked by moving a very high value into the key field or by including a delete field in each record that is initialized to NO when the record is added to the file and changed to YES when the record is deleted. If the record with key 108 were deleted from the ISAM file in Figure 9.24, the key could be replaced with Xs as shown in Figure 9.25. This static approach to deletions requires that sequential and random access to the ISAM file skip over marked records.

The disadvantage of the static approach is the wasted space for deleted records that still reside within the ISAM file and that are merely marked as logically deleted. If the marked records begin to account for a large amount of space, a reorganization of the ISAM file is in order. The organization entails sequentially accessing the ISAM file, skipping marked records, and copying all other records to another file. The reorganization essentially re-creates the ISAM files to physically delete marked records from the file. The advantage to the static approach is that the "garbage collection" of deleted records need not take place with each deletion. If a marked record resides in a prime data area, the space may be used for the next addition to the surface. If a record to be deleted is in the cylinder overflow area, the record can be marked and logically deleted from the linked list of records. The address of the marked record is stored on a free-space list to be used the next time a record is moved into the cylinder overflow area.

Figure 9.23
Cylinder 101 with record 108 added

Surface index for cylinder 101

Normal entry		Overflow entry	
Highest key	Address	Highest key	Address
105	S1	106	S5R0
109	S2	110	S5R1
115	S3	115	S3
121	S4	121	S4

Prime data area for cylinder 101

S1	101	104	105
S2	107	108	109
S3	111	112	115
S4	118	120	121
(Overflow) S5	106	110	

Figure 9.24
Cylinder 101 with record 102

Surface index for cylinder 101

Normal entry		Overflow entry	
Highest key	Address	Highest key	Address
104	S1	106	S5R2
109	S2	110	S5R1
115	S3	115	S3
121	S4	121	S4

Prime data area for cylinder 101

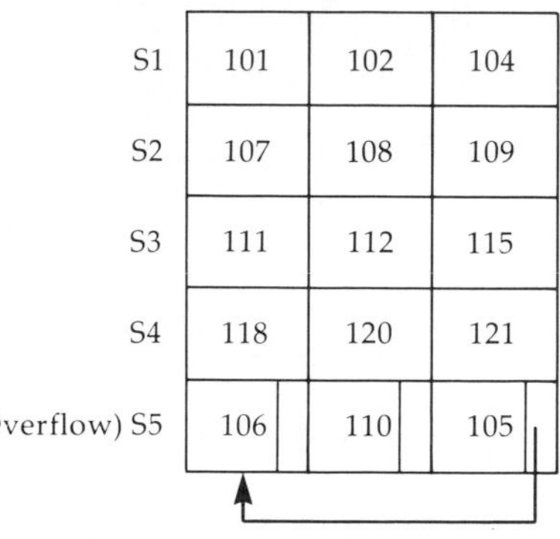

Figure 9.25
Cylinder 101 after deletion of record 108

Surface index for cylinder 101

Normal entry		Overflow entry	
Highest key	Address	Highest key	Address
104	S1	106	S5R2
109	S2	110	S5R1
115	S3	115	S3
121	S4	121	S4

Prime data area for cylinder 101

S1	101	102	104
S2	107	XXX	109
S3	111	112	115
S4	118	120	121
(Overflow) S5	106	110	105

Ada ISAM Package

A generic package for creating, inserting, adding, deleting, and searching an ISAM file can be specified that includes the techniques described in the chapter. The ISAM package specification, which follows, is quite similar to the B$^+$-tree package, but it differs in one way. The difference is in the `Create_ISAM` procedure; its purpose and number of parameters are expanded. The only function of the `Create_BPlus_Tree` procedure in the B$^+$-tree package is to open the index and data files in preparation for insertion of data records, which can be inserted in any random order. The data records in an ISAM file must be presorted in ascending key order before being made available for insertion into an ISAM file. The `Create_ISAM` procedure has four parameters: the external filenames for the sorted sequential data file, the ISAM index file, the ISAM data file, and the ISAM overflow file. The purpose of all of the other procedures listed in the ISAM package specification is the same as for the B$^+$-tree package; only the implementation is different.

```
GENERIC
    INDEX_BLOCK_SIZE : Positive;
    DATA_BLOCK_SIZE : Positive;
    Type key_Type Is Private;
    Type Record_Info Is Private;
    With FUNCTION Key_Of ( a_record : Record_Info ) Return Key_Type;
    With FUNCTION ">" ( left_operand, right_operand : Key_Type )
                        Return Boolean;
PACKAGE ISAM Is
    PROCEDURE Create_ISAM ( external_sequential_filename,
                            external_index_block_filename,
                            external_data_block_filename,
                            external_overflow_filename : String );
    PROCEDURE Open_ISAM ( external_index_block_filename,
                          external_data_block_filename,
                          external_overflow_filename : String );
    PROCEDURE Insert ( data_record : Record_Info );
    PROCEDURE Delete ( key : Key_Type );
    PROCEDURE Retrieve ( key : Key_Type; data_record : Out Record_Info );
    PROCEDURE Replace ( data_record : Record_Info );
    PROCEDURE Close_ISAM;
    key_not_found    : Exception;
    key_not_deleted  : Exception;
    key_not_inserted : Exception;
END ISAM;
```

Implementation in Ada

This section presents a simplified, machine-independent version of the cylinder-and-surface indexing method for the implementation of an indexed sequential file in Ada. Rather than two levels of indexes (cylinder and surface indexes), only one level of index is used. The implementation of ISAM files in Ada requires the use of direct files, which allow rapid access to individual records. The addresses of surfaces are stored in the indexes in terms of relative record numbers.

One index is used for the entire file, and each entry is composed of a normal entry and an overflow entry. Each prime data block contains a fixed number of fixed-size data blocks. Prime data records are maintained in sequence by ascending key values within a data block and within the index. Each overflow block contains a record spilled from a prime data block and the address of the next overflow block in the linked list.

For each prime data block in the file, the index contains a normal entry and an overflow entry. The normal entry contains the address of the prime data block and the largest key in the prime data block. The overflow entry, if different from the normal entry, indicates that records have been added in sequence to the prime data block. The added records cause spilling of data records from the prime data block into overflow blocks. The overflow entry contains: (1) the address of the first block in a linked list of overflow blocks, and (2) the largest key of all the overflow blocks in the linked list. The data records are maintained in sequence from the beginning to the end of a linked list of overflow blocks.

Figure 9.26(a) is a diagram of the data structures (index and prime data blocks) of an indexed sequential file. The maximum number of entries for each prime data block is three. The diagrams in parts (b) through (e) of the figure show the changes in the file as records are added and deleted. Adding key 11 causes key 15 to be moved into overflow. The normal key becomes 11, and the overflow address becomes V1 (Figure 9.26(b)). The link field of –1 in the overflow block V1 indicates the end of the linked list.

The addition of key 6 into prime data block P2 causes key 7 to be moved to an overflow block (V2). The normal key of the index changes to 6, and the overflow address of the index to indicate V2 has an overflow record (Figure 9.26(c)). If key 8 is added next, the indexes are scanned. The scan looks at the normal key and then at the overflow key for each entry to find that the largest key in prime data block P3 is 11. Key 8 is added to prime data block P3, which is full. As a result the last key in the prime data block, key 11, is moved to overflow (Figure 9.26(d)). Notice that prime data block P3 already has key 15 in overflow block V1. Key 11 is stored in the next available overflow block, V3. The link field of overflow block V3 becomes the overflow address from the index, V1. In consequence all records that have overflowed from prime data block P3 are linked (11 points to 15). The address of the beginning of the linked list, V3, is stored in the overflow address in the index for prime data block P3. The normal key in the index is changed to key 10.

The deletion of the last key in a prime data block causes the normal key of an index entry to be changed. In contrast the deletion of key 5—which is in the middle of the prime data block—causes the deleted record to be marked but causes no changes in the index (Figure 9.26(e)).

The pseudocode for creating an indexed sequential file using the cylinder-and-surface indexing method shown in Figure 9.26 is presented in Algorithm 9.6.

Figure 9.26 Indexed sequential file using the cylinder-and-surface indexing method with one level of indexes

Index

Normal		Overflow	
Key	Address	Key	Address
3	P1	3	P1
7	P2	7	P2
15	P3	15	P3

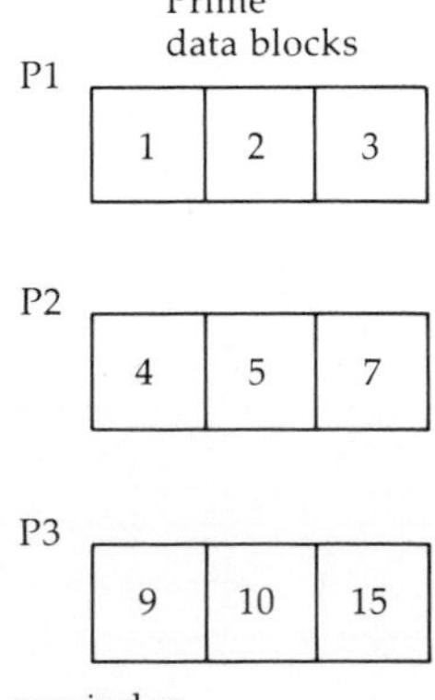

(a) ISAM file with one index

Index

Normal		Overflow	
Key	Address	Key	Address
3	P1	3	P1
7	P2	7	P2
11	P3	15	V1

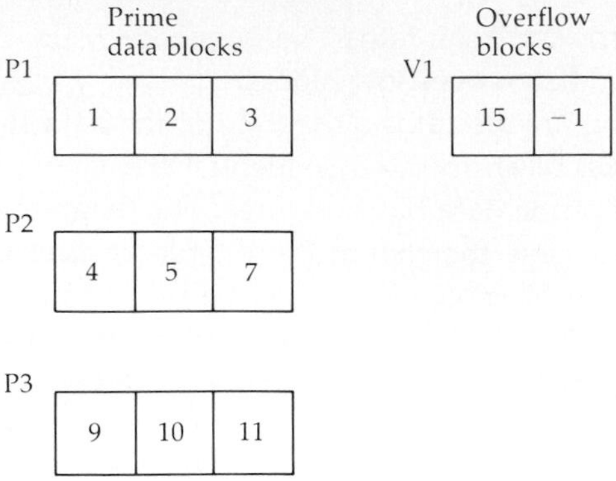

Prime data blocks

P1	1	2	3
P2	4	5	7
P3	9	10	11

Overflow blocks

V1	15	−1

(b) ISAM file with key 11

Index

Normal		Overflow	
Key	Address	Key	Address
3	P1	3	P1
6	P2	7	V2
11	P3	15	V1

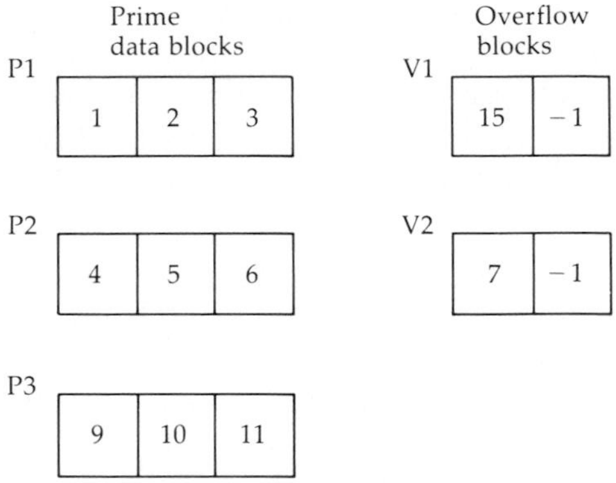

Prime data blocks

P1	1	2	3
P2	4	5	6
P3	9	10	11

Overflow blocks

V1	15	−1
V2	7	−1

(c) ISAM file with key 6

Index

Normal		Overflow	
Key	Address	Key	Address
3	P1	3	P1
6	P2	7	V2
10	P3	15	V3

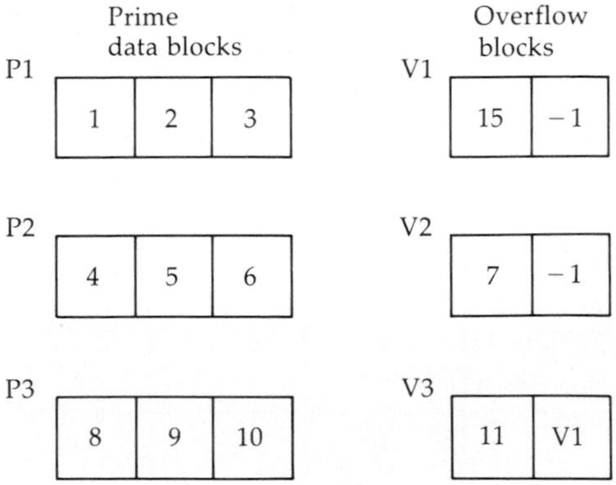

Prime data blocks

P1	1	2	3
P2	4	5	6
P3	8	9	10

Overflow blocks

V1	15	−1
V2	7	−1
V3	11	V1

(d) ISAM file with key 8

(e)

ALGORITHM 9.6 Create ISAM with One Normal Index and One Overflow Index

```
    TYPE An_entry Is Record
                          key      :   Key_Type
                          address  :   Natural
                     End Record
    TYPE Index_entries Is Record
                             normal    :   An_entry
                             overflow  :   An_entry
                         End Record •
    TYPE Tuple_Type Is Array ( 1 .. INDEX_BLOCK_SIZE ) Of Index_entries
    TYPE Index_Type Is Record
                           entries : Natural ← 0
                           tuple : Tuple_Type
                       End Record
    TYPE Data_Status Is ( ACTIVE, DELETED )
    TYPE Data_Type Is Record
                          data : Record_Info
                          status : Data_Status
                      End Record
    TYPE Data_Tuple Is Array ( 1 .. DATA_BLOCK_SIZE ) Of Data_Type
    TYPE Prime_data_block Is Record
                                 data_entries   : Integer
                                 prime_record : Data_Tuple
                             End Record
    TYPE Overflow_block Is Record
                               over_record : Record_Info
                               next_overflow : Natural
                           End Record
    TYPE Status_Type Is ( IN_NORMAL, IN_OVERFLOW )
PROCEDURE Create_ISAM ( seq_file, index_file, data_file,
                        overflow_file : String )
    data_block   : Prime_Data_Block
    db           : Natural ← 0
    indexes      : Index_Type
    location     : Natural ← 0
    over_block   : Overflow_Block
```

```
    Loop
        Exit When End_Of_File ( seq_file )
        db ← db + 1
        Input ( seq_file, data_block.prime_record(db).data )
        data_block.prime_record(db).status ← ACTIVE
        If db = DATA_BLOCK_SIZE
            data_block.data_entries ← db
            increment location
            Full_Data_Block ( data_block, db, location, indexes )
            db ← 0
        End If
    End Loop
    If db /= 0
        data_block.data_entries ← db
        increment location
        Full_Data_Block ( data_block, db, location, indexes )
    End If
    Output ( index_file, indexes )

PROCEDURE Full_Data_Block ( data_block : In Prime_Data_Block
                            db : In Natural
                            location : In Natural
                            indexes : In Out Index_Type )

    Output ( data_file, data_block, location )
    increment indexes.entries
    indexes.tuple(indexes.entries).normal ←
            (data_block.prime_record(db).data.key, location )
    indexes.tuple(indexes.entries).overflow ←
            indexes.tuple(index.entries).normal
```

The algorithm for searching an indexed sequential file created using the cylinder-and-surface method is much simpler than that for searching an indexed sequential file created using the index-and-data-blocks method. The one-level index is scanned until the first key larger than the key sought is found. The corresponding address is the location of a data block (in prime or overflow area). The data block is input to further search for the record being sought. If the record is found that matches the key, the record is returned; otherwise, the exception `key_not_found` is raised. Algorithm 9.7 presents the search routine.

ALGORITHM 9.7 Search Algorithm for Locating a Record in File

```
PROCEDURE Retrieve ( key : In Key_Type
                     data_record : Out Record_Info )
    data_block : Prime_Data_Block
    data_block_number,
    index_location,
    location,
    previous : Natural
```

```
    over_block : Overflow_Block
    status : Status_Type
    successful : Boolean ← FALSE

    Find ( key, status, index_location, data_block_number, location,
           previous, successful )
    If successful
        If status = IN_NORMAL
            Input ( data_file, data_block, data_block_number )
            data_record ← data_block.prime_record(location).data
        Else
            Input ( overflow_file, over_block, data_block_number )
            data_record ← over_block.over_record
    Else
        Raise key_not_found
    End If
```

Maintenance of the indexed sequential file involves changes to and deletions of existing records in the file as well as additions of new records to the file. Algorithm 9.8 is the maintenance algorithm for changing existing records (Procedure `Replace`). Algorithm 9.9 is an expansion of Algorithm 9.8 that allows additions of new records (Procedure `Insert`) as well as changes to existing records. Algorithm 9.10 is a further expansion of Algorithm 9.9 (with new statements indicated with a + to the left). Algorithm 9.10 allows deletions from and changes and additions to the existing file.

ALGORITHM 9.8 Change Indexed Sequential File Created in Algorithm 9.6

```
PROCEDURE Replace ( data_record : Record_Info )

    data_block : Prime_Data_Block
    key : Key_Type
    index_location,
    data_block_number,
    location,
    previous : Natural
    status : Status_Type
    successful : Boolean
    over_block : Overflow_Block

    key ← data_record.key
    Find ( key, status, index_location, data_block_number, location,
           previous, successful )
    If successful
        Case status
            IN_NORMAL →Input ( data_file, data_block,
                                 data_block_number )
                       data_block.prime_record(location).data ←
                           data_record
                       Output ( data_file, data_block,
                                  data_block_number )
```

```
                IN_OVERFLOW → Input ( overflow_file, over_block,
                                      data_block_number )
                              over_block.over_record ← data_record
                              Output ( overflow_file, over_block,
                                       data_block_number )
            End Case
        Else
            Raise key_not_found
        End If
```

ALGORITHM 9.9 User Program to Change and Add Records to Indexed Sequential File Created in Algorithm 9.6

```
    Input_Indexes
    Loop
        Exit When End_Of_File ( transfile )
        Input ( transfile, trans_record )
        Case update_code
            'C' → Retrieve ( key, data_record )
                  Make_Changes ( trans_record, data_record )
                  Replace ( data_record )
            'A' → Insert ( trans_record )
                  Output ( "add successful" )
        End Case
    EXCEPTION
        When key_not_found → Output ( "no matching record" )
            -- key_not_found raised by Retrieve or Replace
        When key_not_inserted → Output ( "duplicate add transaction" )
            -- key_not_inserted raised by Insert
    End Loop
    Output_Indexes  -- sequentially

PROCEDURE Insert ( data_record : Record_Info )
    data_block : Prime_Data_Block
    data_block_number : Natural
    hold_address,
    index_location : Natural
    key : Key_Type
    location : Natural
    new_over_block : Overflow_Block
    next_overflow_location : Natural
    over_block : Overflow_Block
    previous : Natural
    status : Status_Type
    successful : Boolean

    key ← data_record.key
    Find ( key, status, index_location, data_block_number, location,
           previous, successful )
    If successful
        Raise key_not_inserted
    End If
    If data_block_number = 0
        -- key larger than any currently in the file so add to the
        -- next available data block and add new entry to indexes
```

```
        new_over_block.over_record ← data_record
        next_overflow_location ← Size ( overflow_file ) + 1
        hold_address ← indexes.tuple(indexes.entries).overflow.address
        If hold_address = indexes.tuple(indexes.entries).normal.address
            -- no overflow for last data block
            new_over_block.next_overflow ← hold_address
            indexes.tuple(indexes.entries).overflow.address ←
                next_overflow_location
            indexes.tuple(indexes.entries).overflow.key ←
                data_record.key
            Output ( overflow_file, new_over_block,
                    next_overflow_location )
        Else
            Loop
                Input ( overflow_file, over_block, hold_address )
                Exit When over_block.next_overflow = 0
                hold_address ←
                    indexes.tuple(indexes.entries).overflow.address
            End Loop
            new_over_block.next_overflow ← over_block.next_overflow
            over_block.next_overflow ←new_over_block.next_overflow
            indexes.tuple(indexes.entries).overflow.key ←
                data_record.key
            Output ( overflow_file, over_block, hold_address )
            Output ( overflow_file, new_over_block,
                    next_overflow_location )
        End If
    ElsIf status = IN_NORMAL
        Insert_Normal ( index_location, data_block_number, location,
                        data_record )
    Else  -- status = IN_OVERFLOW
        Insert_Overflow ( index_location, previous, data_record )
    End If

PROCEDURE Find ( key : In Key_Type
                 status : In Out Status_Type
                 index_location, data_block_number,
                 location, previous : In Out Natural
                 successful : In Out Boolean )

    Search_Indexes ( key, status, index_location, data_block_number,
                     location, successful )
    If successful
        previous ← 0
        If status = IN_OVERFLOW
            Search_Overflow_Data ( key, data_block_number, previous,
                                   successful )
        Else -- status = IN_NORMAL
            Search_Prime_Data ( key, data_block_number, location,
                                successful )
        End If
    Else
        data_block_number ← 0
    End If
```

```
PROCEDURE Search_Indexes ( key : In Key_Type
                           status : In Out Status_Type
                           index_location, data_block_number,
                           location : Out Natural
                           successful : Out Boolean )

    successful ← FALSE
    index_location ← index.entries + 1
    For count In 1 .. indexes.entries Loop
        If key <= indexes.tuple(count).normal.key
            successful ← TRUE
            status ← IN_NORMAL
            index_location ← count
            data_block_number ← indexes.tuple(count).normal.address
            Exit

        Elsif key <= indexes.tuple(count).overflow.key
            successful ← TRUE
            status ← IN_OVERFLOW
            index_location ← count
            data_block_number ← indexes.tuple(count).overflow.address
            Exit
        End If
    End Loop

PROCEDURE Search_Prime_Data ( trans_key : In Key_Type
                              data_block_number : In Natural
                              location : Out Natural
                              successful : Out Boolean )
    count : Positive
    data_block : Prime_Data_Block
    prime_key : Key_Type
    Input ( data_file, data_block, data_block_number )
    count ← 1
    Loop
        Exit When count > data_block.entries
        If data_block.prime_record(count).status = ACTIVE
            If data_block.prime_record(count).data.key > trans_key
            --
            -- trans_key not found in prime_data_block so return count
            -- as location of first entry greater than transkey.
            -- trans_key belongs immediately prior to location count.
            --
                successful ← FALSE
                Exit
            End If
            If key = data_block.prime_record(count).data.key
                successful ← TRUE
                Exit
            End If
        End If
        increment count
    End Loop
    location ← count
```

```
PROCEDURE Search_Overflow_Data ( key : In Key_Type
                                 over_block_number : In Out Natural
                                 previous : Out Natural
                                 successful : Out Boolean )
    over_block : Overflow_Block

    previous ← 0
    Input ( overflow_file, over_block, over_block_number )
    If key = over_block.over_record.key
        successful ← TRUE
    ElsIf key > over_block.over_record.key
        previous ← over_block_number
        over_block_number ← over_block.next_overflow
        Search_Overflow_Data ( key, over_block_number, previous,
                               successful )
    Else  -- key < overblock.over_record.key
          -- point for insertion
        successful ← FALSE
    End If

PROCEDURE Insert_Normal ( index_location, data_block_number,
                          location : In Out Natural
                          new_record : In Record_Info )
    data_block : Prime_Data_Block
    hold_record : Record_Info
    Input ( data_file, data_block, data_block_number )
    If data_block.entries = DATA_BLOCK_SIZE
      -- data_block full
        hold_record ← data_block.prime_record ( DATA_BLOCK_SIZE ).data
        decrement data_block.data_entries
        Insert_Into_Block (  index_location, data_block_number,
                             location, new_record, data_block )
        If indexes.tuple(index_location).overflow.key >
          indexes.tuple(index_location).normal.key
               -- Find insertion point in overflow
            Find ( key, status, index_location, data_block_number,
                   location, previous, successful )
        End If
        Insert_Overflow ( index_location, previous, hold_record )
    Else  -- block not full
        Insert_Into_Block (  index_location, data_block_number,
                             location, new_record, data_block )
    End If

PROCEDURE Insert_Overflow ( index_location, previous : In Natural
                            new_record : In Record_Info )
    new_over_block, previous_block : Overflow_Block
    new_over_block.over_record ← new_record
    next_overflow_location ← Size ( overflow_blocks_file ) + 1
    If indexes.tuple(index_location).normal.address =
       indexes.tuple(index_location).overflow.address
           -- start overflow linked list
        new_over_block.next_overflow ← 0
        indexes.tuple(index_location).overflow.address ←
                 next_overflow_location
```

```
    Elsif previous = 0
        -- add to front of linked list
        new_over_block.next_overflow ←
                  indexes.tuple(index_location).overflow.address
        indexes.tuple(index_location).overflow.address ←
                  next_overflow_location
    Else
        -- add to middle of linked list
        Input ( overflow_file, previous_block, previous )
        new_over_block.next_overflow ← previous_block.next_overflow
        previous_block.next_overflow ← next_overflow_location
        Output ( overflow_file, previous_block, previous )
    End If
    Output ( overflow_file, new_over_block, next_overflow_location )

PROCEDURE Insert_Into_Block ( index_location,
                              data_block_number, location : In Natural
                              new_record : In Record_Info
                              data_block : In Out Prime_Data_Block )

    For lcv In Reverse location .. data_block.entries Loop
        data_block.prime_record(lcv + 1) ←
                  data_block.prime_record(lcv)
    End Loop
    increment data_block.data_entries
    data_block.prime_record(location).data ← new_record
    data_block.prime_record(location).status ← ACTIVE
    indexes.tuple(index_location).normal.key ←
              data_block.prime_record(data_block.entries).data.key
    Output ( data_file, data_block, data_block_number )
```

ALGORITHM 9.10 User Program to Change, Add, and Delete Records in Indexed Sequential File Created in Algorithm 9.6

```
    Input_Indexes
    Loop
        Exit When End_Of_File ( transfile )
        Input ( transfile, trans_record )
        Case update_code
            'C' → Retrieve ( key, data_record )
                  Make_Changes ( trans_record, data_record )
                  Replace ( data_record )
            'A' → Insert ( trans_key, trans_record )
                  Output ( "add successful" )
+           'D' → Delete ( trans_key )
+                 Output ( "delete successful" )
        End Case

    EXCEPTION
        When key_not_found → Output ( "no matching record")
            -- key_not_found raised by Retrieve or Replace
        When key_not_inserted → Output ( "duplicate add transaction" )
            -- key_not_inserted raised by Insert
        When key_not_deleted → Output ( "no matching record" )
```

```
    End Loop
    Output_Indexes   -- sequentially

+ FUNCTION Delete ( key : In Key_Type ) Return Boolean
+     data_block : Prime_Data_Block
+     data_block_number,
+     index_location,
+     location,
+     previous : Natural
+     previous_block,
+     over_block : Overflow_Block
+     status : Status_Type
+     successful : Boolean
+
+     Find ( key, status, index_location, data_block_number, location,
+            previous, successful )
+     If successful
+         If status = IN_NORMAL
+             Input ( data_file, data_block, data_block_number )
+             data_block.prime_record(location).status ← DELETED
+             Output ( data_file, data_block, data_block_number )
+             If key = indexes.tuple(index_location).normal.key
+                If location > 1
+                   If indexes.tuple(index_location).normal.key =
+                      indexes.tuple(index_location).overflow.key
+                      indexes.tuple(index_location).overflow.key ←
+                          data_block.prime_record(location - 1).data.key
+                   End If
+                   indexes.tuple(index_location).normal.key ←
+                       data_block.prime_record(location - 1).data.key
+                End If
+             End If
+           -- Else status = OVERFLOW
+         ElsIf indexes.tuple(index_location).overflow.address =
+             data_block_number
+           -- first one in linked list
+             Input ( overflow_file, over_block, data_block_number )
+             indexes.tuple(index_location).overflow.address ←
+                 over_block.next_overflow
+         Else  --  middle or last of linked list
+             Input ( overflow_file, previous_block, previous )
+             previous_block.next_overflow ← over_block.next_overflow
+             If over_block.next_overflow = 0
+                 -- last of list so change overflow.key
+             indexes.tuple(index_location).overflow.key ←
+                 previous_block.over_record.key
+         End If
+         Output ( overflow_file, previous_block, previous )
+     Else
+         Raise key_not_deleted
+     End If
```

CASE STUDY 9.2: THE CAR-RENTAL AGENCY

The car-rental agency data used in previous file organizations stored in an ISAM file for comparison. The transaction file T1 in Table 5.1 contains the records to be loaded to the file in sequential order. Each track holds three records. Figure 9.27 shows the ISAM master file after creation. The records are stored sequentially in each prime data block and sequentially in contiguous prime data blocks, and the largest key in each block is recorded in the indexes. Any record can be accessed by searching the cylinder index (not shown) to identify the cylinder to seek, then searching the track index to identify the prime data block (surface), and finally searching through the data block to locate the record. Locating a record in the prime data area involves:

1. seeking the cylinder index
2. scanning the cylinder index
3. seeking the cylinder
4. scanning the track index to identify the prime data block
5. scanning the prime data block (surface)

Accessing the ISAM file sequentially involves scanning the cylinder indexes in order. Each cylinder also scans the track indexes in order. The result is a list of all the records in prime data block P(i), all the overflow blocks for this prime block, all the records in prime data block P(i + 1), all the overflow blocks for this prime block, and so on until all prime data blocks and embedded overflow blocks have been listed in sequential order.

Transaction file T2 contains a single addition to the file, GM6. A search of the indexes indicates that GM6 should be added in prime data block P4, which is full. The last record, H2, from P4 is moved into overflow (V1) and initialized with a link field of –1 (Figure 9.28). The records in the prime data block are moved to allow GM6 to be stored in sequential order in the block. The indexes are changed to reflect the movement of records: The normal key for P4 is now H1, and the overflow address for P4 is now V1.

The transaction file T3 contains several transactions, and they are applied to the file in Figure 9.28. The record with key F1 is to be deleted. A search of the indexes indicates that F1 resides in P1. The key field is marked with Xs to indicate deletion, and, since F1 was the last key in the block, the normal key entry changes to C2 (Figure 9.29). GM7 is added to P4, causing H1 to move to overflow with a link field from the overflow address of P4—namely, V1. H1 is, therefore, linked to H2. The address of H1, which is the beginning of the linked list, is stored in the overflow address for P4 (V2). GM7 is inserted at the end of the prime data block P4, and its key is recorded in the normal key of the entry for P4. The deletion of GM7 causes the key field to be marked with Xs, and, since GM7 was the last key in the block, the normal entry changes to GM6. The subsequent addition of GM7 causes GM7 to be added to overflow, linked ahead of H1. The final transaction deletes T1, which is in P5. Since it is the only record in the block, it is marked as deleted, and the normal and overflow entries for P5 in the index are also marked as deleted. Figure 9.29 illustrates the master file after applying transaction file T3.

Index

Normal		Overflow	
Key	Address	Key	Address
F1	P1	F1	P1
GM1	P2	GM1	P2
GM4	P3	GM4	P3
H2	P4	H2	P4
T1	P5	T1	P5

Prime data blocks

P1

C1	Dodge	2 DR	Omni	25,000	grey
C2	Dodge	2 DR	Aspen	7,000	tan
F1	Ford	2 DR HB	Escort	54,000	white

P2

F2	Lincoln	4 DR	Continental	38,000	black
F3	Ford	2 DR	Thunderbird	35,000	blue
GM1	Cadillac	4 DR	Fleetwood	9,000	red

P3

GM2	Oldsmobile	4 DR	Delta 88	28,050	blue
GM3	Chevrolet	2 DR	Camaro	33,000	silver
GM4	Cadillac	2 DR	Cimarron	63,000	maroon

P4

GM5	Oldsmobile	4 DR	98	11,000	green
H1	Honda	4 DR	Accord	32,000	yellow
H2	Honda	2 DR HB	Accord	11,250	brown

P5

T1	Toyota	2 DR HB	Celica	3,400	white

Figure 9.27
Creation of car-rental agency indexed sequential master file using cylinder-and-surface indexing method

Figure 9.28
Car-rental agency indexed sequential master file after applying transaction file T2

Index

Normal		Overflow	
Key	Address	Key	Address
F1	P1	F1	P1
GM1	P2	GM1	P2
GM4	P3	GM4	P3
H1	P4	H2	V1
T1	P5	T1	P5

Prime data blocks

P1

C1 C2 F1	Dodge Dodge Ford	2 DR 2 DR 2 DR HB	Omni Aspen Escort	25,000 7,000 54,000	grey tan white

P2

F2 F3 GM1	Lincoln Ford Cadillac	4 DR 2 DR 4 DR	Continental Thunderbird Fleetwood	38,000 35,000 9,000	black blue red

P3

GM2 GM3 GM4	Oldsmobile Chevrolet Cadillac	4 DR 2 DR 2 DR	Delta 88 Camaro Cimarron	28,050 33,000 63,000	blue silver maroon

P4

GM5 GM6 H1	Oldsmobile Chevrolet Honda	4 DR 4 DR 4 DR	98 Cimarron Accord	11,000 11,250 32,000	green brown yellow

P5

T1	Toyota	2 DR HB	Celica	3,400	white

Overflow blocks

V1

H2	Honda	2 DR HB	Accord	11,250	brown	−1

Index

Normal		Overflow	
Key	Address	Key	Address
C2	P1	C2	P1
GM1	P2	GM1	P2
GM4	P3	GM4	P3
GM6	P4	H2	V3
XXX	P5	XXX	P5

Prime data blocks

P1

C1	Dodge	2 DR	Omni	25,000	grey
C2	Dodge	2 DR	Aspen	7,000	tan
XX	Ford	2 DR HB	Escort	54,000	white

P2

F2	Lincoln	4 DR	Continental	38,000	black
F3	Ford	2 DR	Thunderbird	35,000	blue
GM1	Cadillac	4 DR	Fleetwood	9,000	red

P3

GM2	Oldsmobile	4 DR	Delta 88	28,050	blue
GM3	Chevrolet	2 DR	Camaro	33,000	silver
GM4	Cadillac	2 DR	Cimarron	63,000	maroon

P4

GM5	Oldsmobile	4 DR	98	11,000	green
GM6	Chevrolet	4 DR	Cimarron	11,250	brown
XXX	Pontiac	2 DR	Fiero	1,500	navy

P4

XXX	Toyota	2 DR HB	Celica	3,400	white

Overflow blocks

V1

H2	Honda	2 DR HB	Accord	11,250	brown	–1

V2

H1	Honda	4 DR	Accord	32,000	yellow	V1

V3

GM7	Pontiac	2 DR	Fiero	1,500	navy	V2

Figure 9.29
Car-rental agency indexed sequential master file after applying transaction file T3

Access to a record in overflow involves:

1. seeking the cylinder index
2. scanning the cylinder index
3. seeking the cylinder
4. scanning the track index to identify the overflow
5. scanning the overflow block
6. if the record is not located, use the link field to find the next overflow block and continue with step 5 until the record is located or a link of –1 is found

Searching for H2 involves scanning the cylinder index, seeking the cylinder, scanning the track index, scanning the overflow blocks V3, V2, and V1 until the record is found. Record H2 in overflow takes six steps to locate; a record in the prime data area takes only five steps to locate. In fact the number of steps translates to I/O operations, and the number increases as the linked list of overflow blocks increases.

After a great many additions to and deletions from the file, a number of records are in overflow blocks, and a number of deleted (marked) records are taking up space in the prime data area. The file can be accessed more efficiently if all the records are in the prime data area. Periodic reorganization of ISAM files is required to ensure efficient access to the data in the file. Reorganization involves accessing the file in sequential order and recreating the ISAM file with all the records stored in prime data blocks and new indexes created.

The Ada implementations of Algorithm 9.6 and Algorithm 9.10 are presented in Appendix B. Figure 9.30 graphically illustrates the interfacing of the program components with each other and the external I/O files. The data structures shared by Algorithm 9.6 (`Create`) and Algorithm 9.10 (`Update`) are encapsulated in a nongeneric package, `Ch5Struc`. The generic `ISAM` package, also used by both algorithms, encapsulates the operations on the ISAM file while hiding the data structures that define the file components. The hiding of these data structures from the instantiator of the `ISAM` package prohibits tampering with file components by the user, thus ensuring the integrity of the ISAM file.

VSAM FILE ORGANIZATION

The cylinder-and-surface indexing method used on IBM machines (ISAM) was replaced in 1972 by Virtual Storage Access Method **(VSAM) file organization** on virtual machines. A VSAM file consists of four areas: (1) **control intervals**, which contain data records; (2) **control areas**, which contain several control intervals; (3) a **sequence set**, which is an index of a control area; and (4) an **index set**, which is a tree containing up to three levels of index blocks. The lowest-level index blocks point to sequence sets. Figure 9.31 illustrates the relationships of the four parts of a VSAM file.

A control interval contains one or more data records, much as the data records are stored in a block in the SIS files or in a single track in the ISAM files. Figure 9.32 depicts the format of a control interval that contains data records at the beginning, free space for later additions, record definition fields **(RDFs)** for each record in the control interval, and finally a control interval definition field **(CIDF)**. The RDF of each record contains the relative byte address **(RBA)** relative to the beginning of the file. The CIDF contains the length in bytes of the free space within the control interval and the position of the free space. The *i*th RDF contains the length in bytes of the *i*th record within the control interval.

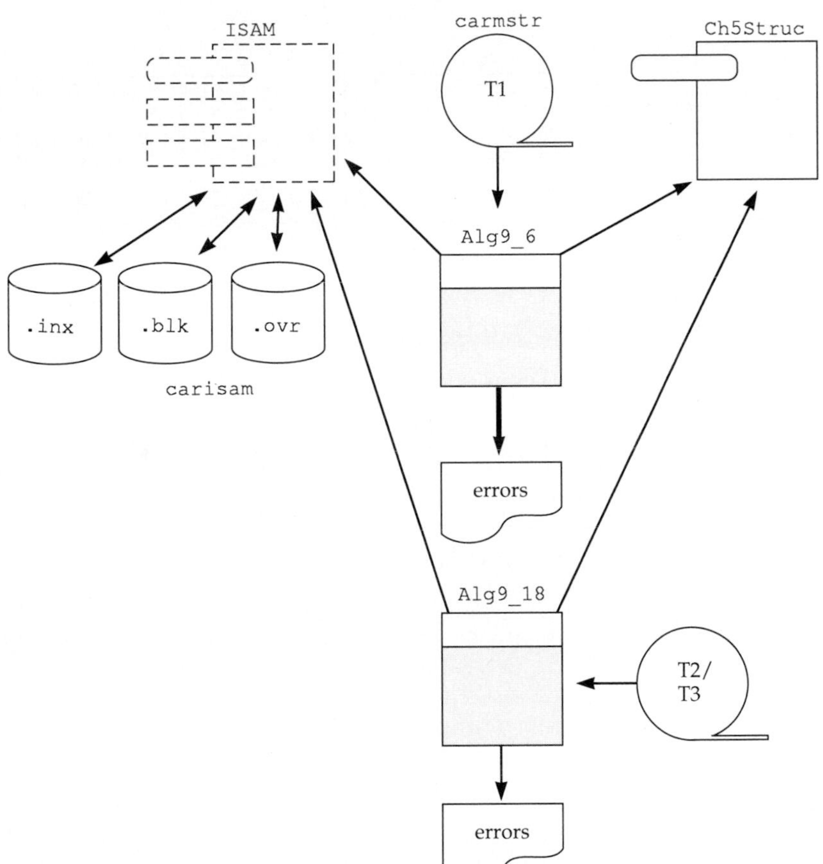

Figure 9.30
Case study 9.2 interfaces

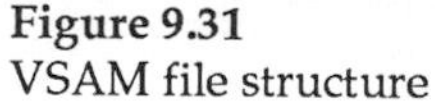

Figure 9.31
VSAM file structure

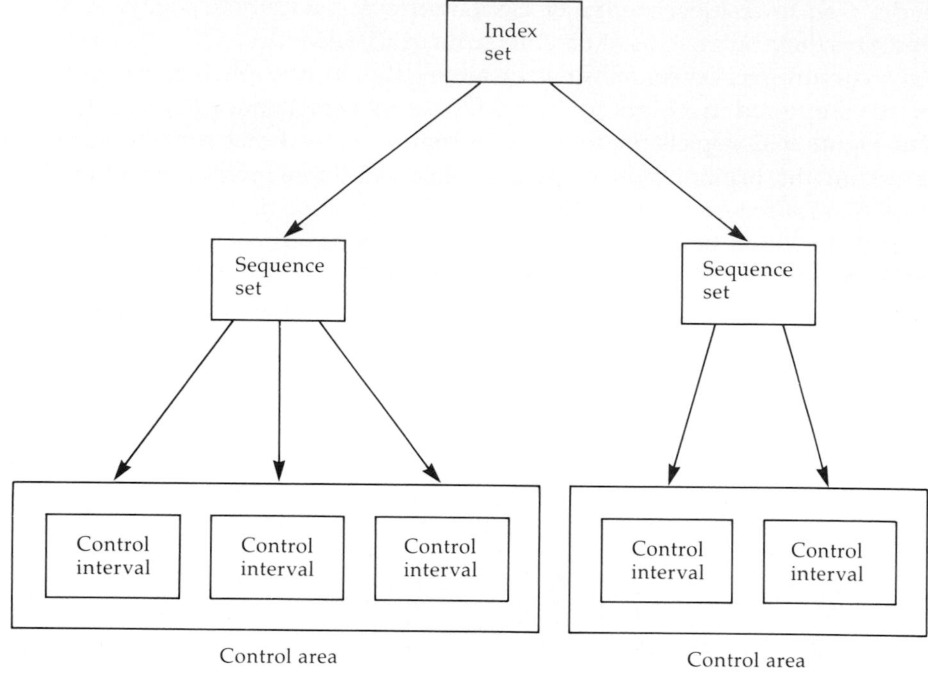

Figure 9.32
Control interval format for a VSAM file

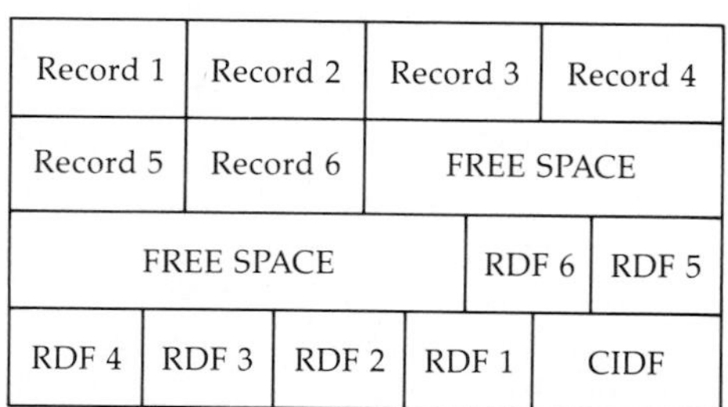

Records are stored physically within the control interval according to the keys of the records. Record 1 is stored at the beginning of the control interval, and the RDF for record 1 is stored to the left of the CIDF. Record 2 is stored to the right of record 1, with the corresponding RDF for record 2 being stored to the left of the RDF for record 1. Thus, the logical records and corresponding RDFs are stored in the control interval as two stacks of information growing toward each other. This method of storing records in one end of the control interval and RDFs in the other end allows the free space to reside in the middle of the control interval. Additions and deletions to the control interval move records and RDFs within the control interval to ensure that all the free space is in contiguous locations.

A control area, which is a collection of control intervals, is synonymous with a cylinder in the ISAM method; it is a collection of tracks. The maximum key in each control interval within a control area is stored in the lowest level of the index known as a sequence set. The control intervals for a given control area need not be physically stored in ascending order by maximum key values. Why? The sequence set has an ordered list of all the maximum key values of all control intervals in the control area along with the address of each control interval. The sequence set elements have pointers to siblings to facilitate easy sequential access.

The index set is a tree structure consisting of index blocks containing key-pointer pairs. The key-pointer pair is the maximum key in an index block at the next lower level in the tree and a pointer to the index block. The lowest level of the index set points to a sequence set. The key-pointer pairs within an index block are stored in order by the key values to facilitate sequencing through the file.

A VSAM file that stores records in order by a key value (a **key-sequenced VSAM file**) must be created sequentially so that the records may be stored physically in order within a control interval. The keys for control intervals may be ordered within sequence sets, and the keys for sequence sets may be ordered within the index set. At the time of creation of a VSAM file, free space is allocated within each control interval to allow for additions to the file later. This space is called **embedded space** or **distributed free space**. Empty control intervals may be allocated at the end of each control area much like the cylinder overflow areas for ISAM files. Figure 9.33 presents a sample VSAM file with two levels of index blocks.

Key-sequenced VSAM files may be accessed sequentially, skip-sequentially, or randomly. Sequential access involves searching through the index to identify the RBA of the first control interval in the file. The linked list formed by the elements of the sequence set is traversed retrieving each control interval referenced. The sequential access need not start with the first record but may start with a specific record key and retrieve sequentially from that point to the end of the file.

Skip-sequential access involves a subset of the records in the file in key order. For a given set of keys that is a subset of the keys in the file, the sequence set is scanned (using the links between sequence set elements) for the RBA of the control interval containing the next key in the given set.

Random access to records in the key-sequenced VSAM file involves traversing the index set down to the sequence set in the same way the B^+-trees in Chapter 8 were traversed to locate information in the leaf nodes. The sequence set identifies the RBA of the control interval to be retrieved that contains the record to be located. Random access may be used to retrieve a record with a specific key, to retrieve the record with the next largest key, and to retrieve the first record to satisfy a generic key. The general form of record retrieval makes VSAM a powerful access mechanism.

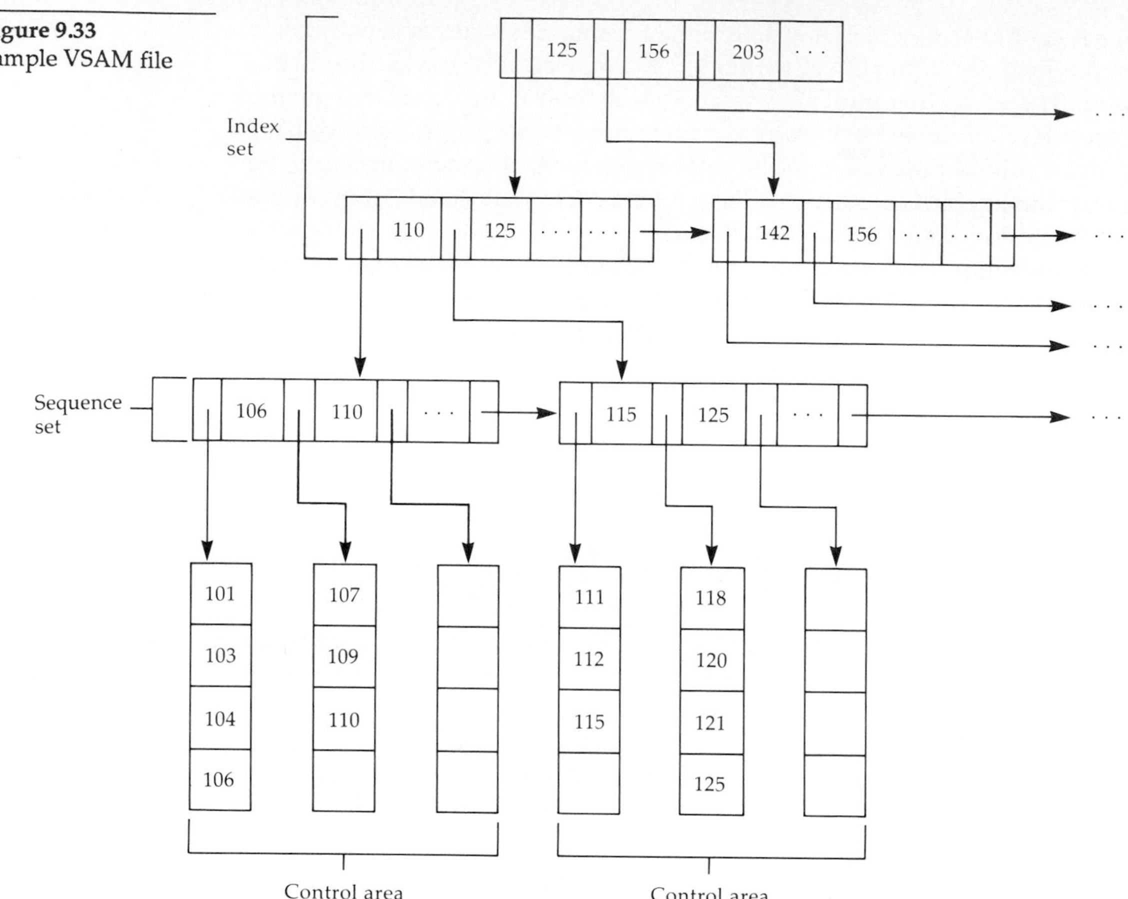

Figure 9.33
Sample VSAM file

Addition of records to a VSAM file involves moving records within the control interval so that the records remain in sequence by the key values. If the free space does not contain enough room to add a record, a **control interval split** takes place. The full control interval is split (by moving half of the records) into one of the empty control intervals at the end of the control area. The control intervals may no longer be in order physically, but the sequence set (index) retains the order for sequencing the control intervals within the control area. If no empty control interval exists within the control area, a **control area split** occurs. Half of the control intervals in the full control area are moved into an empty control area at the end of the file. As with the control interval split, the control areas are no longer in order physically, but the sequence set elements retain the order of control areas.

Suppose a record with the key of 105 is added to the sample VSAM file in Figure 9.33. The search routine scans the top-level index blocks (which are linked for sequencing through the file) for the first key larger than 105. The first entry is 125 with a pointer to the second-level index block. Scanning the second-level index block reveals the key 110 with a pointer to a sequence set. Searching the sequence set for the first key larger than 105 finds a key of 106 with a pointer to a control interval. The control interval containing records with keys 101, 103, 104, and 106 is the block into which record 105 should be added, but there is not sufficient room. The control interval is split, leaving records 101, 103, and 104; 105 is stored in an empty control interval at the end of the control area. Record 106 moves into the same control interval as record 105. Figure 9.34 shows the VSAM file with record 105 inserted. The sequence set for this control area has been modified to include a pointer and the maximum key value of the split control interval. Notice that the keys in the sequence set are moved to maintain the key order.

Suppose that a record with the key 108 is added to the file. A search of the index set and sequence set leads to the same control area. The control interval containing 107, 109, and 110 should now contain 108. Since there is some free space within the control interval, records 110 and 109 are moved toward the end of the control interval so record 108 can be inserted physically in order (Figure 9.35). No change to the sequence set is necessary.

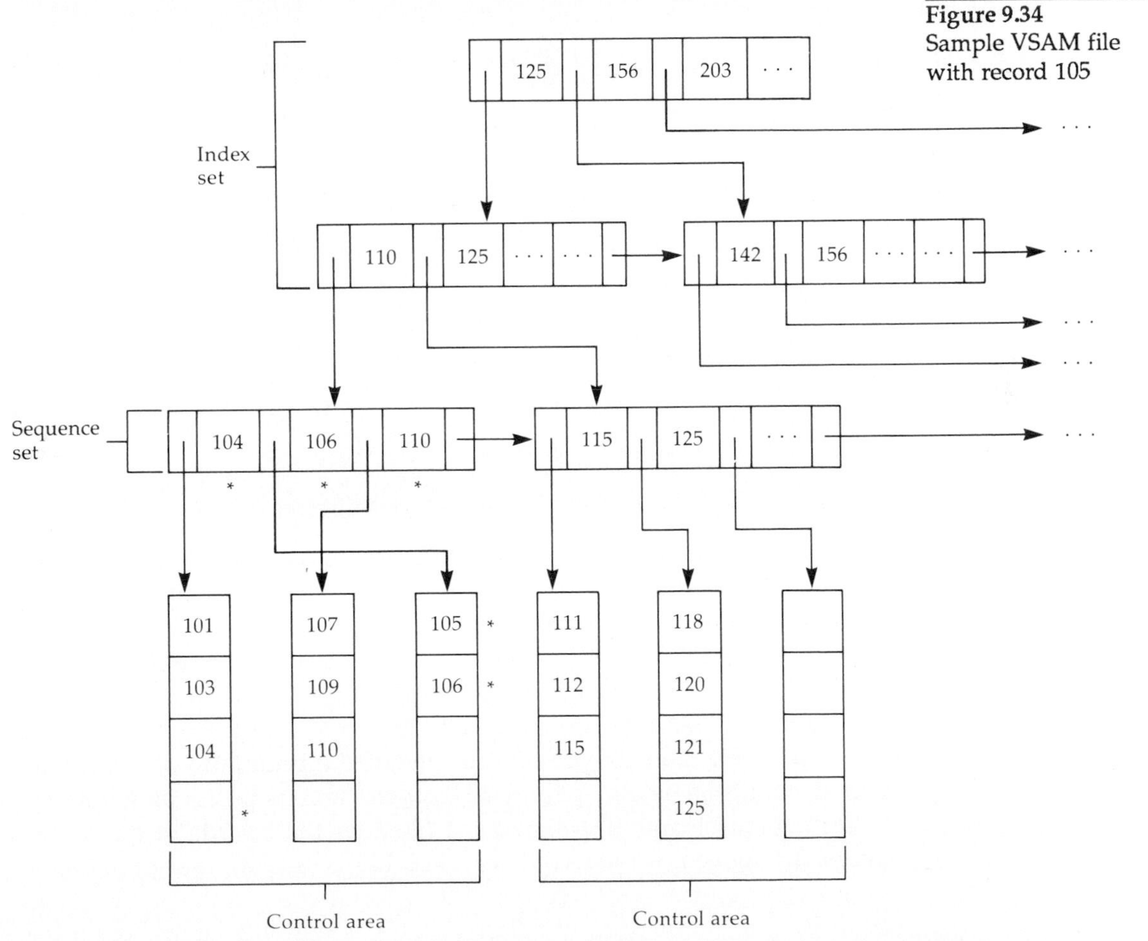

Figure 9.34
Sample VSAM file with record 105

Figure 9.35
VSAM file with record 108

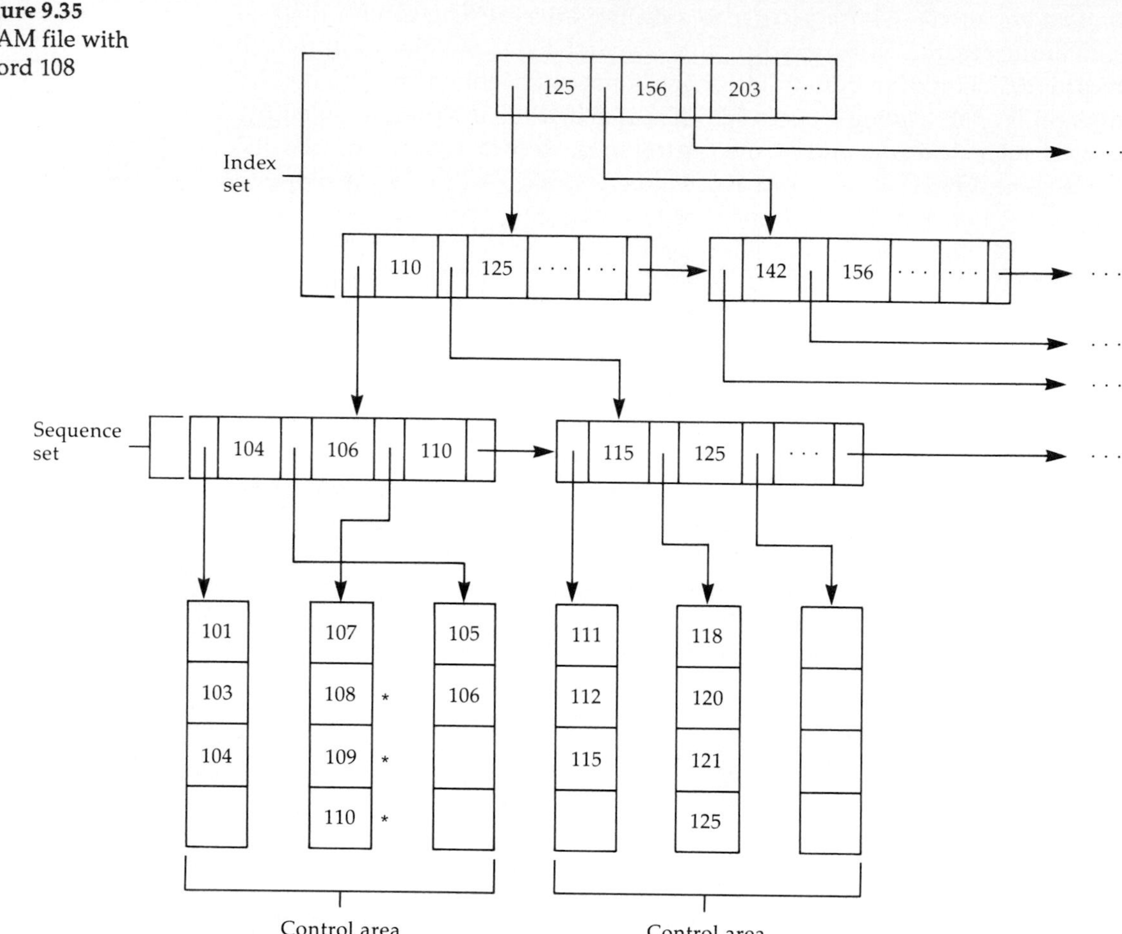

Deletion of records from the VSAM file involves moving all records in the control interval with keys larger than the deleted record up toward the beginning of the control interval (just as we moved the SIS files on the CDC). As a result the deleted space is joined with the free space in the middle of the control interval. Suppose that the record with key 120 is deleted from the VSAM file in Figure 9.35. The records in the control interval with keys larger than 120 are moved toward the beginning of the control interval, so all the empty space resides in contiguous positions within the control interval. Figure 9.36 shows the file after the records in the control interval are moved. If the record with key 125 is deleted, the second entry in the second sequence set record and the second entry in the first index set record have to be changed to reflect that 121 is now the largest key in the control interval.

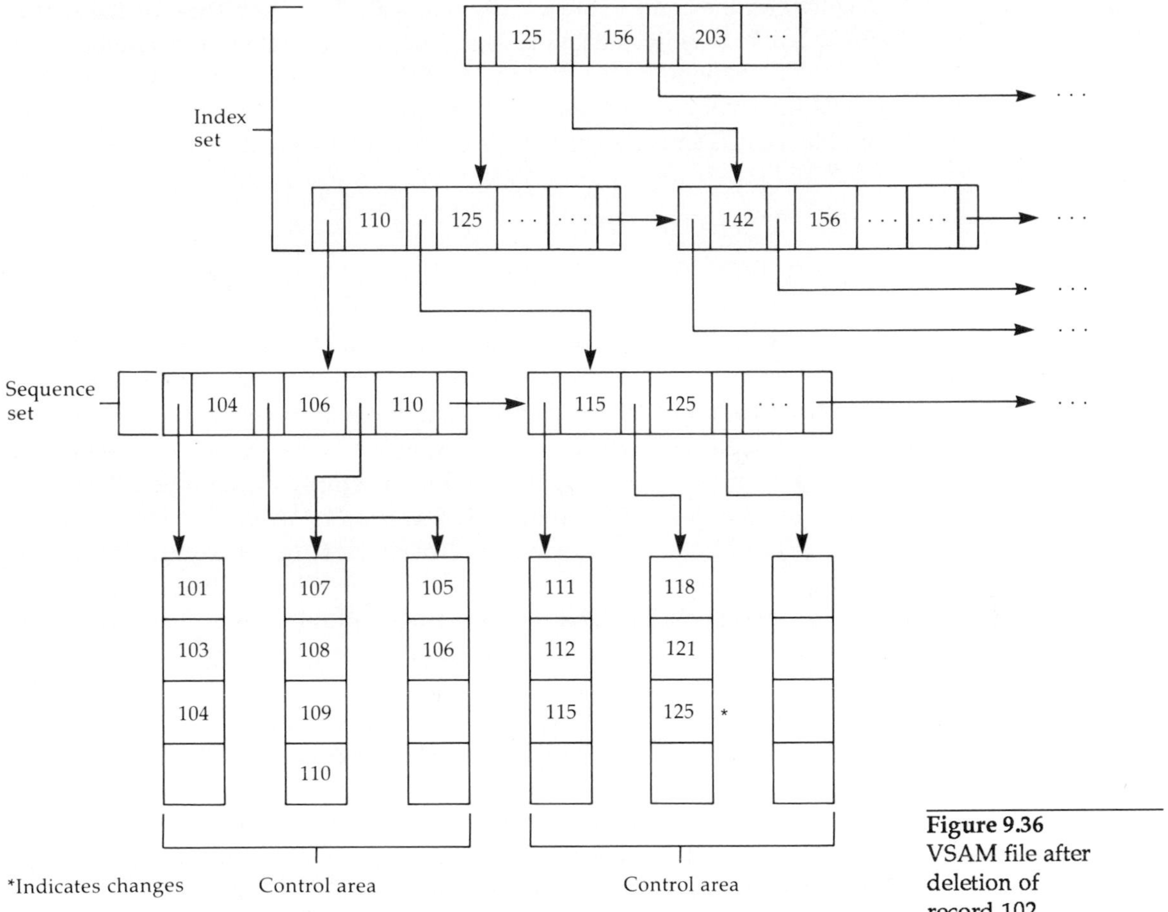

Figure 9.36 VSAM file after deletion of record 102

VSAM also supports **entry-sequenced files** and **relative record files**. An entry-sequenced file is simply a sequential file. The order of the records in the file is determined by the sequence in which records are entered in the file. VSAM keeps no index structure for entry-sequenced files but simply returns to the user the RBA of each record as it is loaded into the file. The user can then use this RBA to build an index to the file.

Relative record files in VSAM are identical to the direct files presented in Chapter 7. VSAM stores records in a relative file in control intervals according to the record's relative record number—a number that is assigned by the user. No index is constructed for relative record files. All records must be fixed in length so that the number of records in each control interval is identical. For example, suppose that each control interval can hold eight relative records. The record indexes for the first control interval are 1 through 8, the locations in the succeeding control interval are relative record numbers 9 through 16, and so on for the whole file.

VSAM performs better than ISAM for two reasons: (1) VSAM does not distinguish between prime data areas and overflow areas and (2) VSAM automatically combines space left after deleting a record with existing free space within the control interval. By using a B^+-tree structure for the index, VSAM is able to split control intervals into free control intervals that are not physically contiguous. By reclaiming deleted record spaces and keeping control information (such as RBAs) on each record in the control interval, variable records can be stored in the control intervals quite easily.

CASE STUDY 9.3: THE CAR-RENTAL AGENCY

The data used in case studies in previous chapters are stored in a VSAM file for comparison. The transaction file T1 in Table 5.1 contains the initial records for creation of the master file. The records are in key order and are loaded into control intervals of size 4 (Figure 9.37). Each control area contains three control intervals, one of which is empty at the time of creation for use in control interval splits. The index entry in the sequence set elements is the largest key in each control interval in the control area. The index entry in the index set is the largest key in each sequence set element.

The transaction file T2 contains a single addition of a record with key GM6. The key GM6 should be stored in the first control interval of the second control area, but the control interval is full. A control interval split occurs. The record to be added, GM6, is stored in the empty control interval in the control area (Figure 9.38), and the keys larger than GM6 are split into the same control interval as GM6. This split moves half of the records out of the original control interval. An index entry for the original control interval (the largest key is GM5) is inserted into the second sequence set element. Figure 9.38 shows the VSAM file after the addition of GM6.

The transaction file T3 contains several changes that result in the deletion of the record with key F1, the addition of a new record with key GM7, and the deletion of the record with key T1. The record with the key F1 is deleted from the first control interval in the first control area, and the records in the same control interval with larger keys are moved forward. As a result all the empty space is left in one large block (Figure 9.39). The record with key GM7 is added to the third control interval in the second control area. The record with the key T1 is deleted from the second control interval of the second control area. The entries in the sequence set elements for these two control areas are adjusted accordingly. Figure 9.39 illustrates the VSAM after applying the transactions in transaction file T3.

The implementation of a VSAM package is not presented because VSAM uses a B^+-tree for its indexes as did case study 9.1. It would differ for the implementation of case study 9.1 only in the fact that VSAM's indexes would reflect the largest key in a data block as opposed to the smallest key as used in case study 9.1.

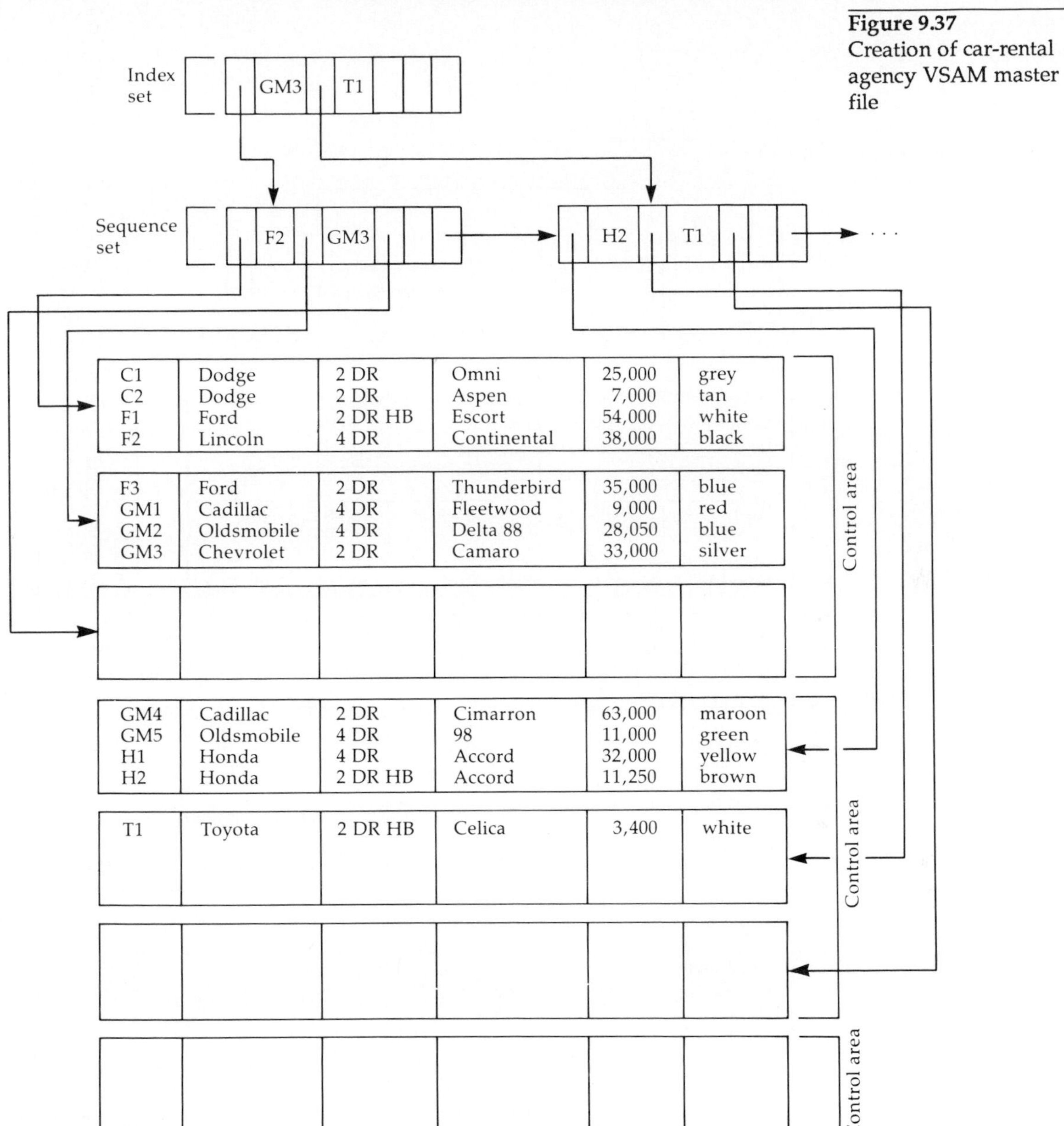

Figure 9.37
Creation of car-rental agency VSAM master file

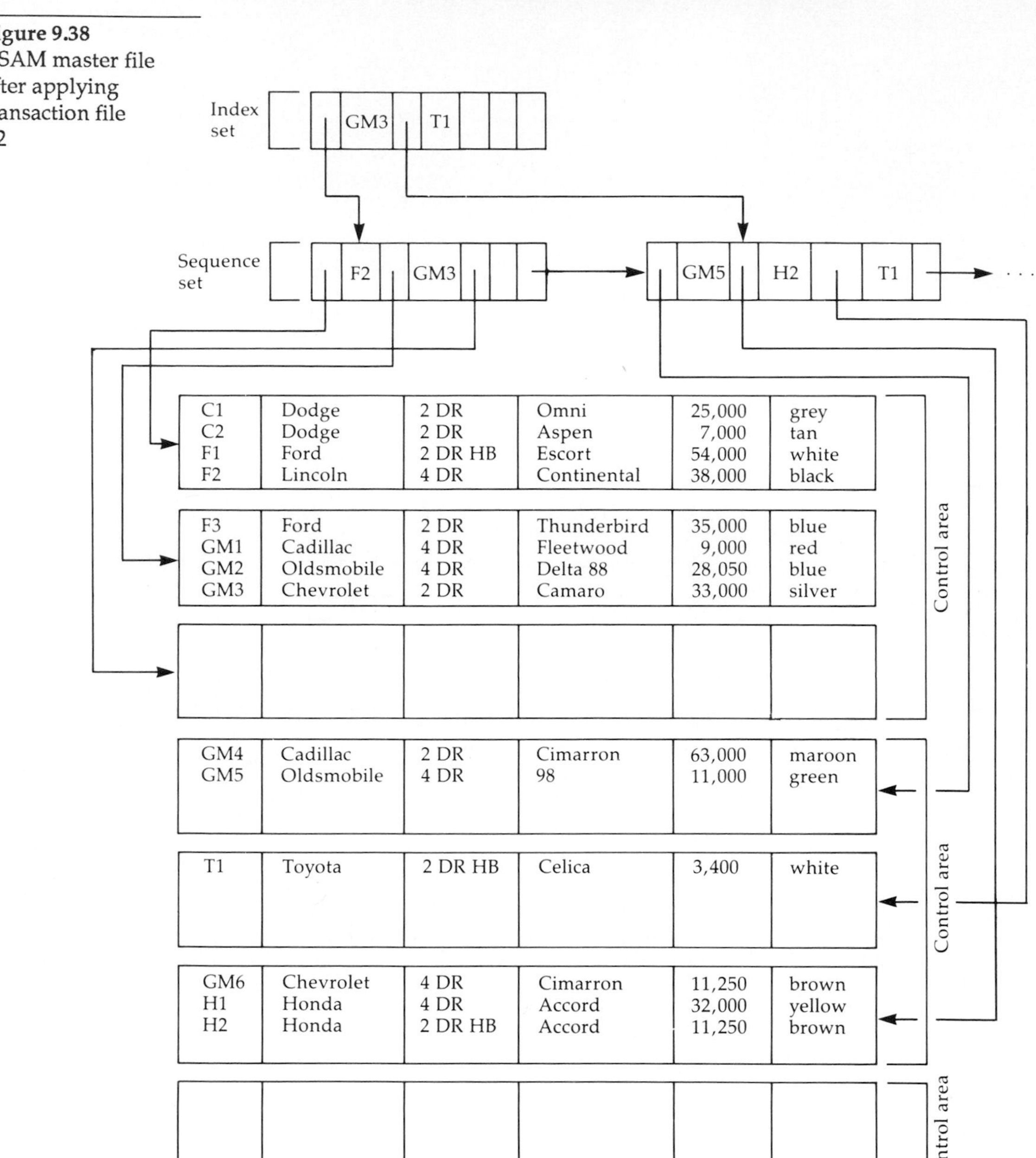

Figure 9.38
VSAM master file after applying transaction file T2

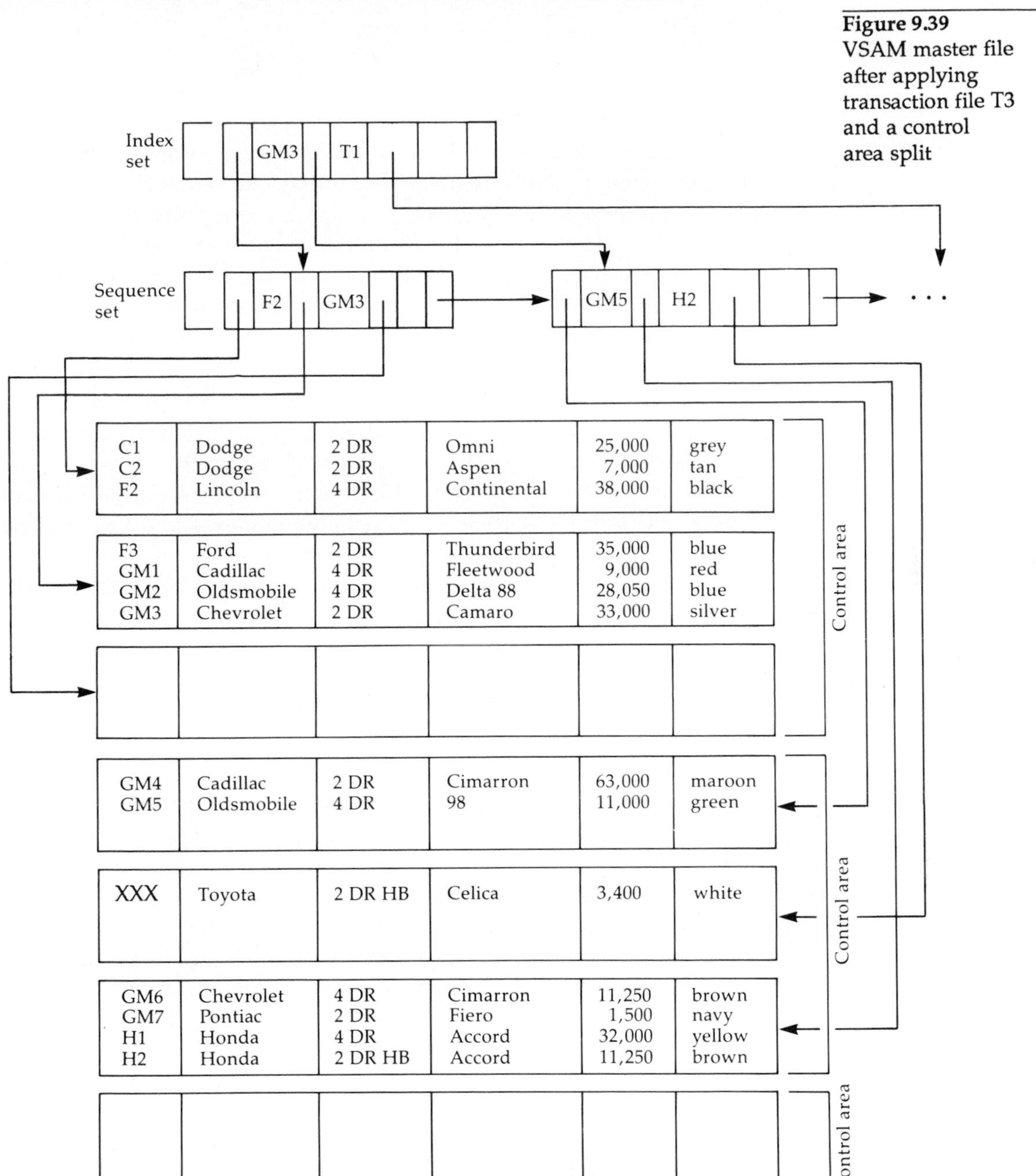

Figure 9.39
VSAM master file after applying transaction file T3 and a control area split

SUMMARY

Indexed sequential file organization for a collection of records in a file provides sequential access to the records in the file by one primary key field as well as random access to an individual record by the same primary key field. Two common methods exist for structuring indexed sequential files: (1) the index-and-data-blocks method (used by CDC computers) and (2) the cylinder-and-surface indexing method (used by IBM computers).

The index-and-data-blocks method organizes the file into data blocks and index blocks. The data blocks contain a fixed number of data records that are maintained in sequence within each data block. The lowest primary key value in each data block is recorded in an index block, which contains a fixed number of references to data blocks. Each reference in an index block contains the lowest key value and the address (relative record number) of a data block. Random access is achieved by searching through several levels of index blocks to locate the one data block that contains the record being sought. Sequential access is achieved by using the indexes to list the file in order by the primary key field. Additions of records to the file cause a data block to split to maintain the sequencing by the primary key field within data blocks. The split of the data block could cause index blocks to split to maintain the sequencing for the whole file. Deletions of records from the file cause movement of records within a data block—movements that keep the unused locations of a data block in one free space.

The cylinder-and-surface indexing method is based on the physical characteristics of a magnetic disk. The indexed file using this method (an ISAM file) consists of an index area, a prime data area, and an independent overflow area. The data are stored sequentially by a primary key field in consecutive cylinders on the magnetic disk. Each cylinder contains a surface index (secondary-level index) to data records stored within the cylinder, a prime data area, and a cylinder overflow area. The first cylinder of the file contains the cylinder index (primary-level index) to the cylinders of data in the file. Each entry in the cylinder indexes contains the largest key value stored in that cylinder. Similarly, each entry in the surface index contains the largest key value stored on that surface. Each entry also contains the largest key value stored in the overflow area that was expanded from that surface of the prime data area. Random access is achieved by first searching the cylinder index to locate the particular cylinder in which the record may reside, then searching the surface index within that cylinder to determine whether the record resides in the prime data area or in the cylinder overflow area. Once the particular area has been determined, that area is searched sequentially to locate the record. Additions of records to the file cause a surface of the prime data area to expand into the cylinder overflow area. The movement of key values is recorded in the surface indexes. Deletions of records from the file cause the record location to be marked for deletion; the record space is wasted until the next reorganization retrieves the unused space.

VSAM file organization is a replacement for ISAM file organization. VSAM organization uses dynamic structures for indexing a data file that resemble the structures used by SIS file organization on CDC computers (a B^+-tree structure).

The car-rental agency case study was repeated for each of the three indexed sequential implementations presented in this chapter.

Key Terms

CIDF
control areas
control area split
control intervals
control interval split
cylinder-and-surface indexing method
cylinder indexes
cylinder overflow area
data block split
distributed free space
embedded overflow
entry-sequenced files
independent overflow area
index-and-data-blocks method
index set
indexed sequential file organization
ISAM file organization
key-sequenced VSAM file
prime data area
RBA
RDFs
relative record files
sequence set
SIS file organization
surface index
track index
VSAM file organization

Exercises

1. What do sequential and indexed sequential files have in common?
2. What facilities do indexed sequential files have for accessing data and updating data files that sequential files do not have?
3. Why is insertion of records into indexed sequential files a problem in theory?
4. List two approaches for handling insertions into an indexed sequential file.
5. Show the SIS file in Figure 9.11(d) after the insertion of keys 19 and 20.
6. Show the SIS file in Figure 9.13(d) after the deletion of keys 10 and 11.
7. Show the ISAM file in Figure 9.26(d) after the insertion of keys 14 and 12.
8. Show the ISAM file in Figure 9.26(e) after the deletion of keys 3 and 11.

9. Show the VSAM file in Figure 9.34 after the addition of keys 123 and 113.
10. Show the VSAM file in Figure 9.35 after the deletion of keys 115 and 105.
11. Why does an ISAM file have to be reorganized more often than an SIS or a VSAM file? What is meant by the reorganization of an ISAM file?
12. Why are fewer accesses expected to an SIS file or a VSAM file as compared to an ISAM file?
13. Identify the exact number of accesses necessary to retrieve a record from an ISAM file.
14. Identify the exact number of accesses necessary to retrieve a record from an SIS file.
15. Identify the exact number of accesses necessary to retrieve a record from a VSAM file.
16. Why is a B^+-tree a better choice than a B-tree for the index structure of an indexed sequential file?
17. Compare the advantages and disadvantages of the index-and-data-blocks method and the cylinder-and-surface indexing method.
18. Describe the actions required to access an SIS file sequentially.
19. Describe the actions required to access an ISAM file sequentially.
20. Describe the actions required to access a VSAM file sequentially.
21. Compare your answers from exercises 18 through 20; which organization is the most efficient?
22. Assume that the maximum time for a seek to a disk is 20 ms and that to search a track is 50 ms. What is the maximum time to access a record in a prime data area in an ISAM file stored on this disk? Assume that the ISAM file has two levels of indexes: cylinder and track.
23. Assume that the maximum time to input an index or data block from an SIS file on disk is 30 ms. If the file has three levels of index blocks, what is the maximum time to access a record in the SIS file.
24. Repeat exercise 23 for a VSAM file with a one-level index set.
25. Rewrite Algorithms 9.1 through 9.5 to implement VSAM file organization.

Programming Problems

1. From a nontext sequential master file, create an indexed sequential master file that describes an inventory of parts. The input file should contain:

   sequential master file
   key field = part number
   a nontext file of part data containing the following in each record:
   part number (10 characters)
   part description (26 characters)
   part price (real)

   The output files should consist of:

   a. Scope Indexed Sequential master file
   key field = part number
   A relative file stores the data physically in sequential order in data blocks. Each relative address should contain the following declaration:

```
TYPE Isamrecord = Record
                      part_number : String ( 1 .. 10 );
                      part_description : String ( 1 .. 26 );
                      part_price : Float;
                  End Record;
TYPE Isamblock = Record
                      part : Array ( 1..3 ) Of Isamrecord;
                      link : Integer;
                 End Record;
```

   two levels of indexes in which each node contains the largest key in five data blocks with a link to each data block (see the diagram that follows). Write the level-one index nodes to a file (`index1`) at the end of the program. Write the level-two index nodes to a file (`index2`) at the end of the program. Each node of the indexes should contain the following declaration:

```
TYPE IndexEntry = Record
                      key : String ( 1 .. 10 );
                      datablock : Integer;
                  End Record;
TYPE Indexnode : Array ( 1..5 ) of IndexEntry;
index1,
index2 : Indexnode;
PACKAGEIndex_File_IO Is New Direct_IO ( Indexnode );
index1_file,
index2_file : Index_File_IO.File_Type;
```

   b. a list produced from a dump of the indexes and data blocks

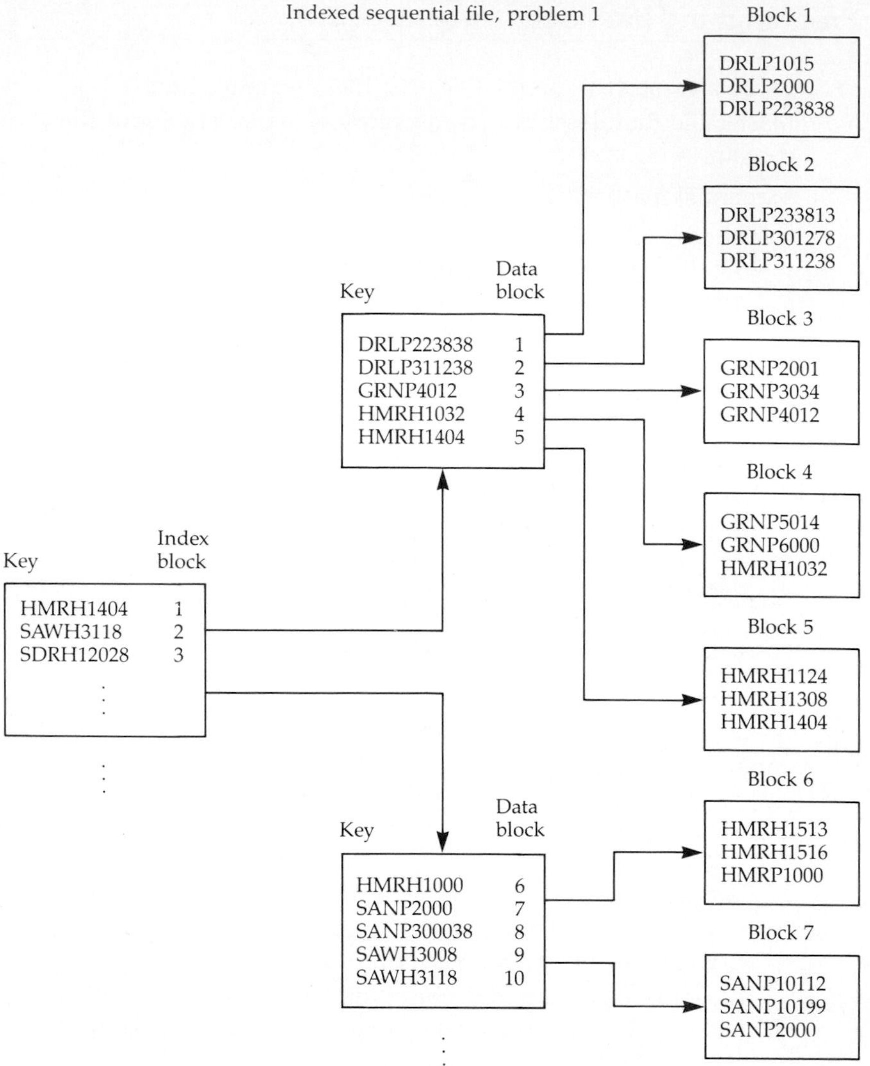

2. In problem 2, you will update the Scope Indexed Sequential master file created in problem 1 with input transaction records. Produce an updated indexed sequential master file (on disk) and an audit/error list (on the printer). Use the SIS you created in problem 1. The transaction file should have the following characteristics:

   a. key fields = part number (major)
      update code (minor)

   b. a text file of update information containing several different formats:

      additions
         update code (A)
         part number (10 characters)

part description (26 characters)
part price (float)
changes
description
update code (C)
part number (10 characters)
change id (D)
new description (26 characters)
price
update code (C)
part number (10 characters)
change id (P)
new price (float)
deletions
update code (D)
part number (10 characters)

The output will consist of:

a. updated indexed sequential master file

b. audit/error list

For each transaction key list:
update code
transaction key
action taken (an addition, a change, a deletion, or an error)
error message if necessary

Your program should perform the following steps:

a. Read each input transaction record (without using standard input). Validate each transaction to ensure that it contains one of the following update codes:
A for add
C for change
D for delete

b. Create a master record for each valid add transaction.

c. Change the appropriate master field for each valid change transaction.

d. Delete the master record for each valid delete transaction.

e. Identify the following error conditions:

ERROR CONDITION	ERROR MESSAGE
Add a transaction that is already on the master file.	INVALID ADD-ALREADY ON MASTER
Change a transaction that is not on the master file.	INVALID CHANGE-NOT ON MASTER
Delete a transaction that is not on the master file.	INVALID DELETE-NOT ON MASTER
Invalid update code	INVALID UPDATE CODE

Employ the following hints to achieve exemplary program style and clarity:

Tally master and transaction record counts and print after audit/error list.

Input the new master file and list on the printer to make sure the information is right.

Count the number of lines output on the page and reprint headings and page numbers at the top of each new page rather than printing across the page perforations.

3. Repeat problem 1, but—this time—create a VSAM key-sequenced file.
4. Repeat problem 2 to update the VSAM file you created in problem 3.
5. Create an ISAM master file from a nontext sequential part master file. The ISAM input file should be like the input file in problem 1. The output files should consist of:

   a. ISAM master file

      key field = part number

      A relative prime data file stores the data physically in sequential order (initially) in data blocks. Each relative address should contain the following declaration:

```
MAX_DATA_ENTRIES : CONSTANT Integer := 5;
TYPE Part_Record Is
        Record
            part_number : String ( 1 .. 10 );
            part_description : String ( 1 .. 26 );
            part_price : Float;
        End Record;

TYPE Prime_Data_Block Is
        Record
            data_entries : Integer;
            prime_record :
                  Array ( 1..MAX_DATA_ENTRIES ) Of Part_Record;
        End Record;

PACKAGE Prime_Data_Block_IO Is
           New Direct_IO ( Prime_Data_Block );
data_file : Prime_Data_Block_IO.File_Type;
```

a relative overflow data file that stores records expanded from the prime data file. Link all records expanded from one prime data block in a singly linked list in sequential order. The overflow linked list for one prime data block should contain records with keys greater than the largest in the prime data block. Each record in the overflow data file should contain the following declaration:

```
TYPE Overflow_Block Is Record
                          over_record : Part_Record;
                          next_overflow : Integer;
                       End Record;
PACKAGE Overflow_Block_IO Is New Direct_IO (Overflow_Block);
over_file : Overflow_Block_IO.File_Type;
```

one level of indexes where each entry in the indexes contains the largest key in one prime data block (normal entry) and the largest key in the overflow file (over entry) that corresponds to the one prime data block with a link to each data block (see the diagram that follows). The indexes should be stored in an array while the indexed sequential file is being built, then written to a sequential data file. Each entry of the indexes should contain the following declaration:

```
TYPE An_Entry Is Record
                    key : String ( 1 .. 10 );
                    address : Integer
                End Record;
TYPE Index_Entries Is Record
                         normal : An_Entry;
                         over   : An_Entry
                     End Record;
indexes    : Array ( 1..30 ) of Index_Entries;
PACKAGE Index_Entries_IO Is New Direct_IO ( Index_Entries );
index_file : Index_Entries_IO.File_Type;
```

b. a listing produced from a dump of the indexes and data blocks

Indexed sequential file, problem 9

Indexes

Normal key	Address	Overflow key	Address
DRLP301278	1	DRLP301278	1
GRNP5014	2	GRNP5014	2
HMRH1404	3	HMRH1404	3
SANP10199	4	SANP10199	4
SAWH116314	5	SAWH116314	5
SAWH3118	6	SAWH3118	6
SAWP43012	7	SAWP43012	7
SAWP5012	8	SAWP5012	8
SDRH12028	9	SDRH12028	9
SDRH215612	10	SDRH215612	10
SDRH25184	11	SDRH25184	11
WWOP5000	12	WWOP5000	12

Prime data blocks

Block 1

5
DRLP1015
DRLP2000
DRLP223838
DRLP233813
DRLP301278

Block 2

5
DRLP311238
DRLP2001
GRNP3034
GRNP4012
GRNP5014

Block 3

5
GRNP6000
HMRH1032
HMRH1124
HMRH1308
HMRH1404

6. Access the ISAM master file you created in problem 5 to retrieve certain records. A sequential transaction text file contains the keys of those records to be retrieved, and each record contains a part number (10 characters). Output should contain a list of each transaction key followed by:

   the record with a matching key retrieved from the indexed sequential file using the indexes, or

   an error message to the effect that the record is not on the master file
7. Repeat problem 2, but—this time—update the ISAM file created in problem 5.
8. Repeat problem 1 but—this time—build a Scope Indexed Sequential file that contains data about vendors. The input file should contain:

   a. key field = vendor number (major)
      vendor date due (minor)

   b. a file of vendor data, where each record contains:
      vendor number (8 characters)
      vendor date due (yymmdd)
      vendor name (20 characters)
      vendor amount due (float)

9. Repeat problem 2, but—this time—update the file created in problem 8 with a transaction file that contains vendor transactions. The input file has the properties:

   a. key field = vendor number (major)
      vendor date due (minor)

   b. a text file of update data that contains several different formats:
      additions
         update code (A)
         vendor number (8 characters)
         vendor date due (yymmdd)
         vendor name (20 characters)
         vendor amount due (float)
      changes
         name
            update code (C)
            vendor number (8 characters)
            vendor date due (yymmdd)
            change id (N)
            new name (20 characters)
         amount due
            update code (C)
            vendor number (8 characters)
            vendor date due (yymmdd)
            change id (A)
            new amount due (float)
      deletions
         update code (D)
         vendor number (8 characters)
         vendor date due (yymmdd)

10. Using the guidelines in problem 1, build a VSAM file using the vendor data in problem 8.
11. Update the VSAM file in problem 10 as you did in problem 9.
12. Using the guidelines in problem 5, build an ISAM file using the vendor data described in problem 12.
13. Update the ISAM file in problem 12 as you did in problem 9.
14. Using the guidelines in problem 1, build an SIS file where the input is now employee data. The file should have the properties:

    a. key field = employee number

b. a file of employee data in which each record contains:
   section id (3 characters)
   department number (integer)
   employee number (integer)
   last name (12 characters)
   first name (9 characters)
   middle initial (1 character)
   sex code (1 character)
   marital status (1 character)
   number of exemptions (integer)
   pay rate (float)
   earnings (float)
   year-to-date earnings (float)

15. Repeat problem 2, but—this time—update the file built in problem 14 with a transaction file containing employee transactions. The input file should have the properties:

a. key field = employee number

b. a file of employee transactions where each record contains one of the following formats:
   additions
      update code (A)
      section id (3 characters)
      department number (integer)
      employee number (integer)
      last name (12 characters)
      first name (9 characters)
      middle initial (1 character)
      sex code (1 character)
      marital status (1 character)
      number of exemptions (integer)
      pay rate (float)
      earnings (float)
      year-to-date earnings (float)
   changes
      employee number (integer)
      one of the following changes:

CHANGE ID	FIELD
L	last name (12 characters)
F	first name (9 characters)
M	middle initial (1 character)
X	sex code (1 character)
S	marital status (1 character)
E	number of exemptions (integer)
P	pay rate (float)

deletions
- update code (D)
- employee number (integer)
- last name (12 characters)

16. Using the guidelines in problem 1, build a VSAM file with the employee data described in problem 14.
17. Repeat problem 2, but—this time—update the file created in problem 16.
18. Using the guidelines in problem 1, build an ISAM file with the employee data described in problem 14.
19. Repeat problem 2, but—this time—update the file created in problem 18.

Chapter 10

Multiple-Key File Organization

CHAPTER CONTENTS

PREVIEW

THIS CHAPTER INVESTIGATES OTHER TYPES of file organization that use linked lists or tree structures to provide multiple-key access to random-access data files. Included in this chapter are discussions of inverted files and multilist files along with creation and manipulation algorithms. The discussions employ the car-rental agency data to illustrate the inverted file and the use of multilist files to provide access by several keys. Quantitative measures of access times provide a basis for comparison to other types of file organization.

TYPES OF MULTIPLE-KEY FILE ORGANIZATION

The field of a record that uniquely identifies the record is known as the **primary key** field. Indexed sequential file organization provides sequential and random access to the records in a file by one primary key field. Many applications require access of records in a file by more than one key field. When using random-access file organization, we can locate a record of data containing a particular key value by specifying that key value. The other fields of a record, which may be used to access the record in **multiple-key file organization**, are known as **secondary key** fields. Two types of multiple-key file organization provide access to the records in a file by several key fields: **inverted file organization** and **multilist file organization.**

Single-key file organization (sequential, random, and indexed sequential) provides access to the data in the record by one primary key field. Given the primary key of a record, the data from the record can be accessed. To locate all records with a given attribute for a field other than the primary key field, all records must be accessed sequentially.

Multiple-key file organizations provide an inverse relationship between the data in a record and the primary key of the record that uniquely identifies it. Multiple-key files allow access to the data file by fields other than the primary key, just as an index for a book allows access to the information within the book by any key word listed in the index. Like the index for a book that lists the page numbers where a particular key word may be found, the multiple-key file index lists the primary keys of all the records in the data file that contain a particular secondary key value. The primary keys are then used to access the records from the data file. In other words, given an attribute for a secondary key field, the primary key field of the records containing the attribute can be found; the records can be accessed.

It is important to realize that the secondary key indexes discussed in this chapter are an additional structure in the sense that the data file is organized according to some underlying structure—either an indexed sequential or relative file—to which the primary key provides access. The secondary key indexes access records according to a particular secondary key value related to a set of primary keys.

The two common approaches to multiple-key file organization, inverted files and multilist files, both build for each secondary key field an index (directory) that is much like an index for a book. The difference between these two approaches is the way in which the list of primary keys for a particular secondary key value is stored. Access to data from a file by secondary keys is achieved in inverted file organization by using a directory of all possible attributes for each secondary key field and the address (primary key) of all records containing those attributes. With multilist file organization, the directory contains all possible attributes for each secondary key field and a pointer to a linked list of all records containing a given attribute.

Primary key	Secondary keys		Nonindexed information		
Id no.	Make	Style	Model	Mileage	Color
C1	Dodge	2 DR	Omni	25,000	grey
C2	Dodge	2 DR	Aspen	7,000	tan
F1	Ford	2 DR HB	Escort	54,000	white
F2	Lincoln	4 DR	Continental	38,000	black
F3	Ford	2 DR	Thunderbird	35,000	blue
GM1	Cadillac	4 DR	Fleetwood	9,000	red
GM2	Oldsmobile	4 DR	Delta 88	28,050	blue
GM3	Chevrolet	2 DR	Camaro	33,000	silver
GM4	Cadillac	2 DR	Cimarron	63,000	maroon
GM5	Oldsmobile	4 DR	98	11,000	green
H1	Honda	4 DR	Accord	32,000	yellow
H2	Honda	2 DR HB	Accord	11,250	brown
T1	Toyota	2 DR HB	Celica	3,400	white

Figure 10.1
Data records for a car-rental agency

Apply multiple-key access to the car-rental agency example. The agency has records for all cars in its inventory and needs access to the inventory data by a unique identification number, by make and by style. The sample inventory in Figure 10.1 is used in all examples in this chapter. The primary key of the data is the unique car identification number (id number). The primary key provides access to the actual record of data within the file. The secondary keys used to access the file are the makes and styles of the cars. The other data fields in the file are nonindexed but are necessary for inventory purposes.

INVERTED FILE ORGANIZATION

The **inversion index** for a record key of a data file contains all the values that the key field contains and a pointer to the records in the file that contain those key values. The data file is considered to be inverted on that key. The index for a book can be considered an inversion on the pages of the book since it lists all the topics contained in the book along with page numbers where the topics can be found.

An inverted file contains two areas: (1) a directory and (2) a data record area. The data records could be stored in a relative file and the primary key hashed to randomly access the records, or the records could be stored in an indexed sequential file to provide random access by the primary key field. The data record area can be organized in any manner as long as random access to the records is provided. The directory contains an inverted list for each secondary key field to be used in accessing the data records in the data record area. The directory provides access to the records in the file using a secondary key field by adding a higher level of indexing over the organization of the data file. A **partially inverted file** is one in which an inverted list is built for each of a number of selected fields. A **fully inverted file** has an inverted list for every field in the record and entries for all attributes in the file. A fully inverted file provides access to the data by any field in the record.

The inverted list for each secondary key field can be stored in individual files, or all inverted lists can be stored in one directory file. Each entry in an inverted list for a secondary key field contains an attribute found in the secondary key field in the file and a list of addresses of records in the file in which this attribute appears. The entries may vary in length because the number of addresses in the list may vary depending on the number of records in the file containing the attribute. Storing the inverted lists for several secondary key fields in one file may be difficult since variable-length records are needed. The inverted list for a single secondary key field can be stored in an individual file. Rather than using variable-length records for storage of inverted lists, each entry is fixed in length and allocated space for the maximum number of addresses for any given entry. Then all inverted lists for an inverted file are stored as a sequential or indexed sequential file.

CASE-STUDY 10.1: THE CAR-RENTAL AGENCY

The process of creating an inverted file from a set of data is called **inverting a data file**. As each record in the data file in this case study is input, the values in the make and style fields are compared to the inverted lists. If the make of the record is not already present in the make inverted list, it is inserted. If the style of the record is not already present in the style inverted list, it is inserted. Once the values for make and style are present in the inverted lists, the primary key of the record input is inserted in the inverted list in the list of addresses for the appropriate secondary key value. After accessing the first record in the data file, the inverted list for make contains the entry Dodge C1, and the style inverted list contains the entry 2 DR C1. Each record in the data file is input in turn, and the make and style values along with the primary keys are inserted into the inverted lists.

Figures 10.2 through Figure 10.10 show several snapshots of the creation of make and style inverted lists. The lists are created by reading a record from the data file in Figure 10.1 and entering the make, style, and primary key values in the inverted directories. Boldface indicates the changes from the previous snapshot. The complete inverted directories for secondary keys make and style are presented in Figure 10.10.

MAKE	PRIMARY KEY(S)
DODGE	**C1**

(a)

STYLE	PRIMARY KEY(S)
2 DR	**C1**

(b)

Figure 10.2
Inverted file directory for (a) make and (b) style with attributes for record with key C1 added

MAKE	PRIMARY KEY(S)
DODGE	**C2**, C1

(a)

STYLE	PRIMARY KEY(S)
2 DR	**C2**, C1

(b)

Figure 10.3
Inverted file directory for (a) make and (b) style from Figure 10.2 with attributes for record with key C2 added

MAKE	PRIMARY KEY(S)
FORD	**F1**
DODGE	C2,C1

(a)

STYLE	PRIMARY KEY(S)
2 DR HB	**F1**
2 DR	C2,C1

(b)

Figure 10.4
Inverted file directory for (a) make and (b) style from Figure 10.3 with attributes for record with key F1 added

MAKE	PRIMARY KEY(S)
LINCOLN	**F2**
FORD	F1
DODGE	C2,C1

(a)

STYLE	PRIMARY KEY(S)
4 DR	**F2**
2 DR HB	F1
2 DR	C2,C1

(b)

Figure 10.5
Inverted file directory for (a) make and (b) style from Figure 10.4 with attributes for record with key F2 added

MAKE	PRIMARY KEY(S)
LINCOLN	F2
FORD	**F3**, F1
DODGE	C2,C1

(a)

STYLE	PRIMARY KEY(S)
2 DR	**F3**,C2,C1
2 DR HB	F1
4 DR	F2

(b)

Figure 10.6
Inverted file directory for (a) make and (b) style from Figure 10.5 with attributes for record with key F3 added

MAKE	PRIMARY KEY(S)
CADILLAC	**GM1**
LINCOLN	F2
FORD	F3,F1
DODGE	C2,C1

(a)

STYLE	PRIMARY KEY(S)
4 DR	**GM1**,F2
2 DR HB	F1
2 DR	F3,C2,C1

(b)

Figure 10.7
Inverted file directory for (a) make and (b) style from Figure 10.6 with attributes for record with key GM1 added

The inverted list for make of car contains eight key values: Toyota, Honda, Chevrolet, Oldsmobile, Cadillac, Lincoln, Ford, and Dodge. The values are entered in the inverted index as they are encountered. For each key value in the inverted list for make, the primary keys of those records containing the corresponding make of car are listed. Two records in the file contain data concerning cars of the make Dodge; namely, the records with primary keys C2 and C1. Five records in the inverted file contain data concerning two-door (2 DR) cars; namely, the records with primary keys GM4, GM3, F3, C2, and C1.

One of the advantages of an inverted file is the ease of answering queries. In answer to the query "What cars are available with a make of Dodge?" the make inverted list is scanned for the make of Dodge. The scan results in a list of two primary keys, C2 and C1. The records C2 and C1 can be accessed from the file, and the answer to the query is that a grey two-door Dodge Omni with 25,000 miles and a tan two-door Dodge Aspen with 7,000 miles are available. Once the secondary key value (make = Dodge) is located in the inverted list, only one access per primary key in the list is needed to satisfy the query.

MAKE	PRIMARY KEY(S)
OLDSMOBILE	**GM2**
CADILLAC	GM1
LINCOLN	F2
FORD	F3,F1
DODGE	C2,C1

(a)

STYLE	PRIMARY KEY(S)
4 DR	**GM2**,GM1,F2
2 DR HB	F1
2 DR	F3,C2,C1

(b)

Figure 10.8
Inverted file directory for (a) make and (b) style from Figure 10.7 with attributes for record with key GM2 added

MAKE	PRIMARY KEY(S)
CHEVROLET	**GM3**
OLDSMOBILE	GM2
CADILLAC	GM1
LINCOLN	F2
FORD	F3,F1
DODGE	C2,C1

(a)

STYLE	PRIMARY KEY(S)
4 DR	GM2,GM1,F2
2 DR HB	F1
2 DR	**GM3**,F3,C2,C1

(b)

Figure 10.9
Inverted file directory for (a) make and (b) style from Figure 10.8 with attributes for record with key GM3 added

Consider an intersecting query such as "How many two-door Dodges are available?" The algorithm searches for the list of all Dodge cars (C2, C1), then searches for the list of all 2 DR cars (GM4, GM3, F3, C2, C1). The intersection of the two lists (C2, C1) satisfies the query with the answer, which is two. If the query is "List all two-door Dodges," the records with the primary keys in the intersection (C2, C1) are accessed. An intersecting query can be answered by the intersection of lists of primary keys from the secondary key entries so that only the records that match the qualifications of the query are accessed from the file. Fewer input and output operations are performed to answer the queries than with other file organizations. If space permits, searching is faster if the inverted lists are retained in main memory during the access of the inverted file.

Figure 10.10 (left) Inverted file directory for (a) make and (b) style from Figure 10.9 with the rest of the records added

MAKE	PRIMARY KEY(S)
TOYOTA	T1
HONDA	H2,H1
CHEVROLET	GM3
OLDSMOBILE	GM5,GM2
CADILLAC	GM4,GM1
LINCOLN	F2
FORD	F3,F1
DODGE	C2,C1

(a)

STYLE	PRIMARY KEY(S)
4 DR	H1,GM5,GM2,GM1,F2
2 DR HB	T1,H2,F1
2 DR	GM4,GM3,F3,C2,C1

(b)

Figure 10.11 (right) Inverted lists and data records for a car-rental agency with no duplication of information

MAKE	PRIMARY KEY(S)
TOYOTA	T1
HONDA	H2,H1
CHEVROLET	GM3
OLDSMOBILE	GM5,GM2
CADILLAC	GM4,GM1
LINCOLN	F2
FORD	F3,F1
DODGE	C2,C1

(a)

STYLE	PRIMARY KEY(S)
4 DR	H1,GM5,GM2,GM1,F2
2 DR HB	T1,H2,F1
2 DR	GM4,GM3,F3,C2,C1

(b)

primary key	data file contents		
	model	mileage	color
C1	Omni	25,000	grey
C2	Aspen	7,000	tan
F1	Escort	54,000	white
F2	Continental	38,000	black
F3	Thunderbird	35,000	blue
GM1	Fleetwood	9,000	red
GM2	Delta 88	28,050	blue
GM3	Camaro	33,000	silver
GM4	Cimarron	63,000	maroon
GM5	98	11,000	green
H1	Accord	32,000	yellow
H2	Accord	11,250	brown
T1	Celica	3,400	white

Another advantage of inverted file organization is the space saved in storing data in the file. Those fields of the records that are primary or secondary keys need not be stored in the data file. The primary key is the address of the record in the file—it does not necessarily need to be stored in the file; it need only be stored in the inverted lists. The actual values for the secondary key fields make and style are stored in the inverted lists with addresses of all records having those values. Storing data about make and style in the inverted lists as well as in the file is a duplication of data. The actual data record need only contain the nonindexed data: model, mileage, and color. Figure 10.11 presents the inverted lists for make and style of car along with the data file that contains only the nonindexed data. The inverted lists and the data file compose the total data concerning all the cars described by the file.

Conserving space in this manner presents a problem if the data file is to be accessed in a sequential manner since the inverted lists for the secondary keys contain only part of the data for the records in the file. Both the data file and the indexes need to be accessed to list all data for all the cars. For example, the first record in the data file contains the primary key C1. To identify the make and style of the car with primary key C1, the lists of primary keys under each value in the inverted directory for make of car are searched sequentially for the primary key C1. C1 is found under the value Dodge. Similarly, the lists of primary keys under each value in the inverted directory for style of car need to be searched to locate the primary key C1 to determine the style. This searching entails a great deal of time, so in this case it is hardly worthwhile to avoid duplicating data in the data file and the inverted directories.

One disadvantage to inverted file organization is the storage of the inverted lists. Each entry contains a secondary key value and a list of record addresses that contain the key value. The list of record addresses varies in length, so it is difficult to store the entries in a file of fixed-length records. For this reason the inverted list for a single secondary key is often stored as an individual file. Access time to the data in the inverted list could be shortened by storing the data as a B-tree rather than a sequential table. Additions to and deletions from the file entail additions to and deletions from the inverted lists for each secondary key field. If the inverted list is a tree, these operations are easier to handle.

Additions to the inverted file result in modifications to the inverted lists. For example, suppose a record is added to the inverted file. The primary key is GM6, the make is Chevrolet, and the style is 4 DR. The modifications to the inverted lists in Figure 10.10 are shown in Figure 10.12. Since Chevrolet already exists as an attribute in the inverted list for make, GM6 is added to the list of addresses containing the attribute Chevrolet for make. Likewise, 4 DR already exists as a style, so GM6 is added to the list of addresses containing 4 DR for style. The addition of a record with attributes that exist in the inverted lists requires that the address (primary key) of the new record be added to the present list of addresses for each secondary key field.

Deletions from the inverted file result in deletions of attributes and/or addresses in the inverted lists. When deleting a record with an attribute that occurs several times in the file, the address of the record to be deleted is removed from each inverted list in which it occurs. If the record with primary key F1 is deleted, all occurrences of F1 are removed from the inverted lists. The make of the car F1 is Ford, and the style is 2 DR HB. Under the attribute Ford in the make inverted list and under the attribute 2 DR HB in the style inverted list, F1 is deleted. The asterisks in Figure 10.13 indicate that data have been deleted for an attribute in order to delete F1 from the inverted file.

MAKE	PRIMARY KEY(S)
TOYOTA	T1
HONDA	H2,H1
CHEVROLET	**GM6**,GM3
OLDSMOBILE	GM5,GM2
CADILLAC	GM4,GM1
LINCOLN	F2
FORD	F3,F1
DODGE	C2,C1

(a)

STYLE	PRIMARY KEY(S)
4 DR	**GM6**,H1,GM5,GM2,GM1,F2
2 DR HB	T1,H2,F1
2 DR	GM4,GM3,F3,C2,C1

(b)

Figure 10.12 (left)
Inverted file directory for (a) make and (b) style from Figure 10.10 with "GM6 Chevrolet 4 DR" added (*)

	MAKE	PRIMARY KEY(S)
	TOYOTA	T1
	HONDA	H2,H1
	CHEVROLET	GM6,GM3
	OLDSMOBILE	GM5,GM2
	CADILLAC	GM4,GM1
	LINCOLN	F2
*	FORD	F3
	DODGE	C2,C1

(a)

	STYLE	PRIMARY KEY(S)
	4 DR	GM6,H1,GM5,GM2,GM1,F2
*	2 DR HB	T1,H2
	2 DR	GM4,GM3,F3,C2,C1

(b)

*Site of latest deletion

Figure 10.13 (right)
Inverted file directory for (a) make and (b) style from Figure 10.12 with "F1" deleted (*)

Suppose an addition of a record with primary key GM7, make of Pontiac, and style of 2 DR is made to the file. Since Pontiac as a make attribute is not present in the inverted list, the new attribute Pontiac must be added to the inverted list for make of car. The primary key GM7 is added as the address of a record with the make Pontiac. Figure 10.14 presents the inverted lists from Figure 10.13 with the addition of GM7. The style 2 DR presently exists in the inverted list for style, so the address GM7 is added to the list of addresses.

Deleting a record with unique attributes in secondary key fields results in the deletion of an entire entry from an inverted list. If the record with primary key T1 is deleted, all occurrences of T1 are removed from the inverted lists. The make of the car T1 is Toyota, and the style is 2 DR HB. The changes to the inverted lists to delete T1 are presented in Figure 10.15. The make Toyota is unique to record T1, so the entire entry for attribute Toyota is removed from the make inverted list. T1 is removed from the list of addresses for 2 DR HB. Only one 2 DR HB remains in the file (primary key H2).

Figure 10.14 (left) Inverted file directory for (a) make and (b) style from Figure 10.13 with "GM7 Pontiac 2 DR" added (*)

MAKE	PRIMARY KEY(S)
PONTIAC	**GM7**
TOYOTA	T1
HONDA	H2,H1
CHEVROLET	GM6,GM3
OLDSMOBILE	GM5,GM2
CADILLAC	GM4,GM1
LINCOLN	F2
FORD	F3
DODGE	C2,C1

(a)

STYLE	PRIMARY KEY(S)
4 DR	GM6,H1,GM5,GM2,GM1,F2
2 DR HB	T1,H2
2 DR	**GM7**,GM4,GM3,F3,C2,C1

(b)

Figure 10.15 (right) Inverted file directory for (a) make and (b) style from Figure 10.14 with "T1" deleted (*)

	MAKE	PRIMARY KEY(S)
	PONTIAC	GM7
*	HONDA	H2,H1
	CHEVROLET	GM6,GM3
	OLDSMOBILE	GM5,GM2
	CADILLAC	GM4,GM1
	LINCOLN	F2
	FORD	F3
	DODGE	C2,C1

(a)

	STYLE	PRIMARY KEY(S)
	4 DR	GM6,H1,GM5,GM2,GM1,F2
*	2 DR HB	H2
	2 DR	GM7,GM4,GM3,F3,C2,C1

(b)

*Site of latest deletion

Inverted Files in Ada

The implementation of inverted files in Ada requires some mechanism for storing the address list for each key value, which may vary in length. One approach for storing the inverted lists is to use a linked-list structure rather than a static structure such as an array. The linked-list structure facilitates the addition and deletion of key values into and from the index and the address list. The make inverted list from Figure 10.10, for example, is stored in the linked structure shown in Figure 10.16. The variant record in Ada can be used to store the inverted lists externally if the nodes in the linked structure are stored in one of the two formats shown in Figure 10.17. The first node in the linked structure in Figure 10.16 is stored in format (a); the key value is Toyota, and the next value field contains a pointer to another node of the same format. (The second node contains Honda for a key value.) The first key field contains a pointer to the linked list of format (b) records, which contains the primary key T1.

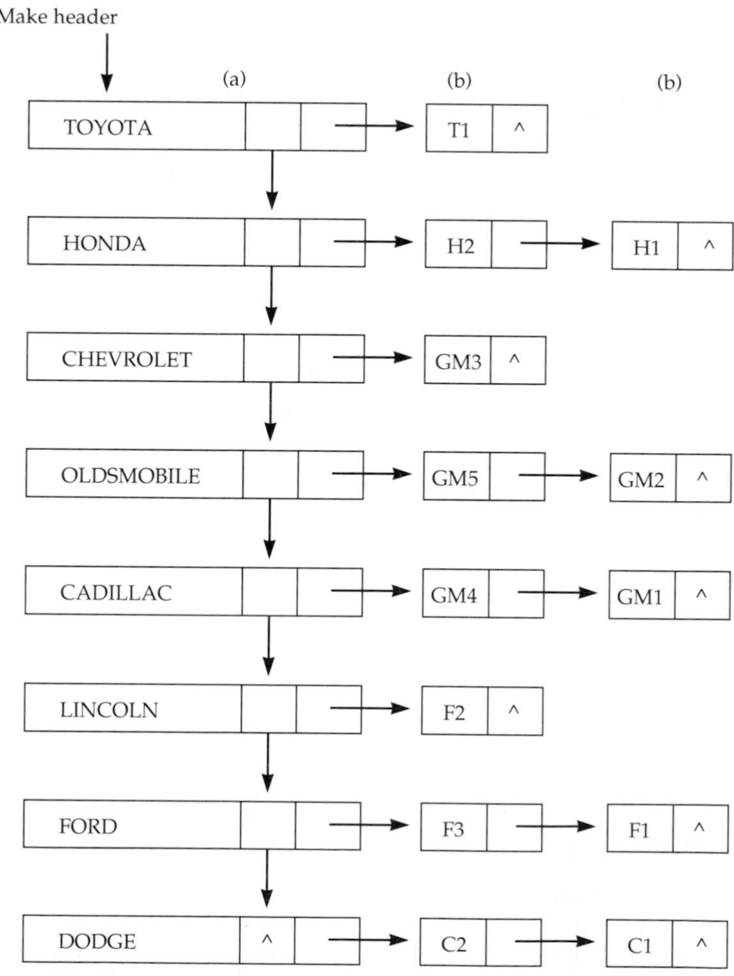

Figure 10.16
"Make" inverted list shown in linked storage structure using formats (a) and (b) from Figure 10.17

key value	next value	first key

(a) Format for storing key_value and a pointer to the first primary key in the address list.

primary key	next key

(b) Format for storing a primary key and a pointer to the next primary key in the address list.

Figure 10.17 (left) Storage formats for linked structure for inverted list

key value	first address

(a) Format for storing key value and a record address of a format (b) record from the index file of the first primary key in the address list.

primary key	next address

(b) Format for storing a primary key and a record address of a format (b) record from the index file of the next primary key in the address list.

Figure 10.18 (right) Storage formats for storing inverted list on external files

The inverted list is built as a linked structure in main memory as the data file is created. At the close of the program, the linked structure containing the inverted list is converted from pointer values to integer record addresses, then stored in a file using the formats shown in Figure 10.18. The first format (a) node, which contains the key value Toyota, is written to record location 1. The first address is record location 2. The first format (b) node (which Toyota points to) contains the primary key T1. The node is stored in record 2. The last address in the address list has a next address value of –1. For example, if the data in the inverted list in Figure 10.16 are written to an external file, the resulting record contents appear as presented in Table 10.1. The first record in the file contains the value Toyota and an address of record 2. Record 2 contains the primary key T1 with a pointer that is –1, indicating the end of the primary key linked list for the make of Toyota. In this way the file is read back into main memory and stored in the linked structure pictured in Figure 10.16.

Locating a certain make of car usually involves searching half the nodes in the linked structure since the values for make of car are inserted in the order in which they appear in the file. With eight different car makes, the average search visits four nodes to successfully locate the primary keys for that make. An unsuccessful search for the make Audi, for example, searches the entire list of eight nodes.

The pseudocode for creating an inverted file using the formats and structures described above is presented in Algorithm 10.1. The `id_no` is the primary key for the car data and is stored in the linked structure of the inverted list. The primary keys are in ascending order to answer intersecting queries more easily.

Table 10.1 File contents of inverted file in Figure 10.16

Format	Record no	File contents	
a	1	TOYOTA	2
b	2	T1	–1
b	3	HONDA	4
a	4	H2	5
b	5	H1	–1
b	6	CHEVROLET	7
a	7	GM3	–1
b	8	OLDSMOBILE	09
b	9	GM5	10
a	10	GM2	–1
b	11	CADILLAC	12
b	12	GM4	13
a	13	GM1	–1
b	14	LINCOLN	15
b	15	F2	–1
a	16	FORD	17
b	17	F3	18
a	18	F1	–1
b	19	DODGE	20
a	20	C2	21
b	21	C1	–1
format a —	key value	first address	
format b —	primary key	next address	

ALGORITHM 10.1 Build Inverted Index as Data File Is Created

```
SUBTYPE Primary_Key_Type Is String ( 1 .. 3 )
SUBTYPE Second_Key_Type Is String ( 1 .. 10 )
TYPE Record_Info Is Record
                        id_no : Primary_Key_Type
                        make : Second_Key_Type
                        style : Second_Key_Type
                        -- other non_indexed_items
                    End Record
TYPE Second_Key_Name_Type Is ( MAKE, STYLE )
TYPE Primary_Key_Access Is Access Primary_Key_Record
TYPE Primary_Key_Record Is Record
                              primary_key : Primary_Key_Type
                              next_key : Primary_Key_Access
                          End Record
TYPE Key_Value_Access Is Access Key_Value_Record
TYPE Key_Value_Record Is Record
                            key_value : Second_Key_Type
                            next_value : Key_Value_Access
                            first_key : Primary_Key_Access
                        End Record
```

```
    TYPE Status_Type Is ( ATTRIBUTE, PRIME_KEY )
    TYPE Index_Record_Type ( status : Status_Type ← ATTRIBUTE )
        Record
            Case status
                When ATTRIBUTE → key_value : Second_Key_Type
                                 first_address : Integer
                When PRIME_KEY → primary_key : Primary_Key_Type
                                 next_address : Integer
            End Case
        End Record
    PACKAGE Data_File_IO Is New Direct_IO ( Record_Info );
    PACKAGE Index_File_IO Is New Sequential_IO ( Index_Record_Type )
    data_file : Data_File_IO.File_Type
    external_file : String
    header : Array ( MAKE..STYLE ) Of Key_Value_Access ← ( NULL, NULL )
    index_file : Index_File_IO.File_Type
    new_record : Record_Info
    record_number : Natural ← 1
    key_not_found : Exception

    Loop
        Exit When End_Of_File ( input_file )
        Input ( input_file, new_record )
        Insert_Index ( MAKE, new_record.make, new_record.id_no )
        Insert_Index ( STYLE, new_record.style, new_record.id_no )
            -- output new_record to data_file
        Output ( data_file, new_record,
                Data_File.Positive_Count ( record_number ) )
        increment record_number
    End Loop
    -- external_file specified by user
    Output_Indexes ( external_file & ".mak", header(MAKE)  )
    Output_Indexes ( external_file & ".sty", header(STYLE) )

PROCEDURE Insert_Index ( second_key_name : In Second_Key_Name_Type)
                         second_key : In Second_Key_Type
                         id_no : In Key_Type )
    -- second_key_name indicates which index is to be built: MAKE or STYLE
    -- second_key is either the make or style that was read into new_record
    previous, where_found : Key_Value_Access

    Search_List ( header(second_key_name), second_key, where_found,
                previous )
        -- Add_To_Key_List
        -- add the record location of new_record to the front of
        -- the list of addresses for the key_value pointed to
        -- by where_found
    where_found.first_key ← New Primary_Key_Record'
                            ( id_no, where_found.first_key )
    EXCEPTION
        When key_not_found → -- Add_To_Directory
            header(second_key_name) ←
                New Key_Value_Record' ( second_key,
                                        header(second_key_name),
                                        New Primary_Key_Record'( id_no, NULL ) )
```

```
PROCEDURE Search_List ( header : In Key_Value_Access
                        second_key : In Second_Key_Type
                        where_found, previous : In Out Key_Value_Access )
    -- returns (in where_found) NULL if
    --      second_key is not found in index
    -- or returns (in where_found) a pointer to the node
    --      in the linked structure if found
    -- previous contains the pointer to the node previous to
    --      the node containing the second_key in case a
    --      deletion is to be made
    previous ← NULL
    where_found ← header
    Loop
        Exit When where_found = NULL
        If where_found.key_value = second_key
            Return
        End If
        previous ← where_found
        where_found ← where_found.next_value
    End Loop
    Raise key_not_found

PROCEDURE Output_Indexes ( index_file : In String
                           header : In Key_Value_Access )
    -- output either the MAKE or the STYLE indexes
    -- (indicated by header) sequentially to an external
    -- file for storage
    --
    -- all pointers must be converted to record
    -- addresses and all "NULL" pointer values must be
    -- converted to –1
    index_record : Index_Record_Type
    key_pointer : Key_Value_Access ← header
    primary_pointer : Primary_Key_Access
    record_number : Positive ← 1
    Loop
        Exit When key_pointer = NULL
        index_record ← ( ATTRIBUTE, key_pointer.key_value, record_number + 1 )
        -- output index_record to location record_number
        -- of index_file
        Output ( index_file, index_record, record_number )
        increment record_number
        primary_pointer ← key_pointer.first_key
        Loop
            Exit When primary_pointer = NULL
            If primary_pointer.next_key /= NULL
                index_record ← ( PRIME_KEY,
                                 primary_pointer.primary_key,
                                 record_number + 1 )
            Else
                index_record ← ( PRIME_KEY,
                                 primary_pointer.primary_key,
                                 –1 )
            End If
```

```
            Output ( index_file, index_record, record_number )
            increment record_number
            primary_pointer ← primary_pointer.next_key
        End Loop
        key_pointer ← key_pointer.next_value
    End Loop
```

The pseudocode for modifying the inverted lists by adding a record to the data file or deleting a record from the data file as discussed previously is presented in Algorithm 10.2. Algorithm 10.2 employs the same formats and structures as Algorithm 10.1. The inverted file is input into a linked structure at the beginning of the algorithm, modified as additions and deletions are made, and output at the end of the algorithm.

ALGORITHM 10.2 Modify Inverted Index (Additions and Deletions)

```
    Input_Indexes ( external_file & ".mak", header(MAKE) )
    Input_Indexes ( external_file & ".sty", header(STYLE) )
    Loop
        Exit When End_Of_File ( transfile )
        Input ( transfile, transaction_code )
        BEGIN
        Case transaction_code
            'A' → Input ( transfile, new_record )
                  Insert_Index ( MAKE, new_record.make,
                                 new_record.id_no )
                  Insert_Index ( STYLE, new_record.style,
                                 new_record.id_no )
                  record_number ← Size ( data_file ) + 1
                  Output ( data_file, new_record, record_number )

            'D' → Input ( trans_file, id_no )
                   -- input record from data file with id = id_no
                   Retrieve ( id_no,  record_number )
                   Input ( data_file, new_record, record_number )
                  Delete_Index ( MAKE, new_record.make, new_record.id_no )
                  Delete_Index ( STYLE, new_record.style, new_record.id_no )
             Others → Null
        End Case
        EXCEPTION
            When key_not_found → Output ( "key not found" );
        END
    End Loop
    Output_Indexes ( external_file & ".mak", header(MAKE) )
    Output_Indexes ( external_file & ".sty", header(STYLE) )

    PROCEDURE Input_Indexes ( index_file : In String
                              header : In Out Key_Value_Access )

        -- input the external file containing the key values and
        -- address pointers into a linked structure
        -- all record addresses must be converted to pointers
        -- and all –1 pointer values must be converted to NULL.
```

```
    index_record : Index_Record_Type
    key_pointer : Key_Value_Access
    next_primary_pointer : Primary_Key_Access ← NULL
    primary_pointer : Primary_Key_Access ← NULL

    Input ( index_file, index_record ) -- ATTRIBUTE
    header ← New Key_Value_Record'
                ( index_record.primary_key, NULL, NULL )
    key_pointer ← header
    Loop
        Input ( index_file, index_record ) -- PRIME_KEY
        primary_pointer ← New Primary_Key_Record'
                                ( index_record.primary_key, NULL )
        key_pointer.first_key ← primary_pointer
        Loop
            Exit When index_record.next_address = -1
            Input ( index_file, index_record ) -- PRIME_KEY
            next_primary_pointer ← New Key_Value_Record'
                                        ( index_record.primary_key, NULL )
            primary_pointer.next_key ← next_primary_pointer
            primary_pointer ← next_primary_pointer
        End Loop
        Exit When End_Of_File ( index_file )
        Input ( index_file, index_record ) -- ATTRIBUTE
        next_key_pointer ← New Key_Value_Record'
                                ( index_record.primary_key, NULL, NULL )
        key_pointer.next_value ← next_key_pointer
        key_pointer ← next_key_pointer
    End Loop

PROCEDURE Delete_Index ( second_key_name : In Second_Key_Name_Type
                         second_key : In String
                         id_no : In Primary_Key_Type )
    -- second_key_name indicates which index is to have a deletion:
    --      MAKE or STYLE
    -- second_key is either the make or style that is
    --      to be deleted from the directory
    previous, where_found : Key_Value_Access
    previous_pointer, primary_pointer : Primary_Key_Access

    Search_List ( header(second_key_name), second_key, where_found,
                  previous )
    If where_found.first_key.primary_key = id_no
        -- delete first key
        where_found.first_key ← where_found.first_key.next_key
        If where_found.first_key = NULL
            -- delete entire entry since the only id_no has been deleted
```

```
                If header(second_key_name) = where_found
                    -- first key value in linked structure
                    header(second_key_name) ← where_found.next_value
                Else
                    previous.next_value ← where_found.next_value
                End If
            End If
        Else    -- search for id_no in list of addresses
            primary_pointer ← where_found.first_key.next_key
            previous_pointer ← where_found.first_key
            Loop
                Exit When primary_pointer = NULL
                If primary_pointer.primary_key = id_no
                    previous_pointer.next_key ←
                        primary_pointer.next_key
                    Return
                Else
                    previous_pointer ← primary_pointer
                    primary_pointer ← primary_pointer.next_key
                End If
            End Loop
            Raise key_not_deleted
        End If
    EXCEPTION
        When key_not_found → Raise key_not_deleted
```

The Ada implementations of Algorithms 10.1 and 10.2 are presented in Appendix B. Figure 10.19 graphically illustrates the interfacing of the program components with each other and the external I/O files. A nongeneric package, `Invert`, encapsulates the data structures and the operations on the inverted files and data files while hiding the details from Algorithm 10.1 (`Create`) and Algorithm 10.2 (`Update`). The generic `B_Tree` package, developed in Chapter 8, is instantiated by the package `Invert` to provide indexing for the data file.

Use of a B-tree provides another approach to storing the inverted lists. A B-tree facilitates modifications but does not require that the structure be built before accessing the data file. The use of a B-tree of some appropriate order reduces the number of nodes required to store the inverted data for make or style of car, thus reducing the number of disk accesses required to search the inverted list. The B-tree is appropriate for an inverted list of a larger, more realistic file that is too large to fit into main memory. Instead of the linked list structure shown in Figure 10.16, the B-tree structure in Figure 10.20 is built externally, and each node of the B-tree represents a disk access. When the B-tree inverted structure for make of car is complete, it already resides in a disk file. The linked structure, as you recall, was built in main memory and had to be copied to a disk file for storage. The B-tree structure that stores the inverted list for style of car is presented in Figure 10.21.

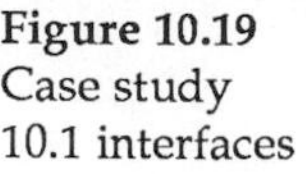

Figure 10.19
Case study 10.1 interfaces

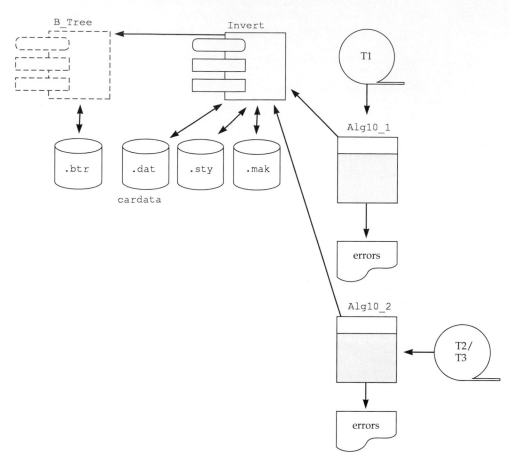

Each tuple in the nodes of the B-tree contains a make value, the address of a record containing the list of primary keys for this make of car, and the address of the record that is the root of the subtree containing values greater than that of this make of car. For example, the first tuple in the root node in Figure 10.20 contains the make Chevrolet, a pointer to the record with primary key GM3, and a pointer to the record that contains tuples Dodge and Ford.

The algorithms for building a B-tree and making additions and deletions of values in the B-tree are presented in Chapter 8. A B-tree package can easily be instantiated to efficiently index the data in the inverted lists. To retrieve data concerning a certain make of car requires, in the worst case, only three accesses: two accesses to visit the two levels of the B-tree and a third access to retrieve the linked list of primary keys for that make of car. This method certainly represents a savings over the previous design in terms of access time, building time, and the time necessary for modification.

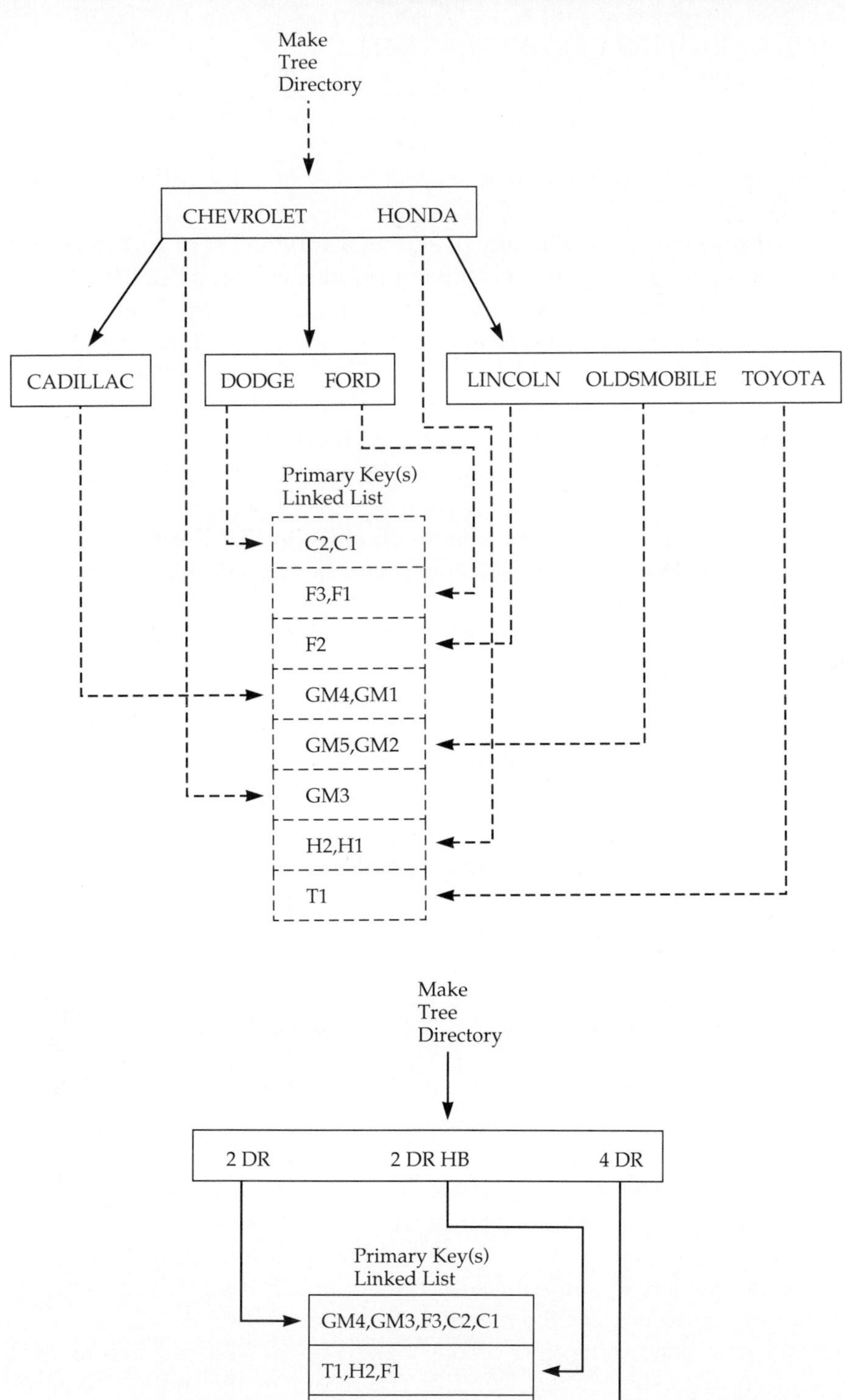

Figure 10.20
B-tree structure of order four for inverted file make of car directory

Figure 10.21
B-tree structure of order four for inverted file style of car directory

MULTILIST FILE ORGANIZATION

Because the length of a list of addresses may vary, the length of an entry in an inverted list may vary. As a previous section discussed, this variance often necessitates storing a single secondary key inverted list in an individual file.

One solution to the difficulty of storing a varying list of addresses with the same secondary key value is linking the elements in a list. The address of the first record in the linked list is stored in the directory. A file that links data records with identical secondary key values is organized as a multilist file. A multilist file contains two areas: (1) a directory and (2) a data record area. The directory contains an inverted list for each secondary key field to be used in accessing the data records in the data record area. The data records are organized in any manner that provides random access to the records.

As in inverted file organization, each entry in the directory for a secondary key field contains an attribute found in this secondary key field in the file. Unlike inverted files, however, each entry in the directory contains the primary key of only one record in the file rather than a list of primary keys of all records containing the attribute. All data records containing the same attribute in a secondary key field are linked in the data file. So the one primary key in the directory is the primary key of the first record in a linked list of records. The list contains the same attribute for a particular secondary key field, and each directory entry also contains an integer indicating the number of records in the linked list for this attribute. If directories are built to provide access to a number of secondary key fields, each data record contains a link field for each secondary key field.

CASE STUDY 10.2: THE CAR-RENTAL AGENCY

The multilist file directory that provides secondary key access by make and style for the sample car-rental agency data is found in Figure 10.22, and so is the corresponding data file for the multilist file organization, expanded to contain link fields for make and style.

Each entry in the directory for make of car contains the make, the primary key of the first record in the linked list of all records containing this make, and the length of the linked list (the number of records in the linked list). As the directory for the inverted file indicates, two records in the file contain data concerning cars of the make Dodge. The first record for a Dodge contains the primary key C2. The record in the multilist data file with the primary key C2 needs to be input so that the link field for make can be accessed to identify the second record in the file for a Dodge. The data record with primary key C2 contains a link field for make of car with the value C1. The record with primary key C1 does contain data for a Dodge, and the link field for make is null (^), which indicates the end of the linked list. Record C2 also contains a style link of C1. Record C1 contains a null style link. The directory indicates that, in fact, the file contains five 2 DR cars beginning with record GM4.

One of the advantages of the multilist file over the inverted file is the fixed length of the entries in the directory. The disadvantage created by the fixed-length directory entries is the increase in the number of record accesses to satisfy queries. Questions that ask "How many Fords are available" can be answered by retrieving the length field of the index entry for the make of Ford.

make	primary key	length
Toyota	T1	1
Honda	H2	2
Chevrolet	GM3	1
Oldsmobile	GM5	2
Cadillac	GM4	2
Lincoln	F2	1
Ford	F3	2
Dodge	C2	2

(a)

style	primary key	length
4 DR	H1	5
2 DR HB	T1	3
2 DR	GM4	5

(b)

Multi-Listed data file

primary key	secondary keys				nonindexed information
id no.	make	link	style	link	
C1	Dodge	^	2 DR	^	
C2	Dodge	C1	2 DR	C1	
F1	Ford	^	2 DR HB	^	
F2	Lincoln	^	4 DR	^	
F3	Ford	F1	2 DR	C2	
GM1	Cadillac	^	4 DR	F2	
GM2	Oldsmobile	^	4 DR	GM1	
GM3	Chevrolet	^	2 DR	F3	
GM4	Cadillac	GM1	2 DR	GM3	
GM5	Oldsmobile	GM2	4 DR	GM2	
H1	Honda	^	4 DR	GM5	
H2	Honda	H1	2 DR HB	F1	
T1	Toyota	^	2 DR HB	H2	

Figure 10.22
Multilist file directories and file with link fields for car-rental agency data

If the query is "How many two-door Dodges are available," the primary keys in the intersection of (1) the list of all Dodges and (2) the list of all two-door cars is the answer. The primary key of one Dodge is listed in the directory for make (C2), but the primary key of the second Dodge can be located only by retrieving the make link field of record C2. The primary key of one 2 DR car is listed in the directory for style (GM4), but the primary key of all other 2 DR cars can be located only by retrieving all records in the following linked list: The style link of record GM4 is GM3, the style link of record GM3 is F3, the style link of record F3 is C2, the style link of record C2 is C1, and the style link of C1 is null. Traversing both lists to find the intersection results in seven accesses to the file. A more efficient solution is to choose the shorter list to traverse and examine records for the other attribute. The length of the Dodge list is only two, while the length of the 2 DR list is five. This method requires only two accesses to the file to answer the query. The answer is two: C2 and C1.

With inverted file organization, the primary keys of all cars having the attribute Dodge for make are listed in the directory as well as cars having the attribute 2 DR for style. In consequence the data file is not accessed to answer a query involving make and style. With multilist file organization, the primary key of one record is listed in the directory, but primary keys of all other records having one of the two attributes must be retrieved from link fields of data records, examining for the other attribute. With multilist file organization, the number of data records that must be retrieved to answer an intersecting query is two: to retrieve primary keys of all Dodge cars and examine for 2 DR cars. With inverted file organization no retrievals are required.

Additions to the multilist file result in modifications to not only the directory but also the link fields of records in the data file. For example, suppose that a record with key fields GM6, Chevrolet, and 4 DR is added to the multilist file. For those attributes that exist in the directories, the length field is incremented. The new record is added to the data file, a make link in the file is changed to include GM6 in the linked list of Chevrolet cars, and a style link in the file is changed to include GM6 in the linked list of 4 DR cars. The required changes are indicated in Figure 10.23 with asterisks.

Deletions from the multilist file result in deletions of keys and/or attributes in the directory as well as changes in the linked lists for all secondary key fields that included the deleted record. If the primary key of the deleted record occurs in the directory, it is deleted, and the next record in the linked list for that attribute is placed in the directory with the length of the list reduced by one. If the primary key of the deleted record does not occur in the directory, the length of the attribute is reduced by one to indicate the removal of one record.

make	primary key	length
Toyota	T1	1
Honda	H2	2
Chevrolet	GM6	2*
Oldsmobile	GM5	2
Cadillac	GM4	2
Lincoln	F2	1
Ford	F3	2
Dodge	C2	2

(a)

style	primary key	length
4 DR	GM6	6*
2 DR HB	T1	3
2 DR	GM4	5

(b)

Figure 10.23
Multilist file directory for (a) make and (b) style car-rental agency data file with "GM6 Chevrolet 4 DR" added

Multi-Listed data file

primary key	secondary keys				nonindexed information
id no.	make	link	style	link	
C1	Dodge	^	2 DR	^	
C2	Dodge	C1	2 DR	C1	
F1	Ford	^	2 DR HB	^	
F2	Lincoln	^	4 DR	^	
F3	Ford	F1	2 DR	C2	
GM1	Cadillac	^	4 DR	F2	
GM2	Oldsmobile	^	4 DR	GM1	
GM3	Chevrolet	^	2 DR	F3	
GM4	Cadillac	GM1	2 DR	GM3	
GM5	Oldsmobile	GM2	4 DR	GM2	
H1	Honda	^	4 DR	GM5	
H2	Honda	H1	2 DR HB	F1	
T1	Toyota	^	2 DR HB	H2	
GM6*	Chevrolet*	GM3*	4 DR*	H1*	*

*latest additions

If the record with primary key F1 in Figure 10.23 is deleted, the record is deleted from the linked list of all cars with make Ford and from the linked list of all cars with style 2 DR HB. The directory for make indicates that Ford occurs in record F1 and that there are two records with Ford. The record F3 is the first record in the linked list, and the make link field of record F3 contains the value F1 (Figure 10.23). Since F1 is the last record in the linked list and is to be deleted, the number of records of Ford make (length) is reduced from two (in Figure 10.23) to one (in Figure 10.24). The first record in Figure 10.23 with the style of 2 DR HB is T1, and three records have that attribute. Since F1 is the last record in the linked list and is to be deleted, the style link field of H2 changes to null, and the entry in the length column changes from 3 (Figure 10.23) to 2 (Figure 10.24). The id number of record F1 is replaced with the string NIL.

Additions of records to the file with new attributes for secondary key fields result in the new attributes being added as new entries in the directory. If the record with fields GM7, Pontiac, 2 DR HB is added to the multilist file, Pontiac is a new attribute for car make. Figure 10.25 presents the multilist file and directory with GM7 added. Pontiac is added as a new entry in the directory for make, and GM7 is added as the first key. The length is 1, and the make link for GM7 is null. Since 2 DR exists in the directory for style, the length is incremented, and the style link field of the GM7 record links to GM4.

Figure 10.24
Multilist file directory for (a) make and (b) style for car-rental agency data file with "F1" deleted

make	primary key	length
Toyota	T1	1
Honda	H2	2
Chevrolet	GM6	2
Oldsmobile	GM5	2
Cadillac	GM4	2
Lincoln	F2	1
Ford	F3	1*
Dodge	C2	2

(a)

style	primary key	length
4 DR	GM6	6
2 DR HB	T1	2*
2 DR	GM4	5

(b)

Multi-Listed data file

primary key	secondary keys				nonindexed information
id no.	make	link	style	link	
C1	Dodge	^	2 DR	^	
C2	Dodge	C1	2 DR	C1	
NIL*	Ford	^	2 DR HB	^	
F2	Lincoln	^	4 DR	^	
F3	Ford	^	2 DR	C2	
GM1	Cadillac	^	4 DR	F2	
GM2	Oldsmobile	^	4 DR	GM1	
GM3	Chevrolet	^	2 DR	F3	
GM4	Cadillac	GM1	2 DR	GM3	
GM5	Oldsmobile	GM2	4 DR	GM2	
H1	Honda	^	4 DR	GM5	
H2	Honda	H1	2 DR HB	^	
T1	Toyota	^	2 DR HB	H2	
GM6	Chevrolet	GM3	4 DR	H1	

*site of deletion

Figure 10.25
Multilist file directory for (a) make and (b) style car-rental agency data file with "GM7 Pontiac 2 DR" added

make	primary key	length
Pontiac*	GM7*	1*
Toyota	T1	1
Honda	H2	2
Chevrolet	GM6	2
Oldsmobile	GM5	2
Cadillac	GM4	2
Lincoln	F2	1
Ford	F3	1
Dodge	C2	2

(a)

style	primary key	length
4 DR	GM6	6
2 DR HB	T1	2
2 DR	GM7	6*

(b)

Multi-Listed data file

primary key	secondary keys				nonindexed information
id no.	make	link	style	link	
C1	Dodge	^	2 DR	^	
C2	Dodge	C1	2 DR	C1	
NIL	Ford	^	2 DR HB	^	
F2	Lincoln	^	4 DR	^	
F3	Ford	^	2 DR	C2	
GM1	Cadillac	^	4 DR	F2	
GM2	Oldsmobile	^	4 DR	GM1	
GM3	Chevrolet	^	2 DR	F3	
GM4	Cadillac	GM1	2 DR	GM3	
GM5	Oldsmobile	GM2	4 DR	GM2	
H1	Honda	^	4 DR	GM5	
H2	Honda	H1	2 DR HB	^	
T1	Toyota	^	2 DR HB	H2	
GM6	Chevrolet	GM3	4 DR	H1	
GM7*	Pontiac*	^*	2 DR*	GM4*	*

*lastest additions

When adding a record to a linked list, the newly added record contains the address of the first record in the linked list. Rather than using five input operations to find the end of the linked list and one output operation to store the last record back to the file, GM7 is added at the beginning of the linked list. Storing the new addition in the beginning of the linked list requires only a change in the directory—no records need be input. It takes one change to the directory and one output operation to add GM7 at the beginning of the linked list as opposed to five inputs and one output to add GM7 at the end of the linked list.

Deleting a record with unique attributes for secondary key fields results in the deletion of an entire entry from the directory of the multilist file. Consider deleting T1 from Figure 10.25. T1 contains the make Toyota, is of the style 2 DR HB, and has a length of 1, which indicates that T1 is the only Toyota in the data file. The entire entry is deleted from the make directory. The style 2 DR HB is not unique, so H2—linked to from T1—becomes the address in the style directory. The length is reduced from 2 to 1. The changes made when deleting T1 from the multilist file are shown in Figure 10.26.

Multilist Files in Ada

The implementation of multilist files in Ada is similar to that of inverted files previously discussed in this chapter. The directories are stored in a linked structure to facilitate the addition and deletion of key values into the directory. Also stored with each key value in the linked structure are the first primary key in the linked list of records that has the same key value and a length field containing the number of records in the linked list. The make directory (Figure 10.22(a)) is stored in a linked structure as shown in Figure 10.27.

Figure 10.26
Multi-List file directory for (a) make and (b) style for car-rental agency data file with "T1" deleted

make	primary key	length
Pontiac	GM7	1
Honda	H2	2
Chevrolet	GM6	2
Oldsmobile	GM5	2
Cadillac	GM4	2
Lincoln	F2	1
Ford	F3	1
Dodge	C2	2

(a)

style	primary key	length
4 DR	GM6	6
2 DR HB	H2	1*
2 DR	GM7	6

(b)

Multi-Listed data file

primary key	secondary keys				nonindexed information
id no.	make	link	style	link	
C1	Dodge	^	2 DR	^	
C2	Dodge	C1	2 DR	C1	
NIL	Ford	^	2 DR HB	^	
F2	Lincoln	^	4 DR	^	
F3	Ford	^	2 DR	C2	
GM1	Cadillac	^	4 DR	F2	
GM2	Oldsmobile	^	4 DR	GM1	
GM3	Chevrolet	^	2 DR	F3	
GM4	Cadillac	GM1	2 DR	GM3	
GM5	Oldsmobile	GM2	4 DR	GM2	
H1	Honda	^	4 DR	GM5	
H2	Honda	H1	2 DR HB	^	
NIL*	Toyota	^	2 DR HB	H2	
GM6	Chevrolet	GM3	4 DR	H1	
NIL	Pontiac	^	2 DR	GM4	
GM7	Pontiac	^	2 DR	GM4	

*site of deletions

Unlike the inverted files discussed earlier, variant records are not needed to store the records externally because the nodes of the linked structure all have three fields. The nodes are stored in the format shown in Figure 10.28. A node of the linked structure with the key value Toyota contains the next value field with a pointer to another node of the same format. The first key field contains the primary key T1 and a length of 1.

The directory of the multilist file is built as a linked structure in main memory as the data file is created. At the close of the program, the linked structure containing the directory is stored in a file using the format shown in Figure 10.28. The next value field is dropped, and the nodes from the linked structure are stored sequentially. Each directory is stored in an individual file since the key value field may vary from one secondary key field to another. For example, the data in the linked storage structure in Figure 10.29 are written to an external file. The resulting record contents are presented in Table 10.2.

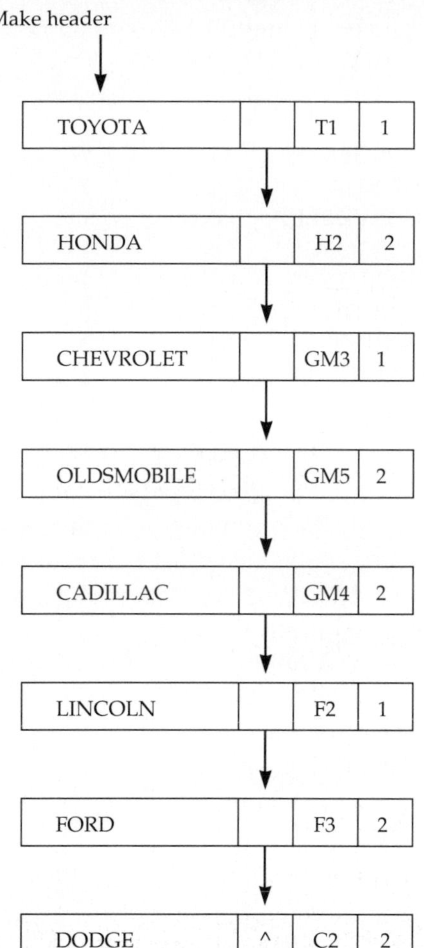

Figure 10.27
Linked storage structure for make directory of multi-listed file using format in Figure 10.28

key value	next value	first key	length

Figure 10.28
Storage formats for linked structure for multilisted file directory for make

key value	first key	length

Figure 10.29
Storage formats for linked structure for multilisted file directory for make on external files

Table 10.2 File contents of multi-list file in Figure 10.26

Record No.	File Contents		
1	TOYOTA	T1	1
2	HONDA	H2	2
3	CHEVROLET	GM3	1
4	OLDSMOBILE	GM5	2
5	CADILLAC	GM4	2
6	LINCOLN	F2	1
7	FORD	F3	2
8	DODGE	C2	2
format	key value	first key	length

Locating a certain make of car involves searching, on the average, half the nodes in the linked structure. In other words the average search visits four nodes to successfully locate the beginning of a linked list of records for that make. Once the beginning of the linked list for a make of car is located, the data file must be accessed to search, on the average, half-way through the linked list of records. This search through the linked list of records is the expensive characteristic of a multilist file. Just as in the inverted list, an unsuccessful search—a search for Audi, for example—requires the search of the entire multilist make directory.

The pseudocode for creating a multilist file using the formats and structures described above is presented in Algorithm 10.3. The `id_no` is the primary key for the car data.

ALGORITHM 10.3 Build Multilist Index as Data File Is Created

```
TYPE Primary_Key_Type Is String(1..3)
TYPE Second_Key_Type Is String(1..10)
TYPE Record_Info Is Record
                        id_no : Primary_Key_Type
                        make : Second_Key_Type
                        make_link : Primary_Key_Type
                        style : Second_Key_Type
                        style_link : Primary_Key_Type
                        -- other non_indexed_items
                     End Record
TYPE Second_Key_Name_Type Is(MAKE, STYLE)
TYPE Key_Value_Access Is Access Key_Value_Record
TYPE Key_Value_Record Is Record
                            key_value : Second_Key_Type
                            next_value : Key_Value_Access
                            first_key : Primary_Key_Type
                            length : Positive
                         End Record
TYPE Index_Record_Type Is Record
                            key_value : Key_Value_Type
                            first_key : Primary_Key_Type
                            length : Positive
                         End Record
```

```
header : Array ( MAKE..STYLE ) Of Key_Value_Access ← ( NULL, NULL)
key_not_found : Exception
new_record : Record_Info
record_number : Positive ← 1
END_OF_LIST : Constant Primary_Key_Type ← "NIL"
Loop
    Exit When End_Of_File ( input_file )
    Input ( input_file, new_record )
    Insert_Index ( MAKE, new_record.make,
                   new_record.make_link, new_record.id_no )
    Insert_Index ( STYLE, new_record.style,
                   new_record.style_link, new_record.id_no )
    Output ( data_file, new_record, record_number )
    increment record_number
End Loop
Output_Indexes ( external_file & ".mak", header(MAKE) )
Output_Indexes ( external_file & ".sty", header(STYLE) )

PROCEDURE Insert_Index ( index_name : In Second_Key_Name_Type
                         second_key : In Second_Key_Type
                         link_field : In Out Primary_Key_Type
                         id_no : In Primary_Key_Type )
    -- index_name indicates which index is to be built:
    --      MAKE or STYLE
    -- second_key is either the make or style that was read
    --      into new_record
    -- link_field is either the make_link or style_link of
    --      new_record
    previous, where_found : Key_Value_Access

    Search_List ( header ( index_name ), second_key, where_found, previous )
        -- Add_To_Key_List
        -- add the primary key of new_record to the list of primary
        -- keys for the key_value pointed to by where_found
    increment where_found.length
    link_field ← where_found.first_key
    where_found.first_key ← id_no
EXCEPTION
    When key_not_found → -- Add_To_Directory
        -- add the second_key as the new value in the linked structure
        -- with the primary key of new_record as the first_key
        header(index_name) ←New Key_Value_Record'
                    ( second_key, header(index_name), id_no, 1 )
        link_field ←  END_OF_LIST

PROCEDURE Search_List ( header : In Key_Value_Access
                        second_key : In Second_Key_Type
                        where_found, previous : In Out Key_Value_Access )
    -- where_found returns NIL if second_key is not found in
    --      index and returns a pointer to the node in the
    --      linked structure if found
    previous ← NULL
    where_found ← header
```

```
Loop
    Exit When where_found = NULL
    If where_found.key_value = second_key
        Return
    End If
    previous ← where_found
    where_found ← where_found.next_value
End Loop
Raise key_not_found

PROCEDURE Output_Indexes ( index_file : In String
                           header : In Key_Value_Access )
    -- output either the MAKE_INDEX or the STYLE_INDEX (index)
    -- sequentially to an external file for storage
    index_record : Index_Record_Type
    lcv : Key_Value_Access

    lcv ← header
    Loop
        Exit When lcv = NULL
        index_record ← ( lcv.key_value, lcv.first_key, lcv.length )
        Output ( index_file, index_record )
        lcv ← lcv.next_value
    End Loop
```

The pseudocode for modifying the multilist file when adding a record to the data file or deleting a record from the data file is presented in Algorithm 10.4. Algorithm 10.4 uses the same formats and structures as Algorithm 10.3. The directory is input at the beginning of the algorithm into the linked structures, modified as additions and deletions are made, and output at the end of the algorithm.

ALGORITHM 10.4 Modify Multilisted Index (Additions and Deletions)

```
id_no : Primary_Key_Type
new_record : Record_Info
transaction_code : Character

Input_Indexes ( external_file & ".mak", header(MAKE) )
Input_Indexes ( external_file & ".sty", header(STYLE) )
Loop
    Exit When End_Of_File ( transfile )
    Input ( transfile, transaction_code )
    BEGIN
        Case transaction_code
        When 'A' → Input ( transfile, new_record )
                   Insert_Index ( MAKE, new_record.make,
                                  new_record.make_link,
                                  new_record.id_no )
                   Insert_Index ( STYLE, new_record.style,
                                  new_record.style_link,
                                  new_record.id_no )
                   record_number ← Size ( data_file ) + 1
                   Output ( data_file, new_record, record_number )
```

```
        When 'D' → Input ( transfile, id_no )
                        -- input record from data_file
                       Retrieve ( id_no, record_number )
                       Input ( data_file, new_record, record_number )
                       Delete_Index ( MAKE, new_record.make, id_no,
                                      new_record )
                       Delete_Index ( STYLE, new_record.style, id_no,
                                      new_record )
        When Others → Null
        End Case
    EXCEPTION
        When key_not_deleted → Output ( "key not found" )
    END
End Loop
Output_Indexes ( external_file & ".mak", header(MAKE) )
Output_Indexes ( external_file & ".sty", header(STYLE) )

PROCEDURE Input_Indexes ( index_file : In String
                          header : In Out Key_Value_Access )
    -- input the external file containing the key values, the
    -- first key and the length into a linked structure
    key_pointer : Key_Value_Access ← New Key_Value_Record

    first: Key_Value_Access ← key_pointer
    Loop
        Exit When End_Of_File ( index_file )
        Input ( index_file, index_record )
        key_pointer.next_value ← New Key_Value_Record'
                                   ( index_record.key_value, NULL,
                                     index_record.first_key
                                     index_record.length )
        key_pointer ← key_pointer.next_value
    End Loop
    key_pointer.next_value ← NULL
    header ← first.next_value

PROCEDURE Delete_Index ( index_name : In Second_Key_Name_Type
                         second_key : In Second_Key_Type
                         id_no : In Primary_Key_Type
                         hold_record : In Record_Info )
    link : Primary_Key_Type
    previous, where_found : Key_Value_Access
    prev_key : Primary_Key_Type
    prev_record : Record_Info

    Search_List ( header(index_name), second_key, where_found, previous )
    If where_found.first_key = id_no
        -- delete first key
        If where_found.length = 1    -- delete entire entry
            If previous = NULL    -- first entry
                header(index_name) ← where_found.next_value
            Else
                previous.next_value ← where_found.next_value
            End If
        Else -- find next primary key to become first_key
```

```
                Case index_name
                    MAKE   → where_found.first_key ← hold_record.make_link
                    STYLE → where_found.first_key ← hold_record.style_link
                End Case
                decrement where_found.length
            End If
        Else -- id_no not = first_key
            prev_key ← where_found.first_key
            Retrieve ( prev_key, record_number )
            Input ( data_file, prev_record, record_number )
            Case index_name
                MAKE → link ← prev_record.make_link
                STYLE→ link ← prev_record.style_link
            End Case
            Loop
                If link = END_OF_LIST
                    Raise key_not_deleted
                End If
                    -- search for id_no in linked list of records
                If link = id_no
                    Case index_name
                        MAKE → prev_record.make_link ←
                                    hold_record.make_link
                        STYLE → prev_record.style_link ←
                                    hold_record.style_link
                    End Case
                    Output ( data_file, prev_record, record_number )
                    decrement where_found.length
                    Exit
                Else
                    prev_key ← link
                    Retrieve ( prev_key, record_number )
                    Input ( data_file, prev_record, record_number )
                    Case index_name
                        MAKE → link  ← prev_record.make_link
                        STYLE → link ← prev_record.style_link
                    End Case
                End If
            End Loop
        End If
    EXCEPTION
        When key_not_found → Raise key_not_deleted
```

The Ada implementations of Algorithms 10.3 and 10.4 are presented in Appendix B. Figure 10.30 illustrates the interfacing of the program components with each other and the external I/O files. A nongeneric package, `Multilist`, encapsulates the data structures and the operations on the multilst files and data files while hiding the details from Algorithm 10.3 (`Create`) and Algorithm 10.4 (`Update`). The generic `B_Tree` package, developed in Chapter 8, is instantiated by the package `Multilist` to provide indexing for the data file.

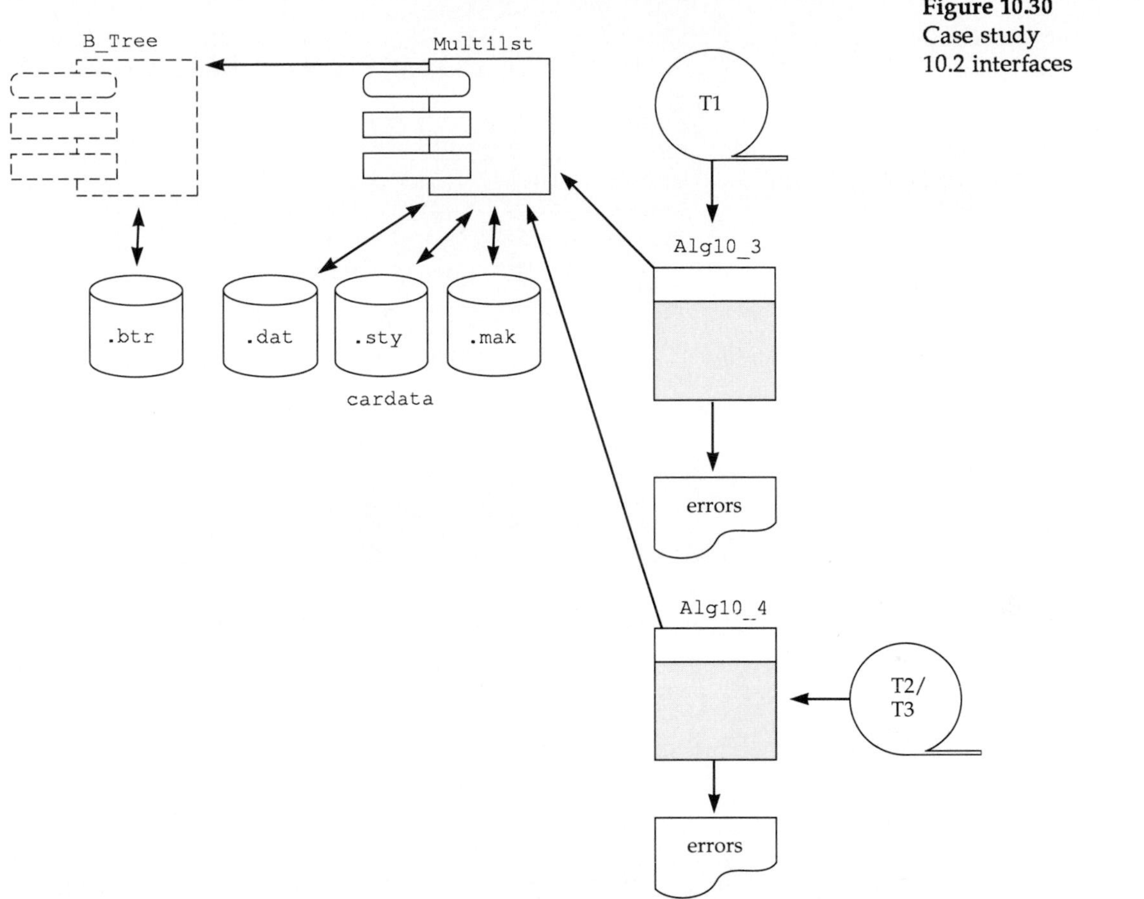

Figure 10.30 Case study 10.2 interfaces

The B-tree presented in Chapter 8 is an appropriate structure in which to store the multilist index. The B-tree allows secondary key values to be stored to facilitate faster searching and easier modification. As with the inverted list, the number of nodes in the B-tree can be reduced by increasing the order of the tree, thus reducing the number of disk accesses to search the multilist directory.

The data in the multilist directories in Figure 10.22 can be stored in a B-tree structure as pictured in Figures 10.31 and 10.32. The B-tree is stored externally, and each node represents a disk access. The whole structure is much simpler than the structure for the inverted list, since each tuple contains the data found in the multilist directory pertaining to one make or style of car. The first tuple in the root node in Figure 10.30 contains the same information found in one entry of the multilist directory of Figure 10.22(a): the make Chevrolet, the first primary key of the linked list (GM3), and the length of the linked list (1). The B-tree also contains a pointer to the record (node) that contains the tuples Dodge and Ford.

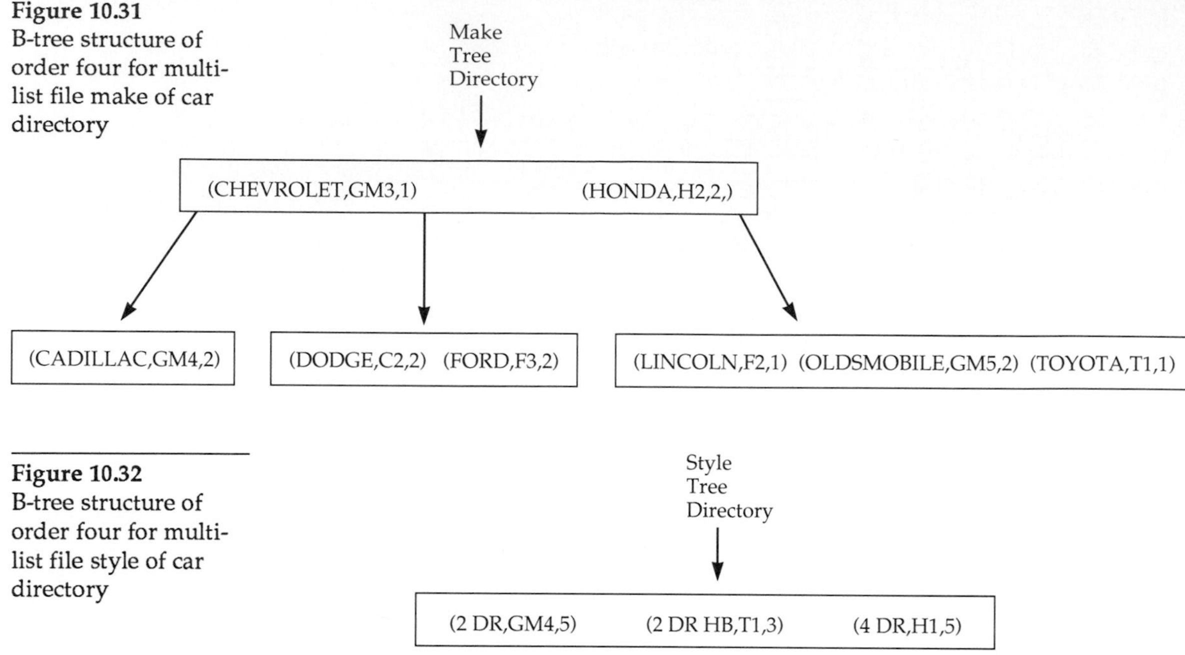

Figure 10.31 B-tree structure of order four for multilist file make of car directory

Figure 10.32 B-tree structure of order four for multilist file style of car directory

SUMMARY

Multiple-key file organization provides access to a data file by one or more secondary key fields in addition to access by a primary key field. Two types of multiple-key file organization are inverted file organization and multilist file organization.

Inverted file organization uses an inverted index of all attributes in the data file for each secondary key field. Each attribute is accompanied by a list of addresses (primary keys) of all records in the data file containing the attribute. Inverted files may be partially inverted (some of the fields in the record are secondary key fields with inverted lists available) or fully inverted (all fields in the record are secondary key fields with inverted lists available). Most queries, including intersecting queries, can be answered from data in the inverted lists for the secondary key fields without access to the data file itself. Additions to and deletions from the file require changes to the directory. The disadvantage of inverted file organization is the variance in length of the list of addresses in the inverted lists.

Multilist file organization overcomes the disadvantage of inverted file organization by linking records in the data file with the same attribute for a secondary key field. Multilist files also retain in the directory the attribute, the address (primary key) of the first record in the linked list, and the length of the linked list. The directory now has fixed-length entries, which are easier to store. However, more space is used for the data file since each field that is a secondary key is accompanied by a link field. A major disadvantage of multilist files is the number of file accesses necessary to answer a query. Since only one primary key is stored in the directory, retrieval of all records in a linked list requires accessing the data file—one record at a time—to retrieve the link field, which specifies the next record in the list. Additions to and deletions from the file require manipulation of all linked lists to properly insert or remove a record.

Key Terms

fully inverted file
inversion index
inverted file organization
multilist file
multilist file organization
multiple-key file organization
partially inverted file
primary key
secondary key

Exercises

1. List the advantages and disadvantages of an inverted index for a multiple-key file.
2. List the advantages and disadvantages of a multilist index for a multiple-key file.
3. Describe the kinds of queries that can be answered by searching the inverted index without searching the data file. Describe the actions necessary to answer the same queries for a multilist index.
4. Describe several applications that might require secondary key access.
5. Of what use is the length field (length of the linked list) in a multilist file?
6. Design an algorithm for answering intersecting queries for the make and style secondary key fields in the car-rental agency data file. A query might be, for example, "List all the four-door Chevrolets," where four-door (4 DR) and Chevrolet are secondary key values for the make and style fields, respectively. Assume that inverted files are used for secondary key access.
7. Repeat exercise 6, but—this time—assume that multilist files are used for secondary key access.
8. Using the inverted files for make and style of car in Figure 10.10, assume the inverted directories are stored in main memory and assume each record in the data file requires a disk access for retrieval.

State the number of disk accesses required to answer the following queries:

a. How many four-door Oldsmobiles are in the data file?

b. List all the four-door cars.

c. What are the colors of the two-door Dodges?

d. Are there any 2-door hatchbacks in the data file?

e. What is the mileage of each of the four-door Cadillacs?

9. Repeat exercise 8 assuming the inverted files for make and style of car are stored as an indexed sequential file and that each attribute requires a disk access. Compare your answers with those to exercise 8.

10. Repeat exercise 8 assuming the inverted files for make and style of car are stored as B-trees as pictured in Figures 10.20 and 10.21. Compare your answers with those to exercises 8 and 9.

11. Repeat exercise 8 assuming the car-rental agency data file is stored with sequential organization and that no secondary key access is available. Compare your answers with those to exercises 8 through 10.

12. Repeat exercises 8 through 11 assuming a multilist file is available for secondary keys make and style of car for a multiple-key car-data file.

13. Use the following data records about a hospital to build inverted lists for secondary key access by the doctor's name and the patient's ward.

Primary Key	Patient's Name	Ward	Room Number	Doctor's Name	Current Medication
121	Novak, T.R.	G	102	White	Hypoch
231	Drew, R.W.	I	123	Rollins	Sulph-3
243	Black, H.J.	I	124	Brown	Sulph-3
354	James, J.K.	P	213	Taylor	Cryol
365	Tasher, R.E.	R	312	Watson	Neoben
467	Andrews, T.B.	G	103	Rollins	Hypoch
587	Black, T.Y.	M	154	Taylor	Tyleph
678	McCarry, C.M	P	215	Taylor	Cryol
767	Jones, T.T.	I	126	Brown	Sulph-3
876	Smith, D.W.	R	313	Watson	Neoben

ward legend:
G = general ward
P = pediatric ward
I = intensive care unit
M = maternity ward
R = recovery room

14. Using the inverted list from exercise 13, how many disk accesses are necessary to answer the following queries? (Assume the inverted list is in main memory.)

    a. What are the names of the patients in the recovery room?

    b. How many patients are currently in the maternity ward?

    c. Is Tom Jones a patient at the hospital?

    d. What drugs are the patients of Dr. Taylor currently taking?

15. Using the hospital data file in exercise 13, draw a multilist file for doctor's name and patient's ward. Also draw the data file with the links included.
16. Repeat exercise 14 for the multilist file built in exercise 15.

Programming Problems

1. Write a program to build an inverted file for the indexed sequential employee data file created in programming problem 14, 16, or 18 in Chapter 9 to provide secondary key access to department number, section id, and marital status. Use the linked structure example shown in Figure 10.16 for the inverted lists, then copy the information to an external file.
2. Repeat problem 1 using a B-tree of order 5 for inverted lists.
3. Write a program to build a multilist file for the indexed sequential employee data file created in programming problem 14, 16, or 18 in Chapter 9 to provide secondary key access to department number, section id, and marital status.
4. Repeat problem 3 using a B-tree of order 5 for the multilists.
5. Write a program to update the file and secondary key indexes created in problem 1.
6. Write a program to update the file and secondary key indexes created in problem 2.
7. Write a program to update the file and secondary key indexes created in problem 3.
8. Write a program to update the file and secondary key indexes created in problem 4.
9. Write a program to count the number of accesses to the file built in problem 1.
10. Modify the program written in problem 1 to eliminate secondary key values from the indexed sequential file.

11. Write a program to count the number of accesses to the file built in problem 10. Compare your answers to those in problem 9.
12. Repeat problem 9 for the file built in problem 3 and compare the counts.

Appendix A

ANSI/MIL-STD-1815A Chapter 14 Input-Output

14. Input-Output

Input-output is provided in the language by means of predefined packages. The generic packages SEQUENTIAL_IO and DIRECT_IO define input-output operations applicable to files containing elements of a given type. Additional operations for text input-output are supplied in the package TEXT_IO. The package IO_EXCEPTIONS defines the exceptions needed by the above three packages. Finally, a package LOW_LEVEL_IO is provided for direct control of peripheral devices. 1

References: direct_io package 14.2 14.2.4, io_exceptions package 14.5, low_level_io package 14.6, sequential_io package 14.2 14.2.2, text_io package 14.3 2

14.1 External Files and File Objects

Values input from the external environment of the program, or output to the environment, are considered to occupy *external files*. An external file can be anything external to the program that can produce a value to be read or receive a value to be written. An external file is identified by a string (the *name*). A second string (the *form*) gives further system-dependent characteristics that may be associated with the file, such as the physical organization or access rights. The conventions governing the interpretation of such strings must be documented in Appendix F. 1

Input and output operations are expressed as operations on objects of some *file type*, rather than directly in terms of the external files. In the remainder of this chapter, the term *file* is always used to refer to a file object; the term *external file* is used otherwise. The values transferred for a given file must all be of one type. 2

Input-output for sequential files of values of a single element type is defined by means of the generic package SEQUENTIAL_IO. The skeleton of this package is given below. 3

4

```
with IO_EXCEPTIONS;
generic
   type ELEMENT_TYPE is private;
package SEQUENTIAL_IO is
   type FILE_TYPE is limited private;

   type FILE_MODE is (IN_FILE, OUT_FILE);
   ...
   procedure OPEN  (FILE : in out FILE_TYPE; ...);
   ...
   procedure READ  (FILE : in FILE_TYPE; ITEM : out ELEMENT_TYPE);
   procedure WRITE (FILE : in FILE_TYPE; ITEM : in ELEMENT_TYPE);
   ...
end SEQUENTIAL_IO;
```

In order to define sequential input-output for a given element type, an instantiation of this generic unit, with the given type as actual parameter, must be declared. The resulting package contains the declaration of a file type (called FILE_TYPE) for files of such elements, as well as the operations applicable to these files, such as the OPEN, READ, and WRITE procedures. 5

5 Input-output for direct access files is likewise defined by a generic package called DIRECT_IO. Input-output in human-readable form is defined by the (nongeneric) package TEXT_IO.

6 Before input or output operations can be performed on a file, the file must first be associated with an external file. While such an association is in effect, the file is said to be *open*, and otherwise the file is said to be *closed*.

7 The language does not define what happens to external files after the completion of the main program (in particular, if corresponding files have not been closed). The effect of input-output for access types is implementation-dependent.

8 An open file has a *current mode*, which is a value of one of the enumeration types

```
type FILE_MODE is (IN_FILE, INOUT_FILE, OUT_FILE);  --  for DIRECT_IO
type FILE_MODE is (IN_FILE, OUT_FILE);              --  for SEQUENTIAL_IO and TEXT_IO
```

9 These values correspond respectively to the cases where only reading, both reading and writing, or only writing are to be performed. The mode of a file can be changed.

10 Several file management operations are common to the three input-output packages. These operations are described in section 14.2.1 for sequential and direct files. Any additional effects concerning text input-output are described in section 14.3.1.

11 The exceptions that can be raised by a call of an input-output subprogram are all defined in the package IO_EXCEPTIONS; the situations in which they can be raised are described, either following the description of the subprogram (and in section 14.4), or in Appendix F in the case of error situations that are implementation-dependent.

Notes:

12 Each instantiation of the generic packages SEQUENTIAL_IO and DIRECT_IO declares a different type FILE_TYPE; in the case of TEXT_IO, the type FILE_TYPE is unique.

13 A bidirectional device can often be modeled as two sequential files associated with the device, one of mode IN_FILE, and one of mode OUT_FILE. An implementation may restrict the number of files that may be associated with a given external file. The effect of sharing an external file in this way by several file objects is implementation-dependent.

14 *References:* create procedure 14.2.1, current index 14.2, current size 14.2, delete procedure 14.2.1, direct access 14.2, direct file procedure 14.2, direct_io package 14.1 14.2, enumeration type 3.5.1, exception 11, file mode 14.2.3, generic instantiation 12.3, index 14.2, input file 14.2.2, io_exceptions package 14.5, open file 14.1, open procedure 14.2.1, output file 14.2.2, read procedure 14.2.4, sequential access 14.2, sequential file 14.2, sequential input-output 14.2.2, sequential_io package 14.2 14.2.2, string 3.6.3, text_io package 14.3, write procedure 14.2.4

14.2 Sequential and Direct Files

1 Two kinds of access to external files are defined: *sequential access* and *direct access*. The corresponding file types and the associated operations are provided by the generic packages SEQUENTIAL_IO and DIRECT_IO. A file object to be used for sequential access is called a *sequential file*, and one to be used for direct access is called a *direct file*.

2 For sequential access, the file is viewed as a sequence of values that are transferred in the order of their appearance (as produced by the program or by the environment). When the file is opened, transfer starts from the beginning of the file.

For direct access, the file is viewed as a set of elements occupying consecutive positions in linear order; a value can be transferred to or from an element of the file at any selected position. The position of an element is specified by its *index*, which is a number, greater than zero, of the implementation-defined integer type COUNT. The first element, if any, has index one; the index of the last element, if any, is called the *current size*; the current size is zero if there are no elements. The current size is a property of the external file. 3

An open direct file has a *current index*, which is the index that will be used by the next read or write operation. When a direct file is opened, the current index is set to one. The current index of a direct file is a property of a file object, not of an external file. 4

All three file modes are allowed for direct files. The only allowed modes for sequential files are the modes IN_FILE and OUT_FILE. 5

References: count type 14.3, file mode 14.1, in_file 14.1, out_file 14.1 6

14.2.1 File Management

The procedures and functions described in this section provide for the control of external files; their declarations are repeated in each of the three packages for sequential, direct, and text input-output. For text input-output, the procedures CREATE, OPEN, and RESET have additional effects described in section 14.3.1. 1

```
procedure CREATE(FILE : in out FILE_TYPE;
                 MODE : in FILE_MODE := default_mode;
                 NAME : in STRING := "";
                 FORM : in STRING := "");
```
2

Establishes a new external file, with the given name and form, and associates this external file with the given file. The given file is left open. The current mode of the given file is set to the given access mode. The default access mode is the mode OUT_FILE for sequential and text input-output; it is the mode INOUT_FILE for direct input-output. For direct access, the size of the created file is implementation-dependent. A null string for NAME specifies an external file that is not accessible after the completion of the main program (a temporary file). A null string for FORM specifies the use of the default options of the implementation for the external file. 3

The exception STATUS_ERROR is raised if the given file is already open. The exception NAME_ERROR is raised if the string given as NAME does not allow the identification of an external file. The exception USE_ERROR is raised if, for the specified mode, the environment does not support creation of an external file with the given name (in the absence of NAME_ERROR) and form. 4

```
procedure OPEN( FILE : in out FILE_TYPE;
                MODE : in FILE_MODE;
                NAME : in STRING;
                FORM : in STRING := "");
```
5

Associates the given file with an existing external file having the given name and form, and sets the current mode of the given file to the given mode. The given file is left open. 6

7 The exception STATUS_ERROR is raised if the given file is already open. The exception NAME_ERROR is raised if the string given as NAME does not allow the identification of an external file; in particular, this exception is raised if no external file with the given name exists. The exception USE_ERROR is raised if, for the specified mode, the environment does not support opening for an external file with the given name (in the absence of NAME_ERROR) and form.

8 **procedure** CLOSE(FILE : **in out** FILE_TYPE);

9 Severs the association between the given file and its associated external file. The given file is left closed.

10 The exception STATUS_ERROR is raised if the given file is not open.

11 **procedure** DELETE(FILE : **in out** FILE_TYPE);

12 Deletes the external file associated with the given file. The given file is closed, and the external file ceases to exist.

13 The exception STATUS_ERROR is raised if the given file is not open. The exception USE_ERROR is raised if (as fully defined in Appendix F) deletion of the external file is not supported by the environment.

14 **procedure** RESET(FILE : **in out** FILE_TYPE; MODE : **in** FILE_MODE);
procedure RESET(FILE : **in out** FILE_TYPE);

15 Resets the given file so that reading from or writing to its elements can be restarted from the beginning of the file; in particular, for direct access this means that the current index is set to one. If a MODE parameter is supplied, the current mode of the given file is set to the given mode.

16 The exception STATUS_ERROR is raised if the file is not open. The exception USE_ERROR is raised if the environment does not support resetting for the external file and, also, if the environment does not support resetting to the specified mode for the external file.

17 **function** MODE(FILE : **in** FILE_TYPE) **return** FILE_MODE;

18 Returns the current mode of the given file.

19 The exception STATUS_ERROR is raised if the file is not open.

20 **function** NAME(FILE : **in** FILE_TYPE) **return** STRING;

21 Returns a string which uniquely identifies the external file currently associated with the given file (and may thus be used in an OPEN operation). If an environment allows alternative specifications of the name (for example, abbreviations), the string returned by the function should correspond to a full specification of the name.

22 The exception STATUS_ERROR is raised if the given file is not open.

function FORM(FILE : **in** FILE_TYPE) **return** STRING; 23

Returns the form string for the external file currently associated with the given file. 24
If an environment allows alternative specifications of the form (for example, abbreviations using default options), the string returned by the function should correspond to a full specification (that is, it should indicate explicitly all options selected, including default options).

The exception STATUS_ERROR is raised if the given file is not open. 25

function IS_OPEN(FILE : **in** FILE_TYPE) **return** BOOLEAN; 26

Returns TRUE if the file is open (that is, if it is associated with an external file), 27
otherwise returns FALSE.

References: current mode 14.1, current size 14.1, closed file 14.1, direct access 14.2, external file 14.1, file 14.1, 28
file_mode type 14.1, file_type type 14.1, form string 14.1, inout_file 14.2.4, mode 14.1, name string 14.1, name_error exception 14.4, open file 14.1, out_file 14.1, status_error exception 14.4, use_error exception 14.4

14.2.2 Sequential Input-Output

The operations available for sequential input and output are described in this section. The excep- 1
tion STATUS_ERROR is raised if any of these operations is attempted for a file that is not open.

procedure READ(FILE : **in** FILE_TYPE; ITEM : **out** ELEMENT_TYPE); 2

Operates on a file of mode IN_FILE. Reads an element from the given file, and 3
returns the value of this element in the ITEM parameter.

The exception MODE_ERROR is raised if the mode is not IN_FILE. The exception 4
END_ERROR is raised if no more elements can be read from the given file. The exception DATA_ERROR is raised if the element read cannot be interpreted as a value of the type ELEMENT_TYPE; however, an implementation is allowed to omit this check if performing the check is too complex.

procedure WRITE(FILE : **in** FILE_TYPE; ITEM : **in** ELEMENT_TYPE); 5

Operates on a file of mode OUT_FILE. Writes the value of ITEM to the given file. 6

The exception MODE_ERROR is raised if the mode is not OUT_FILE. The exception 7
USE_ERROR is raised if the capacity of the external file is exceeded.

function END_OF_FILE(FILE : **in** FILE_TYPE) **return** BOOLEAN; 8

Operates on a file of mode IN_FILE. Returns TRUE if no more elements can be read 9
from the given file; otherwise returns FALSE.

The exception MODE_ERROR is raised if the mode is not IN_FILE. 10

References: data_error exception 14.4, element 14.1, element_type 14.1, end_error exception 14.4, external file 11
14.1, file 14.1, file mode 14.1, file_type 14.1, in_file 14.1, mode_error exception 14.4, out_file 14.1, status_error exception 14.4, use_error exception 14.4

14.2.3 Specification of the Package Sequential_IO

```
with IO_EXCEPTIONS;
generic
   type ELEMENT_TYPE is private;
package SEQUENTIAL_IO is

   type FILE_TYPE  is limited private;

   type FILE_MODE is (IN_FILE, OUT_FILE);


   -- File management

   procedure CREATE (FILE   : in out FILE_TYPE;
                     MODE  : in FILE_MODE := OUT_FILE;
                     NAME  : in STRING := "";
                     FORM  : in STRING := "");

   procedure OPEN   (FILE   : in out FILE_TYPE;
                     MODE  : in FILE_MODE;
                     NAME  : in STRING;
                     FORM  : in STRING := "");

   procedure CLOSE  (FILE : in out FILE_TYPE);
   procedure DELETE (FILE : in out FILE_TYPE);
   procedure RESET  (FILE : in out FILE_TYPE; MODE : in FILE_MODE);
   procedure RESET  (FILE : in out FILE_TYPE);

   function MODE    (FILE : in FILE_TYPE) return FILE_MODE;
   function NAME    (FILE : in FILE_TYPE) return STRING;
   function FORM    (FILE : in FILE_TYPE) return STRING;

   function IS_OPEN (FILE : in FILE_TYPE) return BOOLEAN;

   -- Input and output operations

   procedure READ   (FILE : in FILE_TYPE; ITEM : out ELEMENT_TYPE);
   procedure WRITE  (FILE : in FILE_TYPE; ITEM : in ELEMENT_TYPE);

   function END_OF_FILE(FILE : in FILE_TYPE) return BOOLEAN;

   -- Exceptions

   STATUS_ERROR  : exception renames IO_EXCEPTIONS.STATUS_ERROR;
   MODE_ERROR    : exception renames IO_EXCEPTIONS.MODE_ERROR;
   NAME_ERROR    : exception renames IO_EXCEPTIONS.NAME_ERROR;
   USE_ERROR     : exception renames IO_EXCEPTIONS.USE_ERROR;
   DEVICE_ERROR  : exception renames IO_EXCEPTIONS.DEVICE_ERROR;
   END_ERROR     : exception renames IO_EXCEPTIONS.END_ERROR;
   DATA_ERROR    : exception renames IO_EXCEPTIONS.DATA_ERROR;

private
   -- implementation-dependent
end SEQUENTIAL_IO;
```

References: close procedure 14.2.1, create procedure 14.2.1, data_error exception 14.4, delete procedure 14.2.1, device_error exception 14.4, end_error exception 14.4, end_of_file function 14.2.2, file_mode 14.1, file_type 14.1, form function 14.2.1, in_file 14.1, io_exceptions 14.4, is_open function 14.2.1, mode function 14.2.1, mode_error exception 14.4, name function 14.2.1, name_error exception 14.4, open procedure 14.2.1, out_file 14.1, read procedure 14.2.2, reset procedure 14.2.1, sequential_io package 14.2 14.2.2, status_error exception 14.4, use_error exception 14.4, write procedure 14.2.2. 2

14.2.4 Direct Input-Output

The operations available for direct input and output are described in this section. The exception STATUS_ERROR is raised if any of these operations is attempted for a file that is not open. 1

```
procedure READ(FILE : in FILE_TYPE; ITEM  : out ELEMENT_TYPE;
                                    FROM  : in  POSITIVE_COUNT);
procedure READ(FILE : in FILE_TYPE; ITEM  : out ELEMENT_TYPE);
```
2

Operates on a file of mode IN_FILE or INOUT_FILE. In the case of the first form, sets the current index of the given file to the index value given by the parameter FROM. Then (for both forms) returns, in the parameter ITEM, the value of the element whose position in the given file is specified by the current index of the file; finally, increases the current index by one. 3

The exception MODE_ERROR is raised if the mode of the given file is OUT_FILE. The exception END_ERROR is raised if the index to be used exceeds the size of the external file. The exception DATA_ERROR is raised if the element read cannot be interpreted as a value of the type ELEMENT_TYPE; however, an implementation is allowed to omit this check if performing the check is too complex. 4

```
procedure WRITE(FILE : in FILE_TYPE; ITEM : in ELEMENT_TYPE;
                                     TO   : in POSITIVE_COUNT);
procedure WRITE(FILE : in FILE_TYPE; ITEM : in ELEMENT_TYPE);
```
5

Operates on a file of mode INOUT_FILE or OUT_FILE. In the case of the first form, sets the index of the given file to the index value given by the parameter TO. Then (for both forms) gives the value of the parameter ITEM to the element whose position in the given file is specified by the current index of the file; finally, increases the current index by one. 6

The exception MODE_ERROR is raised if the mode of the given file is IN_FILE. The exception USE_ERROR is raised if the capacity of the external file is exceeded. 7

```
procedure SET_INDEX(FILE : in FILE_TYPE; TO : in POSITIVE_COUNT);
```
8

Operates on a file of any mode. Sets the current index of the given file to the given index value (which may exceed the current size of the file). 9

```
function INDEX(FILE : in FILE_TYPE) return POSITIVE_COUNT;
```
10

Operates on a file of any mode. Returns the current index of the given file. 11

12 **function** SIZE(FILE : **in** FILE_TYPE) **return** COUNT;

13 Operates on a file of any mode. Returns the current size of the external file that is associated with the given file.

14 **function** END_OF_FILE(FILE : **in** FILE_TYPE) **return** BOOLEAN;

15 Operates on a file of mode IN_FILE or INOUT_FILE. Returns TRUE if the current index exceeds the size of the external file; otherwise returns FALSE.

16 The exception MODE_ERROR is raised if the mode of the given file is OUT_FILE.

17 *References:* count type 14.2, current index 14.2, current size 14.2, data_error exception 14.4, element 14.1, element_type 14.1, end_error exception 14.4, external file 14.1, file 14.1, file mode 14.1, file_type 14.1, in_file 14.1, index 14.2, inout_file 14.1, mode_error exception 14.4, open file 14.1, positive_count 14.3, status_error exception 14.4, use_error exception 14.4

14.2.5 Specification of the Package Direct_IO

1
```
with IO_EXCEPTIONS;
generic
   type ELEMENT_TYPE is private;
package DIRECT_IO is

   type FILE_TYPE  is limited private;

   type     FILE_MODE is (IN_FILE, INOUT_FILE, OUT_FILE);
   type     COUNT      is range 0 .. implementation_defined;
   subtype  POSITIVE_COUNT is COUNT range 1 .. COUNT'LAST;


   -- File management

   procedure CREATE ( FILE   : in out FILE_TYPE;
                      MODE   : in FILE_MODE := INOUT_FILE;
                      NAME   : in STRING := "";
                      FORM   : in STRING := "");

   procedure OPEN   ( FILE   : in out FILE_TYPE;
                      MODE   : in FILE_MODE;
                      NAME   : in STRING;
                      FORM   : in STRING := "");

   procedure CLOSE  (FILE : in out FILE_TYPE);
   procedure DELETE (FILE : in out FILE_TYPE);
   procedure RESET  (FILE : in out FILE_TYPE; MODE : in FILE_MODE);
   procedure RESET  (FILE : in out FILE_TYPE);

   function MODE    (FILE : in FILE_TYPE) return FILE_MODE;
   function NAME    (FILE : in FILE_TYPE) return STRING;
   function FORM    (FILE : in FILE_TYPE) return STRING;

   function IS_OPEN  (FILE : in FILE_TYPE) return BOOLEAN;
```

```
    -- Input and output operations

    procedure READ  (FILE : in FILE_TYPE; ITEM : out ELEMENT_TYPE; FROM : POSITIVE_COUNT);
    procedure READ  (FILE : in FILE_TYPE; ITEM : out ELEMENT_TYPE);

    procedure WRITE (FILE : in FILE_TYPE; ITEM : in  ELEMENT_TYPE; TO : POSITIVE_COUNT);
    procedure WRITE (FILE : in FILE_TYPE; ITEM : in ELEMENT_TYPE);

    procedure SET_INDEX(FILE : in FILE_TYPE; TO : in POSITIVE_COUNT);

    function INDEX(FILE : in FILE_TYPE) return POSITIVE_COUNT;
    function SIZE  (FILE : in FILE_TYPE) return COUNT;

    function END_OF_FILE (FILE : in FILE_TYPE) return BOOLEAN;

    -- Exceptions

    STATUS_ERROR  : exception renames IO_EXCEPTIONS.STATUS_ERROR;
    MODE_ERROR    : exception renames IO_EXCEPTIONS.MODE_ERROR;
    NAME_ERROR    : exception renames IO_EXCEPTIONS.NAME_ERROR;
    USE_ERROR     : exception renames IO_EXCEPTIONS.USE_ERROR;
    DEVICE_ERROR  : exception renames IO_EXCEPTIONS.DEVICE_ERROR;
    END_ERROR     : exception renames IO_EXCEPTIONS.END_ERROR;
    DATA_ERROR    : exception renames IO_EXCEPTIONS.DATA_ERROR;

private
   -- implementation-dependent
end DIRECT_IO;
```

References close procedure 14.2.1, count type 14.2, create procedure 14.2.1, data_error exception 14.4, default_mode 14.2.5, delete procedure 14.2.1, device_error exception 14.4, element_type 14.2.4, end_error exception 14.4, end_of_file function 14.2.4, file_mode 14.2.5, file_type 14.2.4, form function 14.2.1, in_file 14.2.4, index function 14.2.4, inout_file 14.2.4 14.2.1, io_exceptions package 14.4, is_open function 14.2.1, mode function 14.2.1, mode_error exception 14.4, name function 14.2.1, name_error exception 14.4, open procedure 14.2.1, out_file 14.2.1, read procedure 14.2.4, set_index procedure 14.2.4, size function 14.2.4, status_error exception 14.4, use_error exception 14.4, write procedure 14.2.4 14.2.1 2

14.3 Text Input-Output

This section describes the package TEXT_IO, which provides facilities for input and output in human-readable form. Each file is read or written sequentially, as a sequence of characters grouped into lines, and as a sequence of lines grouped into pages. The specification of the package is given below in section 14.3.10. 1

The facilities for file management given above, in sections 14.2.1 and 14.2.2, are available for text input-output. In place of READ and WRITE, however, there are procedures GET and PUT that input values of suitable types from text files, and output values to them. These values are provided to the PUT procedures, and returned by the GET procedures, in a parameter ITEM. Several overloaded procedures of these names exist, for different types of ITEM. These GET procedures analyze the input sequences of characters as lexical elements (see Chapter 2) and return the corresponding values; the PUT procedures output the given values as appropriate lexical elements. Procedures GET and PUT are also available that input and output individual characters treated as character values rather than as lexical elements. 2

3 In addition to the procedures GET and PUT for numeric and enumeration types of ITEM that operate on text files, analogous procedures are provided that read from and write to a parameter of type STRING. These procedures perform the same analysis and composition of character sequences as their counterparts which have a file parameter.

4 For all GET and PUT procedures that operate on text files, and for many other subprograms, there are forms with and without a file parameter. Each such GET procedure operates on an input file, and each such PUT procedure operates on an output file. If no file is specified, a default input file or a default output file is used.

5 At the beginning of program execution the default input and output files are the so-called standard input file and standard output file. These files are open, have respectively the current modes IN_FILE and OUT_FILE, and are associated with two implementation-defined external files. Procedures are provided to change the current default input file and the current default output file.

6 From a logical point of view, a text file is a sequence of pages, a page is a sequence of lines, and a line is a sequence of characters; the end of a line is marked by a *line terminator*; the end of a page is marked by the combination of a line terminator immediately followed by a *page terminator*; and the end of a file is marked by the combination of a line terminator immediately followed by a page terminator and then a *file terminator*. Terminators are generated during output; either by calls of procedures provided expressly for that purpose; or implicitly as part of other operations, for example, when a bounded line length, a bounded page length, or both, have been specified for a file.

7 The actual nature of terminators is not defined by the language and hence depends on the implementation. Although terminators are recognized or generated by certain of the procedures that follow, they are not necessarily implemented as characters or as sequences of characters. Whether they are characters (and if so which ones) in any particular implementation need not concern a user who neither explicitly outputs nor explicitly inputs control characters. The effect of input or output of control characters (other than horizontal tabulation) is not defined by the language.

8 The characters of a line are numbered, starting from one; the number of a character is called its *column number*. For a line terminator, a column number is also defined: it is one more than the number of characters in the line. The lines of a page, and the pages of a file, are similarly numbered. The *current column number* is the column number of the next character or line terminator to be transferred. The *current line number* is the number of the current line. The *current page number* is the number of the current page. These numbers are values of the subtype POSITIVE_COUNT of the type COUNT (by convention, the value zero of the type COUNT is used to indicate special conditions).

```
type COUNT is range 0 .. implementation_defined;
subtype POSITIVE_COUNT is COUNT range 1 .. COUNT'LAST;
```

9 For an output file, a *maximum line length* can be specified and a *maximum page length* can be specified. If a value to be output cannot fit on the current line, for a specified maximum line length, then a new line is automatically started before the value is output; if, further, this new line cannot fit on the current page, for a specified maximum page length, then a new page is automatically started before the value is output. Functions are provided to determine the maximum line length and the maximum page length. When a file is opened with mode OUT_FILE, both values are zero: by convention, this means that the line lengths and page lengths are unbounded. (Consequently, output consists of a single line if the subprograms for explicit control of line and page structure are not used.) The constant UNBOUNDED is provided for this purpose.

10 *References:* count type 14.3.10, default current input file 14.3.2, default current output file 14.3.2, external file 14.1, file 14.1, get procedure 14.3.5, in_file 14.1, out_file 14.1, put procedure 14.3.5, read 14.2.2, sequential access 14.1, standard input file 14.3.2, standard output file 14.3.2

14.3.1 File Management

The only allowed file modes for text files are the modes IN_FILE and OUT_FILE. The subprograms 1
given in section 14.2.1 for the control of external files, and the function END_OF_FILE given in section 14.2.2 for sequential input-output, are also available for text files. There is also a version of END_OF_FILE that refers to the current default input file. For text files, the procedures have the following additional effects:

- For the procedures CREATE and OPEN: After opening a file with mode OUT_FILE, the page 2
length and line length are unbounded (both have the conventional value zero). After opening a file with mode IN_FILE or OUT_FILE, the current column, current line, and current page numbers are set to one.

- For the procedure CLOSE: If the file has the current mode OUT_FILE, has the effect of calling 3
NEW_PAGE, unless the current page is already terminated; then outputs a file terminator.

- For the procedure RESET: If the file has the current mode OUT_FILE, has the effect of calling 4
NEW_PAGE, unless the current page is already terminated; then outputs a file terminator. If the new file mode is OUT_FILE, the page and line lengths are unbounded. For all modes, the current column, line, and page numbers are set to one.

The exception MODE_ERROR is raised by the procedure RESET upon an attempt to change the 5
mode of a file that is either the current default input file, or the current default output file.

References: create procedure 14.2.1, current column number 14.3, current default input file 14.3, current line 6
number 14.3, current page number 14.3, end_of_file 14.3, external file 14.1, file 14.1, file mode 14.1, file terminator 14.3, in_file 14.1, line length 14.3, mode_error exception 14.4, open procedure 14.2.1, out_file 14.1, page length 14.3, reset procedure 14.2.1

14.3.2 Default Input and Output Files

The following subprograms provide for the control of the particular default files that are used when 1
a file parameter is omitted from a GET, PUT or other operation of text input-output described below.

procedure SET_INPUT(FILE : **in** FILE_TYPE); 2

> Operates on a file of mode IN_FILE. Sets the current default input file to FILE. 3
>
> The exception STATUS_ERROR is raised if the given file is not open. The exception 4
> MODE_ERROR is raised if the mode of the given file is not IN_FILE.

procedure SET_OUTPUT(FILE : **in** FILE_TYPE); 5

> Operates on a file of mode OUT_FILE. Sets the current default output file to FILE. 6
>
> The exception STATUS_ERROR is raised if the given file is not open. The exception 7
> MODE_ERROR is raised if the mode of the given file is not OUT_FILE.

8 **function** STANDARD_INPUT **return** FILE_TYPE;

9 Returns the standard input file (see 14.3).

10 **function** STANDARD_OUTPUT **return** FILE_TYPE;

11 Returns the standard output file (see 14.3).

12 **function** CURRENT_INPUT **return** FILE_TYPE;

13 Returns the current default input file.

14 **function** CURRENT_OUTPUT **return** FILE_TYPE;

15 Returns the current default output file.

Note:

16 The standard input and the standard output files cannot be opened, closed, reset, or deleted, because the parameter FILE of the corresponding procedures has the mode **in out**.

17 *References:* current default file 14.3, default file 14.3, file_type 14.1, get procedure 14.3.5, mode_error exception 14.4, put procedure 14.3.5, status_error exception 14.4

14.3.3 Specification of Line and Page Lengths

1 The subprograms described in this section are concerned with the line and page structure of a file of mode OUT_FILE. They operate either on the file given as the first parameter, or, in the absence of such a file parameter, on the current default output file. They provide for output of text with a specified maximum line length or page length. In these cases, line and page terminators are output implicitly and automatically when needed. When line and page lengths are unbounded (that is, when they have the conventional value zero), as in the case of a newly opened file, new lines and new pages are only started when explicitly called for.

2 In all cases, the exception STATUS_ERROR is raised if the file to be used is not open; the exception MODE_ERROR is raised if the mode of the file is not OUT_FILE.

3 **procedure** SET_LINE_LENGTH(FILE : **in** FILE_TYPE; TO : **in** COUNT);
procedure SET_LINE_LENGTH(TO : **in** COUNT);

4 Sets the maximum line length of the specified output file to the number of characters specified by TO. The value zero for TO specifies an unbounded line length.

5 The exception USE_ERROR is raised if the specified line length is inappropriate for the associated external file.

procedure SET_PAGE_LENGTH (FILE : **in** FILE_TYPE; TO : **in** COUNT); 6
procedure SET_PAGE_LENGTH (TO : **in** COUNT);

Sets the maximum page length of the specified output file to the number of lines specified by TO. The value zero for TO specifies an unbounded page length. 7

The exception USE_ERROR is raised if the specified page length is inappropriate for the associated external file. 8

function LINE_LENGTH(FILE : **in** FILE_TYPE) **return** COUNT; 9
function LINE_LENGTH **return** COUNT;

Returns the maximum line length currently set for the specified output file, or zero if the line length is unbounded. 10

function PAGE_LENGTH(FILE : **in** FILE_TYPE) **return** COUNT; 11
function PAGE_LENGTH **return** COUNT;

Returns the maximum page length currently set for the specified output file, or zero if the page length is unbounded. 12

References: count type 14.3, current default output file 14.3, external file 14.1, file 14.1, file_type 14.1, line 14.3, line length 14.3, line terminator 14.3, maximum line length 14.3, maximum page length 14.3, mode_error exception 14.4, open file 14.1, out_file 14.1, page 14.3, page length 14.3, page terminator 14.3, status_error exception 14.4, unbounded page length 14.3, use_error exception 14.4 13

14.3.4 Operations on Columns, Lines, and Pages

The subprograms described in this section provide for explicit control of line and page structure; they operate either on the file given as the first parameter, or, in the absence of such a file parameter, on the appropriate (input or output) current default file. The exception STATUS_ERROR is raised by any of these subprograms if the file to be used is not open. 1

procedure NEW_LINE(FILE : **in** FILE_TYPE; SPACING : **in** POSITIVE_COUNT := 1); 2
procedure NEW_LINE(SPACING : **in** POSITIVE_COUNT := 1);

Operates on a file of mode OUT_FILE.

For a SPACING of one: Outputs a line terminator and sets the current column number to one. Then increments the current line number by one, except in the case that the current line number is already greater than or equal to the maximum page length, for a bounded page length; in that case a page terminator is output, the current page number is incremented by one, and the current line number is set to one. 3

For a SPACING greater than one, the above actions are performed SPACING times. 4

The exception MODE_ERROR is raised if the mode is not OUT_FILE. 5

6
```
procedure SKIP_LINE(FILE       : in FILE_TYPE; SPACING : in POSITIVE_COUNT := 1);
procedure SKIP_LINE(SPACING : in POSITIVE_COUNT := 1);
```

7 Operates on a file of mode IN_FILE.

8 For a SPACING of one: Reads and discards all characters until a line terminator has been read, and then sets the current column number to one. If the line terminator is not immediately followed by a page terminator, the current line number is incremented by one. Otherwise, if the line terminator is immediately followed by a page terminator, then the page terminator is skipped, the current page number is incremented by one, and the current line number is set to one.

9 For a SPACING greater than one, the above actions are performed SPACING times.

10 The exception MODE_ERROR is raised if the mode is not IN_FILE. The exception END_ERROR is raised if an attempt is made to read a file terminator.

11
```
function END_OF_LINE(FILE : in FILE_TYPE) return BOOLEAN;
function END_OF_LINE return BOOLEAN;
```

12 Operates on a file of mode IN_FILE. Returns TRUE if a line terminator or a file terminator is next; otherwise returns FALSE.

13 The exception MODE_ERROR is raised if the mode is not IN_FILE.

14
```
procedure NEW_PAGE(FILE : in FILE_TYPE);
procedure NEW_PAGE;
```

15 Operates on a file of mode OUT_FILE. Outputs a line terminator if the current line is not terminated, or if the current page is empty (that is, if the current column and line numbers are both equal to one). Then outputs a page terminator, which terminates the current page. Adds one to the current page number and sets the current column and line numbers to one.

16 The exception MODE_ERROR is raised if the mode is not OUT_FILE.

17
```
procedure SKIP_PAGE(FILE : in FILE_TYPE);
procedure SKIP_PAGE;
```

18 Operates on a file of mode IN_FILE. Reads and discards all characters and line terminators until a page terminator has been read. Then adds one to the current page number, and sets the current column and line numbers to one.

19 The exception MODE_ERROR is raised if the mode is not IN_FILE. The exception END_ERROR is raised if an attempt is made to read a file terminator.

function END_OF_PAGE(FILE : **in** FILE_TYPE) **return** BOOLEAN; 20
function END_OF_PAGE **return** BOOLEAN;

Operates on a file of mode IN_FILE. Returns TRUE if the combination of a line terminator and a page terminator is next, or if a file terminator is next; otherwise returns FALSE. 21

The exception MODE_ERROR is raised if the mode is not IN_FILE. 22

function END_OF_FILE(FILE : **in** FILE_TYPE) **return** BOOLEAN; 23
function END_OF_FILE **return** BOOLEAN;

Operates on a file of mode IN_FILE. Returns TRUE if a file terminator is next, or if the combination of a line, a page, and a file terminator is next; otherwise returns FALSE. 24

The exception MODE_ERROR is raised if the mode is not IN_FILE. 25

The following subprograms provide for the control of the current position of reading or writing in a file. In all cases, the default file is the current output file. 26

procedure SET_COL(FILE : **in** FILE_TYPE; TO : **in** POSITIVE_COUNT); 27
procedure SET_COL(TO : **in** POSITIVE_COUNT);

If the file mode is OUT_FILE: 28

If the value specified by TO is greater than the current column number, outputs spaces, adding one to the current column number after each space, until the current column number equals the specified value. If the value specified by TO is equal to the current column number, there is no effect. If the value specified by TO is less than the current column number, has the effect of calling NEW_LINE (with a spacing of one), then outputs (TO - 1) spaces, and sets the current column number to the specified value. 29

The exception LAYOUT_ERROR is raised if the value specified by TO exceeds LINE_LENGTH when the line length is bounded (that is, when it does not have the conventional value zero). 30

If the file mode is IN_FILE: 31

Reads (and discards) individual characters, line terminators, and page terminators, until the next character to be read has a column number that equals the value specified by TO; there is no effect if the current column number already equals this value. Each transfer of a character or terminator maintains the current column, line, and page numbers in the same way as a GET procedure (see 14.3.5). (Short lines will be skipped until a line is reached that has a character at the specified column position.) 32

The exception END_ERROR is raised if an attempt is made to read a file terminator. 33

34
```
procedure SET_LINE(FILE  : in FILE_TYPE; TO : in POSITIVE_COUNT);
procedure SET_LINE(TO    : in POSITIVE_COUNT);
```

35 If the file mode is OUT_FILE :

36 If the value specified by TO is greater than the current line number, has the effect of repeatedly calling NEW_LINE (with a spacing of one), until the current line number equals the specified value. If the value specified by TO is equal to the current line number, there is no effect. If the value specified by TO is less than the current line number, has the effect of calling NEW_PAGE followed by a call of NEW_LINE with a spacing equal to (TO - 1).

37 The exception LAYOUT_ERROR is raised if the value specified by TO exceeds PAGE_LENGTH when the page length is bounded (that is, when it does not have the conventional value zero).

38 If the mode is IN_FILE :

39 Has the effect of repeatedly calling SKIP_LINE (with a spacing of one), until the current line number equals the value specified by TO ; there is no effect if the current line number already equals this value. (Short pages will be skipped until a page is reached that has a line at the specified line position.)

40 The exception END_ERROR is raised if an attempt is made to read a file terminator.

41
```
function COL(FILE : in FILE_TYPE) return POSITIVE_COUNT;
function COL return POSITIVE_COUNT;
```

42 Returns the current column number.

43 The exception LAYOUT_ERROR is raised if this number exceeds COUNT'LAST.

44
```
function LINE(FILE  : in FILE_TYPE)  return POSITIVE_COUNT;
function LINE return POSITIVE_COUNT;
```

45 Returns the current line number.

46 The exception LAYOUT_ERROR is raised if this number exceeds COUNT'LAST.

47
```
function PAGE(FILE : in FILE_TYPE) return POSITIVE_COUNT;
function PAGE return POSITIVE_COUNT;
```

48 Returns the current page number.

49 The exception LAYOUT_ERROR is raised if this number exceeds COUNT'LAST.

50 The column number, line number, or page number are allowed to exceed COUNT'LAST (as a consequence of the input or output of sufficiently many characters, lines, or pages). These events do not cause any exception to be raised. However, a call of COL, LINE, or PAGE raises the exception LAYOUT_ERROR if the corresponding number exceeds COUNT'LAST.

Note:

51 A page terminator is always skipped whenever the preceding line terminator is skipped. An implementation may represent the combination of these terminators by a single character, provided that it is properly recognized at input.

52 *References:* current column number 14.3, current default file 14.3, current line number 14.3, current page number 14.3, end_error exception 14.4, file 14.1, file terminator 14.3, get procedure 14.3.5, in_file 14.1, layout_error exception 14.4, line 14.3, line number 14.3, line terminator 14.3, maximum page length 14.3, mode_error exception 14.4, open file 14.1, page 14.3, page length 14.3, page terminator 14.3, positive count 14.3, status_error exception 14.4

14.3.5 Get and Put Procedures

1 The procedures GET and PUT for items of the types CHARACTER, STRING, numeric types, and enumeration types are described in subsequent sections. Features of these procedures that are common to most of these types are described in this section. The GET and PUT procedures for items of type CHARACTER and STRING deal with individual character values; the GET and PUT procedures for numeric and enumeration types treat the items as lexical elements.

2 All procedures GET and PUT have forms with a file parameter, written first. Where this parameter is omitted, the appropriate (input or output) current default file is understood to be specified. Each procedure GET operates on a file of mode IN_FILE. Each procedure PUT operates on a file of mode OUT_FILE.

3 All procedures GET and PUT maintain the current column, line, and page numbers of the specified file: the effect of each of these procedures upon these numbers is the resultant of the effects of individual transfers of characters and of individual output or skipping of terminators. Each transfer of a character adds one to the current column number. Each output of a line terminator sets the current column number to one and adds one to the current line number. Each output of a page terminator sets the current column and line numbers to one and adds one to the current page number. For input, each skipping of a line terminator sets the current column number to one and adds one to the current line number; each skipping of a page terminator sets the current column and line numbers to one and adds one to the current page number. Similar considerations apply to the procedures GET_LINE, PUT_LINE, and SET_COL.

4 Several GET and PUT procedures, for numeric and enumeration types, have *format* parameters which specify field lengths; these parameters are of the nonnegative subtype FIELD of the type INTEGER.

5 Input-output of enumeration values uses the syntax of the corresponding lexical elements. Any GET procedure for an enumeration type begins by skipping any leading blanks, or line or page terminators; a *blank* being defined as a space or a horizontal tabulation character. Next, characters are input only so long as the sequence input is an initial sequence of an identifier or of a character literal (in particular, input ceases when a line terminator is encountered). The character or line terminator that causes input to cease remains available for subsequent input.

6 For a numeric type, the GET procedures have a format parameter called WIDTH. If the value given for this parameter is zero, the GET procedure proceeds in the same manner as for enumeration types, but using the syntax of numeric literals instead of that of enumeration literals. If a nonzero value is given, then exactly WIDTH characters are input, or the characters up to a line terminator, whichever comes first; any skipped leading blanks are included in the count. The syntax used for numeric literals is an extended syntax that allows a leading sign (but no intervening blanks, or line or page terminators).

7 Any PUT procedure, for an item of a numeric or an enumeration type, outputs the value of the item as a numeric literal, identifier, or character literal, as appropriate. This is preceded by leading spaces if required by the format parameters WIDTH or FORE (as described in later sections), and then a minus sign for a negative value; for an enumeration type, the spaces follow instead of leading. The format given for a PUT procedure is overridden if it is insufficiently wide.

8 Two further cases arise for PUT procedures for numeric and enumeration types, if the line length of the specified output file is bounded (that is, if it does not have the conventional value zero). If the number of characters to be output does not exceed the maximum line length, but is such that they cannot fit on the current line, starting from the current column, then (in effect) NEW_LINE is called (with a spacing of one) before output of the item. Otherwise, if the number of characters exceeds the maximum line length, then the exception LAYOUT_ERROR is raised and no characters are output.

9 The exception STATUS_ERROR is raised by any of the procedures GET, GET_LINE, PUT, and PUT_LINE if the file to be used is not open. The exception MODE_ERROR is raised by the procedures GET and GET_LINE if the mode of the file to be used is not IN_FILE; and by the procedures PUT and PUT_LINE, if the mode is not OUT_FILE.

10 The exception END_ERROR is raised by a GET procedure if an attempt is made to skip a file terminator. The exception DATA_ERROR is raised by a GET procedure if the sequence finally input is not a lexical element corresponding to the type, in particular if no characters were input; for this test, leading blanks are ignored; for an item of a numeric type, when a sign is input, this rule applies to the succeeding numeric literal. The exception LAYOUT_ERROR is raised by a PUT procedure that outputs to a parameter of type STRING, if the length of the actual string is insufficient for the output of the item.

11 *Examples:*

12 In the examples, here and in sections 14.3.7 and 14.3.8, the string quotes and the lower case letter b are not transferred: they are shown only to reveal the layout and spaces.

```
N : INTEGER;
...
GET(N);

-- Characters at input       Sequence input      Value of N

--        bb-12535b          -12535              -12535
--        bb12_535E1b         12_535E1            125350
--        bb12_535E;          12_535E             (none) DATA_ERROR raised
```

13 *Example of overridden width parameter:*

```
PUT(ITEM => -23, WIDTH => 2);  --  "-23"
```

14 *References:* blank 14.3.9, column number 14.3, current default file 14.3, data_error exception 14.4, end_error exception 14.4, file 14.1, fore 14.3.8, get procedure 14.3.6 14.3.7 14.3.8 14.3.9, in_file 14.1, layout_error exception 14.4, line number 14.1, line terminator 14.1, maximum line length 14.3, mode 14.1, mode_error exception 14.4, new_file procedure 14.3.4, out_file 14.1, page number 14.1, page terminator 14.1, put procedure 14.3.6 14.3.7 14.3.8 14.3.9, skipping 14.3.7 14.3.8 14.3.9, status_error exception 14.4, width 14.3.5 14.3.7 14.3.9

14.3.6 Input-Output of Characters and Strings

For an item of type CHARACTER the following procedures are provided: 1

```
procedure GET(FILE  : in FILE_TYPE; ITEM : out CHARACTER);  2
procedure GET(ITEM  : out CHARACTER);
```

After skipping any line terminators and any page terminators, reads the next character from the specified input file and returns the value of this character in the **out** parameter ITEM. 3

The exception END_ERROR is raised if an attempt is made to skip a file terminator. 4

```
procedure PUT(FILE  : in FILE_TYPE; ITEM : in CHARACTER);  5
procedure PUT(ITEM  : in CHARACTER);
```

If the line length of the specified output file is bounded (that is, does not have the conventional value zero), and the current column number exceeds it, has the effect of calling NEW_LINE with a spacing of one. Then, or otherwise, outputs the given character to the file. 6

For an item of type STRING the following procedures are provided: 7

```
procedure GET(FILE  : in FILE_TYPE; ITEM : out STRING);  8
procedure GET(ITEM  : out STRING);
```

Determines the length of the given string and attempts that number of GET operations for successive characters of the string (in particular, no operation is performed if the string is null). 9

```
procedure PUT(FILE  : in FILE_TYPE; ITEM : in STRING);  10
procedure PUT(ITEM  : in STRING);
```

Determines the length of the given string and attempts that number of PUT operations for successive characters of the string (in particular, no operation is performed if the string is null). 11

```
procedure GET_LINE(FILE : in FILE_TYPE; ITEM : out STRING; LAST : out NATURAL);  12
procedure GET_LINE(ITEM : out STRING; LAST : out NATURAL);
```

Replaces successive characters of the specified string by successive characters read from the specified input file. Reading stops if the end of the line is met, in which case the procedure SKIP_LINE is then called (in effect) with a spacing of one; reading also stops if the end of the string is met. Characters not replaced are left undefined. 13

If characters are read, returns in LAST the index value such that ITEM(LAST) is the last character replaced (the index of the first character replaced is ITEM'FIRST). If no characters are read, returns in LAST an index value that is one less than ITEM'FIRST. 14

The exception END_ERROR is raised if an attempt is made to skip a file terminator. 15

16
```
procedure PUT_LINE(FILE : in FILE_TYPE; ITEM : in STRING);
procedure PUT_LINE(ITEM : in STRING);
```

17 Calls the procedure PUT for the given string, and then the procedure NEW_LINE with a spacing of one.

Notes:

18 In a literal string parameter of PUT, the enclosing string bracket characters are not output. Each doubled string bracket character in the enclosed string is output as a single string bracket character, as a consequence of the rule for string literals (see 2.6).

19 A string read by GET or written by PUT can extend over several lines.

20 *References:* current column number 14.3, end_error exception 14.4, file 14.1, file terminator 14.3, get procedure 14.3.5, line 14.3, line length 14.3, new_line procedure 14.3.4, page terminator 14.3, put procedure 14.3.4, skipping 14.3.5

14.3.7 Input-Output for Integer Types

1 The following procedures are defined in the generic package INTEGER_IO. This must be instantiated for the appropriate integer type (indicated by NUM in the specification).

2 Values are output as decimal or based literals, without underline characters or exponent, and preceded by a minus sign if negative. The format (which includes any leading spaces and minus sign) can be specified by an optional field width parameter. Values of widths of fields in output formats are of the nonnegative integer subtype FIELD. Values of bases are of the integer subtype NUMBER_BASE.

```
subtype NUMBER_BASE is INTEGER range 2 .. 16;
```

3 The default field width and base to be used by output procedures are defined by the following variables that are declared in the generic package INTEGER_IO:

```
DEFAULT_WIDTH  : FIELD := NUM'WIDTH;
DEFAULT_BASE   : NUMBER_BASE := 10;
```

4 The following procedures are provided:

5
```
procedure GET(FILE  : in FILE_TYPE; ITEM : out NUM; WIDTH : in FIELD := 0);
procedure GET(ITEM  : out NUM; WIDTH : in FIELD := 0);
```

6 If the value of the parameter WIDTH is zero, skips any leading blanks, line terminators, or page terminators, then reads a plus or a minus sign if present, then reads according to the syntax of an integer literal (which may be a based literal). If a nonzero value of WIDTH is supplied, then exactly WIDTH characters are input, or the characters (possibly none) up to a line terminator, whichever comes first; any skipped leading blanks are included in the count.

7 Returns, in the parameter ITEM, the value of type NUM that corresponds to the sequence input.

8 The exception DATA_ERROR is raised if the sequence input does not have the required syntax or if the value obtained is not of the subtype NUM.

```
procedure PUT(FILE  : in FILE_TYPE;                                          9
              ITEM  : in NUM;
              WIDTH : in FIELD := DEFAULT_WIDTH;
              BASE  : in NUMBER_BASE := DEFAULT_BASE);

procedure PUT(ITEM  : in NUM;
              WIDTH : in FIELD := DEFAULT_WIDTH;
              BASE  : in NUMBER_BASE := DEFAULT_BASE);
```

Outputs the value of the parameter ITEM as an integer literal, with no underlines, no exponent, and no leading zeros (but a single zero for the value zero), and a preceding minus sign for a negative value. 10

If the resulting sequence of characters to be output has fewer than WIDTH characters, then leading spaces are first output to make up the difference. 11

Uses the syntax for decimal literal if the parameter BASE has the value ten (either explicitly or through DEFAULT_BASE); otherwise, uses the syntax for based literal, with any letters in upper case. 12

```
procedure GET(FROM : in STRING; ITEM : out NUM; LAST : out POSITIVE);       13
```

Reads an integer value from the beginning of the given string, following the same rules as the GET procedure that reads an integer value from a file, but treating the end of the string as a file terminator. Returns, in the parameter ITEM, the value of type NUM that corresponds to the sequence input. Returns in LAST the index value such that FROM(LAST) is the last character read. 14

The exception DATA_ERROR is raised if the sequence input does not have the required syntax or if the value obtained is not of the subtype NUM. 15

```
procedure PUT(TO   : out STRING;                                             16
              ITEM : in NUM;
              BASE : in NUMBER_BASE := DEFAULT_BASE);
```

Outputs the value of the parameter ITEM to the given string, following the same rule as for output to a file, using the length of the given string as the value for WIDTH. 17

Examples: 18

```
package INT_IO is new INTEGER_IO(SMALL_INT); use INT_IO;
-- default format used at instantiation, DEFAULT_WIDTH = 4, DEFAULT_BASE = 10

PUT(126);                                -- "b126"
PUT(-126, 7);                            -- "bbb-126"
PUT(126, WIDTH => 13, BASE => 2);        -- "bbb2#1111110#"
```

References: based literal 2.4.2, blank 14.3.5, data_error exception 14.4, decimal literal 2.4.1, field subtype 14.3.5, file_type 14.1, get procedure 14.3.5, integer_io package 14.3.10, integer literal 2.4, layout_error exception 14.4, line terminator 14.3, put procedure 14.3.5, skipping 14.3.5, width 14.3.5 19

14.3.8 Input-Output for Real Types

1 The following procedures are defined in the generic packages FLOAT_IO and FIXED_IO, which must be instantiated for the appropriate floating point or fixed point type respectively (indicated by NUM in the specifications).

2 Values are output as decimal literals without underline characters. The format of each value output consists of a FORE field, a decimal point, an AFT field, and (if a nonzero EXP parameter is supplied) the letter E and an EXP field. The two possible formats thus correspond to:

```
FORE  .  AFT
```

3 and to:

```
FORE  .  AFT  E  EXP
```

4 without any spaces between these fields. The FORE field may include leading spaces, and a minus sign for negative values. The AFT field includes only decimal digits (possibly with trailing zeros). The EXP field includes the sign (plus or minus) and the exponent (possibly with leading zeros).

5 For floating point types, the default lengths of these fields are defined by the following variables that are declared in the generic package FLOAT_IO:

```
DEFAULT_FORE  : FIELD := 2;
DEFAULT_AFT   : FIELD := NUM'DIGITS-1;
DEFAULT_EXP   : FIELD := 3;
```

6 For fixed point types, the default lengths of these fields are defined by the following variables that are declared in the generic package FIXED_IO:

```
DEFAULT_FORE  : FIELD := NUM'FORE;
DEFAULT_AFT   : FIELD := NUM'AFT;
DEFAULT_EXP   : FIELD := 0;
```

7 The following procedures are provided:

8
```
procedure GET(FILE  : in FILE_TYPE; ITEM : out NUM; WIDTH : in FIELD := 0);
procedure GET(ITEM  : out NUM; WIDTH    : in FIELD := 0);
```

9 If the value of the parameter WIDTH is zero, skips any leading blanks, line terminators, or page terminators, then reads a plus or a minus sign if present, then reads according to the syntax of a real literal (which may be a based literal). If a nonzero value of WIDTH is supplied, then exactly WIDTH characters are input, or the characters (possibly none) up to a line terminator, whichever comes first; any skipped leading blanks are included in the count.

10 Returns, in the parameter ITEM, the value of type NUM that corresponds to the sequence input.

11 The exception DATA_ERROR is raised if the sequence input does not have the required syntax or if the value obtained is not of the subtype NUM.

```
procedure PUT(FILE   : in FILE_TYPE;
              ITEM   : in NUM;
              FORE   : in FIELD := DEFAULT_FORE;
              AFT    : in FIELD := DEFAULT_AFT;
              EXP    : in FIELD := DEFAULT_EXP);
```
12

```
procedure PUT(ITEM   : in NUM;
              FORE   : in FIELD := DEFAULT_FORE;
              AFT    : in FIELD := DEFAULT_AFT;
              EXP    : in FIELD := DEFAULT_EXP);
```

Outputs the value of the parameter ITEM as a decimal literal with the format defined by FORE, AFT and EXP. If the value is negative, a minus sign is included in the integer part. If EXP has the value zero, then the integer part to be output has as many digits as are needed to represent the integer part of the value of ITEM, overriding FORE if necessary, or consists of the digit zero if the value of ITEM has no integer part. 13

If EXP has a value greater than zero, then the integer part to be output has a single digit, which is nonzero except for the value 0.0 of ITEM. 14

In both cases, however, if the integer part to be output has fewer than FORE characters, including any minus sign, then leading spaces are first output to make up the difference. The number of digits of the fractional part is given by AFT, or is one if AFT equals zero. The value is rounded; a value of exactly one half in the last place may be rounded either up or down. 15

If EXP has the value zero, there is no exponent part. If EXP has a value greater than zero, then the exponent part to be output has as many digits as are needed to represent the exponent part of the value of ITEM (for which a single digit integer part is used), and includes an initial sign (plus or minus). If the exponent part to be output has fewer than EXP characters, including the sign, then leading zeros precede the digits, to make up the difference. For the value 0.0 of ITEM, the exponent has the value zero. 16

```
procedure GET(FROM : in STRING; ITEM : out NUM; LAST : out POSITIVE);
```
17

Reads a real value from the beginning of the given string, following the same rule as the GET procedure that reads a real value from a file, but treating the end of the string as a file terminator. Returns, in the parameter ITEM, the value of type NUM that corresponds to the sequence input. Returns in LAST the index value such that FROM(LAST) is the last character read. 18

The exception DATA_ERROR is raised if the sequence input does not have the required syntax, or if the value obtained is not of the subtype NUM. 19

```
procedure PUT(TO     : out STRING;
              ITEM   : in NUM;
              AFT    : in FIELD   := DEFAULT_AFT;
              EXP    : in INTEGER := DEFAULT_EXP);
```
20

Outputs the value of the parameter ITEM to the given string, following the same rule as for output to a file, using a value for FORE such that the sequence of characters output exactly fills the string, including any leading spaces. 21

22 *Examples:*

```
package REAL_IO is new FLOAT_IO(REAL); use REAL_IO;
-- default format used at instantiation, DEFAULT_EXP = 3

X : REAL := -123.4567;  --  digits 8       (see 3.5.7)

PUT(X); -- default format                      "-1.2345670E+02"
PUT(X, FORE => 5, AFT => 3, EXP => 2);    --   "bbb-1.235E+2"
PUT(X, 5, 3, 0);                          --   "b-123.457"
```

Note:

23 For an item with a positive value, if output to a string exactly fills the string without leading spaces, then output of the corresponding negative value will raise LAYOUT_ERROR.

24 *References:* aft attribute 3.5.10, based literal 2.4.2, blank 14.3.5, data_error exception 14.3.5, decimal literal 2.4.1, field subtype 14.3.5, file_type 14.1, fixed_io package 14.3.10, floating_io package 14.3.10, fore attribute 3.5.10, get procedure 14.3.5, layout_error 14.3.5, line terminator 14.3.5, put procedure 14.3.5, real literal 2.4, skipping 14.3.5, width 14.3.5

14.3.9 Input-Output for Enumeration Types

1 The following procedures are defined in the generic package ENUMERATION_IO, which must be instantiated for the appropriate enumeration type (indicated by ENUM in the specification).

2 Values are output using either upper or lower case letters for identifiers. This is specified by the parameter SET, which is of the enumeration type TYPE_SET.

```
type TYPE_SET is (LOWER_CASE, UPPER_CASE);
```

3 The format (which includes any trailing spaces) can be specified by an optional field width parameter. The default field width and letter case are defined by the following variables that are declared in the generic package ENUMERATION_IO:

```
DEFAULT_WIDTH   : FIELD := 0;
DEFAULT_SETTING : TYPE_SET := UPPER_CASE;
```

4 The following procedures are provided:

5
```
procedure GET(FILE  : in FILE_TYPE; ITEM : out ENUM);
procedure GET(ITEM  : out ENUM);
```

6 After skipping any leading blanks, line terminators, or page terminators, reads an identifier according to the syntax of this lexical element (lower and upper case being considered equivalent), or a character literal according to the syntax of this lexical element (including the apostrophes). Returns, in the parameter ITEM, the value of type ENUM that corresponds to the sequence input.

7 The exception DATA_ERROR is raised if the sequence input does not have the required syntax, or if the identifier or character literal does not correspond to a value of the subtype ENUM.

```
procedure PUT(FILE   : in FILE_TYPE;
              ITEM   : in ENUM;
              WIDTH  : in FIELD := DEFAULT_WIDTH;
              SET    : in TYPE_SET := DEFAULT_SETTING);
```
8

```
procedure PUT(ITEM   : in ENUM;
              WIDTH  : in FIELD := DEFAULT_WIDTH;
              SET    : in TYPE_SET := DEFAULT_SETTING);
```

Outputs the value of the parameter ITEM as an enumeration literal (either an identifier or a character literal). The optional parameter SET indicates whether lower case or upper case is used for identifiers; it has no effect for character literals. If the sequence of characters produced has fewer than WIDTH characters, then trailing spaces are finally output to make up the difference. 9

```
procedure GET(FROM : in STRING; ITEM : out ENUM; LAST : out POSITIVE);
```
10

Reads an enumeration value from the beginning of the given string, following the same rule as the GET procedure that reads an enumeration value from a file, but treating the end of the string as a file terminator. Returns, in the parameter ITEM, the value of type ENUM that corresponds to the sequence input. Returns in LAST the index value such that FROM (LAST) is the last character read. 11

The exception DATA_ERROR is raised if the sequence input does not have the required syntax, or if the identifier or character literal does not correspond to a value of the subtype ENUM. 12

```
procedure PUT(TO    : out STRING;
              ITEM  : in ENUM;
              SET   : in TYPE_SET := DEFAULT_SETTING);
```
13

Outputs the value of the parameter ITEM to the given string, following the same rule as for output to a file, using the length of the given string as the value for WIDTH. 14

Although the specification of the package ENUMERATION_IO would allow instantiation for an integer type, this is not the intended purpose of this generic package, and the effect of such instantiations is not defined by the language. 15

Notes:

There is a difference between PUT defined for characters, and for enumeration values. Thus 16

```
TEXT_IO.PUT('A');  --  outputs the character A

package CHAR_IO is new TEXT_IO.ENUMERATION_IO(CHARACTER);
CHAR_IO.PUT('A');  --  outputs the character 'A', between single quotes
```

The type BOOLEAN is an enumeration type, hence ENUMERATION_IO can be instantiated for this type. 17

References: blank 14.3.5, data_error 14.3.5, enumeration_io package 14.3.10, field subtype 14.3.5, file_type 14.1, get procedure 14.3.5, line terminator 14.3.5, put procedure 14.3.5, skipping 14.3.5, width 14.3.5 18

14.3.10 Specification of the Package Text_IO

```
with IO_EXCEPTIONS;
package TEXT_IO is

   type FILE_TYPE  is limited private;

   type FILE_MODE is (IN_FILE, OUT_FILE);

   type COUNT is range 0 .. implementation_defined;
   subtype POSITIVE_COUNT  is COUNT range 1 .. COUNT'LAST;
   UNBOUNDED : constant COUNT := 0; -- line and page length

   subtype FIELD          is INTEGER range 0 .. implementation_defined;
   subtype NUMBER_BASE is INTEGER range 2 .. 16;

   type TYPE_SET is (LOWER_CASE, UPPER_CASE);

   -- File Management

   procedure CREATE  ( FILE   : in out FILE_TYPE;
                       MODE  : in FILE_MODE  := OUT_FILE;
                       NAME  : in STRING     := "";
                       FORM  : in STRING     := "");

   procedure OPEN    ( FILE   : in out FILE_TYPE;
                       MODE  : in FILE_MODE;
                       NAME  : in STRING;
                       FORM  : in STRING := "");

   procedure  CLOSE   (FILE : in out FILE_TYPE);
   procedure  DELETE  (FILE : in out FILE_TYPE);
   procedure  RESET   (FILE : in out FILE_TYPE; MODE : in FILE_MODE);
   procedure  RESET   (FILE : in out FILE_TYPE);

   function   MODE    (FILE : in FILE_TYPE) return FILE_MODE ;
   function   NAME    (FILE : in FILE_TYPE) return STRING;
   function   FORM    (FILE : in FILE_TYPE) return STRING;

   function   IS_OPEN(FILE : in FILE_TYPE) return BOOLEAN;

   -- Control of default input and output files

   procedure  SET_INPUT   (FILE : in FILE_TYPE);
   procedure  SET_OUTPUT (FILE : in FILE_TYPE);


   function   STANDARD_INPUT    return FILE_TYPE;
   function   STANDARD_OUTPUT   return FILE_TYPE;

   function   CURRENT_INPUT     return FILE_TYPE;
   function   CURRENT_OUTPUT    return FILE_TYPE;
```

```
-- Specification of line and page lengths

procedure  SET_LINE_LENGTH   (FILE : in FILE_TYPE; TO : in COUNT);
procedure  SET_LINE_LENGTH   (TO : in COUNT);

procedure  SET_PAGE_LENGTH   (FILE : in FILE_TYPE; TO : in COUNT);
procedure  SET_PAGE_LENGTH   (TO : in COUNT);

function   LINE_LENGTH (FILE : in FILE_TYPE) return COUNT;
function   LINE_LENGTH   return COUNT;

function   PAGE_LENGTH (FILE : in FILE_TYPE) return COUNT;
function   PAGE_LENGTH   return COUNT;

-- Column, Line, and Page Control

procedure  NEW_LINE     (FILE : in FILE_TYPE; SPACING : in POSITIVE_COUNT := 1);
procedure  NEW_LINE     (SPACING : in POSITIVE_COUNT := 1);

procedure  SKIP_LINE    (FILE : in FILE_TYPE; SPACING : in POSITIVE_COUNT := 1);
procedure  SKIP_LINE    (SPACING : in POSITIVE_COUNT := 1);

function   END_OF_LINE  (FILE : in FILE_TYPE) return BOOLEAN;
function   END_OF_LINE   return BOOLEAN;

procedure  NEW_PAGE     (FILE : in FILE_TYPE);
procedure  NEW_PAGE;

procedure  SKIP_PAGE    (FILE : in FILE_TYPE);
procedure  SKIP_PAGE;

function   END_OF_PAGE (FILE : in FILE_TYPE) return BOOLEAN;
function   END_OF_PAGE  return BOOLEAN;

function   END_OF_FILE  (FILE : in FILE_TYPE) return BOOLEAN;
function   END_OF_FILE   return BOOLEAN;


procedure  SET_COL (FILE  : in FILE_TYPE; TO : in POSITIVE_COUNT);
procedure  SET_COL (TO    : in POSITIVE_COUNT);

procedure  SET_LINE (FILE  : in FILE_TYPE; TO : in POSITIVE_COUNT);
procedure  SET_LINE (TO    : in POSITIVE_COUNT);


function COL  (FILE : in FILE_TYPE) return POSITIVE_COUNT;
function COL    return POSITIVE_COUNT;

function LINE  (FILE : in FILE_TYPE) return POSITIVE_COUNT;
function LINE return POSITIVE_COUNT;

function PAGE (FILE : in FILE_TYPE) return POSITIVE_COUNT;
function PAGE   return POSITIVE_COUNT;
```

```
-- Character Input-Output

procedure GET(FILE   : in   FILE_TYPE; ITEM : out CHARACTER);
procedure GET(ITEM   : out  CHARACTER);
procedure PUT(FILE   : in   FILE_TYPE; ITEM : in CHARACTER);
procedure PUT(ITEM   : in   CHARACTER);

-- String Input-Output

procedure GET(FILE   : in   FILE_TYPE; ITEM : out STRING);
procedure GET(ITEM   : out  STRING);
procedure PUT(FILE   : in   FILE_TYPE; ITEM : in STRING);
procedure PUT(ITEM   : in   STRING);

procedure GET_LINE(FILE : in    FILE_TYPE;  ITEM : out STRING; LAST : out NATURAL);
procedure GET_LINE(ITEM : out   STRING; LAST : out NATURAL);
procedure PUT_LINE(FILE : in    FILE_TYPE; ITEM : in STRING);
procedure PUT_LINE(ITEM : in    STRING);

-- Generic package for Input-Output of Integer Types

generic
  type NUM is range <>;
package INTEGER_IO is

  DEFAULT_WIDTH  : FIELD := NUM'WIDTH;
  DEFAULT_BASE   : NUMBER_BASE := 10;

  procedure GET(FILE  : in   FILE_TYPE; ITEM : out NUM; WIDTH : in FIELD := 0);
  procedure GET(ITEM  : out  NUM; WIDTH : in FIELD := 0);

  procedure PUT(FILE    : in FILE_TYPE;
                ITEM    : in NUM;
                WIDTH   : in FIELD := DEFAULT_WIDTH;
                BASE    : in NUMBER_BASE := DEFAULT_BASE);
  procedure PUT(ITEM    : in NUM;
                WIDTH   : in FIELD := DEFAULT_WIDTH;
                BASE    : in NUMBER_BASE := DEFAULT_BASE);

  procedure GET(FROM  : in   STRING; ITEM : out NUM; LAST : out POSITIVE);
  procedure PUT(TO    : out STRING;
                ITEM  : in NUM;
                BASE  : in NUMBER_BASE := DEFAULT_BASE);

end INTEGER_IO;
```

```
-- Generic packages for Input-Output of Real Types

generic
  type NUM is digits <>;
package FLOAT_IO is

  DEFAULT_FORE  : FIELD := 2;
  DEFAULT_AFT   : FIELD := NUM'DIGITS-1;
  DEFAULT_EXP   : FIELD := 3;

  procedure GET(FILE : in FILE_TYPE; ITEM : out NUM; WIDTH : in FIELD := 0);
  procedure GET(ITEM : out NUM; WIDTH : in FIELD := 0);

  procedure PUT(FILE : in FILE_TYPE;
                ITEM : in NUM;
                FORE : in FIELD := DEFAULT_FORE;
                AFT  : in FIELD := DEFAULT_AFT;
                EXP  : in FIELD := DEFAULT_EXP);
  procedure PUT(ITEM : in NUM;
                FORE : in FIELD := DEFAULT_FORE;
                AFT  : in FIELD := DEFAULT_AFT;
                EXP  : in FIELD := DEFAULT_EXP);

  procedure GET(FROM : in STRING; ITEM : out NUM; LAST : out POSITIVE);
  procedure PUT(TO   : out STRING;
                ITEM : in NUM;
                AFT  : in FIELD := DEFAULT_AFT;
                EXP  : in FIELD := DEFAULT_EXP);
end FLOAT_IO;

generic
  type NUM is delta <>;
package FIXED_IO is

  DEFAULT_FORE  : FIELD := NUM'FORE;
  DEFAULT_AFT   : FIELD := NUM'AFT;
  DEFAULT_EXP   : FIELD := 0;

  procedure GET(FILE : in FILE_TYPE; ITEM : out NUM; WIDTH : in FIELD := 0);
  procedure GET(ITEM : out NUM; WIDTH : in FIELD := 0);

  procedure PUT(FILE : in FILE_TYPE;
                ITEM : in NUM;
                FORE : in FIELD := DEFAULT_FORE;
                AFT  : in FIELD := DEFAULT_AFT;
                EXP  : in FIELD := DEFAULT_EXP);
  procedure PUT(ITEM : in NUM;
                FORE : in FIELD := DEFAULT_FORE;
                AFT  : in FIELD := DEFAULT_AFT;
                EXP  : in FIELD := DEFAULT_EXP);

  procedure GET(FROM : in  STRING; ITEM : out NUM; LAST : out POSITIVE);
  procedure PUT(TO   : out STRING;
                ITEM : in NUM;
                AFT  : in FIELD := DEFAULT_AFT;
                EXP  : in FIELD := DEFAULT_EXP);

end FIXED_IO;
```

```
-- Generic package for Input-Output of Enumeration Types

generic
   type ENUM is (<>);
package ENUMERATION_IO is

   DEFAULT_WIDTH    : FIELD := 0;
   DEFAULT_SETTING  : TYPE_SET := UPPER_CASE;

   procedure GET(FILE     : in FILE_TYPE; ITEM : out ENUM);
   procedure GET(ITEM     : out ENUM);

   procedure PUT(FILE     : in FILE_TYPE;
                 ITEM     : in ENUM;
                 WIDTH    : in FIELD      := DEFAULT_WIDTH;
                 SET      : in TYPE_SET   := DEFAULT_SETTING);
   procedure PUT(ITEM     : in ENUM;
                 WIDTH    : in FIELD      := DEFAULT_WIDTH;
                 SET      : in TYPE_SET   := DEFAULT_SETTING);

   procedure GET(FROM  : in   STRING; ITEM : out ENUM; LAST : out POSITIVE);
   procedure PUT(TO    : out  STRING;
                 ITEM  : in   ENUM;
                 SET   : in   TYPE_SET := DEFAULT_SETTING);
end ENUMERATION_IO;

-- Exceptions

STATUS_ERROR  : exception renames IO_EXCEPTIONS.STATUS_ERROR;
MODE_ERROR    : exception renames IO_EXCEPTIONS.MODE_ERROR;
NAME_ERROR    : exception renames IO_EXCEPTIONS.NAME_ERROR;
USE_ERROR     : exception renames IO_EXCEPTIONS.USE_ERROR;
DEVICE_ERROR  : exception renames IO_EXCEPTIONS.DEVICE_ERROR;
END_ERROR     : exception renames IO_EXCEPTIONS.END_ERROR;
DATA_ERROR    : exception renames IO_EXCEPTIONS.DATA_ERROR;
LAYOUT_ERROR  : exception renames IO_EXCEPTIONS.LAYOUT_ERROR;

private
   -- implementation-dependent
end TEXT_IO;
```

14.4 Exceptions in Input-Output

1 The following exceptions can be raised by input-output operations. They are declared in the package IO_EXCEPTIONS, defined in section 14.5; this package is named in the context clause for each of the three input-output packages. Only outline descriptions are given of the conditions under which NAME_ERROR, USE_ERROR, and DEVICE_ERROR are raised; for full details see Appendix F. If more than one error condition exists, the corresponding exception that appears earliest in the following list is the one that is raised.

2 The exception STATUS_ERROR is raised by an attempt to operate upon a file that is not open, and by an attempt to open a file that is already open.

3 The exception MODE_ERROR is raised by an attempt to read from, or test for the end of, a file whose current mode is OUT_FILE, and also by an attempt to write to a file whose current mode is IN_FILE. In the case of TEXT_IO, the exception MODE_ERROR is also raised by specifying a file whose current mode is OUT_FILE in a call of SET_INPUT, SKIP_LINE, END_OF_LINE, SKIP_PAGE, or END_OF_PAGE; and by specifying a file whose current mode is IN_FILE in a call of SET_OUTPUT, SET_LINE_LENGTH, SET_PAGE_LENGTH, LINE_LENGTH, PAGE_LENGTH, NEW_LINE, or NEW_PAGE.

4 The exception NAME_ERROR is raised by a call of CREATE or OPEN if the string given for the parameter NAME does not allow the identification of an external file. For example, this exception is raised if the string is improper, or, alternatively, if either none or more than one external file corresponds to the string.

5 The exception USE_ERROR is raised if an operation is attempted that is not possible for reasons that depend on characteristics of the external file. For example, this exception is raised by the procedure CREATE, among other circumstances, if the given mode is OUT_FILE but the form specifies an input only device, if the parameter FORM specifies invalid access rights, or if an external file with the given name already exists and overwriting is not allowed.

6 The exception DEVICE_ERROR is raised if an input-output operation cannot be completed because of a malfunction of the underlying system.

7 The exception END_ERROR is raised by an attempt to skip (read past) the end of a file.

8 The exception DATA_ERROR may be raised by the procedure READ if the element read cannot be interpreted as a value of the required type. This exception is also raised by a procedure GET (defined in the package TEXT_IO) if the input character sequence fails to satisfy the required syntax, or if the value input does not belong to the range of the required type or subtype.

9 The exception LAYOUT_ERROR is raised (in text input-output) by COL, LINE, or PAGE if the value returned exceeds COUNT'LAST. The exception LAYOUT_ERROR is also raised on output by an attempt to set column or line numbers in excess of specified maximum line or page lengths, respectively (excluding the unbounded cases). It is also raised by an attempt to PUT too many characters to a string.

10 *References:* col function 14.3.4, create procedure 14.2.1, end_of_line function 14.3.4, end_of_page function 14.3.4, external file 14.1, file 14.1, form string 14.1, get procedure 14.3.5, in_file 14.1, io_exceptions package 14.5, line function 14.3.4, line_length function 14.3.4, name string 14.1, new_line procedure 14.3.4, new_page procedure 14.3.4, open procedure 14.2.1, out_file 14.1, page function 14.3.4, page_length function 14.3.4, put procedure 14.3.5, read procedure 14.2.2 14.2.3, set_input procedure 14.3.2, set_line_length 14.3.3, set_page_length 14.3.3, set_output 14.3.2, skip_line procedure 14.3.4, skip_page procedure 14.3.4, text_io package 14.3

14.5 Specification of the Package IO_Exceptions

1 This package defines the exceptions needed by the packages SEQUENTIAL_IO, DIRECT_IO, and TEXT_IO.

2
```
package IO_EXCEPTIONS is

   STATUS_ERROR  : exception;
   MODE_ERROR    : exception;
   NAME_ERROR    : exception;
   USE_ERROR     : exception;
   DEVICE_ERROR  : exception;
   END_ERROR     : exception;
   DATA_ERROR    : exception;
   LAYOUT_ERROR  : exception;

end IO_EXCEPTIONS;
```

14.6 Low Level Input-Output

1 A low level input-output operation is an operation acting on a physical device. Such an operation is handled by using one of the (overloaded) predefined procedures SEND_CONTROL and RECEIVE_CONTROL.

2 A procedure SEND_CONTROL may be used to send control information to a physical device. A procedure RECEIVE_CONTROL may be used to monitor the execution of an input-output operation by requesting information from the physical device.

3 Such procedures are declared in the standard package LOW_LEVEL_IO and have two parameters identifying the device and the data. However, the kinds and formats of the control information will depend on the physical characteristics of the machine and the device. Hence, the types of the parameters are implementation-defined. Overloaded definitions of these procedures should be provided for the supported devices.

4 The visible part of the package defining these procedures is outlined as follows:

5
```
package LOW_LEVEL_IO is
   -- declarations of the possible types for DEVICE and DATA;
   -- declarations of overloaded procedures for these types:
   procedure SEND_CONTROL     (DEVICE : device_type; DATA : in out data_type);
   procedure RECEIVE_CONTROL  (DEVICE : device_type; DATA : in out data_type);
end;
```

6 The bodies of the procedures SEND_CONTROL and RECEIVE_CONTROL for various devices can be supplied in the body of the package LOW_LEVEL_IO. These procedure bodies may be written with code statements.

14.7 Example of Input-Output

The following example shows the use of some of the text input-output facilities in a dialogue with a user at a terminal. The user is prompted to type a color, and the program responds by giving the number of items of that color available in stock, according to an inventory. The default input and output files are used. For simplicity, all the requisite instantiations are given within one subprogram; in practice, a package, separate from the procedure, would be used.

```
with TEXT_IO; use TEXT_IO;
procedure DIALOGUE is
  type COLOR is (WHITE, RED, ORANGE, YELLOW, GREEN, BLUE, BROWN);
  package COLOR_IO is new ENUMERATION_IO(ENUM => COLOR);
  package NUMBER_IO is new INTEGER_IO(INTEGER);
  use COLOR_IO, NUMBER_IO;

  INVENTORY : array (COLOR) of INTEGER := (20, 17, 43, 10, 28, 173, 87);
  CHOICE : COLOR;

  procedure ENTER_COLOR (SELECTION : out COLOR) is
  begin
    loop
      begin
        PUT ("Color selected: ");    --  prompts user
        GET (SELECTION);             --  accepts color typed, or raises exception
        return;
      exception
        when DATA_ERROR =>
          PUT("Invalid color, try again.  ");  --  user has typed new line
          NEW_LINE(2);
          --  completes execution of the block statement
      end;
    end loop;  --  repeats the block statement until color accepted
  end;
begin --  statements of DIALOGUE;

  NUMBER_IO.DEFAULT_WIDTH := 5;

  loop

    ENTER_COLOR(CHOICE);  --  user types color and new line

    SET_COL(5);   PUT(CHOICE); PUT(" items available:");
    SET_COL(40);  PUT(INVENTORY(CHOICE));  --  default width is 5
    NEW_LINE;
  end loop;
end DIALOGUE;
```

Example of an interaction (characters typed by the user are italicized):

```
Color selected:  Black
Invalid color, try again.

Color selected:  Blue
    BLUE  items available:             173
Color selected:  Yellow
    YELLOW  items available:            10
```

Appendix B

Case Study Ada Programs

Case Study 5.1

```
With Sequential_IO;
With Text_IO;
PACKAGE Ch5Struc Is
    SubType Id_String Is String ( 1 .. 3 );
    SubType String10 Is String ( 1 .. 10 );
    Type Car_Master_Record Is
             Record
                 id_number : Id_String;
                 make      : String10;
                 style     : String10;
                 model     : String10;
                 mileage   : String10;
                 color     : String10;
             End Record;
    Type Car_Transaction_Record  Is
             Record
                 update_code : Character;
                 id_number   : Id_String;
                 make        : String10;
                 style       : String10;
                 model       : String10;
                 mileage     : String10;
                 color       : String10;
             End Record;
    PACKAGE Car_IO Is New Sequential_IO ( Car_master_record );
    master_record : Car_master_record;
    masterfile    : Car_IO.File_Type;
    new_record    : Car_Master_Record;
    newfile       : Car_IO.File_Type;
    SENTINEL      : Id_String := "ZZZ";
    transaction   : Car_Transaction_Record;
    transfile     : Text_IO.File_Type;
END Ch5Struc;

With Text_IO;
With Sequential_IO;
With Ch5Struc;
Use Ch5Struc;
PROCEDURE Alg5_4 Is
    PACKAGE Integer_IO Is New Text_IO.Integer_IO ( Integer );
    adds_processed      : Integer := 0;
    BLANKS              : Constant String ( 1 .. 6 ) := "      ";
    changes_processed   : Integer := 0;
    deletefound         : Boolean;
    deletes_processed   : Integer := 0;
```

```
     masters_read,
     new_masters_written : Integer := 0;
     new_record          : Car_Master_Record;
     trans_error         : Integer := 0;
     trans_read          : Integer := 0;

PROCEDURE Get_Next_Trans Is
BEGIN  -- Get_Next_Trans
    If Text_IO.End_Of_File ( transfile ) Then
        transaction.id_number := SENTINEL;
    Else
        trans_read := trans_read + 1;
        Text_IO.Get ( transfile, transaction.update_code );
        Text_IO.Put ( BLANKS );
        Text_IO.Put ( transaction.update_code );
        Text_IO.Put ( ' ' );
        Text_IO.Get ( transfile, transaction.id_number );
        Text_IO.Put ( transaction.id_number );
        Text_IO.Put ( ' ' );
        Case transaction.update_code Is
            When 'A' =>
                Text_IO.Get ( transfile, transaction.make );
                Text_IO.Put ( "  " );
                Text_IO.Put ( transaction.make );
                Text_IO.Get ( transfile, transaction.style );
                Text_IO.Put ( ' ' );
                Text_IO.Put ( transaction.style );
                Text_IO.Get ( transfile, transaction.model );
                Text_IO.Put ( ' ' );
                Text_IO.Put ( transaction.model );
                Text_IO.Get ( transfile, transaction.mileage );
                Text_IO.Put ( ' ' );
                Text_IO.Put ( transaction.mileage );
                Text_IO.Get ( transfile, transaction.color );
                Text_IO.Put ( ' ' );
                Text_IO.Put ( transaction.color );
                Text_IO.Put ( ' ' );
            When 'C' =>
                Text_IO.Get ( transfile, transaction.mileage );
                Text_IO.Put ( "  " );
                Text_IO.Put ( transaction.mileage );
                Text_IO.Put ( "              " );
            When 'D' =>
                Text_IO.Put ( "                                          " );
            When Others =>
                Text_IO.Put ( "                                 " );
                Text_IO.Put ( "invalid update code" );
        End Case;
        Text_IO.Skip_Line ( transfile );
    End If;
END Get_Next_Trans;

PROCEDURE Get_Next_Master Is
BEGIN  -- Get_Next_Master
    If  Car_IO.End_Of_File ( masterfile ) Then
        master_record.id_number := SENTINEL;
    Else
        masters_read := masters_read + 1;
```

```
        Car_IO.Read ( masterfile, master_record );
    End If;
EXCEPTION
    When Car_IO.Status_Error => Null;  -- master file does not exist
END Get_Next_Master;

PROCEDURE Change_Master ( hold_record : In Out Car_master_record ) Is
BEGIN  -- Change_Master
    Text_IO.Put_Line ( "Change_master" );
    hold_record.mileage := transaction.mileage;
    changes_processed := changes_processed + 1;
END Change_Master;

PROCEDURE Build_New_Record Is
                -- Build_new_record moves all the information in the
                -- transaction into new_record
BEGIN  -- Build_New_Record
    Text_IO.Put_Line ( "Build_new_record" );
    new_record :=  ( transaction.id_number, transaction.make, transaction.style,
                    transaction.model, transaction.mileage, transaction.color );
END Build_New_Record;

PROCEDURE Match Is
BEGIN  -- Match
    Case transaction.update_code Is
        When 'A' =>
            Text_IO.Put_Line ( "invalid add; on master file" );
            trans_error := trans_error + 1;
        When 'C' =>
            Change_master ( master_record );
        When 'D' =>
            deletes_processed := deletes_processed + 1;
            Text_IO.Put_Line ( "deleted" );
            Get_next_master;
        When Others =>
            trans_error := trans_error + 1;
            Text_IO.Put_Line ( ";on master file" );
    End Case;
    Get_Next_Trans;
END Match;

PROCEDURE Nomatch Is
    PROCEDURE MatchesToAdds Is
    BEGIN  -- MatchesToAdds
        Case transaction.update_code Is
           When 'A'=>
               Text_IO.Put_Line ( "duplicate add" );
               trans_error := trans_error + 1;
           When 'C' =>
               Change_master ( new_record );
           When 'D' =>
               deletefound := TRUE;
               Text_IO.Put_line ( "Deleted" );
               deletes_processed := deletes_processed + 1;
           When Others =>
               trans_error := trans_error + 1;
               Text_IO.Put_Line ( "& an add in run" );
        End Case;
    END MatchesToAdds;
```

```
        PROCEDURE NoMatchError Is
        BEGIN  -- NoMatchError
            Text_IO.Put_Line ( ";not on master file" );
            trans_error := trans_error + 1;
        END NoMatchError;

    BEGIN  -- Nomatch
        Case transaction.update_code Is
            When 'A' =>
                 Build_new_record;
                 adds_processed := adds_processed + 1;
                 deletefound := FALSE;
                 Get_Next_Trans;
                 Loop
                     Exit When ( transaction.id_number = SENTINEL )
                          Or   ( transaction.id_number /= new_record.id_number )
                          Or   ( deletefound );
                     MatchesToAdds;
                     Get_Next_Trans;
                 End Loop;
                 If Not deletefound Then
                     Car_IO.Write ( newfile, new_record );
                     new_masters_written := new_masters_written + 1;
                 End If;
            When 'C' =>
                NoMatchError;
                Get_Next_Trans;
            When 'D' =>
                NoMatchError;
                Get_Next_Trans;
            When Others =>
                NoMatchError;
                Get_Next_Trans;
        End Case;
    END Nomatch;

    PROCEDURE Print_counts Is

    BEGIN  -- Print_counts
        Text_IO.New_Page;
        Text_IO.Put ( BLANKS );
        Integer_IO.Put ( masters_read );
        Text_IO.Put_Line ( " master records read" );
        Text_IO.Put ( BLANKS );
        Integer_IO.Put ( trans_read );
        Text_IO.Put_Line ( " transactions read" );
        Text_IO.Put ( BLANKS );
        Text_IO.Put ( BLANKS );
        Integer_IO.Put ( trans_error );
        Text_IO.Put_Line ( " transactions in error" );
        Text_IO.Put ( BLANKS );
        Text_IO.Put ( BLANKS );
        Integer_IO.Put ( adds_processed );
        Text_IO.Put_Line ( " add transactions processed" );
        Text_IO.Put ( BLANKS );
        Text_IO.Put ( BLANKS );
        Integer_IO.Put ( changes_processed );
        Text_IO.Put_Line ( " changes processed" );
```

```
     Text_IO.Put ( BLANKS );
     Text_IO.Put ( BLANKS );
     Integer_IO.Put ( deletes_processed );
     Text_IO.Put_Line ( " deletes processed" );
     Text_IO.Put ( BLANKS );
     Integer_IO.Put ( new_masters_written );
     Text_IO.Put_Line ( " new master records written" );
 END Print_counts;

PROCEDURE List_Master Is

BEGIN  -- List_Master
    Car_IO.Open ( newfile, Car_IO.IN_FILE, "NEWMSTR.DAT" );
    masters_read := 0;
    Text_IO.New_Page;
    Text_IO.Put ( BLANKS );
    Text_IO.Put_Line ( "***** dump of new master file *****" );
    Loop
        Exit When Car_IO.End_Of_File (newfile);
        masters_read := masters_read + 1;
        Car_IO.Read ( newfile, new_record );
        Text_IO.Put ( BLANKS );
        Text_IO.Put ( new_record.id_number );
        Text_IO.Put ( "---" );
        Text_IO.Put ( new_record.make );
        Text_IO.Put ( "---" );
        Text_IO.Put ( new_record.style );
        Text_IO.Put ( "---" );
        Text_IO.Put ( new_record.model );
        Text_IO.Put ( "---" );
        Text_IO.Put ( new_record.mileage );
        Text_IO.Put ( "---" );
        Text_IO.Put ( new_record.color );
        Text_IO.New_Line;
    End Loop;
    Text_IO.Put ( BLANKS );
    Integer_IO.Put ( masters_read );
    Text_IO.Put_Line ( "new master records read" );
    Car_IO.Close ( newfile );
END List_master;

BEGIN  -- Alg5_4
    BEGIN
        Car_IO.Open ( masterfile, Car_IO.IN_FILE, "CARMSTR.DAT" );
    EXCEPTION   -- master file does not exist
        When Car_IO.Name_Error => master_record.id_number := SENTINEL;
    END;
    Text_IO.Open ( transfile, Text_IO.IN_FILE, "CARTRANS.TXT" );
    Car_IO.Create ( newfile, Car_IO.OUT_FILE, "NEWMSTR.DAT" );
    Get_Next_Trans;
    Get_Next_Master;
    Loop
        Exit When ( master_record.id_number = SENTINEL )
              And ( transaction.id_number = SENTINEL );
        If ( master_record.id_number < transaction.id_number ) Then
            Car_IO.Write ( newfile, master_record );
            new_masters_written := new_masters_written + 1;
            Get_Next_Master;
```

```
        ElsIf  master_record.id_number = transaction.id_number Then
           Match;
        Else       -- master key > trans key
           Nomatch;
        End If;
    End Loop;
    Text_IO.Close ( transfile );
    Car_IO.Close ( newfile );
    Print_counts;
    List_master;
    Car_IO.Close ( masterfile );
EXCEPTION
    When Car_IO.Status_Error => Null;  -- master file did not exist
END Alg5_4;

With Text_IO;
With Sequential_IO;
With Ch5Struc;
Use Ch5Struc;
PROCEDURE Alg5_5 Is
    PACKAGE Float_IO Is New Text_IO.Float_IO ( Float );
    PACKAGE Integer_IO Is New Text_IO.Integer_IO ( Integer );
    BLANKS            : Constant String (1..6) := "      ";
    current_key       : Id_String;
    hold_master       : Car_Master_Record;
    master_allocated  : Boolean;

    PROCEDURE Get_Next_Trans Is
    BEGIN
        If Text_IO.End_Of_File ( transfile ) Then
            transaction.update_code := ' ';
            transaction.id_number := SENTINEL;
        Else
            Text_IO.Get  ( transfile, transaction.update_code );
            Text_IO.Get ( transfile, transaction.id_number );
        End If;
        Text_IO.Put ( transaction.update_code );
        Text_IO.Put ( " " );
        Text_IO.Put ( transaction.id_number );
    END Get_Next_Trans;

    PROCEDURE Get_Next_Master Is
    BEGIN  -- Get_Next_Master
        If Car_IO.End_Of_File ( masterfile ) Then
            master_record.id_number := sentinel;
        Else
            Car_IO.Read ( masterfile, master_record );
        End If;
    EXCEPTION   -- master file does not exist
        When Car_IO.Status_Error => Null;
    END Get_Next_Master;

    PROCEDURE Choose_Smaller_Key Is
    BEGIN
        If transaction.id_number < master_record.id_number Then
            current_key := transaction.id_number;
        Else
            current_key := master_record.id_number;
```

```
    End If;
END Choose_Smaller_Key;

PROCEDURE Check_Initial_Status_Of_Master Is
BEGIN
    If master_record.id_number = current_key Then
        hold_master := master_record;
        master_allocated := TRUE;
        Get_Next_Master;
    Else
        master_allocated := FALSE;
    End If;
END Check_Initial_Status_Of_Master;

PROCEDURE Check_Final_Status_Of_Master Is
BEGIN
    If master_allocated Then
        Car_IO.Write ( newfile, hold_master );
    End If;
END Check_Final_Status_Of_Master;

PROCEDURE Change Is
BEGIN
    -- Change master record
    Text_IO.Get ( transfile, hold_master.mileage );
END Change;

PROCEDURE Process_One_Transaction Is
BEGIN
    If master_allocated Then
        Case transaction.update_code Is
            When 'A' =>
                Text_IO.Put_Line ( " duplicate add" );
            When 'C' =>
                Change;
                Text_IO.Put_Line ( " change" );
            When 'D' =>
                master_allocated := FALSE;
                Text_IO.Put_Line ( " deleted" );
            When Others =>
                Text_IO.Put ( transaction.update_code );
                Text_IO.Put_Line ( " Illegal update code" );
        End Case;
        Text_IO.Skip_Line ( transfile );
    Else
        Case transaction.update_code Is
            When 'A' =>
                Text_IO.Put ( " addition" );
                Text_IO.Put_Line ( transaction.id_number );
                hold_master.id_number := transaction.id_number;
                Text_IO.Get ( transfile, hold_master.make );
                Text_IO.Get ( transfile, hold_master.style );
                Text_IO.Get ( transfile, hold_master.model );
                Text_IO.Get ( transfile, hold_master.mileage );
                Text_IO.Get ( transfile, hold_master.color );
                master_allocated := TRUE;
            When 'C' | 'D' =>
                Text_IO.Put_Line ( " no matching master record" );
```

```
                When Others =>
                    Text_IO.Put ( transaction.update_code );
                    Text_IO.Put_Line ( " Illegal update code" );
            End Case;
            Text_IO.Skip_Line ( transfile );
        End If;
        Get_Next_Trans;
    END Process_One_Transaction;

  PROCEDURE List_master Is
    masters_read : Integer := 0;
    new_record   : Car_Master_Record;
  BEGIN  -- List_master
      Car_IO.Open ( newfile, Car_IO.IN_FILE, "newmstr.dat" );
      Text_IO.New_Page;
      Text_IO.Put ( BLANKS );
      Text_IO.Put_Line ( "***** dump of new master file *****" );
      Loop
          Exit When Car_IO.End_Of_File (newfile);
          masters_read := masters_read + 1;
          Car_IO.Read ( newfile, new_record );
          Text_IO.Put ( BLANKS );
          Text_IO.Put ( new_record.id_number );
          Text_IO.Put ( "---" );
          Text_IO.Put ( new_record.make );
          Text_IO.Put ( "---" );
          Text_IO.Put ( new_record.style );
          Text_IO.Put ( "---" );
          Text_IO.Put ( new_record.model );
          Text_IO.Put ( "---" );
          Text_IO.Put ( new_record.mileage );
          Text_IO.Put ( "---" );
          Text_IO.Put ( new_record.color );
          Text_IO.New_Line;
      End Loop;
      Text_IO.Put ( BLANKS );
      Integer_IO.Put ( masters_read );
      Text_IO.Put_Line ( " new master records read" );
      Car_IO.Close ( newfile );
  END List_master;

BEGIN  -- Alg5_5
    BEGIN
        Car_IO.Open (masterfile, Car_IO.IN_FILE, "CARMSTR.DAT");
    EXCEPTION        -- master file does not exist
        When Car_IO.Name_Error =>  master_record.id_number := SENTINEL;
    END;
    Car_IO.Create (newfile, Car_IO.OUT_FILE, "NEWMSTR.DAT");
    BEGIN
        Text_IO.Open (transfile, Text_IO.IN_FILE, "CARTRANS.TXT");
    EXCEPTION
        When Text_IO.Name_Error => Null;
    END;
    Get_Next_Trans;
    Get_Next_Master;
    Choose_Smaller_Key;
    Loop
        Exit When current_key = SENTINEL;
```

```
        Check_Initial_Status_Of_Master;
        Loop
            Exit When transaction.id_number /= current_key;
            Process_One_Transaction;
        End Loop;
        Check_Final_Status_Of_Master;
        Choose_Smaller_Key;
    End Loop;
    Car_IO.Close ( newfile );
    Text_IO.Close ( transfile );
    List_Master;
    Text_IO.New_Page;
    Car_IO.Close ( masterfile );
EXCEPTION
    When Car_IO.Status_Error => Null;
END Alg5_5;
```

Case Study 7.1

```
With Direct_IO;
PACKAGE Ch7Struc Is
    prime_file_size : Constant Positive := 17;
    SubType Key_Type Is String ( 1 .. 3 );
    SubType String10 Is String ( 1 .. 10 );
    Type Car_Record_Type Is Record
                            id_number : Key_Type := "   ";
                            make      : String10 := "          ";
                            style     : String10 := "          ";
                            model     : String10 := "          ";
                            mileage   : String10 := "          ";
                            color     : String10 := "          ";
                        End Record;
    Type Rel_Record_Type Is Record
                            info : Car_Record_Type;
                            link : Integer := -1;
                        End Record;

    PACKAGE Rel_IO Is New Direct_IO ( Rel_Record_Type );
    FUNCTION Hash ( key : Key_Type ) Return Positive;
    blank_id_number : Constant Key_Type := "   ";
END Ch7Struc;
PACKAGE Body Ch7Struc Is
    FUNCTION Hash ( key : Key_Type ) Return Positive Is
        sum : Positive;
    BEGIN  -- Hash
        sum := Character'Pos ( key(1) ) * 10;
        For i In 2 .. 3 Loop
            If  ( key(i) >= '0' )
            And ( key(i) <= '9' ) Then
                sum := sum + Character'Pos ( key(i) )
                           - Character'Pos ( '0' );
                Exit;
            End If;
        End Loop;
```

```
        Return sum MOD prime_file_size + 1 ;
    END Hash;
END Ch7Struc;

With Text_IO,
     Ch7Struc;
PROCEDURE Alg7_1 Is

    PACKAGE Integer_IO Is New Text_IO.Integer_IO ( Integer );

    carfile         : Text_IO.File_Type;
    car_record      : Ch7Struc.Car_Record_Type;
    error_flag      : Boolean;
    file_size       : Constant Positive := 18;
    lstfile         : Text_IO.File_Type;
    relative_master : Ch7Struc.Rel_Record_Type;
    relativefile    : Ch7Struc.Rel_IO.File_Type;
    relative_index  : Ch7Struc.Rel_IO.Positive_Count;

    PROCEDURE Input_Car Is
        update_code : Character;
    BEGIN
        Text_IO.Get ( carfile, update_code );
        Text_IO.Get ( carfile, car_record.id_number );
        Text_IO.Put ( lstfile, car_record.id_number );
        Text_IO.Put ( lstfile,  ' ' );
        Text_IO.Get ( carfile, car_record.make );
        Text_IO.Put ( lstfile,  "  " );
        Text_IO.Put ( lstfile,  car_record.make );
        Text_IO.Get ( carfile, car_record.style );
        Text_IO.Put ( lstfile,  ' ' );
        Text_IO.Put ( lstfile,  car_record.style );
        Text_IO.Get ( carfile, car_record.model );
        Text_IO.Get ( carfile, car_record.mileage );
        Text_IO.Get ( carfile, car_record.color );
        Text_IO.Skip_Line ( carfile );
    END Input_Car;

    PROCEDURE Create_File Is
        PROCEDURE Overflow Is
            hold : Ch7Struc.Rel_Record_Type;
            next : Integer;
        BEGIN
            Text_IO.Put ( lstfile, "stored in overflow " );
            next := Integer ( Ch7Struc.Rel_IO.Size ( relativefile ) ) + 1;
            Integer_IO.Put ( lstfile, next, 0 );
            hold := ( car_record, relative_master.link );
            relative_master.link := next;
            Ch7Struc.Rel_IO.Write ( relativefile, relative_master,
                                    relative_index );
            Ch7Struc.Rel_IO.Write ( relativefile, hold,
                                    Ch7Struc.Rel_IO.Positive_Count ( next ) );
        END Overflow;

    BEGIN  -- Create_File
        Loop
            Exit When Text_IO.End_Of_File ( carfile );
            Input_Car;
            Text_IO.Put ( lstfile, car_record.id_number );
```

```
            Text_IO.Put ( lstfile, ' ' );
            relative_index := Ch7Struc.Rel_IO.Positive_Count
                            ( Ch7Struc.Hash ( car_record.id_number ) );
            Text_IO.Put ( lstfile, "hashes to " );
            Integer_IO.Put ( lstfile, Integer ( relative_index ) );
            Text_IO.Put ( lstfile, " " );
            Ch7Struc.Rel_IO.Read ( relativefile, relative_master,
                                   relative_index );
            If relative_master.info.id_number = "     " Then
                relative_master := ( car_record, -1 );
                Ch7Struc.Rel_IO.Write ( relativefile, relative_master,
                                        relative_index );
            Else
                Text_IO.Put ( lstfile, "synonym ");
                Overflow;
            End If;
            Text_IO.New_Line ( lstfile );
        End Loop;
    END Create_File;

    PROCEDURE Dump_File Is
    BEGIN
        Ch7Struc.Rel_IO.Reset ( relativefile );
        Text_IO.New_Page ( lstfile );
        Text_IO.Put_Line ( lstfile, "now list file back" );
        Loop
            Exit When Ch7Struc.Rel_IO.End_Of_File ( relativefile );
            Integer_IO.Put ( lstfile,
                             Integer (Ch7Struc.Rel_IO.Index ( relativefile ) ),
                             3 );
            Ch7Struc.Rel_IO.Read ( relativefile, relative_master );
            Text_IO.Put ( lstfile, "  " );
            Text_IO.Put ( lstfile, relative_master.info.id_number );
            Text_IO.Put ( lstfile, "  " );
            Text_IO.Put ( lstfile, relative_master.info.make );
            Text_IO.Put ( lstfile, "  " );
            Text_IO.Put ( lstfile, relative_master.info.style );
            Text_IO.Put ( lstfile, "  " );
            Text_IO.Put ( lstfile, relative_master.info.model );
            Text_IO.Put ( lstfile, "  " );
            Text_IO.Put ( lstfile, relative_master.info.mileage );
            Text_IO.Put ( lstfile, "  " );
            Text_IO.Put ( lstfile, relative_master.info.color );
            Text_IO.Put ( lstfile, "  " );
            Integer_IO.Put ( lstfile, relative_master.link, 3 );
            Text_IO.New_Line ( lstfile );
        End Loop;
    END Dump_File;

BEGIN  -- Alg7_1
    Text_IO.Create ( lstfile, Text_IO.OUT_FILE, "ALG71OUT.TXT" );
    Ch7Struc.Rel_IO.Create ( relativefile,
                             Ch7Struc.Rel_IO.INOUT_FILE,
                             "RELCAR.DAT" );
    For i In 1 .. file_size Loop
        Ch7Struc.Rel_IO.Write ( relativefile, relative_master );
    End Loop;
    Ch7Struc.Rel_IO.Reset ( relativefile );
```

```
    Text_IO.Open ( carfile, Text_IO.IN_FILE, "T1.TXT" );
    Create_FIle;
    Text_IO.Close ( carfile );
    Dump_File;
    Ch7Struc.Rel_IO.Close ( relativefile );
    Text_IO.Close ( lstfile );
END Alg7_1;

With Text_IO,
     Ch7Struc;
PROCEDURE Alg7_4 Is

    PACKAGE  Int_IO Is New Text_IO.Integer_IO ( Integer );
    blank_id_number   : Constant Ch7Struc.Key_Type := "    ";
    error             : Boolean;
    location,
    previous          : Ch7Struc.Rel_IO.Positive_Count;
    relativefile      : Ch7Struc.Rel_IO.File_Type;
    relative_index    : Ch7Struc.Rel_IO.Positive_Count;
    relative_master   : Ch7Struc.Rel_Record_Type;
    trans             : Text_IO.File_Type;
    trans_record      : Ch7Struc.Rel_Record_Type;
    trans_update_code : Character;

PROCEDURE Initialize Is

BEGIN  -- Initialize
    Text_IO.Put_Line ( "           ***** AUDIT/ERROR LIST *****" );
    Text_IO.New_Line;
    Text_IO.Put_Line
    ( "ID NUMBER MAKE   STYLE   MODEL  MILEAGE   COLOR" );
    Text_IO.New_Line;
    Text_IO.Put_Line
    ( "**********************************************************************" );
END Initialize;

PROCEDURE Input_Trans_Record ( trans : IN OUT Text_IO.File_Type;
                               trans_record : IN OUT Ch7Struc.Rel_Record_Type ) Is
    trans_record_info : Ch7Struc.Car_Record_Type Renames trans_record.info;
BEGIN  -- Input_Trans_Record
    Text_IO.Get ( trans, trans_update_code );
    Text_IO.Get ( trans, trans_record_info.id_number );
    Text_IO.Put ( trans_update_code );
    Text_IO.Put ( ' ' );
    Text_IO.Put ( trans_record_info.id_number );
    Text_IO.Put ( "  " );
    Case trans_update_code Is
        When 'A' =>
            Text_IO.Get ( trans, trans_record_info.make );
            Text_IO.Get ( trans, trans_record_info.style );
            Text_IO.Get ( trans, trans_record_info.model );
            Text_IO.Get ( trans, trans_record_info.mileage );
            Text_IO.Get ( trans, trans_record_info.color );
            Text_IO.Put ( trans_record_info.make );
            Text_IO.Put ( trans_record_info.style );
            Text_IO.Put ( trans_record_info.model );
            Text_IO.Put ( trans_record_info.mileage );
            Text_IO.Put ( trans_record_info.color );
```

```
        When 'C' =>
            Text_IO.Get ( trans, trans_record_info.mileage );
            Text_IO.Put ( trans_record_info.mileage );
            Text_IO.Put ( "          " );
        When 'D' =>
            Text_IO.Put ( "                                  " );
        When Others =>
            Text_IO.Put ( "                                  " );
            Text_IO.Put_Line ( "  INVALID UPDATE CODE" );
    End Case;
    Text_IO.Skip_Line ( trans );
END Input_Trans_Record;

PROCEDURE Find_Record ( key : In Ch7Struc.Key_Type;
                        relative_master : In Out Ch7Struc.Rel_Record_Type;
                        relative_index,
                        previous : In Out Ch7Struc.Rel_IO.Positive_Count;
                        found : In Out Boolean ) Is
BEGIN  -- Find_Record
    Ch7Struc.Rel_IO.Read ( relativefile, relative_master, relative_index );
    If relative_master.info.id_number = key Then
        found := TRUE;
    ElsIf relative_master.link = -1 Then
        found := FALSE;
    Else
        previous := relative_index;
        relative_index := Ch7Struc.Rel_IO.Positive_Count ( relative_master.link );
        Find_Record ( key, relative_master, relative_index, previous, found );
    End If;
END Find_Record;

PROCEDURE Add Is
    overflow : Integer;
BEGIN
    Text_IO.Put_Line ( "  VALID ADD" );
    If relative_master.info.id_number = blank_id_number Then
        trans_record.link := -1;
        Ch7Struc.Rel_IO.Write ( relativefile, trans_record, relative_index );
    Else
        Ch7Struc.Rel_IO.Read ( relativefile, relative_master, location );
        trans_record.link := relative_master.link;
        overflow := Integer ( Ch7Struc.Rel_IO.Size ( relativefile ) ) + 1;
        relative_master.link := overflow;
        Ch7Struc.Rel_IO.Write ( relativefile, relative_master, location );
        Ch7Struc.Rel_IO.Write ( relativefile, trans_record,
                                Ch7Struc.Rel_IO.Positive_Count ( overflow ) );
    End If;
END Add;

PROCEDURE Change Is

BEGIN
    Text_IO.Put_Line ( "  VALID CHANGE" );
    relative_master.info.mileage := trans_record.info.mileage;
    Ch7Struc.Rel_IO.Write ( relativefile, relative_master, relative_index );
END Change;

PROCEDURE Delete Is
    null_record : Ch7Struc.Rel_Record_Type;
```

```
    synonym   : Ch7Struc.Rel_IO.Positive_Count;
BEGIN
    Text_IO.Put_Line ( "  VALID DELETE" );
    If Positive ( relative_index ) = Positive ( location ) Then
        If relative_master.link = -1 Then
            Ch7Struc.Rel_IO.Write ( relativefile, null_record, location );
        Else
            synonym := Ch7Struc.Rel_IO.Positive_Count ( relative_master.link );
            Ch7Struc.Rel_IO.Read ( relativefile, relative_master, synonym );
            Ch7Struc.Rel_IO.Write ( relativefile, relative_master, relative_index );
            Ch7Struc.Rel_IO.Write ( relativefile, null_record, synonym );
        End If;
    Else
        synonym := Ch7Struc.Rel_IO.Positive_Count ( relative_master.link );
        Ch7Struc.Rel_IO.Read ( relativefile, relative_master, previous );
        relative_master.link := Integer ( synonym );
        Ch7Struc.Rel_IO.Write ( relativefile, relative_master, previous );
        Ch7Struc.Rel_IO.Write ( relativefile, null_record, relative_index );
    End If;
END Delete;

PROCEDURE List_Master Is

    i : Integer := 1;

    PROCEDURE Print_Heading Is
    BEGIN
        Text_IO.New_Line;
        Text_IO.Put_Line ( "***** UPDATED RELATIVE MASTER *****" );
        Text_IO.New_Line;
        Text_IO.Put_Line ( "LOCATION   ID  NUMBER  MAKE  STYLE    POINTER" );
        Text_IO.New_Line;
    END Print_Heading;

BEGIN  -- List_Master
    Print_Heading;
    Loop
        Exit When Ch7Struc.Rel_IO.End_of_File ( relativefile );
        Ch7Struc.Rel_IO.Read ( relativefile, relative_master );
        DECLARE
            relative_master_info : Ch7Struc.Car_Record_Type Renames relative_master.info;
        BEGIN
            If relative_master_info.id_number /= blank_id_number
            Or i = 1   Then
                Int_IO.Put ( i, 10 );
                Text_IO.Put ( "      " );
                Text_IO.Put ( relative_master_info.id_number );
                Text_IO.Put ( "    " );
                Text_IO.Put ( relative_master_info.make );
                Text_IO.Put ( relative_master_info.style );
                Int_IO.Put ( relative_master.link, 8 );
                Text_IO.New_Line;
            End If;
            i := i + 1;
        END;  -- Declare
    End Loop;
END List_Master;
```

```
BEGIN  -- Alg7_4
    Ch7Struc.Rel_IO.Open ( relativefile, Ch7Struc.Rel_IO.INOUT_FILE, "RELCAR.DAT" );
    Text_IO.Open ( trans, Text_IO.IN_FILE, "CARTRANS.TXT" );
    Initialize;
    Loop
        Input_Trans_Record ( trans, trans_record );
        location := Ch7Struc.Rel_IO.Positive_Count
                    ( Ch7Struc.Hash ( trans_record.info.id_number ) );
        relative_index := location;
        Find_Record ( trans_record.info.id_number, relative_master,
                      relative_index, previous, found );
        Case trans_update_code Is
            When 'A'=>
                If found Then
                    Text_IO.Put_Line ( "  INVALID ADD; ALREADY ON MASTER" );
                Else
                    Add;
                End If;
            When 'C'=>
                If found Then
                    Change;
                Else
                    Text_IO.Put_Line ( "  INVALID CHANGE; NOT ON MASTER" );
                End If;
            When 'D' =>
                If found Then
                    Delete;
                Else
                    Text_IO.Put_Line ( "  INVALID DELETE; NOT ON MASTER" );
                End If;
            When Others =>
                Text_IO.Put_Line ( "  INVALID TRANSACTION CODE" );
        End Case;
        Exit When Text_IO.End_of_File ( trans );
    End Loop;
    Ch7Struc.Rel_IO.Reset ( relativefile );
    List_Master;
    Ch7Struc.Rel_IO.Close ( relativefile );
    Text_IO.New_Page;
END Alg7_4;
```

Case Study 8.1

```
With Direct_IO;
GENERIC
    degree : Positive;
    Type Key_Type Is Private;
    With FUNCTION ">" ( left_operand, right_operand : Key_Type )
                    Return Boolean;
PACKAGE B_Tree Is
    PROCEDURE Create_B_Tree ( external_b_tree_filename : String );
    PROCEDURE Open_B_Tree ( external_b_tree_filename : String );
```

```
    PROCEDURE Insert ( key : Key_Type; key_position : Positive );
    PROCEDURE Delete ( key : Key_Type );
    PROCEDURE Search ( key : Key_Type; key_position : Out Positive );
    PROCEDURE Close_B_Tree ;
    key_not_inserted : Exception;
    key_not_deleted  : Exception;
    key_not_found    : Exception;
END B_Tree;

PACKAGE Body B_Tree Is

    Type A_Tuple Is Record
                        key     : Key_Type;
                        address : Positive;
                        subtree : Natural;
                    End Record;
    Type Tuple_Array Is Array ( Integer Range <>  ) Of A_Tuple;
    Type Node_Type Is Record
                         number_of_tuples : Natural;
                         first_subtree    : Natural;
                         tuple            : Tuple_Array ( 1 .. degree - 1 );
                      End Record;
    Type BigNode_Type Is Record
                            number_of_tuples : Natural;
                            first_subtree    : Natural;
                            tuple            : Tuple_Array ( 1 .. degree );
                         End Record;
    Type Operation_Type Is ( INSERT_KEY, DELETE_KEY, NIL, SEARCH_KEY );
    Package B_Tree_IO Is New Direct_IO ( Node_Type );

    b_tree_file : B_Tree_IO.File_Type;
    hold_tuple  : A_Tuple;
    key_found   : Exception;
    next        : Positive;

    PROCEDURE Create_B_Tree ( external_b_tree_filename : String ) Is
        node : Node_Type;
    BEGIN
        B_Tree_IO.Create ( b_tree_file, B_Tree_IO.INOUT_FILE,
                           external_b_tree_filename );
        node.number_of_tuples := 0;
        B_Tree_IO.Write ( b_tree_file, node, 1 );
        next := 1;
    END Create_B_Tree;

    PROCEDURE Open_B_Tree ( external_b_tree_filename : String ) Is
    BEGIN
        B_Tree_IO.Open ( b_tree_file, B_Tree_IO.INOUT_FILE,
                         external_b_tree_filename );
        next := Positive ( B_Tree_IO.Size ( b_tree_file ) );
    END Open_B_Tree;

    PROCEDURE Find_node ( hold_tuple : IN OUT A_Tuple;
                          p : In Natural;
                          operation : In Out Operation_Type ) Is
        ith_position : Integer;
        node         : Node_Type;
```

```
PROCEDURE Insert_Tuple ( hold_tuple : IN OUT A_Tuple;
                         ith_position  : Positive;
                         node : In Out Node_Type;
                         operation : In Out Operation_Type ) Is

    PROCEDURE Split   ( hold_tuple : IN OUT A_Tuple;
                        ith_position  : Positive;
                        node : In Out Node_Type ) Is
        bignode    : BigNode_Type;
        index      : Integer;
        middle     : Positive;
        newnode    : Node_Type;
        temp_tuple : A_Tuple;

    BEGIN  -- Split
        bignode.number_of_tuples := node.number_of_tuples;
        bignode.first_subtree := node.first_subtree;
        For lcv In 1 .. ith_position  - 1 Loop
            bignode.tuple(lcv) := node.tuple(lcv);
        End Loop;
        bignode.tuple(ith_position) := hold_tuple;
        For lcv In ith_position .. node.number_of_tuples Loop
            bignode.tuple(lcv + 1) := node.tuple(lcv);
        End Loop;
        bignode.number_of_tuples := bignode.number_of_tuples + 1;

        middle := ( degree - 1 ) / 2 + 1;  -- withdraw middle tuple
        hold_tuple := bignode.tuple(middle);
        next := next + 1;
        hold_tuple.subtree := next;

        node.first_subtree := bignode.first_subtree;
        For lcv In 1 .. middle - 1 Loop
                node.tuple(lcv) := bignode.tuple(lcv);
        End Loop;
        node.number_of_tuples := middle - 1;

        B_Tree_IO.Write ( b_tree_file, node,
                          B_Tree_IO.Positive_Count ( p ) );

        newnode.first_subtree := bignode.tuple(middle).subtree;
        index := 0;
        For lcv In middle + 1 .. bignode.number_of_tuples Loop
            index := index + 1;
            newnode.tuple(index) := bignode.tuple(lcv);
        End Loop;
        newnode.number_of_tuples := index;

        B_Tree_IO.Write ( b_tree_file, newnode,
                          B_Tree_IO.Positive_Count ( next ) );

   END Split;

BEGIN  --  Insert_Tuple
           -- insert hold_tuple into position ith position of node ( address p )
    If node.number_of_tuples < degree - 1 Then
           -- resulting node is not too big
        operation := NIL;
        For lcv In Reverse ith_position .. node.number_of_tuples Loop
            node.tuple(lcv + 1) := node.tuple(lcv);
        End Loop;
```

```
            node.number_of_tuples := node.number_of_tuples + 1;
            node.tuple(ith_position) := hold_tuple;
            B_Tree_IO.Write ( b_tree_file, node,
                              B_Tree_IO.Positive_Count ( p ) );
        Else
            Split ( hold_tuple, ith_position, node );
        End If;
    END Insert_Tuple;

BEGIN  -- Find_Node
    If p = 0 Then
        Return;
    Else
        B_Tree_IO.Read ( b_tree_file, node,
                         B_Tree_IO.Positive_Count ( p ) );
        If hold_tuple.key > node.tuple(node.number_of_tuples).key Then
            ith_position := node.number_of_tuples + 1;
            Find_Node ( hold_tuple, node.tuple(node.number_of_tuples).subtree,
                        operation );
            If operation = INSERT_KEY Then
                Insert_Tuple ( hold_tuple, ith_position, node, operation );
            End If;
        Else  -- hold_tuple.key <= node.tuple(ith_position)
            ith_position := 1;
            Loop
                If hold_tuple.key > node.tuple(ith_position).key Then
                    ith_position := ith_position + 1;
                ElsIf hold_tuple.key = node.tuple(ith_position).key Then
                    hold_tuple.address := node.tuple(ith_position).address;
                    Raise key_found;
                Else
                --  hold_tuple.key < node.tuple(ith_position).key
                    If ith_position = 1 Then
                        Find_Node ( hold_tuple,
                                    node.first_subtree,
                                    operation );
                    Else
                        Find_Node ( hold_tuple,
                                    node.tuple(ith_position - 1).subtree,
                                    operation );
                    End If;
                    If operation = INSERT_KEY Then
                        Insert_Tuple ( hold_tuple, ith_position, node, operation );
                    End If;
                    Exit;
                End If;
            End Loop;
        End If;
    End If;
END Find_Node;

PROCEDURE Insert ( key : Key_Type; key_position : Positive ) Is
    new_node  : Node_Type;
    new_tuple : A_Tuple;
    root_node : Node_Type;
    operation : Operation_Type := INSERT_KEY;
BEGIN  -- Insert
    B_Tree_IO.Read ( b_tree_file, root_node, 1 );
```

```
    new_tuple := ( key, key_position, 0 );
    Find_Node ( new_tuple, root_node.number_of_tuples, operation );
    If operation = INSERT_KEY Then
        new_node.number_of_tuples := 1;
        B_Tree_IO.Read ( b_tree_file, root_node, 1 );
        new_node.first_subtree := root_node.number_of_tuples;
        new_node.tuple(1) := ( new_tuple.key,
                               new_tuple.address,
                               new_tuple.subtree );
        next := next + 1;
        B_Tree_IO.Write ( b_tree_file, new_node,
                          B_Tree_IO.Positive_Count ( next ) );
        root_node.number_of_tuples := next;
        B_Tree_IO.Write ( b_tree_file, root_node, 1 );
    End If;
EXCEPTION
    When key_found => Raise key_not_inserted;
END Insert;

PROCEDURE Delete ( key : Key_Type ) Is
    MINIMUM          :  Positive := degree / 2;
    node_undersized : Boolean := FALSE;
    operation        : Operation_Type := DELETE_KEY;
    root_address     : Positive;
    root_node        : Node_Type;

    PROCEDURE Delete_Tuple ( delete_value : Key_Type;
                             p : In Natural;
                             node_undersized : In Out Boolean ) Is
            -- search node with address p for key
        child_address : Natural;
        ith_position  : Natural;
        node          : Node_Type;

        PROCEDURE Under_Flow ( parent_address,
                               child_address : In Positive;
                               tuple_index : In Out Natural;
                               node_undersized : Out Boolean ) Is

        child_node    : Node_Type;
        left          : Positive;
        left_extras   : Integer;
        left_node     : Node_Type;
        parent_node   : Node_Type;
        right_address : Positive;
        right_extras  : Integer;
        right_node    : Node_Type;

        PROCEDURE Balance_From_Right Is
        BEGIN
            For j In 1 .. right_extras - 1 Loop
                child_node.tuple ( child_node.number_of_tuples + j )
                    := right_node.tuple( j );
            End Loop;
            child_node.number_of_tuples := MINIMUM - 1 + right_extras;
            B_Tree_IO.Write ( b_tree_file, child_node,
                              B_Tree_IO.Positive_Count ( child_address ) );
            parent_node.tuple(tuple_index) := right_node.tuple(right_extras);
            parent_node.tuple(tuple_index).subtree := right_address;
```

```
    B_Tree_IO.Write ( b_tree_file, parent_node,
                      B_Tree_IO.Positive_Count ( parent_address ) );
    right_node.first_subtree
        := right_node.tuple(right_extras).subtree;
    right_node.number_of_tuples
        := right_node.number_of_tuples - right_extras;
    For j In 1 .. right_node.number_of_tuples Loop
        right_node.tuple(j)
            := right_node.tuple(right_extras + j);
    End Loop;
    B_Tree_IO.Write ( b_tree_file, right_node,
                      B_Tree_IO.Positive_Count ( right_address ) );
    node_undersized := FALSE;
END Balance_From_Right;

PROCEDURE Balance_From_Left Is
BEGIN
    For j In Reverse 1 .. MINIMUM Loop
            -- move tuples over 'left_extras' places to make
            -- room for tuples at lower end
        child_node.tuple(j + left_extras) :=
            child_node.tuple ( j );
    End Loop;
    child_node.tuple(left_extras) := parent_node.tuple(tuple_index);
    child_node.tuple(left_extras).subtree
        := child_node.first_subtree;
    left_node.number_of_tuples := MINIMUM + 1;
    For j In Reverse 1 .. left_extras - 1 Loop
        child_node.tuple(j)
            := left_node.tuple(left_node.number_of_tuples + j);
    End Loop;
    child_node.first_subtree
        := left_node.tuple(left_node.number_of_tuples).subtree;
    child_node.number_of_tuples := MINIMUM - 1 + left_extras;
    parent_node.tuple(tuple_index)
        := left_node.tuple(left_node.number_of_tuples);
    parent_node.tuple(tuple_index).subtree:= child_address;
    left_node.number_of_tuples := left_node.number_of_tuples - 1;
    B_Tree_IO.Write ( b_tree_file, parent_node,
                      B_Tree_IO.Positive_Count ( parent_address ) );
    B_Tree_IO.Write ( b_tree_file, left_node,
                      B_Tree_IO.Positive_Count ( left ) );
    B_Tree_IO.Write ( b_tree_file, child_node,
                      B_Tree_IO.Positive_Count ( child_address ) );
    node_undersized := FALSE;
END Balance_From_Left;

PROCEDURE Merge_With_Right Is
BEGIN
    For j In 1 .. MINIMUM Loop
        child_node.tuple(MINIMUM + j) := right_node.tuple(j);
    End Loop;
    For j In tuple_index .. parent_node.number_of_tuples - 1 Loop
        parent_node.tuple(j) := parent_node.tuple(j + 1);
    End Loop;
    child_node.number_of_tuples := degree - 1;
    right_node.number_of_tuples := 0;
```

```
        B_Tree_IO.Write ( b_tree_file, right_node,
                          B_Tree_IO.Positive_Count ( right_address ) );
        parent_node.number_of_tuples :=
            parent_node.number_of_tuples - 1;
        node_undersized := parent_node.number_of_tuples < MINIMUM;
        B_Tree_IO.Write ( b_tree_file, child_node,
                          B_Tree_IO.Positive_Count ( child_address ) );
        B_Tree_IO.Write ( b_tree_file, parent_node,
                          B_Tree_IO.Positive_Count ( parent_address ) );
    END Merge_With_Right;

    PROCEDURE Merge_With_Left Is
    BEGIN
        left_node.number_of_tuples := left_node.number_of_tuples + 1;
        left_node.tuple(left_node.number_of_tuples)
            := parent_node.tuple(tuple_index);
        left_node.tuple(left_node.number_of_tuples).subtree
            := child_node.first_subtree;
        For j In 1 .. child_node.number_of_tuples Loop
            left_node.tuple(left_node.number_of_tuples + j)
                := child_node.tuple (j);
        End Loop;
        left_node.number_of_tuples := degree - 1;
        parent_node.number_of_tuples := parent_node.number_of_tuples - 1;
        node_undersized := parent_node.number_of_tuples < MINIMUM;
        B_Tree_IO.Write ( b_tree_file, left_node,
                          B_Tree_IO.Positive_Count ( left ) );
        B_Tree_IO.Write ( b_tree_file, parent_node,
                          B_Tree_IO.Positive_Count ( parent_address ) );
    END Merge_With_Left;

    PROCEDURE Choose_Left_Sibling Is
    BEGIN
        If tuple_index = 1 Then
            left := parent_node.first_subtree;
        Else
            left := parent_node.tuple(tuple_index - 1).subtree;
        End If;
        B_Tree_IO.Read ( b_tree_file, left_node,
                         B_Tree_IO.Positive_Count ( left ) );
        left_extras := ( left_node.number_of_tuples - MINIMUM + 1 ) / 2;
    END Choose_Left_Sibling;

BEGIN  -- Under_Flow
    B_Tree_IO.Read ( b_tree_file, child_node,
                     B_Tree_IO.Positive_Count ( child_address ) );
    B_Tree_IO.Read ( b_tree_file, parent_node,
                     B_Tree_IO.Positive_Count ( parent_address ) );
    If tuple_index < parent_node.number_of_tuples Then
            -- a right sibling exists
        tuple_index := tuple_index + 1;
        right_address := parent_node.tuple(tuple_index).subtree;
        B_Tree_IO.Read ( b_tree_file, right_node,
                         B_Tree_IO.Positive_Count ( right_address ) );
        right_extras := (right_node.number_of_tuples
                         - MINIMUM + 1) / 2;
            -- right_extras = number of tuples over the MINIMUM
            -- that can be balanced between child_node
```

```
            -- and right_node
        child_node.number_of_tuples := child_node.number_of_tuples + 1;
        child_node.tuple(child_node.number_of_tuples)
            := parent_node.tuple(tuple_index);
        child_node.tuple(child_node.number_of_tuples).subtree
            := right_node.first_subtree;
            --  replace predecessor of node to original location
        If right_extras > 0 Then
            -- move right_extras number of tuples from right_node
            -- to child_node
            Balance_From_Right;
        ElsIf tuple_index /= 0 Then
              -- check to see if left sibling exists and has extras
              -- left sibling exists
                Choose_Left_Sibling;
                If left_extras > 0 Then
                    Balance_From_Left;
                Else
                    -- left sibling has no extras so merge child_node
                    -- and right_node into child_node
                    Merge_With_Right;
                End If;
        Else
            -- left sibling does not exist so merge child_node
            -- and right_node into child_node
            Merge_With_Right;
        End If;
    Else
        -- no right sibling exists; choose left sibling
        Choose_Left_Sibling;
        If left_extras > 0 Then
            Balance_From_Left;
        Else
            Merge_With_Left;
        End If;
    End If;

END Under_Flow;

PROCEDURE Found_Delete_Value Is
    PROCEDURE Find_Predecessor ( descendant_address : In Positive;
                                 node_undersized : In Out Boolean ) Is
        descendant_node : Node_Type;
        n, q : Natural;
    BEGIN  -- Find_Predecessor
        B_Tree_IO.Read ( b_tree_file, descendant_node,
                 B_Tree_IO.Positive_Count ( descendant_address ) );
        n := descendant_node.number_of_tuples;
        q := descendant_node.tuple(n).subtree;
        If q = 0 Then
            descendant_node.tuple(n).subtree :=
                node.tuple(ith_position).subtree;
            node.tuple(ith_position) := descendant_node.tuple(n);
            descendant_node.number_of_tuples
                := descendant_node.number_of_tuples - 1;
            node_undersized := descendant_node.number_of_tuples
                                   < MINIMUM;
```

```
            B_Tree_IO.Write ( b_tree_file, node,
                              B_Tree_IO.Positive_Count ( p ) );
            B_Tree_IO.Write ( b_tree_file, descendant_node,
                              B_Tree_IO.Positive_Count
                                  ( descendant_address ) );
        Else  -- look deeper in the tree for predecessor
            Find_Predecessor ( q, node_undersized );
            If node_undersized Then
                Under_Flow ( descendant_address, q,
                             descendant_node.number_of_tuples,
                             node_undersized );
            End If;
        End If;
    End Find_Predecessor;

BEGIN  -- Found_Delete_Value
    If ith_position = 1 Then
        child_address := node.first_subtree;
    Else
        child_address := node.tuple(ith_position - 1).subtree;
    End If;
    If child_address = 0 Then
          -- delete key( ith_position ) from leaf node
        node.number_of_tuples := node.number_of_tuples - 1;
        node_undersized := node.number_of_tuples < MINIMUM;
        For j In ith_position .. node.number_of_tuples Loop
            node.tuple(j) := node.tuple(j + 1);
        End Loop;
        B_Tree_IO.Write ( b_tree_file, node,
                          B_Tree_IO.Positive_Count ( p ) );
    Else  --    delete key( ith_position ) from nonterminal node;
          --    find predecessor to replace key( ith_position )
        Find_Predecessor ( child_address, node_undersized );
        If node_undersized Then
            ith_position := ith_position - 1;
            Under_Flow ( p, child_address, ith_position,
                         node_undersized );
        End If;
    End If;
END Found_Delete_Value;

BEGIN  -- Delete_Tuple
    If p = 0 Then  --  not found
        Raise key_not_deleted;
    Else
        B_Tree_IO.Read ( b_tree_file, node,
                         B_Tree_IO.Positive_Count ( p ) );
        If delete_value > node.tuple(node.number_of_tuples).key Then
            ith_position := node.number_of_tuples;
            child_address := node.tuple(ith_position).subtree;
            Delete_Tuple ( delete_value, child_address, node_undersized );
            If node_undersized Then
                Under_Flow ( p, child_address, ith_position, node_undersized );
            End If;
        Else
            ith_position := 1;
            Loop
                If delete_value > node.tuple(ith_position).key Then
```

```
                        ith_position := ith_position + 1;
                    ElsIf delete_value = node.tuple(ith_position).key Then
                        Found_Delete_Value;
                        Exit;
                    Else
                    -- delete_value < node.tuple(ith_position).key Then

                        If ith_position > 1 Then
                            child_address := node.tuple(ith_position - 1).subtree;
                        Else
                            child_address := node.first_subtree;
                        End If;
                        Delete_Tuple ( delete_value, child_address,
                                       node_undersized );
                        If node_undersized Then
                            ith_position := ith_position - 1;
                            Under_Flow ( p, child_address, ith_position,
                                         node_undersized );
                        End If;
                        Exit;
                    End If;
                End Loop;
            End If;
        End If;
    END Delete_Tuple;

BEGIN  -- Delete
    If degree / 2 * 2 = degree Then  -- test for even numbered degree
        MINIMUM := MINIMUM - 1;
    End If;
    B_Tree_IO.Read ( b_tree_file, root_node, 1 );
    root_address := root_node.number_of_tuples;
    Delete_Tuple ( key, root_address, node_undersized );
    If node_undersized
    And Then root_node.number_of_tuples = 0 Then
            -- reducing the height of the B_tree
        root_node.number_of_tuples := root_node.first_subtree;
        B_Tree_IO.Write ( b_tree_file, root_node, 1 );
    End If;
END Delete;

PROCEDURE Search ( key : Key_Type; key_position : Out Positive ) Is
    new_tuple : A_Tuple := (Key, 1, 0);
    root_node : Node_Type;
    operation : Operation_Type := SEARCH_KEY;
BEGIN
    B_Tree_IO.Read ( b_tree_file, root_node, 1 );
    Find_Node ( new_tuple, root_node.number_of_tuples, operation );
    key_position := 1;
    Raise key_not_found;
EXCEPTION
    When key_found => key_position := new_tuple.address;
END Search;

PROCEDURE Close_B_Tree Is
BEGIN
        B_Tree_IO.Close ( b_tree_file );
END Close_B_Tree;
END B_Tree;
```

```
With Text_IO,
     B_Tree,
     Ch5Struc,
     Direct_IO;
PROCEDURE Alg8_2 Is

    Package Rel_Car_IO Is New Direct_IO ( Ch5Struc.Car_Master_Record );

    relative_file      : Rel_Car_IO.File_Type;
    transaction_file   : Text_IO.File_Type;
    transaction_record: Ch5Struc.Car_Master_Record;

    Package Car_B_Tree Is New B_Tree ( 5, Ch5Struc.Id_String, ">" );

    PROCEDURE Get_Next_Trans (transaction : In Out Ch5Struc.Car_Master_Record)  Is
        update_code :  Character;
    BEGIN  -- Get_Next_Trans
        Text_IO.Get ( transaction_file, update_code);
        Text_IO.Put ( ' ' );
        Text_IO.Put ( update_code );
        Text_IO.Put ( ' ' );
        Text_IO.Get ( transaction_file, transaction.id_number);
        Text_IO.Put ( transaction.id_number );
        Text_IO.Put ( ' ' );
        Case update_code Is
            When 'A' =>
                Text_IO.Get ( transaction_file, transaction.make);
                Text_IO.Put ( ' ' );
                Text_IO.Put ( transaction.make );
                Text_IO.Get ( transaction_file, transaction.style);
                Text_IO.Put ( ' ' );
                Text_IO.Put ( transaction.style );
                Text_IO.Get ( transaction_file, transaction.model );
                Text_IO.Put ( ' ' );
                Text_IO.Put ( transaction.model );
                Text_IO.Get ( transaction_file, transaction.mileage );
                Text_IO.Put ( ' ' );
                Text_IO.Put ( transaction.mileage );
                Text_IO.Get ( transaction_file, transaction.color );
                Text_IO.Put ( ' ' );
                Text_IO.Put ( transaction.color );
                Text_IO.Put ( ' ' );
            When Others =>
                Text_IO.Put ( "                                   " );
                Text_IO.Put ( "invalid update code" );
        End Case;
        Text_IO.Skip_Line ( transaction_file );
    END Get_Next_Trans;

BEGIN  -- Alg8_2
    Rel_Car_IO.Create ( relative_file, Rel_Car_IO.INOUT_FILE, "RELCAR.DAT" );
    Text_IO.Open ( transaction_file, Text_IO.IN_FILE, "T1.TXT");
    Car_B_Tree.Create_B_Tree ( "CARBTREE.DAT" );
    Loop
        Exit When Text_IO.End_of_File ( transaction_file );
        Get_Next_Trans ( transaction_record );
```

```
        Rel_Car_IO.Write ( relative_file, transaction_record );
        Text_IO.Put ( transaction_record.id_number );
        Car_B_Tree.Insert ( transaction_record.id_number,
                            Positive ( Rel_Car_IO.Index ( relative_file ) ) - 1 );
        Text_IO.New_Line;
    End Loop;
    Rel_Car_IO.Close ( relative_file );
    Text_IO.Close ( transaction_file );
    Car_B_Tree.Close_B_Tree;
END Alg8_2;

With Text_IO,
     B_Tree,
     Ch5Struc,
     Direct_IO;
PROCEDURE Alg8_3 Is

    PACKAGE Rel_Car_IO Is New Direct_IO ( Ch5Struc.Car_Master_Record );

    record_number     : Positive;
    relative_file     : Rel_Car_IO.File_Type;

    PACKAGE Car_B_Tree Is New B_Tree ( 5, Ch5Struc.Id_String, ">" );

    PROCEDURE Get_Next_Trans ( transaction : In Out Ch5Struc.Car_Transaction_Record ) Is
    BEGIN  -- Get_Next_Trans
        Text_IO.Get ( Ch5Struc.transfile, transaction.update_code );
        Text_IO.Put ( ' ' );
        Text_IO.Put ( transaction.update_code );
        Text_IO.Put ( ' ' );
        Text_IO.Get ( Ch5Struc.transfile, transaction.id_number );
        Text_IO.Put ( transaction.id_number );
        Text_IO.Put ( ' ' );
        Case transaction.update_code Is
            When 'A' =>
                Text_IO.Get ( Ch5Struc.transfile, transaction.make );
                Text_IO.Put ( "  " );
                Text_IO.Put ( transaction.make );
                Text_IO.Get ( Ch5Struc.transfile, transaction.style );
                Text_IO.Put ( ' ' );
                Text_IO.Put ( transaction.style );
                Text_IO.Get ( Ch5Struc.transfile, transaction.model );
                Text_IO.Put ( ' ' );
                Text_IO.Put ( transaction.model );
                Text_IO.Get ( Ch5Struc.transfile, transaction.mileage );
                Text_IO.Put ( ' ' );
                Text_IO.Put ( transaction.mileage );
                Text_IO.Get ( Ch5Struc.transfile, transaction.color );
                Text_IO.Put ( ' ' );
                Text_IO.Put ( transaction.color );
                Text_IO.Put ( ' ' );
            When 'C' =>
                Text_IO.Get ( Ch5Struc.transfile, transaction.mileage );
                Text_IO.Put ( "  " );
                Text_IO.Put ( transaction.mileage );
                Text_IO.Put ( "           " );
            When 'D' =>
                Text_IO.Put ( "                                   " );
```

```
            When Others =>
                Text_IO.Put ( "                                   " );
                Text_IO.Put ( "invalid update code" );
        End Case;
        Text_IO.Skip_Line ( Ch5Struc.transfile );
    END Get_Next_Trans;

BEGIN  -- Alg8_3
    Rel_Car_IO.Open ( relative_file, Rel_Car_IO.INOUT_FILE, "RELCAR.DAT" );
    Text_IO.Open ( Ch5Struc.transfile, Text_IO.IN_FILE, "CARTRANS.TXT");
    Car_B_Tree.Open_B_Tree ( "CARBTREE.DAT" );
    Loop
        Exit When Text_IO.End_of_File ( Ch5Struc.transfile );
        Get_Next_Trans ( Ch5Struc.transaction );
        Text_IO.Put ( Ch5Struc.transaction.id_number );
        Case Ch5Struc.transaction.update_code Is
            When 'A' =>
                BEGIN
                    Ch5Struc.master_record :=
                           ( Ch5Struc.transaction.id_number,
                             Ch5Struc.transaction.make,
                             Ch5Struc.transaction.style,
                             Ch5Struc.transaction.model,
                             Ch5Struc.transaction.mileage,
                             Ch5Struc.transaction.color );
                    record_number := Positive ( Rel_Car_IO.Size ( relative_file ) ) + 1;
                    Car_B_Tree.Insert ( Ch5Struc.master_record.id_number,
                                        record_number );
                    Rel_Car_IO.Write ( relative_file, Ch5Struc.master_record,
                                       Rel_Car_IO.Positive_Count ( record_number ) );
                    Text_IO.Put_Line ( " add    ");
                EXCEPTION
                    When Car_B_Tree.key_not_inserted =>
                        Text_IO.Put_Line ("  duplicate add");
                END;
            When 'C' =>
                BEGIN
                    Car_B_Tree.Search ( Ch5Struc.transaction.id_number,
                                        record_number );
                    Rel_Car_IO.Read ( relative_file, Ch5Struc.master_record,
                                      Rel_Car_IO.Positive_Count ( record_number ) );
                    Ch5Struc.master_record.mileage := Ch5Struc.transaction.mileage;
                    Rel_Car_IO.Write ( relative_file, Ch5Struc.master_record,
                                       Rel_Car_IO.Positive_Count ( record_number ) );
                    Text_IO.Put_Line ( "  changed" );
                EXCEPTION
                    When Car_B_Tree.key_not_found =>
                       Text_IO.Put_Line ( " no matching master for change");
                END;
            When 'D' =>
                BEGIN
                    Car_B_Tree.Delete ( Ch5Struc.transaction.id_number );
                    Text_IO.Put_Line ( " deleted");
                EXCEPTION
                    When Car_B_Tree.key_not_deleted =>
                       Text_IO.Put_Line ("  no matching master for delete");
                END;
            When Others = > Text_IO.Put_Line ( " invalid update code");
```

```
        End Case;
        Text_IO.New_Line;
    End Loop;
    Rel_Car_IO.Close ( relative_file );
    Text_IO.Close ( Ch5Struc.transfile );
    Car_B_Tree.Close_B_Tree;
END Alg8_3;
```

Case Study 9.1

```
GENERIC
    Type Stack_Entry Is Private;
    size : Integer := 50;
PACKAGE StackPkg is
    Type Status_Type is ( EMPTY, OK, FULL );
    BOTTOM : Constant := 1;
    Type Space_Type is Array ( BOTTOM .. SIZE ) Of Stack_Entry;
    Type Stack_Type is Record
                           top : Integer;
                           space : Space_Type;
                       End Record;
    PROCEDURE Create ( stack : in out Stack_Type );
    PROCEDURE Push ( stack : in out Stack_Type; info : in Stack_Entry );
    PROCEDURE Pop  ( stack : in out Stack_Type; info : out Stack_Entry );
    FUNCTION Status ( stack : Stack_Type ) Return Status_Type;
    FUNCTION Tos ( stack : Stack_Type ) Return Stack_Entry;
END StackPkg;
PACKAGE Body StackPkg is
    PROCEDURE Create ( stack : in out Stack_Type ) is
    BEGIN   -- Create
        stack.top := 0;
    END Create;

    PROCEDURE Push ( stack : in out Stack_Type;
                     info : in Stack_Entry ) is
    BEGIN   -- Push
            stack.top := stack.top + 1;
            stack.space(stack.top) := info;
    END Push;

    PROCEDURE Pop  ( stack : in out Stack_Type;
                     info : out Stack_Entry ) is
    BEGIN   -- Pop
            info := stack.space(stack.top);
            stack.top := stack.top - 1;
    END Pop;

    FUNCTION Status ( stack : Stack_Type ) Return Status_Type is
    BEGIN   -- Status
        If stack.top < BOTTOM Then
            Return EMPTY;
        Elsif stack.top = SIZE Then
            Return FULL;
        Else
            Return OK;
```

```
        End If;
    END Status;

    FUNCTION Tos ( stack : Stack_Type ) Return Stack_Entry is
    BEGIN   -- Tos
        Return stack.space ( stack.top );
    END Tos;
END StackPkg;

GENERIC
    INDEX_BLOCK_SIZE : Positive;
    DATA_BLOCK_SIZE  : Positive;
    Type key_Type Is Private;
    Type Record_Info Is Private;
    With FUNCTION Key_Of ( a_record : Record_Info ) Return Key_Type;
    With FUNCTION ">" ( left_operand, right_operand : Key_Type )
                    Return Boolean;
PACKAGE BPlus_Tree Is
    PROCEDURE Create_BPlus_Tree ( external_bplus_tree_filename,
                                  external_data_block_file : String );
    PROCEDURE Open_BPlus_Tree ( external_bplus_tree_filename,
                                external_data_block_file : String );
    PROCEDURE Insert ( data_record : Record_Info );
    PROCEDURE Delete ( key : Key_Type );
    PROCEDURE Retrieve ( key : Key_Type; data_record : Out Record_Info );
    PROCEDURE Replace ( data_record : Record_Info );
    PROCEDURE Close_BPlus_Tree ( external_bplus_tree_filename,
                                 external_data_block_file : String );
    key_not_found    : Exception;
    key_not_inserted : Exception;
    key_not_deleted  : Exception;
END BPlus_Tree;

With IO_Exceptions;
With Direct_IO;
With StackPkg;
PACKAGE Body BPlus_Tree Is
    PACKAGE Stack_Package Is New StackPkg ( Positive );
    Use Stack_Package;
    stack : Stack_Package.Stack_Type;
    Type Index_Entry Is Record
                            key     : Key_Type;
                            address : Positive;
                        End Record;
    Type Index_Tuple Is Array ( 1 .. INDEX_BLOCK_SIZE ) Of Index_Entry;
    Type Level_Indicator Is ( DATA, INDEX );
    Type Index_Node Is Record
                           entries : Natural;
                           level : Level_Indicator;
                           tuple   : Index_Tuple;
                       End Record;
    PACKAGE Index_Block_IO Is New Direct_IO ( Index_Node );
    index_blocks_file : Index_Block_IO.File_Type;
    Type Data_Tuple Is Array ( 1 .. DATA_BLOCK_SIZE ) Of Record_Info;
```

```
Type Data_Block_Type Is Record
                            entries : Natural;
                            tuple   : Data_Tuple;
                            link    : Natural;
                        End Record;
PACKAGE Data_Block_IO Is New Direct_IO ( Data_Block_Type );
data_blocks_file : Data_Block_IO.File_Type;

PROCEDURE Create_BPlus_Tree ( external_bplus_tree_filename,
                              external_data_block_file : String ) Is
    first_node : Index_Node;
BEGIN -- Create_BPlus_Tree
    Index_Block_IO.Create ( index_blocks_file,
                            Index_Block_IO.INOUT_File,
                            external_bplus_tree_filename );
    first_node.entries := 0;
    Index_Block_IO.Write ( index_blocks_file, first_node, 1 );
    Data_Block_IO.Create ( data_blocks_file,
                           Data_Block_IO.INOUT_FILE,
                           external_data_block_file );
END Create_BPlus_Tree;

PROCEDURE Open_BPlus_Tree ( external_bplus_tree_filename,
                            external_data_block_file : String ) Is
BEGIN  -- Open_BPlus_Tree

    Index_Block_IO.Open  ( index_blocks_file,
                           Index_Block_IO.INOUT_File,
                           external_bplus_tree_filename );
    Data_Block_IO.Open ( data_blocks_file,
                         Data_Block_IO.INOUT_FILE,
                         external_data_block_file );
END Open_BPlus_Tree;

PROCEDURE Find_Node ( key : Key_Type;
                      data_block_number : In Out Natural;
                      location : Out Natural;
                      data_block : In Out Data_Block_Type;
                      successful : In Out Boolean ) Is
    first_node   : Index_Node;
    root_address : Natural;

    PROCEDURE Search_Indexes ( key : Key_Type;
                               index_block_address : Natural;
                               successful : Out Boolean;
                               data_block_number : Out Natural ) Is
        found       : Boolean := FALSE;
        index_block : Index_Node;
        lcv         : Natural := 1;
    BEGIN -- Search_Indexes
        If index_block_address = 0 Then
            successful := FALSE;
            data_block_number := 0;
        Else
            Index_Block_IO.Read ( index_blocks_file, index_block,
                  Index_Block_IO.Positive_Count ( index_block_address ) );
```

```
        Loop
            Exit When lcv > index_block.entries;
            If key > index_block.tuple(lcv).key Then
                lcv := lcv + 1;
            Elsif key = index_block.tuple(lcv).key Then
                found := TRUE;
                Exit;
            Else -- key < index_block.tuple(lcv).key
                found := TRUE;
                lcv := lcv - 1;
                Exit;
            End If;
        End Loop;
        If lcv > index_block.entries Then
            -- key was > last key in index_block so look in last address
            found := TRUE;
            lcv := lcv - 1;
        End If;
        Stack_Package.Push ( stack, lcv );
        Stack_Package.Push ( stack, index_block_address );
        successful := found;
        If found Then
            If lcv = 0 Then
                -- key was < first key in index_block so is not
                -- in the file
                data_block_number := 0;
                found := FALSE;
                successful := found;
            Else
                -- search next level down
                If index_block.level = DATA Then
                    data_block_number := index_block.tuple(lcv).address;
                Else  -- index_block.level = INDEX
                    Search_Indexes ( key, index_block.tuple(lcv).address,
                                     successful, data_block_number );
                End If;
            End If;
        End If;
    End If;
END Search_Indexes;

PROCEDURE Search_Data_Block ( key : Key_Type;
                              data_block : Data_Block_Type;
                              location : Out Natural;
                              successful : Out Boolean ) Is
    lcv : Natural := 1;
BEGIN -- Search_Data_Block
    successful := FALSE;
    Loop
        Exit When lcv > data_block.entries;
        If key > Key_Of ( data_block.tuple(lcv) ) Then
            lcv := lcv + 1;
        Elsif key = Key_Of ( data_block.tuple(lcv) ) Then
            successful := TRUE;
            Exit;
```

```
            Else  -- key < Key_Of ( data_block.tuple(lcv) )
                Exit;
                -- key not found in data block so return lcv as the
                -- location of the first entry > key.
                -- key belongs immediately prior to location lcv
            End If;
        End Loop;
        location := lcv;
    END Search_Data_Block;

BEGIN -- Find_Node
      Index_Block_IO.Read ( index_blocks_file, first_node, 1 );
      root_address := first_node.entries;
      Search_Indexes ( key, root_address, successful, data_block_number );
      If successful Then
          Data_Block_IO.Read ( data_blocks_file, data_block,
               Data_Block_IO.Positive_Count ( data_block_number ) );
          Search_Data_Block ( key, data_block, location, successful );
      Else
          data_block.entries := 0;
          data_block.link := 0;
          location := 1;
      End If;
  END Find_Node;

PROCEDURE Insert ( data_record : Record_Info ) Is
    data_block        : Data_Block_Type;
    data_block_number : Natural;
    hold_tuple        : Index_Entry;
    key               : Key_Type;
    location          : Natural;
    new_block         : Data_Block_Type;
    successful        : Boolean;

    PROCEDURE New_Root ( hold_tuple : Index_Entry ) Is
        first_node          : Index_Node;
        next_index_location : Positive;
        new_node            : Index_Node;
        root_address        : Natural;
        root_node           : Index_Node;
    BEGIN -- New_Root
        Index_Block_IO.Read ( index_blocks_file, first_node, 1 );
        root_address := first_node.entries;
        If root_address = 0 Then  -- no root exists yet
            new_node.level := DATA;
            new_node.tuple(1) := hold_tuple;
            new_node.entries := 1;
        Else
            Index_Block_IO.Read ( index_blocks_file, root_node,
                  Index_Block_IO.Positive_Count ( root_address ) );
            new_node.level := INDEX;
            new_node.tuple(1) := ( root_node.tuple(1).key, root_address );
            new_node.tuple(2) := hold_tuple;
            new_node.entries := 2;
        End If;
```

```
        next_index_location :=
            Positive ( Index_Block_IO.Size ( index_blocks_file ) ) + 1;
        Index_Block_IO.Write ( index_blocks_file, new_node,
             Index_Block_IO.Positive_Count ( next_index_location ) );
        first_node.entries := next_index_location;
        Index_Block_IO.Write ( index_blocks_file, first_node, 1 );
    END New_Root;

    PROCEDURE Split_Data_Block ( data_block : In Out Data_Block_Type;
                                 location : In Positive;
                                 new_block : In Out Data_Block_Type ) Is
         -- Splits records from positions location..entries of
         -- data block into a new data block and adjusts indexes
       entry_position : Positive := 1;
       next_data_location : Natural;

       PROCEDURE Insert_Into_Index_Blocks ( key : Key_Type;
                                            address : Positive ) Is
           Type Operation_Type Is ( INSERT_KEY, NIL );
           hold_tuple          : Index_Entry;
           index,
           index_block_address : Positive;
           node                : Index_Node;
           operation           : Operation_Type := INSERT_KEY;
           PROCEDURE Insert_Tuple ( hold_tuple : In Out Index_Entry;
                                    node : In Out Index_Node;
                                    index_block_address : In Positive;
                                    index : In Positive;
                                    operation : In Out Operation_Type ) Is

               PROCEDURE Split Is
                   j                   : Natural := 1;
                   new_node            : Index_Node;
                   next_index_location : Positive;
               BEGIN
                   new_node.tuple(1) := hold_tuple;
                   For count In index + 1 .. node.entries Loop
                       j := j + 1;
                       new_node.tuple(j) := node.tuple(count);
                   End Loop;
                   new_node.entries := j;
                   new_node.level := node.level;
                   node.entries := index;
                   next_index_location :=
                       Positive ( Index_Block_IO.Size ( index_blocks_file ) )
                                                    + 1;
                   hold_tuple := ( new_node.tuple(1).key,
                                   next_index_location );
                   Index_Block_IO.Write ( index_blocks_file, new_node,
                       Index_Block_IO.Positive_Count ( next_index_location ) );
                   Index_Block_IO.Write ( index_blocks_file, node,
                       Index_Block_IO.Positive_Count ( index_block_address ) );
               END Split;
           BEGIN -- Insert_Tuple
                If node.entries < INDEX_BLOCK_SIZE Then
                       -- resulting node is large enough for addition
                    operation := NIL;
```

```
                    For count In Reverse index + 1 .. node.entries Loop
                        node.tuple(count + 1) := node.tuple(count);
                    End Loop;
                    node.entries := node.entries + 1;
                    node.tuple(index + 1) := hold_tuple;
                    Index_Block_IO.Write ( index_blocks_file, node,
                        Index_Block_IO.Positive_Count ( index_block_address ) );
               Else   --  node is full so addition will cause a split
                   Split;
                   -- operation retains INSERT_KEY upon return
               End If;
           END Insert_Tuple;
       BEGIN --Insert_Into_Index_Blocks
           hold_tuple := ( key, address );
           Loop
               Exit When Stack_Package.Status ( stack ) = EMPTY;
                -- pop off ancestors
               Stack_Package.Pop ( stack, index_block_address );
               Stack_Package.Pop ( stack, index );
                 -- index_block_address is the address of the index_block
                 -- at the next higher level; insert into position index + 1
               If operation = INSERT_KEY Then
                   Index_Block_IO.Read ( index_blocks_file, node,
                       Index_Block_IO.Positive_Count ( index_block_address ) );
                   Insert_Tuple ( hold_tuple, node, index_block_address,
                                  index, operation );
               End If;
           End Loop;
           If operation = INSERT_KEY Then
             -- new root contains hold_tuple with old root as
             -- tuple(1); tuple = ( key, addr(key) )
               New_Root ( hold_tuple );
           End If;
       END Insert_Into_Index_Blocks;

    BEGIN -- Split_Data_Block
        For lcv In location .. data_block.entries Loop
            entry_position := entry_position + 1;
            new_block.tuple(entry_position) := data_block.tuple(lcv);
        End Loop;

        new_block.entries := entry_position;
        data_block.entries := location - 1;

        new_block.link := data_block.link;
        next_data_location :=
            Natural ( Data_Block_IO.Size ( data_blocks_file ) ) + 1;
        data_block.link := next_data_location;
        Data_Block_IO.Write ( data_blocks_file, new_block,
            Data_Block_IO.Positive_Count ( next_data_location ) );
        Insert_Into_Index_Blocks ( Key_Of ( new_block.tuple(1) ),
                                   next_data_location );
    END Split_Data_Block;

BEGIN  -- Insert
    -- Create Indexed Sequential File
    key := Key_Of ( data_record );
    Find_Node ( key, data_block_number, location, data_block, successful );
```

```
    If successful Then
        Raise key_not_inserted;
    End If;
    If data_block_number = 0 Then
        data_block_number := 1;
        hold_tuple := ( key, 1 );
        New_Root ( hold_tuple );
    End If;
    If data_block.entries = DATA_BLOCK_SIZE Then
        new_block.tuple(1) := data_record;
        Split_Data_Block ( data_block, location, new_block );
    Else
        data_block.entries := data_block.entries + 1;
        For lcv In Reverse  location + 1 .. data_block.entries Loop
            data_block.tuple(lcv) := data_block.tuple(lcv - 1);
        End Loop;
        data_block.tuple(location) := data_record;
        Stack_Package.Create ( stack ); -- clear the stack
    End If;
    Data_Block_IO.Write ( data_blocks_file, data_block,
        Data_Block_IO.Positive_Count ( data_block_number ) );
END Insert;

PROCEDURE Delete ( key : Key_Type ) Is
    Type Operation_Type Is ( REPLACE, DELETE, NIL );
    action            : Operation_Type;
    data_block        : Data_Block_Type;
    data_block_number : Natural;
    first_key         : Key_Type;
    hold_tuple        : Index_Entry;
    location          : Natural;
    successful        : Boolean;

    PROCEDURE Delete_Index_Entry ( action : In Out Operation_Type;
                                   key : Key_Type;
                                   hold_tuple : In Out Index_Entry ) Is

        index,
        index_block_address : Positive;
        index_block         : Index_node;
        predecessor_found   : Boolean := FALSE;

        PROCEDURE Locate_Predecessor ( previous : Positive ) Is
            data_block         : Data_Block_Type;
            hold_address       : Natural;
            index_block        : Index_Node;
            next_block         : Data_Block_Type;
            next_block_address : Natural;
        BEGIN -- Locate_Predecessor
            hold_address := index_block.tuple(previous).address;
            Index_Block_IO.Read ( index_blocks_file, index_block,
                Index_Block_IO.Positive_Count ( hold_address ) );
            Loop
                Exit When index_block.level = DATA;
                hold_address := index_block.tuple(index_block.entries).address;
                Index_Block_IO.Read ( index_blocks_file, index_block,
                    Index_Block_IO.Positive_Count ( hold_address ) );
            End Loop;
```

```
        hold_address := index_block.tuple(index_block.entries).address;
        Data_Block_IO.Read ( data_blocks_file, data_block,
             Data_Block_IO.Positive_Count ( hold_address ) );
        next_block_address := data_block.link;
        Data_Block_IO.Read ( data_blocks_file, next_block,
             Data_Block_IO.Positive_Count ( next_block_address ) );
        data_block.link := next_block.link;
        Data_Block_IO.Write ( data_blocks_file, data_block,
             Data_Block_IO.Positive_Count ( hold_address ) );
    END Locate_Predecessor;

    PROCEDURE Replace_Entry ( key : Key_Type;
                              hold_tuple : In Out Index_Entry;
                              index_block : In Out Index_Node;
                              index_block_address : Positive;
                              index : Positive;
                              action : In Out Operation_Type ) Is
    BEGIN  -- Replace_Entry
        If index_block.tuple(index).key = key Then
            index_block.tuple(index) := hold_tuple;
            Index_Block_IO.Write ( index_blocks_file, index_block,
                  Index_Block_IO.Positive_Count ( index_block_address ) );
        End If;
        If index = 1 Then
            hold_tuple := ( index_block.tuple(1).key,
                            index_block_address );
            -- action remains REPLACE
        Else
            action := NIL;
        End If;
    END Replace_Entry;

    PROCEDURE Delete_Entry ( index_block : In Out Index_Node;
                             index_block_address : Positive;
                             index : Positive;
                             action : In Out Operation_Type;
                             predecessor_found : In Out Boolean ) Is
        key      : Key_Type;
        previous : Natural;
    BEGIN  -- Delete_Entry
        key := index_block.tuple(1).key;
        If index_block.level = DATA Then
            If index = 1 Then
                predecessor_found := FALSE;
            Else
              --   link around deleted data block
                previous := index_block.tuple(index - 1).address;
                Data_Block_IO.Read ( data_blocks_file, data_block,
                   Data_Block_IO.Positive_Count ( previous ) );
                data_block.link := index_block.tuple(index + 1).address;
                Data_Block_IO.Write ( data_blocks_file, data_block,
                     Data_Block_IO.Positive_Count ( previous ) );
                predecessor_found := TRUE;
            End If;
        Else -- index_block.level = INDEX
            If Not predecessor_found And index > 1 Then
                Locate_Predecessor ( index - 1 );
                predecessor_found := TRUE;
```

```
            End If;
        End If;
        If index_block.entries = 1 Then  -- delete only entry
           Return;
        Else
            index_block.entries := index_block.entries - 1;
            For count In index .. index_block.entries Loop
                 index_block.tuple(count) := index_block.tuple(count + 1);
            End Loop;
            Index_Block_IO.Write ( index_blocks_file, index_block,
                Index_Block_IO.Positive_Count ( index_block_address ) );
            If index = 1 Then
                hold_tuple := ( index_block.tuple(1).key,
                                index_block_address );
                -- replace key with hold_tuple entry in parent
                action := REPLACE;
            Else
                action := NIL;
            End If;
        End If;
    END Delete_Entry;

BEGIN -- Delete_Index_Entry
    Loop
        Exit When Stack_Package.Status ( stack ) = EMPTY;
        Stack_Package.Pop ( stack, index_block_address );
        Stack_Package.Pop ( stack, index );
        Index_Block_IO.Read ( index_blocks_file, index_block,
              Index_Block_IO.Positive_Count ( index_block_address ) );
        Case action Is
            When REPLACE =>
                 Replace_Entry ( key, hold_tuple, index_block,
                                 index_block_address, index, action);

            When DELETE  =>
                 Delete_Entry ( index_block, index_block_address,
                                index, action, predecessor_found );
            When NIL => Null;
        End Case;
    End Loop;
    If action = DELETE Then   -- last data block has been deleted
        index_block.entries := 0;
        Index_Block_IO.Write ( index_blocks_file, index_block, 1 );
    End If;
END Delete_Index_Entry;

BEGIN  -- Delete
    Find_Node ( key, data_block_number, location, data_block, successful );
    If successful Then
        first_key := Key_Of ( data_block.tuple(1) );
        If data_block.entries = 1  Then  -- delete only entry
            action := DELETE;
            Delete_Index_Entry ( action, key, hold_tuple );
        Else
            For lcv In location + 1 .. data_block.entries Loop
                data_block.tuple(lcv - 1) := data_block.tuple(lcv);
            End Loop;
```

```
            data_block.entries := data_block.entries - 1;
            Data_Block_IO.Write ( data_blocks_file, data_block,
                 Data_Block_IO.Positive_Count ( data_block_number ) );

            If location = 1 Then --  delete first entry
                hold_tuple := ( Key_Of ( data_block.tuple(1)),data_block_number);
                -- replace key with hold_tuple entry in parent
                action := REPLACE;
                Delete_Index_Entry ( action, key, hold_tuple );
            End If;
        End If;
        Stack_Package.Create ( stack ); -- clear the stack
    Else
        Stack_Package.Create ( stack ); -- clear the stack
        Raise key_not_deleted;
    End If;
END Delete;

PROCEDURE Retrieve ( key : Key_Type; data_record : Out Record_Info ) Is
    data_block        : Data_Block_Type;
    data_block_number : Natural;
    location          : Natural;
    successful        : Boolean;
BEGIN
    Find_Node ( key, data_block_number, location, data_block, successful );
    Stack_Package.Create ( stack ); -- clear the stack
    If successful Then
        data_record := data_block.tuple(location);
    Else
        Raise key_not_found;
    End If;
END Retrieve;

PROCEDURE Replace ( data_record : Record_Info ) Is
    data_block : Data_Block_Type;
    data_block_number,
    location   : Natural;
    key        : Key_Type;
    successful : Boolean;
BEGIN -- Replace
    key := Key_Of ( data_record );
    Find_Node ( key, data_block_number, location, data_block, successful );
    Stack_Package.Create ( stack ); -- clear the stack
    If successful Then
        data_block.tuple(location) := data_record;
        Data_Block_IO.Write ( data_blocks_file, data_block,
             Data_Block_IO.Positive_Count ( data_block_number ) );
    Else
        Raise key_not_found;
    End If;
END Replace;

PROCEDURE Close_BPlus_Tree ( external_bplus_tree_filename,
                             external_data_block_file : String ) Is
BEGIN -- Close_BPlus_Tree
    Index_Block_IO.Close  ( index_blocks_file );
    Data_Block_IO.Close ( data_blocks_file );
END Close_BPlus_Tree;
```

```
BEGIN -- BPlus_Tree;
    Stack_Package.Create ( stack );
END BPlus_Tree;

With Sequential_IO,
     Text_IO,
     BPLus_Tree,
     Ch5Struc;
PROCEDURE Alg9_1 Is
    FUNCTION Car_Key ( car : Ch5Struc.Car_Master_Record )
             Return Ch5Struc.Id_String Is
    BEGIN
        Text_IO.Put_Line ( car.id_number );
        Return car.id_number;
    END Car_Key;
    PACKAGE Car_BPlus Is New BPlus_Tree ( 3, 3,
                                          Ch5Struc.Id_String,
                                          Ch5Struc.Car_Master_Record,
                                          Car_Key, ">" );

    PROCEDURE Get_Next_Trans ( transaction : In Out Ch5Struc.Car_Master_Record )  Is
        update_code :  Character;
    BEGIN  -- Get_Next_Trans
        Text_IO.Get ( Ch5Struc.transfile, update_code );
        Text_IO.Put ( ' ' );
        Text_IO.Put ( update_code );
        Text_IO.Put ( ' ' );
        Text_IO.Get ( Ch5Struc.transfile, transaction.id_number );
        Text_IO.Put ( transaction.id_number );
        Text_IO.Put ( ' ' );
        Case update_code Is
            When 'A' =>
                Text_IO.Get ( Ch5Struc.transfile, transaction.make );
                Text_IO.Put ( ' ' );
                Text_IO.Put ( transaction.make );
                Text_IO.Get ( Ch5Struc.transfile, transaction.style );
                Text_IO.Put ( ' ' );
                Text_IO.Put ( transaction.style );
                Text_IO.Get ( Ch5Struc.transfile, transaction.model );
                Text_IO.Put ( ' ' );
                Text_IO.Put ( transaction.model );
                Text_IO.Get ( Ch5Struc.transfile, transaction.mileage );
                Text_IO.Put ( ' ' );
                Text_IO.Put ( transaction.mileage );
                Text_IO.Get ( Ch5Struc.transfile, transaction.color );
                Text_IO.Put ( ' ' );
                Text_IO.Put ( transaction.color );
                Text_IO.Put ( ' ' );
            When Others =>
                Text_IO.Put ( "                                  " );
                Text_IO.Put ( "invalid update code" );
        End Case;
        Text_IO.Skip_Line ( Ch5Struc.transfile );
    END Get_Next_Trans;

BEGIN  -- Alg9_1
    Text_IO.Open ( Ch5Struc.transfile, Text_IO.IN_FILE, "CARTRANS.TXT" );
    Car_BPlus.Create_BPlus_Tree ( "CARDATA.BPT", "CARDATA.BLK" );
```

```
    Loop
        Exit When Text_IO.End_Of_File ( Ch5Struc.transfile );
        Get_Next_Trans ( Ch5Struc.master_record );
        BEGIN
            Car_BPlus.Insert ( Ch5Struc.master_record );
            Text_IO.Put ( Ch5Struc.master_record.id_number );
            Text_IO.Put_Line ( " inserted" );
        EXCEPTION
            When Car_BPlus.key_not_inserted =>
                Text_IO.Put ( Ch5Struc.master_record.id_number );
                Text_IO.Put_Line ( " is a duplicate id number." );
        END;
    End Loop;
    Car_BPlus.Close_BPlus_Tree ( "CARDATA.BPT", "CARDATA.BLK" );
END Alg9_1;

With Sequential_IO,
     Text_IO,
     BPLus_Tree,
     Ch5Struc;
PROCEDURE Alg9_5 Is
    FUNCTION Car_Key ( car : Ch5Struc.Car_Master_Record )
             Return Ch5Struc.Id_String Is
    BEGIN
        Return car.id_number;
    END Car_Key;
    PACKAGE Car_BPlus Is New BPlus_Tree ( 3, 3,
                                          Ch5Struc.Id_String,
                                          Ch5Struc.Car_Master_Record,
                                          Car_Key, ">" );
PROCEDURE Get_Next_Trans ( transaction : In Out Ch5Struc.Car_Transaction_Record ) Is
BEGIN  -- Get_Next_Trans
    Text_IO.Get ( Ch5Struc.transfile, transaction.update_code );
    Text_IO.Put ( ' ' );
    Text_IO.Put ( transaction.update_code );
    Text_IO.Put ( ' ' );
    Text_IO.Get ( Ch5Struc.transfile, transaction.id_number );
    Text_IO.Put ( transaction.id_number );
    Text_IO.Put ( ' ' );
    Case transaction.update_code Is
        When 'A' =>
            Text_IO.Get ( Ch5Struc.transfile, transaction.make );
            Text_IO.Put ( "  " );
            Text_IO.Put ( transaction.make );
            Text_IO.Get ( Ch5Struc.transfile, transaction.style );
            Text_IO.Put ( ' ' );
            Text_IO.Put ( transaction.style );
            Text_IO.Get ( Ch5Struc.transfile, transaction.model );
            Text_IO.Put ( ' ' );
            Text_IO.Put ( transaction.model );
            Text_IO.Get ( Ch5Struc.transfile, transaction.mileage );
            Text_IO.Put ( ' ' );
            Text_IO.Put ( transaction.mileage );
            Text_IO.Get ( Ch5Struc.transfile, transaction.color );
            Text_IO.Put ( ' ' );
            Text_IO.Put ( transaction.color );
            Text_IO.Put ( ' ' );
```

```
        When 'C' =>
            Text_IO.Get ( Ch5Struc.transfile, transaction.mileage );
            Text_IO.Put ( "  " );
            Text_IO.Put ( transaction.mileage );
            Text_IO.Put ( "           " );
        When 'D' =>
            Text_IO.Put ("                                           " );
        When Others =>
            Text_IO.Put ( "                                  " );
            Text_IO.Put ( "invalid update code" );
    End Case;
    Text_IO.Skip_Line ( Ch5Struc.transfile );
END Get_Next_Trans;

BEGIN  -- Alg9_5
    Car_BPlus.Open_BPlus_Tree ( "CARDATA.BPT", "CARDATA.BLK" );
    Text_IO.Open ( Ch5Struc.transfile, Text_IO.IN_FILE, "CARTRANS.TXT" );
    Loop
        Exit When Text_IO.End_Of_File ( Ch5Struc.transfile );
        Get_Next_Trans (Ch5Struc.transaction);
        Case Ch5Struc.transaction.update_code Is
            When 'A' => DECLARE
                            trans : Ch5Struc.Car_Transaction_Record
                                        Renames Ch5Struc.transaction;
                        BEGIN
                            Ch5Struc.master_record := ( trans.id_number,
                                                        trans.make,
                                                        trans.style,
                                                        trans.model,
                                                        trans.mileage,
                                                        trans.color );
                            Car_BPlus.Insert ( Ch5Struc.master_record );
                            Text_IO.Put_Line ( " add");
                        EXCEPTION
                            When Car_BPlus.key_not_inserted =>
                                Text_IO.Put_Line ("  duplicate add");
                        END;
            When 'C' => BEGIN
                            Car_BPlus.Retrieve ( Ch5Struc.transaction.id_number,
                                                 Ch5Struc.master_record );
                            Ch5Struc.master_record.mileage :=
                                Ch5Struc.transaction.mileage;
                            Car_BPLus.Replace ( Ch5Struc.master_record );
                            Text_IO.Put_Line ( "  changed");
                        EXCEPTION
                             When Car_BPlus.key_not_found =>
                                 Text_IO.Put_Line ( " no matching master for change" );
                        END;
            When 'D' => BEGIN
                            Car_BPlus.Delete ( Ch5Struc.transaction.id_number );
                            Text_IO.Put_Line ( " deleted");
                        EXCEPTION
                            When Car_BPlus.key_not_deleted =>
                                Text_IO.Put_Line ("  no matching master for delete");
                        END;
            When Others => Text_IO.Put_Line ( " invalid update code");
        End Case;
    End Loop;
```

```
    Car_BPlus.Close_BPlus_Tree ( "CARDATA.BPT", "CARDATA.BLK" );
    Text_IO.Close ( Ch5Struc.transfile );
END Alg9_5;
```

Case Study 9.2

```
GENERIC
    INDEX_BLOCK_SIZE : Positive;
    DATA_BLOCK_SIZE : Positive;
    Type Key_Type Is Private;
    Type Record_Info Is Private;
    With FUNCTION Key_Of ( a_record : Record_Info ) Return Key_Type;
    With FUNCTION ">" ( left_operand, right_operand : Key_Type )
                       Return Boolean;
PACKAGE ISAM Is
    PROCEDURE Create_ISAM ( external_sequential_filename,
                            external_index_block_filename,
                            external_data_block_filename,
                            external_overflow_filename : String );
    PROCEDURE Open_ISAM ( external_index_block_filename,
                          external_data_block_filename,
                          external_overflow_filename : String );
    PROCEDURE  Insert ( data_record : Record_Info );
    PROCEDURE Delete ( key : Key_Type );
    PROCEDURE Retrieve ( key : Key_Type; data_record : Out Record_Info );
    PROCEDURE Replace ( data_record : Record_Info );
    PROCEDURE Close_ISAM;
    key_not_found    : Exception;
    key_not_deleted  : Exception;
    key_not_inserted : Exception;
END ISAM;

With Text_IO;
With Direct_IO;
With Sequential_IO;
PACKAGE Body ISAM Is
    Type An_entry Is Record
                        key     : Key_Type;
                        address : Natural;
                    End Record;
    Type Index_entries Is Record
                             normal   : An_entry;
                             overflow : An_entry;
                         End Record;
    Type Tuple_Type Is Array ( 1 .. INDEX_BLOCK_SIZE ) Of Index_entries;
    Type Index_Type Is Record
                          entries : Natural := 0;
                          tuple   : Tuple_Type;
                      End Record;
    Type Data_Status Is ( ACTIVE, DELETED );
    Type Data_Type Is Record
                         data   : Record_Info;
                         status : Data_Status;
                     End Record;
```

```
Type Data_Tuple Is Array ( 1 .. DATA_BLOCK_SIZE ) Of Data_Type;
Type Prime_data_block Is Record
                             data_entries : Integer;
                             prime_record : Data_Tuple;
                         End Record;
Type Overflow_block Is Record
                           over_record   : Record_Info;
                           next_overflow : Natural;
                       End Record;
Type Status_Type Is ( IN_NORMAL, IN_OVERFLOW );
PACKAGE Index_IO    Is New Direct_IO     ( Index_type );
PACKAGE Data_IO     Is New Direct_IO     ( Prime_Data_Block );
PACKAGE Overflow_IO Is New Direct_IO     ( Overflow_Block );
index_file    : Index_IO.File_Type;
data_file     : Data_IO.File_Type;
overflow_file : Overflow_IO.File_Type;
indexes     : Index_Type;

PROCEDURE Create_ISAM ( external_sequential_filename,
                        external_index_block_filename,
                        external_data_block_filename,
                        external_overflow_filename : String ) Is

    PACKAGE Seq_IO Is New Sequential_IO ( Record_Info );
    data_block  : Prime_Data_Block;
    db          : Natural := 0;
    location    : Natural := 0;
    over_block  : Overflow_Block;
    seq_file    : Seq_IO.File_Type;

    PROCEDURE Full_Data_Block ( data_block : In Prime_Data_Block;
                                db : In Natural;
                                location : In Natural;
                                indexes : In Out Index_Type ) Is
    BEGIN  -- Full_Data_Block
        Data_IO.Write ( data_file, data_block,
                        Data_IO.Positive_Count ( location ) );
        indexes.entries := indexes.entries + 1;
        indexes.tuple(indexes.entries).normal :=
                ( Key_Of ( data_block.prime_record(db).data ), location );
        indexes.tuple(indexes.entries).overflow :=
           indexes.tuple(indexes.entries).normal;
    END Full_Data_Block;

BEGIN  -- Create_ISAM
    Seq_IO.Open ( seq_file, Seq_IO.IN_FILE, external_sequential_filename );
    Index_IO.Create ( index_file,
                      Index_IO.INOUT_FILE,
                      external_index_block_filename );
    Data_IO.Create ( data_file,
                     Data_IO.INOUT_FILE,
                     external_data_block_filename );
    Overflow_IO.Create ( overflow_file,
                         Overflow_IO.INOUT_FILE,
                         external_overflow_filename );

    Loop
        Exit When Seq_IO.End_Of_File ( seq_file );
        db := db + 1;
```

```
            Seq_IO.Read ( seq_file, data_block.prime_record(db).data );
            data_block.prime_record(db).status := ACTIVE;
            If db = DATA_BLOCK_SIZE Then
                data_block.data_entries := db;
                location := location + 1;
                Full_Data_Block ( data_block, db, location, indexes );
                db := 0;
            End If;
        End Loop;
        If db /= 0 Then
            data_block.data_entries := db;
            location := location + 1;
            Full_Data_Block ( data_block, db, location, indexes );
        End If;
        Seq_IO.Close ( seq_file );
    END Create_ISAM;

    PROCEDURE Open_ISAM ( external_index_block_filename,
                          external_data_block_filename,
                          external_overflow_filename : String ) Is
    BEGIN
        Index_IO.Open ( index_file,
                        Index_IO.INOUT_FILE,
                        external_index_block_filename );
        Index_IO.Read ( index_file, indexes );
        Data_IO.Open ( data_file,
                       Data_IO.INOUT_FILE,
                       external_data_block_filename );
        Overflow_IO.Open ( overflow_file,
                           Overflow_IO.INOUT_FILE,
                           external_overflow_filename );
    END Open_ISAM;

    PROCEDURE Find ( key : Key_Type;
                     status : In Out Status_Type;
                     index_location, data_block_number,
                     location, previous : In Out Natural;
                     successful : In Out Boolean ) Is

        PROCEDURE Search_Indexes ( key : Key_Type;
                                   status : In Out Status_Type;
                                   index_location, data_block_number,
                                   location : Out Natural;
                                   successful : Out Boolean ) Is
        BEGIN
            successful := FALSE;
            index_location := indexes.entries + 1;
            For count In 1 .. indexes.entries Loop
                If Not ( key > indexes.tuple(count).normal.key ) Then
                    successful := TRUE;
                    status := IN_NORMAL;
                    index_location := count;
                    data_block_number := indexes.tuple(count).normal.address;
                    Exit;
                Elsif Not ( key > indexes.tuple(count).overflow.key ) Then
                    successful := TRUE;
                    status := IN_OVERFLOW;
                    index_location := count;
```

```
            data_block_number := indexes.tuple(count).overflow.address;
            Exit;
        End If;
    End Loop;
END Search_Indexes;
PROCEDURE Search_Prime_Data ( trans_key : Key_Type;
                              data_block_number : Natural;
                              location : Out Natural;
                              successful : Out Boolean ) Is
    count      : Positive := 1;
    data_block : Prime_Data_Block;
    prime_key  : Key_Type;
BEGIN
    Data_IO.Read ( data_file, data_block,
        Data_IO.Positive_Count ( data_block_number ) );
    Loop
        Exit When count > data_block.data_entries;
        If data_block.prime_record(count).status = ACTIVE Then
            prime_key := Key_OF ( data_block.prime_record(count).data );
            If trans_key > prime_key Then
                Null;
            Elsif  key = prime_key Then
                successful := TRUE;
                Exit;
            Else -- trans_key < prime_key
              -- trans_key not found in prime_data_block so return count
              -- as location of first entry greater than transkey.
              -- trans_key belongs immediately prior to location count.
                successful := FALSE;
                Exit;
            End If;
        End If;
        count := count + 1;
    End Loop;
    location := count;
END Search_Prime_Data;

PROCEDURE Search_Overflow_Data ( key : Key_Type;
                                 over_block_number : In Out Natural;
                                 previous : Out Natural;
                                 successful : Out Boolean ) Is

    over_block   : Overflow_Block;
    overflow_key : Key_Type;
BEGIN  -- Search_Overflow_Data
    previous := 0;
    Overflow_IO.Read ( overflow_file, over_block,
                   Overflow_IO.Positive_Count ( over_block_number ) );
    overflow_key := Key_Of ( over_block.over_record );
    If key > overflow_key Then
        previous := over_block_number;
        over_block_number := over_block.next_overflow;
        Search_Overflow_Data ( key, over_block_number, previous,
                               successful );
    Elsif  key = overflow_key Then
          -- point for insertion
        successful := TRUE;
```

```
        Else -- key < overflow_key
            successful := FALSE;
        End If;
    END Search_Overflow_Data;

BEGIN  -- Find
    Search_Indexes ( key, status, index_location, data_block_number,
                     location, successful );
    If successful Then
        previous := 0;
        If status = IN_OVERFLOW Then
            Search_Overflow_Data ( key, data_block_number, previous,
                                   successful );
        Else -- status = IN_NORMAL
            Search_Prime_Data ( key, data_block_number, location,
                                successful );
        End If;
    Else
        data_block_number := 0;
    End If;
END Find;

PROCEDURE Insert ( data_record : Record_Info ) Is
    data_block             : Prime_Data_Block;
    data_block_number,
    hold_address,
    index_location         : Natural;
    key                    : Key_Type;
    location               : Natural;
    new_over_block         : Overflow_Block;
    next_overflow_location : Natural;
    over_block             : Overflow_Block;
    previous               : Natural;
    status                 : Status_Type;
    successful             : Boolean;

    PROCEDURE Insert_Overflow ( index_location,
                                previous : Natural;
                                new_record : Record_Info ) Is
        new_over_block, previous_block : Overflow_Block;
    BEGIN  -- Insert_Overflow
        new_over_block.over_record := new_record;
        next_overflow_location :=
            Natural ( Overflow_IO.Size ( overflow_file ) ) + 1;
        If indexes.tuple(index_location).normal.address =
           indexes.tuple(index_location).overflow.address Then
          -- start overflow linked list
           new_over_block.next_overflow := 0;
           indexes.tuple(index_location).overflow.address :=
               next_overflow_location;
       Elsif previous = 0 Then
         -- add to front of linked list
           new_over_block.next_overflow :=
               indexes.tuple(index_location).overflow.address;
           indexes.tuple(index_location).overflow.address :=
               next_overflow_location;
```

```
   Else
     -- add to middle of linked list
       Overflow_IO.Read ( overflow_file, previous_block,
           Overflow_IO.Positive_Count ( previous ) );
       new_over_block.next_overflow := previous_block.next_overflow;
       previous_block.next_overflow := next_overflow_location;
       Overflow_IO.Write ( overflow_file, previous_block,
           Overflow_IO.Positive_Count ( previous ) );
   End If;
   Overflow_IO.Write ( overflow_file, new_over_block,
       Overflow_IO.Positive_Count ( next_overflow_location ) );
END Insert_Overflow;

PROCEDURE Insert_Normal ( index_location,
                          data_block_number,
                          location : In Out Natural;
                          new_record : Record_Info ) Is
    data_block  : Prime_Data_Block;
    hold_record : Record_Info;

    PROCEDURE Insert_Into_Block ( index_location,
                                  data_block_number,
                                  location : Natural;
                                  new_record : In Record_Info;
                                  data_block : In Out Prime_Data_Block ) Is
    BEGIN  -- Insert_Into_Block
        For lcv In Reverse location .. data_block.data_entries Loop
            data_block.prime_record(lcv + 1) :=
                data_block.prime_record(lcv);
        End Loop;
        data_block.data_entries := data_block.data_entries + 1;
        data_block.prime_record(location).data := new_record;
        data_block.prime_record(location).status := ACTIVE;
        indexes.tuple(index_location).normal.key :=
           Key_Of( data_block.prime_record(data_block.data_entries).data );
        Data_IO.Write ( data_file, data_block,
            Data_IO.Positive_Count ( data_block_number ) );
    END Insert_Into_Block;

BEGIN  -- Insert_Normal
    Data_IO.Read ( data_file, data_block,
        Data_IO.Positive_Count ( data_block_number ) );
    If data_block.data_entries = DATA_BLOCK_SIZE Then
        -- data_block full
        hold_record := data_block.prime_record( DATA_BLOCK_SIZE).data;
        data_block.data_entries := data_block.data_entries - 1;
        Insert_Into_Block ( index_location, data_block_number,
                            location, new_record, data_block );
        If indexes.tuple(index_location).overflow.key >
           indexes.tuple(index_location).normal.key Then
            -- Find insertion point in overflow
            Find ( key, status, index_location, data_block_number,
                   location, previous, successful );
        End If;
        Insert_Overflow ( index_location, previous, hold_record );
    Else  -- block not full
        Insert_Into_Block ( index_location, data_block_number,
                            location, new_record, data_block );
```

```
        End If;
    END Insert_Normal;

BEGIN  -- Insert
    key := Key_Of ( data_record );
    Find ( key, status, index_location, data_block_number, location,
           previous, successful );
    If successful Then
        Raise key_not_inserted;
    End If;
    If data_block_number = 0 Then
        -- key larger than any currently in the file so add to the
        -- next available data block and add new entry to indexes
        new_over_block.over_record := data_record;
        next_overflow_location :=
            Natural ( Overflow_IO.Size ( overflow_file ) ) + 1;
        hold_address := indexes.tuple(indexes.entries).overflow.address;
        If hold_address = indexes.tuple(indexes.entries).normal.address Then
            -- no overflow for last data block
            new_over_block.next_overflow := hold_address;
            indexes.tuple(indexes.entries).overflow.address :=
                next_overflow_location;
            indexes.tuple(indexes.entries).overflow.key :=
                Key_Of ( data_record );
            Overflow_IO.Write ( overflow_file, new_over_block,
                Overflow_IO.Positive_Count ( next_overflow_location ) );
        Else
            Loop
                Overflow_IO.Read ( overflow_file, over_block,
                    Overflow_IO.Positive_Count ( hold_address ) );
                Exit When over_block.next_overflow = 0;
                hold_address :=
                    indexes.tuple(indexes.entries).overflow.address;
            End Loop;
            new_over_block.next_overflow := over_block.next_overflow;
            over_block.next_overflow := new_over_block.next_overflow;
            indexes.tuple(indexes.entries).overflow.key :=
                Key_Of ( data_record );
            Overflow_IO.Write ( overflow_file, over_block,
                Overflow_IO.Positive_Count ( hold_address ) );
            Overflow_IO.Write ( overflow_file, new_over_block,
                 Overflow_IO.Positive_Count ( next_overflow_location ) );
        End If;
    ElsIf status = IN_NORMAL Then
        Insert_Normal ( index_location, data_block_number, location,
                        data_record );
    Else  -- status = IN_OVERFLOW
        Insert_Overflow ( index_location, previous, data_record );
    End If;
END Insert;

PROCEDURE Delete ( key : Key_Type ) Is
    data_block         : Prime_Data_Block;
    data_block_number,
    index_location,
    location,
    previous           : Natural;
    previous_block,
```

```
    over_block          : Overflow_Block;
    status              : Status_Type;
    successful          : Boolean;
BEGIN  -- Delete
    Find ( key, status, index_location, data_block_number,
           location, previous, successful );
    If successful Then
        If status = IN_NORMAL Then
            Data_IO.Read ( data_file, data_block,
                Data_IO.Positive_Count ( data_block_number ) );
            data_block.prime_record(location).status := DELETED;
            Data_IO.Write ( data_file, data_block,
                Data_IO.Positive_Count ( data_block_number ) );
            If key = indexes.tuple(index_location).normal.key Then
                If location > 1 Then
                    -- will not delete the last one in the block
                    If indexes.tuple(index_location).normal.key =
                          indexes.tuple(index_location).overflow.key Then
                       indexes.tuple(index_location).overflow.key :=
                          Key_Of ( data_block.prime_record(location - 1).data );
                    End If;
                    indexes.tuple(index_location).normal.key :=
                        Key_Of ( data_block.prime_record(location - 1).data );
                End If;
            End If;
        ElsIf indexes.tuple(index_location).overflow.address
              = data_block_number Then
            --  status = IN_OVERFLOW; first one in linked list
            Overflow_IO.Read ( overflow_file, over_block,
                Overflow_IO.Positive_Count ( data_block_number ) );
            indexes.tuple(index_location).overflow.address :=
                over_block.next_overflow;
        Else  -- middle or last of linked list
            Overflow_IO.Read ( overflow_file, previous_block,
                Overflow_IO.Positive_Count ( previous ) );
            previous_block.next_overflow := over_block.next_overflow;
            If over_block.next_overflow = 0 Then
                -- last of list so change overflow.key
                indexes.tuple(index_location).overflow.key :=
                    Key_Of ( previous_block.over_record );
            End If;
            Overflow_IO.Write (overflow_file, previous_block,
                Overflow_IO.Positive_Count ( previous ) );
        End If;
    Else
        Raise key_not_deleted;
    End If;
END Delete;

PROCEDURE Retrieve ( key : Key_Type; data_record : Out Record_Info) Is
data_block          : Prime_Data_Block;
data_block_number,
index_location,
location,
previous            : Natural;
over_block          : Overflow_Block;
status              : Status_Type;
successful          : Boolean := FALSE;
```

```
BEGIN -- Retrieve
    Find ( key, status, index_location, data_block_number, location,
           previous, successful );
    If successful Then
        If status = IN_NORMAL Then
            Data_IO.Read ( data_file, data_block,
                Data_IO.Positive_Count ( data_block_number ) );
            data_record := data_block.prime_record(location).data;
        Else
            Overflow_IO.Read ( overflow_file, over_block,
                Overflow_IO.Positive_Count ( data_block_number ) );
            data_record := over_block.over_record;
        End If;
    Else
        Raise key_not_found;
    End If;
END Retrieve;

PROCEDURE Replace ( data_record : Record_Info ) Is
    data_block          : Prime_Data_Block;
    key                 : Key_Type;
    index_location,
    data_block_number,
    location,
    previous            : Natural;
    status              : Status_Type;
    successful          : Boolean;
    over_block          : Overflow_Block;

BEGIN  -- Replace
    key := Key_Of ( data_record );
    Find ( key, status, index_location, data_block_number, location,
           previous, successful );
    If successful Then
        Case status Is
            When IN_NORMAL   =>
                Data_IO.Read ( data_file, data_block,
                        Data_IO.Positive_Count ( data_block_number ) );
                data_block.prime_record(location).data := data_record;
                Data_IO.Write ( data_file, data_block,
                        Data_IO.Positive_Count ( data_block_number ) );
            When IN_OVERFLOW =>
                Overflow_IO.Read ( overflow_file, over_block,
                        Overflow_IO.Positive_Count ( data_block_number ) );
                over_block.over_record := data_record;
                Overflow_IO.Write ( overflow_file, over_block,
                         Overflow_IO.Positive_Count ( data_block_number ) );
        End Case;
    Else
        Raise key_not_found;
    End If;
END Replace;

PROCEDURE Close_ISAM Is
BEGIN
    Index_IO.Write ( index_file, indexes, 1 );
    Index_IO.Close ( index_file );
```

```
        Data_IO.Close ( data_file );
        Overflow_IO.Close ( overflow_file );
    END Close_ISAM;

END ISAM;

With ISAM,
     Ch5Struc;
PROCEDURE Alg9_6 Is
    FUNCTION Car_Key ( car_data : Ch5Struc.Car_Master_Record )
             Return Ch5Struc.Id_String Is
    BEGIN
        Return car_data.id_number;
    END Car_Key;
    PACKAGE Car_ISAM Is New ISAM ( 30,
                                   3,
                                   Ch5Struc.Id_String,
                                   Ch5Struc.Car_Master_Record,
                                   Car_Key,
                                   ">" );
BEGIN
    Car_ISAM.Create_ISAM ( "CARMSTR.DAT",
                           "CARISAM.INX",
                           "CARISAM.BLK",
                           "CARISAM.OVR" );
    Car_ISAM.Close_ISAM;
END Alg9_6;

With ISAM,
     Text_IO,
     Ch5Struc;
PROCEDURE Alg9_10 Is
    FUNCTION Car_Key ( car_data : Ch5Struc.Car_Master_Record )
             Return Ch5Struc.Id_String Is
    BEGIN
        Return car_data.id_number;
    END Car_Key;
    PACKAGE Car_ISAM Is New ISAM ( 30, 3,
                                   Ch5Struc.Id_String,
                                   Ch5Struc.Car_Master_Record,
                                   Car_Key,
                                   ">" );
    PROCEDURE Get_Next_Trans
              (transaction : In Out Ch5Struc.Car_Transaction_Record) Is
    BEGIN  -- Get_Next_Trans
        Text_IO.Get ( Ch5Struc.transfile, transaction.update_code );
        Text_IO.Put ( ' ' );
        Text_IO.Put ( transaction.update_code );
        Text_IO.Put ( ' ' );
        Text_IO.Get ( Ch5Struc.transfile, transaction.id_number );
        Text_IO.Put ( transaction.id_number );
        Text_IO.Put ( ' ' );
        Case transaction.update_code Is
            When 'A' =>
                Text_IO.Get ( Ch5Struc.transfile, transaction.make );
                Text_IO.Put ( "  " );
                Text_IO.Put ( transaction.make );
                Text_IO.Get ( Ch5Struc.transfile, transaction.style );
```

```
                Text_IO.Put ( ' ' );
                Text_IO.Put ( transaction.style );
                Text_IO.Get ( Ch5Struc.transfile, transaction.model );
                Text_IO.Put ( ' ' );
                Text_IO.Put ( transaction.model );
                Text_IO.Get ( Ch5Struc.transfile, transaction.mileage );
                Text_IO.Put ( ' ' );
                Text_IO.Put ( transaction.mileage );
                Text_IO.Get ( Ch5Struc.transfile, transaction.color );
                Text_IO.Put ( ' ' );
                Text_IO.Put ( transaction.color );
                Text_IO.Put ( ' ' );
            When 'C' =>
                Text_IO.Get ( Ch5Struc.transfile, transaction.mileage );
                Text_IO.Put ( "  " );
                Text_IO.Put ( transaction.mileage );
                Text_IO.Put ( "            " );
            When 'D' =>
                Text_IO.Put ( "                                       " );
            When Others =>
                Text_IO.Put ( "                             " );
                Text_IO.Put ( "invalid update code" );
        End Case;
        Text_IO.Skip_Line ( Ch5Struc.transfile );
    END Get_Next_Trans;

BEGIN -- Alg9_10
    Car_ISAM.Open_ISAM ( "CARISAM.INX",
                         "CARISAM.BLK",
                         "CARISAM.OVR" );
    Text_IO.Open ( Ch5Struc.transfile, Text_IO.IN_FILE, "CARTRANS.TXT" );
    Loop
        Exit When Text_IO.End_Of_File ( Ch5Struc.transfile );
        Get_Next_Trans ( Ch5Struc.transaction );
        Case Ch5Struc.transaction.update_code Is
            When 'A' => DECLARE
                            trans : Ch5Struc.Car_Transaction_Record
                                        renames Ch5Struc.transaction;
                        BEGIN
                            Ch5Struc.master_record := ( trans.id_number,
                                                        trans.make,
                                                        trans.style,
                                                        trans.model,
                                                        trans.mileage,
                                                        trans.color );
                            Car_ISAM.Insert ( Ch5Struc.master_record );
                            Text_IO.Put_Line ( " add");
                        EXCEPTION
                            When Car_ISAM.key_not_inserted =>
                                Text_IO.Put_Line ( "  duplicate add" );
                        END;
            When 'C' => BEGIN
                            Car_ISAM.Retrieve ( Ch5Struc.transaction.id_number,
                                                Ch5Struc.master_record );
                            Ch5Struc.master_record.mileage :=
                                Ch5Struc.transaction.mileage;
                            Car_ISAM.Replace ( Ch5Struc.master_record );
                            Text_IO.Put_Line ( "  changed");
```

```
                        EXCEPTION
                             When Car_ISAM.key_not_found =>
                                 Text_IO.Put_Line ( " no matching master for change" );
                        END;
            When 'D' => BEGIN
                            Car_ISAM.Delete ( Ch5Struc.transaction.id_number );
                            Text_IO.Put_Line ( " deleted" );
                        EXCEPTION
                            When Car_ISAM.key_not_deleted =>
                                Text_IO.Put_Line ("  no matching master for delete" );
                        END;
            When Others => Text_IO.Put_Line ( " invalid update code" );
        End Case;
    End Loop;
    Car_ISAM.Close_ISAM;
    Text_IO.Close ( Ch5Struc.transfile );
END Alg9_10;
```

Case Study 10.1

```
PACKAGE Invert Is
    SubType Primary_Key_Type Is String ( 1 .. 3 );
    SubType Secondary_Key_Type Is String ( 1 .. 10 );
    Type Record_Info Is Record
                            id_no   : Primary_Key_Type;
                            make    : Secondary_Key_Type;
                            style   : Secondary_Key_Type;
                            model   : Secondary_Key_Type;
                            mileage : Secondary_Key_Type;
                            color   : Secondary_Key_Type;
                        End Record;
    Type Secondary_Key_Name_Type Is ( MAKE, STYLE );

    PROCEDURE Create ( external_filename_prefix : String );
    PROCEDURE Open   ( external_filename_prefix : String );
    PROCEDURE Close  ( external_filename_prefix : String );
    PROCEDURE Insert ( new_record : Record_Info );
    PROCEDURE Delete ( id_no : In Primary_Key_Type );
    key_not_inserted,
    key_not_deleted : Exception;
END Invert;

With B_Tree;
With Direct_IO;
With Sequential_IO;
PACKAGE Body Invert Is
    Type Primary_Key_Record;
    Type Primary_Key_Access Is Access Primary_Key_Record;
    Type Primary_Key_Record Is Record
                                  primary_key : Primary_Key_Type;
                                  next_key    : Primary_Key_Access;
                               End Record;
    SubType Key_Value_Type Is String ( 1 .. 10 );
    Type Key_Value_Record;
```

```
Type Key_Value_Access Is Access Key_Value_Record;
Type Key_Value_Record Is Record
                             key_value  : Key_Value_Type;
                             next_value : Key_Value_Access;
                             first_key  : Primary_Key_Access;
                        End Record;

Type Status_Type Is ( ATTRIBUTE, PRIME_KEY );
Type Index_Record_Type ( status : Status_Type := ATTRIBUTE ) Is
     Record
         Case status Is
             When ATTRIBUTE => key_value     : Key_Value_Type;
                               first_address : Integer;
             When PRIME_KEY => primary_key   : Primary_Key_Type;
                               next_address  : Integer;
         End Case;
     End Record;

PACKAGE Data_File_IO Is New Direct_IO ( Record_Info );
PACKAGE B_Tree_IO Is New B_Tree ( 3, Primary_Key_Type, ">" );
PACKAGE Index_File_IO Is New Sequential_IO ( Index_Record_Type );
index_file    : Index_File_IO.File_Type;
data_file     : Data_File_IO.File_Type;
key_not_found : Exception;
header        : Array ( Secondary_Key_Name_Type ) Of Key_Value_Access
                                       := ( Others => NULL );
record_number : Natural := 1;

PROCEDURE Create ( external_filename_prefix : String ) Is
BEGIN  -- Create
    Data_File_IO.Create ( data_file,
                          Data_File_IO.INOUT_FILE,
                          external_filename_prefix & ".DAT" );
    B_Tree_IO.Create_B_Tree ( external_filename_prefix & ".BTR" );
END Create;

PROCEDURE Search_List ( header : In Key_Value_Access;
                        secondary_key : In Secondary_Key_Type;
                        where_found, previous : In Out Key_Value_Access ) Is
    -- returns (in where_found) NULL if
    --     secondary_key is not found in index
    -- or returns (in where_found) a pointer to the node
    --     in the linked structure if found
    -- previous contains the pointer to the node previous to
    --     the node containing the secondary_key in case a
    --     deletion is to be made
BEGIN  -- Search_List
    previous := NULL;
    where_found := header;
    Loop
        Exit When where_found = NULL;
        If where_found.key_value = secondary_key Then
            Return;
        End If;
        previous := where_found;
        where_found := where_found.next_value;
    End Loop;
    Raise key_not_found;
END Search_List;
```

```
PROCEDURE Insert ( new_record : Record_Info ) Is
    next_record_location : Natural;
    PROCEDURE Insert_Index ( secondary_key_name : In Secondary_Key_Name_Type;
                             secondary_key : In Secondary_Key_Type;
                             id_no : In Primary_Key_Type ) Is
        -- secondary_key_name indicates which index is to be built:
        --      MAKE or STYLE
        -- secondary_key is either the make or style that was read
        --      into new_record
        previous,
        where_found   : Key_Value_Access;
    BEGIN -- Insert_Index
        Search_List ( header(secondary_key_name), secondary_key,
                      where_found, previous );
            -- Add_To_Key_List
            -- add the record location of new record to the front of
            -- the list of addresses for the key_value pointed to
            -- by where_found
        where_found.first_key := New Primary_Key_Record'
                                ( id_no, where_found.first_key );

    EXCEPTION
        When key_not_found =>
                -- Add_To_Directory
                -- add the secondary_key as a first Key_Value_Record in the
                -- linked structure with the address of the primary key
                -- of new record as the first_key
            header ( secondary_key_name ) :=
                New Key_Value_Record' ( secondary_key,
                                        header(secondary_key_name),
                                        New Primary_Key_Record'( id_no, NULL ) );
    END Insert_Index;

BEGIN -- Insert
    next_record_location := Natural ( Data_File_IO.Index ( data_file ) ) + 1;
    B_Tree_IO.Insert ( new_record.id_no, Positive ( next_record_location ) );
    Insert_Index ( MAKE, new_record.make, new_record.id_no );
    Insert_Index ( STYLE, new_record.style, new_record.id_no );
    Data_File_IO.Write ( data_file,
                         new_record,
                         Data_File_IO.Positive_Count ( next_record_location ) );
EXCEPTION
    When B_Tree_IO.key_not_inserted => Raise key_not_inserted;
END Insert;

PROCEDURE Delete ( id_no : In Primary_Key_Type ) Is
    location   : Positive;
    new_record : Record_Info;
    PROCEDURE Delete_Index ( secondary_key_name : In Secondary_Key_Name_Type;
                             secondary_key : In Secondary_Key_Type;
                             id_no : In Primary_Key_Type ) Is
        -- secondary_key_name indicates which index is to have a deletion:
        --      MAKE or STYLE index
        -- secondary_key is either the make or style that is
        --      to be deleted from the directory
        previous_pointer,
        primary_pointer : Primary_Key_Access;
```

```
            previous,
            where_found     : Key_Value_Access;
        BEGIN -- Delete_Index
            Search_List ( header(secondary_key_name), secondary_key, where_found,
                          previous );
            If where_found.first_key.primary_key = id_no Then
                -- delete first key
                where_found.first_key := where_found.first_key.next_key;
                If where_found.first_key = NULL Then
                    -- delete entire entry since the only id_no has been deleted
                    If header(secondary_key_name) = where_found Then
                        -- first key value in linked structure
                         header(secondary_key_name) := where_found.next_value;
                    Else
                        previous.next_value := where_found.next_value;
                    End If;
                End If;
            Else    -- search for id_no in list of addresses
                primary_pointer := where_found.first_key.next_key;
                previous_pointer := where_found.first_key;
                Loop
                    Exit When primary_pointer = NULL;
                    If primary_pointer.primary_key = id_no Then
                        previous_pointer.next_key :=
                             primary_pointer.next_key;
                        Return;
                    Else
                        previous_pointer := primary_pointer;
                        primary_pointer := primary_pointer.next_key;
                    End If;
                End Loop;
                Raise key_not_deleted;
            End If;
        EXCEPTION
            When key_not_found => Raise key_not_deleted;
        END Delete_Index;

    BEGIN -- Delete
        B_Tree_IO.Search ( id_no, location );
        Data_File_IO.Read ( data_file,
                            new_record,
                            Data_File_IO.Positive_Count ( location ) );
        Delete_Index ( MAKE, new_record.make, new_record.id_no );
        Delete_Index ( STYLE, new_record.style, new_record.id_no );
        new_record.id_no := "NIL";
        Data_File_IO.Write ( data_file,
                             new_record,
                             Data_File_IO.Positive_Count ( location ) );
        B_Tree_IO.Delete ( id_no );
    EXCEPTION
        When B_Tree_IO.key_not_found
           | B_Tree_IO.key_not_deleted => Raise key_not_deleted;
    END Delete;
    PROCEDURE Open  ( external_filename_prefix : String ) Is
        PROCEDURE Input_Indexes ( external_filename : String;
                                  header : In Out Key_Value_Access ) Is
            key_index_record     : Index_Record_Type; -- ( ATTRIBUTE );
            key_pointer          : Key_Value_Access;
```

```
        next_key_pointer      : Key_Value_Access;
        next_primary_pointer  : Primary_Key_Access;
        primary_index_record  : Index_Record_Type; -- ( PRIME_KEY );
        primary_pointer       : Primary_Key_Access;
    BEGIN  -- Input_Indexes
        Index_File_IO.Open ( index_file,
                             Index_File_IO.IN_FILE,
                             external_filename );
        Index_File_IO.Read ( index_file, key_index_record );
        header := New Key_Value_Record'
                      ( key_index_record.key_value, NULL, NULL );
        key_pointer := header;
        Loop
            Index_File_IO.Read ( index_file, primary_index_record );
            primary_pointer := New Primary_Key_Record'
                                  ( primary_index_record.primary_key, NULL );
            key_pointer.first_key := primary_pointer;
            Loop
                Exit When primary_index_record.next_address = -1;
                Index_File_IO.Read ( index_file, primary_index_record );
                next_primary_pointer := New Primary_Key_Record'
                                  ( primary_index_record.primary_key, NULL );
                primary_pointer.next_key := next_primary_pointer;
                primary_pointer := next_primary_pointer;
            End Loop;
            Exit When Index_File_IO.End_Of_File ( index_file );
            Index_File_IO.Read ( index_file, key_index_record );
            next_key_pointer := New Key_Value_Record'
                                  ( key_index_record.key_value, NULL, NULL );
            key_pointer.next_value := next_key_pointer;
            key_pointer := next_key_pointer;
        End Loop;
        Index_File_IO.Close ( index_file );
    END Input_Indexes;

BEGIN  -- Open
    Data_File_IO.Open ( data_file,
                        Data_File_IO.INOUT_FILE,
                        external_filename_prefix & ".DAT" );
    B_Tree_IO.Open_B_Tree ( external_filename_prefix & ".BTR" );
    Input_Indexes ( external_filename_prefix & ".MAK", header(MAKE) );
    Input_Indexes ( external_filename_prefix & ".STY", header(STYLE) );
END Open;

PROCEDURE Close  ( external_filename_prefix : String ) Is
    PROCEDURE Output_Indexes ( external_filename : String;
                               header : In Out Key_Value_Access ) Is
        -- output either the MAKE or the STYLE indexes
        -- (indicated by secondary_key_name) sequentially  to an external
        -- file for  storage
        --
        -- all  pointers  must  be  converted  to  record
        -- addresses and all "NULL" pointer values must be
        -- converted to -1
        key_pointer      : Key_Value_Access;
        lcv              : Positive;
        primary_pointer  : Primary_Key_Access;
        one_index_record : Index_Record_Type;  -- (ATTRIBUTE);
```

```
            two_index_record : Index_Record_Type;  -- (PRIME_KEY);
            record_number    : Positive := 1;
        BEGIN  -- Output_Indexes
            Index_File_IO.Create ( index_file,
                                   Index_File_IO.OUT_FILE,
                                   external_filename );
            key_pointer := header;
            Loop
                Exit When key_pointer = NULL;
                one_index_record.key_value := key_pointer.key_value;
                one_index_record.first_address := record_number + 1;
                    -- output index_record to location record_number
                    -- of index_file
                Index_File_IO.Write ( index_file, one_index_record );
                record_number := record_number + 1;
                primary_pointer := key_pointer.first_key;
                Loop
                    Exit When primary_pointer = NULL;
                    two_index_record.primary_key := primary_pointer.primary_key;
                    If primary_pointer.next_key /= NULL Then
                        two_index_record.next_address := record_number + 1;
                    Else
                        two_index_record.next_address := -1;
                    End If;
                    Index_File_IO.Write ( index_file, two_index_record );
                    record_number := record_number + 1;
                    primary_pointer := primary_pointer.next_key;
                End Loop;
                key_pointer := key_pointer.next_value;
            End Loop;
            Index_File_IO.Close ( index_file );
        END Output_Indexes;
    BEGIN  -- Close
        Data_File_IO.Close ( data_file );
        B_Tree_IO.Close_B_Tree;
        Output_Indexes ( external_filename_prefix & ".MAK", header(MAKE) );
        Output_Indexes ( external_filename_prefix & ".STY", header(STYLE) );
    END Close;
END Invert;

With Text_IO,
     Invert;
PROCEDURE Alg10_1 Is
    input_file : Text_IO.File_Type;
    new_record : Invert.Record_Info;
    code       : Character;
BEGIN -- Alg10_1
    Text_IO.Open ( input_file, Text_IO.IN_FILE, "CARDATA.TXT" );
    Invert.Create ( "CARDATA" );
    Loop
        Exit When Text_IO.End_Of_File ( input_file );
        Text_IO.Get ( input_file, code );
        Text_IO.Get ( input_file, new_record.id_no );
        Text_IO.Put_Line ( new_record.id_no );
        Text_IO.Get ( input_file, new_record.make );
        Text_IO.Get ( input_file, new_record.style );
        Text_IO.Get ( input_file, new_record.model );
        Text_IO.Get ( input_file, new_record.mileage );
```

```
        Text_IO.Get ( input_file, new_record.color );
        Text_IO.Skip_Line ( input_file );
        BEGIN
            Invert.Insert ( new_record );
        EXCEPTION
            When Invert.key_not_inserted =>
                Text_IO.Put ( new_record.id_no );
                Text_IO.Put_Line ( "    Duplicate Key" );
        END;
    End Loop;
    Text_IO.Close ( input_file );
    Invert.Close ( "CARDATA" );
END Alg10_1;

With Text_IO,
     Invert;
PROCEDURE Alg10_2 Is

    id_no            : Invert.Primary_Key_Type;
    new_record       : Invert.Record_Info;
    transaction_code : Character;
    transfile        : Text_IO.File_Type;

BEGIN -- Alg10_2
    Text_IO.Open ( transfile, Text_IO.IN_FILE, "CARTRANS.TXT" );
    Invert.Open ( "CARDATA" );
    Loop
        Exit When Text_IO.End_Of_File ( transfile );
        Text_IO.Get ( transfile, transaction_code );
        Text_IO.Put ( transaction_code );
        Text_IO.Put ( " " );
        Text_IO.Get ( transfile, id_no );
        Text_IO.Put_Line ( id_no );
        BEGIN
            Case transaction_code Is
                When 'A' =>
                    new_record.id_no := id_no;
                    Text_IO.Get ( transfile, new_record.make );
                    Text_IO.Get ( transfile, new_record.style );
                    Text_IO.Get ( transfile, new_record.model );
                    Text_IO.Get ( transfile, new_record.mileage );
                    Text_IO.Get ( transfile, new_record.color );
                    Invert.Insert ( new_record );
                When 'D' =>
                    Invert.Delete ( id_no );
                When Others =>
                    Text_IO.Put_Line ( " Invalid Update Code" );
            End Case;
        EXCEPTION
            When Invert.key_not_inserted => Text_IO.Put_Line("   Duplicate key" );
            When Invert.key_not_deleted => Text_IO.Put_Line("   key not deleted" );
        END;
        Text_IO.Skip_Line ( transfile );
    End Loop;
    Invert.Close ( "CARDATA" );
    Text_IO.Close ( transfile );
END Alg10_2;
```

Case Study 10.2

```
PACKAGE MultiLst Is
    SubType Primary_Key_Type Is String ( 1 .. 3 );
    SubType Secondary_Key_Type Is String ( 1 .. 10 );
    Type Record_Info Is Record
                        id_no       : Primary_Key_Type;
                        make        : Secondary_Key_Type;
                        make_link   : Primary_Key_Type;
                        style       : Secondary_Key_Type;
                        style_link  : Primary_Key_Type;
                        model       : Secondary_Key_Type;
                        mileage     : Secondary_Key_Type;
                        color       : Secondary_Key_Type;
                    End Record;

    PROCEDURE Create ( external_filename_prefix : String );
    PROCEDURE Open   ( external_filename_prefix : String );
    PROCEDURE Close  ( external_filename_prefix : String );
    PROCEDURE Insert ( new_record : In Out Record_Info );
    PROCEDURE Delete ( id_no : In Primary_Key_Type );
    key_not_inserted,
    key_not_deleted : Exception;
END MultiLst;

With Sequential_IO,
     Direct_IO,
     B_Tree;
PACKAGE Body MultiLst Is

    Type Key_Value_Record;
    Type Key_Value_Access Is Access Key_Value_Record;
    Type Key_Value_Record Is Record
                             key_value  : Secondary_Key_Type;
                             next_value : Key_Value_Access;
                             first_key  : Primary_Key_Type;
                             length     : Positive;
                         End Record;
    Type Index_Type Is ( MAKE, STYLE );
    Type Index_Record_Type Is Record
                              key_value : Secondary_Key_Type;
                              first_key : Primary_Key_Type;
                              length    : Positive;
                          End Record;
    PACKAGE Data_File_IO Is New Direct_IO ( Record_Info );
    PACKAGE B_Tree_IO Is New B_Tree ( 3, Primary_Key_Type, ">" );
    PACKAGE Index_IO Is New Sequential_IO ( Index_Record_Type );
    data_file     : Data_File_IO.File_Type;
    index_file    : Index_IO.File_Type;
    header        : Array ( Index_Type ) Of Key_Value_Access := ( Others => NULL );
    key_not_found : Exception;

    PROCEDURE Create ( external_filename_prefix : String ) Is
    BEGIN  -- Create
        Data_File_IO.Create ( data_file,
                              Data_File_IO.INOUT_FILE,
                              external_filename_prefix & ".DAT" );
```

```
    B_Tree_IO.Create_B_Tree ( external_filename_prefix & ".BTR" );
END Create;

PROCEDURE Search_List ( header : In Key_Value_Access;
                        secondary_key : In Secondary_Key_Type;
                        where_found, previous : In Out Key_Value_Access ) Is
    -- where_found returns NIL if secondary_key is not found in
    --     index and returns a pointer to the node in the
    --     linked structure if found
BEGIN -- Search_List
    previous := NULL;
    where_found := header;
    Loop
        Exit When where_found = NULL;
        If where_found.key_value = secondary_key Then
            Return;
        End If;
        previous := where_found;
        where_found := where_found.next_value;
    End Loop;
    Raise key_not_found;
END Search_List;

PROCEDURE Insert ( new_record : In Out Record_Info ) Is
    next_record_number : Natural;
    PROCEDURE Insert_Index ( index_name : In Index_Type;
                             secondary_key : In Secondary_Key_Type;
                             link_field : In Out Primary_Key_Type;
                             id_no : In Primary_Key_Type ) Is
        -- index_name indicates which index is to be built:
        --     MAKE or STYLE
        -- secondary_key is either the make or style that was read
        --     into new_record
        -- link_field is either the make_link or style_link of
        --     new_record
        previous,
        where_found : Key_Value_Access;

    BEGIN -- Insert_Index
        Search_List ( header(index_name), secondary_key, where_found,
                      previous );
            -- Add_To_Key_List
            -- add the primary key of new_record to the list of primary
            --     keys for the key_value pointed to by where_found
            where_found.length := where_found.length + 1;
            link_field := where_found.first_key;
            where_found.first_key := id_no;
    EXCEPTION
        When key_not_found =>
            -- Add_To_Index
            -- add the secondary_key as the new value in the linked
            --     structure with the primary key of new_record as the
            --     first_key
            header(index_name) := New Key_Value_Record'
                        ( secondary_key, header(index_name), id_no, 1 );
            link_field := "NIL";
    END Insert_Index;
```

```
BEGIN -- Insert
    next_record_number := Natural ( Data_File_IO.Size ( data_file ) ) + 1;
    B_Tree_IO.Insert ( new_record.id_no, Positive ( next_record_number ) );
    Insert_Index ( MAKE, new_record.make, new_record.make_link,
                   new_record.id_no );
    Insert_Index ( STYLE, new_record.style, new_record.style_link,
                   new_record.id_no );
    Data_File_IO.Write ( data_file,
                         new_record,
                         Data_File_IO.Positive_Count ( next_record_number ) );
EXCEPTION
    When B_Tree_IO.key_not_inserted => Raise key_not_inserted;
END Insert;

PROCEDURE Delete ( id_no : In Primary_Key_Type ) Is
    location   : Positive;
    new_record : Record_Info;
    PROCEDURE Delete_Index ( index : In Index_Type;
                             secondary_key : In Secondary_Key_Type;
                             id_no : In Primary_Key_Type;
                             hold_record : Record_Info ) Is

        link          : Primary_Key_Type;
        previous      : Key_Value_Access;
        prev_key      : Primary_Key_Type;
        prev_record   : Record_Info;
        record_number : Positive;
        where_found   : Key_Value_Access;
    BEGIN -- Delete_Index
        Search_List ( header(index),
                      secondary_key,
                      where_found,
                      previous );
        If where_found.first_key = id_no Then
              -- delete first key
            If where_found.length = 1 Then  -- delete entire entry
                If previous = NULL Then  -- first entry
                    header(index) := where_found.next_value;
                Else
                    previous.next_value := where_found.next_value;
                End If;
            Else -- find next primary key to become first_key
                Case index Is
                    When MAKE  =>
                        where_found.first_key := hold_record.make_link;
                    When STYLE =>
                        where_found.first_key := hold_record.style_link;
                End Case;
                where_found.length := where_found.length - 1;
            End If;

        Else -- id_no not = first_key
            prev_key := where_found.first_key;
            B_Tree_IO.Search ( prev_key, record_number );
            Data_File_IO.Read ( data_file,
                                prev_record,
                                Data_File_IO.Positive_Count ( record_number ) );
```

```
            Case index Is
                When MAKE  => link := prev_record.make_link;
                When STYLE => link := prev_record.style_link;
            End Case;
            Loop
                If link = "NIL" Then
                    Raise key_not_deleted;
                End If;
                    -- search for id_no in linked list of records
                If link = id_no Then
                    Case index Is
                        When MAKE => prev_record.make_link :=
                                        hold_record.make_link;
                        When STYLE => prev_record.style_link :=
                                        hold_record.style_link;
                   End Case;
                   Data_File_IO.Write ( data_file, prev_record,
                       Data_File_IO.Positive_Count ( record_number ) );
                   where_found.length := where_found.length - 1;
                   Exit;
               Else
                   prev_key := link;
                   B_Tree_IO.Search ( prev_key, record_number );
                   Data_File_IO.Read ( data_file, prev_record,
                       Data_File_IO.Positive_Count ( record_number ) );
                   Case index Is
                       When MAKE  => link := prev_record.make_link;
                       When STYLE => link := prev_record.style_link;
                   End Case;
                End If;
            End Loop;
        End If;
    EXCEPTION
        When B_Tree_IO.key_not_found => Raise key_not_deleted;
    END Delete_Index;

BEGIN  -- Delete
    B_Tree_IO.Search ( id_no, location );
    Data_File_IO.Read ( data_file,
                        new_record,
                        Data_File_IO.Positive_Count ( location ) );
    Delete_Index ( MAKE, new_record.make, new_record.id_no, new_record );
    Delete_Index ( STYLE, new_record.style, new_record.id_no, new_record );
    new_record.id_no := "NIL";
    Data_File_IO.Write ( data_file, new_record,
                        Data_File_IO.Positive_Count ( location ) );
    B_Tree_IO.Delete ( id_no );
EXCEPTION
    When B_Tree_IO.key_not_found
       | B_Tree_IO.key_not_deleted => Raise key_not_deleted;
END Delete;

PROCEDURE Open ( external_filename_prefix : String ) Is
    PROCEDURE Input_Indexes ( external_filename : In String;
                              header : Out Key_Value_Access ) Is
        -- input either the MAKE_INDEX or the STYLE_INDEX (index)
        --     sequentially from an external file
```

```
          first,
          lcv,
          next         : Key_Value_Access;
          index_record : Index_Record_Type;
      BEGIN -- Input_Indexes
          Index_IO.Open ( index_file, Index_IO.IN_FILE, external_filename );
          lcv := New Key_Value_Record;
          first := lcv;
          Loop
              Exit When Index_IO.End_Of_File ( index_file );
              Index_IO.Read ( index_file, index_record );
              lcv.next_value := New Key_Value_Record'
                                  ( index_record.key_value, null,
                                    index_record.first_key,
                                    index_record.length );
              lcv := lcv.next_value;
          End Loop;
          lcv.next_value := Null;
          header := first.next_value;
          Index_IO.Close ( index_file );
      END Input_Indexes;
  BEGIN  -- Open
      Data_File_IO.Open ( data_file,
                          Data_File_IO.INOUT_FILE,
                          external_filename_prefix & ".DAT" );
      B_Tree_IO.Open_B_Tree ( external_filename_prefix & ".btr" );
      Input_Indexes ( external_filename_prefix & ".MAK", header(MAKE) );
      Input_Indexes ( external_filename_prefix & ".STY", header(STYLE) );
  END Open;

  PROCEDURE Close ( external_filename_prefix : String ) Is
      PROCEDURE Output_Indexes ( external_filename : In String;
                                 header : In Key_Value_Access ) Is
          -- output either the MAKE or the STYLE index
          --     sequentially to an external file for storage
          index_record : Index_Record_Type;
          lcv : Key_Value_Access;
      BEGIN  -- Output_Indexes
          Index_IO.Create ( index_file, Index_IO.OUT_FILE, external_filename );
          lcv := header;
          Loop
              Exit When lcv = NULL;
              index_record := ( lcv.key_value, lcv.first_key, lcv.length );
              Index_IO.Write ( index_file, index_record );
              lcv := lcv.next_value;
          End Loop;
         Index_IO.Close ( index_file );
      END Output_Indexes;

  BEGIN  -- Close
      Data_File_IO.Close ( data_file );
      B_Tree_IO.Close_B_Tree;
      Output_Indexes ( external_filename_prefix & ".MAK", header(MAKE) );
      Output_Indexes ( external_filename_prefix & ".STY", header(STYLE) );
  END Close;
END MultiLst;
```

```
With Text_IO,
     MultiLst;
PROCEDURE Alg10_3 Is

     char          : Character;
     input_file    : Text_IO.File_Type;
     new_record    : MultiLst.Record_Info;

BEGIN  -- Alg10_3
    Text_IO.Open ( input_file, Text_IO.IN_FILE, "T1.TXT");
    MultiLst.Create ( "CARDATA" );
    Loop
        Exit When Text_IO.End_Of_File ( input_file );
        Text_IO.Get ( input_file, char );
        Text_IO.Get ( input_file, new_record.id_no );
        Text_IO.Put_Line ( new_record.id_no );
        Text_IO.Get ( input_file, new_record.make );
        Text_IO.Get ( input_file, new_record.style );
        Text_IO.Get ( input_file, new_record.model );
        Text_IO.Get ( input_file, new_record.mileage );
        Text_IO.Get ( input_file, new_record.color );
        Text_IO.Skip_Line ( input_file );
        BEGIN
            MultiLst.Insert ( new_record );
        EXCEPTION
            When MultiLst.key_not_inserted =>
                 Text_IO.Put_Line ( " Duplicate Key" );
        END;
    End Loop;
    Text_IO.Close ( input_file );
    MultiLst.Close ( "cardata" );
END Alg10_3;

With Text_IO,
     MultiLst;
PROCEDURE Alg10_4 Is

    id_no            : MultiLst.Primary_Key_Type;
    new_record       : MultiLst.Record_Info;
    transaction_code : Character;
    transfile        : Text_IO.File_Type;

BEGIN -- Alg10_4
    MultiLst.Open ( "CARDATA" );
    Text_IO.Open ( transfile, Text_IO.IN_FILE, "CARTRANS.TXT" );
    Loop
        Exit When Text_IO.End_Of_File ( transfile );
        Text_IO.Get ( transfile, transaction_code );
        Text_IO.Put ( transaction_code );
        Text_IO.Put ( " " );
        Text_IO.Get ( transfile, id_no );
        Text_IO.Put_Line ( id_no );
        BEGIN
            Case transaction_code Is
                When 'A' => new_record.id_no := id_no;
                            Text_IO.Get ( transfile, new_record.make );
                            Text_IO.Get ( transfile, new_record.style );
                            Text_IO.Get ( transfile, new_record.model );
                            Text_IO.Get ( transfile, new_record.mileage );
```

```
                        Text_IO.Get ( transfile, new_record.color );
                        MultiLst.Insert ( new_record );
                        Text_IO.Put_Line ( "    added" );
                When 'D' => MultiLst.Delete ( id_no );
                        Text_IO.Put_Line ( "   deleted" );
                When Others => Text_IO.Put_Line ( " invalid update code" );
            End Case;
        EXCEPTION
            When MultiLst.key_not_inserted =>
                    Text_IO.Put_Line ( "   duplicate key" );
            When MultiLst.key_not_deleted =>
                    Text_IO.Put_Line ( "   key not found on delete" );
        END;
        Text_IO.Skip_Line ( transfile );
    End Loop;
    Text_IO.Close ( transfile );
    MultiLst.Close ( "CARDATA" );
END Alg10_4;
```

Glossary

abort An Ada statement that terminates an active task.

absolute address A machine-dependent address: cylinder number, surface-number, and record number for cylinder-addressable devices; sector number and record number for sector-addressable devices.

abstract data type Defines a structure and a set of values for data objects of this type.

accept An Ada statement that serves as the rendezvous point for a task named entry and that specifies the actions to be performed when the entry is called.

activity of a file A measure of the percentage of existing master file components changed during a maintenance run.

additions Transactions that cause a new record to be added to an existing master file.

aggregate A basic operation that combines component values into a composite value of a record or array type.

ancestor A node that is at one or more levels higher than the current node.

array A collection of data items of the same type, each accessed by a name and an index. See **record.**

ASCII A 7-bit code for representing characters.

audit/error listing One output of a maintenance run that includes all transactions processed, update actions (additions, changes, deletions) taken for each transaction (*audit* portion), and any errors that occurred during the run (*error* portion).

AVL tree A height-balanced binary tree introduced by Adelson-Velskii and Landis in 1962.

B-tree An *m*-way search tree, stored externally, in which all nodes (except the root node) have at least half as many keys and subtree pointers as indicated by the order *m*.

B^*-tree An *m*-way search tree, stored externally, in which all nodes (except the root node) have at least two-thirds as many keys and subtree pointers as the maximum (indicated by the order).

B^+-tree A B-tree with interior nodes that contain only keys and subtree pointers and with addresses of records in terminal nodes only.

balanced *k*-way sort/merge Each cycle involves merging sorted runs from *k* files into larger sorted runs stored alternately on *k* empty files. The cycle is repeated until all data are in one sorted run.

balanced tree A tree in which the height is a minimum for the number of nodes.

balanced two-way sort/merge Each cycle involves merging sorted runs from two files into larger sorted runs stored alternately on two empty files. The cycle is repeated until all data are in one sorted run.

balance factor (of a node)—The difference between the height of the left subtree and the height of the right subtree of a node (equals 0 if both heights are the same).

batch processing Updates to a master file are accumulated over a period of time in a transaction file, then periodically sorted into the same order as the master file and applied to the master file in a maintenance run. See **maintenance run**.

binary search tree A tree in which each node contains a left pointer to a subtree with lower values and a right pointer to a subtree with higher values than that of the current node.

block The smallest amount of data that can be input from or output to a secondary storage device during one access.

blocking The software interface between a program and a blocked file that groups several components into a block with memory accesses to be output to a file during one output operation.

bucket addresses A collision-resolution method where a group of record locations are associated with one hash address.

bucket chaining Synonyms that overflow a bucket are stored in a separate overflow area, and the overflow location is linked to the home bucket for easy access.

buffering The software interface between a program that accesses one component of a file at a time and a file of blocked components. See **blocking** and **deblocking**.

ceiling (of x)—The next integer greater than x.

changes Transactions that cause information in an existing master record to be changed.

child A node that is one level below and pointed to by the current node.

collision Occurs when the hashing function results in the same relative address for two keys that are not the same.

consecutive spill addressing Used with bucket addressing. Overflow from one bucket spills into the nearest bucket with available locations.

control file An output of a maintenance run containing information concerning the run.

current index A property of a direct file in Ada; used by the next I/O operation to indicate the position in the file for access.

current size A property of a direct file in Ada; the index of the last element of a direct file. The size is zero if there is no element.

cylinder A collection of vertically aligned tracks on a disk pack.

deblocking The software interface that inputs one block of file components from a blocked file and allows a program to access only one component at a time with memory accesses.

degree of a node The number of subtrees pointed to by the node.

degree of a tree The maximum degree of the nodes in the tree.

deletions Transactions that cause existing master records to be deleted from the file.

descendant A node that is at one or more levels lower than the current node.

digit extraction A hashing function.

direct file organization A file organization in which there exists a predictable relationship between the key used to identify an individual component and that component's location in an external file. The location is a device-specific absolute address. See **random file organization**.

discriminant The data object that serves as a tag in the variant part of a record.

displacement Occurs with linear probing when a synonym of location i is stored in location k, displacing a later record that hashes to location k, where i and k are different. The displaced record is displaced by a non-synonym.

double buffering Allocating two file buffer variables for a file instead of one to improve the access time.

double hashing A collision-resolution method where a second hash function is applied to synonyms and added to the first hash value to distribute synonyms into a separate overflow area. Double hashing eliminates the sequential searching for an available location.

double-sided Describing a floppy disk on which information can be recorded on both sides. See **single-sided**.

dummy runs Empty or null runs that are added to files during the sort phase (initial distribution of sorted runs) to obtain an nth-level perfect Fibonacci distribution.

dynamic hashing A collision-resolution method that dynamically changes the hashing function to access a hashed file that increases in size as records are added.

EBCDIC An 8-bit code for representing characters.

editing The process of identifying invalid data values in a transaction file prior to the maintenance run so that the invalid values can be corrected and, thus, more transactions will be accepted during the maintenance run.

encapsulated The definition of an abstract data type and the implementation of the operations on that data type are isolated in a package body and thereby hidden from the user.

end-of-tape marker A reflective aluminum strip near the end of a tape indicating the end of recordable surface, followed by a section of leader for winding around the tape reel. It is sensed by the tape drive so that the tape does not unwind from the reel.

entry Used only in a task specification to declare entry point names for corresponding accept statements which appear in the task body.

exception An error or exceptional situation that might arise during the execution of an Ada program.

exception handler A portion of a program specifying a response to a raised exception.

field A component of a record data stucture.

file buffer Contains one component of a file. It is initialized to the first file component by the Read procedure, filled with a file component by the Open procedure, accessed by the Write procedure.

file header label Precedes every file on tape or disk; contains file identification information.

file organization Refers to the way in which components are stored on an external file; determines the type of access.

file size Determined by the number of components in the file and the length (in bytes) of each component.

file trailer label Follows every file on tape or disk; contains record and block counts for the file.

fixed-head disk A disk with a permanently sealed pack and a read/write head for every track. See **removable disk**.

floor (of *x*)—The largest integer contained in *x*.

floppy disk A single plastic platter that resembles a 45-rpm phonograph record. A floppy disk is common secondary storage for microcomputers. See **single-sided** and **double-sided**.

folding A hashing function.

generic I/O packages Templates for generating file manipulation modules.

gigabyte 2^{30} (1,073,741,824) bytes.

hard disk A collection of rigid aluminum platters stacked to form a disk pack; a common secondary storage for large-scale computers.

hard-sectored A floppy disk containing a ring of tiny index holes, one at each sector boundary, punched near the center of the disk. A beam of light senses the holes to determine the beginning of a sector.

hashing The application of a function to a key value that will result in mapping the range of possible key values into a smaller range of relative (or absolute) addresses.

head activation time The time necessary to electrically switch on the read/write head for a particular track on a disk to be accessed. Essentially, head activation time is 0 relative to other factors involved in access time.

head settle time The time necessary for the read/write heads to settle onto the floppy disk surface and make contact. Settling must occur before access is possible.

height The number of levels of nodes contained in a tree.

height-balanced binary tree A tree in which the heights of the subtrees of each node are the same.

history file A collection of the old master files, old transaction files, and control files from past maintenance runs.

index A property of a direct file in Ada; the relative record number of a record in a direct file.

indexed sequential file organization A file organization that combines the sequential access and ordering of file components provided in sequential file organization and the random-access capabilities of random file organization.

interblock gap (IBG) Separates blocks of information on tape and disk; allows the tape to start and stop between read/write requests without stopping on information; allows information to be processed by CPU before the next block is accessed from disk.

interrecord gap (IRG) Another term for **interblock gap (IBG)**.

I/O-bound A program or computer system which is limited in processing speed by its I/O devices.

I/O channel The part of the operating system that provides input and output control to peripheral devices. See **processor-bound**.

I/O exceptions A group of predefined exceptions designed specifically for I/O operations.

latency Rotational delay; the time required for the beginning of the block to be accessed to rotate around to the read/write heads (on removable disks).

leaf nodes Nodes that point to no other node. See **terminal nodes**.

level The distance a node is from the root of the tree, where the root is on level 1, the root's child nodes are on level 2, etc.

lg x The logarithm to the base 2 of x.

linear probing A collision-resolution method in which the file is scanned sequentially until an empty location is found for a synonym.

LL rotation Rotation performed to balance an AVL tree that has had an insertion in the *L*eft subtree of the *L*eft subtree of the root, causing the tree to no longer be height-balanced.

load factor The ratio of the number of key values to be stored in a relative file to the number of file locations allocated for the file.

load point marker A reflective aluminum strip following a section of leader at the beginning of a tape indicating the beginning of recordable surface. The marker is sensed by a beam of light when loading a tape into a tape drive.

logical record The amount of data requested and processed by a program at a time. A logical record is grouped into blocks for more efficient use of space and access time on tape and disk. See **physical record**.

LR rotation Rotation performed to balance an AVL tree that has had an insertion in the *R*ight subtree of a node that is the *L*eft child of its parent node, causing the tree to no longer be height-balanced.

***m*-way search tree** A balanced search tree in which all nodes are of degree *m* or less.

magnetic disk A direct-access storage device (DASD) that allows a particular record to be accessed randomly, without reference to preceding records.

magnetic tape A sequential-access storage device in which blocks of information are stored serially along the length of the tape and can only be accessed in a serial manner.

maintenance run The application of transactions of additions, changes, and deletions to a master file in order to keep the master file information current.

master file Contains permanent information.

megabyte 2^{20} (1,048,576) bytes.

merge phase The second of two phases of an external sort/merge algorithm. A merge phase involves merging the sorted runs produced by the sort phase repeatedly until all data are in one sorted run. See **sort phase**.

mid-square A hashing function.

millisecond One-thousandth of a second.

multikey file organization Allows access to a data file by several different key fields.

named aggregate Associates values with components of a record by specifying both the name of the component and the associated value.

nontext file A file of components, each component being the same type, with noncharacter data stored in internal (computational) form.

***n*th-level Fibonacci distribution** A distribution of sorted runs on file where *n* indicates the number of passes of the merge cycle that must be performed in order to merge all data into one run.

order of a tree The maximum degree of any node in the tree.

overflow technique A technique used in B^*-trees of rotating keys from a full node into a sibling node that is less than full; used instead of splitting.

package body The implementation of the subprograms provided by the package. This part of the package is not visible to the user.

package specification The package interface. It provides visibility to the types, exceptions, variables, and subprograms implemented in the package.

packing density See **load factor.**

packing factor See **load factor.**

parent The node in a tree that points to the current node (node at one level higher in the tree).

parity bit An addition bit for each character that is used to detect errors that occur when reading or writing data. Even parity makes the parity bit 1, so the number of bits for a character is even and 0 if the number of bits is already even. Odd parity ensures that each character has an odd number of bits by making the parity bit 1 when necessary.

perfect Fibonacci distribution The distribution of sorted runs to files that ensures that there is only one run on each of *k* files to be merged during the last merge pass, regardless of the number of initial runs.

perfect hashing function A hashing function that provides a one-to-one mapping from a key into a location.

physical record The amount of information that can be transferred at any one access. See **block.**

polyphase sort/merge Each cycle involves merging sorted runs from *k* files into one empty file until one file becomes empty. The empty file becomes the output file for the next cycle. The merge is most efficient when the *p*th order perfect Fibonacci distribution is used in the sort phase. See ***p*****th order Fibonacci distribution.**

positional aggregate Associates the values with the components of a record according to the position of the value in the list of values.

prime-number division remainder A hashing function.

processor-bound A program or computer system which is limited in processing speed by the speed of the CPU. See **I/O-bound.**

p**th order Fibonacci distribution** The distribution of sorted runs to files where the *n*th term in the *p*th order Fibonacci series is computed as the sum of the previous *p* terms.

quotient reduction A perfect hashing function.

radix conversion A hashing function.

raise The Ada statement that explicitly raises an exception. To raise an exception is to abandon normal program execution. See **exception handler.**

random file organization A file organization in which there exists a predictable relationship between the key used to identify an individual component and that component's location in an external file. The location is an integer relative to the beginning of the file. See **direct file organization.**

randomizing scheme See **hashing.**

random update The maintenance process consists of randomly locating the master record that matches the transaction key, applying the transaction, and rewriting the updated master record to the original location from which it was read. The transaction need not be in the key order. Random updating is available only on direct access storage devices (disks). See **sequential update.**

readable radius The radius of the readable portion of the surface of a disk. The outermost track is not on the very edge of the disk, and the innermost track is not on the very center of the disk, so the distance between the two is the readable portion. (See Figure 4.9.)

reciprocal hashing A perfect hashing function.

record A collection of data items of similar or different types, accessed by a single name. See **array.**

record aggregate See **aggregate, named aggregate, positional aggregate.**

recording density The number of characters or bytes of information that can be stored in 1 inch of storage media.

relative file organization A common implementation of random file organization in which a component's location is specified as an integer relative to the beginning of the file.

relative record number A relative address representing the location of a record within a file, relative to the beginning of the file.

remainder reduction A perfect hashing function.

removable disk A disk pack that may be mounted on the disk drive to access information and subsequently unmounted for storage. It contains movable read/write heads, one per surface. See **fixed head disk.**

renames An Ada clause that declares a new name for an existing entity.

rendezvous The synchronization of a program unit issuing an entry call and a task accepting the call.

report file A file containing information drawn from a master file that has been prepared for a user.

RL rotation A rotation performed to balance an AVL tree that has had an insertion in the *L*eft subtree of a node that is the *R*ight child of its parent node, causing the tree to no longer be height-balanced.

root The top node of a tree that is pointed to by no other node in the tree except an external pointer.

rotational delay Latency.

RR rotation Rotation performed to balance an AVL tree that has had an insertion in the *R*ight subtree of the *R*ight subtree of the root, causing the tree to no longer be height-balanced.

run A sorted partition of a file to be sorted but which is larger than main memory, requiring an external sort.

secondary collision The second collision that occurs when looking for an empty location for a synonym. Such a collision may occur during linear probing and double hashing.

sector A portion of a track on a disk pack. Each sector has a unique address for access.

seek time The time required to move the read/write heads (access arm) to a particular track on movable head disk drives with removable disk packs. Seek time is eliminated for fixed-head disks.

separate overflow area A collision-resolution method where a storage separate from the home area is allocated for synonyms so displacement is eliminated. This method offers an alternative to linear probing.

sequential file organization A file organization in which components are written and accessed consecutively, and in which the physical order of information is the same as the logical order.

sequential update The maintenance process that is restricted to sequential access whereby the transactions must be in the same sorted order as the master file. The process is similar to a file merge process. See **random update**.

sibling nodes Nodes in a tree that are at the same level of the tree.

single-sided Describing a floppy disk on which information can be recorded on only one side. See **double-sided**.

skewed Describing a tree with more levels of nodes on one subtree of a node than in the other subtree.

soft-sectored Describing a floppy disk with one index hole for allowing the read/write heads to access the disk where the boundaries between sectors are determined by the computer software.

sort phase The first of two phases of a sort/merge algorithm. This phase involves accessing a partition of the file to be sorted into main memory on which an internal sort is applied. The sorted result written to one or more files as a sorted run. See **merge phase**.

spanned record A block that is stored on a sector-addressable disk and that is longer than a sector.

spill addressing Used with bucket addressing. An overflowed bucket "spills" over into the next bucket.

start/stop time The time necessary to start the tape moving up to speed to access a block of information, or the time necessary to stop the tape after accessing a block of information. Usually the stop time and start time are exactly the amount of time to traverse an IBG.

substrate An underlying layer; the layer below the surface on which CD-ROM data are written.

synonym chaining A collision-resolution method where synonyms are linked together to provide faster access with fewer I/O accesses.

synonyms Two or more keys that have hashed to the same relative address.

table file A file containing a table of information that is static and referenced by other files.

task An Ada program unit that operates independently (in parallel) and has facilities for communicating with other program units.

task body Contains executable statements that implement the task specification.

task specification Specifies the name of the task and the names and formal parameters of the task entries.

terminal nodes Nodes in a tree that point to no other node in the tree. See **leaf nodes.**

text file A file of characters grouped into lines, each line being terminated by an end of line marker.

track A row of bits (one bit for each character) on a tape that is parallel to the edges of the tape. A circle of bits on a disk contains the bits for characters stored serially along the track.

transaction file Contains changes, additions, and deletions to be applied to a master file.

transfer rate Time required to transfer information to or from a disk.

two-way sort/merge Each cycle merges two files containing sorted runs into one output file; the runs from the output file are redistributed back to the input file, and the cycle repeats until all data are in one sorted run.

variant part A portion of a record data structure that varies in the number of fields allocated, depending on the value of a tag field.

variant record A record data structure containing a variant part.

volatility of a file A measure of the number of file components added and deleted during a maintenance run compared to the number of components in the file originally.

volume label Contains the serial number of the tape or disk and other identifying information for the reel or pack.

Winchester disk A hard disk used with microcomputers consisting of one platter that is sealed in the drive. This type of disk offers higher densities, higher storage capacities, and faster access speeds than floppy disks.

Bibliography

Alberte-Hallam, Teresa; Hallam, Stephen F.; and Hallam, James. *Microcomputer Use: Word Processors, Spreadsheets, and Data Bases.* Academic Press, Inc., Orlando, Florida, 1985.

Barnes, J. *Programming in Ada.* Addison-Wesley, London, 1984.

Bayer, R. and McCreight, E. "Organization and maintenance of large ordered indexes," *Acta Informatica*, 1(3):173–189, 1972.

Booch, G. *Software Components with Ada.* Benjamin/Cummings Publishing Co., Menlo Park, California, 1987.

Booch, G. *Software Engineering With Ada.* Benjamin/Cummings, Menlo Park, California, 1983.

Bradley, James. *File and Data Base Techniques.* Holt, Rinehart & Winston, New York, 1981.

Buchholz, W. "File organization and addressing," *IBM Systems Journal*, 2(6):86–111, 1963.

Chang, C. C. "The study of an ordered minimal perfect hashing scheme," *Communications of the ACM*, 27(4):384–387, 1984.

Chaturvedi, Atindra. "Tree structures: A tutorial on using tree structures for random data storage and retrieval," *PC Tech Journal*, (2):78–87, 1985.

Chaturvedi, Atindra. "Tree structures: Part 2," *PC Tech Journal*, (3):131–142, 1985.

Choen, Norman H. *Ada as a Second Language.* McGraw-Hill Book Company, New York, 1986.

Cichelli, R. J. "Minimal perfect hash functions made simple," *Communications of the ACM*, 23(1):17–19, 1980.

Claybrook, Billy G. *File Management Techniques.* John Wiley & Sons, New York, 1983.

Cook, C. R. "A letter oriented minimal perfect hashing function," *Sigplan Notices*, 17(9):18–27, 1982.

Dijkstra, E. W. *A Discipline of Programming.* Prentice-Hall, Inc., Englewood Cliffs, New Jersey, 1976.

Doty, Roy. "Dazzling data discs," *Popular Science*, 231(12):38–39,46, 1987.

Dwyer, Barry. "One more time—how to update a master file," *Communications of the ACM*, 24(1):3–8, 1981.

Fagin, R. et al. "Extendable hashing: A fast access method for dynamic files," *ACM Transactions on Database Systems*, 4(3):315–344, 1979.

Finger, Susan, and Finger, Ellen. *PASCAL with Applications in Science and Engineering.* D. C. Heath and Company, Lexington, Massachusetts, 1986.

Folk, M. J. and Zoellick, B. *File Structures: A Conceptual Toolkit.* Addison-Wesley, Reading, Massachusetts, 1987.

Ghosh, S. P. and Lum, V. Y. "An analysis of collisions when hashing by division," IBM Research Report RJ1218, May 1973.

Guibas, L. U. "The analysis of hashing techniques that exhibit *k*-ary clustering," *Journal of ACM*, 25(4):544–555, 1978.

Hanson, Owen J. *Design of Computer Data Files.* Computer Science Press, Rockville, Maryland, 1982.

Helman, Paul and Veroff, Robert. *Intermediate Problem Solving and Data Structures.* Benjamin/Cummings Publishing Co., Menlo Park, California, 1986.

Horowitz, Ellis and Sahni, Sartaj. *Fundamentals of Data Structures in PASCAL.* Computer Science Press, Rockville, Maryland, 1984.

Introduction to Computer Architecture. Edited by Harold S. Stone. Science Research Associates, Chicago, 1980.

Introduction to IBM Direct Access Storage Devices and Organization Methods. IBM Manual No. GC 20-1649-10.

Jackson, M. A. *Principles of Program Design.* Academic Press, New York, 1975.

Jaeschke, G. "Reciprocal hashing: A method for generating minimal perfect hashing functions," *Communications of the ACM,* 24(12):829–833, 1981.

Jaeschke, G. and Osterburg, G. "On Cichelli's minimal perfect hash functions method," *Communications of the ACM,* 23(12):728–729, 1980.

Jensen, Kathleen and Wirth, Nicklaus. *Pascal User Manual and Report.* Third Edition. Revised by Andrew B. Mickel and James F. Miner. Springer-Verlag, New York, 1985.

Johnson, Leroy F. and Cooper, Rodney H. *File Techniques for Data Base Organization in COBOL.* Prentice-Hall, Englewood Cliffs, New Jersey, 1981.

Knott, G. D. "Hashing functions," *Computer Journal,* 18(3):265–278, 1975.

Knuth, Donald E. *The Art of Computer Programming, Vol. 3, Sorting and Searching.* Addison-Wesley, Reading, Massachusetts, 1973.

Litwin, W. "Virtual hashing: A dynamically changing hashing," *Proceedings of the Fourth Conference on Very Large Databases,* West Berlin, September 1978, pp. 517–523.

Loomis, Mary E. S. *Data Management and File Processing.* Prentice-Hall, Englewood Cliffs, New Jersey, 1983.

Lum, V. Y. "General performance analysis of key-to-address transformation methods using an abstract file concept," *Communications of the ACM,* 16(10):603–612, 1973.

Lum, V. Y., and Yuen, P. S. T. "Additional results on key-to-address transform techniques," *Communications of the ACM,* 15(11):996–997, 1972.

Lum, V. Y. et al. "Key-to-address transform techniques," *Communications of the ACM,* 14(4):228–229, 1971.

Maurer, W. D. and Lewis, T. G. "Hash table methods," *ACM Computing Surveys,* 7(1):5–20, 1975.

Microcomputer Interfaces Handbook. Digital Equipment Corporation, Marlboro, Massachusetts, 1981.

OS/VS1 and VS2 Access Method Services. IBM Manuals No. GC 26-3840 and GC 26-3841.

Peterson, W. Wesley and Lew, Art. *File Design And Programming.* John Wiley & Sons, New York, 1986.

Powers, Michael J.; Adams, David R.; and Mills, Harlan D. *Computer Information Systems Development: Analysis and Design.* South-Western Publishing Co., Cincinnati, 1984.

Programming in VAX PASCAL. Order #AA-L369B-TE. Digital Equipment Corporation, Maynard, Massachusetts, 1985.

Reference Manual for the Ada Programming Language, ANSI/MIL-STD-1815A. Department of Defense, Ada Joint Program Office. Government Printing Office, Washington, D.C., 1983.

Saib, S. *Ada: An Introduction*. Holt, Rinehart & Winston, New York, 1985.

Scholl, M. "New file organization based on dynamic hashing," *ACM Transactions on Database Systems*, 6(1):194–211, 1981.

Sloan, M. E. *Computer Hardware and Organization*. Science Research Associates, Chicago, 1983.

Sprugnoli, R. "Perfect hashing functions: A single probe retrieving method for static sets," *Communications of the ACM*, 20(11):841–850, 1977.

Texel, Putnam. *Introductory Ada Packages for Programming*. Wadsworth Publishing Company, Belmont, California, 1986.

Tremblay, Jean-Paul and Sorenson, Paul G. *An Introduction to Data Structures with Applications*. McGraw-Hill Book Company, New York, 1984.

Tyre, Terian. "New CD-ROM drive offered for Apple IIs and Macintosh," *T.H.E. Journal*, 15(9):56–59, 1988.

Vasilescu, E. N. *Ada Programming with Applications*. Allyn & Bacon, Boston, 1987.

Vasudeva, Anil. "Drive design optimizes optical disks for use in archival storage," *Computer Technology Review*, 7(5):49–53, 1987.

Weiderhold, Gio. *File Organization for Database Design*. McGraw-Hill Book Company, New York, 1987.

Welburn, Tyler. *Advanced Structured COBOL, Batch, On-line, and Data-Base Concepts*. Mayfield Publishing Co., Palo Alto, California. 1983.

Wirth, Nicklaus. *Algorithms + Data Structures = Programs*. Prentice-Hall, Englewood Cliffs, New Jersey, 1976.

Zaks, Rodnay. *Introduction to PASCAL (Including UCSD PASCAL)*. Sybex, Inc., Berkeley, California, 1981.

Index